McDougal Littell

MODERN WORLD HISTORY

PATTERNS OF INTERACTION

CURRICULUM

Formal Assessment

McDougal Littell
A DIVISION OF HOUGHTON MIFFLIN COMPANY

ISBN-13 978-0-618-40985-3   ISBN-10 0-618-40985-8

Printed in the United States of America.

5 6 7 8 9 CKI   09 08 07 06

To the Teacher

This *Formal Assessment* book contains the test material for *Modern World History: Patterns of Interaction*, as described below.

SECTION QUIZZES

A one-page quiz is provided for each chapter section. Each quiz consists of two parts. The first part uses multiple-choice, matching, sentence completion, or other formats to test students' understanding of the terms and names taught in the section. The second part tests students' critical thinking skills with an extended-response question about major events, trends, conflicts, or conditions covered in the section. Quizzes should be administered after students have completed the Guided Reading pages.

CHAPTER TESTS

The *Formal Assessment* book offers teachers the flexibility of three leveled tests for each chapter in the textbook. The Chapter Tests—identified as Forms A, B, and C—cover equivalent content but vary in the level of difficulty of the items. Form A is the most basic, with questions that require students to demonstrate literal understanding of facts and concepts. Form B is more difficult, with a mix of literal and inferential questions. Form C is the most challenging, with most items requiring students to use higher-order thinking skills.

The three forms are identical in format and consist of four sections that total 100 points. Part 1 covers the main ideas, using multiple choice, modified true/false, or matching questions. Part 2 uses a map related to the chapter content and tests map skills through multiple choice, matching, or constructed response questions.

Most Part 3 sections present a prompt—such as a chart, graph, or political cartoon—that students must interpret. Students then answer multiple-choice or constructed-response items about the prompts. Some Part 3 sections, however, consist of document-based questions, which are explained below.

Part 4 presents two extended-response questions—or essay questions—that test critical thinking and conceptual understanding of the content. In Forms A and B, students' writing is scaffolded in the form of several "Think About" points for each question.

Answers for all test questions appear in the back of the book. As essays for the extended response will vary, models are provided that include the necessary points students should cover.

DOCUMENT-BASED QUESTIONS

Once per unit, Part 3 of the Chapter Test consists of document-based questions. Document-based questions focus on several primary resources—both visual and written—of the historical period. The introduction of each document-based question describes the historical context so that students can better understand the documents and accompanying questions. After the historical context appears the task—a brief overview of what the students must do.

The task is followed by three primary source documents, which may be excerpts, political cartoons, photographs, artifacts, or other types of primary sources. Each document is followed by a short-answer question.

The final part of the document-based question is an essay question that students answer in one to two paragraphs. In writing the essay, the students must synthesize by using the primary sources and their answers to the short-answer questions.

ANSWER KEYS

This section includes answer keys for Section Quizzes, Chapter Tests, and ACT/SAT I Standardized Test Practice passages.

TEST GENERATOR CD-ROM

All of the Section Quizzes and Chapter Tests in this booklet are available in electronic form on the Test Generator CD-ROM. Each question is assigned a difficulty level—basic, intermediate, or advanced. Using the Test Generator, you can make customized Chapter Tests based on your students' levels and needs. See the *Test Generator User's Guide* for details about how to construct and edit your tests.

Section Quizzes and Tests for *Modern World History: Patterns of Interaction*

PROLOGUE: THE RISE OF DEMOCRATIC IDEAS QUIZ 1

The Legacy of Greece and Rome

A. Terms and Names Write the letter or letters of the terms or names that best complete each statement. Each term or name is used one time.

a. Justinian
b. Cleisthenes
c. Romans
d. aristocracy
e. Pericles
f. government

g. Solon
h. Senate
i. city–states
j. Twelve Tables
k. direct democracy
l. republic

_____ 1. Greek civilization began as separate _____, each of which had its own system of _____.

_____ 2. At first Athens was governed by a king who was replaced by a(n) _____ made up of three nobles who were chosen by an assembly of citizens.

_____ 3. _____ initiated policies of political reform, including the determination of class of citizenship according to income rather than heredity.

_____ 4. Partly because he allowed all citizens to propose laws to the Athenian assembly, _____ is regarded as the founder of democracy in Athens.

_____ 5. _____ strengthened Athenian democracy by increasing the number of paid public officials which allowed poorer citizens to serve in the government.

_____ 6. The _____ learned about Greek democracy when they defeated the Greeks in a war for control of the Italian peninsula.

_____ 7. In contrast to Greece's _____, which allowed all citizens to participate in the decision-making of government, the Romans set up a _____, in which citizens chose representatives to make the decisions.

_____ 8. Like the Athenians, the Romans established a government made up of separate branches, including a _____, which controlled foreign and financial policies.

_____ 9. The Romans demonstrated their respect for the democratic principles of justice and reason by adhering to written laws known as the _____.

_____ 10. Rome's early written laws were expanded by _____ into a legal code which has had a profound impact on the laws of most Western countries.

B. Extended Response Briefly answer the following question on the back of this paper.

How is a democracy limited by the way the government defines who is and who is not a citizen?

PROLOGUE: THE RISE
OF DEMOCRATIC IDEAS *Judeo-Christian Tradition*
QUIZ 2

A. Terms and Names Write the letter of the best answer.

_____ 1. The religion of the Hebrew people was called
        a. polytheism.   c. Judaism.
        b. Christianity.   d. Protestantism.

_____ 2. The first five books of the Hebrew Bible are called the
        a. Torah.   c. New Testament.
        b. Old Testament.   d. Book of the Covenant.

_____ 3. Jesus' followers believed that he was
        a. the Messiah.   c. a non-Jew.
        b. a prophet.   d. a Roman Catholic.

_____ 4. According to the Torah, God's choice to be "father" of the Hebrews was
        a. Jesus.   c. Abraham.
        b. Moses.   d. Paul.

_____ 5. The earliest religion to develop from the teaching of Jesus was
        a. Judaism.   c. monotheism.
        b. Lutheranism.   d. Christianity.

_____ 6. During the Middle Ages, the Roman Catholic Church became
        a. democratic.   c. experimental.
        b. authoritarian.   d. ineffectual.

_____ 7. The renewed interest in non-Church matters which arose in 14th century
      Italy was called the
        a. Reformation.   c. Renaissance.
        b. Enlightenment.   d. Peasants' Revolt.

_____ 8. Protestants wanted to reform the Catholic Church in the 16th century because
      they believed that the Church
        a. was too weak.   c. rejected the Bible.
        b. was too powerful.   d. opposed the clergy.

B. Extended Response Briefly answer the following question on the back of this paper.

Compare and contrast the ways in which the Renaissance and the Reformation threatened the authority of the Roman Catholic Church.

6

Name _____ Date _____

Democratic Developments in England

A. Terms and Names
Write the letter of the term or name that best each statement.
Each term or name is used one time.

a. Magna Carta
b. Parliament
c. divine right
d. Charles Stuart
e. Henry II
f. Restoration
g. common law

h. Provisions of Oxford
i. constitutional monarchy
j. Oliver Cromwell
k. King James II
l. Glorious Revolution
m. the Protectorate
n. "power of the purse"

_____ 1. Before _____ developed the jury trial, feudal lords determined the guilt
or innocence of an accused person without benefit of the due process of law.

_____ 2. England's legal system built on precedents determined by the decisions of
royal justices and became known as _____.

_____ 3. England's monarchy began to lose its power when King John was forced by
English nobles to sign the _____.

_____ 4. The _____ gave English barons the right to rule along with the King
Edward I in exchange for financial aid.

_____ 5. Because _____ had _____, it could influence the governing of
England by withholding or granting financial support to the king.

_____ 6. European monarchs claimed that their authority to rule was given to them by
_____ and that any opposition to them was a sin.

_____ 7. For a brief period in the mid-1600's, _____ replaced England's monarchy
with a government that he called _____.

_____ 8. In 1660, the monarchy was reinstated by Parliament which placed _____
on the throne, beginning the period known as the _____.

_____ 9. By ousting _____ and placing William and Mary on the throne,
Parliament established its right to limit the power of the English monarchy, an
event which became known as the _____.

_____ 10. By accepting the English Bill of Rights from Parliament, William and Mary
agreed to limit their authority and England at last became a _____.

B. Extended Response
Briefly answer the following question on the back of this paper.

Why do you think Oliver Cromwell's overthrow of the monarchy failed to win the
support of the English people?

Name _____   Date _____

PROLOGUE: THE RISE
OF DEMOCRATIC IDEAS

The Enlightenment and Democratic Revolutions

QUIZ 4

A. Terms and Names If the statement is true, write "true" on the line. If it is false, change the underlined word or words to make it true.

Example: Intellectuals during the "<u>Enlightenment</u>" tried to apply the principles

of reason and the methods of science to all aspects of society.

_____ *true* _____

Example: <u>John Locke</u> believed that the best government to maintain peace in a society

was absolute monarchy. _____ *Thomas Hobbes* _____

1. Rousseau believed that the only government that was legitimate came from <u>divine</u>

   <u>right</u>. _____

2. <u>Baron de Montesquieu</u> concluded that government could best be kept under control if

   it were divided into three separate branches. _____

3. The American colonists resented the taxes assessed against them by <u>King George</u>

   <u>III</u>._____

4. Before the present U.S. Constitution was framed, the states were organized according

   to the <u>Declaration of Independence</u>. _____

5. In France, the commoners abandoned the Estates General and formed a <u>National</u>

   <u>Assembly</u>. _____

6. After the French Revolution, Napoleon Bonaparte created a <u>democracy</u>._____

7. One of the branches of the UN, the <u>Security Council</u> operates like a

   democracy._____

B. Extended Response Briefly answer the following questions on the back of this paper.

Should Native Americans have been invited to participate in the formation of the new government? Why do you think they weren't?

⬤ **PROLOGUE: THE RISE
OF DEMOCRATIC IDEAS
FORM A**   *The Rise of Democratic Ideas*

Part 1: Main Ideas

Write the letter of the best answer. (4 points each)

_____ 1. What form of government is based on the idea that people can govern themselves?
     a. absolute rule   c. democracy
     b. constitutional monarchy   d. dictatorship

_____ 2. How are powers divided in a federal system?
     a. The power is divided between the House of Commons and House of Lords.
     b. The power is divided among the judicial, legislative, and executive branches.
     c. The power is divided between the monarchy and the Parliament.
     d. The power is divided between the central and state governments.

_____ 3. What is a republic?
     a. a government in which citizens elect leaders who make government
        decisions
     b. a government in which citizens rule directly and not through representatives
     c. a government in which one person rules
     d. a government in which the noble class rules

_____ 4. Which Enlightenment thinker believed that all human beings had a right to life,
liberty, and property?
     a. Thomas Hobbes   c. John Locke
     b. Jean-Jacques Rousseau   d. Baron de Montesquieu

_____ 5. When did the Reformation begin?
     a. when William and Mary were crowned co-rulers and Parliament established
        limits on royal rule
     b. when Martin Luther began criticizing the Catholic Church's practice of
        selling pardons for sins
     c. when people began restoring old monuments and works of art and began
        believing in individualism
     d. when Parliament restored the monarch, Charles II, to the throne

_____ 6. What Hebrew code focused more on morality and ethics and less on politics?
     a. Roman law   c. Petition of Right
     b. divine right   d. Ten Commandments

_____ 7. What was the Magna Carta?
     a. the formal summary of the rights and liberties of the people
     b. the laws that reflected the customs and principles established over time
     c. the document signed by King John, guaranteeing certain English rights
     d. the assertion that the power of kings came from God

_____ 8. What form of government did England establish during the Glorious Revolution?
     a. constitutional monarchy   c. absolute monarchy
     b. direct democracy   d. feudalism

_____ 9. What tradition, developed in southwest Asia, helped to shape democratic rule?
        a. Roman law
        b. religious prophets
        c. emphasis on community
        d. monotheistic religion

_____ 10. Which war led to the creation of a short-lived republic whose leaders resorted to a
        Reign of Terror during a national crisis?
        a. the American Revolution   c. the English Civil War
        b. the French Revolution   d. the Seven Years' War

Part 2: Map Skills

Use the map to choose the best possible answer (4 points each)

The Greek World Before Alexander

_____ 11. What was Greece's largest island?
        a. Rhodes   c. Crete
        b. Marathon   d. Knossos

_____ 12. What sea separates Greece from Asia Minor?
        a. Mediterranean   c. Aegean
        b. Ionian   d. all of the above

_____ 13. Which is Greece's easternmost city?
        a. Byzantium   b. Pella   c. Troy   d. Athens

_____ 14. Troy lies near what narrow waterway that separates Europe from Asia Minor?
        a. Sea of Marmara   c. Ionian Sea
        b. Aegean Sea   d. Dardanelles

_____ 15. What is the largest area named on the map that was not part of the Greek World?
  a. Knossos   c. Byzantium
  b. Asia Minor   d. Crete

Part 3: Interpreting Charts

Use the chart to answer the following questions. (4 points each)

Forms of Government

Monarchy	Aristocracy
• State ruled by a king. • Rule is hereditary. • Some rulers claim divine right. • Form practiced in Mycenae (1450 B.C.).	• State ruled by nobility. • Rule is hereditary and based on land ownership. • Social status and wealth support rulers' authority. • Form practiced in Athens (594 B.C.).
Oligarchy	**Direct Democracy**
• State ruled by a small group of citizens. • Rule is based on wealth. • Ruling group controls the military. • Form practiced in Sparta (800-600 B.C.).	• State ruled by its citizens. • Rule is based on citizenship. • Majority vote decides rule. • Form practiced in Athens (461 B.C.).

_____ 16. In which form of government did social status play a role?
  a. monarchy   c. oligarchy
  b. aristocracy   d. direct democracy

_____ 17. What form of government was practiced in Sparta?
  a. monarchy   c. oligarchy
  b. aristocracy   d. direct democracy

_____ 18. Where was monarchy the form of government around 1450 B.C.?
  a. Athens   c. Sparta
  b. Mycenae   d. all of the above

_____ 19. Which form of government sometimes had a ruler who claimed divine right?
  a. monarchy
  b. aristocracy
  c. oligarchy
  d. direct democracy

_____ 20. Which form of government was ruled by citizens?
  a. monarchy
  b. aristocracy
  c. oligarchy
  d. direct democracy

Part 4: Extended Response

Answer the following questions on the back of this paper or on a separate sheet of paper.
(10 points each)

21. **Recognizing Effects** How did the Renaissance and the Reformation influence democracy
    and the shaping of the modern world?

    Think about:
    • role of the individual
    • questioning of power
    • emphasis on reading

22. **Drawing Conclusions** What two events in English history had a great impact on
    democracy in England? Which other areas of the world did these events also impact?

    Think about:
    • rights of the people
    • limits to power
    • democratic revolutions

PROLOGUE: THE RISE OF DEMOCRATIC IDEAS FORM B
The Rise of Democratic Ideas

Part 1: Main Ideas

If the statement is true, write "true" on the line. If the statement is false, change the underlined word or words to make it true. (4 points each)

Example: The first great Greek philosopher was <u>Plato</u>. _____ *Socrates* _____

1. Greek philosophers used reason and intelligence to discover predictable patterns that they called <u>common laws</u>. _____

2. The <u>Renaissance</u> was a cultural movement marked by renewed interest in classical culture. _____

3. The framers of the U.S. Constitution set up a <u>direct democracy</u> and created a federal system of government. _____

4. Rome adopted from the Greeks the idea that an individual is a <u>citizen</u> in a state rather than the subject of a ruler. _____

5. The <u>Petition of Right</u> limited the power of the monarchy and was a formal summary of the rights and liberties considered essential to the people. _____

6. The <u>Protestant and Anglican</u> beliefs about the worth of individuals and the responsibility of individuals had a strong impact on the development of democracy. _____

7. By the Middle Ages, the <u>Lutheran Church</u> influenced religious, social, and political aspects of life. _____

8. The <u>Magna Carta</u> was a contract between the king and the nobles of England, and it established basic legal rights for individuals. _____

9. Baron de Montesquieu concluded that liberty was safeguarded by a <u>separation of powers</u>, or the division of government into three separate branches. _____

10. A modern example of a struggle toward democracy was the breakup of <u>Eastern Europe</u> in the early 1990s. _____

Part 2: Map Skills

Use the map to choose the best possible answer. (4 points each)

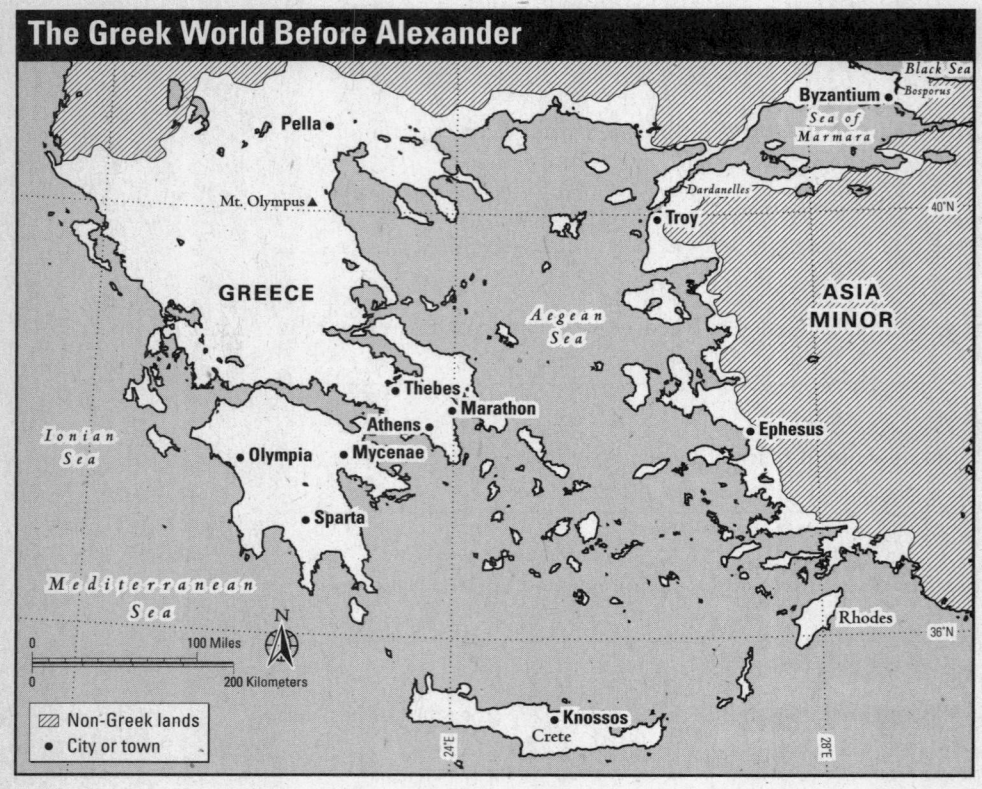

The Greek World Before Alexander

_____ 11. What are the longitude and latitude (to the nearest whole degree) of Olympia,
the site of the first Olympic Games?
a. 40°N 28°E
b. 38°N 22°E
c. 42°N 22°E
d. 38°N 24°E

_____ 12. The Mycenaeans traveled approximately how many miles to reach Knossos, Crete,
from Mycenae?
a. 95
b. 120
c. 175
d. 210

_____ 13. What narrow waterway was used to travel from Byzantium to Troy?
a. Black Sea
b. Bosporus
c. Dardanelles
d. Aegean Sea

_____ 14. What was the direct distance in miles between Sparta and Athens?
  a. 70
  b. 83
  c. 95
  d. 110

_____ 15. Judging from the map, what conclusion can you draw about the economy of ancient Greece?
  a. It probably relied heavily on fishing and trade.
  b. It probably relied on agriculture.
  c. It probably relied on its colonies.
  d. All of the above are true.

Part 3: Interpreting Charts

Write the letter of the best answer. (4 points each)

Forms of Government

Monarchy	Aristocracy
• State ruled by a king. • Rule is hereditary. • Some rulers claim divine right. • Form practiced in Mycenae (1450 B.C.).	• State ruled by nobility. • Rule is hereditary and based on land ownership. • Social status and wealth support rulers' authority. • Form practiced in Athens (594 B.C.).
Oligarchy	**Direct Democracy**
• State ruled by a small group of citizens. • Rule is based on wealth. • Ruling group controls the military. • Form practiced in Sparta (800-600 B.C.).	• State ruled by its citizens. • Rule is based on citizenship. • Majority vote decides rule. • Form practiced in Athens (461 B.C.).

_____ 16. In which forms of government was rule based at least partially on wealth?
  a. oligarchy and monarchy
  b. democracy and aristocracy
  c. aristocracy and oligarchy
  d. monarchy and aristocracy

_____ 17. In which forms of government did heredity play no role in the selection of rulers?
  a. monarchy and oligarchy
  b. aristocracy and monarchy
  c. oligarchy and aristocracy
  d. democracy and oligarchy

_____ 18. Which form of government does not involve rule by a group?
  a. monarchy
  b. aristocracy
  c. oligarchy
  d. democracy

_____ 19. How did government in Athens evolve?
    a. from a monarchy to an aristocracy
    b. from an aristocracy to a democracy
    c. from a city-state to an oligarchy
    d. from an oligarchy to a democracy

_____ 20. Which form of government was the earliest in this region?
    a. monarchy
    b. aristocracy
    c. oligarchy
    d. direct democracy

Part 4: Extended Response

Answer the following questions on the back of this paper or on a separate sheet of paper.
(10 points each)

21. **Drawing Conclusions** What led to the French Revolution, and why did the country end up as a dictatorship rather than a democracy?

Think about:
• debt and threat of increased taxes
• unfair representation
• fear of spreading ideas

22. **Making Inferences** What was the Magna Carta, and how was it the first step in a democratic form of government in England?

Think about:
• individual rights
• limits of power
• rule by law

PROLOGUE: THE RISE
OF DEMOCRATIC IDEAS
FORM C

The Rise of Democratic Ideas

Part 1: Main Ideas

Write the letter of the best answer. (4 points each)

_____ 1. How did Pericles' decisions to increase the number of paid public officials and to
pay jurors affect democracy in Greece?
   a. It allowed poorer citizens to participate in government.
   b. It gave more power to the aristocracy.
   c. It allowed even the lowest class of citizens to vote in the assembly.
   d. It gave the lower class of citizens the power to set up the Senate.

_____ 2. How did the Hebrew code of justice differ from other law codes of the time?
   a. The Hebrew code was strict and oppressive.
   b. The Hebrew code focused more on morality and ethics.
   c. The Hebrew code focused only on politics and economic issues.
   d. The Hebrew code did not focus on the individual.

_____ 3. What was the long-term effect of Henry II's development of the jury trial?
   a. All English-speaking countries used juries in their legal systems.
   b. England was unified under common law.
   c. Judges were no longer necessary since people were tried by their peers.
   d. Court was held only once a year.

_____ 4. What was Rome's influence on government and democracy?
   a. Rome gave the world the idea of a republic.
   b. Rome adopted the idea that individuals were citizens not subjects.
   c. Rome left its written legal code and the idea of equal and impartial justice.
   d. All of the above are true.

_____ 5. What was the significance of England's Bill of Rights?
   a. It returned the power to the monarchy and the Catholic Church.
   b. It ensured that England would forever be ruled by Protestants.
   c. It limited the power of the monarch and guaranteed rights of the people.
   d. It gave all of the power to Parliament and reduced the need for a monarch.

_____ 6. What did John Locke consider to be people's natural rights, and how did he say
these rights should be protected?
   a. the right to be selfish and ambitious; protected by a social contract
   b. the right to life, liberty, and property; protected by forming governments
   c. the right to overthrow a government; protected by a constitution
   d. the right to freedoms of religion and speech; protected by a republic

_____ 7. How did the U.S. Constitution set up a strong but not tyrannical government?
   a. They set up a representative government, created a federal system, and
      balanced the powers.
   b. They set up a direct democracy in which all citizens could vote.
   c. They set up a union of states that limited the federal government.
   d. They set up a social contract in which people agreed to be ruled in order
      to prevent disorder.

_____ 8. How was the French Revolution an example of why democracies sometimes fail?
  a. The new assembly was not accepted, so the people revolted again.
  b. France did not tolerate new ideas, so the revolution didn't last.
  c. The people of France were too diverse to agree on a government.
  d. Equality was a promise made but not backed up by practice.

_____ 9. How did the Reformation and the Renaissance influence the modern world?
  a. They placed an emphasis on the importance of the individual.
  b. They taught that people should not question God or authorities.
  c. They supported the theory of the divine right of kings.
  d. All of the above are true.

_____ 10. How was South Africa a modern example of a struggle for democracy?
  a. It broke up into 15 republics that asserted separate national identities.
  b. Apartheid was abolished, and an all–race election was held.
  c. It created the Universal Declaration of Human Rights.
  d. It created the General Assembly and gave each city equal representation.

Part 2: Map Skills—Constructed Response

Answer the following questions on the lines provided. (4 points each)

11. What is the approximate direct distance in miles between Athens and Troy?

_____

12. Geographically what military advantage did Sparta have that Athens did not?

_____

13. What was the economic advantage of Greece's geographic location?

_____

14. What does the location of Greek cities suggest about inland Greece?

_____

15. What were the advantages of Troy's location?

_____

Part 3: Interpreting Charts

Write the letter of the best answer. (4 points each)

Forms of Government	
Monarchy	**Aristocracy**
• State ruled by a king. • Rule is hereditary. • Some rulers claim divine right. • Form practiced in Mycenae (1450 B.C.).	• State ruled by nobility. • Rule is hereditary and based on land ownership. • Social status and wealth support rulers' authority. • Form practiced in Athens (594 B.C.).
Oligarchy	**Direct Democracy**
• State ruled by a small group of citizens. • Rule is based on wealth. • Ruling group controls the military. • Form practiced in Sparta (800-600 B.C.).	• State ruled by its citizens. • Rule is based on citizenship. • Majority vote decides rule. • Form practiced in Athens (461 B.C.).

_____ 16. In which form of government was rule sometimes justified by religion?
        a. monarchy   c. oligarchy
        b. aristocracy   d. direct democracy

_____ 17. Why is the government during the Age of Pericles referred to as a "direct democracy"?
        a. A group of directors governed by majority rule.
        b. Citizens ruled directly; they did not elect representatives.
        c. Those who could not vote—women, enslaved persons, and foreigners—experienced "indirect" democracy.
        d. Citizens in a democracy had sufficient means to meet their needs in a "direct" way.

_____ 18. How do you know that Sparta's rulers would be hard to overthrow?
        a. As long as they didn't lose their wealth, they were safe.
        b. Their rulers claimed divine right.
        c. They had control of the military.
        d. The rulers took oaths to protect each other.

_____ 19. In which city-state was power most widely shared?
        a. Mycenea (1450 B.C.)
        b. Sparta (800 B.C.)
        c. Athens (594 B.C.)
        d. Athens (461 B.C.)

_____ 20. Which of the following did Athenians do to transform an aristocracy into a direct democracy?
        a. eliminate the military
        b. offer citizenship to all people living in Athens
        c. break up the power of the rich nobility
        d. give up the claim to divine right

Part 4: Extended Response

Answer the following questions on the back of this paper or on a separate sheet of paper.
(10 points each)

21. **Recognizing Effects** How did the Enlightenment thinkers influence the American colonies and the framers of America's eventual government?

22. **Synthesizing** How did England's Glorious Revolution and Bill of Rights help give rise to the American and French Revolutions nearly 100 years later?

SECTION QUIZ *Italy: Birthplace of the Renaissance*

Section 1

A. Terms and Names Write the letter of the best answer.

_____ 1. The period of European history known as the Renaissance roughly covers the time from
      a. 1100 to 1400.
      b. 1200 to 1500.
      c. 1300 to 1600.
      d. 1400 to 1700.

_____ 2. The best synonym for *secular* is
      a. *new.*
      b. *worldly.*
      c. *humane.*
      d. *religious.*

_____ 3. To become known as an important patron, one most needed to be
      a. wealthy.
      b. creative.
      c. religious.
      d. intellectual.

_____ 4. The technique known as perspective is most useful in the creation of
      a. drama.
      b. sculpture.
      c. two-dimensional art.
      d. the sonnet form in poetry.

_____ 5. A person who produces work "in the vernacular" is one who
      a. relies on realism.
      b. uses only natural light.
      c. uses a verse form of writing.
      d. writes in a local, rather than a classical, language.

_____ 6. The intellectual and cultural movement known as humanism arose from the study of
      a. medieval scholarship.
      b. original Christian writings.
      c. classical Greek and Roman culture.
      d. the contributions of the Tang and Song dynasties.

B. Extended Response Briefly answer the following question on the back of this paper.

What do you think were the major causes of the European Renaissance? Explain your answer.

CHAPTER 1

SECTION QUIZ *The Northern Renaissance*

Section 2

A. Terms and Names Write the letter of the best answer.

_____ 1. Renaissance painters in Flanders, as in Italy, tended to produce work that was
      a. realistic.
      b. idealistic.
      c. distorted.
      d. formal and tightly structured.

_____ 2. In Greek, the word *utopia* means
      a. "highest."
      b. "no place."
      c. "everywhere."
      d. "an ideal place."

_____ 3. The first use of movable type was in
      a. Greece.
      b. Germany.
      c. Italy.
      d. China.

_____ 4. The printing press was invented by
      a. Jan van Eyck.
      b. Johann Gutenberg.
      c. Peter Bruegel the Elder.
      d. Hans Holbein the Younger.

_____ 5. Which of the following correctly matches the author with something he or
she wrote?
      a. Thomas More and *Utopia*
      b. Christine de Pizan and *Hamlet*
      c. William Shakespeare and *The Praise of Folly*
      d. Desiderius Erasmus and *Gargantua and Pantagruel*

_____ 6. Which of the following did Desiderius Erasmus and Thomas More have in
common?
      a. Both were French.
      b. Both wrote only in English.
      c. Both were considered humanists.
      d. Both rejected religion and the Bible.

B. Extended Response Briefly answer the following question on the back of this paper.

What was one important and lasting result of the invention of the printing press?
Explain why it came about.

Name _____ Date _____

SECTION QUIZ *Luther Leads the Reformation*

CHAPTER 1

Section 3

A. Terms and Names Write the letter of the term or name that best answers the question.
A term or name may be used more than once or not at all.

a. Lutheran   f. Pope Leo X   k. Anne Boleyn
b. Protestant   g. Emperor Charles V   l. Elizabeth I
c. Anglican   h. Catherine of Aragon   m. annul
d. Edict of Worms   i. Peace of Augsburg   n. recant
e. indulgence   j. Act of Supremacy   o. Edward VI

_____ 1. Who was the last of Henry VIII's children to rule England?

_____ 2. Which official measure made the king, instead of the pope, the head of the
English Church?

_____ 3. Who was the wife of a king of England, the mother of a queen of England, and
the aunt of an emperor of the Holy Roman Empire?

_____ 4. Whom did Henry VIII want to marry badly enough to prompt his break with
the Roman Catholic Church and the pope?

_____ 5. Which term originally referred to a German prince who was not loyal to the
pope?

_____ 6. Which term means "to take back a statement"?

_____ 7. Who was the first of Henry VIII's children to rule England?

_____ 8. Which official measure made it a crime to give Martin Luther food or shelter?

_____ 9. Which term refers to a pardon that releases a sinner from a penalty for
committing a sin?

_____ 10. Who was beheaded after being unable to produce a male heir for Henry VIII?

_____ 11. Which term means "to set aside"?

_____ 12. Who ruled England beginning in 1558?

B. Extended Response Briefly answer the following question on the back of this paper.

Why do you think some of the German princes supported the pope while others
supported Luther's ideas?

CHAPTER
1

Section 4

SECTION QUIZ *The Reformation Continues*

A. Terms and Names Write the letter of the best answer.

_____ 1. The followers of John Knox became known as
  a. Amish.
  b. Quakers.
  c. Lutherans.
  d. Presbyterians.

_____ 2. Predestination was one of the main doctrines of
  a. theocracy.
  b. Calvinism.
  c. Lutheranism.
  d. the Catholic Reformation.

_____ 3. The founder of the religious order known as the Jesuits was
  a. Matthew Zell.
  b. St. Bartholomew.
  c. Ignatius of Loyola.
  d. Marguerite of Navarre.

_____ 4. The education of children and missionaries was the principal goal of
  a. the Jesuits.
  b. the Huguenots.
  c. the Anabaptists.
  d. the Presbyterians.

_____ 5. The Council of Trent agreed that
  a. Christians need only faith for salvation.
  b. the Church's interpretation of the Bible is final.
  c. priests cannot pardon sinners for committing sins.
  d. the Bible is the only authority for guiding Christian life.

_____ 6. Only the baptism of adults was valid to the
  a. Jesuits.
  b. Anglicans.
  c. Calvinists.
  d. Anabaptists.

B. Extended Response Briefly answer the following question on the back of this paper.

Although Calvinism was severely restrictive, many people admired the way of life in Geneva, where it controlled the society. Why do you think this was so?

CHAPTER **1**

CHAPTER TEST *European Renaissance and Reformation*

Form A

Part 1: Main Ideas

Write the letter of the best answer. (4 points each)

_____ 1. What was the Renaissance a rebirth of?
a. Christian devotion
b. art and learning
c. chivalry and tournaments
d. good health after the plague

_____ 2. The study of classical texts caused humanists to focus on what subject?
a. human potential and achievements
b. an understanding of early Christianity
c. an understanding of ancient Muslim values
d. Roman law and government

_____ 3. For what is the Medici family famous?
a. for being artists
b. for being writers
c. for being rulers and supporters of the arts
d. for being religious reformers

_____ 4. What were Desiderius Erasmus and Thomas More?
a. German painters
b. Flemish painters
c. patrons of the arts
d. Christian humanists

_____ 5. What was the first full-sized book Gutenberg printed?
a. *Utopia*
b. *Romeo and Juliet*
c. the Bible
d. *The Prince*

_____ 6. In what way did Leonardo da Vinci represent the Renaissance Man?
a. He was a painter, sculptor, inventor, and scientist.
b. He painted the *Mona Lisa* while holding scientific discussions.
c. He lived in Italy during the 1500s.
d. He used perspective in all of his drawings and paintings.

_____ 7. Luther protested the practice of selling indulgences. What was that practice?
a. Clergy members bought indulgences to reach higher offices.
b. The clergy sold pardons that released people from performing penalties for their sins.
c. Charles V told his people that buying indulgences was a way to earn a way to heaven.
d. Indulgences permitted priests to marry and have children.

_____ 8. Who declared himself the head of the English Church?
a. Henry VIII
b. John Knox
c. Martin Luther
d. Emperor Charles V

_____ 9. What was one of John Calvin's major teachings?

   a. humanism   c. indulgences

   b. adult baptism   d. predestination

_____ 10. Who was the important Catholic Reformer who founded the Jesuit order?

   a. Katarina Zell   c. Ignatius of Loyola

   b. Girolamo Savonarola   d. Pope Paul III

Part 2: Map Skills

Use the map to choose the best possible answer. (4 points each)

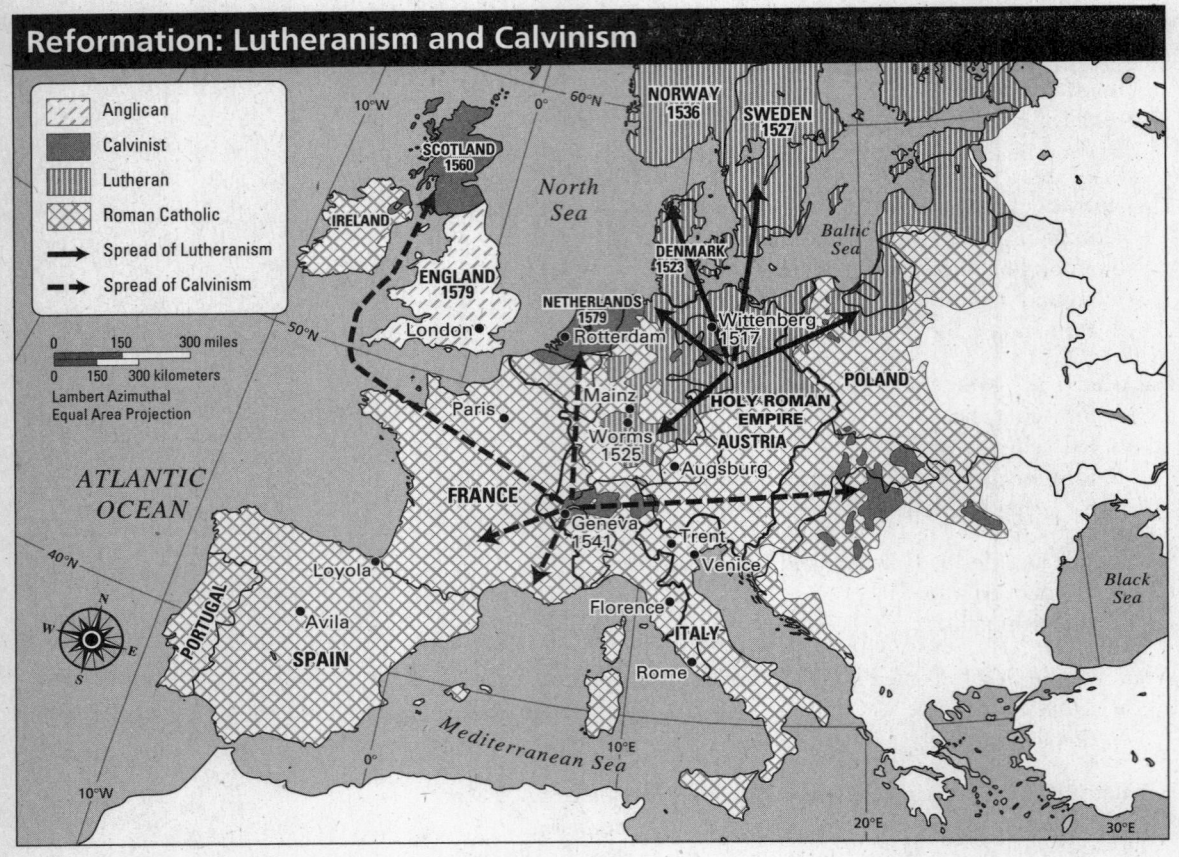

Reformation: Lutheranism and Calvinism

_____ 11. Which cities were the centers of Calvinism and Lutheranism?

   a. Rotterdam and London

   b. Geneva and Wittenberg

   c. Wittenberg and Rotterdam

   d. Worms and Geneva

_____ 12. In which two countries was Calvinism the dominant religion?

   a. England and Ireland

   b. France and Poland

   c. Scotland and the Netherlands

   d. Sweden and Norway

_____ 13. Between 1500 and 1600, which religion was dominant in the greatest number
of countries?
a. Anglican   c. Lutheran
b. Calvinist   d. Roman Catholic

_____ 14. In what year did Denmark adopt Lutheranism as its chief religion?
a. 1517   b. 1523   c. 1527   d. 1579

_____ 15. Around which body of water did the Lutherans dominate?
a. Mediterranean Sea   c. Baltic Sea
b. Black Sea   d. North Sea

Part 3: Document-Based Questions
Introduction

Historical Context During the Renaissance, scholars and artists began to seek other sources
of inspiration beyond the Catholic faith. Many studied the classical past and adopted a
humanistic outlook–focusing on the potential and the achievements of human beings. The
Renaissance ideal became a person who used his or her potential to excel in many areas, either
as a "Renaissance man" or a strong ruler. In addition, art changed, becoming more realistic
than the art of the Middle Ages. This was also due to the influence of classical models.

Task: Discuss the view of human beings that developed during the Renaissance.

A. Short Answer

Study each document carefully and answer the questions that follow. (4 points each)

Document 1: Excerpt from *The Prince* by Niccolò Machiavelli, translated by Daniel Donno

Here a question arises [for a prince, or ruler]: whether it is better to be loved than feared,
or the reverse. The answer is, of course, that it would be best to be both loved and feared.
But since the two rarely come together, anyone compelled to choose will find greater
security in being feared than loved. . . . Men are less concerned about offending someone
they have cause to love than someone they have cause to fear. Love endures by a bond
which men, being scoundrels, may break whenever it serves their advantage to do so;
but fear is supported by the dread of pain, which is ever present. . . . Returning to the
question, then, of being loved or feared, I conclude that since men love as they themselves
determine but fear as their ruler determines, a wise prince must rely upon what he and not
others can control.

16. According to Machiavelli, what is the best answer to whether it is better for a prince
to be loved or feared?

_____

Document 2: Excerpt from a letter to Sigismund of Austria by Aeneas Silvius (Pius II) *Selected Letters of Aeneas Silvius Piccolomini,* **translated by Charles S. Singleton**

Nothing can help you in guiding your life more than the study of literature. . . . Yet it is my understanding that you have thrown off your studies like some yoke which obliges me to try to induce you to take them up again. . . . We ought to study literature because it offers us models of behavior after which we can pattern out lives; knowing these will be helpful. And one must know literature deeply, not superficially, if real progress is to be made. Contemporary rulers are happy with a smattering of knowledge and leave detailed study to philosophers and jurisconsultants, just as if it were less important for them to know the principles of a good life. I entreat you not to fall into this pattern of thinking which will block your developing into a good man and a famous ruler.

17. What is the main idea Aeneas Silvius wants Sigismund to understand?

_____

Document 3: Two drawings by Leonardo da Vinci: *Study of Hands*

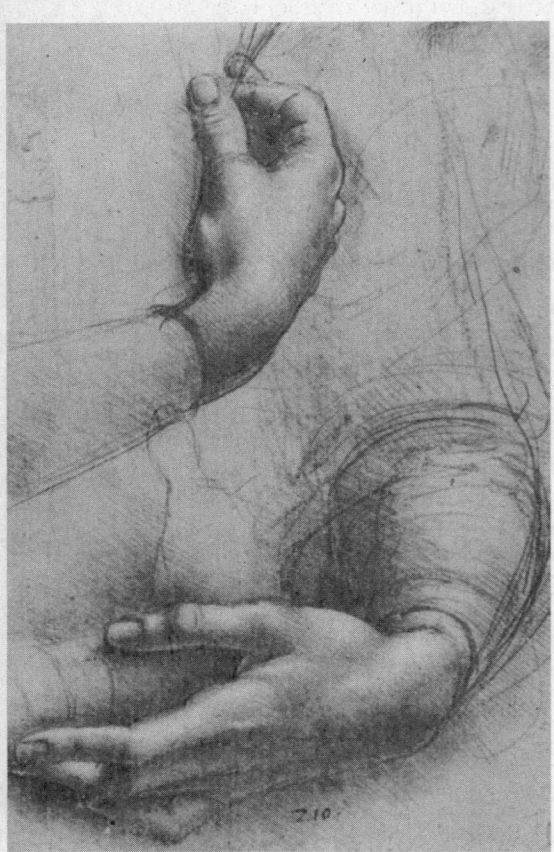

Source: *Study of Hands* (c. 1485), Leonardo da Vinci. Silverpoint, 21.6 cm x 15.2 cm. Royal Library (RL 12558), Windsor Castle. The Royal Collection © 2002, Her Majesty Queen Elizabeth II

18. How are Leonardo da Vinci's drawings an expression of humanistic ideals?

_____

B. Essay

19. Using information from the documents, your answers to the questions in Part A, and your knowledge of world history, write an essay on your own paper that discusses how Renaissance thinkers and artists viewed human beings. (8 points)

Part 4: Extended Response

Answer the following questions on the back of this paper or on a separate sheet. (10 points each)

20. **Recognizing Efffects** What were the effects of Gutenberg's printing press?

Think about:
- the effect on culture and society
- the effect on language
- the effect on learning

21. **Analyzing Issues** What were Luther's chief objections to the Roman Catholic Church?

Think about:
- his objections to Church practices
- his objections to Church teaching
- his objections to Church leaders

CHAPTER
1
Form B

CHAPTER TEST *European Renaissance and*
Reformation

Part 1: Main Ideas

If the statement is true, write "true" on the line. If it is false, change the underlined word or
words to make it true. (4 points each)

Example: In 1559, the Anglican Church became the official church of <u>France.</u>
_____ *England* _____

1. *Utopia*, the title of a book by Thomas More, has come to mean an ideal place._____
_____

2. The Renaissance in northern Europe lagged behind the Renaissance in Italy because of the
<u>printing press.</u> _____

3. When <u>Jerusalem</u> fell to the Ottoman Turks in 1453, scholars fled to Rome with ancient
Greek manuscripts. _____

4. The Act of Supremacy was passed during the reign of <u>Henry VIII.</u> _____

5. During the Renaissance, artists were often supported by wealthy people known as
<u>humanists.</u> _____

6. Gutenberg's invention of <u>the vernacular</u> made possible the quick spread of ideas._____
_____

7. To set aside a marriage as having not been legal is to <u>recant</u> the marriage. _____
_____

8. The name *Anabaptist* is from the Greek for <u>baptize again.</u> _____
_____

9. In England, the king was declared to be the head of the <u>Lutheran Church</u> . _____

_____

10. The term Protestant comes from the name given some <u>German princes</u> who protested

against joining forces with the pope against Luther's ideas. _____

_____

Part 2: Map Skills
Use the map to choose the best possible answer. (4 points each)

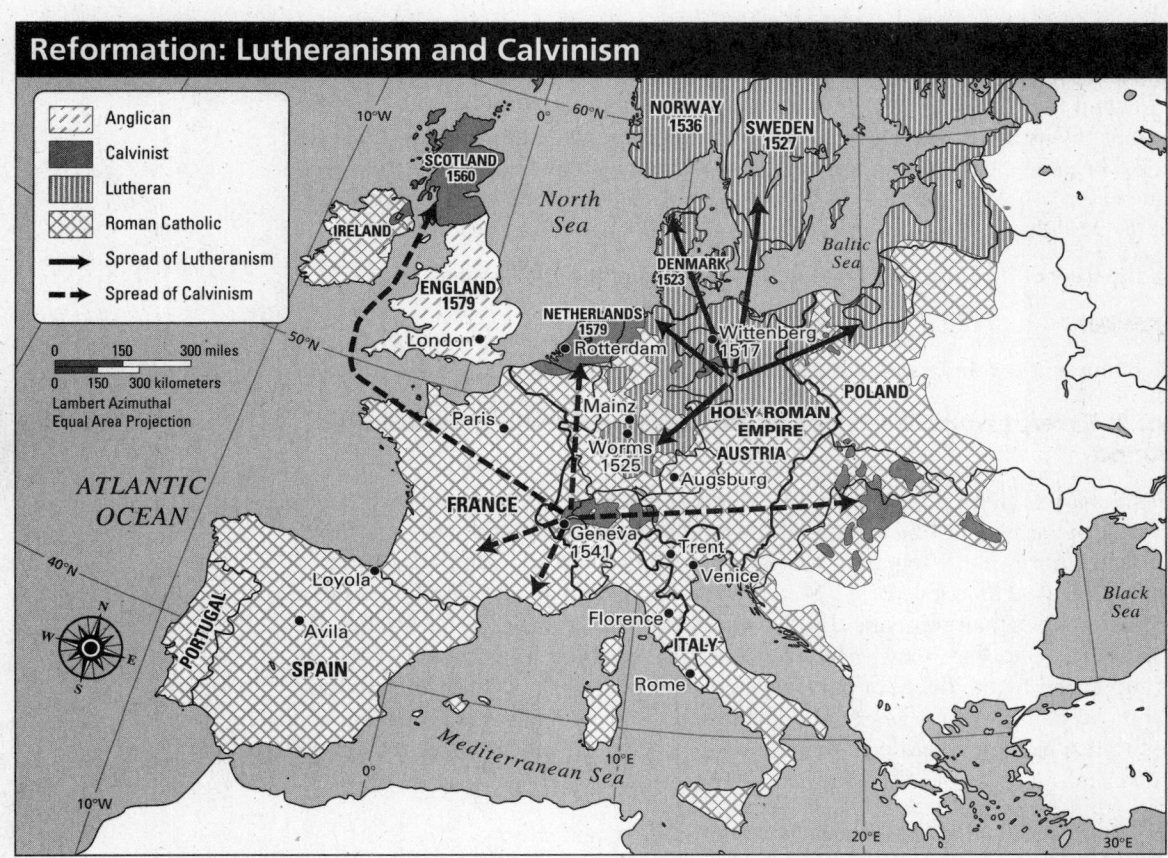

_____ 11. In which state were three different religions practiced?
      a. France   c. Netherlands
      b. Holy Roman Empire   d. Italy

_____ 12. What was the northernmost country where Calvinism spread?
      a. Norway   c. Scotland
      b. Netherlands   d. Poland

_____ 13. During what time period did Lutheranism win the most followers?
      a. 1517–1536   c. 1559
      b. 1541–1579   d. 1527–1536

_____ 14. Judging from this map, how many miles east of Geneva did Calvinism spread?

       a. 350   b. 500   c. 900   d. 1050

_____ 15. What geographic pattern can you observe from the way Catholicism and the Protestant faiths were distributed?

       a. Lutheranism was more widely distributed than Catholicism.

       b. The lands closest to Rome, center of the Catholic Church, remained mostly Catholic.

       c. People who lived in harsh northern lands were drawn to strict Calvinism.

       d. Eastern Europe remained completely Catholic because reformers did not cross the mountains.

Part 3: Document-Based Questions

Introduction

Historical Context During the Renaissance, scholars and artists began to seek other sources of inspiration beyond the Catholic faith. Many studied the classical past and adopted a humanistic outlook–focusing on the potential and the achievements of human beings. The Renaissance ideal became a person who used his or her potential to excel in many areas, either as a "Renaissance man" or a strong ruler. In addition, art changed, becoming more realistic than the art of the Middle Ages. This was also due to the influence of classical models.

Task: Discuss the view of human beings that developed during the Renaissance.

A. Short Answer

Study each document carefully and answer the questions that follow. (4 points each)

Document 1: Excerpt from *The Prince* by Niccolò Machiavelli, translated by Daniel Donno

Here a question arises [for a prince, or ruler]: whether it is better to be loved than feared, or the reverse. The answer is, of course, that it would be best to be both loved and feared. But since the two rarely come together, anyone compelled to choose will find greater security in being feared than loved. . . . Men are less concerned about offending someone they have cause to love than someone they have cause to fear. Love endures by a bond which men, being scoundrels, may break whenever it serves their advantage to do so; but fear is supported by the dread of pain, which is ever present. . . . Returning to the question, then, of being loved or feared, I conclude that since men love as they themselves determine but fear as their ruler determines, a wise prince must rely upon what he and not others can control.

16. What recommendation does Machiavelli make to rulers, and why?

_____

Document 2: Excerpt from a letter to Sigismund of Austria by Aeneas Silvius (Pius II) *Selected Letters of Aeneas Silvius Piccolomini,* **translated by Charles S. Singleton**

Nothing can help you in guiding your life more than the study of literature. . . . Yet it is my understanding that you have thrown off your studies like some yoke which obliges me to try to induce you to take them up again. . . . We ought to study literature because it offers us models of behavior after which we can pattern out lives; knowing these will be helpful. And one must know literature deeply, not superficially, if real progress is to be made. Contemporary rulers are happy with a smattering of knowledge and leave detailed study to philosophers and jurisconsultants, just as if it were less important for them to know the principles of a good life. I entreat you not to fall into this pattern of thinking which will block your developing into a good man and a famous ruler.

17. Why does Aeneas Silvius recommend studying literature?

Document 3: Two drawings by Leonardo da Vinci: *Study of Hands*

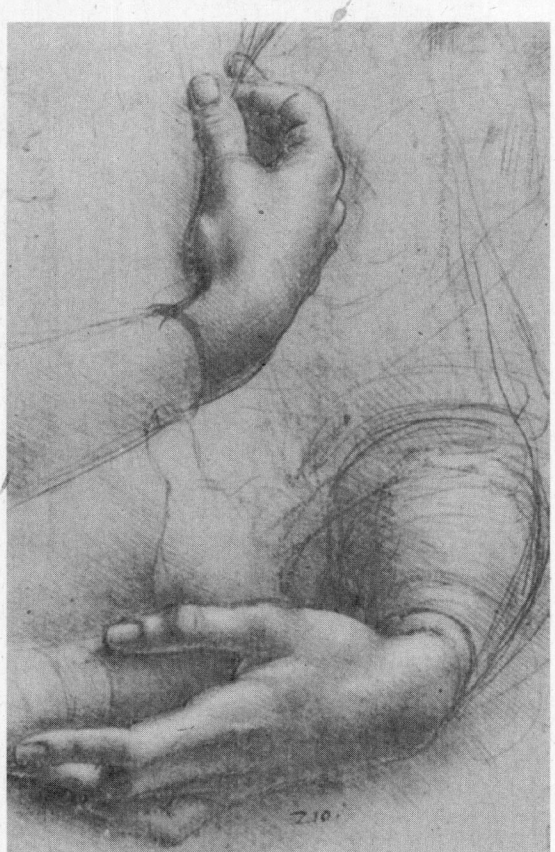

Source: *Study of Hands* (c. 1485), Leonardo da Vinci. Silverpoint, 21.6 cm x 15.2 cm. Royal Library (RL 12558), Windsor Castle. The Royal Collection © 2002, Her Majesty Queen Elizabeth II

18. What Renaissance values do you think motivated Leonardo to make this drawing?

B. Essay

19. Using information from the documents, your answers to the questions in Part A, and your knowledge of world history, write an essay on your own paper that discusses how Renaissance thinkers and artists viewed human beings. (8 points)

Part 4: Extended Response

Answer the following questions on the back of this paper or on a separate sheet. (10 points each)

20. **Drawing Conclusions** Based on what you learned in this chapter, what are three words or phrases you would use to describe Martin Luther? Defend each choice in a paragraph.

   Think about:
   • what he thought
   • what he did
   • how other people reacted to him and his views

21. **Contrasting** How was the shift from medieval to Renaissance values reflected in the art and learning of the two periods?

   Think about:
   • focus of interest
   • painting, architecture, sculpture, literature

CHAPTER TEST *European Renaissance and Reformation*

Form C

Part 1: Main Ideas
Write the letter of the best answer. (4 points each)

_____ 1. What kind of person represented the ideal of the "Renaissance man"?
    a. someone who enjoyed worldly pleasures
    b. someone who excelled in many areas of study
    c. someone who specialized in a particular field of study
    d. someone who supported and appreciated the arts without creating art

_____ 2. How did Italy's location help it become the birthplace of the Renaissance?
    a. Ideas could be spread easily by means of Italy's fleet.
    b. Italy was protected from the rest of Europe by the Alps.
    c. Italy had access to Roman ruins and ancient manuscripts from Constantinople.
    d. The bubonic plague had not reached the southern tip of Europe.

_____ 3. What was an important effect of the invention of the printing press?
    a. Gutenberg used his wealth from the invention to support artists.
    b. It led to the development of public libraries.
    c. It led to a renewed study of Latin and Greek.
    d. It increased literacy and the use of the vernacular.

_____ 4. Why was block printing more useful in Europe than in China?
    a. Chinese paper was difficult to print on.
    b. The Chinese had invented movable type but not the printing press.
    c. European languages had a smaller number of characters than Chinese.
    d. All of the above are true.

_____ 5. Which of the following was a major reason for the Reformation?
    a. Northern merchants resented paying taxes to the Church in Rome.
    b. The Church was threatening to excommunicate the king of France.
    c. The pope in Rome insisted on speaking only Latin.
    d. Martin Luther said he could interpret the Bible better than the pope.

_____ 6. Which of the following was one of Luther's main beliefs?
    a. Men and women are naturally sinful.
    b. Christians needed to be baptized again as adults.
    c. Good works were required for salvation.
    d. All people with faith were equal.

_____ 7. What was the main reason for Henry VIII's split with the Roman Catholic Church?
    a. his religious beliefs
    b. his desire for a male heir
    c. his treatment of Catherine of Aragon
    d. his unwillingness to pay Church taxes

_____ 8. Which of the following was agreed upon at the Council of Trent?
       a. The Church's interpretation of the Bible was final.
       b. Selling indulgences was an appropriate practice.
       c. Local priests had to originate the process of excommunication.
       d. Church and state should be separate.

_____ 9. The Peace of Augsburg ended a war between supporters of which two groups?
       a. England and Spain
       b. Catholic and Protestant German princes
       c. Roman Catholics and Anglicans
       d. French Catholics and Huguenots

_____ 10. Which idea of Luther's most influenced John Calvin?
       a. Humans cannot earn a place in heaven.
       b. There was no hierarchy of believers.
       c. The Church should not sell indulgences.
       d. People did not need priests to interpret the Bible for them.

Part 2: Map Skills

Using the map, answer the questions on the lines provided. (4 points each)

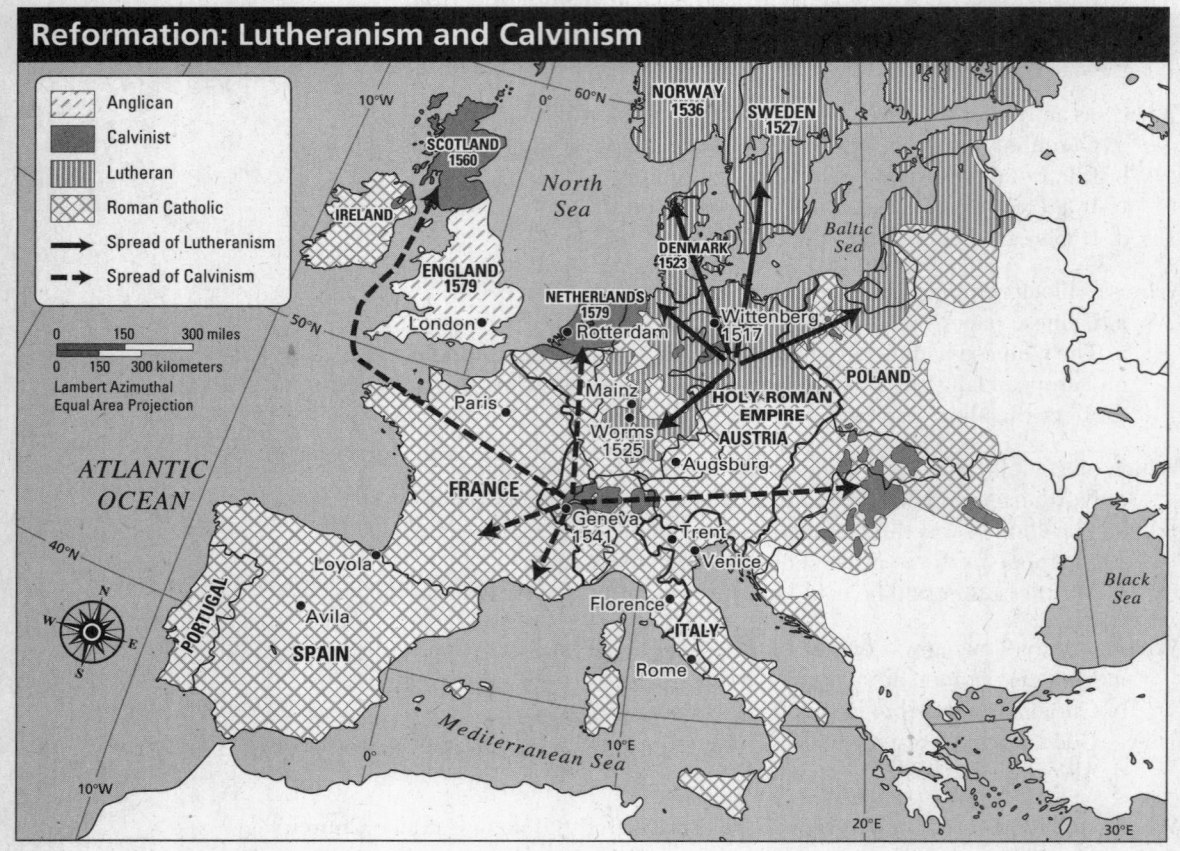

11. During what period of time did Calvinism attract the most followers?

_____

12. Judging from the map, about how many miles north did Calvinism spread from Geneva?

_____

13. Judging from the map, why might Ireland have problems in the future?

_____

14. How did distance from Rome affect a region's chances of becoming Protestant? Why might that be?

_____

15. Which of the three Protestant faiths shown here spread the least? Why might that be?

_____

Part 3: Document-Based Questions
Introduction

Historical Context During the Renaissance, scholars and artists began to seek other sources of inspiration beyond the Catholic faith. Many studied the classical past and adopted a humanistic outlook—focusing on the potential and the achievements of human beings. The Renaissance ideal became a person who used his or her potential to excel in many areas, either as a "Renaissance man" or a strong ruler. In addition, art changed, becoming more realistic than the art of the Middle Ages. This was also due to the influence of classical models.

Task: Discuss the view of human beings that developed during the Renaissance.

A. Short Answer

Study each document carefully and answer the questions that follow. (4 points each)

Document 1: Excerpt from *The Prince* by Niccolò Machiavelli, translated by Daniel Donno

Here a question arises [for a prince, or ruler]: whether it is better to be loved than feared, or the reverse. The answer is, of course, that it would be best to be both loved and feared. But since the two rarely come together, anyone compelled to choose will find greater security in being feared than loved. . . . Men are less concerned about offending someone they have cause to love than someone they have cause to fear. Love endures by a bond which men, being scoundrels, may break whenever it serves their advantage to do so; but fear is supported by the dread of pain, which is ever present. . . . Returning to the question, then, of being loved or feared, I conclude that since men love as they themselves determine but fear as their ruler determines, a wise prince must rely upon what he and not others can control.

16. How would you describe Machiavelli's view of human beings?

_____

Document 2: Excerpt from a letter to Sigismund of Austria by Aeneas Silvius (Pius II) *Selected Letters of Aeneas Silvius Piccolomini,* **translated by Charles S. Singleton**

Nothing can help you in guiding your life more than the study of literature. . . . Yet it is my understanding that you have thrown off your studies like some yoke which obliges me to try to induce you to take them up again. . . . We ought to study literature because it offers us models of behavior after which we can pattern out lives; knowing these will be helpful. And one must know literature deeply, not superficially, if real progress is to be made. Contemporary rulers are happy with a smattering of knowledge and leave detailed study to philosophers and jurisconsultants, just as if it were less important for them to know the principles of a good life. I entreat you not to fall into this pattern of thinking which will block your developing into a good man and a famous ruler.

17. What does Aeneas Silvius's statement imply about his view of human nature?

Document 3: Two drawings by Leonardo da Vinci: *Study of Hands*

Source: *Study of Hands* (c. 1485), Leonardo da Vinci. Silverpoint, 21.6 cm x 15.2 cm. Royal Library (RL 12558), Windsor Castle. The Royal Collection © 2002, Her Majesty Queen Elizabeth II

18. Judging from these drawings, how do you think Leonardo viewed human beings?

B. Essay

19. Using information from the documents, your answers to the questions in Part A, and your knowledge of world history, write an essay on your own paper that discusses how Renaissance thinkers and artists viewed human beings. (8 points)

Part 4: Extended Response

Answer the following questions on the back of this paper or on a separate sheet. (10 points each)

20. **Drawing Conclusions** Which authority figures lost the most as a result of the Protestant Reformation? Which ones gained the most from it? Explain your answers.

21. **Synthesizing** Which aspects of the Renaissance contributed to the environment that made the Reformation possible?

CHAPTER 2

Section 1

SECTION QUIZ   *The Ottomans Build a Vast Empire*

A. Terms and Names Write the letter of the person who matches the description. A person may be used more than once.

a. Timur
b. Osman
c. Mehmed II
d. Suleyman I
e. Selim the Grim

_____ 1. The Ottoman Empire reached its peak size and grandeur during his reign.

_____ 2. In the West, he was called Othman, and his followers were known as Ottomans.

_____ 3. He was known both as "the Lawgiver" and as "the Magnificent."

_____ 4. He earned the title "the Conqueror" by leading the Ottomans in conquering Constantinople.

_____ 5. He was a warrior who became an able ruler. He turned the Hagia Sophia into a mosque and changed the name of Constantinople to Istanbul.

_____ 6. In the 15th century, this warrior and conqueror from Samarkand in Central Asia briefly interrupted the rise of the Ottoman Empire.

_____ 7. He conquered Russia, Persia, and northern India. He died on his way to conquer China.

_____ 8. He captured Mecca and Medina, the holiest cities of Islam, and Cairo, the intellectual center of the Muslim world. He also expanded the Ottoman Empire into Syria, Palestine, and North Africa.

_____ 9. As the first Ottoman leader, he built a small state in Anatolia that his successors would expand. He died not realizing that his conquests marked the birth of one of history's largest and longest-lived empires.

_____ 10. As a military leader, he expanded the Ottoman Empire into Central Europe, North Africa, and Central Asia. As a political leader, he streamlined the government bureaucracy, simplified the system of taxation, and revamped the laws of the empire.

B. Extended Response Briefly answer the following question on the back of this paper.

Compare the ghazi with the janissary, and the role that each played in the Ottoman Empire. Which was part of the *devshirme* system?

CHAPTER
2

Section 2

SECTION QUIZ   *Cultural Blending* CASE STUDY: *The Safavid Empire*

A. Terms and Names Write the letter of the best answer.

_____ 1. All of the following contributed to the cultural blending that created Ottoman culture EXCEPT
        a. trade.
        b. conquest.
        c. migration.
        d. the pursuit of religious converts.

_____ 2. Originally, the Safavids were members of
        a. the janissary forces.
        b. the Ottoman Dynasty.
        c. a powerful Turkish family.
        d. an Islamic religious brotherhood.

_____ 3. Isma'il was all of the following EXCEPT
        a. a shah.
        b. a Safavid.
        c. a Shi'i Muslim.
        d. an Anatolian Turk.

_____ 4. Isma'il conquered most of what is now
        a. Iran.
        b. Iraq.
        c. Egypt.
        d. Turkey.

_____ 5. The person who rebuilt Esfahan was
        a. Isma'il.
        b. Suleyman.
        c. Shah Abbas.
        d. Nadir Shah Afshar.

_____ 6. The group that provided the model on which the Safavids based their government was
        a. the Uzbek.
        b. the Chinese.
        c. the Ottomans.
        d. the "redheads."

B. Extended Response Briefly answer the following question on the back of this paper.

What did Shah Abbas do to bring on a golden age for the Safavid Empire?

SECTION QUIZ *The Mughals Empire in India*

A. Terms and Names
Write the letter of the term or name that matches the description. Not all terms will be used.

a. Sikhs
b. Babur
c. Akbar
d. Hindus
e. Jahangir
f. Mughals
g. Muslims
h. Nur Jahan
i. Aurangzeb
j. Shah Jahan

_____ 1. This is the religious group to which the Mughal emperors belonged.

_____ 2. This Mughal emperor built the Taj Mahal in memory of his beloved wife.

_____ 3. Their religious beliefs are a mixture of the doctrines of Buddhism, Hinduism, and Sufism.

_____ 4. Although this son of Akbar was an extremely weak ruler, he wisely left the affairs of state to his more capable wife.

_____ 5. Known as the "Great One," he added more territory to the lands conquered by Babur than did any other Mughal emperor.

_____ 6. It was under this Mughal emperor that the empire expanded to its greatest size. Even so, the power of the empire weakened greatly during his reign.

_____ 7. His kingdom was stolen from him when he was a boy. As a young man, he regained it along with other lands, thus laying the foundation for the vast Mughal Empire.

_____ 8. This is the group to whom Khusrau turned for aid when he rebelled against his father. As a result, this group became the target of the Mughals' particular hatred.

_____ 9. She was a Persian princess who married a son of Akbar's and became a brilliant politician. When her husband proved weak, she took the opportunity to rule India in his name.

B. Extended Response
Briefly answer the following question on the back of this paper.

Why is the reign of Akbar considered a golden age of the Mughal Empire?

CHAPTER TEST *The Muslim World Expands*

Form A

Part 1: Main Ideas
Write the letter of the term or name that best matches the description. (4 points each)

a. Akbar
b. Constantinople
c. cultural blending
d. *devshirme*
e. ghazi
f. Esfahan
g. Isma'il
h. Shah Abbas
i. Shah Jahan
j. Timur the Lame

_____ 1. He encouraged religious tolerance in the Mughal Empire and presided over a great cultural and artistic age.

_____ 2. Christian boys were taken as slaves, converted to Islam, and turned into warriors and government officials as part of this Ottoman policy.

_____ 3. He built the Taj Mahal in memory of his wife, Mumtaz Mahal.

_____ 4. This interaction of two or more cultures produces new languages and new ideas in art, religion, and society.

_____ 5. This was the term for a warrior for Islam who belonged to a military society with a strict code of conduct.

_____ 6. He drew from many cultural influences and reformed civilian and military life in the Safavid Empire.

_____ 7. This Shi'a warrior led the Safavids to conquer what is now Iran.

_____ 8. This Central Asian conqueror interrupted the growth of the Ottoman Empire.

_____ 9. Artists from many cultures worked together in this capital city of the Safavid Empire.

_____ 10. Mehmed II was able to conquer this Byzantine city using cannons and military strategy.

Part 2: Map Skills

Use the map to choose the best possible answer. (4 points each)

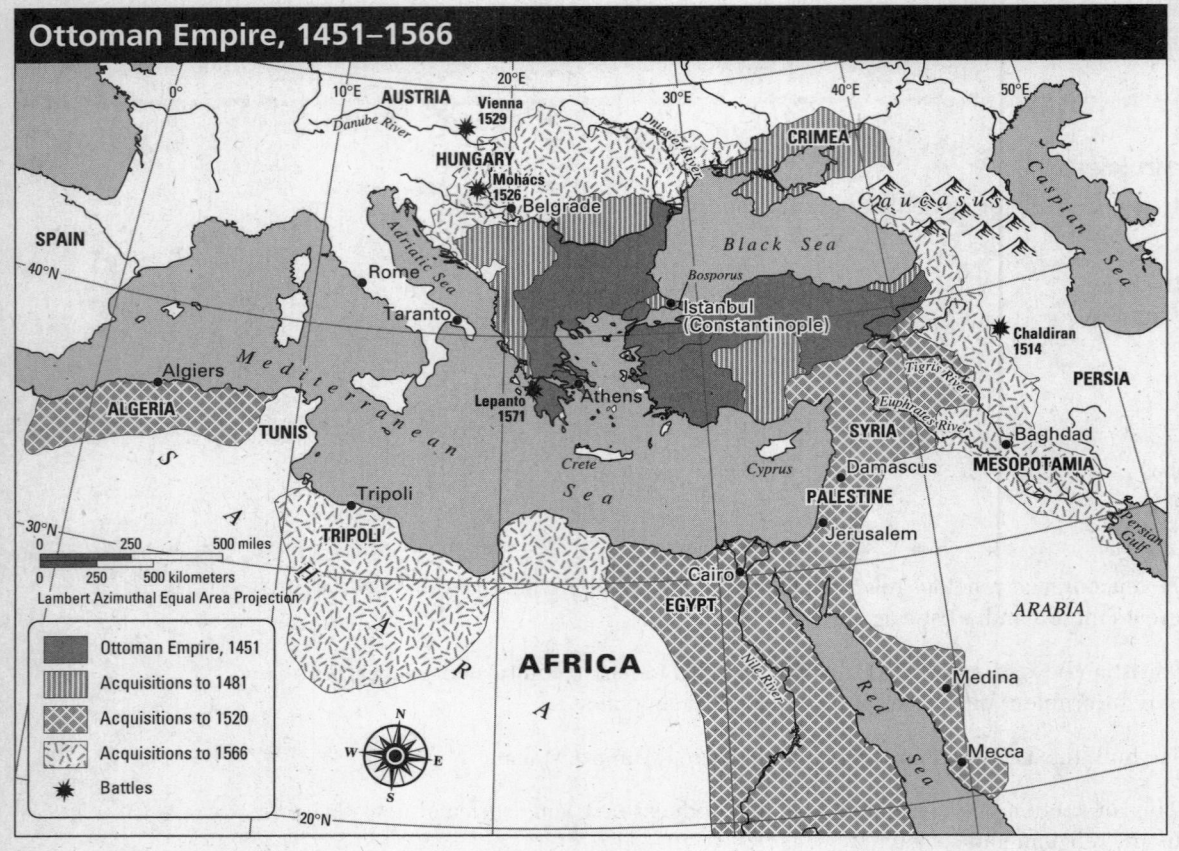

Ottoman Empire, 1451–1566

_____ 11. Which of the following did the Ottomans conquer first?
     a. Damascus
     b. Baghdad
     c. Athens
     d. Belgrade

_____ 12. On which continents had the Ottomans gained territory by 1481?
     a. Europe and Asia
     b. Europe and Africa
     c. Asia and Africa
     d. Europe, Asia, and Africa

_____ 13. By what year had the Ottoman Empire reached its farthest southern extent?
     a. 1451
     b. 1481
     c. 1520
     d. 1566

_____ 14. By what year did the Ottomans control Hungary?
          a. 1451
          b. 1481
          c. 1520
          d. 1566

_____ 15. In 1520, what region of the Ottoman Empire was separated from its main territories?
          a. Mesopotamia
          b. Algeria
          c. Greece
          d. Balkans

Part 3: Interpreting Graphs

Use the graph to choose the best possible answer. (4 points each)

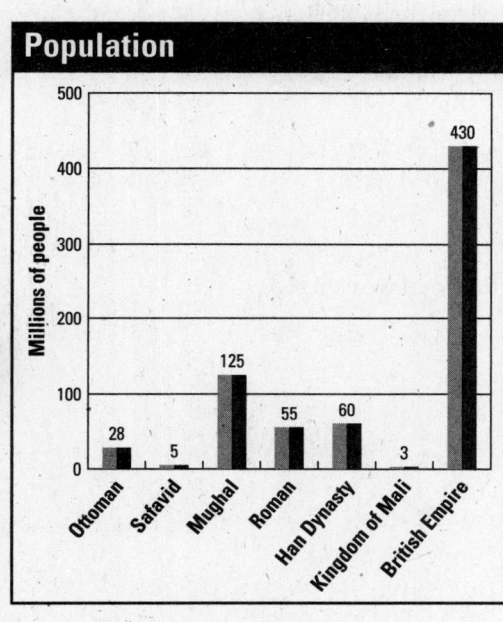

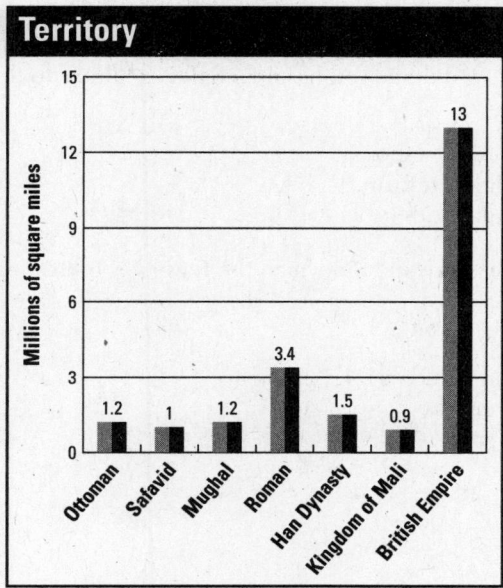

_____ 16. Which empire had the smallest territory?
          a. Ottoman Empire
          b. Safavid Empire
          c. Kingdom of Mali
          d. Mughal Empire

_____ 17. Which empire had the second largest population?
          a. Roman Empire
          b. Han Dynasty
          c. Han Dynasty
          d. Mughal Empire

_____ 18. How many people were in the British Empire at its height?
          a. 13 million people
          b. 60 million people
          c. 125 million people
          d. 430 million people

_____ 19. How much larger was the Roman Empire's territory than the Mughal Empire's
       territory?
       a. 1.9 million square miles
       b. 2.2 million square miles
       c. 2.6 million square miles
       d. 3.1 million square miles

_____ 20. How much larger was the population of the Han Dynasty at its height than the
       population of the Ottoman Empire?
       a. 21 million people
       b. 26 million people
       c. 29 million people
       d. 32 million people

Part 4: Extended Response

Answer the following questions on the back of this paper or on a separate sheet. (10 points
each)

21. **Analyzing Causes** How did Shah Abbas help Safavid culture to flourish?

   Think about:
   • relationships with foreign nations
   • government and military reform
   • the effects of cultural blending

22. **Drawing Conclusions** How did Suleyman the Lawgiver both strengthen and weaken the
   Ottoman Empire?

   Think about:
   • the effects of cultural blending
   • the structure of the empire
   • his treatment of his sons

CHAPTER TEST *The Muslim World Expands*

Form B

Part 1: Main Ideas

Write the letter of the best answer. (4 points each)

_____ 1. What was the *devshirme* system designed to do?
    a. turn Christian boys into Muslim soldiers
    b. do away with all possible rivals to the throne
    c. make the tax system fairer and more efficient
    d. divide political power equally between Christians and Muslims

_____ 2. How did Timur the Lame's military activities affect the growth of the Ottoman Empire?
    a. They had no effect on it.
    b. They interrupted its growth.
    c. They helped it grow more rapidly.
    d. They permanently ended its growth.

_____ 3. Why did Shah Jahan order the building of the Taj Mahal?
    a. to honor his grandfather, Akbar
    b. to encourage Hindus and Muslims to worship together
    c. in memory of his wife, Mumtaz Mahal
    d. as a memorial for Guru Arjun, the Sikh leader

_____ 4. Which of the following was a result of Western influences on the Safavid Empire?
    a. The military weakened in power.
    b. Carpet weaving became a national industry.
    c. The division between Sunni and Shi'a decreased.
    d. Suleiman invited Shah Abbas to rule with him.

_____ 5. What contributed to the decline of both the Ottoman and Safavid Empires?
    a. natural disasters
    b. disruption in trade
    c. religious rebellions
    d. incompetent leadership

_____ 6. What change did the Sikhs undergo during the course of the Mughal Empire?
    a. They transformed from a nonviolent group into a militant group.
    b. They gained the support of the Mughal government.
    c. They moved their nonviolent society to Marathas' state.
    d. Because of persecution, they rejected all Muslim aspects of their faith.

_____ 7. What did Mehmed II do after he conquered Constantinople?
    a. He forced conversion upon Constantinople's Christian inhabitants.
    b. He opened the city to new citizens of many religions and backgrounds.
    c. He chipped marble from the Hagia Sophia and sank it in the Black Sea.
    d. He captured Cairo, Mecca, and Medina.

_____ 8. Which of the following is NOT true about Isma'il?
      a. He took the title Shah.
      b. He established Shi'a Islam as the Safavid state religion.
      c. He promoted religious tolerance in areas conquered by his troops.
      d. By the age of sixteen, he had conquered what is now Iran.

_____ 9. What did Suleyman the Lawgiver support?
      a. government reform and cultural achievements
      b. the military conquest of India
      c. equality for people of all faiths in his empire
      d. the conquest of Constantinople

_____ 10. Who ruled India for Jahangir?
      a. Akbar   c. Shah Jahan
      b. Aurangzeb   d. Nur Jahan

Part 2: Map Skills

Use the map to choose the best possible answer. (4 points each)

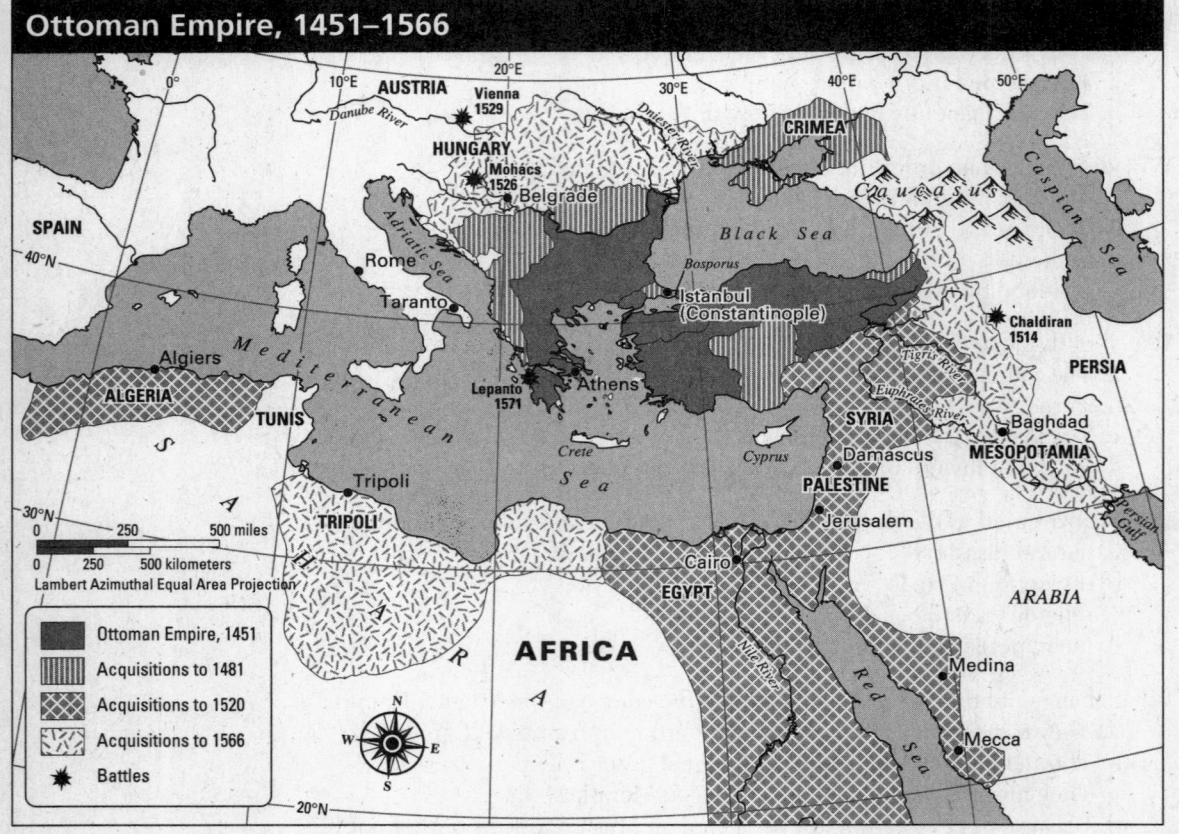

Ottoman Empire, 1451–1566

_____ 11. What might have prevented the Ottomans from controlling the Caspian Sea?
      a. deserts   c. mountains
      b. Persian Gulf   d. Tigris River

_____ 12. Which of the following generalizations is true?
　　　　　a. By 1481, the Ottoman Empire was established on three continents.
　　　　　b. By 1481, the Ottomans had access to the Red Sea and the Indian Ocean.
　　　　　c. By 1520, the Ottomans controlled trade in the Eastern Mediterranean.
　　　　　d. By 1566, the Ottomans controlled all of the Black Sea.

_____ 13. What regions did the Ottomans gain control of between 1481 and 1520?
　　　　　a. Syria, Egypt, and Algeria
　　　　　b. Hungary, Tripoli, and Mesopotamia
　　　　　c. the Balkans, Greece, and Crimea
　　　　　d. Hungary, the Balkans, and Mesopotamia

_____ 14. How was the outcome of the battle at Vienna different from the outcome of the
　　　　　battle at Mohács?
　　　　　a. The Ottomans ruled Vienna until 1570, when they were defeated.
　　　　　b. The battle at Mohács gave the Ottomans control of Belgrade.
　　　　　c. The Ottoman success at Vienna allowed them to control central Europe.
　　　　　d. The Ottomans gained control of the region around Mohács, but not Vienna.

_____ 15. What did the Ottomans achieve when they attacked Constantinople?
　　　　　a. a better position for　　　　　　　c. control of Greece
　　　　　　　attacking Hungary　　　　　　　　d. control of Hungary
　　　　　b. control of the Bosporus

Part 3: Interpreting Graphs

Use the graph to choose the best possible answer. (4 points each)

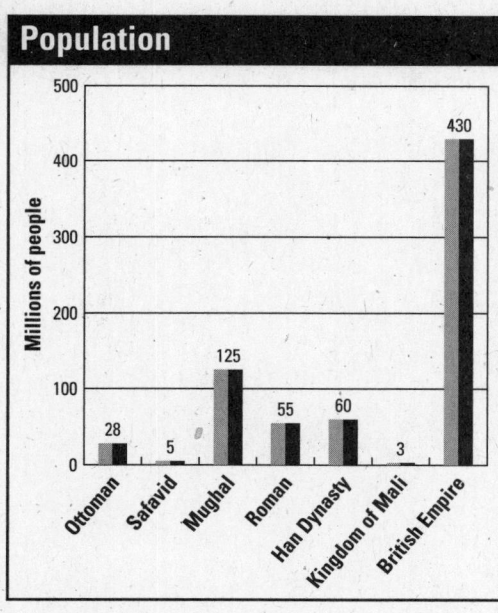

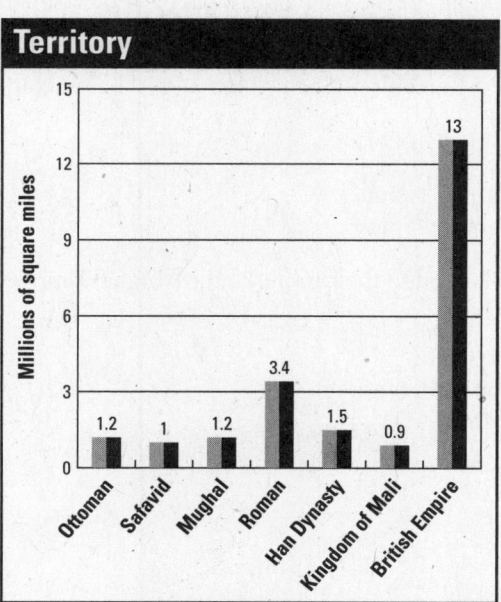

_____ 16. Which empire had the second largest population at its height?
　　　　　a. British Empire　　　　　　　　　c. Mughal Empire
　　　　　b. Roman Empire　　　　　　　　　d. Han Dynasty

_____ 17. Which two empires had the same amount of territory?
                a. Safavid and Han Dynasty
                b. Ottoman and Mughal
                c. Safavid and Mughal
                d. Ottoman and Safavid

_____ 18. How much larger was the Roman Empire's territory than the Han Dynasty's territory?
                a. 1.2 million square miles
                b. 1.5 million square miles
                c. 1.9 million square miles
                d. 2.3 million square miles

_____ 19. How much more territory did the British Empire have than the Ottoman Empire?
                a. 9.3 million square miles
                b. 10.2 million square miles
                c. 10.9 million square miles
                d. 11.8 million square miles

_____ 20. What was the population density (population divided by land area) of Mali?
                a. approximately 3 people per square mile
                b. approximately 4 people per square mile
                c. approximately 5 people per square mile
                d. approximately 6 people per square mile

Part 4: Extended Response

Answer the following questions on the back of this paper or on a separate sheet. (10 points each)

21. **Comparing** How did the actions of Shah Abbas and Akbar encourage cultural blending in their empires?

   Think about:
   • relationships with foreign nations
   • influences of conquered peoples

22. **Analyzing Causes** What led to the decline of the Mughal Empire?

   Think about:
   • treatment of other religions
   • the effects of taxation and spending
   • succession to the throne

CHAPTER TEST *The Muslim World Expands*

Form C

Part 1: Main Ideas
Write the letter of the term or name that best matches the description. (4 points each)

_____ 1. How were ghazis and janissaries similar?
      a. They were slaves.
      b. They were warriors.
      c. They were born into Islam.
      d. They converted to Islam.

_____ 2. Which of the following did NOT adopt a policy of religious tolerance?
      a. Shah Abbas   c. Mehmed II
      b. Suleyman I   d. Isma'il

_____ 3. Why did the Mughal rulers turn against the Sikhs in India?
      a. The Sikhs formed a militant society that threatened the court of Jahangir.
      b. The Sikhs disagreed with Akbar's policies on religious tolerance.
      c. The Sikhs protected Jahangir's rebellious son, so the Mughals killed their
         leader.
      d. The Sikhs sided with Aurangzeb against his father, Shah Jahan.

_____ 4. Which of the following led to the cultural blending in the Ottoman Empire?
      a. migration, trade, and conquest
      b. pursuit of religious converts, trade, and conquest
      c. pursuit of religious freedom, migration, and trade
      d. pursuit of religious converts, conquest, and migration

_____ 5. Which Mughal ruler was most like Shah Abbas in his views on cultural blending?
      a. Akbar   c. Aurangzeb
      b. Nur Jahan   d. Jahangir

_____ 6. Why did Shah Jahan ignore his people's needs?
      a. He cared only about conquering new territory.
      b. He was more interested in architecture and his wife.
      c. He cared only about painting and writing poetry.
      d. He received poor advice from his mother, Nur Jahan.

_____ 7. What did Isma'il do that enraged the Ottomans?
      a. He captured Sunni slaves to train as warriors.
      b. He captured Shi'a slaves to train as warriors.
      c. He destroyed the Shi'a population of Medina.
      d. He destroyed the Sunni population of Baghdad.

_____ 8. What language, meaning "from the soldier's camp," was an example of cultural
    blending during the Mughal Empire?
      a. Marathi   b. Sanskrit   c. Urdu   d. Hindi

_____ 9. What did Suleyman the Lawgiver and Akbar have in common?
      a. Architecture, the arts, and literature flourished under their rule.
      b. Specially trained foreign slaves formed the core of their armies.
      c. Both appointed Hindus to high government positions.
      d. Both killed their sons to eliminate competition.

_____ 10. Which of the following was NOT true of Aurangzeb?
      a. He oppressed his people and levied heavy taxes.
      b. He was intolerant of non-Muslim religions.
      c. He built the greatest monuments of the Mughal era.
      d. Millions of his people died in a famine while he was waging war.

Part 2: Map Skills—Constructed Response

Using the map, answer the questions below. You do not need to write complete sentences.
(4 points each)

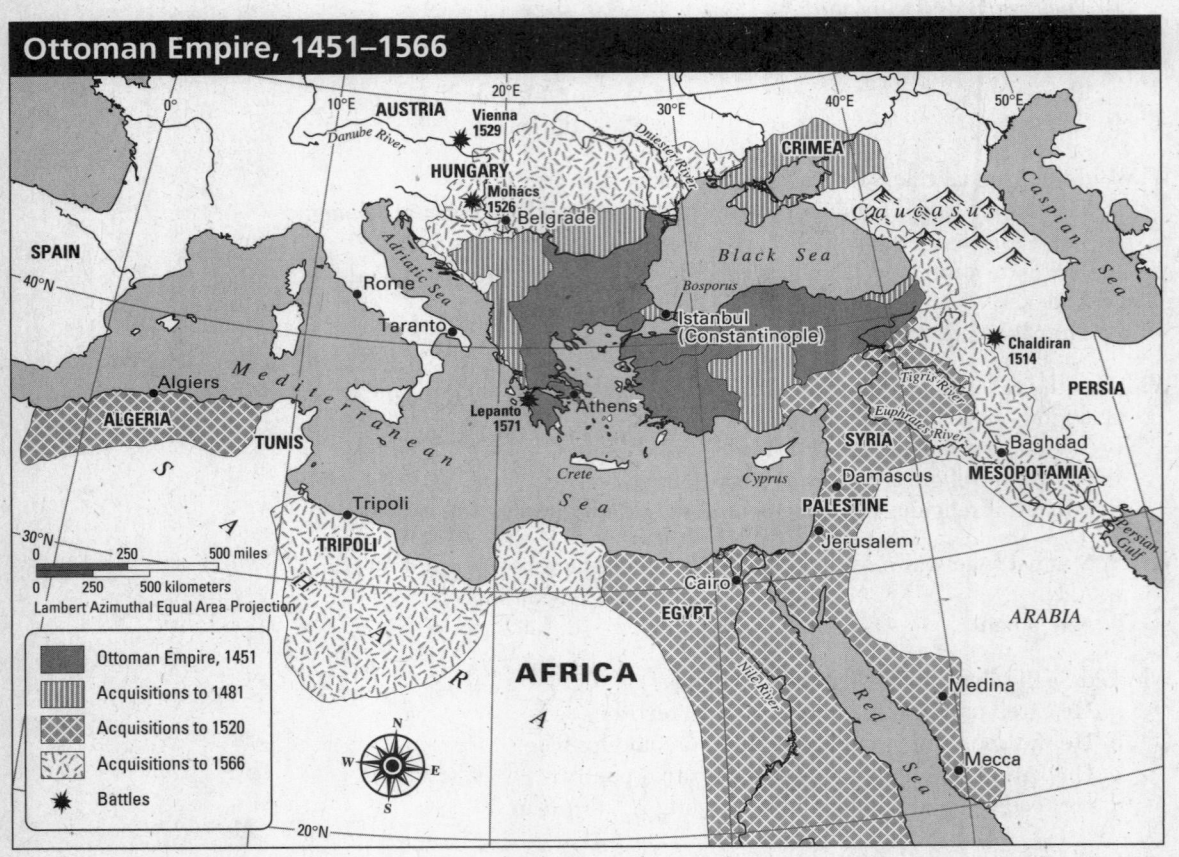

11. What regions did the Ottomans conquer between 1520 and 1566?

_____

12. Why was control of Constantinople important to Mehmed II?

_____

13. How did the lands acquired between 1451 and 1481 compare to previous acquisitions?

_____

14. How did the lands acquired between 1481 and 1520 compare to previous acquisitions?

_____

15. What geographic pattern describes the regions the Ottomans conquered? Why would they want those regions?

_____

Part 3: Interpreting Graphs

Use the graph to choose the best possible answer. (4 points each)

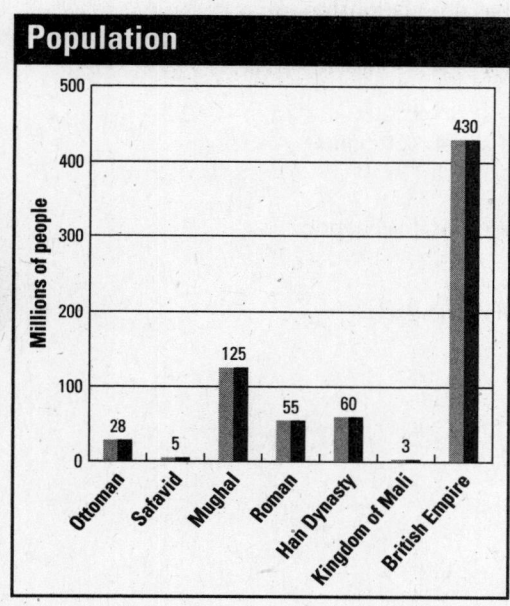

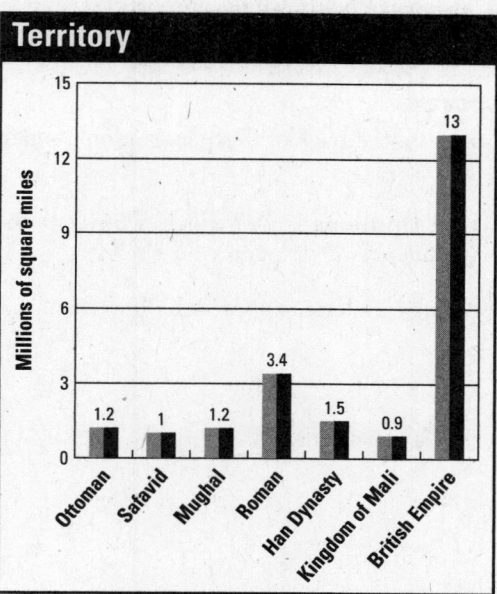

_____ 16. What was true of the Ottoman and Mughal empires?
   a. The Ottoman Empire had a higher population than did the Mughal Empire.
   b. The Mughal Empire was twice the size of the Ottoman Empire.
   c. They were the same size, but the Mughal empire had a higher population.
   d. They had the same number of people, but the Ottoman Empire was larger.

_____ 17. What was the population density (population divided by land area) of the empire with the largest territory?
   a. 27 people per square mile
   b. 29 people per square mile
   c. 31 people per square mile
   d. 33 people per square mile

_____ 18. Of the three empires studied in this chapter, which would have an advantage in war, and why?
    a. the Ottoman, because it was the largest of the three
    b. the Mughal, because it could afford to lose the most people
    c. the Safavid, because it had the least land to defend
    d. the Safavid, because it had the fewest people to protect

_____ 19. Which empire had the greatest amount of territory per person?
    a. Kingdom of Mali
    b. Safavid Empire
    c. Ottoman Empire
    d. Roman Empire

_____ 20. What conclusion can be drawn about the quality of life in the empire with the most territory per person?
    a. It was peaceful because the empire did not need to make war for land.
    b. It was prosperous because the empire had plenty of land to farm.
    c. No conclusion can be drawn because the quality of the land is unknown.
    d. No conclusion can be drawn because land ownership has no relationship to quality of life.

Part 4: Extended Response

Answer the following questions on the back of this paper or on a separate sheet. (10 points each)

21. **Forming and Supporting Opinions** Under which two rulers discussed in this chapter did the most cultural blending occur? Explain your choices.

22. **Contrasting** How did Akbar's leadership approach differ from that of Aurangzeb?

Name _____ Date _____

A. Terms and Names Write the letter of the best answer.

_____ 1. What European nation profited most from trade with the East in the years
directly following the Crusades?
    a. Italy   c. France
    b. Spain   d. England

_____ 2. Which nation did Prince Henry help to take the lead in overseas exploration?
    a. Italy   c. Portugal
    b. Spain   d. the Netherlands

_____ 3. In the 1400s, what was the most important trade good from the East?
    a. tea   c. spices
    b. silk   d. porcelain

_____ 4. Bartolomeu Dias captained the first European ship to sail what route?
    a. west across the Atlantic Ocean
    b. along the West Coast of Africa
    c. across the Indian Ocean to India
    d. around the southern tip of Africa

_____ 5. What did Vasco da Gama succeed in gaining for Portugal?
    a. control of the Spice Islands
    b. a sea route between Portugal and India
    c. a sea route between Portugal and China
    d. profitable trade with the Philippine Islands

_____ 6. The Line of Demarcation established a boundary between which two regions?
    a. Portugal and Spain
    b. claimed and unclaimed lands
    c. new lands Portugal could claim and those Spain could claim
    d. the part of the world that was under the pope's control and the part
       that was not

_____ 7. By the 1700s, which nation's East India Company dominated the Indian Ocean
trade?
    a. France   c. Portugal
    b. England   d. the Netherlands

B. Extended Response Briefly answer the following question on the back of this paper.

What inspired Europeans to begin exploring foreign lands in the 1400s? What made it
possible for them to begin these explorations?

CHAPTER **3**

Section 2

SECTION QUIZ *China Limits European Contacts*

A. Terms and Names
Write the letter of the term or name that matches the description. A term may be used more than once or not at all.

a. Korea
b. Dutch
c. Kangxi
d. Yonglo
e. Chinese
f. Hongwu
g. Mongols

h. Manchus
i. Zheng He
j. Qian-long
k. Netherlands
l. Great Britain
m. Qing Dynasty
n. Ming Dynasty

_____ 1. This dynasty was founded in the mid 1600s.

_____ 2. The Qing Dynasty was founded by a member of this group.

_____ 3. This son of peasants founded the Ming Dynasty.

_____ 4. This dynasty included the rulers Kangxi and Qian-long.

_____ 5. This dynasty ruled China following the end of Mongol rule.

_____ 6. This nation was a vassal state of China during the Qing Dynasty.

_____ 7. This Chinese ruler attempted to expand China's tribute system by sponsoring voyages of exploration.

_____ 8. This Chinese ruler moved the Chinese capital to Beijing, where he built the palace complex known as the Forbidden City.

_____ 9. This nation's trade representatives won the favor of Chinese emperors by accepting restrictions on trade, paying tribute, and kowtowing.

_____ 10. This Chinese Muslim explorer led seven voyages of exploration to places such as Southeast Asia, India, Arabia, and eastern Africa.

_____ 11. This emperor ruled China for 60 years. He won popularity with the people by reducing government expenses and cutting taxes and won the support of the intellectuals by offering them government positions.

B. Extended Response
Briefly answer the following question on the back of this paper.

What were the main aspects of everyday life under China's Ming and Qing dynasties? Be sure to note some of the changes that affected the Chinese people during this period.

CHAPTER
3
Section 3

SECTION QUIZ *Japan Returns to Isolation*

A. Terms and Names Write the letter of the best answer.

_____ 1. Under Japan's new system of feudalism, the daimyo were
      a. warlords.
      b. emperors.
      c. religious leaders.
      d. peasant foot soldiers.

_____ 2. The Tokugawa Shogunate was a type of
      a. cultural institution.
      b. religious authority.
      c. military government.
      d. commercial partnership or organization.

_____ 3. Kabuki is a type of
      a. music.   c. poetry.
      b. drama.   d. religion.

_____ 4. The leader whose rule ended the "warring states" period, even though he did not succeed in unifying Japan, was
      a. Oda Nobunaga.
      b. Toyotomi Hideyoshi.
      c. Tokugawa Ieyasu.
      d. Tokugawa Hidetada.

_____ 5. In 1600, the person who finally completed the long process of unifying Japan was
      a. Matsuo Basho.   c. Tokugawa Ieyasu.
      b. Oda Nobunaga.   d. Toyotomi Hideyoshi.

_____ 6. Haiku is a type of
      a. literature.
      b. ritual suicide.
      c. fortified castle.
      d. riddle in Zen Buddhism.

_____ 7. Tokugawa Ieyasu used the "alternate attendance policy" to control the
      a. daimyo.   c. merchants.
      b. peasants.   d. foreign traders.

B. Extended Response Briefly answer the following question on the back of this paper.

What was the "closed country policy," and how did it affect Japan?

CHAPTER

3

Form A

CHAPTER TEST *An Age of Explorations and Isolation*

Part 1: Main Ideas

Write the letter of the best answer. (4 points each)

_____ 1. Which European country was the leader in developing and applying 15th century
sailing innovations?
  a. Italy   c. Portugal
  b. Spain   d. the Netherlands

_____ 2. Who were the first Europeans to arrive on Japanese soil?
  a. Italians who traded firearms
  b. shipwrecked Portuguese sailors
  c. Christian missionaries
  d. Dutch merchants from the Dutch East India Company

_____ 3. Why was the caravel an important development in navigation?
  a. It was able to sail against the wind.
  b. It was able to sail in shallow waters.
  c. It was able to withstand storms at sea.
  d. It was able to carry large numbers of crew members.

_____ 4. Korea was a vassal state of which country during the 1700s?
  a. Japan   c. Portugal
  b. China   d. the Netherlands

_____ 5. During the 1500s, what was China's official trade policy?
  a. China openly traded with all European countries.
  b. Only the government was allowed to trade with foreign countries.
  c. China traded only with Japan and other Asian countries.
  d. The government lowered taxes to promote trade.

_____ 6. Why did Lord Macartney give a letter from King George III to Qian-long?
  a. Great Britain wanted China to follow certain trade rituals.
  b. Great Britain wanted China to stop trade with the Dutch.
  c. Great Britain wanted to import manufactured goods from China.
  d. Great Britain wanted to increase trade with China.

_____ 7. Who captained the first European ship to sail around the tip of Africa, now known
as the Cape of Good Hope?
  a. Prince Henry   c. Bartolomeu Dias
  b. Vasco da Gama   d. Christopher Columbus

_____ 8. What did Hongwu do first to help China become a dominant power?
  a. He sent explorers to western Europe to learn about science and medicine.
  b. He overthrew the Mongols and established the Ming Dynasty.
  c. He reduced government expenses and lowered taxes.
  d. He opened all ports to trade with European countries.

_____ 9. What type of policy did Japan institute to control foreign ideas?
  a. a closed country policy
  b. a policy of persecution
  c. a policy of colonization
  d. a Zen Buddhist policy

_____ 10. What type of poetry presents images rather than expresses an idea?
  a. kabuki   c. haiku
  b. kowtow   d. Saikaku

Part 2: Map Skills

Write the letter of the best answer. (4 points each)

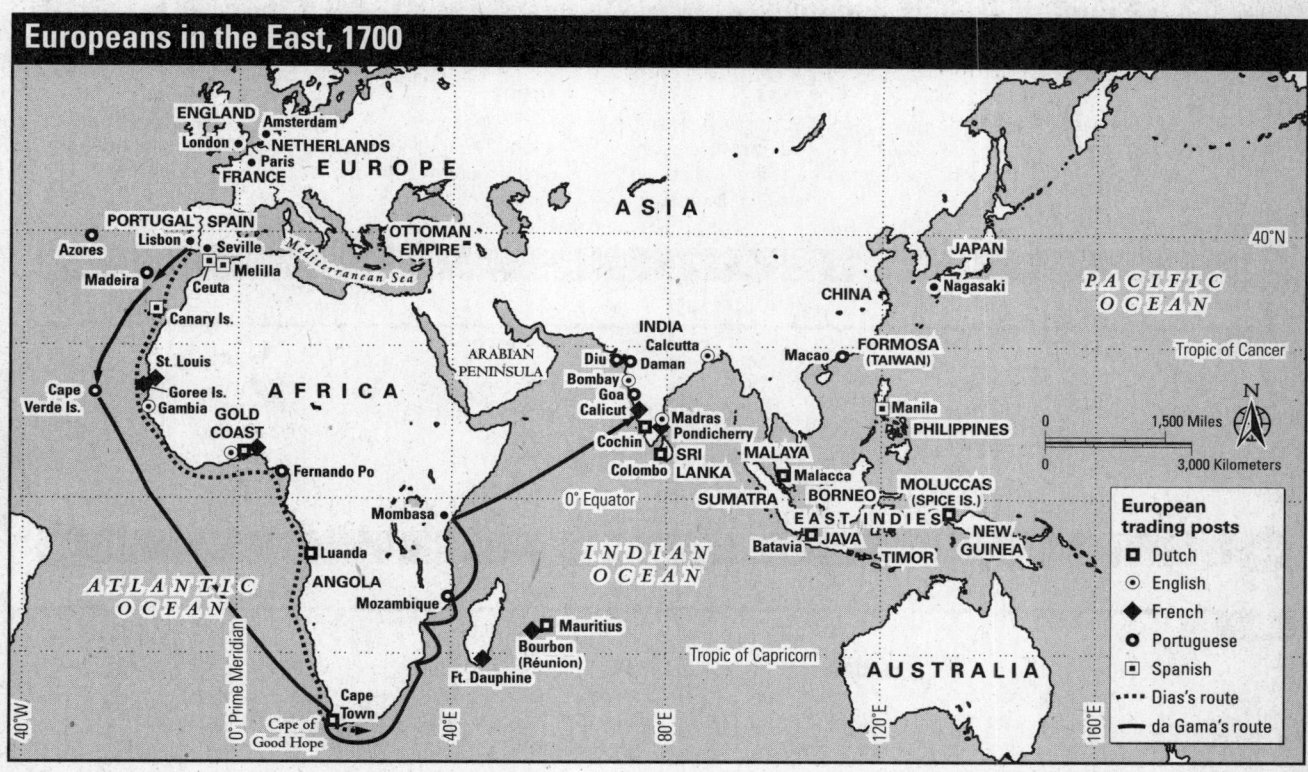

Europeans in the East, 1700

_____ 11. What was the easternmost city da Gama reached?
  a. Nagasaki   b. Macao   c. Malacca   d. Calicut

_____ 12. Which European country controlled trade in the East Indies?
  a. Portugal   c. England
  b. the Netherlands   d. France

_____ 13. Which European countries had the most trading posts in India?
  a. Portugal and England
  b. Spain and France
  c. France and the Netherlands
  d. England and the Netherlands

_____ 14. About how many miles did a trader sail to go from Mombasa, Africa, to Calicut, India?

        a. 3,500   c. 4,000

        b. 2,000   d. 2,800

_____ 15. Where did Dias' route stop?

        a. east of Calicut   c. east of Cape Town

        b. south of Mombasa   d. west of Fernando Po

Part 3: Interpreting Time Lines

Write the letter of the best answer. (4 points each)

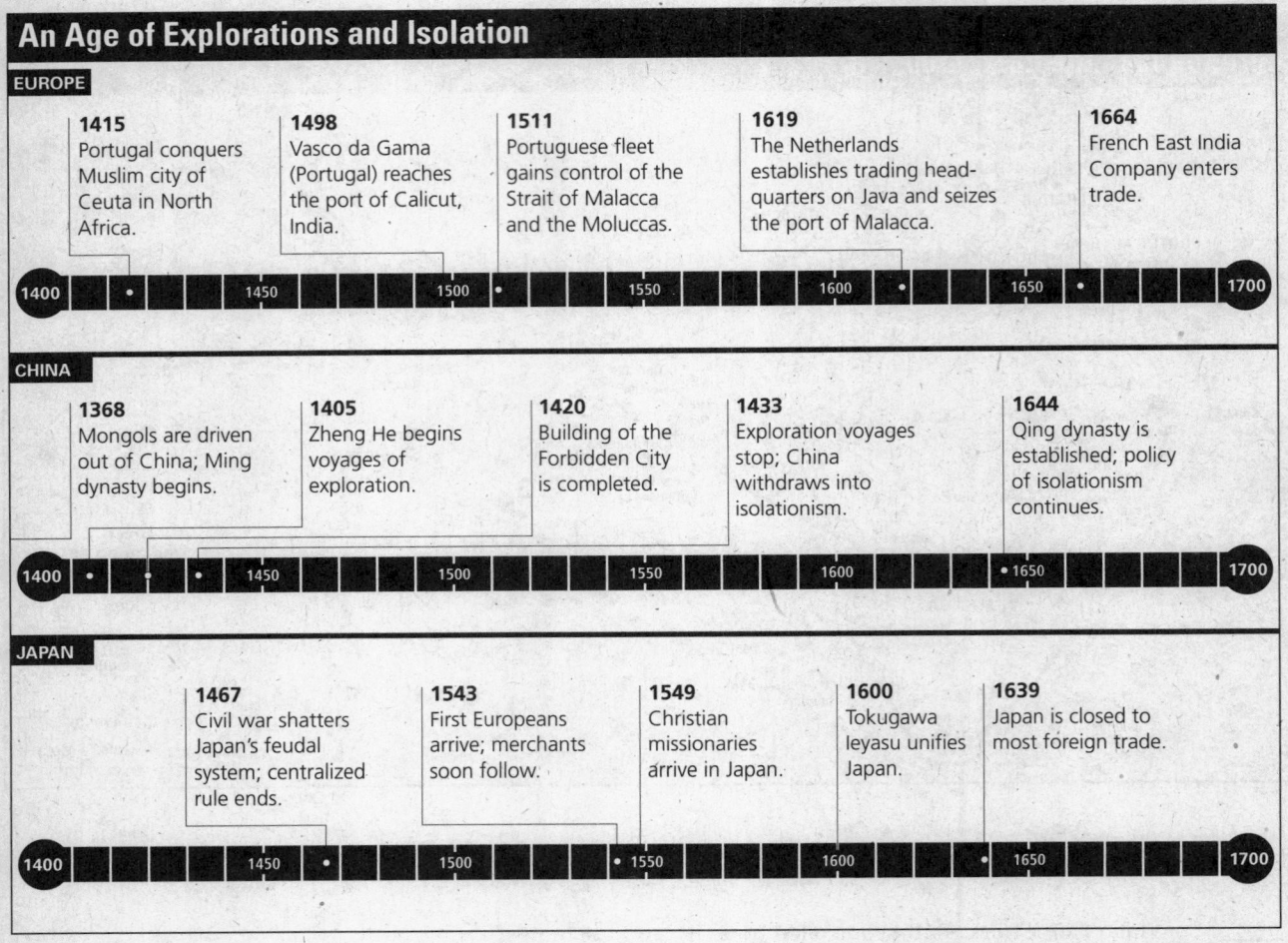

An Age of Explorations and Isolation

EUROPE

1415 Portugal conquers Muslim city of Ceuta in North Africa.

1498 Vasco da Gama (Portugal) reaches the port of Calicut, India.

1511 Portuguese fleet gains control of the Strait of Malacca and the Moluccas.

1619 The Netherlands establishes trading headquarters on Java and seizes the port of Malacca.

1664 French East India Company enters trade.

1400 — 1450 — 1500 — 1550 — 1600 — 1650 — 1700

CHINA

1368 Mongols are driven out of China; Ming dynasty begins.

1405 Zheng He begins voyages of exploration.

1420 Building of the Forbidden City is completed.

1433 Exploration voyages stop; China withdraws into isolationism.

1644 Qing dynasty is established; policy of isolationism continues.

1400 — 1450 — 1500 — 1550 — 1600 — 1650 — 1700

JAPAN

1467 Civil war shatters Japan's feudal system; centralized rule ends.

1543 First Europeans arrive; merchants soon follow.

1549 Christian missionaries arrive in Japan.

1600 Tokugawa Ieyasu unifies Japan.

1639 Japan is closed to most foreign trade.

1400 — 1450 — 1500 — 1550 — 1600 — 1650 — 1700

_____ 16. How many years after China began voyages of exploration did Portugal conquer the city of Ceuta in North Africa?

        a. 5   b. 93   c. 10   d. 52

_____ 17. How many years did it take Europeans to reach Japan after they conquered Ceuta?

        a. 128   b. 122   c. 132   d. 154

_____ 18. Which European nation had the latest entry into the Asian trade?

        a. Portugal   c. France

        b. Italy   d. the Netherlands

_____ 19. How many years after Portugal gained control of the Strait of Malacca did the
Netherlands seize the port?

      a. 13   b. 108   c. 121   d. 45

_____ 20. Which event happened before the other events in China?

      a. policy of isolation

      b. exploration of foreign lands

      c. completion of the Forbidden City

      d. Mongols driven out

Part 4: Extended Response

Answer the following questions on the back of this paper or on a separate sheet of paper.
(10 points each)

21. **Identifying Problems** What problems did Europeans have to overcome in order to
find an all-water route to Asia?

Think about:
- ships and sails
- navigational tools
- southern tip of Africa

22. **Drawing Conclusions** What were some of the things that improved the quality of life in
China and Japan during the 1600s and 1700s?

Think about:
- quality of leadership
- trade with Europe
- improvements in agriculture

CHAPTER **3**

Form B

CHAPTER TEST *An Age of Explorations and Isolation*

Part 1: Main Ideas

If the statement is true, write "true" on the line. If the statement is false, change the underlined word or words to make it true. (4 points each)

Example: <u>French</u> settlers in South Africa were known as Boers. _____*Dutch*_____

1. The Tokugawa Shogunate ruled during a time of <u>peace</u>. _____

2. Portugal explored the <u>African coast</u> to find an all-water route to Asia._____

3. Portugal, the Netherlands, England, and France competed for control of the <u>Atlantic Ocean</u> trade._____

4. The Chinese Muslim explorer <u>Zheng He</u> led seven voyages of exploration that ranged from southeast Asia to eastern Africa. _____

5. Unlike the British, the Dutch were able to win the favor of the <u>Japanese</u> emperors by accepting trade restrictions, paying tribute, and kowtowing._____

6. Under Japan's system of feudalism, the <u>daimyo</u> functioned most similarly to what, in Europe's system of feudalism, were the lords._____

7. The <u>Italians</u> established good trade relations with Japan, partly because they had introduced the musket and cannon to this nation._____

8. Kangxi and Qian-long were emperors of China's <u>Ming Dynasty</u>._____

9. In 1612, Tokugawa Ieyasu began a successful campaign to rid Japan of all <u>Buddhist</u> belief._____

10. After the Crusades ended, the <u>Spanish and Portuguese</u> controlled the trade of goods from East to West. _____

_____

Part 2: Map Skills

Write the letter of the best answer. (4 points each)

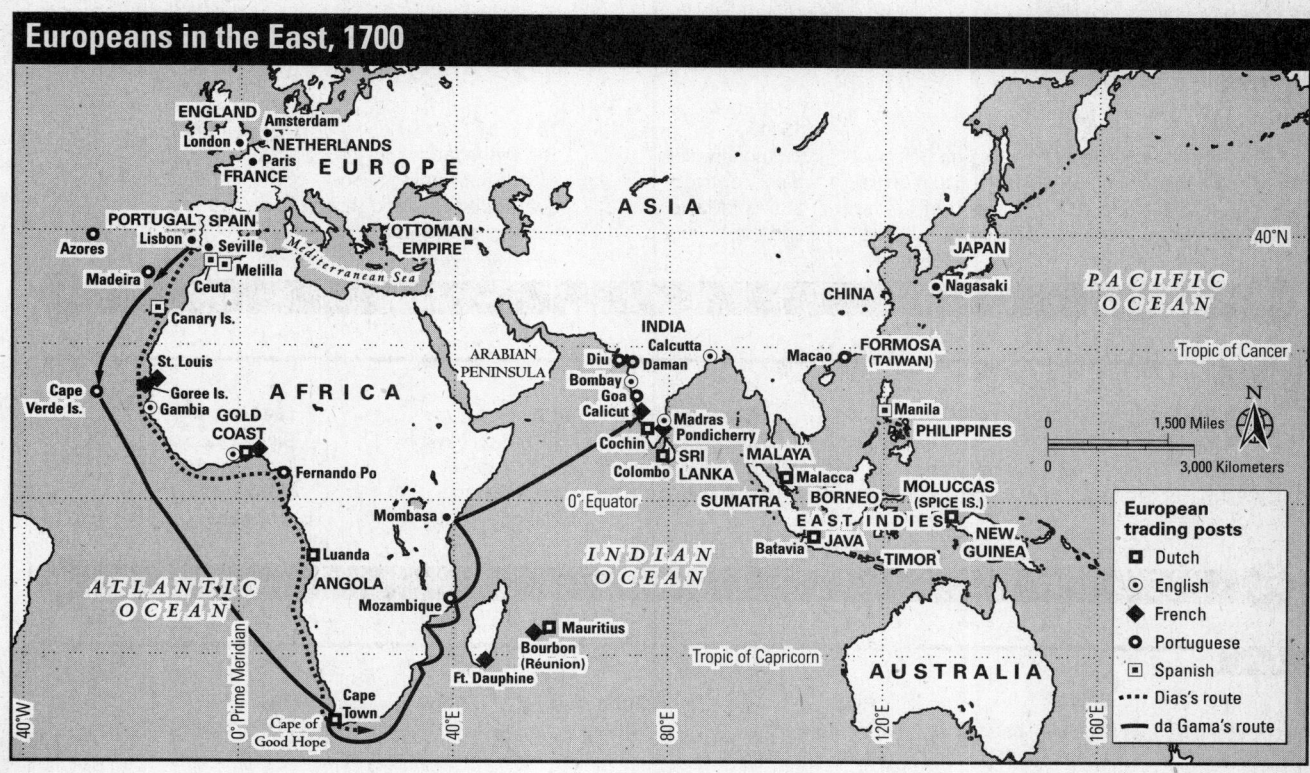

Europeans in the East, 1700

_____ 11. Both Dias and da Gama sailed from which city?
        a. Seville   c. Melilla
        b. Lisbon   d. Madeira

_____ 12. Which European country had trading posts in the Canary Islands and the Philippines?
        a. Spain   c. France
        b. England   d. the Netherlands

_____ 13. How many trading posts were located east of the longitude line 80°E?
        a. 9   b. 10   c. 6   d. 12

_____ 14. Which European countries had the most trading posts in Africa?
        a. Portugal and Spain
        b. France and the Netherlands
        c. Spain and England
        d. Portugal and the Netherlands

_____ 15. Approximately how many miles did da Gama have to travel to get from Mombasa, Africa, to his last destination?
        a. 2,000 miles
        b. 1,000 miles
        c. 750 miles
        d. 3,000 miles

Part 3: Interpreting Time Lines

Write the letter of the best answer. (4 points each)

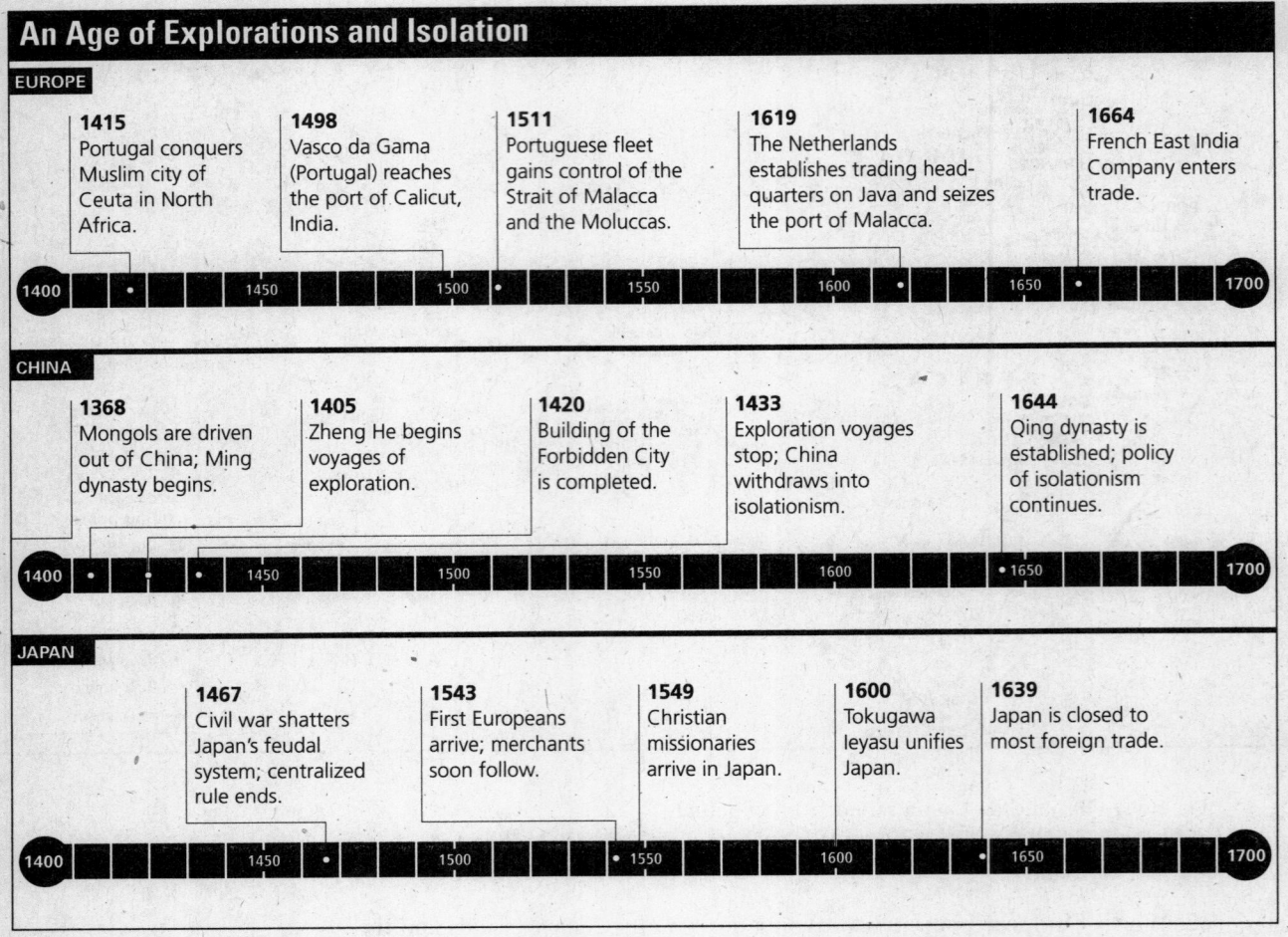

An Age of Explorations and Isolation

EUROPE

1415 Portugal conquers Muslim city of Ceuta in North Africa.

1498 Vasco da Gama (Portugal) reaches the port of Calicut, India.

1511 Portuguese fleet gains control of the Strait of Malacca and the Moluccas.

1619 The Netherlands establishes trading headquarters on Java and seizes the port of Malacca.

1664 French East India Company enters trade.

1400 · 1450 1500 · 1550 1600 · 1650 · 1700

CHINA

1368 Mongols are driven out of China; Ming dynasty begins.

1405 Zheng He begins voyages of exploration.

1420 Building of the Forbidden City is completed.

1433 Exploration voyages stop; China withdraws into isolationism.

1644 Qing dynasty is established; policy of isolationism continues.

1400 · · 1450 1500 1550 1600 · 1650 1700

JAPAN

1467 Civil war shatters Japan's feudal system; centralized rule ends.

1543 First Europeans arrive; merchants soon follow.

1549 Christian missionaries arrive in Japan.

1600 Tokugawa Ieyasu unifies Japan.

1639 Japan is closed to most foreign trade.

1400 1450 · 1500 · 1550 1600 · 1650 1700

_____ 16. What might be one result of Europeans reaching Japan?
   a. the unification of Japan
   b. the borders of Japan closing
   c. the end of the feudal system
   d. Christian missionaries arriving in Japan

_____ 17. Which country began explorations first?
   a. the Netherlands   c. China
   b. Portugal   d. Japan

_____ 18. Which two countries did NOT actively seek trade?
   a. Portugal and France
   b. France and the Netherlands
   c. China and Portugal
   d. China and Japan

_____ 19. How many years after Europeans gained control of the Moluccas did they reach Japan?
   a. 32   b. 22   c. 52   d. 12

_____ 20. Why was Japan most likely NOT exploring new lands at the time the other countries were?
     a. Japan felt it didn't need to explore other countries or find other trading partners.
     b. Japan didn't have the technology to build ships or travel to far away lands.
     c. Japan was not unified, so its priority was solving internal problems.
     d. Japan had already explored and was done exploring when the other countries began.

Part 4: Extended Response

Answer the following questions on the back of this paper or on a separate sheet of paper.
(10 points each)

21. **Comparing** How were the Europeans' reasons for overseas exploration similar to the reasons the Chinese had for overseas exploration in the early 1400s?

     Think about:
     • what could be gained
     • what could be shared

22. **Analyzing Motives** Why did China and Japan react as they did to the Europeans' desire to trade with them?

     Think about:
     • Europeans reasons for trade
     • cultural traditions
     • financial gain

CHAPTER

3

Form C

CHAPTER TEST **An Age of Explorations and Isolation**

Part 1: Main Ideas
Write the letter of the best answer. (4 points each)

_____ 1. What were Europeans' main motives for making voyages of exploration?
    a. to test their new technology
    b. to grow wealthy and spread Christianity
    c. to break the Portuguese monopoly on trade
    d. to gain extra land for a growing population

_____ 2. Why was Zheng He important?
    a. He was China's first Chinese emperor.
    b. He was China's first non-Chinese emperor.
    c. He led seven Chinese overseas explorations.
    d. He overthrew the Mongol rule.

_____ 3. Why was the introduction of European firearms in Japan successful?
    a. It corresponded with the end of the closed country policy.
    b. It corresponded with the warring states period of new feudalism.
    c. It corresponded with the attempts of powerful shoguns to unify Japan.
    d. It corresponded with the civil war that destroyed the old feudal system.

_____ 4. What were China's main reasons for rejecting British offers of trade?
    a. British merchants refused to kowtow to the emperor.
    b. Britain wanted to be the exclusive trading partner with China.
    c. China's emperor did not like the gifts the British merchants offered.
    d. China believed it was self-sufficient and didn't need outside goods.

_____ 5. How did Prince Henry of Portugal influence exploration?
    a. He was the first to sail around the southern tip of Africa.
    b. He founded a navigational school on the coast of Portugal.
    c. He invented the caravel, a sturdier ship with triangular sails.
    d. He improved the astrolabe and invented the compass.

_____ 6. Which of the following was NOT an attitude reflected by China's Forbidden City and the way it was used?
    a. the nation's isolationism
    b. the power and wealth of the emperor
    c. the importance of Confucianism in China
    d. the distinction between social classes in China

_____ 7. What major barrier hindered effective centralized government in Japan?
    a. the power of the daimyo
    b. the difficulties of collecting taxes
    c. the dissatisfaction of the peasant class
    d. the interference from Christian missionaries

_____ 8. Why was Tokugawa Ieyasu upset by the success of Christian missionaries?
   a. The missionaries refused to pay taxes to him.
   b. The missionaries refused to kowtow and follow the rules of his court.
   c. He believed the missionaries were barbarians and would harm his people.
   d. He feared religious uprisings and Christian interference in politics.

_____ 9. What was the purpose of the Treaty of Tordesillas signed by Portugal and Spain?
   a. to divide up the trade routes to the East
   b. to decrease conflict over the claiming of new lands
   c. to promote cooperation in the sharing of technological advances
   d. to create an alliance that would offset Dutch domination of sea routes

_____ 10. What two main reasons kept China from becoming highly industrialized?
   a. The idea of commerce offended Confucian beliefs, and taxes on manufactured goods were high.
   b. Missionaries made little impact, and economic policy favored agriculture.
   c. Demand for Chinese goods was low, so merchants traded grain.
   d. Merchants had to smuggle cargo to trade, and the silver that bought smuggled goods forced inflation.

Part 2: Map Skills

Write the letter of the best answer. (4 points each)

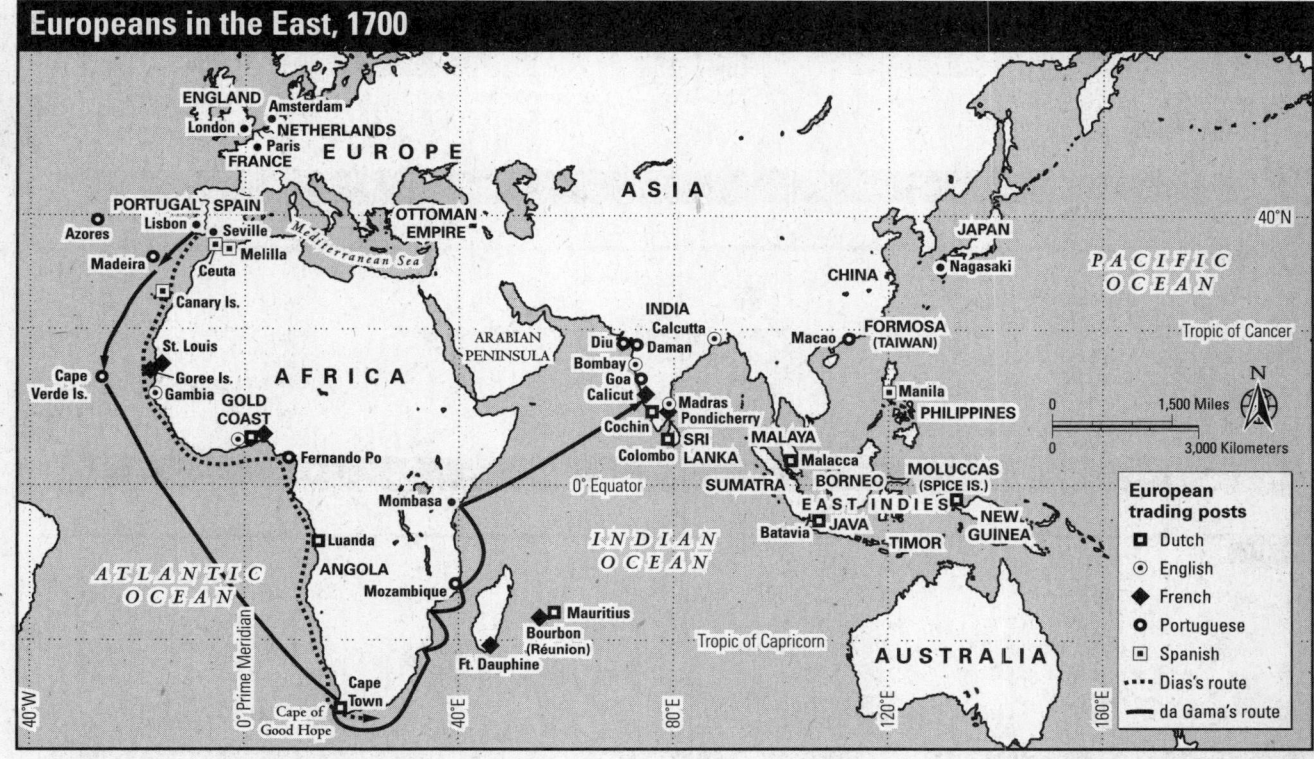

Europeans in the East, 1700

_____ 11. About how far in miles did da Gama travel from Lisbon, Portugal, to Calicut, India?
   a. 3,200   b. 6,500   c. 16,000   d. 20,000

_____ 12. About how far in miles was it from Seville to Spain's most distant trading post?
   a. 1,000   b. 4,500   c. 10,000   d. 16,000

_____ 13. Besides Dias' route being shorter, how did the two explorers' routes differ?
    a. Dias sailed near the coast of Africa; da Gama sailed out in the Atlantic.
    b. Da Gama sailed near the coast of Africa; Dias sailed out in the Atlantic.
    c. Da Gama stopped at more trading ports than Dias had.
    d. Da Gama encountered more danger on his trip because of storms.

_____ 14. What reason might explain the difference between the two explorers' routes?
    a. Dias aroused French anger, so da Gama avoided their trading posts.
    b. Da Gama visited trading posts that were founded after Dias' voyage.
    c. Dias and da Gama hated each other and would not sail the same waters.
    d. Da Gama did not hug the coast because Dias had already mapped it.

_____ 15. In what region did the Netherlands have the majority of its trading posts?
    a. Africa   c. East Indies
    b. India   d. China

Part 3: Interpreting Time Lines—Constructed Response

Use the time lines to answer the following questions. (4 points each)

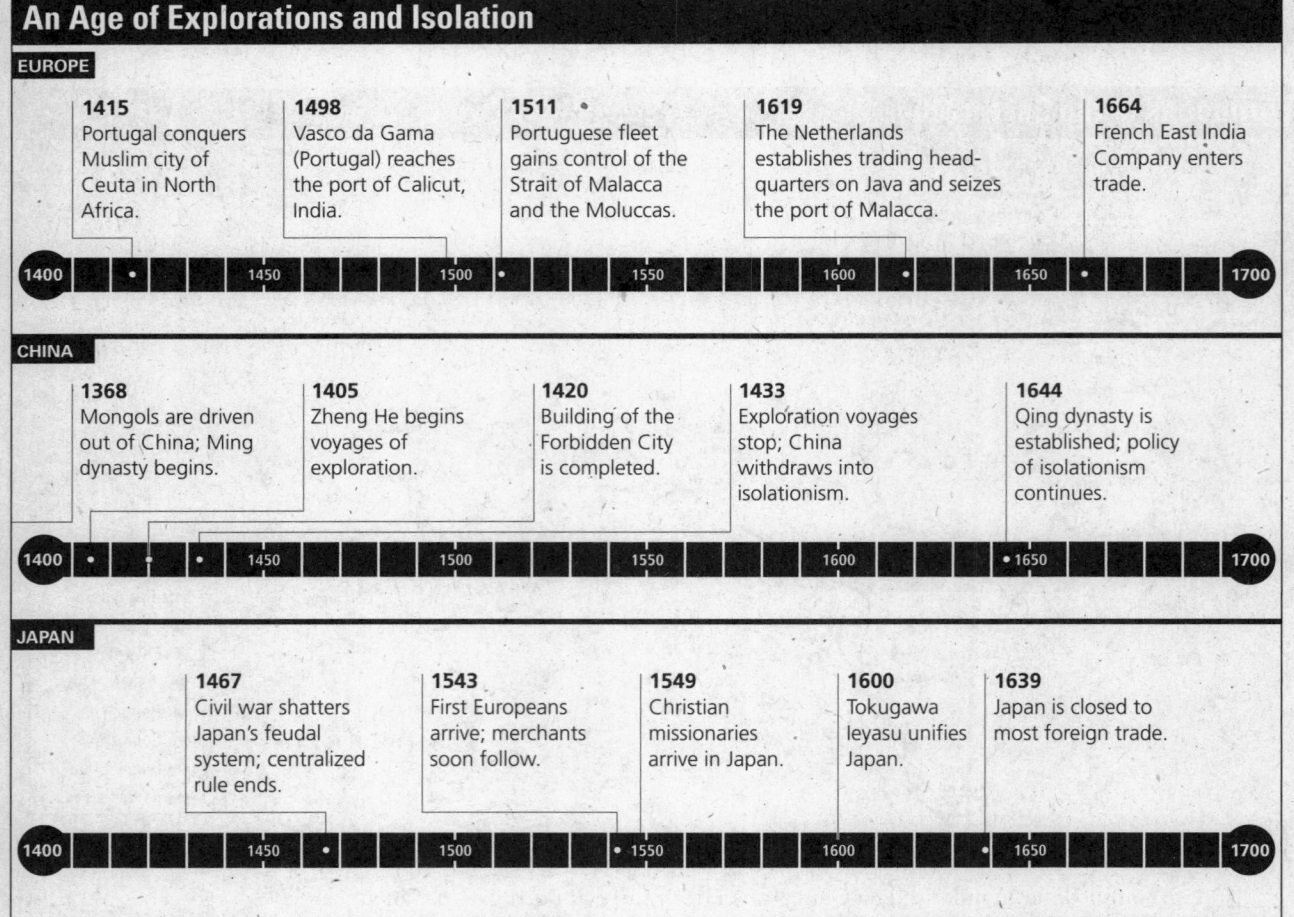

An Age of Explorations and Isolation

EUROPE

1415 Portugal conquers Muslim city of Ceuta in North Africa.

1498 Vasco da Gama (Portugal) reaches the port of Calicut, India.

1511 Portuguese fleet gains control of the Strait of Malacca and the Moluccas.

1619 The Netherlands establishes trading headquarters on Java and seizes the port of Malacca.

1664 French East India Company enters trade.

1400 — 1450 — 1500 — 1550 — 1600 — 1650 — 1700

CHINA

1368 Mongols are driven out of China; Ming dynasty begins.

1405 Zheng He begins voyages of exploration.

1420 Building of the Forbidden City is completed.

1433 Exploration voyages stop; China withdraws into isolationism.

1644 Qing dynasty is established; policy of isolationism continues.

1400 — 1450 — 1500 — 1550 — 1600 — 1650 — 1700

JAPAN

1467 Civil war shatters Japan's feudal system; centralized rule ends.

1543 First Europeans arrive; merchants soon follow.

1549 Christian missionaries arrive in Japan.

1600 Tokugawa Ieyasu unifies Japan.

1639 Japan is closed to most foreign trade.

1400 — 1450 — 1500 — 1550 — 1600 — 1650 — 1700

16. What happened in China about the same time it withdrew into isolation?

_____

17. What does the time line reveal about relations among the various European nations pursuing exploration and trade?

_____

18. Why might Japan have been the only country NOT to explore new lands during this time period?

_____

19. What might have been the attitudes of Europeans and Chinese toward each other in 1600? Why?

_____

20. Why might Japan have closed its borders in 1639?

_____

Part 4: Extended Response

Answer the following questions on the back of this paper or on a separate sheet of paper. (10 points each)

21. **Making Inferences** Why might Europe have been more eager to trade with China and Japan during this time than China and Japan were to trade with Europe?

22. **Contrasting** Why might China's reaction to trading with Europeans differed from Japan's initial reaction to European trade? How did these attitudes change over time?

CHAPTER
4

SECTION QUIZ   *Spain Builds an American Empire*

Section 1

A. Terms and Names If the statement is true, write "true" on the line. If it is false, change the underlined word or words to make it true.

Example: In 1680, Popé led a successful revolt against the <u>Spanish</u>. _____ *true* _____

Example: As a result of Popé's uprising, the <u>Apache</u> regained control of their lands.
_____ *Pueblo* _____

1. Today's mestizos are descendants of <u>Portuguese colonists</u> and Native

   Americans. _____

2. <u>Hernándo Cortés</u> marched his force of about 600 men through Mexico to conquer the

   Aztec Empire. _____

3. In 1492, Christopher Columbus set sail <u>east across the Indian Ocean</u> in search of a

   trade route to Asia and its riches. _____

4. The purpose of Christopher Columbus's second voyage to the Americas was to establish

   <u>Spanish colonies</u> on the islands of the Caribbean. _____

5. The <u>*encomiendas*</u> were Spanish explorers who conquered and colonized areas of what

   are now Mexico, South America, and the United States._____

6. Montezuma II, the leader of the <u>Arawak people of Brazil</u>, fell out of favor with his

   subjects over his response to the Spanish conquest. _____

7. <u>Francisco Pizarro</u> and his army defeated the Inca by killing a largely unarmed group

   and then kidnapping and murdering their king._____

B. Extended Response Briefly answer the following question on the back of this paper.

   Do you think the native peoples of the Americas could have successfully defended their
   civilizations if they had been more suspicious of the first Spanish to arrive? Explain.

CHAPTER
4

Section 2

SECTION QUIZ *European Nations Settle North America*

A. Terms and Names If the statement is true, write "true" on the line. If it is false, change the underlined word or words to make it true.

Example: The Treaty of Tordesillas divided new lands between the <u>Spanish and the Portuguese</u>. _____ true _____

Example: The French and the English largely <u>honored</u> the Treaty of Tordesillas.

_____ ignored _____

1. The Dutch were ousted from North America by the <u>English</u>. _____

2. <u>Quebec</u> was the first permanent English settlement in North America. _____

3. <u>New Netherland</u> covered much of what is now the midwestern United States and eastern Canada. _____

4. The Pilgrim settlers who founded <u>Jamestown</u> were mainly interested in religious freedom. _____

5. The group known as the <u>Puritans</u> founded the colony known as Massachusetts Bay.

_____

6. <u>The French and Indian War</u> began in 1675 when Metacom led an attack on colonial villages in Massachusetts. _____

7. As a result of the French and Indian War, the <u>French</u> seized control of nearly the entire eastern half of North America. _____

B. Extended Response Briefly answer the following question on the back of this paper.

What were the chief reasons that the French, English, and Dutch each were interested in North America during this time? How did the occupations and activities of the French, English, and Dutch compare?

The Atlantic Slave Trade

_____

A. Terms and Names Answer the following questions on the lines provided.

1. Why did the trade in African slaves increase dramatically in the seventh century?

   _____

2. What are some ways in which slavery in African and Muslim societies was different
   from slavery in the Americas?

   _____

   _____

3. What are some reasons that Africans were considered ideal laborers for the plantations
   and mines of the European colonists in the Americas?

   _____

   _____

4. What are three nations, continents, or regions that were an essential part of the
   triangular trade network?

   _____

5. What are some of the goods that were essential to the triangular trade network?

   _____

6. What was the starting point and what were the ending points of the middle passage?

   _____

B. Extended Response Briefly answer the following question on the back of this paper.

   What were some of the ways in which the Atlantic slave trade affected African and
   American societies from the 1400s to the 1800s?

CHAPTER 4

Section 4

SECTION QUIZ *The Columbian Exchange and Global Trade*

A. **Terms and Names** If the statement is true, write "true" on the line. If it is false, change the underlined word or words to make it true.

Example: The Columbian Exchange began with the arrival of <u>Christopher Columbus</u> in

the Caribbean. _____ *true* _____

Example: The transfer of disease that was part of the Columbian Exchange was most

deadly to the native peoples of <u>Europe</u>. _____ *the Americas* _____

1. The joint-stock company of the 1500s and 1600s was very similar to today's

    <u>corporation</u>. _____

2. Capitalism is an economic system based on <u>public</u> ownership of property and the

    investment of wealth to earn profit. _____

3. Most European joint-stock companies of the 1500s and 1600s were founded for the

    purpose of <u>fighting wars</u>. _____

4. New business and trade practices in Europe during the 16th and 17th centuries took

    place <u>before</u> the establishment of colonial empires in the Americas. _____

5. As part of the Columbian Exchange, corn and potatoes were carried <u>west across the</u>

    <u>Pacific Ocean</u> for the first time. _____

6. As part of the Columbian Exchange, tobacco and tomatoes were carried <u>west across</u>

    <u>the Pacific Ocean</u> for the first time_____

7. According to mercantilism, a favorable balance of trade results when the value of the

    goods sold by a country <u>equals</u> the value of the goods bought by that country. _____

B. **Extended Response** Briefly answer the following question on the back of this paper.

    What was mercantilism? How and why did it encourage European colonization of
    the Americas?

CHAPTER
4
Form A

CHAPTER TEST *The Atlantic World*

Part 1: Main Ideas

Write the letter of the best answer. (4 points each)

_____ 1. What was the main economic activity in New France?
     a. finding gold and spices
     b. building a fur trade
     c. finding religious freedom
     d. creating long-term colonial investments

_____ 2. Who conquered the Aztec empire?
     a. Hernando Cortés
     b. Francisco Pizarro
     c. Ferdinand Magellan
     d. Vasco Núñez de Balboa

_____ 3. Why did Europeans see Africans as a better a source of labor than Native Americans?
     a. Africans had complete immunity to all diseases, so they wouldn't die off.
     b. Africans had no experience in farming, so they wouldn't try to do things their way.
     c. Africans were strangers in the Americas, so they wouldn't have allies or places to hide.
     d. Africans were already Christians, so they didn't have to be converted.

_____ 4. What was the purpose of most of the joint-stock companies of the 1500s and 1600s?
     a. financing wars in Africa
     b. funding colonies in the Americas
     c. paying for the building of slave ships
     d. funding the digging of gold mines

_____ 5. Where in the Americas did Christopher Columbus land first?
     a. an island in the Caribbean Sea
     b. the southern tip of South America
     c. the coast of what is today Panama
     d. the eastern coast of North America

_____ 6. What did the *encomienda* system provide for New Spain?
     a. more land   c. military protection
     b. more settlers   d. a cheap labor source

_____ 7. What prompted a wave of new businesses and trade practices in Europe in the 16th and 17th centuries?
     a. the global transfer of foods, plants, and animals during colonization
     b. new wealth from the Americas and the growth in overseas trade
     c. people pooling their wealth for a common purpose
     d. European countries becoming able to sell more goods than they bought

_____ 8. Which European country was the first to import enslaved Africans to the Americas?
       a. the Netherlands   c. England
       b. France   d. Spain

_____ 9. As part of the Columbian Exchange, which of the following was carried west
across the Atlantic?
       a. livestock   b. tobacco   c. potatoes   d. tomatoes

_____ 10. Which of the following areas was originally founded as a settlement by the Dutch?
       a. Quebec   c. New York
       b. Montreal   d. Massachusetts

Part 2: Map Skills

Use the maps to answer the following questions. Write the letter or letters of the best answer.
(4 points each)

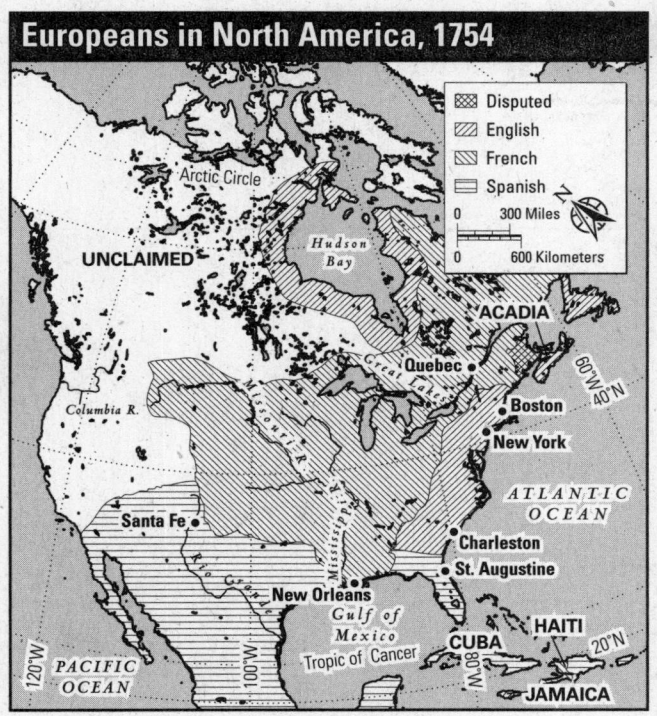

a. England
b. France
c. Russia
d. Spain
e. none of the above

_____ 11. In 1754, which nation(s) held part of what is now the United States?

_____ 12. In 1754, which nation(s) controlled Quebec?

_____ 13. After 1763, which nation(s) had direct access to the Pacific Ocean?

_____ 14. By 1763, which nation(s) won control of territory that had been disputed in 1754?

_____ 15. In 1754, which nation(s) held part of what is now Canada?

Part 3: Interpreting Charts

Use the charts to answer the following questions. (4 points each)

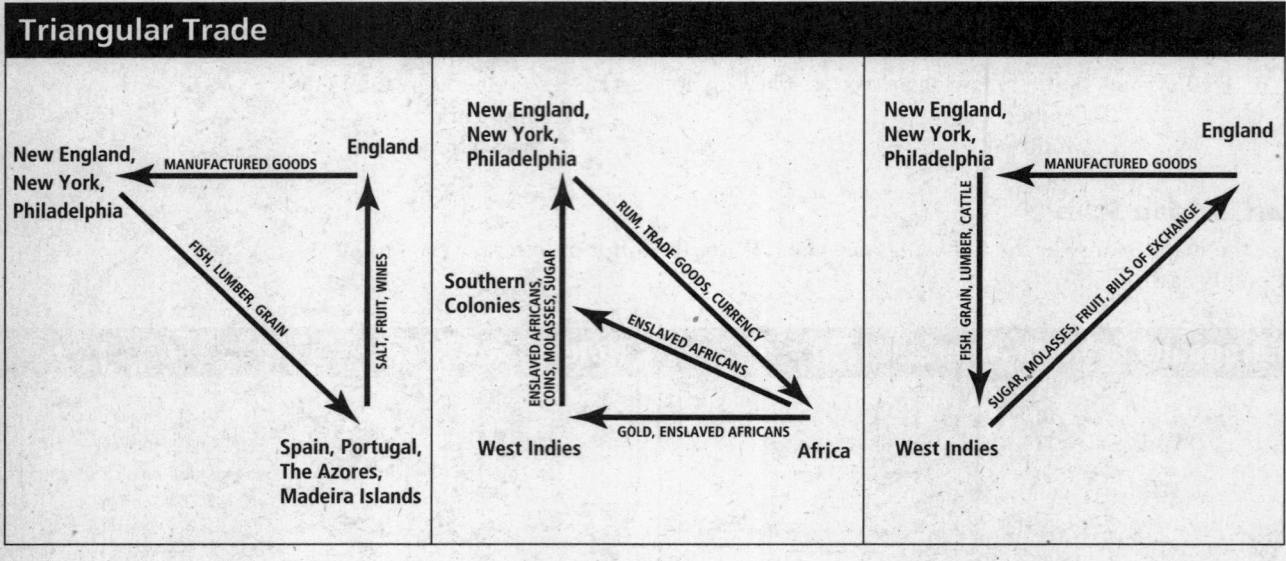

Triangular Trade

_____ 16. What did ships transport on the "middle passage"?
     a. coins, enslaved Africans, and sugar
     b. gold and enslaved Africans
     c. rum, trade goods, and currency
     d. sugar, molasses, and enslaved Africans

_____ 17. Which places were part of all three triangular trade routes?
     a. England
     b. West Indies and southern colonies
     c. New England, New York, and Philadelphia
     d. Africa

_____ 18. What did England export?
     a. salt, fruit, and wines
     b. sugar, molasses, and fruit
     c. bills of exchange
     d. manufactured goods

_____ 19. What did the West Indies export both to England and to New England, New York, and Philadelphia?
     a. sugar and molasses
     b. coins and enslaved Africans
     c. fruit and bills of exchange
     d. sugar, coins, molasses, and enslaved Africans

_____ 20. What did New England, Philadelphia, and New York export to both the West
Indies and Spain, Portugal, the Azores, and Madeira Islands?
   a. cattle and grain
   b. lumber and cattle
   c. fish, lumber, and grain
   d. fish and cattle

Part 4: Extended Response

Answer the following questions on the back of this paper or on a separate sheet of paper.
(10 points each)

21. **Analyzing Causes and Recognizing Effects** What enabled the Spanish forces to
conquer the Aztec people?

   Think about:
   • weapons used by each side
   • allies and enemies
   • forces that weakened the Aztec

22. **Analyzing Motives** How did the English gain control of Dutch and French interests in
North America, and why did England want to gain control of that land?

   Think about:
   • location of colonies
   • the Seven Years' War
   • growing populations

CHAPTER 4

Form B

CHAPTER TEST *The Atlantic World*

Part 1: Main Ideas

If the statement is true, write "true" on the line. If it is false, change the word or words to make it true. (4 points each)

Example: The triangular trade network centered on the <u>Pacific Ocean</u>.

                                  Atlantic Ocean
_____

1. The colony of <u>Plymouth</u> was the first English settlement established in the Americas. _____

2. The middle passage of the triangular trade system began in <u>Europe</u> and ended in the West Indies, North America, or South America. _____

3. To maintain a favorable balance of trade, in comparing exports and imports, it is the value of the <u>imports</u> that must be higher. _____

4. The French lost their North American holdings to the English because they were defeated in <u>King Philips War</u>. _____

5. Mestizos are the descendants of <u>French</u> colonists in the Americas and Native Americas. _____

6. One of the long-term effects of the African slave trade was the <u>introduction of guns</u> into the African continent. _____

7. The main purpose of a joint-stock company during the 1500s and 1600s was to share the risks and profits of <u>colonial investments</u>. _____

8. The global transfer of foods, plants, and animals during the colonization of the Americas is known as the <u>Columbian Exchange</u>. _____

9. The economic system of <u>mercantilism</u> is based on private ownership and the investment of wealth for profit. _____

10. The first Spanish settlers in the Americas were brought on a ship captained by <u>Christopher Columbus</u>. _____

Part 2: Map Skills

Use the maps to answer the following questions. (4 points each)

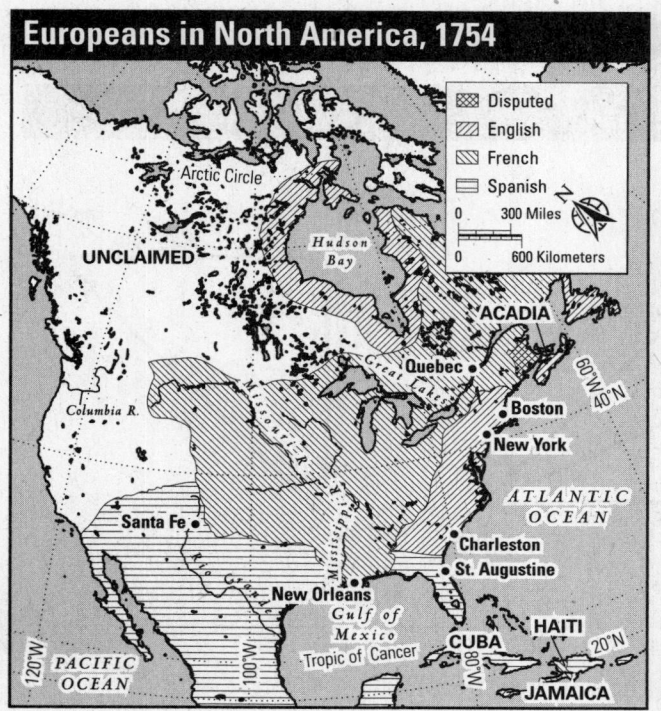

_____ 11. In 1754, which nation controlled the Great Lakes region?
        a. England   c. France
        b. Spain   d. none of the above

_____ 12. In 1754, which colony was near disputed territory?
        a. Cuba   c. Haiti
        b. Acadia   d. Jamaica

_____ 13. After 1763, which geographic feature separated much of the English and Spanish territory?
        a. Rio Grande   c. Mississippi River
        b. Hudson Bay   d. Great Lakes

_____ 14. What two cities did France lose to England by 1763?
        a. St. Augustine and Quebec
        b. New Orleans and Santa Fe
        c. Santa Fe and Quebec
        d. New Orleans and Quebec

_____ 15. By 1763, which country had lost the most territory to which other country?
  a. France lost territory to Spain.
  b. Spain lost territory to England.
  c. England lost territory to Spain.
  d. France lost territory to England.

Part 3: Interpreting Charts

Use the charts to answer the following questions. (4 points each)

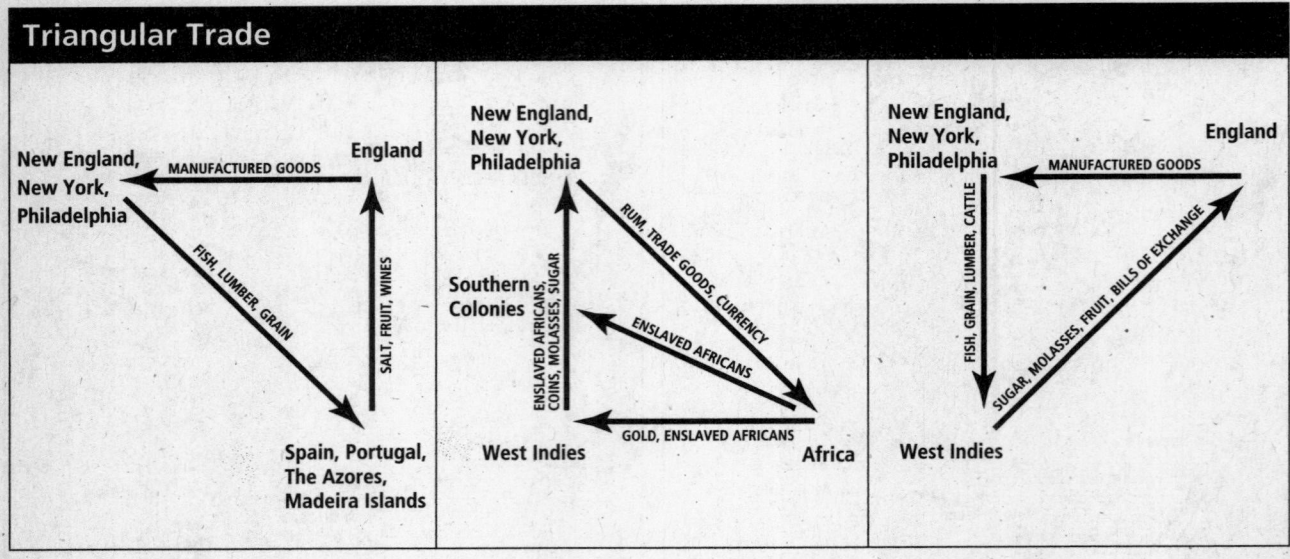

_____ 16. According to the charts, from where did New England, New York, and Philadelphia import enslaved Africans?
  a. West Indies
  b. southern colonies and Africa
  c. Africa
  d. West Indies and southern colonies

_____ 17. Where were sugar plantations located?
  a. West Indies
  b. Africa
  c. Spain, Portugal, the Azores, Madeira Islands
  d. New England, New York, Philadelphia

_____ 18. According to the charts, what did New England, New York, and Philadelphia primarily export?
  a. manufactured goods   c. natural resources
  b. raw materials   d. crops and fish

_____ 19. How might the "middle passage" have gotten its name?
  a. It traveled through the middle of the Atlantic Ocean.
  b. It traveled in between, or in the middle of, all the continents.
  c. It was the second part, or middle part, of the triangular trade.
  d. The enslaved Africans traveled in the middle of the ship.

_____ 20. What conclusion about manufacturing can be drawn from the charts?
  a. The southern colonies did all the manufacturing, which is why they needed enslaved persons.
  b. England did the manufacturing while other places supplied raw materials.
  c. New England, Philadelphia, and New York imported raw materials to make manufactured goods.
  d. The West Indies and Africa sent enslaved persons to England to make manufactured goods.

Part 4: Extended Response

Answer the following questions on the back of this paper or on a separate sheet of paper. (10 points each)

21. **Drawing Conclusions** What was the general pattern of conquest and settlement followed by the Spanish in the Americas?

    Think about:
    • the roles of conquistadors and priests
    • relationships between Spanish and natives
    • the *encomienda* system

22. **Comparing and Contrasting** How did slavery in the Americas differ from slavery in most African and Muslim societies?

    Think about:
    • the duties of enslaved persons
    • the way they were treated
    • their future prospects

CHAPTER
4

Form C

CHAPTER TEST   *The Atlantic World*

Part 1: Main Ideas
Write the letter of the best answer. (4 points each)

_____ 1. What helped to increase the slave trade in Africa during the seventh century?
  a. the crusades and holy wars
  b. the spread of Islam into Africa
  c. an increase in trade between Europe and Asia
  d. the establishment of trade networks between Africa and Portugal

_____ 2. Which of the following did NOT aid the Spanish in conquering the Aztecs?
  a. disease   c. native enemies
  b. larger forces   d. superior weapons

_____ 3. On what assumption was the *encomienda* system based?
  a. that Europeans had the right to demand labor from Native Americans
  b. that exposure to European culture would help educate Native Americans
  c. that living on Spanish plantations would convert Native Americans to Christianity
  d. that mestizos had more rights than full-blooded Native Americans

_____ 4. Why did the English want to take control of New Netherland?
  a. As they pushed west into the continent, they collided with New Netherland.
  b. The Dutch and the English were longtime enemies.
  c. New Netherland separated England's northern and southern colonies.
  d. The English wanted to take control of the fur trade and the Hudson Bay.

_____ 5. What was one result of the loss of native lives to disease?
  a. the ruin of several tobacco and sugar cane plantations
  b. a growing tolerance between the colonists and the natives
  c. fewer battles between the colonists and natives over land
  d. a severe shortage of labor in the colonies

_____ 6. How did slavery in African and Muslim societies differ from slavery in the Americas?
  a. People in African and Muslim societies could not escape their slavery.
  b. Slavery in the Americas was based on race and heredity.
  c. Enslaved people in African and Muslim societies could not rise socially.
  d. The slavery in Africa and Muslim societies was based primarily on race.

_____ 7. What was one effect in Europe of the financial success of American colonies?
  a. The prices of goods steadily increased.
  b. The prices of goods steadily decreased.
  c. The supply of goods increased to meet demand.
  d. Both the prices and supply of goods steadily increased.

_____ 8. How did Bartolemé de Las Casas affect race relations in the Americas?
     a. He urged better treatment of Native Americans but proposed using African laborers.
     b. He led a well-organized uprising against the Spanish to protest the treatment of Native Americans.
     c. He started a colony in present-day Arizona based on equality of all men.
     d. He visited the king of Spain to protest the treatment of Native Americans.

_____ 9. According to the policy of mercantilism, how could a nation increase its wealth?
     a. It should center its wealth and power in its government.
     b. It should spread its wealth and power among private individuals.
     c. It should sell more goods than it buys from other countries.
     d. It should buy more goods than it sells to other countries.

_____ 10. How was Africa affected by the Atlantic slave trade?
     a. Many cultures lost their fittest members, and families were torn apart.
     b. All African countries prospered and grew to be world powers.
     c. Kings were able to stop rebellions with the firearms they received in trade.
     d. African empires became safer because they traded away their criminals.

Part 2: Map Skills

Use the maps to answer the following questions. (4 points each)

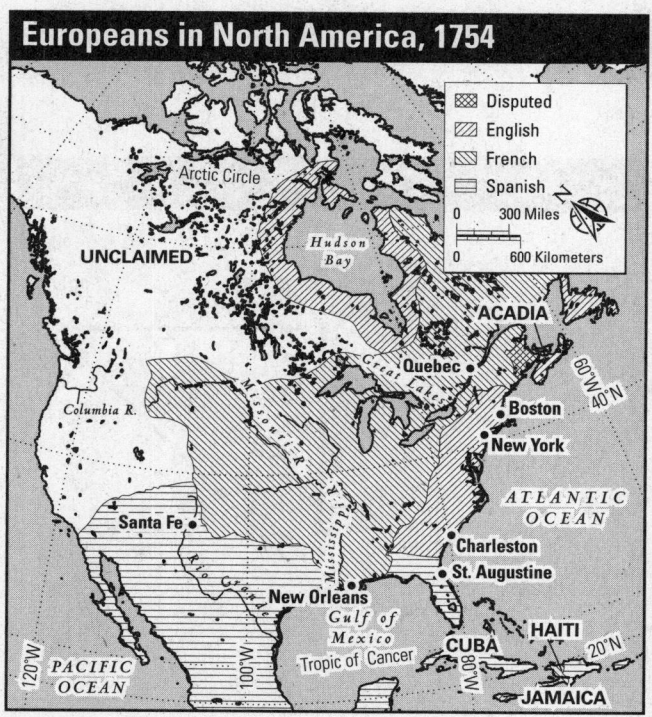

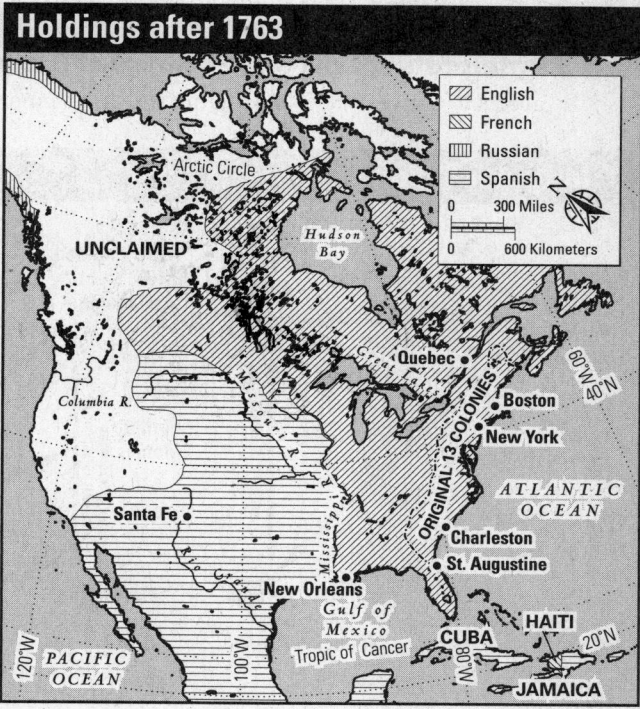

_____ 11. How did the European powers who controlled the Americas change by 1763?
     a. France had large holdings in the Americas.
     b. England controlled all of the holdings in the present-day United States.
     c. Russia gained control of territory along the far northwest coast.
     d. Spain's holdings were cut in half.

_____ 12. Which city would most likely become a source of conflict between the Americas
and the Spanish after 1763?
      a. New Orleans   c. New York
      b. Boston   d. St. Augustine

_____ 13. Which of the following U.S. cultural traits can NOT be explained by the colonial
patterns shown on these two maps?
      a. English became the main language spoken across the United States.
      b. The U.S. and Russian governments often distrust each other.
      c. The central United States has many French place names.
      d. The southwestern United States has a strong Spanish heritage.

_____ 14. How did territorial holdings west of the Mississippi River change after 1763?
      a. Only a small part of previously unclaimed territory had been claimed.
      b. Spain claimed much of the previously unclaimed territory in the southwest.
      c. Russia claimed most of the previously unclaimed territory in the region
         that became Canada.
      d. England claimed all of the previously unclaimed territory.

_____ 15. Which region did NOT undergo territorial changes between 1754 and 1763?
      a. the islands of Jamaica, Cuba, and Haiti
      b. the Gulf of Mexico region, including Florida
      c. the Great Lakes region
      d. the northwest region (unclaimed territory)

Part 3: Interpreting Charts—Constructed Response

Use the charts to answer the following questions. (4 points each)

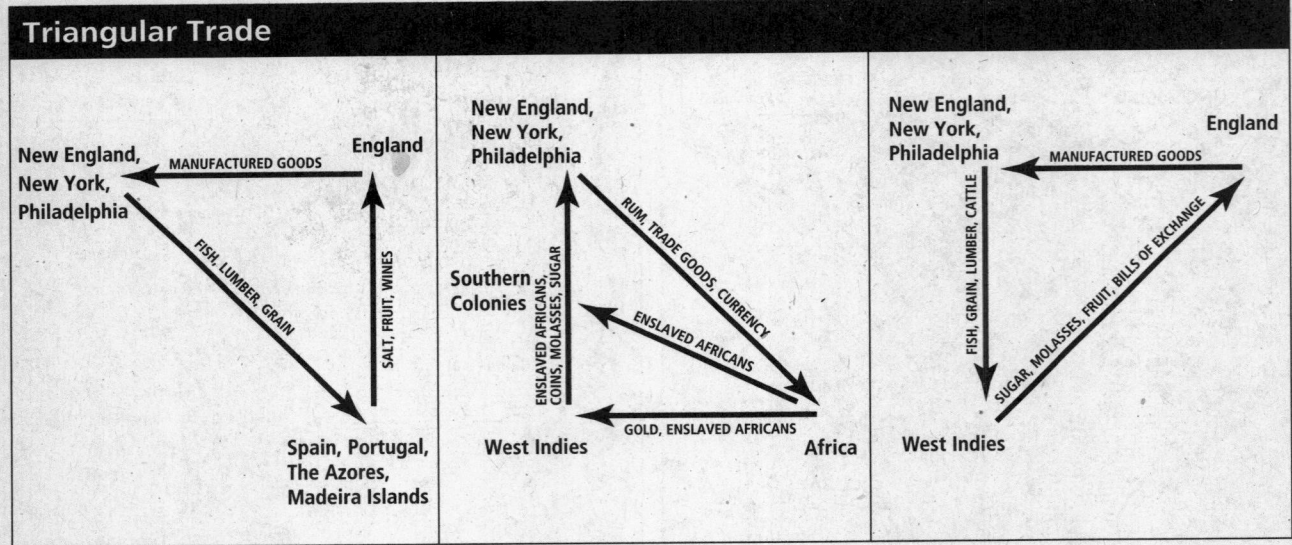

Triangular Trade

16. According to the charts, how did New England, Philadelphia, and New York trade for

enslaved Africans?

_____

17. According to the charts, what role did England play in the triangular trade?

    _____

18. Other than being part of the triangular trade, how were enslaved Africans essential to
    the triangular trade?

    _____

19. What became of the gold transported from Africa?

    _____

20. Why was the system called the triangular trade?

    _____

Part 4: Extended Response

Answer the following questions on the back of this paper or on a separate piece of paper.
(10 points each)

21. **Comparing and Contrasting** How were the French, Dutch, and English interests and
    activities in North America similar, and how were they different?

22. **Analyzing Causes and Recognizing Effects** What effects did the establishment of
    colonial empires in the Americas and the dramatic increase in overseas trade and the
    world's wealth have on Europe?

CHAPTER 5

SECTION QUIZ   *Spain's Empire and European Absolutism*

Section 1

_____

A. Terms and Names If the statement is true, write "true" on the line. If it is false, change the underlined word or words to make it true.

Example: Rembrandt van Rijn was a <u>Dutch</u> painter. _____ *true* _____

Example: In *The Night Watch*, <u>Jan Vermeer</u> portrayed a group of city guards.
_____ *Rembrandt van Rijn* _____

1. Philip II of Spain lived within the walls of his gray, granite palace called <u>the Escorial</u>.
_____

2. The <u>Portuguese</u> Armada was defeated in 1588 by stormy weather and the English navy.
_____

3. During the 1600s, the <u>Spanish</u> gradually replaced the Italians as the bankers of Europe.
_____

4. The republic formed by the United Provinces of <u>Spain</u> was an unusual type of government for 16th-century Europe. _____

5. In his novel, *Don Quixote de la Mancha*, <u>Miguel de Cervantes</u> wrote about a poor Spanish nobleman who chases after windmills. _____

6. Philip II believed it was his duty to defend <u>Protestantism</u> from its enemies in Europe and the Ottoman Empire. _____

7. <u>England</u> failed to develop a middle class in the 1500s because the tax burden on the lower classes prevented their ability to begin businesses. _____

B. Extended Response Briefly answer the following question on the back of this paper.

What is an absolute monarch? How was absolutism encouraged by the belief in the divine right of monarchs and the upheavals of the times?

The Reign of Louis XIV

Section 2

A. Terms and Names Write the letter of the term or name that matches the description. A term may be used more than once or not at all.

a. Versailles
b. intendants
c. Huguenots
d. Louis XIII
e. Louis XIV
f. René Descartes

g. Edict of Nantes
h. Cardinal Mazarin
i. Thirty Years' War
j. Cardinal Richelieu
k. Treaty of Nijmegen
l. Jean Baptiste Colbert

m. Michel de Montaigne
n. Henry IV (Henry of Navarre)
o. War of the Spanish Succession

_____ 1. was known as the Sun King.

_____ 2. became first king of the Bourbon dynasty.

_____ 3. is the magnificent palace built for Louis XIV.

_____ 4. was a Protestant prince who became a Catholic king.

_____ 5. was a writer who became a skeptic and developed the essay form.

_____ 6. were government agents who collected taxes and administered justice.

_____ 7. was the conflict that was waged to prevent the union of the French and Spanish thrones.

_____ 8. fought against Catholics in eight wars in France between 1562 and 1598.

_____ 9. was the king who increased the power of the intendants at the expense of the nobility.

_____ 10. was a declaration of religious tolerance issued by Henry IV and canceled by Louis XIV.

_____ 11. was the minister to Louis XIV whose policies drove nobles to rebel against the boy king.

_____ 12. was the minister of finance under Louis XIV whose policies of mercantilism caused France's economy to grow and prosper.

_____ 13. was the minister to Louis XIII who took steps to strengthen the power of the monarchy at the expense of the Huguenots and the nobility.

B. Extended Response Briefly answer the following question on the back of this paper.

How did religious and political turmoil in France encourage absolutism? How did it encourage skepticism?

CHAPTER 5

SECTION QUIZ   *Central European Monarchs Clash*

Section 3

_____

A. Terms and Names Write the letter of the best answer.

_____ 1. Most of the early battles of the Thirty Years' War were won by the
   a. Calvinists.
   b. Hapsburgs.
   c. French Catholics.
   d. German Protestants.

_____ 2. In the mid-1600s, the group that was LEAST dependent on the labor of serfs
   was
   a. the Ottoman Empire.
   b. the kingdom of Poland.
   c. the Holy Roman Empire.
   d. the nations of western Europe.

_____ 3. Under Maria Theresa, Austria's greatest enemy was
   a. Prussia.
   b. Hungary.
   c. Bohemia.
   d. the Ottoman Empire.

_____ 4. Frederick II came to power as the
   a. king of Prussia.
   b. king of Austria.
   c. elector of Brandenburg.
   d. emperor of the Holy Roman Empire.

_____ 5. The War of the Austrian Succession was fought over the possession of lands
   belonging to
   a. Charles VI.
   b. Frederick II.
   c. Ferdinand II.
   d. Maria Theresa.

_____ 6. In Europe, the Seven Years' War resulted in
   a. no exchange of territories in Europe.
   b. Germany's becoming part of France.
   c. Bohemia's becoming part of Austria.
   d. Hungary's becoming part of the Ottoman Empire.

B. Extended Response Briefly answer the following question on the back of this paper.

What were some of the most important results of the Thirty Years' War?

Name _____   Date _____

SECTION QUIZ   *Absolute Rulers of Russia*

A. Terms and Names Write the letter of the best answer.

_____ 1. The first Russian ruler to adopt the title *czar*, meaning "caesar," was
  a. Peter the Great.
  b. Ivan the Terrible.
  c. Michael Romanov.
  d. Anastasia Romanov.

_____ 2. Ivan the Terrible's cruelty was aimed mainly at
  a. serfs.
  b. priests.
  c. nobles.
  d. merchants.

_____ 3. In Russia, the boyars were
  a. merchants.
  b. career soldiers.
  c. slave-like laborers.
  d. landowning nobles.

_____ 4. Peter the Great's main reason for visiting the West was to
  a. gain allies for Russia.
  b. gain a warm-water seaport for Russia.
  c. learn about Western customs and technology.
  d. impress the West with Russia's learning and technology.

_____ 5. At the time that Peter the Great took the throne, the most essential part of the
Russian economy was
  a. serfs.
  b. colonies.
  c. trade relations with Europe.
  d. merchants and bankers.

_____ 6. The site for St. Petersburg was chosen because it was near
  a. Moscow.
  b. Peter's favorite palace.
  c. water routes to Europe.
  d. major roadways to Europe.

B. Extended Response Briefly answer the following question on the back of this paper.

Why did Peter the Great decide to westernize Russia, and what are some things he
did to accomplish this?

CHAPTER 5

SECTION QUIZ *Parliament Limits the English Monarchy*

A. Terms and Names Write the letter of the term or name that matches the description. A term may be used more than once or not at all.

a. James I
b. James II
c. William
d. Charles I
e. Charles II
f. Parliament

g. Restoration
h. Bill of Rights
i. habeas corpus
j. cabinet system
k. Petition of Right
l. Oliver Cromwell

m. English Civil War
n. absolute monarchy
o. constitutional monarchy

_____ 1. This began when Charles II took the throne.

_____ 2. This king of England lost the English Civil War.

_____ 3. This king of England was tried and then put to death.

_____ 4. This Catholic king of England was replaced by William and Mary.

_____ 5. Parliament's financial power was an obstacle to this type of government.

_____ 6. This Puritan leader ruled England after the end of the English Civil War.

_____ 7. This Puritan leader abolished the monarchy and ruled as a military dictator.

_____ 8. This document made clear the limits on royal power after the Glorious Revolution.

_____ 9. This king of England came to power as a result of the Glorious Revolution.

_____ 10. This king of Scotland inherited Elizabeth I's throne as well as her conflicts with Parliament.

_____ 11. This prevented monarchs from jailing people for purely political reasons and from indefinitely holding prisoners without trial.

_____ 12. This was adopted to prevent disagreements between the monarchy and Parliament from bringing government to a standstill.

B. Extended Response Briefly answer the following question on the back of this paper.

What were some of the most important political changes that resulted from the Glorious Revolution?

CHAPTER TEST **Absolute Monarchs in Europe**

Form A

Part 1: Main Ideas

Write the letter of the best answer. (4 points each)

_____ 1. What concept was the belief in "divine right" used to support?
a. absolute rule
b. freedom of religion
c. separation of church and state
d. waging war for religious purposes

_____ 2. Which war was sparked by religious conflict and resulted in the increased power of France, the weakening of Spain and Austria, and the devastation of Germany?
a. the Seven Years' War
b. the Thirty Years' War
c. the War of the Spanish Succession
d. the War of the Austrian Succession

_____ 3. Who inherited the Austrian throne only after Charles VI had the other European powers sign an agreement declaring they would recognize the heir?
a. Frederick the Great   c. William of Orange
b. Anastasia Romanov   d. Maria Theresa

_____ 4. Which of the following did the Glorious Revolution bring to England's throne?
a. James I   c. James II
b. Charles I   d. William and Mary

_____ 5. By the end of the 1600s, what had England's system of government become?
a. an absolute monarchy   d. a constitutional
b. a military dictatorship   democracy
c. a constitutional monarchy

_____ 6. During the reign of Ivan the Terrible, which of the following groups suffered the greatest loss of power?
a. the serfs   d. the Russian Orthodox
b. the boyars   church
c. the monarchy

_____ 7. What were some of Philip II's accomplishments as king of Spain?
a. He built up the strongest army in the world with 80,000 men.
b. He won territory in the Seven Years' War.
c. He reformed the culture and made Spain a power to be reckoned with.
d. He defended Roman Catholicism and helped stimulate the arts.

_____ 8. What was the main cause of the eight civil wars that were fought in France between 1562 and 1598?
    a. class differences
    b. economic hardship
    c. religious differences
    d. the lack of a clear heir to the throne

_____ 9. What king became France's most powerful ruler and boasted "I am the state"?
    a. Henry II   c. Louis IX
    b. Henry IV   d. Louis XIV

_____ 10. Why did Peter the Great build the city of St. Petersburg?
    a. He wanted a city named after himself so that he would be remembered.
    b. He wanted a city on a seaport that would make it easier to travel to the West.
    c. He didn't like Moscow, so he decided to build a new city.
    d. He wanted to build a city that was just like the European cities he visited.

Part 2: Map Skills

Use the maps to answer the questions. (4 points each)

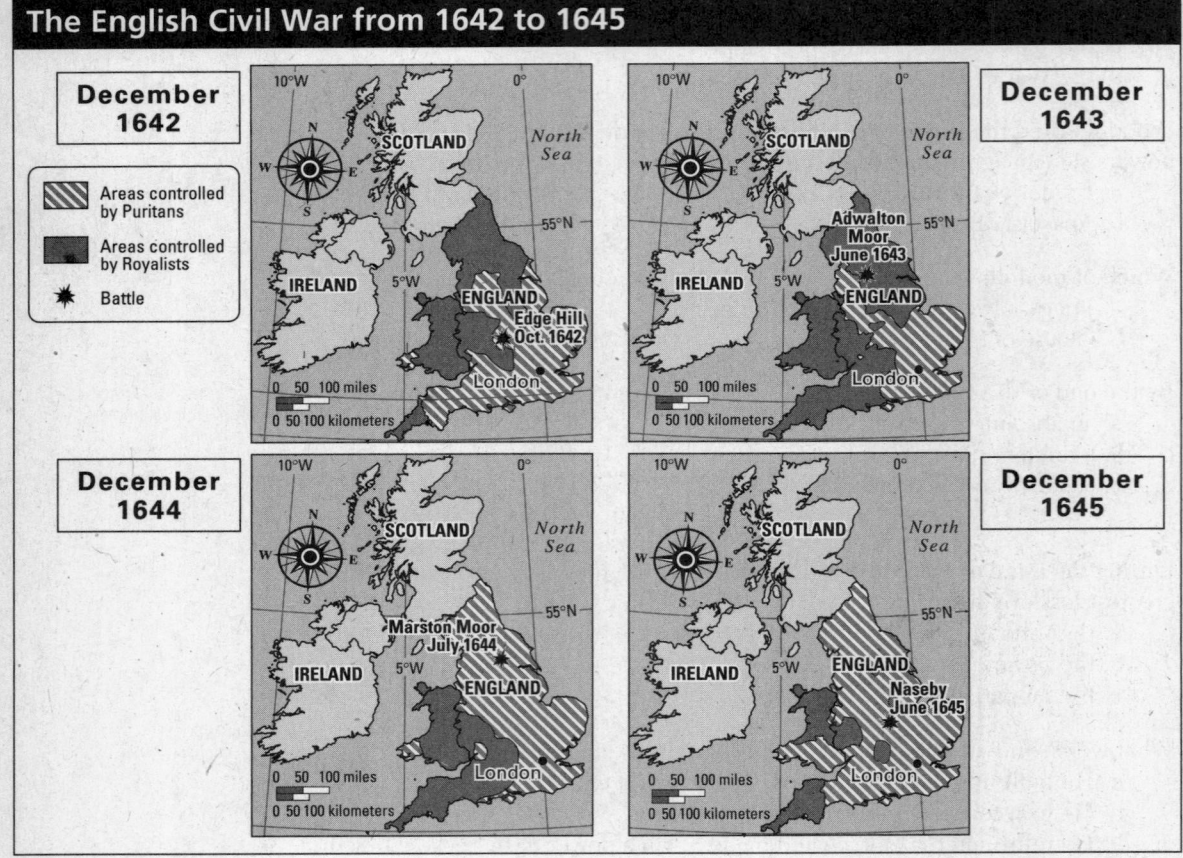

The English Civil War from 1642 to 1645

December 1642
December 1643
December 1644
December 1645

Areas controlled by Puritans
Areas controlled by Royalists
Battle

Edge Hill Oct. 1642
Adwalton Moor June 1643
Marston Moor July 1644
Naseby June 1645

_____ 11. In which year did the Royalists control the most land?
    a. 1642   b. 1643   c. 1644   d. 1645

_____ 12. Which part of England did the Royalists control during all four years?
a. the northern part
b. the southwest peninsula
c. the western shore
d. the southeast part

_____ 13. During which years did the Puritans control the capital city of London?
a. 1642–1643
b. 1643–1644
c. 1643–1645
d. 1642–1645

_____ 14. Which battle was closest to the capital city of London?
a. Adwalton Moor
b. Marston Moor
c. Naseby
d. Edge Hill

_____ 15. In which year did the Puritans control most of England?
a. 1642   b. 1643   c. 1644   d. 1645

Part 3: Interpreting Charts

Use the chart to answer the questions. (4 points each)

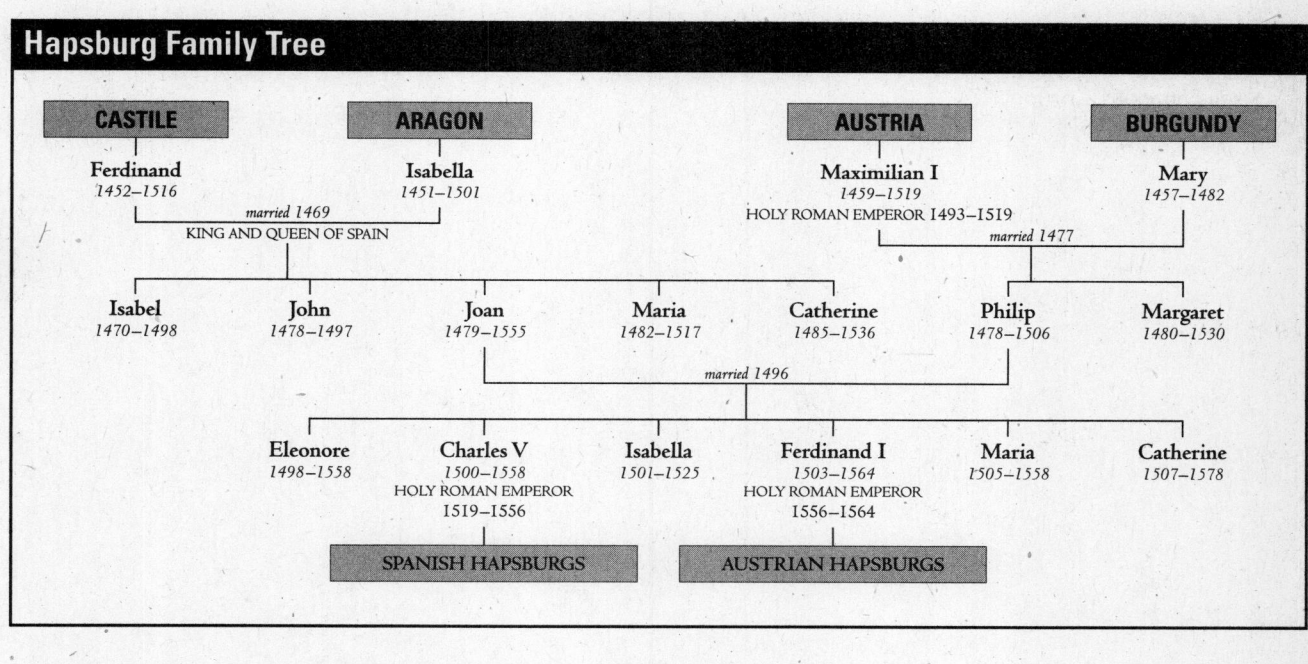

Hapsburg Family Tree

_____ 16. How many descendants of Isabella and Ferdinand are shown?
a. 5   b. 2   c. 11   d. 8

_____ 17. What was the relationship between Joan and Philip?
a. They were cousins.
b. They were brother and sister.
c. They were husband and wife.
d. They were mother and son.

_____ 18. Who was the founder of the Spanish Hapsburgs and also was Holy Roman Emperor?
a. Maximilian I
b. Charles V
c. Ferdinand I
d. Ferdinand

_____ 19. How many grandchildren did Maximilian I and Mary have?
      a. 2   b. 5   c. 6   d. 0

_____ 20. How old was the king of Spain when he died?
      a. 64   b. 47   c. 60   d. 58

Part 4: Extended Response

Answer the following questions on the back of this paper or on a separate sheet of paper.
(10 points each)

21. **Comparing and Contrasting** How were the central characteristics of the English and French governments of the late 1600s similar or different?

Think about:
- power of the rulers
- organization of the governments
- restraints on power

22. **Drawing Conclusions** What important changes took place in Russia in the late 1600s and early 1700s?

Think about:
- westernization and Europe
- sea routes to Europe
- styles and culture

CHAPTER 5

Form B

CHAPTER TEST *Absolute Monarchs in Europe*

Part 1: Main Ideas

Write the letter of the best answer. (4 points each)

_____ 1. European monarchs became absolute rulers in response to which of the following?
   a. heavy tax burdens that were levied to support trade and colonial growth
   b. the growth and increased power of nobilities and representative bodies
   c. the increased size of courts and new government bureaucracies
   d. religious and territorial conflicts that caused warfare and revolts

_____ 2. After the northern Dutch gained their freedom from Spain, what type of government did the United Provinces of the Netherlands establish?
   a. a republic   c. a constitutional monarchy
   b. a military dictatorship   d. an absolute monarchy

_____ 3. What was the Edict of Nantes issued in an effort to do?
   a. break the power of the French nobility
   b. increase the political power of the Huguenots
   c. increase the political power of the French Catholics
   d. bring an end to violent religious conflicts in France

_____ 4. What political purpose did the splendid palace at Versailles serve?
   a. to aid the artists of the time by displaying their works for others to see
   b. to show the power of Louis XIV and arouse the envy of the other monarchs
   c. to reflect the religious faith of Louis XIV and give the appearance of strength and virtue
   d. to reflect Louis XIV's ideas of westernization and his desire to modernize his country

_____ 5. Which of the following did the Restoration "restore" to power in England?
   a. Parliament
   b. the Catholics
   c. the monarchy, as an institution
   d. the king who had been overthrown in the civil war

_____ 6. Which war resulted in the beginning of the modern state system in Europe?
   a. Seven Years' War
   b. Thirty Years' War
   c. War of the Spanish Succession
   d. War of the Austrian Succession

_____ 7. What did Frederick the Great believe a ruler should be?
   a. a father to his people
   b. all-powerful and unrelenting
   c. suspicious of his advisers
   d. a military commander

_____ 8. What was Peter the Great the first Russian ruler to make an effort to do?
    a. westernize Russia
    b. reduce the power of the nobles
    c. add territory to the Russian state
    d. organize and utilize a secret police force

_____ 9. Which of the following reflects the chronological order of events in English history?
    a. the Glorious Revolution—the Restoration—the English Civil War
    b. the English Civil War—the Restoration—the Glorious Revolution
    c. the English Civil War—the Glorious Revolution—the Restoration
    d. the Restoration—the English Civil War—the Glorious Revolution

_____ 10. How did the economy of central Europe differ from that of western Europe?
    a. The feudal system ended earlier in central Europe.
    b. A middle class and a system of capitalism developed in central Europe.
    c. Monarchs in central Europe taxed the middle class to pay for armies.
    d. Serfs in central Europe did not move to cities and become the middle class.

Part 2: Map Skills

Use the maps to answer the questions. (4 points each)

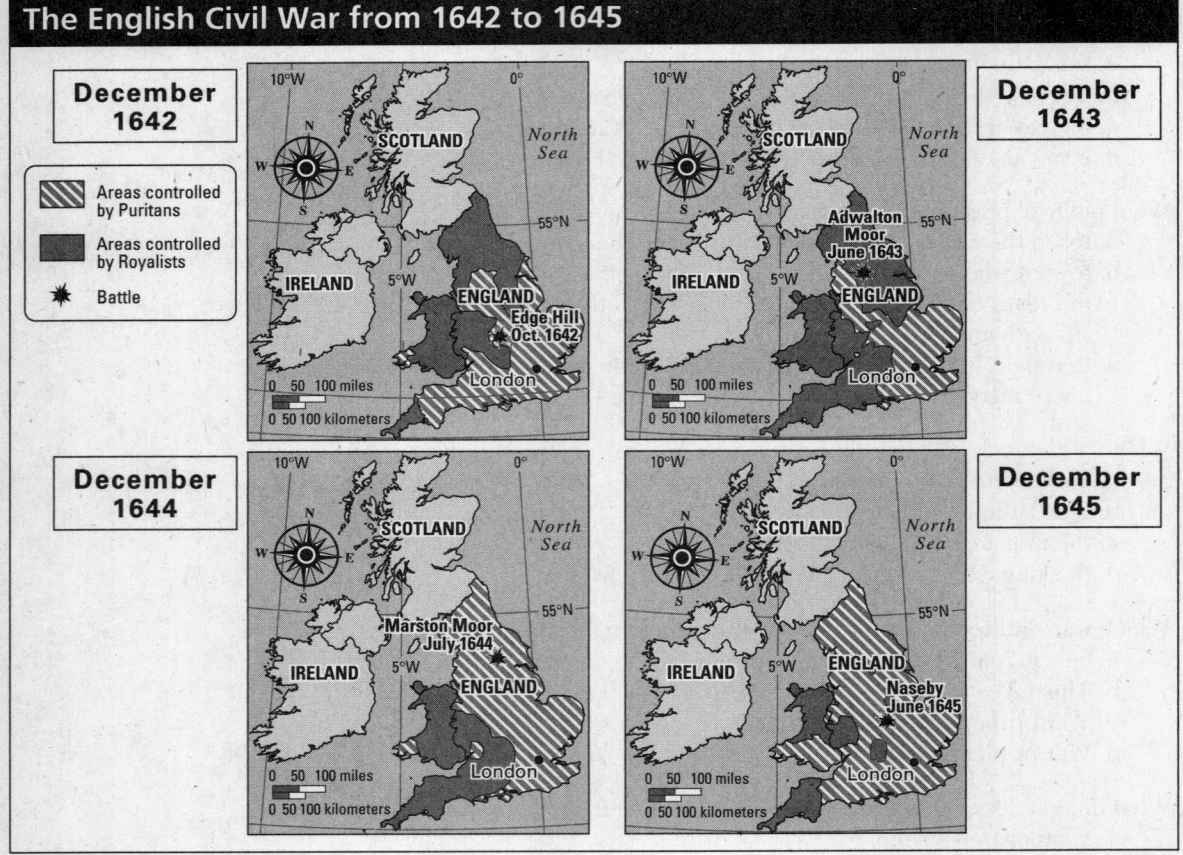

The English Civil War from 1642 to 1645

_____ 11. Approximately how many miles away from London was the Battle of Naseby?
        a. 50   b. 60   c. 75   d. 100

_____ 12. In which years was the land controlled by the Royalists closest to the capital London?
        a. 1642 and 1643
        b. 1643, 1644, and 1645
        c. 1642 and 1645
        d. 1642, 1643, and 1645

_____ 13. According to the map, how many battles were fought in land controlled by the Royalists?
        a. 1   b. 2   c. 3   d. 4

_____ 14. Judging from this map, what is one reason the Royalists lost the war?
        a. They never controlled as much land as the Puritans.
        b. Their holdings grew smaller every year from 1642 to 1645.
        c. They never captured the capital city of London.
        d. All of the above are true.

_____ 15. Which regions did the Royalists control in 1645?
        a. the northern and eastern shores
        b. the central and eastern regions
        c. the region including London and the northern shore
        d. the southwest peninsula and part of the western shore

Part 3: Interpreting Charts

Use the chart to answer the questions. (4 points each)

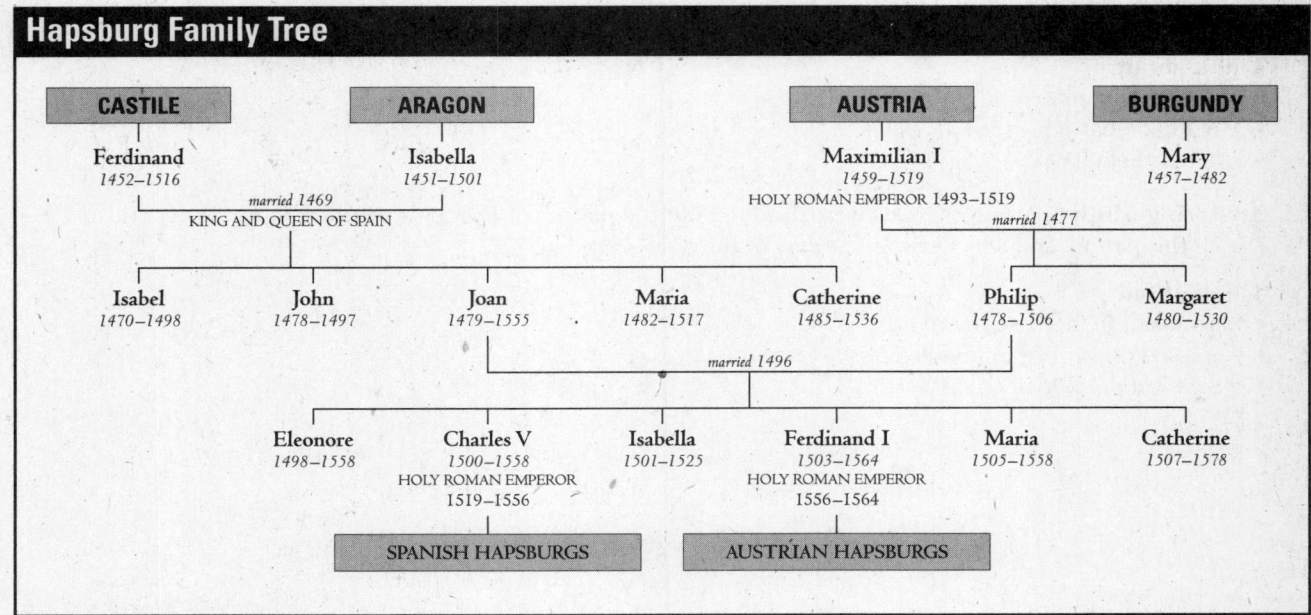

Hapsburg Family Tree

_____ 16. How many years did Charles V rule as Holy Roman Emperor?
        a. 36   b. 37   c. 8   d. 21

_____ 17. What was the relationship between Philip and Margaret?
        a. They were brother and sister.
        b. They were husband and wife.
        c. They were father and daughter.
        d. They were cousins.

_____ 18. Which three people connect the House of Aragon to the Austrian Hapsburgs?
        a. Ferdinand, Isabella, and Joan
        b. Isabella, Joan, and Charles V
        c. Mary, Philip, and Charles V
        d. Isabella, Joan, and Ferdinand I

_____ 19. How old were Maximilian I and Mary when they were married?
        a. Maximilian I was 18, and Mary was 20.
        b. Maximilian I was 20, and Mary was 18.
        c. Maximilian I was 18, and Mary was 17.
        d. They were both 17.

_____ 20. How could two brothers both have the title of Holy Roman Emperor?
        a. They split the empire into Spain and Austria.
        b. Ferdinand I was Charles V's heir.
        c. That title was given to all sons in that family.
        d. Charles V killed Ferdinand I to gain the title.

Part 4: Extended Response

Answer the following questions on the back of this paper or on a separate sheet of paper.
(10 points each)

21. **Drawing Conclusions** How was Russia different from western Europe? How did Peter the Great want to change Russia?

    Think about:
    • economic systems
    • geographic barriers
    • religious beliefs

22. **Analyzing Motives** What methods were used to limit the powers of Europe's nobles during this period, and why were the powers of the nobles limited?

    Think about:
    • steps taken to increase the monarchs' power
    • increased power of the middle class
    • redistribution of land

Name _____ Date _____

CHAPTER
5

Form C

CHAPTER TEST *Absolute Monarchs in Europe*

Part 1: Main Ideas

Write the letter of the best answer. (4 points each)

_____ 1. What problem helped to weaken the Spanish Empire?
    a. Spain experienced a period of severe inflation and heavy taxes.
    b. Spain developed a highly influential middle class and lost its nobility.
    c. Spanish kings borrowed money from England and France to finance wars.
    d. Spanish kings refused to declare bankruptcy or repay their debts.

_____ 2. How did the United Provinces of the Netherlands differ from neighboring states?
    a. It was a constitutional monarchy.
    b. It had elected governors whose power depended on landowners and merchants.
    c. It had an unstable government that did not focus on economic growth.
    d. It continued the feudal system and did not allow a middle class to grow.

_____ 3. How did Cardinal Richelieu work to increase the power of the Bourbon monarchy?
    a. He dissolved Parliament and refused to make Puritan reforms.
    b. He executed nobles and gave their land to the middle class.
    c. He moved against the Huguenots and weakened the power of the nobles.
    d. He excluded nobles from his councils and demanded they live at court.

_____ 4. What event led to the War of the Spanish Succession?
    a. Charles II made Louis XIV's grandson his heir, adding to Bourbon power.
    b. The Dutch prince William of Orange became king of England.
    c. Great Britain took control of the entrance to the Mediterranean Sea.
    d. The Austrian Hapsburgs took control of the Spanish Netherlands.

_____ 5. What was the Thirty Years' War a conflict over?
    a. the closing of Catholic churches by Ferdinand II
    b. the alliance of Maria Theresa and the French kings
    c. the invasion of Silesia by the king of Prussia
    d. religion, territory, and power among European ruling families

_____ 6. Why did strong states form more slowly in central Europe than in western Europe?
    a. They experienced terrible losses during the Thirty Years' War.
    b. They had weak empires and poor economies without a middle class.
    c. The citizens in the empires overthrew one ruler after another.
    d. The rulers wore too many crowns and ruled too much land.

_____ 7. What was the significance of the English Bill of Rights?
    a. It established the group of government ministers known as the cabinet.
    b. It allowed for the bloodless overthrow of King James II.
    c. It made clear the limits of royal power.
    d. It restored power to the monarch.

_____ 8. What were some of the things Peter the Great did to westernize Russia?
        a. He raised women's status and made nobles wear Western fashions.
        b. He introduced the potato and tobacco, both of which became staples.
        c. He moved the capital of Russia to Moscow, which has a seaport.
        d. He established the outdoor market and promoted the arts.

_____ 9. What was one reason Ivan IV was called Ivan the Terrible?
        a. He poisoned his wife Anastasia because she was from a boyar family.
        b. He organized a police force that murdered people he considered traitors.
        c. He made the nobility dependent on him and gave power to the middle class.
        d. He was in debt to several countries and had to declare bankruptcy.

_____ 10. How did the Puritans finally win the English Civil War?
        a. Cromwell's army defeated the Royalists, and the Puritans held the king prisoner.
        b. Cromwell killed Charles I and appointed himself dictator.
        c. Cromwell stormed the castle and seized Charles I.
        d. Cromwell won support of Parliament and was appointed dictator.

Part 2: Map Skills—Constructed Response

Use the maps to answer the questions. (4 points each)

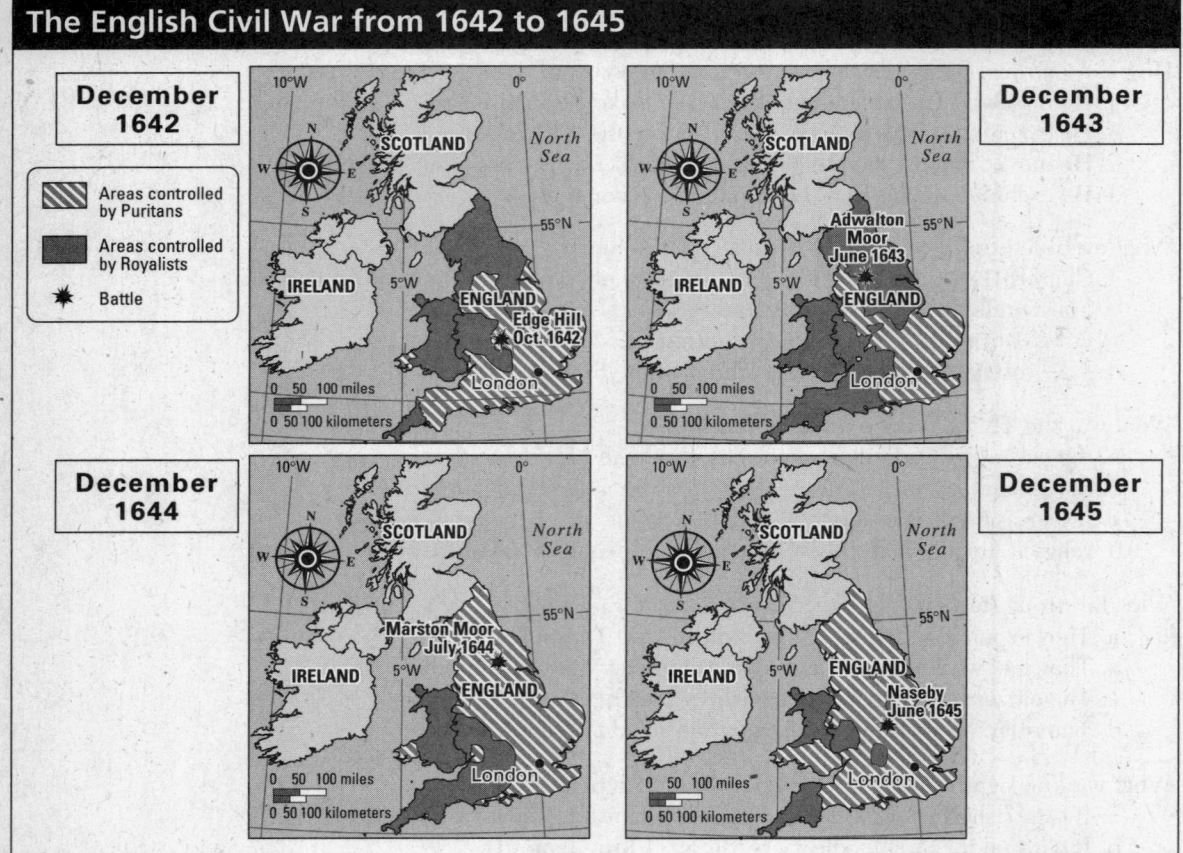

The English Civil War from 1642 to 1645

December 1642

Areas controlled by Puritans
Areas controlled by Royalists
✹ Battle

SCOTLAND
North Sea
55°N
IRELAND
ENGLAND
Edge Hill Oct. 1642
London
0 50 100 miles
0 50 100 kilometers

December 1643

SCOTLAND
North Sea
Adwalton Moor June 1643
55°N
IRELAND
ENGLAND
London
0 50 100 miles
0 50 100 kilometers

December 1644

SCOTLAND
North Sea
55°N
Marston Moor July 1644
IRELAND
ENGLAND
London
0 50 100 miles
0 50 100 kilometers

December 1645

SCOTLAND
North Sea
55°N
IRELAND
ENGLAND
Naseby June 1645
London
0 50 100 miles
0 50 100 kilometers

11. Which battles were fought on land controlled by the Puritans?

    _____

12. How did the territorial control of the Royalists change during the four years?

    _____

13. What major strategic site did the Puritans control for the whole war?

    _____

14. Which regions of England did the Royalist control for the entire civil war?

    _____

15. Which side controlled the most important territory for the entire war, and why?

    _____

Part 3: Interpreting Charts

Use the chart to answer the questions. (4 points each)

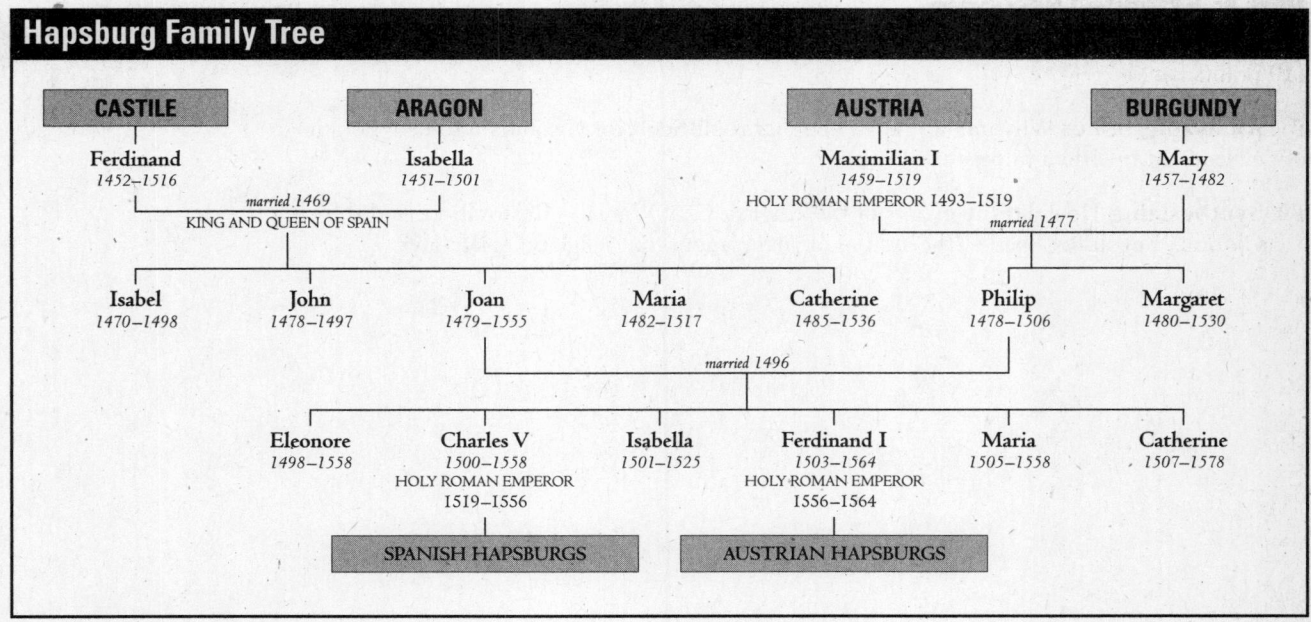

_____ 16. Which three people connect the House of Burgundy to the Spanish Hapsburgs?
  a. Mary, Philip, and Ferdinand I
  b. Mary, Joan, and Charles V
  c. Isabella, Joan, and Ferdinand I
  d. Mary, Philip, and Charles V

_____ 17. What is the significance of this family tree?
  a. It shows the relationship of the Spanish Hapsburgs and the Austrian Hapsburgs.
  b. It shows the relationship of the House of Burgundy and the House of Austria.
  c. It shows the relationship of the House of Aragon and the House of Castile.
  d. It shows how many children the king and queen of Spain had.

_____ 18. What event joined the Houses of Burgundy, Austria, Aragon, and Castile?
  a. the marriage of Maximilian I and Mary
  b. the marriage of Ferdinand and Isabella
  c. the birth of Charles V
  d. the marriage of Joan and Philip

_____ 19. Which Holy Roman Emperor ruled for the longest amount of time?
  a. Maximilian I
  b. Ferdinand I
  c. Charles V
  d. Philip

_____ 20. Which grandchild of Isabella and Ferdinand lived the longest?
  a. Joan
  b. Eleonore
  c. Ferdinand I
  d. Catherine

Part 4: Extended Response

Answer the following questions on the back of this paper or on a separate sheet of paper. (10 points each)

21. **Analyzing Issues** Why might it have been more difficult for absolutism to take hold in central Europe than in western Europe?

22. **Synthesizing** How did the events of the English Civil War, the Restoration, and the Glorious Revolution lead to the system of government that England has today?

SECTION QUIZ *The Scientific Revolution*

CHAPTER
6

Section 1

A. Terms and Names Write the letter of the name that matches the description. Not all names will be used.

a. Galen
b. Aristotle
c. Tycho Brahe
d. Robert Boyle
e. Isaac Newton
f. Francis Bacon

g. Edward Jenner
h. Galileo Galilei
i. Anders Celsius
j. René Descartes
k. Johannes Kepler
l. Nicolaus Copernicus

_____ 1. This brilliant mathematician used the data of Tycho Brahe to prove the accuracy of Copernicus's basic ideas about the motion of the planets.

_____ 2. This great mathematician and physicist brought together some of the theories and discoveries of Copernicus, Kepler, and Galileo under a single theory of motion known as the law of universal gravitation.

_____ 3. This pioneer of the use of the scientific method in chemistry is considered the founder of modern chemistry. He is best known for the discovery of a law that helps to explain characteristics of gases.

_____ 4. This English politician and writer had a passionate interest in science. In his writings, he criticized the techniques of the ancient and medieval scholars. He argued forcefully for the adoption of new scientific techniques such as the experimental method.

_____ 5. After studying planetary movements for many years, this astronomer reasoned that the stars and planets revolved around the sun, an idea that became known as the heliocentric theory. Fearing ridicule or persecution, he didn't publish his findings until 1543, the year of his death.

_____ 6. This mathematician developed analytical geometry, which links algebra and geometry. Of his own existence, he was sure; everything else was doubtful until proved by reason. In his writings, he urged scientists to rely on mathematics and logic to reach fundamental truths about the natural world.

_____ 7. Among his many scientific discoveries are the law of the pendulum and the fact that falling objects accelerate at fixed and predictable rates. Despite his genius, he lived the last years of his life under house arrest because his scientific findings did not go along with the Church authorities' interpretation of the Bible.

B. Extended Response Briefly answer the following question on the back of this paper.

What was so revolutionary about the Scientific Revolution? In your answer, be sure to discuss the scientific method.

Name _____ Date _____

CHAPTER 6

Section 2

SECTION QUIZ *The Enlightenment in Europe*

A. Terms and Names Write the letter of the name that matches the description. Not all names will be used.

a. Voltaire
b. John Locke
c. Montesquieu
d. Thomas Hobbes
e. Emilie du Châtelet
f. Mary Wollstonecraft
g. Jean Jacques Rousseau
h. Cesare Bonesana Beccaria

_____ 1. In *A Vindication of the Rights of Women,* this political thinker presented an argument for the education of women. She also declared that women should have the same political rights as men.

_____ 2. This philosopher's ideas greatly influenced criminal law reformers in Europe and North America. He argued against the use of torture and other common abuses of justice.

_____ 3. This aristocratic philosophe was devoted to the study of political liberty. In his famous book *On the Spirit of the Laws,* he proposed that separation of powers would keep any individual or group from gaining total control of a government.

_____ 4. This philosophe strongly disagreed with other philosophes on a number of matters. For instance, although most philosophes believed that reason, science, and art improve the lives of all people, he argued that civilization corrupts people's natural goodness.

_____ 5. This philosophe's masterful use of satire got him into frequent trouble with the clergy, the aristocracy, and the government of France. Despite serving two prison terms and being exiled, he never stopped fighting for tolerance, reason, freedom of religion, and freedom of speech.

_____ 6. This political thinker felt that people are reasonable beings. He supported self-government and argued that the purpose of government is to protect the natural rights of people. If government fails to protect these natural rights, he said, citizens have the right to overthrow it.

_____ 7. This political thinker believed that all humans are naturally selfish and wicked. He argued, therefore, that strong governments are necessary to control human behavior. To avoid chaos, he said, people enter into a social contract. They give up their rights in exchange for law and order.

B. Extended Response Briefly answer the following question on the back of this paper.

What were some of the most important effects of the Enlightenment?

CHAPTER
6

Section 3

SECTION QUIZ   *The Enlightenment Spreads*

A. Terms and Names Write the letter of the name or group of names that matches the description. A name or group of names may be used more than once or not at all.

a. Joseph II
b. Denis Diderot
c. Frederick the Great
d. Catherine the Great
e. Marie-Thérèse Geoffrin
f. Elisabeth-Louise Vigée-Le Brun
g. Samuel Richardson and Henry Fielding
h. Franz Joseph Haydn, Wolfgang Amadeus Mozart, and Ludwig van Beethoven

_____ 1. abolished serfdom.

_____ 2. composed classical music.

_____ 3. ruled Russia as an enlightened despot.

_____ 4. ruled Prussia as an enlightened despot.

_____ 5. ruled Austria as an enlightened despot.

_____ 6. edited and published the *Encyclopedia*.

_____ 7. brutally crushed a massive uprising of serfs.

_____ 8. gave the nobility absolute power over the serfs.

_____ 9. developed many of the features of the modern novel.

_____ 10. ran the most influential of Paris salons during the Enlightenment.

B. Extended Response Briefly answer the following question on the back of this paper.

What are some of the ways that western culture changed in response to Enlightenment ideas? Be sure to mention the baroque, neoclassical, and classical styles.

CHAPTER 6 — **SECTION QUIZ**   *The American Revolution*

Section 4

A. Terms and Names Write the letter of the best answer.

_____ 1. Which of the following occurred last?
   a. the repeal of the Stamp Act
   b. the adoption of the Bill of Rights
   c. the end of the French and Indian War
   d. the calling of the Second Continental Congress

_____ 2. Who wrote the Declaration of Independence?
   a. John Locke
   b. Samuel Adams
   c. Thomas Jefferson
   d. Benjamin Franklin

_____ 3. Which of the following documents created the first national government of the
   13 individual states in North America?
   a. Constitution
   b. Navigation Acts
   c. Articles of Confederation
   d. Declaration of Independence

_____ 4. Which of the following was a major reason for the colonists' victory over
   Britain was?
   a. superior weaponry
   b. a stronger motivation to fight
   c. military support from Italy
   d. more experience generals

_____ 5. Which of the following was created by the Articles of Confederation?
   a. the Congress
   b. the Supreme Court
   c. the office of president
   d. the office of vice-president

B. Extended Response Briefly answer the following question on the back of this paper.

In what ways did the U.S. Constitution and the Bill of Rights reflect Enlightenment
ideas? In your answer, be sure to discuss the system of checks and balances and the
federal system.

CHAPTER **6** Form A

CHAPTER TEST *Enlightenment and Revolution*

Part 1: Main Ideas
Write the letter of the correct answer next to each question. (4 points each)

_____ 1. The heliocentric, or sun-centered, theory was proposed by
     a. Galileo Galilei.   c. Francis Bacon.
     b. Nicolaus Copernicus.   d. Isaac Newton.

_____ 2. Francis Bacon helped to develop
     a. the microscope.   c. the scientific method.
     b. the law of the pendulum.   d. the barometer.

_____ 3. Isaac Newton explained the
     a. law of universal gravitation.
     b. anatomy of the human body.
     c. chemical composition of matter.
     d. function of blood vessels.

_____ 4. In general, the philosophes believed in which of the following?
     a. expanding women's rights   c. progress for society
     b. all Church decrees   d. authoritarian rule

_____ 5. The idea of a direct democracy is explained in
     a. *A Vindication of the Rights of Woman.*
     b. *The Social Contract.*
     c. *Starry Messenger.*
     d. *On the Spirit of Laws.*

_____ 6. European art of the 1600s and early 1700s was dominated by a grand, ornate style called
     a. neoclassical.   b. classical.   c. baroque.   d. gothic.

_____ 7. The philosophes influenced Catherine the Great's
     a. architectural plans for her palace.
     b. military campaign against Poland.
     c. diplomatic relations with France
     d. proposal on reforms to Russia's laws.

_____ 8. The Declaration of Independence was written by
     a. John Adams.   c. Thomas Jefferson.
     b. Benjamin Franklin.   d. Patrick Henry.

_____ 9. The Bill of Rights was influenced by
     a. Voltaire.   c. Jean Jacques Rousseau.
     b. John Locke.   d. all of the above.

_____ 10. Henry Fielding was a writer who
   a. turned out many popular poems in the 1700s.
   b. wrote a novel about the life of a young servant girl.
   c. developed many features of the modern novel.
   d. did all of the above.

Part 2: Map Skills

Using the map, answer the following questions. (4 points each)

North America, 1783

British Territory
French Territory
Russian Territory
Spanish Territory
Claimed by the U.S. and Great Britain
Claimed by the U.S. and Spain

0   500   1000 miles
0   500   1000 kilometers
Azimuthal Equal-Area Projection

_____ 11. What is the approximate distance in miles between Quebec and Charleston?
   a. 1,000   b. 500   c. 1,500   d. 750

_____ 12. Which of the following cities was NOT located in the United States in 1783?
        a. Boston   c. New Orleans
        b. New York   d. Charleston

_____ 13. Which of the following islands did the British own?
        a. Puerto Rico   b. Hispaniola   c. Cuba   d. Jamaica

_____ 14. Who owned most of the territory west of the Mississippi in 1783?
        a. Spain   c. Russia
        b. the United States   d. Great Britain

_____ 15. Which of the following regions did both the United States and Spain claim in 1783?
        a. the region between Canada, the Louisiana Territory, and the United States
        b. the region north of New Orleans and northwestern Florida
        c. the region along the coast of Alaska
        d. the region around Hudson Bay

Part 3: Interpreting Charts

Using the chart below, answer the questions. (4 points each)

Enlightenment and Revolution, 1550-1789

SCIENTIFIC REVOLUTION
- Heliocentric theory challenges geocentric theory.
- Mathematics and observation support heliocentric theory.
- Scientific method develops.
- Scientists make discoveries in many fields.

A new way of thinking about the world develops—based on observation and a willingness to question assumptions.

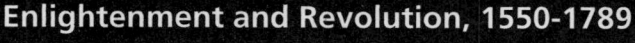

ENLIGHTENMENT
- People try to apply the scientific approach to all aspects of society.
- Political scientists propose new ideas about government.
- Philosophers urge using reason to discover truths.
- Philosophers address social issues through reason.

Enlightenment writers challenge many accepted ideas about government and society.

SPREAD OF ENLIGHTENMENT IDEAS
- Enlightenment ideas appeal to thinkers and artists across Europe.
- Salons help spread Enlightenment thinking.
- Ideas spread to literate middle class.
- Enlightened despots attempt reforms.

Enlightenment ideas sweep through European society and also to colonial America.

AMERICAN REVOLUTION
- Enlightenment ideas influence colonists.
- Britain taxes colonies after French and Indian War.
- Colonists denounce taxation without representation.
- War begins in Lexington and Concord.

Colonists declare independence, defeat Britain, and establish a republic.

_____ 16. The heliocentric theory challenged the
        a. political scientists.   c. geocentric theory.
        b. observed patterns.   d. mathematical theories.

_____ 17. Between 1550 and 1789, Enlightenment ideas swept
   a. only through France and colonial America.
   b. only through European society.
   c. through European society and colonial America.
   d. throughout the world.

_____ 18. Salons helped to spread
   a. the geocentric theory.
   b. only the ideas of the philosophes.
   c. only the ideas of political scientists.
   d. Enlightenment thinking.

_____ 19. The philosophes used reason to address
   a. British taxes.   c. abusive rulers
   b. social issues.   d. all of the above.

_____ 20. The American Revolution was influenced by
   a. British policies.   c. the philosophes.
   b. political scientists.   d. all of the above.

Part 4: Extended Response

Answer the following questions on the back of this paper or on a separate sheet. (10 points each)

21. **Contrasting** What is the scientific method? How does it differ from the methods used by scholars in medieval times?

   Think about:
   • questioning authority
   • gathering data
   • the basis for conclusions

22. **Recognizing Effects** What influence did the ideas of John Locke have on the Declaration of Independence? Support your answer with specific details.

   Think about:
   • natural rights
   • the purpose of government
   • the right of citizens

Name _____ Date _____

CHAPTER TEST *Enlightenment and Revolution*

CHAPTER
6

Form B

Part 1: Main Ideas

Write the letter of the correct answer next to each question. (4 points each)

_____ 1. Which of the following is true of the neoclassical style of art?
a. It emphasized elegance and simplicity.
b. It tended to be ornate, highly detailed, and rich in color.
c. It was the dominant style of art during the Middle Ages.
d. It was based on ideas and themes from ancient Japan.

_____ 2. What reflects the correct sequence of steps used in the scientific process?
a. observation, question, experimentation, hypothesis, conclusion
b. question, experimentation, hypothesis, observation, conclusion
c. question, observation, hypothesis, experimentation, conclusion
d. observation, question, hypothesis, experimentation, conclusion

_____ 3. Which of the following events occurred after the American Revolution?
a. Constitutional   c. Stamp Act
   Convention   d. Navigation Acts
b. French and Indian War

_____ 4. What was Montesquieu's influence on the U.S. Constitution?
a. public elections   c. the Bill of Rights
b. branches of government   d. representatives

_____ 5. How did the Baroque style and the neoclassical style differ?
a. Baroque was used for music; neoclassical was used for painting.
b. Baroque was used by Mozart; neoclassical was used by Bach.
c. Baroque was grand and ornate; neoclassical was simple and elegant.
d. All of the above are true.

_____ 6. Frederick II supported which of the following?
a. freedom of worship   c. wealthy landowners
b. Christian religion   d. direct democracy

_____ 7. How were Thomas Hobbes and Catherine the Great similar?
a. Both were influenced by John Locke.
b. Both were affected by the horrors of the English Civil War.
c. Both were influenced by Voltaire and Baron de Montesquieu.
d. Both believed that a monarch should have absolute authority.

_____ 8. What was the law of universal gravitation?
a. The earth and other planets revolve around the sun.
b. All physical objects are affected equally by the same forces.
c. A falling object accelerates at a fixed and predictable rate.
d. The physical world consists of four elements—earth, air, fire, and water.

_____ 9. Which of the following did the Enlightenment promote?
        a. a belief in progress   c. faith in science
        b. a more secular outlook   d. all of the above

_____ 10. What did American colonists protest as "taxation without representation"?
        a. French and Indian War   c. Stamp Act
        b. Navigation Acts   d. import tax on tea

Part 2: Map Skills

Using the map, answer the following questions. (4 points each)

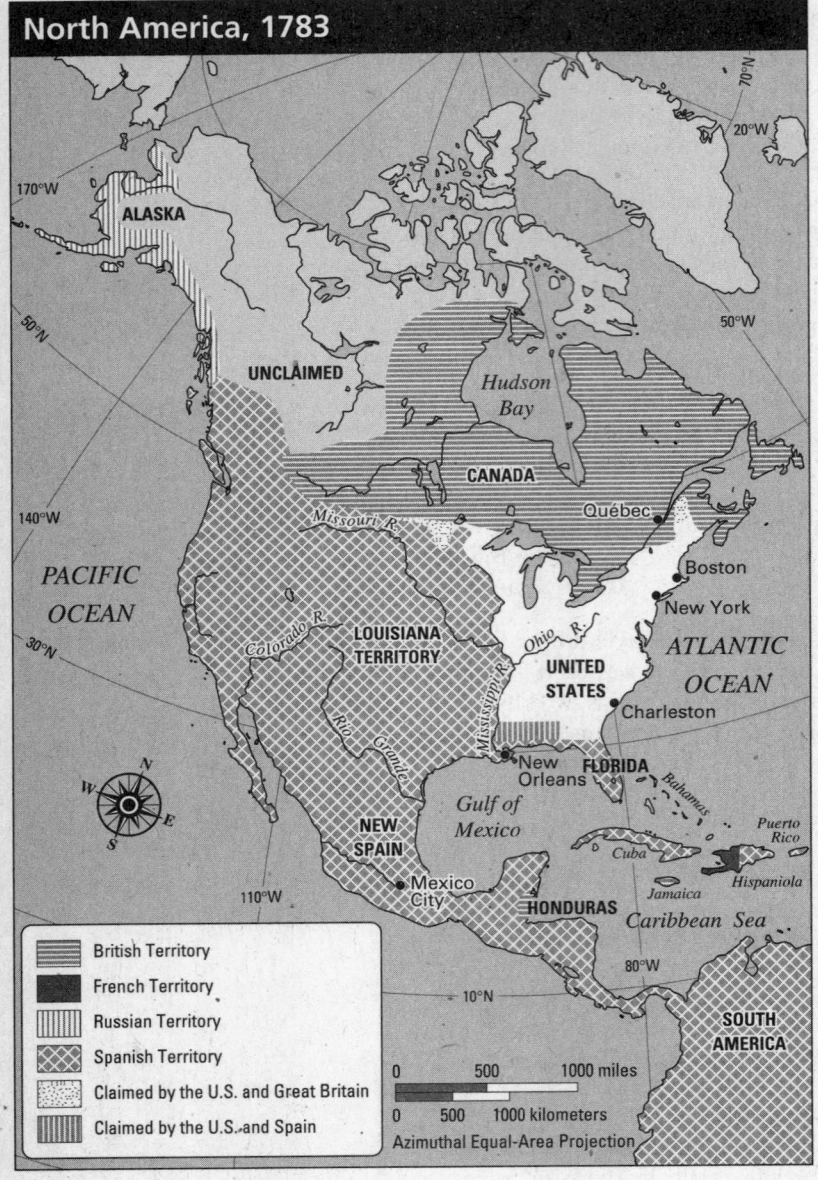

North America, 1783

Legend:
- British Territory
- French Territory
- Russian Territory
- Spanish Territory
- Claimed by the U.S. and Great Britain
- Claimed by the U.S. and Spain

_____ 11. Which of the following countries claimed land close to Asia?
        a. Russia   b. Britain   c. Spain   d. France

_____ 12. If a ship was sailing at a rate of 20 miles per hour, about how many hours would it take to deliver sugar from Puerto Rico to New York?

      a. 25   b. 50   c. 75   d. 95

_____ 13. Which country could ship goods down the Mississippi River to New Orleans without seeking permission from a foreign power?

      a. Great Britain   b. Spain   c. Russia   d. France

_____ 14. Which country posed the biggest threat to invade the United States in 1783?

      a. Russia   c. France

      b. Great Britain   d. all of the above

_____ 15. Which of the following bodies of water bordered Spanish territory?

      a. the Pacific Ocean   c. the Caribbean Sea

      b. the Gulf of Mexico   d. all of the above

Part 3: Interpreting Charts

Using the charts below, answer the questions. (4 points each)

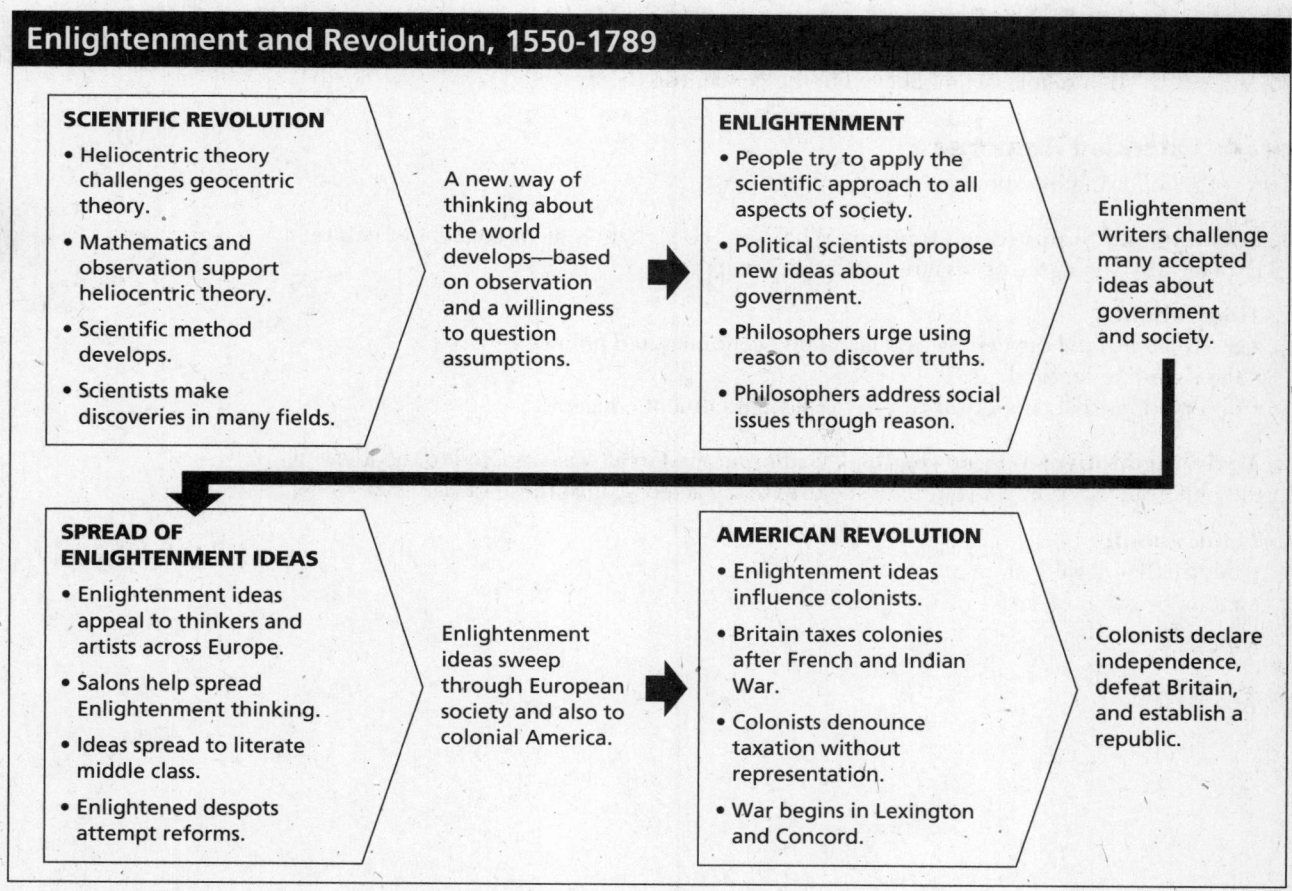

Enlightenment and Revolution, 1550-1789

SCIENTIFIC REVOLUTION
- Heliocentric theory challenges geocentric theory.
- Mathematics and observation support heliocentric theory.
- Scientific method develops.
- Scientists make discoveries in many fields.

A new way of thinking about the world develops—based on observation and a willingness to question assumptions.

ENLIGHTENMENT
- People try to apply the scientific approach to all aspects of society.
- Political scientists propose new ideas about government.
- Philosophers urge using reason to discover truths.
- Philosophers address social issues through reason.

Enlightenment writers challenge many accepted ideas about government and society.

SPREAD OF ENLIGHTENMENT IDEAS
- Enlightenment ideas appeal to thinkers and artists across Europe.
- Salons help spread Enlightenment thinking.
- Ideas spread to literate middle class.
- Enlightened despots attempt reforms.

Enlightenment ideas sweep through European society and also to colonial America.

AMERICAN REVOLUTION
- Enlightenment ideas influence colonists.
- Britain taxes colonies after French and Indian War.
- Colonists denounce taxation without representation.
- War begins in Lexington and Concord.

Colonists declare independence, defeat Britain, and establish a republic.

_____ 16. Which of the following was influenced by Enlightenment Ideas?

      a. literate middle class   c. American colonists

      b. thinkers and artists   d. all of the above

_____ 17. How did the Scientific Revolution influence the American Revolution?
     a. Questioning assumptions led to challenging ideas about government.
     b. Scientific discoveries influenced British foreign policies.
     c. The heliocentric theory caused unrest among the colonists.
     d. The salons influenced the French and Indian War.

_____ 18. Which of the following attempted social reforms?
     a. the philosophes
     b. scholars
     c. enlightened despots
     d. all of the above

_____ 19. Which of the following occurred after the salons spread enlightenment ideas?
     a. The scientific method develops.
     b. The heliocentric theory develops.
     c. The scientific method begins to affect society.
     d. The colonists denounce taxation without representation.

_____ 20. Which person would probably NOT have been influenced by the philosophes?
     a. a European artist living during the 1700s
     b. a leader of a salon
     c. an American patriot denouncing taxation without representation
     d. a scholar who believed in the geocentric theory

Part 4: Extended Response
Answer the following questions. (10 points each)

21. **Forming and Supporting Opinions** What was the Enlightenment concept of nature? Explain why you agree or disagree with this concept.

Think about:
- the relationship between natural laws and economics and politics
- the scientific method
- observations that support or refute the Enlightenment concept

22. **Analyzing Motives** Why do you think Catherine the Great was attracted to the ideas of the philosophes? Why do you think she eventually acted against these ideas?

Think about:
- the Russian legal system
- the oppression of serfs
- loss of power

CHAPTER TEST *Enlightenment and Revolution*

Part 1: Main Ideas
Write the letter of the correct answer next to each question. (4 points each)

_____ 1. What did Andreas Vesalius and Voltaire both do?
a. write drama and fiction   c. challenge existing ideas
b. analyze human anatomy   d. spend time in jail

_____ 2. How did Zacharias Janssen make Anton van Leeuwenhoek's discoveries possible?
a. He invented the microscope.
b. He offered Leeuwenhoek financial support.
c. He provided valuable research information to Leeuwenhoek.
d. He invented the thermometer.

_____ 3. Which of the following men contradicted the ideas in the U.S. Constitution?
a. Baron de Montesquieu   c. John Locke
b. Thomas Hobbes   d. Denis Diderot

_____ 4. How does the main character in Richardson's *Pamela* reflect Enlightenment ideas?
a. She was a monarch who became enlightened.
b. She used the scientific method.
c. She resisted an abuse of authority.
d. She worked as a servant girl.

_____ 5. In the 1700s, which of the following showed the influence of Enlightenment ideas?
a. a woman reading a novel
b. a woman allowing her child to have a smallpox vaccination
c. a man attending a salon
d. all of the above

_____ 6. Which of the following did the censors of the Catholic Church ban?
a. *Don Giovanni*   c. *Tom Jones*
b. the *Encyclopedia*   d. all of the above

_____ 7. How did the taxation problem in America differ before and after independence?
a. Before were too many British taxes; after were not enough federal taxes.
b. Before were too few British taxes; after were too many federal taxes.
c. Before were too many British taxes; after were too many federal taxes.
d. Before were too few British taxes; after were not enough federal taxes.

_____ 8. How did the Declaration of Independence embody Enlightenment ideals?
a. It stated that all titles of nobility should be abolished.
b. It protected the rights of the accused and prohibited cruel punishment.
c. It set up a system of checks and balances for the U.S. government.
d. It said that people have rights of life, liberty, and the pursuit of happiness.

_____ 9. Which of the following might reflect the neoclassical style?
      a. an ornate palace   c. a simple, elegant church
      b. an elaborate painting   d. a complex composition

_____ 10. Which of the following were caused by the scientific revolution?
      a. the belief that the earth was at the center of the universe
      b. improvements in medicine and scientific instruments
      c. reliance on ancient authorities to explain the physical world
      d. the belief that the human body was similar to the anatomy of animals

Part 2: Map Skills

Using the map, answer the following questions. (4 points each)

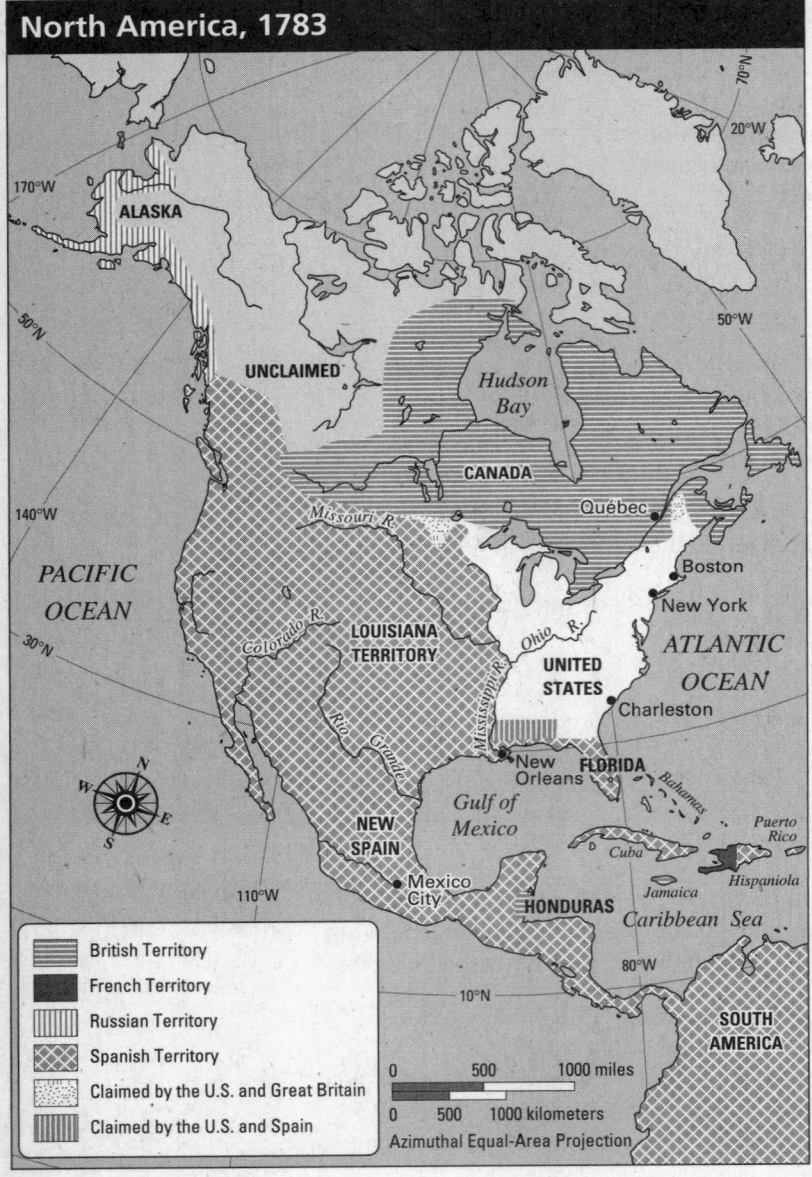

North America, 1783

Legend:
- British Territory
- French Territory
- Russian Territory
- Spanish Territory
- Claimed by the U.S. and Great Britain
- Claimed by the U.S. and Spain

0   500   1000 miles
0   500   1000 kilometers
Azimuthal Equal-Area Projection

_____ 11. Which region of North America was the last to be explored?
    a. central   b. eastern   c. southern   d. northern

_____ 12. Which region probably had both Spanish and U.S. settlers in 1783?
    a. the region about 200 miles east of Quebec
    b. the region about 100 miles east of New York
    c. the region about 100 miles north of New Orleans
    d. the region about 300 miles north of Mexico City

_____ 13. If soldiers were marching by land at 3 miles per hour, 10 hours a day, about how many days would it take them to travel from Mexico City to New Orleans?
    a. 25   b. 40   c. 70   d. 100

_____ 14. Which of the following regions had the highest potential for international conflict?
    a. New York City   c. Hudson Bay
    b. the Caribbean islands   d. central New Spain

_____ 15. Which of the following did NOT claim land in or on the Caribbean Sea in 1783?
    a. Great Britain   c. Spain
    b. France   d. Russia

Part 3: Interpreting Charts—Constructed Response

Using the chart below, answer the questions. (4 points each)

Enlightenment and Revolution, 1550-1789

SCIENTIFIC REVOLUTION
- Heliocentric theory challenges geocentric theory.
- Mathematics and observation support heliocentric theory.
- Scientific method develops.
- Scientists make discoveries in many fields.

A new way of thinking about the world develops—based on observation and a willingness to question assumptions.

ENLIGHTENMENT
- People try to apply the scientific approach to all aspects of society.
- Political scientists propose new ideas about government.
- Philosophers urge using reason to discover truths.
- Philosophers address social issues through reason.

Enlightenment writers challenge many accepted ideas about government and society.

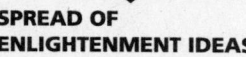

SPREAD OF ENLIGHTENMENT IDEAS
- Enlightenment ideas appeal to thinkers and artists across Europe.
- Salons help spread Enlightenment thinking.
- Ideas spread to literate middle class.
- Enlightened despots attempt reforms.

Enlightenment ideas sweep through European society and also to colonial America.

AMERICAN REVOLUTION
- Enlightenment ideas influence colonists.
- Britain taxes colonies after French and Indian War.
- Colonists denounce taxation without representation.
- War begins in Lexington and Concord.

Colonists declare independence, defeat Britain, and establish a republic.

16. What part of the middle-class was strongly influenced by Enlightenment ideas? Why?

_____

17. Based on the charts, what methods were used to spread Enlightenment ideas? Give examples.

_____

18. How were the Scientific Revolution and the American Revolution similar?

_____

19. How were the philosophes influenced by the Scientific Revolution?

_____

20. Why were many American colonists attracted to Enlightenment ideas?

_____

Part 4: Extended Response

Answer the following questions. (10 points each)

21. **Making Inferences** How did Enlightenment ideas influence the arts and literature in Europe during the 1700s? Give examples.

22. **Synthesizing** How did the ideas of Locke, Montesquieu, Rousseau, Voltaire, and Beccaria influence the U.S. Constitution?

CHAPTER **7**

SECTION QUIZ   *The French Revolution Begins*

Section 1

A. Terms and Names

Write the letter or letters of the terms or names that best complete each statement. A term or name may be used more than once or not at all.

a. Estates-General
b. First Estate
c. Second Estate
d. Third Estate
e. Louis XVI
f. Marie Antoinette
g. Old Regime
h. National Assembly
i. Emmanuel-Joseph Sieyès
j. bourgeoisie
k. Tennis Court Oath
l. Great Fear

_____ 1. The social and political system in use in France in the 1770s, called the _____, had been in place since the Middle Ages.

_____ 2. A financial crisis, brought on in part by excessive spending and huge gambling losses by _____, resulted in forcing _____ to call the _____ into session for the first time in 175 years.

_____ 3. The delegates of the _____, who represented 98 percent of the French population, felt they should have as much say in the decision-making process as the _____ and the _____ combined.

_____ 4. Although not a member of the Third Estate, _____ was a spokesman for this group who recommended that its delegates should name themselves the _____ and pass laws and make reforms in the name of the French people.

_____ 5. When Third Estate delegates were forced to find a new meeting place, they made a pledge, called the _____, to continue their meeting until they had drawn up a new constitution.

_____ 6. The noblemen of the _____ and the clergy of the _____ were forced by the king to join the National Assembly.

_____ 7. Expecting trouble, _____ called up mercenary troops. This action caused a rebellion that fueled a widespread emotional reaction called the _____.

B. Extended Response

Briefly answer the following question on the back of this paper.

What event or events signified the end of absolute monarchy and the beginning of representative government? Explain your answer.

CHAPTER 7

Section 2

SECTION QUIZ *Revolution Brings Reform and Terror*

A. Terms and Names Match each name or term with its description. One term will not be used.

a. Legislative Assembly
b. émigrés
c. sans-culottes
d. left-wing
e. right-wing
f. National Assembly
g. Olympe de Gouges
h. Maximilien Robespierre
i. guillotine
j. Jean-Paul Marat
k. National Convention
l. Georges Danton

_____ 1. This describes the most conservative members of the Legislative Assembly.

_____ 2. This was a radical group, named for the style of breeches its members wore.

_____ 3. This refers to the nobles who fled France but still hoped to restore the monarchy.

_____ 4. This is the name of the government body that replaced the National Assembly.

_____ 5. This describes the most radical members of the Legislative Assembly.

_____ 6. This person wrote a strong response to "A Declaration of the Rights of Man and of the Citizen" because it did not give the same rights to women that it gave to men.

_____ 7. This person claimed it was possible to build a "republic of virtue" by means of what came to be known as the Reign of Terror.

_____ 8. This radical revolutionary was fatally stabbed by another revolutionary.

_____ 9. This was invented to further humane goals, though often used in contradiction to such goals.

_____ 10. Just before being beheaded, this person suggested that his severed head would be "well worth seeing."

_____ 11. Out of fear for their own safety, members of this group finally put an end to the Reign of Terror.

B. Extended Response Briefly answer the following question on the back of this paper.

Why do you think the Reign of Terror occurred and went on as long as it did?

CHAPTER 7 SECTION QUIZ *Napoleon Forges an Empire*

Section 3

A. Terms and Names If the statement is true, write "true" on the line. If it is false, change the underlined word or words to make it true.

Example: Napoleon became a hero of the French republic when he led troops against a group of <u>royalists.</u> _____*true*_____

Example: Napoleon introduced a system of laws called the <u>Declaration of Rights</u>.
_____*Napoleonic Code*_____

1. A <u>coup d'état</u> describes a sudden, forceful seizure of governmental control._____

2. At first, in an attempt to appear to be a constitutionally chosen leader, Napoleon held a vote of the people or <u>plebiscite.</u> _____

3. As part of his reform program, Napoleon set up lycées, or <u>national banks</u>. _____

4. In 1804, Napoleon Bonaparte made himself the <u>president</u> of France._____

5. To restore good relations between France and the Roman Catholic Church, Napoleon and the pope signed a <u>concordat</u>, or agreement. _____

6. In Egypt and later in the Battle of <u>Saint Domingue</u>, Napoleon suffered rare military defeats at the hands of the same man, British Admiral Horatio Nelson. _____

B. Extended Response Briefly answer the following question on the back of this paper.

Why do you think Napoleon became as popular as he did?

CHAPTER
7

SECTION QUIZ *Napoleon's Empire Collapses*

Section 4

A. Terms and Names Write the letter or letters of the terms or names that best complete each statement. A term or name may be used more than once or not at all.

  a. blockade
  b. guerrillas
  c. Hundred Days
  d. Peninsular War
  e. scorched-earth policy
  f. King Louis XVIII
  g. Battle of Waterloo
  h. Continental System
  i. Elba
  j. Creoles
  k. Czar Alexander I
  l. St. Helena

_____ 1. In 1806, Napoleon attempted to make Europe more self-sufficient through the use of what he termed the _____.

_____ 2. Great Britain responded with a _____ against France, which became the major cause of a war between Great Britain and the United States.

_____ 3. Because Portugal refused to honor the _____, Napoleon sent an army through Spain to invade Portugal.

_____ 4. French actions in Spain led to armed resistance by _____ and a long and draining conflict called the _____.

_____ 5. In 1812, Napoleon and 400,000 troops encountered severe difficulties as a result of the _____ used by the Russian leader in response to France's invasion.

_____ 6. After suffering defeat at the hands of King Frederick William III of Prussia and _____ of Russia, Napoleon was exiled to the island of _____.

_____ 7. After escaping from exile, Napoleon gathered volunteers from the French countryside and seized power from _____.

_____ 8. Napoleon's last bid for power, called _____, ended with his defeat at the _____.

B. Extended Response Briefly answer the following question on the back of this paper.

What aspect of Napoleon's character or personality do you think was most responsible for the collapse of his empire? Explain.

Name _____ Date _____

SECTION QUIZ *The Congress of Vienna*

Section 5

A. Terms and Names Write the letter of the best answer.

_____ 1. The person most responsible for the accomplishments of the Congress of
Vienna was
     a. Czar Alexander I of Russia.
     b. Emperor Francis I of Austria.
     c. King Frederick William III of Prussia.
     d. Prince Klemens von Metternich of Austria.

_____ 2. The accomplishments of the Congress of Vienna included all of the following
EXCEPT
     a. reinstating the royal families dethroned by Napoleon.
     b. creating a balance of power among European nations.
     c. surrounding France with strong neighboring countries.
     d. signing the alliances that made up the Concert of Europe.

_____ 3. The actions of the Congress of Vienna helped to generate an independence
movement in
     a. Africa.
     b. North America.
     c. South America.
     d. Asia.

_____ 4. All of the following were members of the Holy Alliance EXCEPT
     a. Italy.
     b. Russia.
     c. Austria.
     d. Prussia.

_____ 5. As a result of actions taken by the Congress of Vienna, the monarchy was
restored on the basis of "legitimacy" in
     a. Spain.
     b. Russia.
     c. Prussia.
     d. Great Britain.

B. Extended Response Briefly answer the following question on the back of this paper.

What did the Congress of Vienna accomplish that had real and lasting value for the
welfare of Europe, and which of its accomplishments were harmful to Europe's future?

CHAPTER **7**

CHAPTER TEST *The French Revolution and Napoleon*

Form A

_____

Part 1: Main Ideas

Write the letter of the best answer. (4 points each)

_____ 1. About what percentage of France's population belonged to the Third Estate?
       a. 1   b. 10   c. 50   d. 98

_____ 2. What happened on July 14, Bastille Day?
       a. Robespierre was executed by guillotine.
       b. French women marched all the way to Versailles.
       c. A mob stormed a prison looking for gunpowder.
       d. All of the above are true.

_____ 3. Which goal was NOT stated in the "slogan of the Revolution"?
       a. liberty   c. justice
       b. equality   d. brotherhood

_____ 4. Which document stated that "men are born and remain free and equal in rights"?
       a. Holy Alliance
       b. Declaration of the Rights of Man
       c. Declaration of Independence
       d. Napoleonic Code

_____ 5. During the Reign of Terror, who was safe from the guillotine?
       a. no one
       b. the nobility
       c. known revolutionaries
       d. only Maximilien Robespierre

_____ 6. What was Napoleon able to accomplish during peacetime?
       a. He set up government-run public schools.
       b. He set up a comprehensive system of laws.
       c. He established a fairer tax code.
       d. All of the above are true.

_____ 7. How did Admiral Nelson win the Battle of Trafalgar?
       a. He bombed the French ships with cannonballs.
       b. He divided the French fleet and attacked smaller groups of ships.
       c. He got help from the Prussians.
       d. All of the above are true.

_____ 8. Why did Napoleon attack Portugal?
       a. to force Portugal to trade with France
       b. to enforce the terms of the Continental System
       c. to prove he was stronger than the Pope
       d. All of the above are true.

_____ 9. Which of the following was an important goal of the Congress of Vienna?
        a. to destroy France
        b. to execute Napoleon by guillotine
        c. to establish a balance of power in Europe
        d. to establish Vienna as the new capital of Europe

_____ 10. Who was the most influential leader at the Congress of Vienna?
        a. Czar Alexander I of Russia
        b. Emperor Francis I of Austria
        c. King Frederick William III of Prussia
        d. Prince Klemens von Metternich of Austria

Part 2: Map Skills

Using the map, place the letter of the correct answer next to each question. (4 points each)

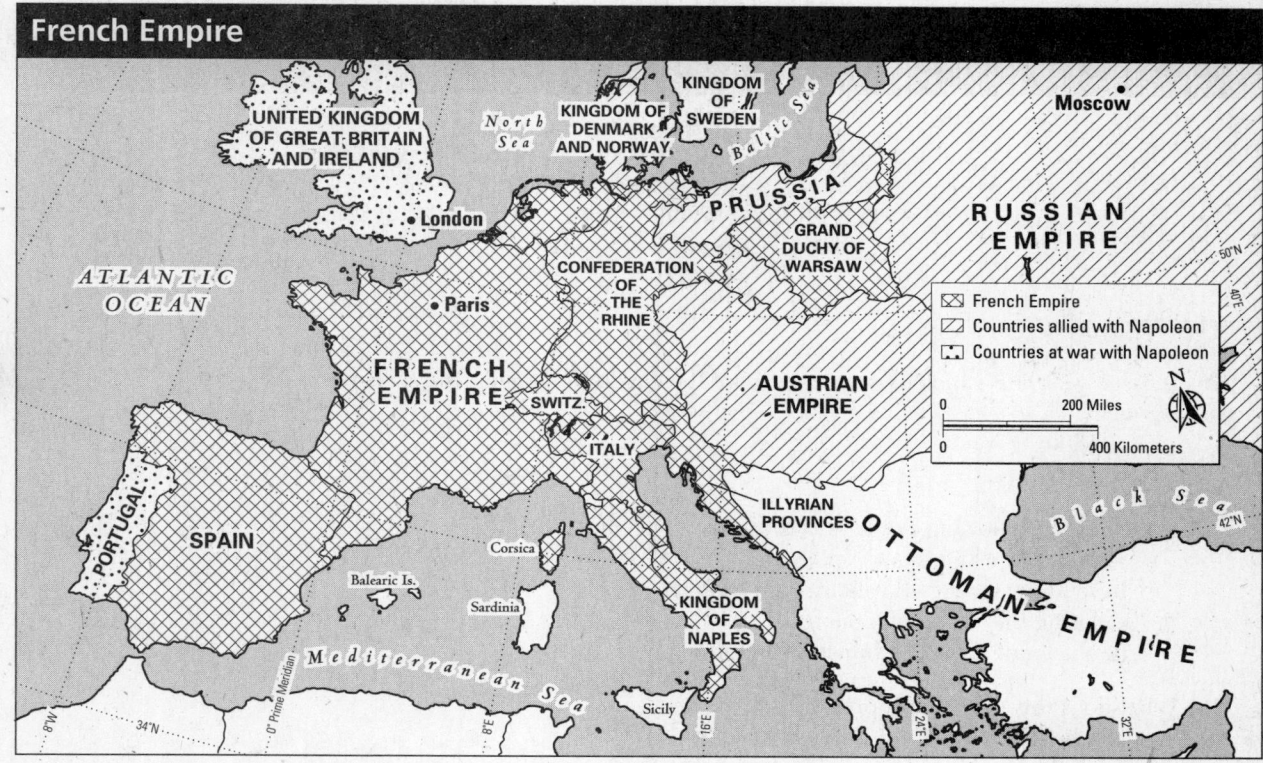

a. Russian Empire
b. Kingdom of Sweden
c. United Kingdom of Great Britain
d. Corsica
e. Portugal

_____ 11. _____ had a coastline on the Baltic Sea and was neither allied nor at war with Napoleon.

_____ 12. _____ had a coastline on the North Sea and was Napoleon's chief rival.

_____ 13. _____ was a Mediterranean island that belonged to the French Empire.

_____ 14. _____ was a peninsular country at war with Napoleon.

_____ 15. _____ had a coastline on the Black Sea and was an ally of Napoleon in 1810.

Part 3: Interpreting Time Lines

Using the time line below, place the letter of the best answer in the space provided. (4 points each)

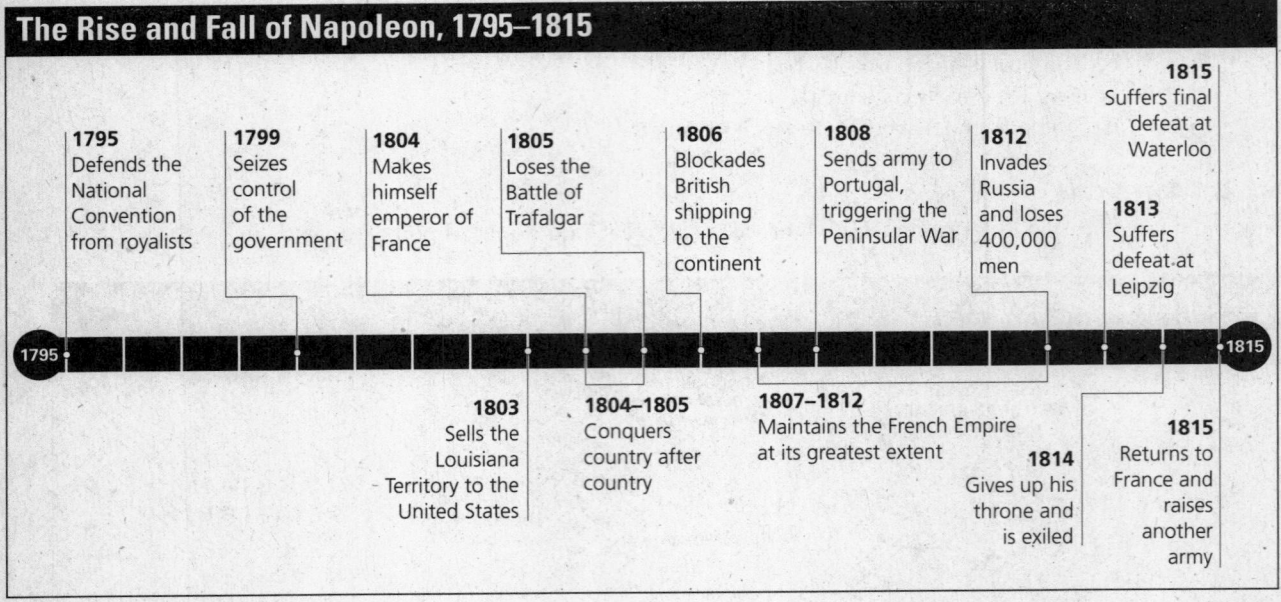

The Rise and Fall of Napoleon, 1795–1815

1795 Defends the National Convention from royalists

1799 Seizes control of the government

1804 Makes himself emperor of France

1805 Loses the Battle of Trafalgar

1806 Blockades British shipping to the continent

1808 Sends army to Portugal, triggering the Peninsular War

1812 Invades Russia and loses 400,000 men

1815 Suffers final defeat at Waterloo

1813 Suffers defeat at Leipzig

1803 Sells the Louisiana Territory to the United States

1804–1805 Conquers country after country

1807–1812 Maintains the French Empire at its greatest extent

1814 Gives up his throne and is exiled

1815 Returns to France and raises another army

_____ 16. In what year did Napoleon seize control of the government and assume dictatorial
        powers?
        a. 1800   c. 1805
        b. 1799   d. 1804

_____ 17. Which of the following events was the latest to occur?
        a. sale of the Louisiana Territory
        b. sending an army through Spain to Portugal
        c. losing the Battle of Trafalgar
        d. Napoleon's making himself Emperor

_____ 18. What does this time line represent?
        a. a brief history of the French Revolution
        b. all the battles Napoleon fought in
        c. highlights of Napoleon's political and military career
        d. all of the above are true

_____ 19. In what year did Napoleon sell the Louisiana Territory to the United States?
        a. 1805   c. 1800
        b. 1796   d. 1803

_____ 20. Which event happened earliest?
        a. Battle of Trafalgar
        b. invasion of Russia
        c. sale of the Louisiana Territory
        d. invasion of Portugal

Part 4: Extended Response
Answer the following questions on the back of this paper or on a separate sheet. (10 points each)

21. **Analyzing Causes; Recognizing Effects** Why did the people of the Third Estate revolt?

    Think about:
    • who paid taxes
    • food supplies
    • political power

22. **Making Decisions** Napoleon invaded Russia in June of 1812. Why was this military decision so unwise?

    Think about:
    • the Russian strategy
    • Alexander I's reaction
    • weather

CHAPTER TEST *The French Revolution and Napoleon*

Form B

Part 1: Main Ideas
Write the letter of the best answer. (4 points each)

_____ 1. About what percent of France's population belonged to the First and Second Estates?
      a. 2   b. 10   c. 50   d. 98

_____ 2. Which group most strongly embraced the ideals and principles of the Enlightenment?
      a. the nobility   c. the peasant class
      b. the bourgeoisie   d. the urban class

_____ 3. What issue led to the first meeting of the Estates-General in 175 years?
      a. proposed taxation of the Second Estate
      b. political representation in the government
      c. food shortages and riots among the peasants
      d. equalizing the tax burden among the Three Estates

_____ 4. Why did the National Assembly lose the support of many French peasants?
      a. It taxed the bourgeoisie.
      b. It made peasants and noblemen equals.
      c. It adopted "A Declaration of the Rights of Man and of the Citizen."
      d. It took away the Catholic Church's lands and independence.

_____ 5. Which group imposed the Reign of Terror?
      a. the Second Coalition
      b. the Committee of Public Safety
      c. the National Assembly
      d. the king's Swiss guard

_____ 6. Which group finally forced Robespierre from power?
      a. royalists   c. the clergy
      b. the peasants   d. his fellow revolutionaries

_____ 7. Which of the following was NOT a reason for Napoleon to sell the Louisiana Territory?
      a. to raise money
      b. to cut his losses in America
      c. to punish the sugar growers in Saint Domingue
      d. to increase America's power as a British rival

_____ 8. What was one important consequence of the Battle of Trafalgar?
   a. Portugal became part of the French Empire.
   b. Napoleon conquered Russia.
   c. Napoleon gave up his plans of invading Britain.
   d. Napoleon became emperor.

_____ 9. How did Great Britain react to the Continental System?
   a. It invaded France.
   b. It organized its own blockade.
   c. It negotiated a peace agreement with France.
   d. It formed an alliance with Austria and Prussia.

_____ 10. What was the main goal of the participants in the Congress of Vienna?
   a. to create constitutional monarchies in Europe
   b. to restore royal families to the thrones of Europe
   c. to establish security and stability for the nations of Europe
   d. to prevent nations outside Europe from interfering in European affairs

Part 2: Map Skills

Using the map, place the letter of the correct answer next to each question. (4 points each)

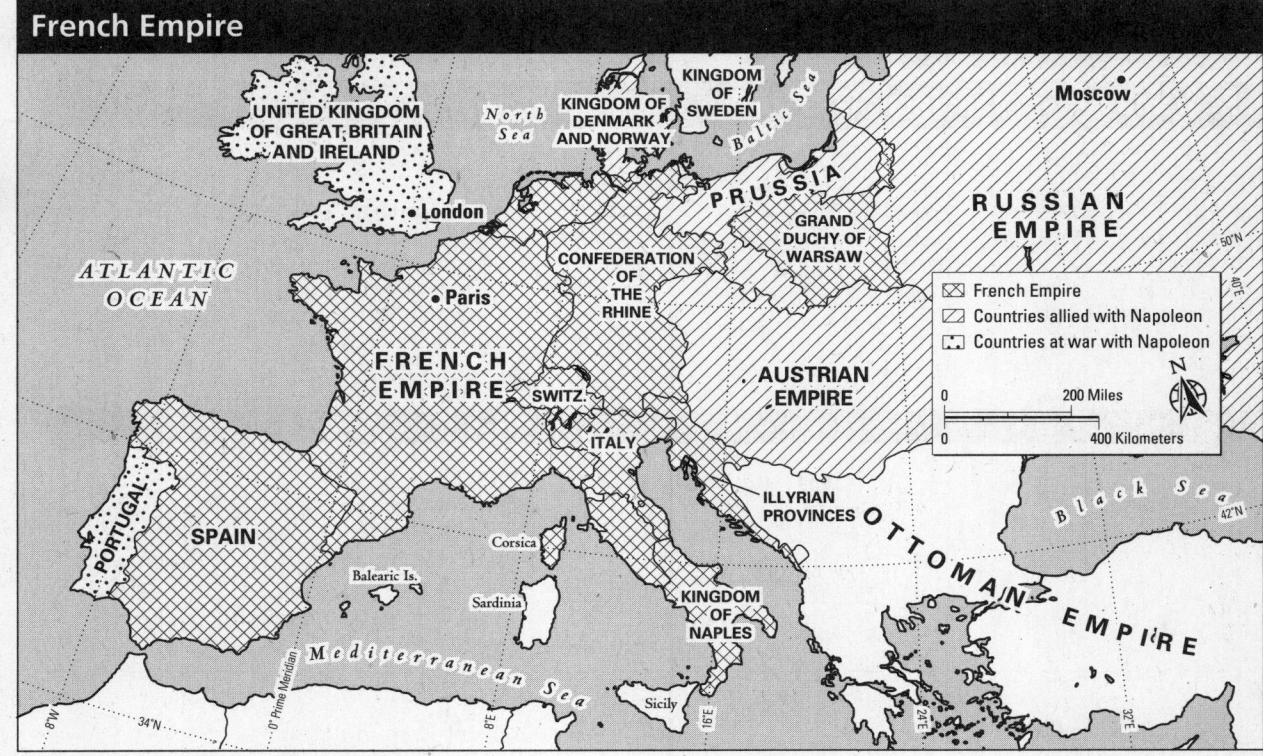

_____ 11. What is the approximate distance, in miles, between Paris and London?
   a. 90   b. 200   c. 50   d. 125

_____ 12. What geographic advantage helped Britain resist conquest?
   a. It was farther north.
   b. It was larger.
   c. It was an island.
   d. It was far from France.

_____ 13. What pattern best describes Napoleon's conquests?
   a. conquering islands for French shipping
   b. conquering Asia and Africa
   c. conquering countries that surrounded France
   d. conquering the nations with the largest amount of land

_____ 14. Which state neither belonged to the French Empire nor was at war with it?
   a. Portugal   c. Ottoman Empire
   b. Switzerland   d. Kingdom of Naples

_____ 15. Which of Napoleon's allies shared the longest border with the area he controlled?
   a. Austrian Empire   c. Kingdom of Naples
   b. Portugal   d. Ottoman Empire

Part 3: Interpreting Time Lines

Using the timeline below, place the letter of the best answer in the space provided. (4 points each)

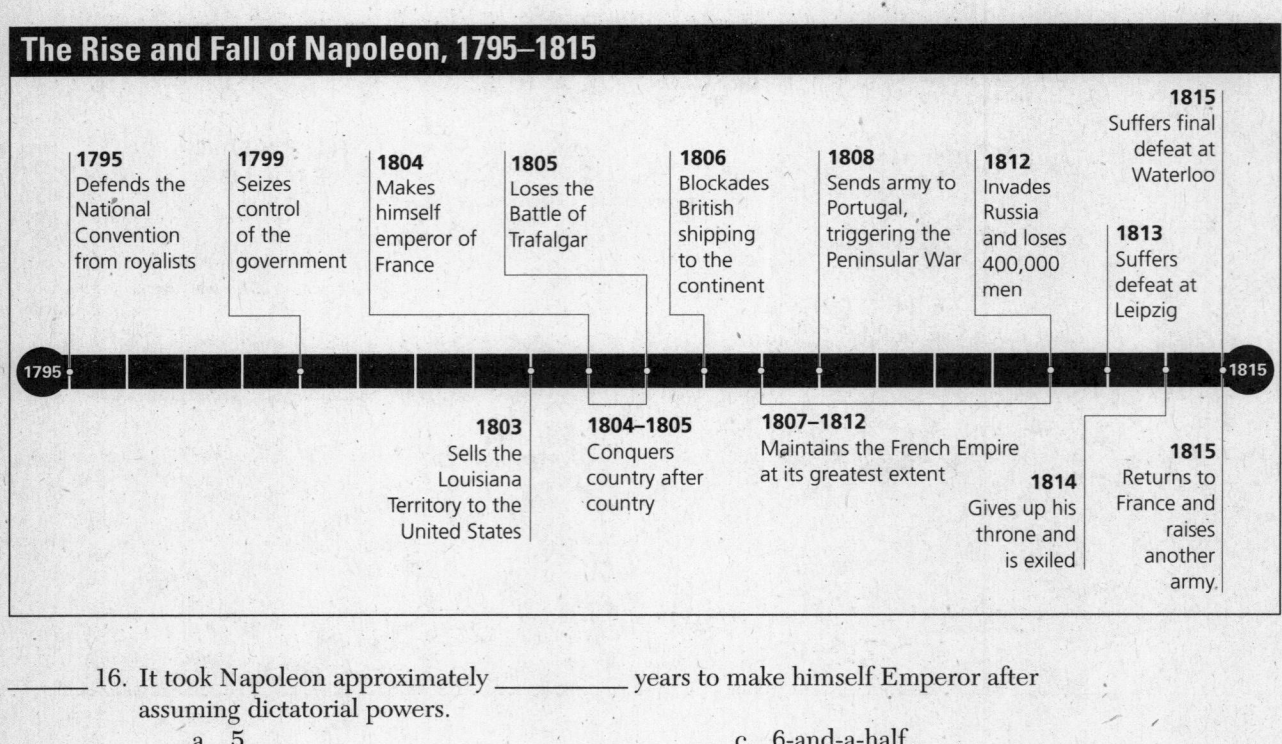

The Rise and Fall of Napoleon, 1795–1815

1795 Defends the National Convention from royalists

1799 Seizes control of the government

1804 Makes himself emperor of France

1805 Loses the Battle of Trafalgar

1806 Blockades British shipping to the continent

1808 Sends army to Portugal, triggering the Peninsular War

1812 Invades Russia and loses 400,000 men

1815 Suffers final defeat at Waterloo

1813 Suffers defeat at Leipzig

1803 Sells the Louisiana Territory to the United States

1804–1805 Conquers country after country

1807–1812 Maintains the French Empire at its greatest extent

1814 Gives up his throne and is exiled

1815 Returns to France and raises another army.

_____ 16. It took Napoleon approximately _____ years to make himself Emperor after assuming dictatorial powers.
   a. 5   c. 6-and-a-half
   b. 3   d. 4

_____ 17. Napoleon's career finally ended in _____
   a. 1812.   b. 1815.   c. 1795.   d. 1800.

_____ 18. Napoleon was able to maintain the Empire at its greatest extent for _____
         a. 2 years.
         b. 10 years.
         c. 7 years.
         d. 5 years.

_____ 19. An important aspect of Napoleon's character was his unwillingness to accept defeat. What action best shows that trait?
         a. He gives up his throne and is exiled.
         b. He returns to France and raises another army.
         c. He loses the Battle of Trafalgar to British navy.
         d. He sells the Louisiana Territory to the United States.

_____ 20. The action of Napoleon's that caused the greatest human losses was _____
         a. the Battle of Trafalgar
         b. the invasion of Russia
         c. the sale of the Louisiana Territory
         d. the Peninsular War

Part 4: Extended Response

Answer the following questions on the back of this paper or on a separate sheet. (10 points each)

21. **Drawing Conclusions** What were some of Napoleon's most enduring achievements during the years of peace following his government takeover? Why were they important?

    Think about:
- the economy
- education and religion
- laws

22. **Analyzing Causes; Recognizing Effects** What events led to Napoleon's downfall?

    Think about:
- Britain
- Spain
- Russia

CHAPTER 7

Form C

CHAPTER TEST *The French Revolution and Napoleon*

Part 1: Main Ideas
Write the letter of the best answer. (4 points each)

_____ 1. Which of the following is an accurate description of the tax system in France in the years preceding the French Revolution?
    a. Only peasants and the clergy paid taxes.
    b. Only about 2 percent of the nobility paid any taxes.
    c. The nobility paid taxes only on land, not on income.
    d. The members of the Third Estate paid almost all of the taxes.

_____ 2. In what way did the bourgeoisie differ from other members of the Third Estate?
    a. They believed in Enlightenment ideals.
    b. They had more political power.
    c. They were poor.
    d. They were fond of expensive clothing and elegant living.

_____ 3. What issue arose after the king called for the Estates-General to meet?
    a. where to meet
    b. what would be discussed
    c. how many votes each Estate would get
    d. whether the Third Estate would be represented

_____ 4. What does the word *plebiscite* mean?
    a. an agreement   c. a seizure of power
    b. a vote of the people   d. a public school

_____ 5. Which of the following did Napoleon NOT accomplish?
    a. a uniform set of laws
    b. a stabilization of the economy
    c. an expansion of freedom of speech
    d. an equal-opportunity public education system

_____ 6. How did Admiral Nelson defeat the French-Spanish fleet in the Battle of Trafalgar?
    a. He ordered the British fleet to surround the French fleet.
    b. He bombed Napoleon's fleet.
    c. He divided the French fleet into smaller groups and then attacked them.
    d. He pretended to retreat and then attacked them from behind.

_____ 7. What strategy did Czar Alexander I use to defeat Napoleon in Russia?
    a. endless negotiations   c. frontal attack
    b. guns and cannons   d. scorched-earth policy

_____ 8. Which of the following traits did Napoleon NOT possess?
    a. courage   c. a brilliant military mind
    b. humility   d. an ability to inspire others

_____ 9. What did Klemens von Metternich NOT want to accomplish at the Congress
of Vienna?
   a. create a balance of power in Europe
   b. strengthen countries surrounding France to prevent future French
      aggression
   c. restore Europe's royal families to their thrones
   d. create the beginnings of a European democracy

_____ 10. What was one important effect resulting from the political changes made at the
Congress of Vienna?
   a. Russia and Prussia joined forces to control France.
   b. Nationalistic feelings grew in countries placed under foreign rule.
   c. Monarchs in Austria, Russia, and Prussia agreed to share power with
      elected officials.
   d. France managed to retain control over the Netherlands.

Part 2: Map Skills

Using the map, place the letter of the correct answer next to each question. (4 points each)

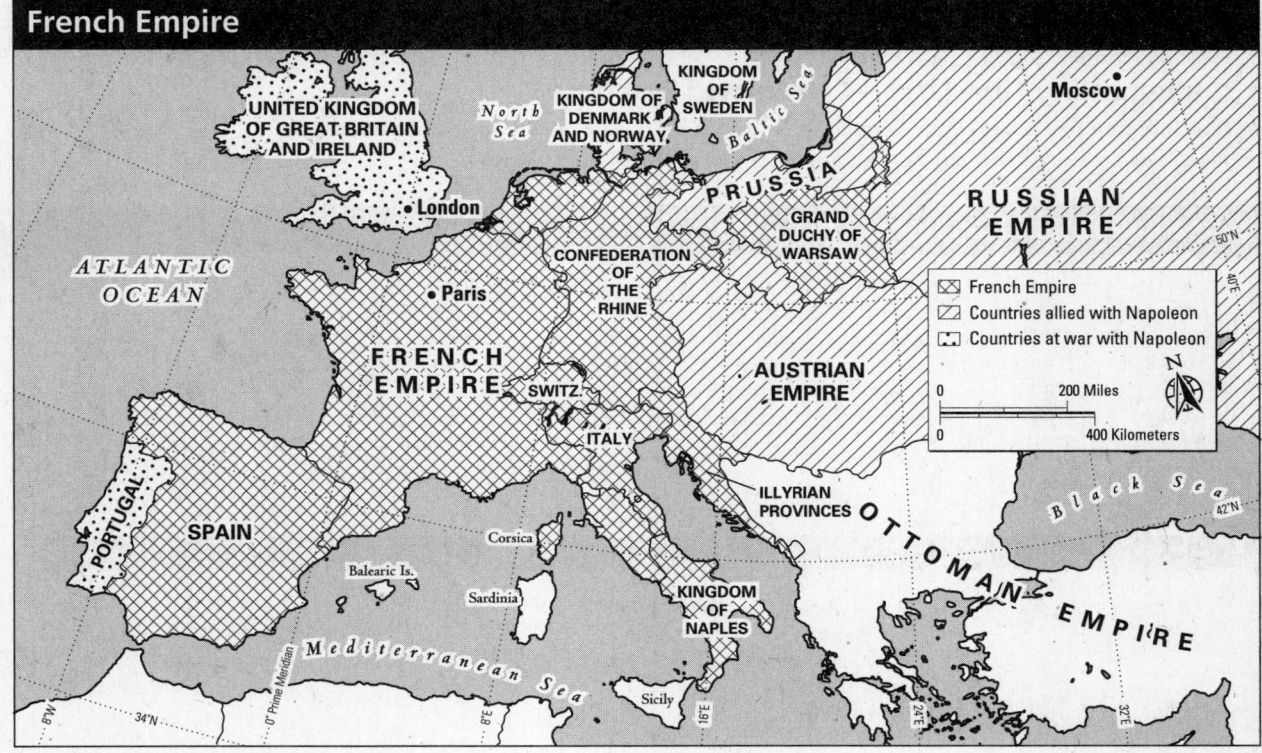

_____ 11. What is the approximate distance, in kilometers, between Paris and Moscow?
   a. 2,500   b. 900   c. 1,200   d. 1,950

_____ 12. Great Britain and Moscow lie above which line of latitude?
   a. 40°   b. 8°   c. 50°   d. 8°
      E   W   N   E

_____ 13. How did Napoleon's conquests affect the size of French-controlled territory?
   a. It approximately doubled.
   b. It approximately tripled.
   c. It stayed approximately the same.
   d. It got smaller.

_____ 14. Which route would enable French troops to stay within the French Empire for the majority of the journey to the Russian border?
   a. crossing through Switzerland, Italy, the Illyrian Provinces, Austrian Empire
   b. crossing the Confederation of the Rhine, Austrian Empire
   c. crossing the Confederation of the Rhine, Prussia
   d. crossing the Confederation of the Rhine, Prussia, the Grand Duchy of Warsaw

_____ 15. What major geographical advantage did Alexander I have over Napoleon's Grand Army?
   a. The Grand Army had no access to the Baltic Sea.
   b. The Grand Army was far from its enemies.
   c. The Grand Army was not accustomed to Russian winters.
   d. The Grand Army had great difficulty navigating the Black Sea.

Part 3: Interpreting Time Lines—Constructed Response

Using the time line below and your knowledge of the time period to answer the following questions. Your answers need not be in complete sentences. (4 points each)

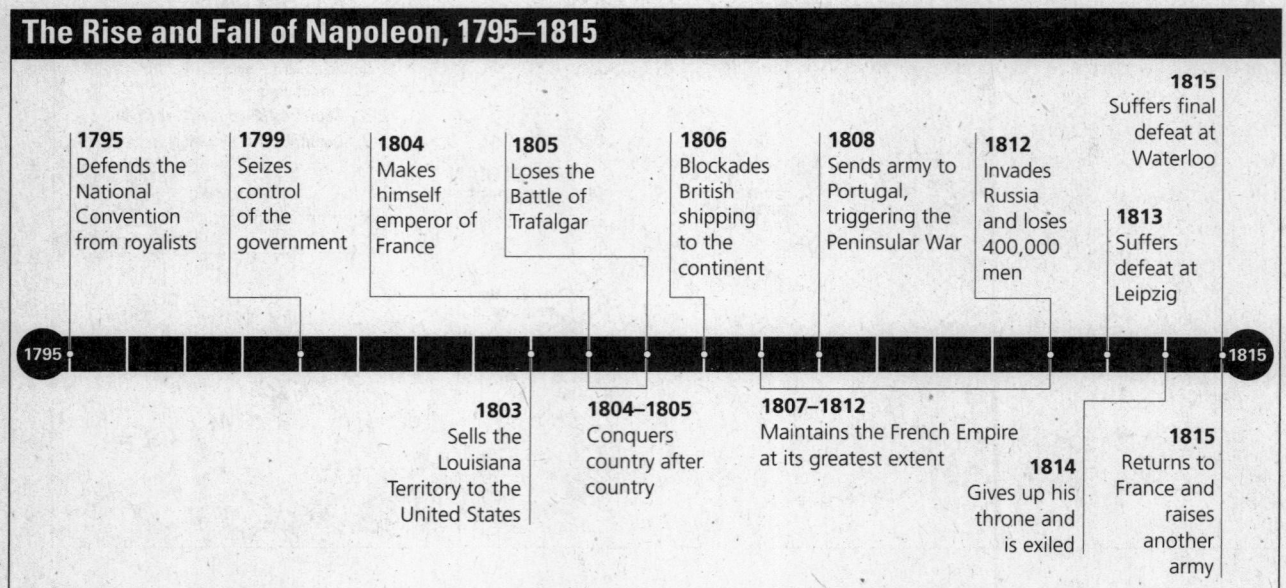

The Rise and Fall of Napoleon, 1795–1815

1795 Defends the National Convention from royalists

1799 Seizes control of the government

1804 Makes himself emperor of France

1805 Loses the Battle of Trafalgar

1806 Blockades British shipping to the continent

1808 Sends army to Portugal, triggering the Peninsular War

1812 Invades Russia and loses 400,000 men

1815 Suffers final defeat at Waterloo

1813 Suffers defeat at Leipzig

1803 Sells the Louisiana Territory to the United States

1804–1805 Conquers country after country

1807–1812 Maintains the French Empire at its greatest extent

1814 Gives up his throne and is exiled

1815 Returns to France and raises another army

16. For approximately how many years was Napoleon emperor?

_____

17. Which two events directly led to Napoleon's fall from power?

    _____

18. In 1815 Napoleon escaped from exile, returned to France, and raised another army. For a "Hundred Days" he reigned as emperor. Name one conclusion you can draw about Napoleon's character.

    _____

19. What was the relationship between the blockade against Britain and the attack on Portugal?

    _____

20. Looking at the events that happened between 1803–1805, why do you think Napoleon might have sold the Louisiana Territory to the United States?

    _____

Part 4: Extended Response
Answer the following questions on the back of this paper or on a separate sheet. (10 points each)

21. **Forming and Supporting Opinions** Do you think the causes of the French Revolution were more economic or political in nature? Explain your answer.

22. **Analyzing Causes; Recognizing Effects** What might have caused the French people to embrace Napoleon as emperor so soon after fighting a revolution that rid them of a king? Support your answer with evidence.

SECTION QUIZ *Latin American Peoples Win Independence*

A. Terms and Names Write the letter of the term or name that best matches the description. A term or name may be used more than once or not at all.

a. creoles
b. Simón Bolívar
c. mestizos
d. José María Morelos
e. mulattos
f. Miguel Hidalgo

g. Bernardo O'Higgins
h. Saint-Domingue
i. *peninsulares*
j. Toussaint L'Ouverture
k. José de San Martín
l. Santo Domingo

_____ 1. He was a priest who issued the *Grito de Dolores,* a call for a peasant rebellion in Mexico.

_____ 2. This was the name of the French third of the island of Hispaniola.

_____ 3. He led a slave revolt that ended slavery on the island of Hispaniola.

_____ 4. This term was used in Latin America to describe people of mixed European and Indian ancestry.

_____ 5. This term was used in Latin America to describe Latin Americans born in Spain.

_____ 6. He was known as *Libertador*.

_____ 7. After winning independence for Argentina and Chile, he gave up command of his army.

_____ 8. This term was used in Latin America to describe people of mixed European and African ancestry.

_____ 9. He was a priest who was also a skillful military leader.

_____ 10. He led his forces against the Spanish army in the Battle of Ayacucho, the last major battle in the Spanish colonies' war for independence.

_____ 11. This term was used in Latin America to describe Spaniards born in Latin America.

_____ 12. This term names the people at the top of Spanish American society.

B. Extended Response Briefly answer the following question on the back of this paper.

Why do you think that Latin-American-born Spaniards, a group that suffered far less oppression than other groups, would be the group to lead the revolution against Spain?

CHAPTER 8

SECTION QUIZ *Europe Faces Revolutions*

Section 2

A. Terms and Names Write the letter of the best answer.

_____ 1. In the first half of the 1800s, a political liberal was most likely to be
   a. a peasant.
   b. a revolutionary.
   c. a middle-class merchant.
   d. a wealthy property owner.

_____ 2. A key characteristic of nationalism is
   a. a shared culture.
   b. a flag.
   c. a president.
   d. a supply of weapons.

_____ 3. The elected ruler of France who declared himself emperor was
   a. Louis Blanc.
   b. Louis-Philippe.
   c. Louis-Napoleon.
   d. Alphonse de Lamartine.

_____ 4. By 1849, most of Europe was under the control of the
   a. liberals.
   b. radicals.
   c. peasants.
   d. conservatives.

_____ 5. The Edict of Emancipation was issued by
   a. Nicholas I.
   b. Alexander II.
   c. Alexander III.
   d. the Decembrists.

_____ 6. How successful were the Revolutions of 1830 and 1848?
   a. Very successful—each revolutionary group achieved its goals.
   b. Only the Greek Revolution was successful.
   c. The liberals won in the Ottoman Empire.
   d. None achieved their goals.

B. Extended Response Briefly answer the following question on the back of this paper.

What conditions and realities of life made it difficult for supporters of constitutional government to succeed in Europe in the early 1800s?

CHAPTER

8

Section 3

SECTION QUIZ *Nationalism*
Case Study: Italy and Germany

A. Terms and Names Write the letter of the best answer.

_____ 1. Which country suffered the most lost territory as a result of the unification
of Italy?
   a. France
   b. Russia
   c. Prussia
   d. Austria

_____ 2. What city became the capital of the Kingdom of Italy after the conquest of
the Papal States?
   a. Venice
   b. Lombardy
   c. Rome
   d. Piedmont-Sardinia

_____ 3. Which of the following was the leader of the Red Shirts?
   a. King William I
   b. Camillo di Cavour
   c. Otto von Bismark
   d. Giuseppe Garibaldi

_____ 4. Which event did Otto von Bismark use to gain support from Germans in
the south?
   a. the Franco-Prussia War
   b. the German confederation
   c. the Seven Weeks War
   d. the defeat of the Junkers

_____ 5. Who originated the political style known as realpolitik?
   a. King Victor EEmmanuel II
   b. Camillo di Cavour
   c. Otto von Bismarck
   d. Giuseppe Garibaldi

_____ 6. What was the title given to the ruler of the new, unified German empire?
   a. czar
   b. reich
   c. kaiser
   d. Junker

B. Extended Response Briefly answer the following question on the back of this paper.

How influential do you think feelings of nationalism are in terms of conflicts around the
world today? Explain.

Name _____   Date _____

CHAPTER
8

SECTION QUIZ *Revolutions in the Arts*

Section 4

A. Terms and Names Write the letter of the best answer.

_____ 1. Which of the following is largely identified with the artistic movement known
as romanticism?
   a. chamber music   c. the Gothic novel
   b. the daguerreotype   d. the scientific method

_____ 2. Which of the following ideas is associated with romanticism?
   a. political importance of the working class
   b. wild emotions and feelings
   c. mass distribution of books
   d. impressions of the moment

_____ 3. In the first practical process of reproducing photographs for books, on what
were photographs printed?
   a. glass   c. metal
   b. wood   d. paper

_____ 4. Which of the following was NOT a realist writer?
   a. Victor Hugo   c. Gustave Flaubert
   b. Charles Dickens   d. Honoré de Balzac

_____ 5. Which of the following descriptions is accurate for Goethe, Chopin, Coleridge,
and Constable?
   a. writer   c. realist
   b. painter   d. romantic

_____ 6. Which of the following is NOT properly matched with the artistic movement to
which he or she contributed?
   a. Louis Daguerre—realism
   b. Emile Zola—romanticism
   c. Charles Dickens—realism
   d. Ludwig van Beethoven—romanticism

_____ 7. Which of the following is a characteristic of impressionism?
   a. creation of mental   c. folk traditions
      pictures   d. realist views of life
   b. reformist ideas

B. Extended Response Briefly answer the following question on the back of this paper.

How did the industrialization of Europe help to bring about a change from romanticism
to realism in art and literature?

Name _____   Date _____

CHAPTER
8

Form A

CHAPTER TEST *Nationalist Revolutions Sweep the West*

Part 1: Main Ideas

Write the letter of the correct answer next to each question. (4 points each)

_____ 1. The independence movement in Latin America was spearheaded in large part by
      a. the mulattos.
      b. the Creoles.
      c. the Spanish.
      d. the *peninsulares*.

_____ 2. José de San Martín was a military officer who
      a. liberated parts of Mexico.
      b. liberated parts of Brazil.
      c. liberated parts of Spanish-speaking South America.
      d. liberated Spanish-speaking islands in the Caribbean.

_____ 3. The independence movement in Mexico was led, in part, by a priest named
      a. Miguel Hidalgo.
      b. Simón Bolívar.
      c. Dom Pedro.
      d. Toussaint L'Ouverture.

_____ 4. In early 19th century Europe, one political goal that liberals had was to
      a. to limit the influence of business leaders and merchants.
      b. to protect the traditional monarchies of Europe.
      c. to give more power to elected parliaments.
      d. to abolish formal government and replace it with anarchy.

_____ 5. Nationalism was a force that
      a. tore apart centuries-old empires.
      b. gave rise to the nation-state.
      c. was opposed by conservatives.
      d. accomplished all of the above

_____ 6. The uprisings in 1848 resulted in
      a. the resignation of Metternich.
      b. the liberation of Greece.
      c. the emancipation of Russian serfs.
      d. the victory of liberals throughout Europe.

_____ 7. In the 1860s, the expansion of the state of Prussia was achieved under the
leadership of
      a. King Victor Emmanuel II.
      b. Frederick William IV.
      c. Otto von Bismarck.
      d. Giuseppe Garibaldi.

_____ 8. During the mid–1800s, Count Camillo di Cavour expanded Piedmont-Sardinia's power and also
       a. conquered part of France.
       b. unified Italy.
       c. took control of Venetia.
       d. did all of the above.

_____ 9. Mary Shelley wrote
       a. an early Gothic horror story about a monster created from corpses.
       b. realistic stories about everyday life in the coal mines of Yorkshire.
       c. novels that showed the struggle of middle-class individuals against society.
       d. a novel about two star–crossed lovers who live on the moors of England.

_____ 10. One of the first European composers to experiment with romanticism in music was
       a. Wolfgang Amadeus Mozart.
       b. Ludwig van Beethoven.
       c. Joseph Turner.
       d. Johann Sebastian Bach.

Part 2: Map Skills

Using the maps, write the letter of the correct answer next to each question. (4 points each)

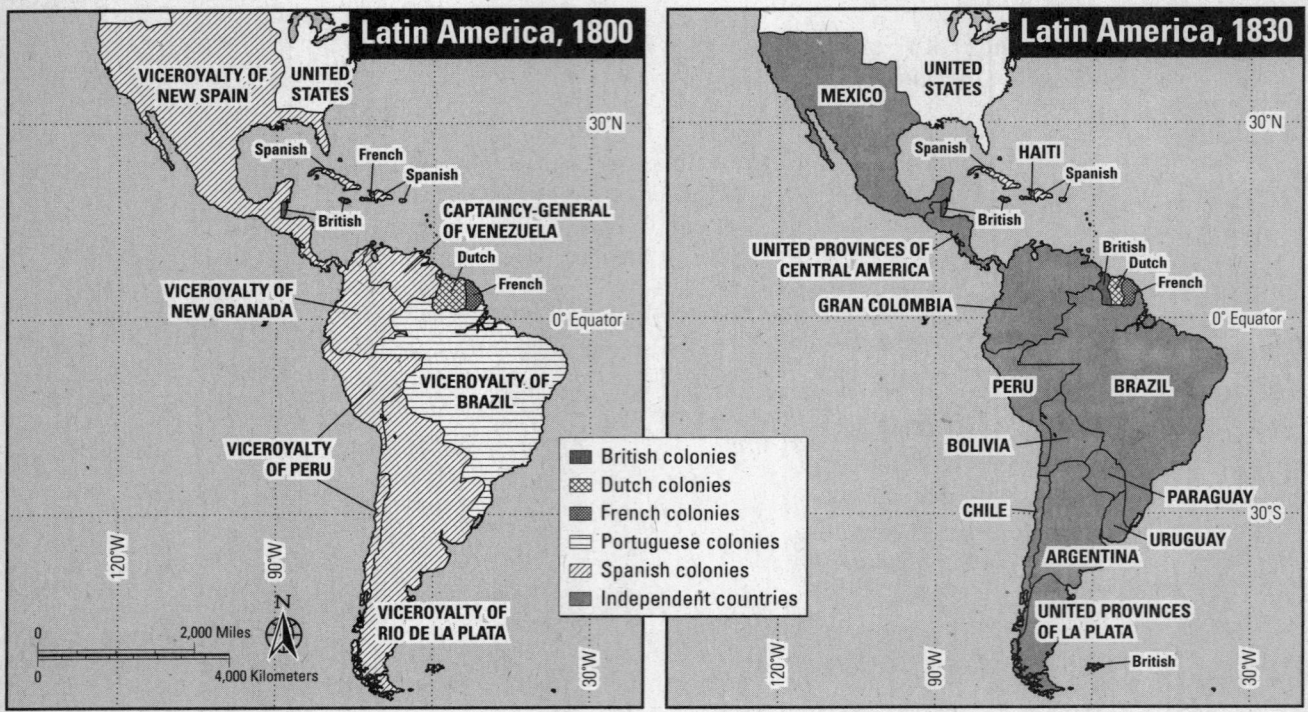

a. Chile
b. Viceroyalty of Brazil
c. Viceroyalty of New Spain

d. United Provinces of Central America
e. Spain

_____ 11. In 1800, this region was west of the United States.

_____ 12. This region was a Portuguese colony in 1800.

_____ 13. By 1830, this independent country extended along the southwest coast of South America.

_____ 14. In 1800, this country had colonies in North America, the Caribbean, and South America.

_____ 15. In 1830, this country was bordered by both Mexico and Gran Colombia.

Part 3: Document-Based Questions

Introduction

Historical Context: From the early 1500s to the early 1800s, the Latin American people had been oppressed by Spain. Spaniards born in Latin America could not hold high offices in government. People of mixed ancestry had even fewer privileges. Most Africans were enslaved, and Native Americans were severely oppressed. Inspired by democratic ideals, Simón Bolívar and José de San Martín gained independence for Spanish South America. This independence brought a sudden and dramatic change in government for millions of Latin Americans.

Task: Discuss the difficulties that the people of Spanish South America faced in the transition from oppressive Spanish control to democracy.

A. Short Answer

Study each document carefully and answer the question that follows. (4 points each)

Document 1: Excerpt from the Jamaican Letter by Simón Bolívar

We have been harassed by a conduct which has not only deprived us of our rights but has kept us in a sort of permanent infancy with regard to public affairs. . . . Among the popular and representative systems, I do not favor the federal system. It is overperfect, and it demands political virtues and talents far superior to our own. For the same reason I reject a monarchy that is part aristocracy and part democracy, although with such a government England has achieved much fortune and splendor. . . . I say: Do not adopt the best system of government, but the one that is most likely to succeed.

16. Did Bolívar believe that the federal system of government would work well in Spanish South America? Explain your answer.

_____

Document 2: Excerpt from José de San Martín's Farewell Address to the People of Peru

My promises to the countries in which I warred are fulfilled: to make them independent, and to leave to their will the election of their governments. The presence of a fortunate soldier, however disinterested he may be, is dangerous to newly constituted states. I am also disgusted with hearing that I wish to make myself a sovereign. Nevertheless, I shall always be ready to make the last sacrifice for the liberty of the country—but in the capacity of a private individual and no other. . . . Peruvians! I leave your national representation established: if you repose implicit confidence in it, you will triumph; if not, anarchy will swallow you up.

17. Why does San Martín believe he has fulfilled his promise to Latin Americans?

_____

Document 3: The Divisions in Spanish Colonial Society in 1789

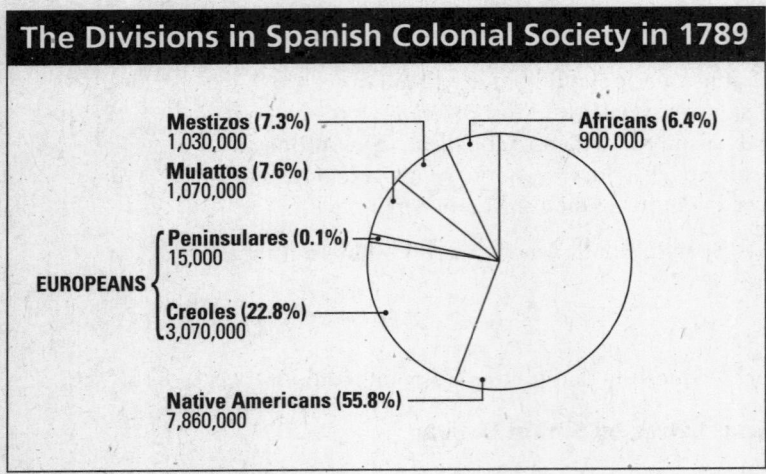

The Divisions in Spanish Colonial Society in 1789

- Mestizos (7.3%) 1,030,000
- Mulattos (7.6%) 1,070,000
- EUROPEANS
  - Peninsulares (0.1%) 15,000
  - Creoles (22.8%) 3,070,000
- Africans (6.4%) 900,000
- Native Americans (55.8%) 7,860,000

18. Which group made up the largest part of Spanish America? Which made up the smallest?

_____

B. Essay

19. Using the information from the documents, your answers to the questions in Part A, and your knowledge of world history, write an essay on your own paper that discusses the difficulties that were involved in establishing democratic governments in Latin America and the solutions that were needed to overcome these difficulties. (8 points)

Part 4: Extended Response

Answer the following questions on the back of this page or on a separate sheet.. (10 points each)

20. **Analyzing Issues** In the first half of the 1800s, what three groups struggled to gain a political advantage in European societies? Define each group.

    Think about:
    • who had power and who lacked it
    • political divisions
    • the influence of democratic ideals

21. **Recognizing Effects** How did nationalism affect the Austro-Hungarian and Russian empires?

    Think about:
    • nationalism's power both to unite and tear apart
    • attempts to suppress nationalism
    • the ultimate result of nationalism

Name _____   **Date** _____

CHAPTER TEST *Nationalist Revolutions Sweep the West*

Form B

Part 1: Main Ideas
Write the letter of the correct answer next to each question. (4 points each)

_____ 1. Which of the following men led a revolt of enslaved Africans in Saint Domingue?
- a. José de san Martín
- b. José Maria Morelos
- c. Toussaint L'Ouverture
- d. Giuseppe Garibaldi

_____ 2. In which of the following ways did the liberation of Mexico and Brazil differ?
- a. Mexico's liberation was violent; Brazil's liberation was nonviolent.
- b. Mexico was liberated from Spanish control; Brazil was liberated from French control.
- c. Mexico's liberation involved Creoles; Brazil's liberation did not involve Creoles.
- d. All of the above are true.

_____ 3. In which of the following ways were France and Russia similar during the 1800s?
- a. Both had bloody but unsuccessful revolutions.
- b. Both had reforms halted by an assassination.
- c. Both had policies that encouraged industrialization.
- d. Both had movements that tried to establish a democracy.

_____ 4. Which of the following was probably NOT influenced by nationalism during the 1800s?
- a. groups uniting against an oppressive monarchy
- b. an empire that crumbles into independent states
- c. an empire granting long-needed social reforms
- d. groups accepting a long-established form of government

_____ 5. Which of the following was true about nationalism?
- a. One's greatest loyalty should not be to a king.
- b. One's greatest loyalty should be to a nation of people.
- c. The nation of people should have a common culture.
- d. All of the above are true.

_____ 6. Which of the following statements would Otto von Bismarck probably NOT agree with?
- a. It is the destiny of the weak to be devoured by the strong.
- b. A ruler should never violate the constitution of his or her country.
- c. Military force should be used to achieve political gain.
- d. Manufacturing political "incidents" is acceptable if it achieves a worthy goal.

_____ 7. By 1871 there was a shift in power in Europe, which nation changed?
         a. Prussia became Germany.
         b. Italy replaced Prussia.
         c. Germany replaced France.
         d. Britain replaced Germany.

_____ 8. Which of the following ideals was NOT a major component of romanticism?
         a. the love of nature's untamed beauty
         b. the value of common people
         c. the promotion of established ideas
         d. the glorification of heroes and heroic actions

_____ 9. How did music change during the Romantic period?
         a. It became more structured.
         b. It lost popularity.
         c. It focused on creating impressions of a moment.
         d. It became a part of the middle class life.

_____ 10. What was the goal of impressionistic artists and composers?
         a. to show the ugly conditions created by industrialization
         b. to illustrate a moment in time
         c. to protest the growing wealth of the middle class
         d. to glorify national heroes

Part 2: Map Skills

Using the maps, answer the following questions. (4 points each)

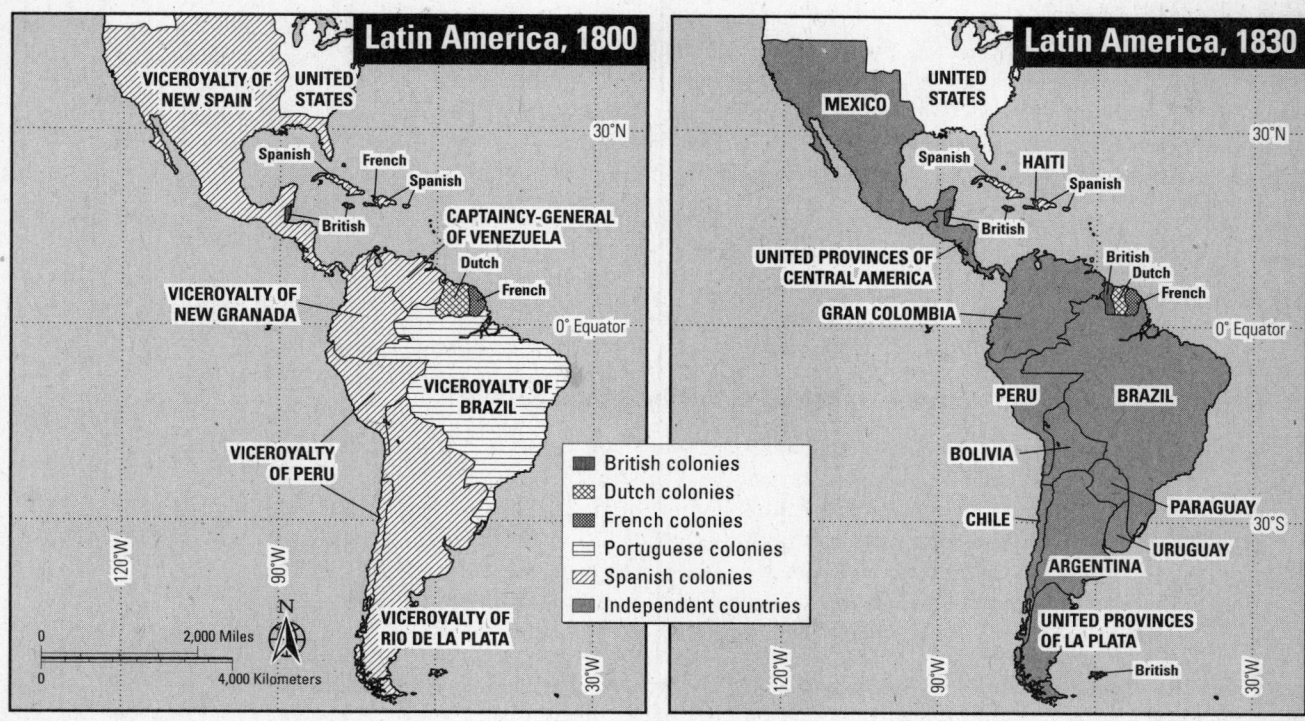

_____ 11. Which of the following combined to form Gran Colombia?
          a. the Viceroyalty of Brazil and the Captaincy-General of Venezuela
          b. the Viceroyalty of New Granada and the Viceroyalty of Peru
          c. the Viceroyalty of New Granada and the Captaincy-General of Venezuela
          d. the Viceroyalty of Peru and the Viceroyalty of Brazil

_____ 12. In the early 1800s, which region was least affected by independence movements?
          a. the Caribbean
          b. Central America
          c. Spanish-speaking North America
          d. Spanish-speaking South America

_____ 13. What does the political division of the Viceroyalty of Rio de la Plata by 1830 show?
          a. There were many distinct groups within the Viceroyalty of Rio de la Plata.
          b. Nationalism united the people of this region into one country.
          c. The people of this region did not fight effectively against the Spanish.
          d. All of the above are true.

_____ 14. By 1830, which of the following had lost all of their colonies in South America?
          a. the British   c. the Dutch
          b. the Spanish   d. the French

_____ 15. Which of the following countries gained independence from France by 1830?
          a. Mexico   b. Haiti   c. Bolivia   d. Brazil

Part 3: Document-Based Questions
Introduction

Historical Context: From the early 1500s to the early 1800s, the Latin American people had been oppressed by Spain. Spaniards born in Latin America could not hold high offices in government. People of mixed ancestry had even fewer privileges. Most Africans were enslaved, and Native Americans were severely oppressed. Inspired by democratic ideals, Simón Bolívar and José de San Martín gained independence for Spanish South America. This independence brought a sudden and dramatic change in government for millions of Latin Americans.

Task: Discuss the difficulties that the people of Spanish South America faced in the transition from oppressive Spanish control to democracy.

A. Short Answer

Study each document carefully and answer the question that follows. (4 points each)

Document 1: Excerpt from the Jamaican Letter by Simón Bolívar

We have been harassed by a conduct which has not only deprived us of our rights but has kept us in a sort of permanent infancy with regard to public affairs. . . . Among the popular and representative systems, I do not favor the federal system. It is overperfect, and it demands political virtues and talents far superior to our own. For the same reason I reject a monarchy that is part aristocracy and part democracy, although with such a government England has achieved much fortune and splendor. . . . I say: Do not adopt the best system of government, but the one that is most likely to succeed.

16. Bolívar believed that Latin Americans lacked the virtues and talents needed for the federal system of government. What reason does he give for this situation?

_____

Document 2: Excerpt from José de San Martín's Farewell Address to the People of Peru

My promises to the countries in which I warred are fulfilled: to make them independent, and to leave to their will the election of their governments. The presence of a fortunate soldier, however disinterested he may be, is dangerous to newly constituted states. I am also disgusted with hearing that I wish to make myself a sovereign. Nevertheless, I shall always be ready to make the last sacrifice for the liberty of the country—but in the capacity of a private individual and no other. . . . Peruvians! I leave your national representation established: if you repose implicit confidence in it, you will triumph; if not, anarchy will swallow you up.

17. How does San Martín feel about the future of democracy in Peru? Explain your answer.

_____

Document 3: The Divisions in Spanish Colonial Society in 1789

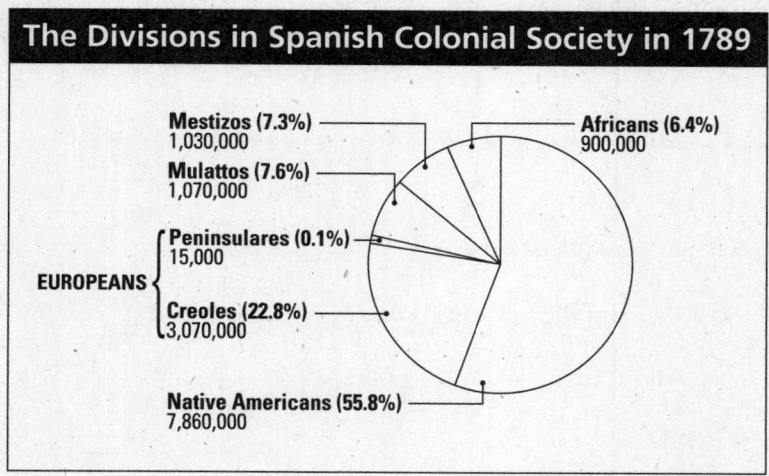

The Divisions in Spanish Colonial Society in 1789

Mestizos (7.3%)
1,030,000

Mulattos (7.6%)
1,070,000

EUROPEANS
{ Peninsulares (0.1%)
15,000

Creoles (22.8%)
3,070,000 }

Africans (6.4%)
900,000

Native Americans (55.8%)
7,860,000

18. Which groups combined to make up 44.2% of the population of Spanish America?

_____

B. Essay

19. Using the information from the documents, your answers to the questions in Part A, and your knowledge of world history, write an essay on your own paper that discusses the difficulties that were involved in establishing democratic governments in Latin America and the solutions that were needed to overcome these difficulties. (8 points)

Part 4: Extended Response

Answer the following questions on the back of this page or on a separate sheet. (10 points each)

20. **Forming and Supporting Opinions** Do you approve or disapprove of Otto von Bismark's policy of realpolitik? Give reasons and examples from the text.

Think about:
- his attitude toward the German parliament
- his accomplishments
- his relationship with France

21. **Contrasting** How did romantic and realistic literature differ? Give examples.

Think about:
- the subject matter of the two
- the main characters of the two
- the goals of each

CHAPTER **8**

Form C

CHAPTER TEST *Nationalist Revolutions Sweep the West*

Part 1: Main Ideas

Write the letter of the correct answer next to each question. (4 points each)

_____ 1. In Latin America during the early 1800s, which of the following probably belonged to the Creole class?
a. a colonel in the Spanish colonial army
b. a governor of a Spanish colony
c. an enslaved person working on a plantation
d. a person who never had a formal education

_____ 2. How were the liberation movements in Spanish South America and Brazil similar?
a. Both were headed by José de San Martín.
b. Both involved the Creole class.
c. Both used violence.
d. Both used two armies.

_____ 3. Which of the following artistic styles would be used to accurately depict the oppressive working conditions of Latin Americans under Spanish control?
a. romanticism
b. impressionism
c. realism
d. Gothic horror

_____ 4. Which of the following people would most likely have been a radical in the 1800s?
a. a nobleman who is related to his country's king
b. a prosperous land owner who owns less than 10,000 acres
c. a wealthy business man who wants to give his country's parliament more power
d. a poor student who has read extensively about democracy

_____ 5. During the 19th century, which of the following occurred in Europe?
a. conflict between conservative and liberal movements
b. the resurgence of conservatives over liberals
c. the decline of established empires
d. all of the above

_____ 6. How were the unifications of Italy and Germany similar?
a. Both involved a war with France.
b. Both took over territory controlled by the Catholic Church.
c. Both used military force to unify various territories.
d. Both unified into an empire.

_____ 7. Which of the following events was NOT strongly influenced by economic problems?
        a. the peasant revolt in Italy
        b. the election of Louis-Napoleon
        c. the independence movement of Latin America
        d. the declaration of war by France on Prussia

_____ 8. Which of the following political trends helped lead to the formation of the Second Reich?
        a. ruthless leadership
        b. friendly diplomatic relations with France
        c. the power of the German parliament
        d. all of the above

_____ 9. How were romanticism and nationalism linked?
        a. National heroes and cultural pride were themes.
        b. Both rejected the ideas of the liberals.
        c. They were not linked to each other.
        d. They both focuses on solving real world problems.

_____ 10. Which of the following works of art can be seen as a reaction against realism?
        a. a Dickens novel
        b. a Renoir painting
        c. a Talbot daguerreotype
        d. a Balzac story

Part 2: Map Skills

Using the map, answer the following questions. (4 points each)

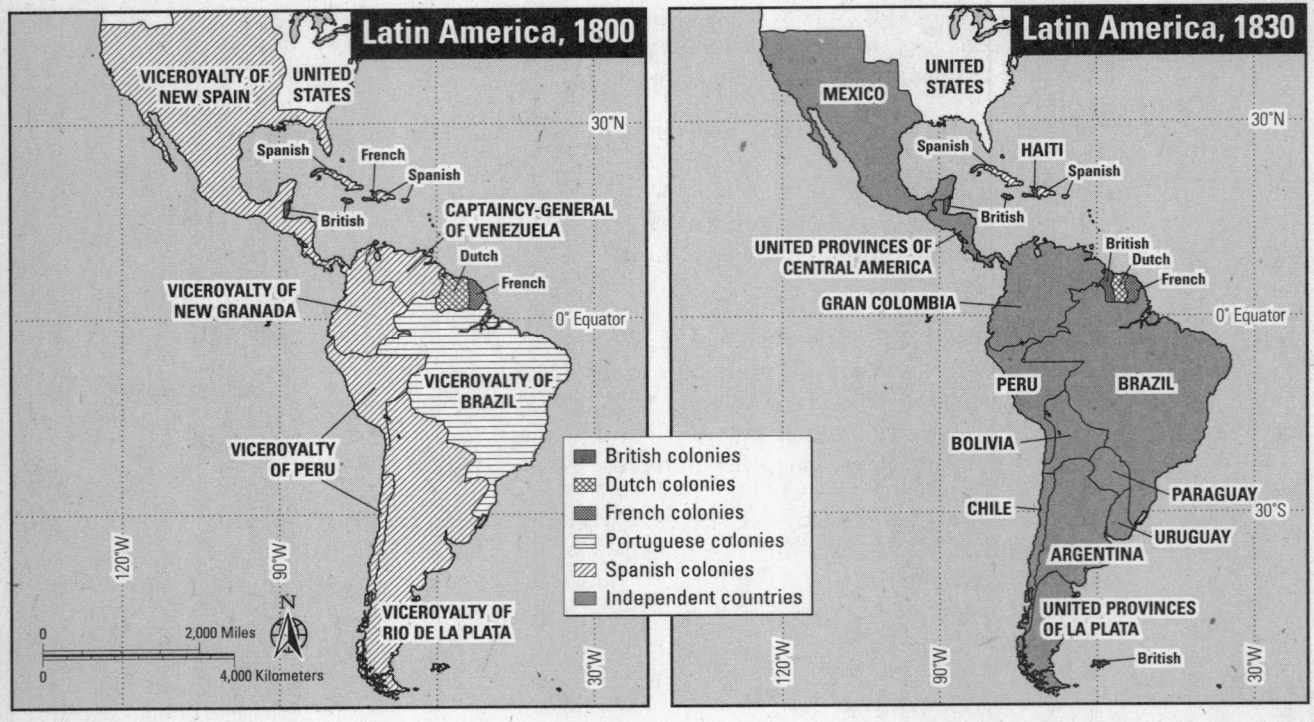

_____ 11. The economy of which country was most severely affected by the liberation of Latin America?
        a. France   c. Spain
        b. Holland   d. Great Britain

_____ 12. Which of the following countries probably benefited the most territorially from the liberation of Latin America?
        a. Great Britain   c. Holland
        b. the United States   d. France

_____ 13. If a ship was traveling at 5 miles per hour, how many hours would it take to sail from Haiti to the Dutch colony in South America?
        a. 150   b. 200   c. 300   d. 450

_____ 14. After 1830, Mexico probably had the most conflict with which of the following country?
        a. the United States
        b. Brazil
        c. the British colony in South America
        d. Gran Colombia

_____ 15. In 1830, fishing probably provided the smallest income for which of the following countries?
        a. Brazil   c. Peru
        b. Chile   d. Paraguay

Part 3: Document-Based Questions
Introduction

Historical Context: From the early 1500s to the early 1800s, the Latin American people had been oppressed by Spain. Spaniards born in Latin America could not hold high offices in government. People of mixed ancestry had even fewer privileges. Most Africans were enslaved, and Native Americans were severely oppressed. Inspired by democratic ideals, Simón Bolívar and José de San Martín gained independence for Spanish South America. This independence brought a sudden and dramatic change in government for millions of Latin Americans.

Task: Discuss the difficulties that the people of Spanish South America faced in the transition from oppressive Spanish control to democracy.

A. Short Answer

Study each document carefully and answer the question that follows. (4 points each)

Document 1: Excerpt from the Jamaican Letter by Simón Bolívar

We have been harassed by a conduct which has not only deprived us of our rights but has kept us in a sort of permanent infancy with regard to public affairs. . . . Among the popular and representative systems, I do not favor the federal system. It is overperfect, and it demands political virtues and talents far superior to our own. For the same reason I reject a monarchy that is part aristocracy and part democracy, although with such a government England has achieved much fortune and splendor. . . . I say: Do not adopt the best system of government, but the one that is most likely to succeed.

16. Do you think the part aristocracy and part democracy form of government would have been more or less successful than the federal system (used in the United States) in Latin America? Why?

_____

Document 2: Excerpt from José de San Martín's Farewell Address to the People of Peru

My promises to the countries in which I warred are fulfilled: to make them independent, and to leave to their will the election of their governments. The presence of a fortunate soldier, however disinterested he may be, is dangerous to newly constituted states. I am also disgusted with hearing that I wish to make myself a sovereign. Nevertheless, I shall always be ready to make the last sacrifice for the liberty of the country—but in the capacity of a private individual and no other. . . . Peruvians! I leave your national representation established: if you repose implicit confidence in it, you will triumph; if not, anarchy will swallow you up.

17. Why do you think San Martín felt that the presence of a successful military leader (fortunate soldier) was dangerous to newly constituted states? Explain your answer.

_____

Document 3: The Divisions in Spanish Colonial Society in 1789

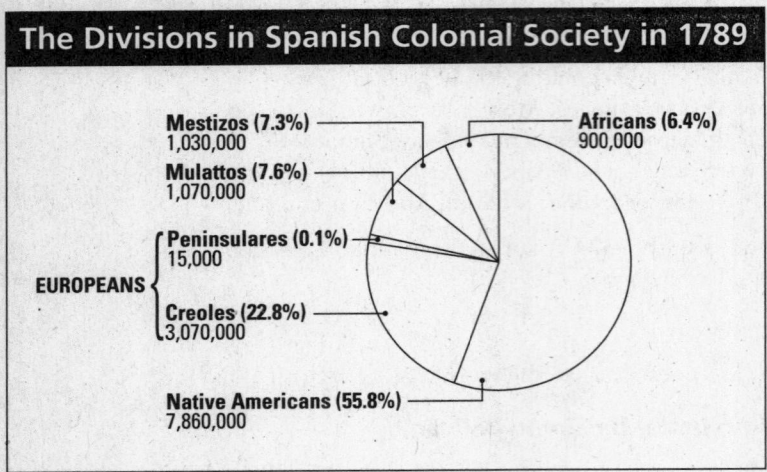

The Divisions in Spanish Colonial Society in 1789

- Mestizos (7.3%) 1,030,000
- Mulattos (7.6%) 1,070,000
- Peninsulares (0.1%) 15,000
- EUROPEANS — Creoles (22.8%) 3,070,000
- Native Americans (55.8%) 7,860,000
- Africans (6.4%) 900,000

18. Based on the pie chart, why do you think the liberation movement in Spanish South America was successful?

_____

B. Essay

19. Using the information from the documents, your answers to the questions in Part A, and your knowledge of world history, write an essay on your own paper that discusses the difficulties that were involved in establishing democratic governments in Latin America and the solutions that were needed to overcome these difficulties. (8 points)

Part 4: Extended Response

Answer the following questions on the back of this page or on a separate sheet. (10 points each)

20. **Making Inferences** How did nationalism and industrialization influence the romantic movement in art and literature? Support your answer with examples from the text.

21. **Hypothesizing** Why were some nationalistic movements successful and others failures? Give reasons and examples from the text.

CHAPTER 9

SECTION QUIZ   *The Beginnings of Industrialization*

Section 1

A. Terms and Names Write the letter of the best answer.

_____ 1. In the 1700s, the process of enclosure tended to increase
   a. farming efficiency.
   b. farmers' reliance on a single cash crop.
   c. the use of the broadcast method of seeding.
   d. the amount of common land available for grazing.

_____ 2. The crop rotation system that developed in Britain during the agricultural
   revolution increased crop yields
   a. by allowing more land to rest.
   b. by increasing nutrients in the soil.
   c. by ensuring that more of the seeds that were planted actually sprouted.
   d. by decreasing the amount of land used to grow nutrient-depleting crops.

_____ 3. All of the following were results of the agricultural revolution in Britain
   EXCEPT that
   a. food prices decreased.
   b. population increased.
   c. the number of farmers increased.
   d. the average size of farms increased.

_____ 4. The first area to undergo major industrialization was
   a. banking.
   b. railroads.
   c. coal mining.
   d. textile production.

_____ 5. By the late 1700s, the best place to find a water frame and a spinning mule
   was in
   a. a barn.
   b. a factory.
   c. a farm house.
   d. an urban home.

_____ 6. An entrepreneur is a type of
   a. scientist.
   b. inventor.
   c. business person.
   d. personal secretary.

B. Extended Response Briefly answer the following question on the back of this paper.

What were the factors of production present in Britain that encouraged the Industrial
Revolution?

CHAPTER
9

Section 2

SECTION QUIZ   *Industrialization*
Case Study: Manchester

A. Terms and Names Write the letter of the best answer.

_____ 1. Which of the following did NOT improve as an early result of the Industrial
Revolution?
   a. factory working conditions
   b. the quality of clothing
   c. the average person's diet
   d. transportation

_____ 2. Which of the follwing did NOT increase as an early result of the Industrial
Revolution?
   a. urbanization
   b. the size of the middle class
   c. the length of the average work day
   d. the life expectancy of the average worker

_____ 3. Which of the following did NOT improve as a result of the Industrial
Revolution?
   a. living conditions for the average worker
   b. educational opportunities
   c. preservation of the environment
   d. affordability of consumer goods

B. Extended Response Briefly answer the following question on the back of this paper.

Think about all of the various groups of people who were involved in the Industrial
Revolution, from rural aristocrats to skilled workers to the children of the poor. What
one group would you say benefitted the most from the Industrial Revolution in the
short term? What one group would you say benefitted the least in the short term?
Support your opinions.

Name _____   Date _____

CHAPTER 9

Section 3

SECTION QUIZ *Industrialization Spreads*

A. Terms and Names If the statement is true, write "true" on the line. If it is false, change the underlined word or words to make it true.

Example: Imperialism was a <u>result</u> of industrialization. _____ *true* _____

Example: The country where the Industrial Revolution began was <u>the United States</u>.
_____ *England* _____

1. In the United States, the Industrial Revolution began with the industrialization of the <u>railroad</u> industry. _____

2. The country of <u>Belgium</u> led Europe in adopting the industrial technology of Britain.

    _____

3. The French Revolution and the Napoleonic Wars <u>accelerated</u> the process of industrialization in Europe. _____

4. Being blockaded during the War of 1812 encouraged <u>France</u> to use its own resources to develop independent industries. _____

5. A <u>corporation</u> is a type of business owned by stockholders who share in its profits but are not personally responsible for its debts. _____

6. In the 19th century, industrialization had the effect of <u>closing</u> the gap between industrialized and non-industrialized countries. _____

7. Under the Meiji rulers, <u>Japan</u> began to industrialize. _____

B. Extended Response Briefly answer the following question on the back of this paper.

What are some of the factors that discouraged the growth of industrialization in certain European countries?

CHAPTER
9

Section 4

SECTION QUIZ   *An Age of Reforms*

A. Terms and Names Write the letter of the best answer.

_____ 1. The free-market system of capitalism was defended in the book *The Wealth of Nations* by
  a. Adam Smith.
  b. John Stuart Mill.
  c. Jeremy Bentham.
  d. William Wilberforce.

_____ 2. Utilitarianism held that government policies should promote
  a. wars and epidemics to kill off excess people.
  b. public ownership of the means of production.
  c. the complete independence of each individual.
  d. the greatest good for the greatest number of people.

_____ 3. Nineteenth-century socialists argued that government should
  a. leave the economy alone.
  b. actively plan the economy.
  c. destroy the economy.
  d. allow the economy to be controlled by the bourgeoise.

_____ 4. Karl Marx is most closely associated with
  a. socialism.
  b. communism.
  c. utilitarianism.
  d. trade unionism.

_____ 5. In the 19th century, collective bargaining was carried out between
  a. government and unions.
  b. employers and employees.
  c. communists and capitalists.
  d. political and financial leaders.

_____ 6. When the trade union movement began in Britain, the strike was an illegal action taken against
  a. child laborers by factory owners.
  b. union workers by factory owners.
  c. factory owners by union workers.
  d. non-union workers by union workers.

B. Extended Response Briefly answer the following question on the back of this paper.

In the 19th century, what were some of the main differences between the beliefs of laissez-faire capitalists and communists?

CHAPTER **9** Form A

CHAPTER TEST *The Industrial Revolution*

Part 1: Main Ideas
Write the letter of the best answer. (4 points each)

_____ 1. What was the Industrial Revolution?
    a. increased purchases of land by wealthy landowners to cultivate larger fields
    b. an increase in machine-made goods beginning in England during the 1700s
    c. widespread use of teenagers as factory laborers who worked long hours
    d. increased populations of urban areas during the 1800s

_____ 2. Which of the following was a result of the agricultural revolution?
    a. Many small farmers became tenant farmers or moved to cities.
    b. Enclosures became landmarks of wealthy landowners.
    c. Landowners experimented with new agricultural methods.
    d. All of the above are true.

_____ 3. What were the three factors of production required for industrialization?
    a. land, labor, capital
    b. government, military, colonies
    c. raw materials, natural resources, man-made goods
    d. road, railway, and water transport

_____ 4. What was the main cause of the process of urbanization that occurrred in
    19th-century Britain and elsewhere in western Europe?
    a. poor crop yields
    b. industrialization
    c. improved living conditions in cities
    d. more efficient transportation systems

_____ 5. How did landowners and aristocrats view wealthy members of the middle class?
    a. regarded highly   c. saw as equals
    b. looked down upon   d. saw as outcasts

_____ 6. What did Britain do to keep industrial secrets from the United States?
    a. blockaded the United States from engaging in international trade
    b. sent messengers with misleading information to the United States
    c. forbade engineers, mechanics, and toolmakers from leaving the country
    d. charged impossible fees for the secrets to industrialization

_____ 7. What was the benefit of being a stockholder in a corporation?
    a. complete ownership of branch corporations
    b. free goods produced by the corporation
    c. not personally responsible for its debts
    d. all of the above

_____ 8. What is the laissez-faire policy?
    a. a policy that allowed labor to set working conditions based on votes on issues relevant to their industry
    b. a policy where labor created a committee to set working standards without interference from industry owners
    c. a policy that taught owners of industry how to set working conditions based on government standards
    d. a policy that let owners of industry set working conditions without government interference

_____ 9. What is the name for the voluntary associations of workers seeking labor reforms?
    a. unions   c. collective bargaining
    b. strikes   d. utilitarianism

_____ 10. Which of the following is an example of a reform movement?
    a. abolition of slavery   c. public education
    b. women's rights   d. all of the above

Part 2: Map Skills

Use the map to choose the best possible answer. (4 points each)

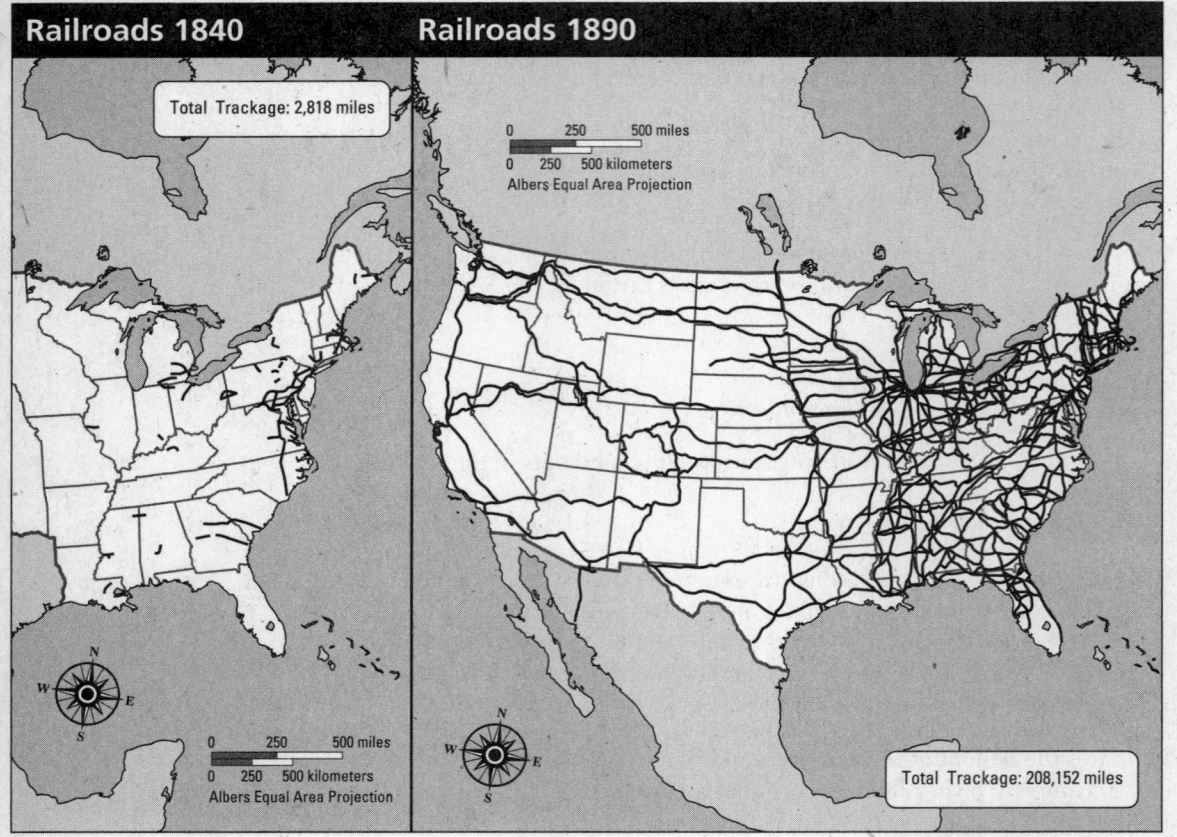

_____ 11. Which region of the country had the most miles of railroad track in 1890?
    a. East Coast   c. West
    b. Midwest   d. Pacific Coast

_____ 12. Which of the following is a true comparison of the two maps?
      a. The railroad system in 1840 was less developed than that in 1890.
      b. The railroad system had 205,334 more miles of track in 1890 than in 1840.
      c. The railroad system in 1840 carried goods great distances but not as far
         as in 1890.
      d. All of the above are true.

_____ 13. In which region were there no railroads in 1840?
      a. West   b. Midwest   c. Northeast   d. Southeast

_____ 14. In which two directions did railroads transport goods and people in the West
      in 1890?
      a. north   b. south   c. east   d. west
         and   and   and   and
         south   east   west   south

_____ 15. Approximately how many miles of tracks were laid from northern Washington to
      the southernmost point in California?
      a. 2,500   b. 1,000   c. 550   d. 100

Part 3: Interpreting Charts

Write the letter of the best answer. (4 points each)

Population Growth of Five Cities

_____ 16. Which of the following shows the cities ranked from smallest to largest in 1850?
     a. London, Liverpool, Glasgow, Birmingham, Edinburgh
     b. Edinburgh, Birmingham, Glasgow, Liverpool, London
     c. Birmingham, Glasgow, Liverpool, London, Edinburgh
     d. Edinburgh, Liverpool, Birmingham, Glasgow, London

_____ 17. Which of the following cities had about 320,000 people in 1850?
     a. Birmingham   c. Glasgow
     b. Liverpool   d. Edinburgh

_____ 18. Which two cities had approximately the same population in 1800?
     a. Birmingham and Liverpool
     b. Edinburgh and Glasgow
     c. Glasgow and Liverpool
     d. Edinburgh and Birmingham

_____ 19. Which cities had fewer than 100,000 people in 1800?
     a. Birmingham, Liverpool, Edinburgh, Glasgow
     b. London, Liverpool, Edinburgh, Glasgow
     c. Birmingham and Glasgow
     d. Liverpool and Edinburgh

_____ 20. Which of the smaller cities showed the most population growth between 1800 and 1850?
     a. Birmingham   c. Edinburgh
     b. Liverpool   d. Glasgow

Part 4: Extended Response

Answer the following questions on the back of this paper or on a separate sheet. (10 points each)

21. **Drawing Conclusions** Why did the Industrial Revolution occur in Great Britain before it occurred elsewhere in Europe?

Think about:
- resources (land and people) that allow for industrialization
- exportation of goods from Great Britain
- the political situation

22. **Recognizing Effects** What were some economic, social, and political effects that the Industrial Revolution had on Great Britain? Describe at least one economic, social, and political effect.

Think about:
- impact on trade
- impact on social classes
- impact on ideas

CHAPTER TEST   *The Industrial Revolution*

Form B

Part 1: Main Ideas

Write the letter of the best answer. (4 points each)

_____ 1. How did the Agricultural Revolution lead to the Industrial Revolution?
   a. It led to population growth.
   b. It increased food supplies.
   c. It caused farmers to lose land and seek other work.
   d. All of the above are true.

_____ 2. How did Britain's economy affect the process of industrialization?
   a. positively, by Britain's highly developed banking system, availability of loans, and climate of progress
   b. positively, by Britain allowing women and children to work long hours
   c. negatively, by Britain's decision to forbid engineers, mechanics, and toolmakers to leave the country
   d. negatively, by Britain's overseas expansion, which took jobs away from British citizens

_____ 3. What was the impact of the steam engine on the production of British goods?
   a. It enabled mines to work efficiently without more workers.
   b. It allowed small ferries to monopolize the English canals.
   c. It launched the railway age, which brought transportation to a new level.
   d. All of the above are true.

_____ 4. How did the Industrial Revolution affect cities?
   a. It created technology to clean them.
   b. It made them lose valuable sources of food.
   c. It made the population grow faster than the housing supply.
   d. It made the crime rate drop.

_____ 5. Which of the following factors most contributed to the shorter life span of those living in cities as opposed to those in the country?
   a. long working hours   c. inadequate housing
   b. illness caused by   d. excessive garbage
   unhealthy living
   conditions

_____ 6. In what way did the new middle class change British society?
   a. The power structure in London shifted from the city to the country.
   b. The middle class became the new ruling class in society.
   c. Aristocrats and wealthy landowners looked down on the middle class.
   d. Some members of the middle class achieved top positions in society.

_____ 7. Which of the following was a key idea in the free-market system?
       a. protect the nation's industries from foreign competition
       b. establish minimum wages and maximum working hours
       c. give government complete control of the means of production
       d. refuse to interfere in any economic matters

_____ 8. Which factor played a major role in the industrialization of the United States?
       a. end of the Civil War   c. railroad expansion
       b. Native American slaves   d. all of the above

_____ 9. Which of the following was NOT a legislative reform in the 1800s?
       a. In England, it became illegal to hire children under the age of nine.
       b. The Mines Act prevented women and children from working underground.
       c. The U.S. Supreme Court objected to a federal child labor law.
       d. The U.S. Supreme Court created social security for retired workers.

_____ 10. What did William Wilberforce fight for in the 1800s?
       a. to establish public schools
       b. to limit the length of the workday
       c. to abolish child labor in factories
       d. to abolish slavery and the slave trade

Part 2: Map Skills

Use the map to choose the best possible answer. (4 points each)

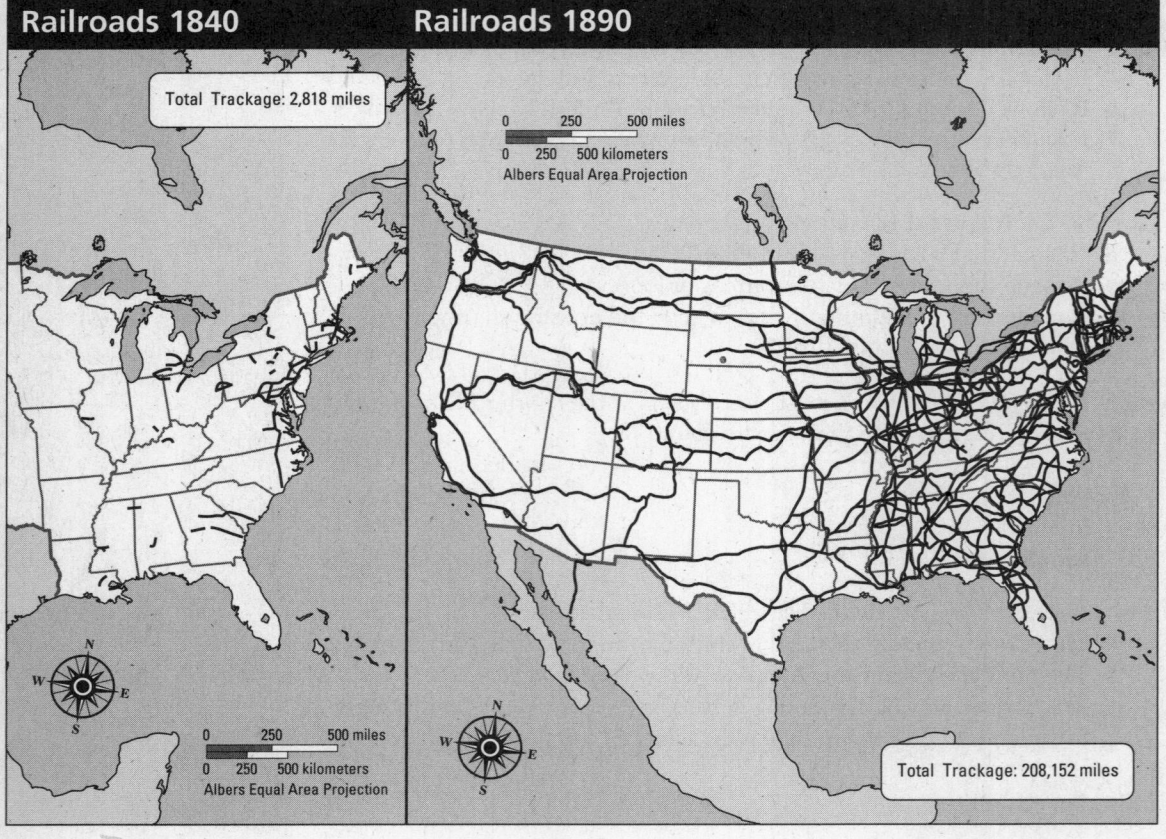

Railroads 1840   **Railroads 1890**

Total Trackage: 2,818 miles

0 250 500 miles
0 250 500 kilometers
Albers Equal Area Projection

0 250 500 miles
0 250 500 kilometers
Albers Equal Area Projection

Total Trackage: 208,152 miles

_____ 11. How many miles of track were added between 1840 and 1890?
        a. 2,818   b. 93,745   c. 100,225   d. 205,334

_____ 12. In which two directions did railroads mostly transport goods and people in 1890?
        a. north and south   c. east and west
        b. south and east   d. west and south

_____ 13. Which of the following states had mostly east and west railroad routes in 1890?
        a. New York   c. Illinois
        b. Texas   d. California

_____ 14. Approximately how many miles of tracks were laid across the state of Texas
by 1890?
        a. 2,600   b. 1,800   c. 1,300   d. 1,000

_____ 15. What might be a reason that the West had fewer miles of railroad track than
the East did in 1890?
        a. The western territories were still new.
        b. Industry was more developed in the East and Midwest.
        c. East coast ports were part of major trade routes.
        d. All of the above are true.

Part 3: Interpreting Charts

Write the letter of the best answer. (4 points each)

Population Growth of Five Cities

BIRMINGHAM	1800	(icons)
	1850	(icons)
LIVERPOOL	1800	(icons)
	1850	(icons)
LONDON	1800	(icons)
	1850	(icons)
EDINBURGH	1800	(icons)
	1850	(icons)
GLASGOW	1800	(icons)
	1850	(icons)

= 10,000 people

_____ 16. Which of the following cities had more than two million people in 1850?

      a. Birmingham   c. Glasgow

      b. Liverpool   d. London

_____ 17. Which of the following cities showed the greatest percentage increase in population?

      a. Liverpool   c. Edinburgh

      b. London   d. Glasgow

_____ 18. Which three cities more than tripled in population?

      a. London, Edinburgh, Glasgow

      b. Birmingham, Liverpool, Glasgow

      c. Liverpool, London, Edinburgh

      d. Edinburgh, Liverpool, Birmingham

_____ 19. What was the approximate population difference between Liverpool and Glasgow in 1850?

      a. 60,000   c. 250,000

      b. 95,000   d. 320,000

_____ 20. What is the most probable reason for the population growth in all cities between 1800 and 1850?

      a. agricultural revolution

      b. Industrial Revolution

      c. new middle class

      d. railroads

Part 4: Extended Response

Answer the following questions on the back of this paper or on a separate sheet. (10 points each)

21. **Analyzing Causes** What made 18th-century Great Britain ideal for rapid and revolutionary industrialization?

Think about:
- factors of industrialization
- population growth
- economic and political stability

22. **Drawing Conclusions** Why might the philosophy of communism have appealed to many 19th-century factory workers?

Think about:
- factory workers' conditions and lives
- beliefs of communism
- social status of the factory worker

CHAPTER
9

Form C

CHAPTER TEST   *The Industrial Revolution*

Part 1: Main Ideas

Write the letter of the best answer. (4 points each)

_____ 1. How might small farmers of the agricultural revolution be compared to the
working class of the Industrial Revolution?
    a. Both endured long working hours.
    b. Both suffered job losses due to progress.
    c. Both lived in climates of social restructuring.
    d. All of the above are true.

_____ 2. What impact did technological advances have on industry?
    a. Production of goods was increased.
    b. Quality of products was decreased.
    c. Number of factory workers decreased.
    d. All of the above are true.

_____ 3. What was a benefit of the railroad in Britain?
    a. It encouraged people to emigrate to other countries.
    b. It eliminated hundreds of thousands of jobs.
    c. It displaced England's agricultural and fishing industries.
    d. It offered cheap transportation for materials and goods.

_____ 4. Which of the following was NOT a positive aspect of industrialization?
    a. more jobs   c. cleaner cities
    b. increased wealth   d. more goods

_____ 5. How did the War of 1812 pave the way for the United States to industrialize?
    a. The British blockade forced it to develop its own industries.
    b. Materials from the war influenced new American inventions.
    c. British prisoners from the war greatly increased the U.S. work force.
    d. Under the Treaty of Ghent, Britain assisted U.S. industry.

_____ 6. How did the Napoleonic wars and French Revolution impact the industrialization
of Continental Europe?
    a. Trade was halted in many parts of Europe.
    b. Communications between countries were interrupted.
    c. Inflation was on the rise in some areas of Europe, disrupting the economy.
    d. All of the above are true.

_____ 7. What was a worldwide impact of industrialization?
    a. It was the driving force behind imperialism.
    b. It weakened economic ties between nations.
    c. Industrialized nations exploited their overseas colonies for slaves.
    d. All of the above are true.

_____ 8. How did the philosophy of laissez-faire influence early industrialists?
      a. with ideas of a free market governed by natural laws, not government rules
      b. with ideas of an economy supported by tariffs on foreign goods
      c. with ideas that the elite had a responsibility to give to charities
      d. all of the above

_____ 9. What were the long-term effects of Marx and Engels's *The Communist Manifesto*?
      a. Working classes worldwide demanded a "dictatorship of the proletariat."
      b. Marx and Engels proved correct as economic forces alone ruled society.
      c. In the 1900s, Marxism inspired revolutionaries such as Russia's Lenin.
      d. The 1848 and 1849 revolts shook Europe but were suppressed.

_____ 10. Which of the following statements is true?
      a. Socialism and communism are two words for the same ideology.
      b. Socialism and communism are two completely unrelated ideologies.
      c. Communism is complete socialism where the people own all property.
      d. Communism seeks political control; socialism seeks economic control.

Part 2: Map Skills

Using the map, answer the following questions. (4 points each)

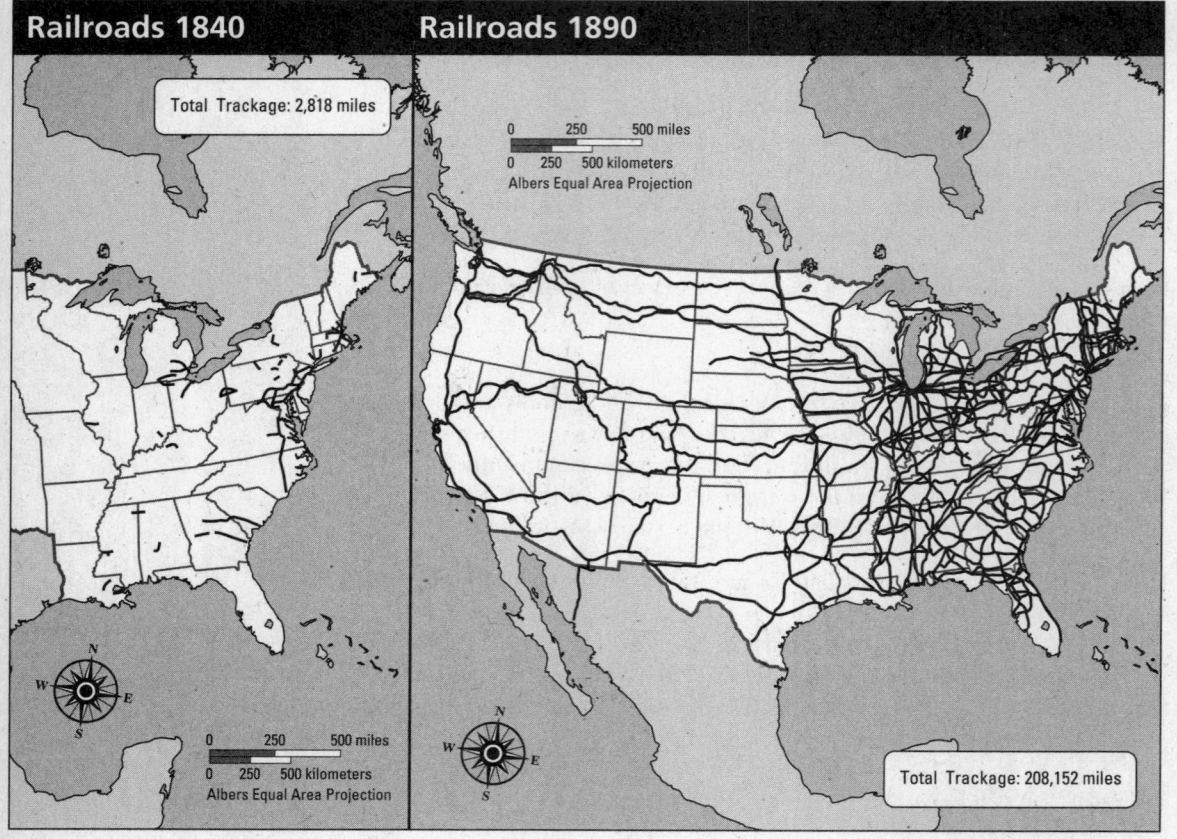

Railroads 1840 — Total Trackage: 2,818 miles
Railroads 1890 — Total Trackage: 208,152 miles
0 250 500 miles
0 250 500 kilometers
Albers Equal Area Projection

11. How might railroad expansion have influenced U.S. growth from 1840 to 1890?

_____

12. What might explain the mostly north and south route along the Pacific Coast?

_____

13. What might be the purpose of the short railroad lines in the Midwest in 1840?

_____

14. How does the number of miles of track in the West and the East compare in 1890?

_____

15. What geographic reasons might explain the difference you identified in question 14?

_____

Part 3: Interpreting Charts

Write the letter of the best answer. (4 points each)

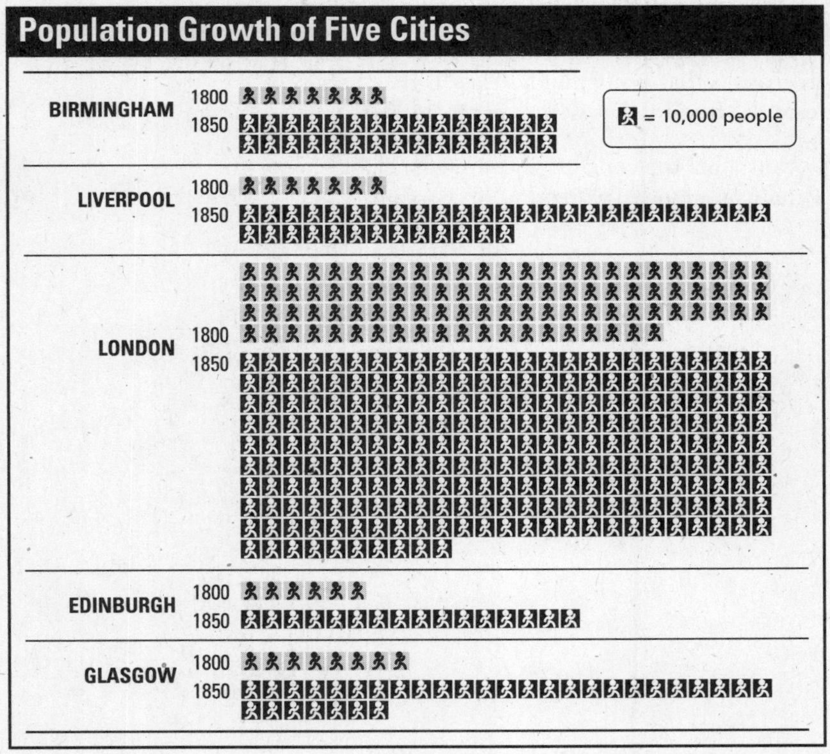

Population Growth of Five Cities

_____ 16. Which city showed the smallest percentage increase in population?
     a. Liverpool   b. London   c. Edinburgh   d. Glasgow

_____ 17. What reason might account for the city that had the smallest increase in growth?
      a. Industry was slow to grow in that city.
      b. Sickness was widespread in that city.
      c. Natural resources were scarce in that city.
      d. Population was already high in that city.

_____ 18. Which three cities increased in population by at least 300%?
      a. London, Edinburgh, Glasgow
      b. Birmingham, Liverpool, Glasgow
      c. Liverpool, London, Edinburgh
      d. Edinburgh, Liverpool, Birmingham

_____ 19. Which city would be ranked with the second largest population in 1850?
      a. Birmingham   c. Edinburgh
      b. Liverpool   d. Glasgow

_____ 20. Which of the following cities had the fewest people in 1800 and again in 1850?
      a. Birmingham   c. Edinburgh
      b. Liverpool   d. Glasgow

Part 4: Extended Response

Answer the following questions on the back of this paper or on a separate sheet. (10 points each)

21. **Analyzing Motives** What are some likely reasons that many middle-class British believed in the theories of laissez-faire capitalism and the free-market system in the 1800s?

22. **Forming and Supporting Opinions** Do you think the concept of complete reliance on a free-market system, using 19th-century Britain as a model, worked well? Explain.

Name _____ Date _____

SECTION QUIZ *Democratic Reform and Activism*

CHAPTER 10

Section 1

_____

A. Terms and Names Write the letter of the best answer.

_____ 1. Before the passage of the Reform Bill of 1832, the percentage of the British
population that had voting rights was about
   a. 5%.   b. 12%.   c. 20%.   d. 35%.

_____ 2. The Reform Bill of 1832 lowered the property requirements for voting in
order to give voting rights to
   a. poor men.   c. urban working class
   b. rural working class   men.
      men.   d. wealthy middle class
                                          men.

_____ 3. The Chartist movement pressed for all of the following EXCEPT
   a. a secret ballot.
   b. universal male suffrage.
   c. universal woman suffrage.
   d. pay for members of Parliament.

_____ 4. Queen Victoria was forced to
   a. share power with Parliament.
   b. preside over a shrinking empire.
   c. accept a less powerful role for the monarchy.
   d. die without providing an heir to the throne.

_____ 5. Alfred Dreyfus was a French army officer who was unjustly accused of
   a. disobeying orders.
   b. selling military secrets.
   c. cruelty toward his men.
   d. cowardice under enemy fire.

_____ 6. The pogroms that took place in Russia were fueled by
   a. Zionism.
   b. anti-Semitism.
   c. anti-communism.
   d. demands for voting rights.

_____ 7. The only country to allow women to vote before 1900 was
   a. Britain.   c. Canada.
   b. Ireland.   d. New Zealand.

B. Extended Response Briefly answer the following question on the back of this paper.

Why do you think French political leadership was so concerned about conflict that the
best form of government seemed to be the one that divided France the least?

CHAPTER
10

Section 2

SECTION QUIZ *Self-Rule for British Colonies*

A. Terms and Names Write the letter of the best answer.

_____ 1. Canada received the right to control its own domestic affairs when it
   a. became a dominion.
   b. became part of the British Empire.
   c. was reunited as the Province of Canada.
   d. persuaded frontier territories to join the Canadian union.

_____ 2. The first country to give full voting rights to women was
   a. Ireland.   c. Australia.
   b. Canada.   d. New Zealand.

_____ 3. Most Protestants opposed the idea of home rule in
   a. Ireland.   c. Australia.
   b. Canada.   d. New Zealand.

_____ 4. The people known as the Maori are
   a. inhabitants of the Arctic.
   b. nomadic inhabitants of Australia.
   c. French speaking Roman Catholic Canadians.
   d. a Polynesian people that settled in New Zealand.

_____ 5. The British colony originally set up as a penal colony was
   a. Ulster.   c. Australia.
   b. Nunavut.   d. Upper Canada.

_____ 6. The Catholic Emancipation Act of 1829 affected the rights of Roman Catholics
   who lived in
   a. Ireland.   c. Australia.
   b. Canada.   d. New Zealand.

_____ 7. The Great Famine was a time of widespread starvation in Ireland caused
   by the destruction of
   a. cattle herds.   c. wheat crops.
   b. sheep herds.   d. potato crops.

B. Extended Response Briefly answer the following question on the back of this paper.

How did the treatment of native people by British settlers in Australia and New Zealand
compare with the actions of the British settlers in North America?

CHAPTER **10**

Section 3

SECTION QUIZ *War and Expansion in the United States*

A. Terms and Names Write the letter of the best answer.

_____ 1. The term "manifest destiny" describes something that is both inevitable and
   a. proper.   c. the will of God.
   b. common to all.   d. clearly apparent.

_____ 2. Americans used the term "manifest destiny" to justify
   a. westward expansion.
   b. preserving the Union.
   c. both sides of the slavery issue.
   d. government support for industrial expansion.

_____ 3. The outbreak of the Civil War was a direct result of the
   a. election of Abraham Lincoln.
   b. secession of the Southern states.
   c. Confederate attack on Fort Sumter.
   d. issuance of the Emancipation Proclamation.

_____ 4. In the Gadsden Purchase, the United States purchased land from
   a. Spain.   c. Mexico.
   b. France.   d. Great Britain.

_____ 5. Parts of all of the following present-day states were included in the territory
   ceded by Mexico as a result of the Mexican-American War EXCEPT
   a. Texas.   c. California.
   b. Arizona.   d. New Mexico.

_____ 6. The Trail of Tears was the forced westward migration of the Cherokee from
   Georgia to
   a. Nevada.   c. Kansas.
   b. Oklahoma.   d. Arizona.

_____ 7. In 1836, Texas fought for its independence from
   a. Spain.   c. Mexico.
   b. France.   d. the United States.

B. Extended Response Briefly answer the following question on the back of this paper.

What was the point of issuing the Emancipation Proclamation when the United States government was not able, at that time, to enforce it?

CHAPTER 10

Section 4

SECTION QUIZ *Nineteenth-Century Progress*

A. Terms and Names Write the letter of the name that best matches the description. A name may be used more than once or not at all.

a. Thomas Edison
b. Guglielmo Marconi
c. Alexander Graham Bell
d. Henry Ford
e. Ivan Pavlov
f. Marie Curie
g. Charles Darwin
h. Louis Pasteur
i. Wilbur Wright
j. Sigmund Freud

_____ 1. Who developed the theory of evolution?

_____ 2. Who made use of the assembly line to make his factory highly efficient?

_____ 3. Who developed the germ theory of disease along with discovering and naming bacteria?

_____ 4. Who invented the first practical electric light bulb?

_____ 5. Who invented the telephone?

_____ 6. Who participated in identifying and naming radioactivity?

_____ 7. Who won Nobel Prizes for both Physics and Chemistry?

_____ 8. Who invented the first radio?

_____ 9. Who started a well-staffed research laboratory in Menlo Park, New Jersey?

_____ 10. Who helped to invent the first airplane?

_____ 11. Who believed that human actions were often unconscious reactions to experiences and could be changed by training?

_____ 12. Who wrote the controversial book *On the Origin of Species by Means of Natural Selection*?

_____ 13. Who was a pioneer in the field of making motion pictures?

_____ 14. Who created psychoanalysis, based on the idea that the unconscious mind has a powerful influence on behavior?

B. Extended Response Briefly answer the following question on the back of this paper.

What were the major factors in the development of a mass culture?

CHAPTER TEST *An Age of Democracy and Progress*

Form A

Part 1: Main Ideas

Write the letter of the best answer. (4 points each)

_____ 1. What did The People's Charter of 1838 petition for?
a. suffrage for non-landowning men
b. suffrage for men and women
c. suffrage for all men and annual parliamentary elections
d. suffrage for women and annual parliamentary elections

_____ 2. Who were the Zionists?
a. founders of France's Third Republic
b. supporters of the British Parliament
c. Jews who worked for a homeland in Palestine
d. French journalists who opposed an army cover-up

_____ 3. What was Captain Alfred Dreyfus accused of in the Dreyfus affair?
a. Zionist activity   c. covering up a scandal
b. being anti-Semitic   d. selling military secrets

_____ 4. What did it mean to be a dominion?
a. It meant that a country pledged its allegiance to the Catholic Church.
b. It meant that a country was domestically self-governing but part of the British Empire.
c. It meant that a country paid tariffs to another country for protection.
d. It meant that a country could not take part in international trade due to war.

_____ 5. Why did Great Britain establish a penal colony in Australia?
a. to claim it before the Americans could
b. to further their industrialization overseas
c. to have a trading colony close to Asia
d. to relieve overcrowding in English prisons

_____ 6. To which country did the most Irish emigrants go during the Great Famine?
a. Canada   c. Australia
b. England   d. the United States

_____ 7. How was most of the territory west of Texas obtained by the United States?
a. Texas Annexation   c. Louisiana Purchase
b. Gadsen Purchase   d. Mexican-American War

_____ 8. Who was the American inventor and industrialist who made factory production more efficient by introducing the assembly line?
a. Thomas Edison   c. Marie Curie
b. Henry Ford   d. Orville Wright

_____ 9. What did the Emancipation Proclamation do?
      a. guaranteed former slaves the right to vote
      b. forever abolished slavery in all parts of the United States
      c. declared all slaves in the Confederate states as free
      d. all of the above

_____ 10. What concept is the theory of evolution based on?
      a. special creation
      b. natural selection
      c. manifest destiny
      d. power of the subconscious

Part 2: Map Skills

Use the map to choose the best possible answer. (4 points each)

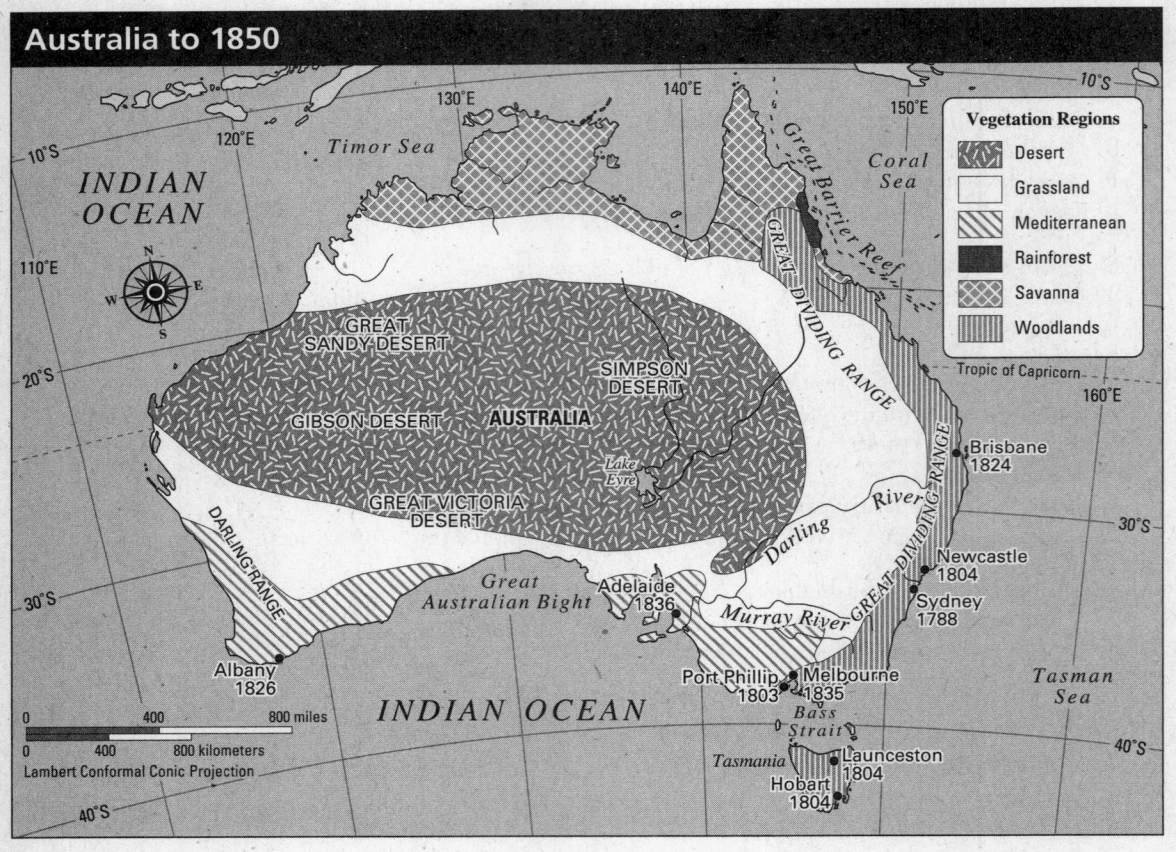

Australia to 1850

_____ 11. Which of the following cities falls within a Mediterranean vegetation zone?
      a. Newcastle   c. Adelaide
      b. Brisbane   d. Sydney

_____ 12. Which of the following geographic features crosses three vegetation zones?
      a. Simpson Desert   c. Darling Range
      b. Murray River   d. all of the above

_____ 13. Which cities were founded first and last, in that order?
      a. Sydney, Adelaide   c. Newcastle, Albany
      b. Hobart, Melbourne   d. Launceston, Brisbane

_____ 14. What might have kept colonists from settling deeper into the interior of Australia?
      a. Coasts gave ready access to drinking water.
      b. Grasslands were excellent areas to farm.
      c. Deserts were difficult places to live.
      d. All of the above are true.

_____ 15. What characterizes the location of Australia's main cities?
      a. They are all near a coast.
      b. They are all on the Coral Sea.
      c. They are all within the Great Dividing Range.
      d. They are all on the Murray River.

Part 3: Document Based Questions
Introduction

Historical Context: The growth of cities and the spread of industrialization around the world in the early 19th century created many problems. To solve these problems, people began to want a larger role in politics, greater individual freedoms, and changes in the way business was conducted. These desires led to various reform movements that over time would bring about tremendous changes in the ways that governments interacted with their citizens and in the rights available to those citizens.

Task: Discuss what the various reform movements sought and their effectiveness overall.

A. Short Answer

Study each document carefully and answer the questions that follow. (4 points each)

Document 1: An excerpt from "The Great Charter," a petition to Parliament

That your honourable House, as at present constituted, has not been elected by, and acts irresponsibly of, the people; and hitherto has only represented parties, and benefited the few, regardless of the miseries, grievances, and petitions of the many. Your honourable House has enacted laws contrary to the expressed wishes of the people, and by unconstitutional means enforced obedience to them, hereby creating an unbearable despotism on the one hand, and degrading slavery on the other.

That if your honourable House is of opinion that the people of Great Britain and Ireland ought not to be fully represented, your petitioners pray that such opinion may be unequivocally made known, that the people may fully understand what they can or cannot expect from your honourable House; because if such be the decision of your honourable House, your petitioners are of opinion that where representation is denied, taxation ought to be resisted.

16. What type of laws were passed by the British Parliament and how were they enforced?

_____

Document 2: An excerpt from *The Jewish State* by Theodore Herzl

Thus, whether we like it or not, we are now, and shall henceforth remain, a historic group with unmistakable characteristics common to us all.

We are one people—our enemies have made us one without our consent, as repeatedly happens in history. Distress binds us together, and, thus united, we suddenly discover our strength. Yes, we are strong enough to form a State, and, indeed, a model State. We possess all human and material resources necessary for the purpose. . . . Let the sovereignty be granted us over a portion of the globe large enough to satisfy the rightful requirements of a nation; the rest we shall manage for ourselves.

17. According to Herzl, what were the Jewish people strong enough to do?

_____

Document 3: woman suffrage poster

Source: Library of Congress, Prints and Photographs Division

18. Why is the word "handicapped" in capital letters with an exclamation point?

_____

B. Essay

19. Using information from the documents, your answers to the questions in Part A, and your knowledge of world history, write an essay that discusses what changes the reform movements sought and the effects they had on the 1800s and later time periods. Students may also cite quotes or visual descriptions from the documents and cite information they may recall from the chapter. (8 points)

Part 4: Extended Response

Answer the following questions on the back of this paper or on a separate sheet. (10 points each)

20. **Analyzing Issues** What led to self-rule for the British colonies in Canada, Australia, and New Zealand, and what form did their governments take?

   Think about:
   • growing populations
   • economic changes
   • political choices and reforms

21. **Analyzing Causes and Recognizing Effects** What were the three significant changes that occurred in the late 1800s because of inventions and discoveries made at that time?

   Think about:
   • exchange of ideas
   • culture of a nation
   • new sciences

CHAPTER 10 **Form B**

CHAPTER TEST *An Age of Democracy and Progress*

Part 1: Main Ideas

Write the letter of the best answer. (4 points each)

_____ 1. Before the reform act of 1832, who were the only British citizens who could vote?
    a. wealthy men
    b. owners of large landholdings
    c. members of the House of Lords
    d. members of the middle and upper classes

_____ 2. Which of the following reforms did NOT occur in Great Britain by the early 1900s?
    a. The secret ballot came into use.
    b. Working-class men received voting rights.
    c. Members of Parliament were paid a salary.
    d. Annual elections to the House of Commons were held.

_____ 3. During the early 1900s, who was the British woman who formed the Women's Social and Political Union?
    a. Emmeline Parkhurst
    b. Queen Victoria
    c. Sylvia Parkhurst
    d. Marie Curie

_____ 4. What form of government did France adopt in 1875?
    a. monarchy   c. dictatorship
    b. republic   d. socialist state

_____ 5. Which two lands did Captain Cook claim for Great Britain in 1770?
    a. Ireland and Scotland
    b. Canada and Nova Scotia
    c. Australia and New Zealand
    d. Hawaii and New Zealand

_____ 6. Which of the following political reforms occurred in New Zealand in 1893?
    a. secret ballot   c. home rule
    b. woman suffrage   d. all of the above

_____ 7. How did California and much of the Southwest become part of the United States?
    a. Texas annexation   c. Mexican Cession
    b. Gadsden Purchase   d. Louisiana Purchase

_____ 8. What policy or action led to the Trail of Tears?
    a. Texas annexation
    b. Emancipation Proclamation
    c. Indian Removal Act of 1830
    d. building of the transcontinental railroad

_____ 9. What event provoked the secession of the Southern states from the United States?
  a. attack on Fort Sumter
  b. election of Abraham Lincoln
  c. issuance of the Emancipation Proclamation
  d. formation of the Confederate States of America

_____ 10. Why was the work of Louis Pasteur important in the history of medicine?
  a. He published *The Origin of Species*.
  b. He discovered radium and polonium.
  c. He found that bacteria caused diseases.
  d. He created psychoanalysis.

Part 2: Map Skills

Use the map to choose the best possible answer. (4 points each)

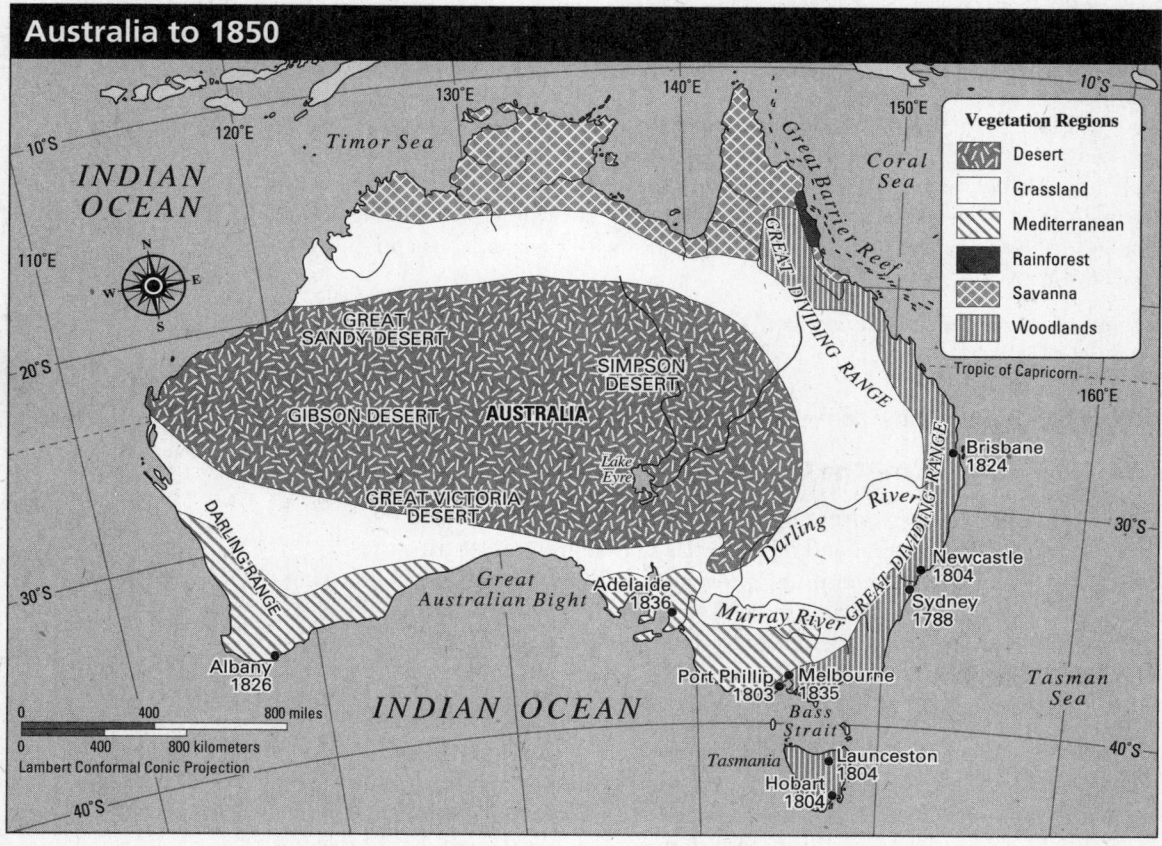

_____ 11. How many years passed between the founding of Sydney and the founding of
  Adelaide?
    a. 52   b. 48   c. 37   d. 25

_____ 12. Approximately how many miles did ships travel between Albany and Brisbane?
    a. 2,600   b. 3,500   c. 4,250   d. 5,575

_____ 13. Why were all the settlements founded in southern and eastern Australia?
        a. The western region is entirely desert.
        b. The native populations inhabit the north.
        c. They were closer to shipments from New Zealand.
        d. The climate was more favorable.

_____ 14. Which region lies directly on the Tropic of Capricorn?
        a. Great Sandy Desert
        b. Great Victoria Desert
        c. Simpson Desert
        d. Gibson Desert

_____ 15. Which Australian settlement can be found at approximately 138° E by 35° S?
        a. Adelaide   c. Port Phillip
        b. Melbourne   d. Sydney

Part 3: Document Based Questions
Introduction

Historical Context: The growth of cities and the spread of industrialization around the world in the early 19th century created many problems. To solve these problems, people began to want a larger role in politics, greater individual freedoms, and changes in the way business was conducted. These desires led to various reform movements that over time would bring about tremendous changes in the ways that governments interacted with their citizens and in the rights available to those citizens.

Task: Discuss what the various reform movements sought and their effectiveness overall.

A. Short Answer

Study each document carefully and answer the questions that follow. (4 points each)

Document 1: An excerpt from "The Great Charter," a petition to Parliament

That your honourable House, as at present constituted, has not been elected by, and acts irresponsibly of, the people; and hitherto has only represented parties, and benefited the few, regardless of the miseries, grievances, and petitions of the many. Your honourable House has enacted laws contrary to the expressed wishes of the people, and by unconstitutional means enforced obedience to them, hereby creating an unbearable depotism on the one hand, and degrading slavery on the other.

That if your honourable House is of opinion that the people of Great Britain and Ireland ought not to be fully represented, your petitioners pray that such opinion may be unequivocally made known, that the people may fully understand what they can or cannot expect from your honourable House; because if such be the decision of your honourable House, your petitioners are of opinion that where representation is denied, taxation ought to be resisted.

16. What do the petitioners think should be done if their demands are not met?

_____

Document 2: An excerpt from *The Jewish State* by Theodore Herzl

Thus, whether we like it or not, we are now, and shall henceforth remain, a historic group with unmistakable characteristics common to us all.

We are one people—our enemies have made us one without our consent, as repeatedly happens in history. Distress binds us together, and, thus united, we suddenly discover our strength. Yes, we are strong enough to form a State, and, indeed, a model State. We possess all human and material resources necessary for the purpose. . . . Let the sovereignty be granted us over a portion of the globe large enough to satisfy the rightful requirements of a nation; the rest we shall manage for ourselves.

17. How have the Jewish people been made "one people" without their consent?

_____

Document 3: woman suffrage poster

Source: Library of Congress, Prints and Photographs Division

18. How does this poster illustrate the struggle for woman suffrage?

_____

B. Essay

19. Using information from the documents, your answers to the questions in Part A, and your knowledge of world history, write an essay that discusses what changes the reform movements sought and the effects they had on the 1800s and later time periods. Students may also cite quotes or visual descriptions from the documents and cite information they may recall from the chapter. (8 points)

Part 4: Extended Response

Answer the following questions on the back of this paper or on a separate sheet. (10 points each)

20. **Drawing Conclusions** Which of the inventions discussed in this chapter do you think was the most important? Explain your answer.

   Think about:
   - impacts on work and daily life
   - inventions used by more than one nation
   - systems still in use today

21. **Comparing and Contrasting** How are the histories of Australia and New Zealand similar and different?

   Think about:
   - native peoples
   - which settlers came and why
   - self-government

Name _____ Date _____

Part 1: Main Ideas
Write the letter of the best answer. (4 points each)

_____ 1. How did the democratic reforms in Great Britain change the government?
     a. Most adult males gained the right to vote by 1884.
     b. British monarchs became symbolic rulers with no political power.
     c. Political power shifted greatly to the elected House of Commons.
     d. All of the above are true.

_____ 2. Which of the following was true of women's fight for suffrage?
     a. The secret ballot came into use.
     b. Some women participated in hunger strikes.
     c. Women won the right to vote prior to WWI.
     d. Women's suffrage began in France.

_____ 3. How might the French government of the late 1800s and early 1900s be
characterized?
     a. harsh   b. radical   c. unstable   d. idealistic

_____ 4. Which of the following influenced the formation of Upper and Lower Canada?
     a. abolition of slavery in half of Canada
     b. a war between France and Britain
     c. Native American land rights
     d. cultural conflicts between the British and French

_____ 5. Why did Australia and New Zealand want to become dominions of Great Britain
rather than independent nations?
     a. They were unable to defeat the native peoples.
     b. They wanted the protection of the British Empire.
     c. They needed help establishing a government.
     d. They wanted British convicts as laborers.

_____ 6. What does the phrase *manifest destiny* mean?
     a. Native Americans should keep all their lands from coast to coast.
     b. The American people had the right and the duty to rule North America
from coast to coast.
     c. The British government should always have a say in U.S. foreign affairs, but
not domestic.
     d. The United States had the right to expand its territory to any continent.

_____ 7. What promise by Abraham Lincoln frightened Southern states into seceding?
     a. to stop the spread of slavery
     b. to build factories in the South
     c. to offer women the right to vote
     d. to create the Confederate States of America

_____ 8. What impact did the Civil War have on the postwar American economy?
  a. The economy sagged because of widespread deaths.
  b. The war caused massive railroad expansion.
  c. The economy suffered from mass emigration.
  d. The war speeded up the pace of industrialization

_____ 9. What effect did the major inventions of the 19th-century have on people's lives in
  industrialized nations?
  a. Life was made harder through increased demand for goods.
  b. Car, telephone, and electricity helped ease ways of living.
  c. Work days increased because of higher technological demands.
  d. All of the above are true.

_____ 10. Which of the following was NOT a reason for the rise of mass culture?
  a. the assembly line   c. increase in literacy
  b. public education   d. shorter work day

Part 2: Map Skills

Use the map to choose the best possible answer. (4 points each)

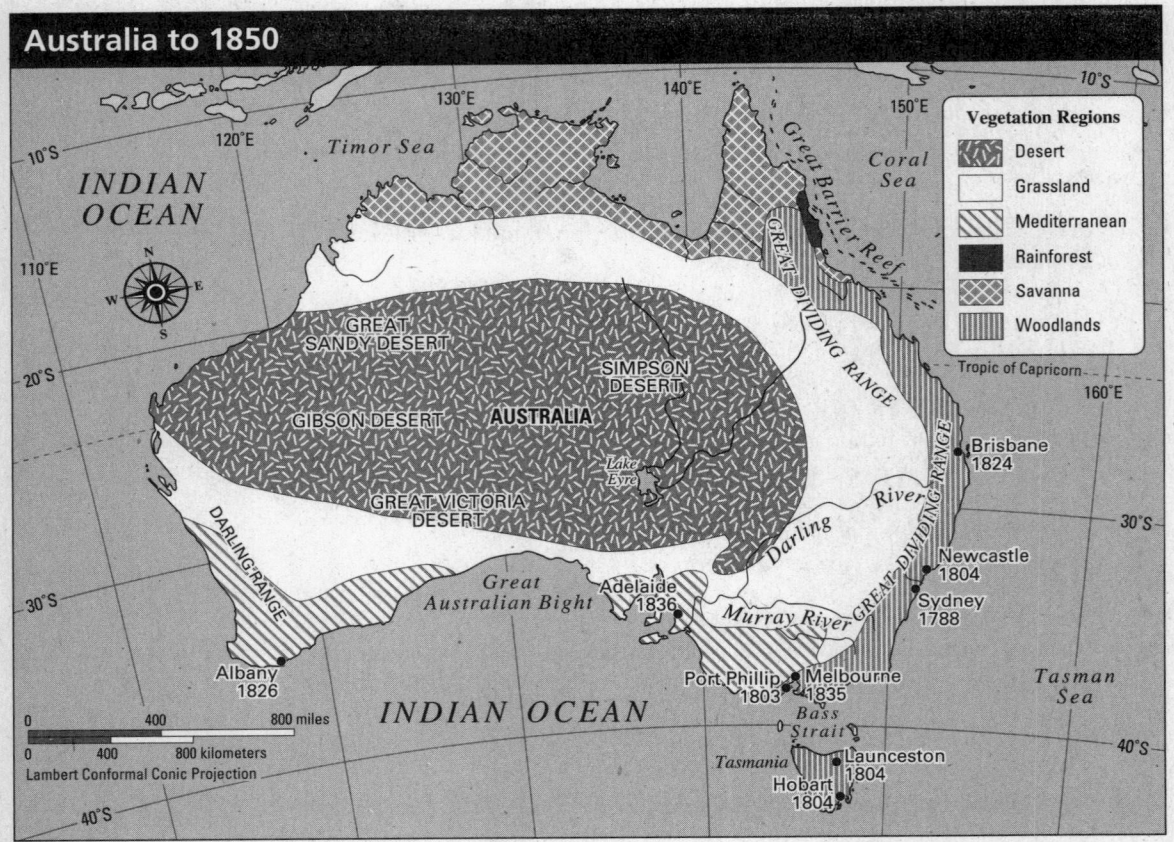

_____ 11. What would be the most efficient mode of travel from Brisbane to Adelaide in
  1850?
  a. horseback   c. railroad
  b. river   d. on foot

_____ 12. Why might a settler choose to live in Albany as opposed to one of the other cities?
  a. The Indian Ocean offered better fishing than the Coral Sea.
  b. The climate was more favorable for farming in Albany.
  c. It was easier to trade with the British colony of India from Albany.
  d. It was on a peninsula that was good for defense.

_____ 13. What is the approximate width in miles of the continent at its widest point?
  a. 1,500   b. 2,000   c. 2,500   d. 3,000

_____ 14. What vegetation type covers most areas?
  a. savanna   c. rainforest
  b. mediterranean   d. desert

_____ 15. What geographic pattern do Australian cities follow?
  a. They are all near a mountain range.
  b. They are all located on the coasts.
  c. They are all on the southern side of the continent.
  d. They are all along the Tropic of Cancer.

Part 3: Document Based Questions
Introduction

Historical Context: The growth of cities and the spread of industrialization around the world in the early 19th century created many problems. To solve these problems, people began to want a larger role in politics, greater individual freedoms, and changes in the way business was conducted. These desires led to various reform movements that over time would bring about tremendous changes in the ways that governments interacted with their citizens and in the rights available to those citizens.

Task: Discuss what the various reform movements sought and their effectiveness overall.

A. Short Answer

Study each document carefully and answer the questions that follow. (4 points each)

Document 1: An excerpt from "The Great Charter," a petition to Parliament

That your honourable House, as at present constituted, has not been elected by, and acts irresponsibly of, the people; and hitherto has only represented parties, and benefited the few, regardless of the miseries, grievances, and petitions of the many. Your honourable House has enacted laws contrary to the expressed wishes of the people, and by unconstitutional means enforced obedience to them, hereby creating an unbearable depotism on the one hand, and degrading slavery on the other.

That if your honourable House is of opinion that the people of Great Britain and Ireland ought not to be fully represented, your petitioners pray that such opinion may be unequivocally made known, that the people may fully understand what they can or cannot expect from your honourable House; because if such be the decision of your honourable House, your petitioners are of opinion that where representation is denied, taxation ought to be resisted.

16. What is meant by the statement that Parliament has created an unbearable depotism on one hand and degraded slavery on the other?

_____

Document 2: An excerpt from _The Jewish State_ by Theodore Herzl

Thus, whether we like it or not, we are now, and shall henceforth remain, a historic group with unmistakable characteristics common to us all.

We are one people—our enemies have made us one without our consent, as repeatedly happens in history. Distress binds us together, and, thus united, we suddenly discover our strength. Yes, we are strong enough to form a State, and, indeed, a model State. We possess all human and material resources necessary for the purpose. . . . Let the sovereignty be granted us over a portion of the globe large enough to satisfy the rightful requirements of a nation; the rest we shall manage for ourselves.

17. What do you suppose are the human and material resources necessary to form a State?

_____

Document 3: woman suffrage poster

Source: Library of Congress, Prints and Photographs Division

18. What does this cartoon imply about the attitude of most 19th-century men toward women?

_____

B. Essay

19. Using information from the documents, your answers to the questions in Part A, and your knowledge of world history, write an essay that discusses what changes the reform movements sought and the effects they had on the 1800s and later time periods. Students may also cite quotes or visual descriptions from the documents and cite information they may recall from the chapter. (8 points)

Part 4: Extended Response

Answer the following questions on the back of this paper or on a separate sheet. (10 points each)

20. **Identifying Problems and Solutions** What did the Dreyfus affair reveal about problems in France? Give specific examples.

21. **Forming and Supporting Opinions** How did the following U.S. policies advance or hinder democratic progress: manifest destiny, emancipation, and segregation? Explain your answer.

CHAPTER
11

Section 1

SECTION QUIZ *The Scramble for Africa*

A. Terms and Names If the statement is true, write "true" on the line. If it is false, change the underlined word or words to make it true.

Example: In 1871, reporter <u>Henry Stanley</u> found Scottish minister David Livingstone on the shores of Lake Tanganyika. _____ *true* _____

Example: In 1882, Henry Stanley signed treaties with local chiefs of the Congo River valley that gave <u>Britain</u> control over these lands. _____ *Belgium* _____

1. <u>Belgian</u> settlers in South Africa were known as Boers. _____

2. Racism is the name for the belief that <u>one race is superior to others</u>. _____

3. In 1884 and 1885, 14 <u>African</u> nations met at the Berlin Conference to discuss the future of Africa. _____

4. The theory of Social Darwinism was used to <u>attack</u> the actions and beliefs of European imperialists. _____

5. The major source of wealth in Africa was the continent's <u>agricultural</u> resources. _____

6. The Boer War, which involved guerrilla warfare tactics and the use of concentration camps, was fought between the <u>Zulu</u> and the Boers. _____

7. Shaka was a Zulu chief who used highly disciplined warriors and good military organization to create a large centralized state in <u>southern Africa</u>. _____

8. The Great Trek was undertaken by the <u>French</u> in an attempt to escape the British but led them into conflict with the Zulu and other Africans. _____

B. Extended Response Briefly answer the following question on the back of this paper.

What motivated European imperialism, and why were European imperialists so successful in Africa?

Name _____   Date _____

A. Terms and Names Write the letter of the best answer.

_____ 1. The main difference between European colonies and protectorates in Africa had to do with their
      a. economies.
      b. governments.
      c. social organizations.
      d. levels of technology.

_____ 2. The European policy of paternalism reflected the belief that Africans should be
      a. separated into ethnic groups.
      b. trained to function as leaders.
      c. watched over and taken care of.
      d. granted more rights and freedoms.

_____ 3. The policy of assimilation in Africa was adapted and then largely abandoned by
      a. France.
      b. Britain.
      c. Ethiopia.
      d. the United States.

_____ 4. Menelik II differed from other 19th-century African leaders because
      a. he managed to maintain his nation's independence.
      b. he established colonies in Africa for his own nation.
      c. he eagerly adopted European methods of governing.
      d. he aggressively rebelled against European imperialism.

_____ 5. The national boundaries that existed in Africa at the end of the 19th century can best be described as
      a. ancient.
      b. unnaturally imposed.
      c. geographically logical.
      d. traditionally established.

B. Extended Response Briefly answer the following question on the back of this paper.

What were two of the steps taken by the British to gain economic, political, or social control over Nigeria?

CHAPTER 11

SECTION QUIZ *Europeans Claim Muslim Lands*

Section 3

A. Terms and Names Write the letter of the best answer.

_____ 1. By 1914, the Ottoman Empire had
   a. ceased to exist.
   b. achieved its greatest size.
   c. begun to experience a decline.
   d. declined to about a third of its greatest size.

_____ 2. The Crimean War was lost by
   a. Russia.
   b. France.
   c. Britain.
   d. the Ottoman Empire.

_____ 3. Muhammad Ali instituted a series of reforms in the military and in the economy of
   a. Egypt.
   b. Persia.
   c. Herzegovina.
   d. the Ottoman Empire.

_____ 4. The Suez Canal was built through the combined efforts of the
   a. French and British.
   b. French and Egyptians.
   c. Russians and Persians.
   d. Egyptians and Persians.

_____ 5. In 1907, Russia and Britain agreed to spheres of influence in
   a. India.
   b. Egypt.
   c. Persia.
   d. Afghanistan.

B. Extended Response Briefly answer the following question on the back of this paper.

What role did geopolitics play in the outbreak of the Crimean War?

CHAPTER
11

Section 4

SECTION QUIZ *British Imperialism in India*

A. Terms and Names Write the letter of the best answer.

_____ 1. The term *Raj* is used to refer to the period of Indian history during which India was
        a. independent.
        b. dominated by Britain.
        c. torn apart by civil war.
        d. loosely ruled by the British East India Company.

_____ 2. The sepoys were
        a. Indian soldiers.
        b. Bengal Hindus.
        c. Mughal princes.
        d. Sikh civil servants.

_____ 3. All of the following were causes of the Sepoy Mutiny EXCEPT
        a. famine.
        b. nationalism.
        c. religious beliefs.
        d. resentment of British rule.

_____ 4. One result of the Sepoy Mutiny was that
        a. the British East India Company went bankrupt.
        b. the British government tightened its control over India.
        c. the British stopped trying to convert Indians to Christianity.
        d. British officials became more sensitive to the needs of Indians.

_____ 5. According to Ram Mohun Roy, in order to successfully move towards independence, Indians had to
        a. convert to Christianity.
        b. hold firmly to traditional ideas.
        c. take up arms against their British rulers.
        d. change some of their cultural and religious practices.

B. Extended Response Briefly answer the following question on the back of this paper.

What does it mean that India was the "jewel in the crown" of the British Empire? Why did the British view India in this way?

CHAPTER

11

Section 5

SECTION QUIZ *Imperialism in Southeast Asia*

A. Terms and Names Write the letter of the best answer.

_____ 1. All of the following places were located on the Pacific Rim EXCEPT
        a. China.   c. Singapore.
        b. Indochina.   d. the Philippine Islands.

_____ 2. Malaysia became the world's leading exporter of
        a. tea.   c. rubber.
        b. teak.   d. sugar cane.

_____ 3. The main reason for British colonization of Singapore was to obtain use of its
        a. harbor.
        b. tin mines.
        c. plantations.
        d. sources of cheap labor.

_____ 4. Queen Liliuokalani was the last monarch of
        a. Java.   c. Borneo.
        b. Hawaii.   d. the Philippine Islands.

_____ 5. King Mongkut modernized
        a. Siam.   c. Hawaii.
        b. Guam.   d. New Guinea.

_____ 6. As a direct result of the Spanish-American War, the United States acquired all of the following EXCEPT
        a. Guam.   c. Puerto Rico.
        b. Hawaii.   d. the Philippine Islands.

_____ 7. Emilio Aguinaldo fought for the independence of
        a. Java.   c. Indonesia.
        b. Malacca.   d. the Philippine Islands.

_____ 8. The annexation of Hawaii was pushed by U.S.
        a. steel makers.   c. railroad builders.
        b. shipbuilders.   d. sugar-cane planters.

B. Extended Response Briefly answer the following question on the back of this paper.

What were the negative and positive results of European colonization of Southeast Asia?

Name _____   Date _____

CHAPTER TEST   *The Age of Imperialism*

Form A

Part 1: Main Ideas
Write the letter of the term or name that best matches the description. (4 points each)

a. Boer War
b. Crimean War
c. Emilio Aguinaldo
d. Sepoy Mutiny
e. Menelik II
f. Nigeria
g. Persia
h. Queen Liliuokalani
i. Raj
j. Shaka

_____ 1. The main cause of the_____ was Russia's desire to gain land on the Black
Sea from the Ottoman Empire.

_____ 2. The part of India that was under direct British rule was known as the _____.
This term is also used to refer to the period of British rule over India.

_____ 3. In 1907, _____ lost a long fight to maintain its independence when Britain
and Russia took over the country and divided it into spheres of influence.

_____ 4. In the 1800s, the Zulu chief _____ used highly disciplined warriors and good
military organization to create a large state in southern Africa.

_____ 5. _____ was the leader of the Filipino nationalists who claimed that the United
States had promised immediate independence of the Philippine Islands after
the end of the Spanish-American War.

_____ 6. The opposition of Dutch settlers to British policy in South Africa turned violent
during the _____.

_____ 7. The _____began after rumors spread among Indian soldiers that the
cartridges of their rifles were sealed with beef and pork fat.

_____ 8. The overthrow of _____, the last monarch of Hawaii, was accomplished in
the late 1800s by a group of American sugar planters.

_____ 9. _____ managed to maintain the independence of Ethiopia by exploiting
imperialistic rivalries between European nations and by building up a modern
arsenal that helped his forces defeat an Italian army.

_____ 10. _____ was a British colony in Africa that combined diverse cultures and
long-term rival groups.

Part 2: Map Skills

Use the map to choose the best possible answer. (4 points each)

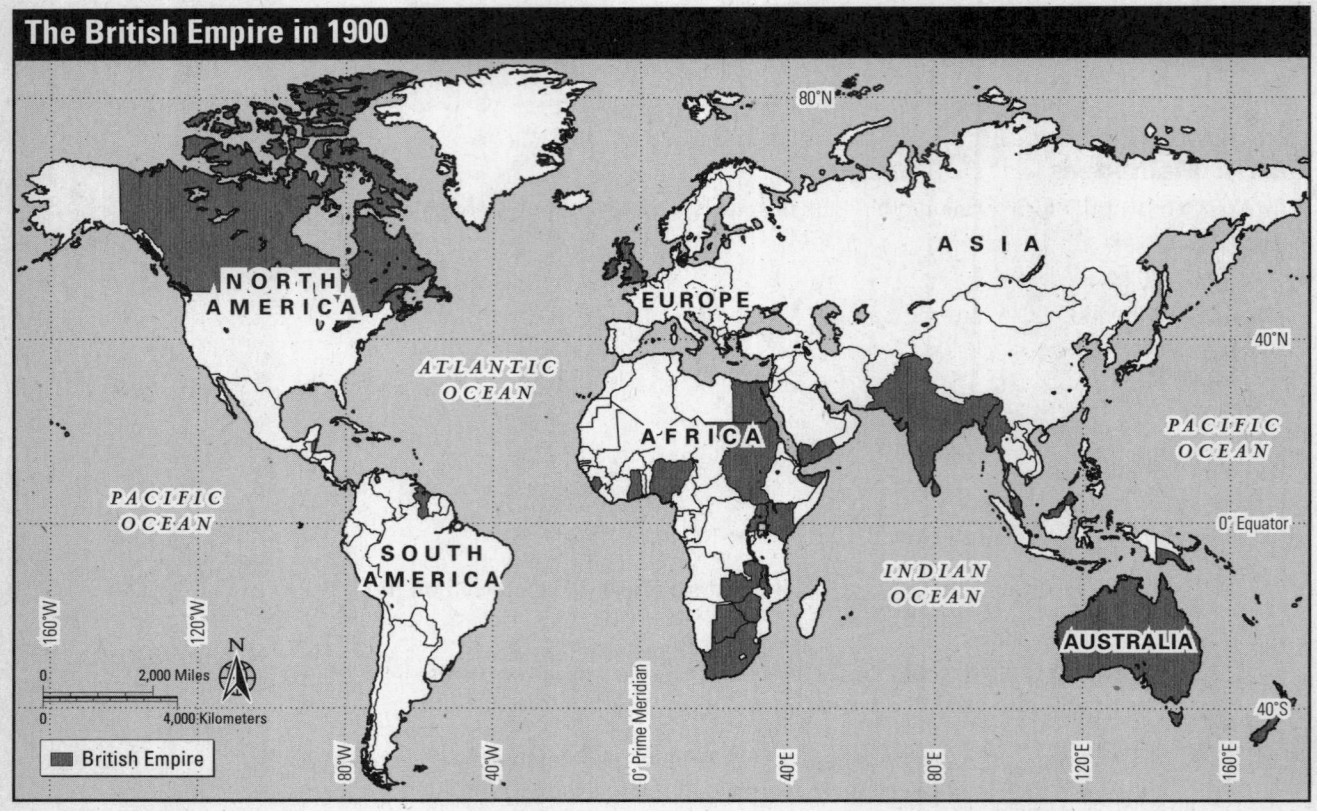

The British Empire in 1900

_____ 11. Where did the British Empire control an entire continent?
   a. North America
   b. Africa
   c. Europe
   d. Australia

_____ 12. Which continent had the greatest number of British colonies?
   a. Asia
   b. Africa
   c. North America
   d. South America

_____ 13. On which of these continents did Britain control the smallest land area?
   a. Asia
   b. Africa
   c. North America
   d. South America

_____ 14. What was the approximate distance between Britain and its North American colony?
   a. 1,500 miles
   b. 2,800 miles
   c. 3,700 miles
   d. 4,900 miles

CHAPTER 12

Section 3

SECTION QUIZ *U.S. Economic Imperialism*

A. Terms and Names If the statement is true, write "true" on the line. If it is false, change the underlined word or words to make it true.

Example: The Panama Canal is about <u>50</u> miles long. _____ *true* _____

Example: It took engineers and laborers from the United States about <u>50</u> years to build the Panama Canal. _____ *ten* _____

1. After independence from colonial rule, <u>caudillos</u> ruled many Latin American nations as dictators. _____

2. After Latin America gained independence, <u>France</u> became its largest European trading partner. _____

3. After losing the <u>War of 1812</u>, Spain ceded its last colonies to the United States.

   _____

4. Use of the Panama Canal reduced the sea route from the west coast of the United States to the east coast by about <u>9,000 miles</u>. _____

5. The Roosevelt Corollary gave the United States the right to be "an international police power" in the <u>Western</u> hemisphere. _____

6. The Monroe Doctrine was intended to reduce the threat of <u>U.S.</u> interference in the affairs of the new Latin American republics. _____

7. Panama allowed the United States to build a canal across its territory in exchange for U.S. aid in helping Panama <u>build a modern navy</u>. _____

B. Extended Response Briefly answer the following question on the back of this paper.

What were some of the main problems facing Latin American nations in the early years of independence?

CHAPTER
12

Section 4

SECTION QUIZ *Turmoil and Change in Mexico*

_____

A. Terms and Names Write the letter of the name that best completes the statement. A name may be used once or not at all.

a. Maximilian
b. Napoleon III
c. Porfirio Díaz
d. Benito Juárez
e. Alvaro Obregón
f. Emiliano Zapata

g. Ponciano Arriaga
h. Francisco Madero
i. Victoriano Huerta
j. Venustiano Carranza
k. "Pancho" Villa
l. Antonio López de Santa Anna

_____ 1. _____ played leading roles in Mexico's fight for independence from Spain and, after independence, Mexico's fight to hold on to Texas. He also served four times as the president of Mexico.

_____ 2. During the Mexican Revolution, the former cowboy _____ was immensely popular in northern Mexico because of his reputation for being a Robin Hood.

_____ 3. The caudillo _____ came to power in Mexico in the mid-1870s and ruled until he was forced from office in 1910 by the Mexican Revolution. The order and progress that he brought Mexico was not enough for those who cared more about liberal reforms.

_____ 4. In the 1840s and 1850s, _____ worked for acceptance of *La Reforma*. Although he served as the president of Mexico several times, it was only in his last presidency that he was able to institute *La Reforma* during a period of relative peace and prosperity.

_____ 5. Born into one of Mexico's ten richest families, _____ was a strong supporter of democracy. When his attempt to run for Mexico's presidency forced him into exile, he called for revolution. In 1911, he became president but resigned soon after.

_____ 6. _____ was a popular leader who raised a powerful army to fight in the Mexican Revolution. *"Tierra y Libertad"* (Land and Liberty) was his battle cry. He helped to overthrow Díaz and Huerta and, in 1919, was himself lured into a trap and murdered by forces loyal to Carranza.

B. Extended Response Briefly answer the following question on the back of this paper.

Identify any two reforms of the Mexican Constitution of 1917. Why did reformers feel that they were needed in Mexico at that time?

CHAPTER 12
Form A

CHAPTER TEST   *Transformations Around the Globe*

Part 1: Main Ideas
Write the letter of the term or name that best matches the description. (4 points each)

a. Antonio López de Santa Anna
b. Benito Juárez
c. Boxer Rebellion
d. "Pancho" Villa
e. José Martí
f. Open Door Policy
g. Russo-Japanese War
h. sphere of influence
i. Spanish-American War
j. Treaty of Kanagawa

_____ 1. The _____ proposed that all nations have equal opportunities to trade in China.

_____ 2. _____ was a writer who died while fighting for Cuba's independence from Spain.

_____ 3. Chinese people fought against the Dowager Empress Cixi's rule and foreign privilege in the _____.

_____ 4. In the late 1840s and early 1850s, _____ started a liberal reform movement, called *La Reforma*, in Mexico.

_____ 5. _____ fought for Mexican independence from Spain, and he fought to retain the territory of Texas.

_____ 6. Because of the _____, Japan opened two ports to U.S. ships, and the United States set up an embassy in Japan.

_____ 7. The Mexican revolutionary fighter _____ took money from the rich and gave it to the poor.

_____ 8. After losing the _____, Spain lost its colonies of Puerto Rico, Guam, Cuba, and the Philippines.

_____ 9. A _____ is a region in which a foreign nation controls trade and investment.

_____ 10. Two great powers fought over Korea during the _____.

Part 2: Map Skills

Use the map to choose the best possible answer. (4 points each)

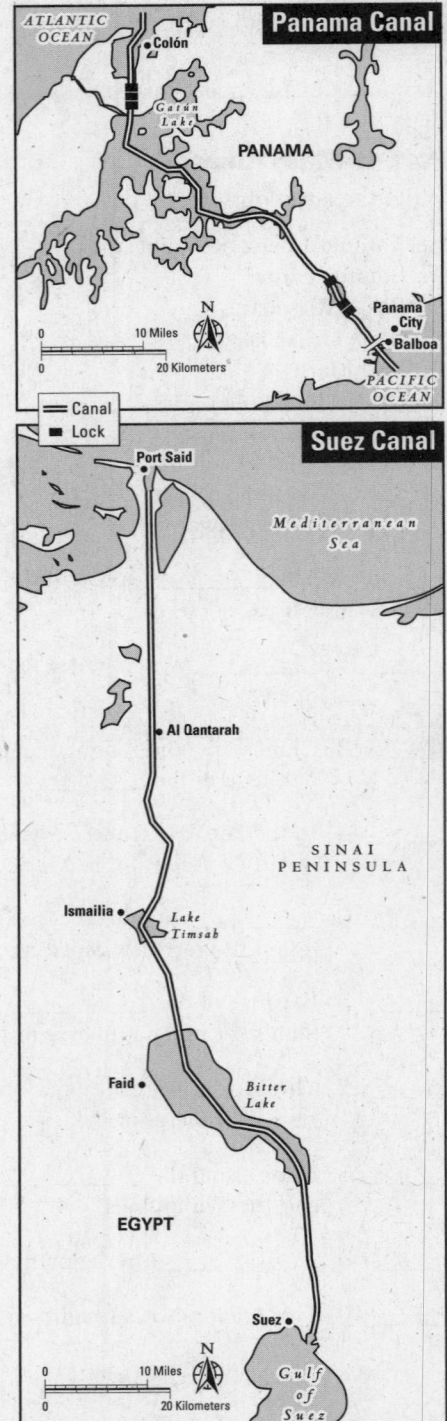

_____ 11. What was the approximate length in miles of
the Panama Canal?
a. 35
b. 50
c. 65
d. 80

_____ 12. What was the approximate length in miles of
the Suez Canal?
a. 60
b. 75
c. 95
d. 105

_____ 13. If a ship is using the Suez Canal to reach the
Gulf of Suez, in what direction does it mainly
travel?
a. north
b. south
c. east
d. west

_____ 14. What waterway or body of water provided part
of the route for the Panama Canal?
a. Pacific Ocean
b. Atlantic Ocean
c. Panama River
d. Gatún Lake

_____ 15. If a ship is using the Panama Canal to reach
the Pacific Ocean, in which direction does
it mainly travel?
a. northeast
b. southeast
c. northwest
d. southwest

Part 3: Document-Based Questions

Introduction

Historical Context: During the 19th century, Europeans and the Chinese had strained trade relations. British merchants began smuggling opium into China. Within a few decades, 12 million Chinese people were addicted to the drug. Britain refused to stop bringing opium into China despite pleas to do so by the Chinese government. The result was the Opium War of 1839, which the Chinese lost, thus growing weaker internationally. In the late 19th century, several European countries gained economic control over regions in China. The United States was worried that the European colonization of China would shut out U.S. traders. In 1899 the United States proposed the Open Door Policy so that China's "doors" would be open to merchants of all nations.

Task: Discuss the ways that Europe and the United States tried to trade.
(4 points each)

A. Short Answer

Study each document carefully and answer the question that follows. (8 points each)

Document 1: Excerpt from the "Letter to Queen Victoria" by Lin Zexu

Among the unscrupulous are those who bring opium to China to harm the Chinese; they succeed so well that this poison has spread far and wide in all the provinces. . . . The products that foreign countries need and have to import from China are too numerous to enumerate. . . . The imported goods from foreign countries, on the other hand, are merely playthings which can be easily dispensed with without causing any ill effect. Since we do not need these things really, what harm would come if we should decide to stop foreign trade altogether? . . . A murderer of one person is subject to the death sentence; just imagine how many people opium has killed! This is the rationale behind the new law which says that any foreigner who brings opium to China will be sentenced to death by hanging or beheading.

16. What was Lin Zexu's opinion about the trading of opium? Why did he feel this way?

_____

Document 2: Excerpt from "First Open Door Note" by John Hay

The Government of the United States would be pleased to see His German Majesty's Government give formal assurances, and lend its cooperation in securing like assurances from the other interested powers, that each, within its respective sphere of whatever influence—

First. Will in no way interfere with any treaty port or any vested interest within any so-called "sphere of interest" or leased territory it may have in China.

Second. That the Chinese treaty tariff of the time being shall apply to all merchandise landed or shipped to all such ports as are within said "sphere of interest" (unless they be "free ports"), no matter to what nationality it may belong, and that duties so leviable shall be collected by the Chinese Government.

Third. That it will levy no higher harbor dues on vessels of another nationality frequenting any port in such "sphere" than shall be levied on vessels of its own nationality.

17. Why was John Hay concerned about Germany's use of harbor dues in its sphere of influence?

_____

Document 3: Foreign Influence in China, 1850–1911

Foreign Influence in China, 1850–1911

Spheres of Influence and Colonies
British   German   Russian   — — Qing Empire, 1850
French   Japanese   —— China, 1911

18. What country's sphere of influence included southern China? What country's sphere of
    influence included the northwestern tip of China?

_____

B. Essay

19. Using the information from the documents, your answers to the questions in Part A,
    and your knowledge of world history, write an essay on your own paper that discusses
    the methods the European powers and the United States used to establish trade
    relations with China during the 19th century. (8 points)

Part 4: Extended Response

Answer the following questions on the back of this paper or on a separate sheet. (10 points
each)

20. **Drawing Conclusions** What changes occurred in Japan during the Meiji era? Discuss
    their effect on the country.

    Think about:
    • the reasons for modernization
    • the results of modernization
    • the stance on imperialism

21. **Contrasting** What were the differences between Benito Juárez and Porfirio Díaz? Contrast both their ideas and their actions.

   Think about:
   • their accomplishments
   • their views on reform
   • their goals for government

CHAPTER
12
Form B

CHAPTER TEST *Transformations Around the Globe*

Part 1: Main Ideas

Write the letter of the best answer. (4 points each)

_____ 1. Who benefited the most from the granting of extraterritorial rights in 19th century China?
　　　　a. foreigners in China
　　　　b. Chinese peasants
　　　　c. Chinese Christians
　　　　d. Chinese government officials

_____ 2. Why did Britain sell opium to China?
　　　　a. to weaken the Chinese people
　　　　b. to keep the drug out of Britain
　　　　c. to improve the balance of trade between Britain and China
　　　　d. to encourage the Chinese government to buy British products

_____ 3. Which of the following resulted in the establishment of a rebel government in southeastern China that lasted about ten years?
　　　　a. the Boxer Rebellion
　　　　b. the Guangxu reforms
　　　　c. the self-strengthening movement
　　　　d. the Taiping Rebellion

_____ 4. What did the Sino-Japanese War and Russo-Japanese War have in common?
　　　　a. Japan lost both wars.
　　　　b. Theodore Roosevelt negotiated the treaties ending both wars.
　　　　c. Both were fought over control of Korea.
　　　　d. Both occurred in the early 1900s.

_____ 5. What American system did the Japanese adopt during the Meiji era?
　　　　a. a military draft
　　　　b. universal public education
　　　　c. separation of local and central governments
　　　　d. the development of naval and land-based military operations

_____ 6. What was the purpose of the Monroe Doctrine?
　　　　a. to open trade in China to all nations
　　　　b. to annex Texas to the United States
　　　　c. to establish the right of the United States to be an international policeman
　　　　d. to discourage European nations from establishing colonies in Latin America

_____ 7. During the 19th century, how did Latin American countries spend most of the income they received from imports?
      a. fighting wars
      b. purchasing imported products
      c. developing manufacturing industries
      d. building roads, schools, and hospitals

_____ 8. Which of the following was a result of the Spanish-American War?
      a. Spain lost control of Cuba.
      b. Panama gained its independence.
      c. Cuba broke free of U.S. influence.
      d. The United States granted independence to the last of its colonies.

_____ 9. Why was the Mexican Revolution fought?
      a. to free Mexico from Spanish rule
      b. to gain back the lands Mexico had lost to the United States
      c. to overthrow the dictator ruling Mexico
      d. to overthrow the emperor imposed by Napoleon III

_____ 10. For what is Benito Juárez remembered?
      a. for defeating Texans at the siege of the Alamo
      b. for instituting *La Reforma* while he was president of Mexico
      c. for luring Emiliano Zapata into a trap and killing him
      d. for using strong-arm methods that kept him in power for 25 years

Part 2: Map Skills

Use the map to choose the best possible answer. (4 points each)

_____ 11. About how much longer than the Panama Canal
is the Suez Canal?
   a. 35 miles
   b. 45 miles
   c. 55 miles
   d. 65 miles

_____ 12. What is the direct distance between Port Said
and Suez?
   a. 37 miles
   b. 50 miles
   c. 69 miles
   d. 88 miles

_____ 13. Judging from the top map, what is true of the
Panama Canal?
   a. It only took advantage of bodies of salt
      water.
   b. It used a system of locks to raise and
      lower ships.
   c. It worked only at high tide.
   d. It had fewer curves than the Suez Canal.

_____ 14. If a ship is using the Panama Canal to reach
the Atlantic Ocean, in what direction does
it mainly travel?
   a. northeast
   b. southeast
   c. northwest
   d. southwest

_____ 15. What did the Panama Canal take advantage of
for nearly half its length?
   a. natural waterways
   b. the Panama Canyon
   c. the tunnel of the isthmus
   d. salt marshes

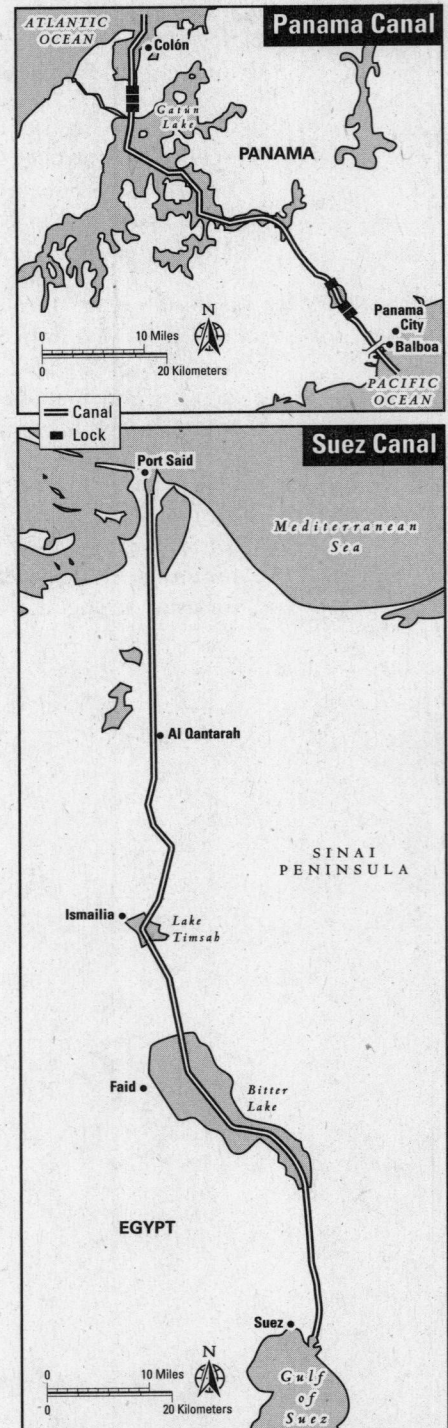

Part 3: Document-Based Questions
Introduction

Historical Context: During the 19th century, Europeans and the Chinese had strained trade relations. British merchants began smuggling opium into China. Within a few decades, 12 million Chinese people were addicted to the drug. Britain refused to stop bringing opium into China despite pleas to do so by the Chinese government. The result was the Opium War of 1839, which the Chinese lost, thus growing weaker internationally. In the late 19th century, several European countries gained economic control over regions in China. The United States was worried that the European colonization of China would shut out U.S. traders. In 1899 the United States proposed the Open Door Policy so that China's "doors" would be open to merchants of all nations.

Task: Discuss the ways that Europe and the United States tried to trade.

A. Short Answer

Study each document carefully and answer the question that follows. (4 points each)

Document 1: Excerpt from the "Letter to Queen Victoria" by Lin Zexu

Among the unscrupulous are those who bring opium to China to harm the Chinese; they succeed so well that this poison has spread far and wide in all the provinces. . . . The products that foreign countries need and have to import from China are too numerous to enumerate. . . . The imported goods from foreign countries, on the other hand, are merely playthings which can be easily dispensed with without causing any ill effect. Since we do not need these things really, what harm would come if we should decide to stop foreign trade altogether? . . . A murderer of one person is subject to the death sentence; just imagine how many people opium has killed! This is the rationale behind the new law which says that any foreigner who brings opium to China will be sentenced to death by hanging or beheading.

16. What was Lin Zexu's view on the self-sufficiency of China? Support your answer based on the document.

_____

Document 2: Excerpt from "First Open Door Note" by John Hay

The Government of the United States would be pleased to see His German Majesty's Government give formal assurances, and lend its cooperation in securing like assurances from the other interested powers, that each, within its respective sphere of whatever influence—

First. Will in no way interfere with any treaty port or any vested interest within any so-called "sphere of interest" or leased territory it may have in China.

Second. That the Chinese treaty tariff of the time being shall apply to all merchandise landed or shipped to all such ports as are within said "sphere of interest" (unless they be "free ports"), no matter to what nationality it may belong, and that duties so leviable shall be collected by the Chinese Government.

Third. That it will levy no higher harbor dues on vessels of another nationality frequenting any port in such "sphere" than shall be levied on vessels of its own nationality.

17. What negative effect could European powers have on the United States by using their spheres of influence? Use the document to support your answer.

_____

Document 3: Foreign Influence in China, 1850–1911

Foreign Influence in China, 1850–1911

18. Which nation was best able to obtain goods from the interior of China? Why?

_____

B. Essay

19. Using the information from the documents, your answers to the questions in Part A, and your knowledge of world history, write an essay on your own paper that discusses the methods the European powers and the United States used to establish trade relations with China during the 19th century. (8 points)

Part 4: Extended Response

Answer the following questions on the back of this page or your own paper. (10 points each)

20. **Contrasting** What differences existed in Japan and China's status as world powers?

Think about:
- military strength
- economy and government

21. **Analyzing Issues** Why did the United States get involved in Latin America?

Think about:
- official U.S. policies
- transportation and industry

Part 1: Main Ideas
Write the letter of the best answer. (4 points each)

_____   1. What led to problems within the self-strengthening movement in China in the 1860s?
   a. Empress Cixi did not support it.
   b. Political rebellions interrupted its progress.
   c. Chinese officials feared that their positions would be threatened.
   d. China suffered increasing foreign influence.

_____   2. What did NOT happen as a result of the Opium War?
   a. The treaty of Nanjing was signed.
   b. Britain stopped selling opium to China.
   c. China suffered a humiliating defeat.
   d. China gave up the island of Hong Kong.

_____   3. What did the Opium War and the Boxer Rebellion have in common?
   a. Both were fought against Great Britain.
   b. Resentment of foreigners contributed to both.
   c. In both, Hong Xiuquan led the Chinese forces.
   d. Both were uprisings against the rule of Dowager Empress Cixi.

_____   4. What effect did the visit of Commodore Perry have on the Japanese?
   a. Japan closed its ports to all Western traders.
   b. Japan declared war on Russia to gain Korea as a buffer zone.
   c. Japan and the United States signed the Treaty of Kanagawa.
   d. Japan tried to build its own modern navy before Perry's return.

_____   5. Which of the following pairs of rulers tried to modernize their countries?
   a. Guangxu and Mutsuhito
   b. Cixi and Mutsuhito
   c. Guangxu and José Martí
   d. José Martí and Porfirio Díaz

_____   6. What action did the United States take to gain the right to build the Panama Canal?
   a. It fought the Spanish-American War, defeated Spain, and gained Panama as a result.
   b. It bought the isthmus of Panama from Colombia.
   c. It invaded Mexico and forced the Mexican president to give up Panama.
   d. It aided Panama's fight for independence from Colombia.

_____   7. Which of the following was NOT a reason for political instability in Latin America?
   a. caudillos who used their countries to grow wealthy
   b. lack of experience with democracy
   c. caudillos who implemented untested reforms that backfired
   d. upper classes who supported caudillos to keep power from the lower classes

_____ 8. What was one major result of the Spanish-American War?
  a. The United States became an imperial power in Latin America and the Pacific.
  b. The United States established friendly relations with Cuba.
  c. The United States completely ended colonialism in Latin America.
  d. The United States convinced Latin Americans that it would defend their liberties.

_____ 9. Which two Mexican leaders were most alike in their goals for reforming Mexico?
  a. Benito Juárez and Porfirio Díaz
  b. Benito Juárez and Alvaro Obregón
  c. Porfirio Díaz and Alvaro Obregón
  d. Francisco Madero and Porfirio Díaz

_____ 10. Which of the following statements best summarizes Santa Anna's career?
  a. He won the battle of the Alamo and later served as Mexican ambassador to the United States.
  b. After serving as president, he lost a bitter war to the United States and then became a permanent exile.
  c. He helped win independence from Spain, and served as Mexico's president, but lost much territory to the United States.
  d. After losing a war to the United States, he seized power at home and served as dictator of Mexico for 20 years.

Part 2: Map Skills

Use the map to choose the best possible answer. (4 points each)

_____ 11. Judging from the map, what geographic features
were used by the builders of the Suez Canal?
- a. rivers
- b. canyons
- c. lakes
- d. waterfalls

_____ 12. What does the Panama Canal use to raise and
lower ships?
- a. the oceans' tides
- b. the wake from ships
- c. electric pulleys on cranes
- d. a system of locks

_____ 13. Travelling north on the Suez Canal at a rate
of ten miles per hour, how long would it take
to reach the Mediterranean Sea from the Gulf
of Suez?
- a. 9.5 hours
- b. 11 hours
- c. 12.5 hours
- d. 14.5 hours

_____ 14. Judging from the map, why wasn't the Panama
Canal built in a straight line?
- a. to avoid mountains
- b. to use Gatún Lake
- c. to avoid swamps
- d. to connect with Panama City

_____ 15. What did the Suez Canal and the Panama Canal
have in common?
- a. They both used a series of locks.
- b. They both connected two oceans.
- c. They both made more direct voyages
for traders possible.
- d. They both used existing waterways for
at least half their length.

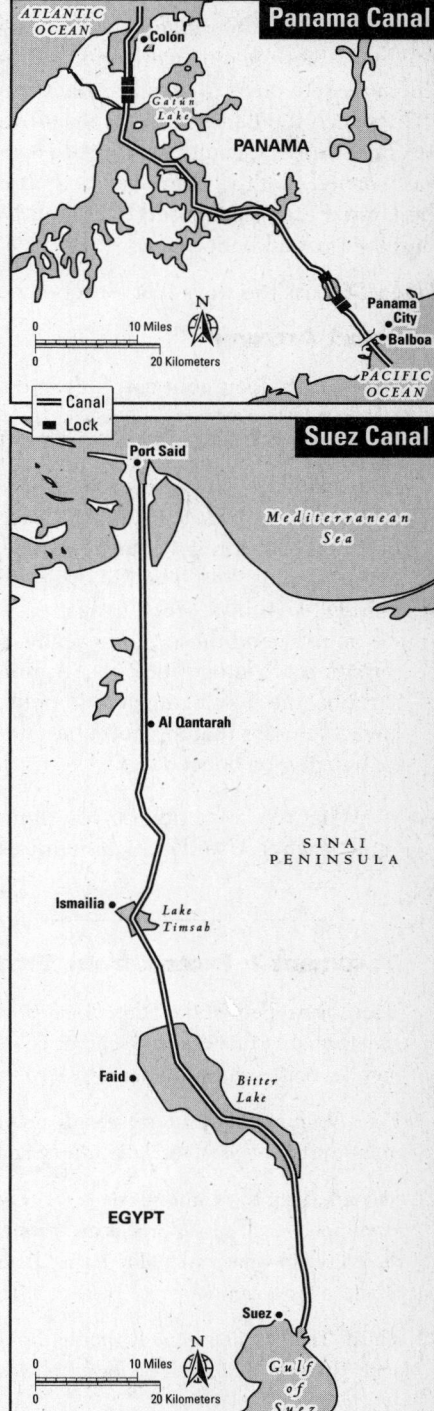

Part 3: Document-Based Questions
Introduction

Historical Context: During the 19th century, Europeans and the Chinese had strained trade relations. British merchants began smuggling opium into China. Within a few decades, 12 million Chinese people were addicted to the drug. Britain refused to stop bringing opium into China despite pleas to do so by the Chinese government. The result was the Opium War of 1839, which the Chinese lost, thus growing weaker internationally. In the late 19th century, several European countries gained economic control over regions in China. The United States was worried that the European colonization of China would shut out U.S. traders. In 1899 the United States proposed the Open Door Policy so that China's "doors" would be open to merchants of all nations.

Task: Discuss the ways that Europe and the United States tried to trade.

A. Short Answer

Study each document carefully and answer the question that follows. (4 points each)

Document 1: Excerpt from the "Letter to Queen Victoria" by Lin Zexu

Among the unscrupulous are those who bring opium to China to harm the Chinese; they succeed so well that this poison has spread far and wide in all the provinces. . . . The products that foreign countries need and have to import from China are too numerous to enumerate. . . . The imported goods from foreign countries, on the other hand, are merely playthings which can be easily dispensed with without causing any ill effect. Since we do not need these things really, what harm would come if we should decide to stop foreign trade altogether? . . . A murderer of one person is subject to the death sentence; just imagine how many people opium has killed! This is the rationale behind the new law which says that any foreigner who brings opium to China will be sentenced to death by hanging or beheading.

16. What type of action do you think China took when Britain ignored the above letter, and why? Use the document to support your answer.

_____

Document 2: Excerpt from "First Open Door Note" by John Hay

The Government of the United States would be pleased to see His German Majesty's Government give formal assurances, and lend its cooperation in securing like assurances from the other interested powers, that each, within its respective sphere of whatever influence—

First. Will in no way interfere with any treaty port or any vested interest within any so-called "sphere of interest" or leased territory it may have in China.

Second. That the Chinese treaty tariff of the time being shall apply to all merchandise landed or shipped to all such ports as are within said "sphere of interest" (unless they be "free ports"), no matter to what nationality it may belong, and that duties so leviable shall be collected by the Chinese Government.

Third. That it will levy no higher harbor dues on vessels of another nationality frequenting any port in such "sphere" than shall be levied on vessels of its own nationality.

17. Judging from the document, how do you think China viewed John Hays' "First Open Door Note"? Why?

_____

Document 3: Foreign Influence in China, 1850–1911

18. What country posed the greatest threat to invade China? Why?

_____

B. Essay

19. Using the information from the documents, your answers to the questions in Part A, and your knowledge of world history, write an essay on your own paper that discusses the methods the European powers and the United States used to establish trade relations with China during the 19th century. (8 points)

Part 4: Extended Response

Answer the following questions on the back of this paper or on a separate sheet. (10 points each)

20. **Analyzing Issues** Why was China vulnerable to interference by European powers and the United States?

21. **Comparing** What similarities existed between the political and social conditions in 19th century China and Latin America? Support your answers with examples from the text.

CHAPTER
13

Section 1

SECTION QUIZ   *Marching Toward War*

A. Terms and Names Write the letter of the nation or territory that answers the question. A nation may be used more than once or not at all. Where noted, there is more than one answer.

   a. Italy
   b. Serbia
   c. Russia
   d. France
   e. Greece
   f. Germany
   g. Great Britain
   h. Austria-Hungary

_____ 1. Which THREE nations belonged to the Triple Entente?

_____ 2. Which THREE nations belonged to the Triple Alliance?

_____ 3. Which nation annexed Bosnia and Herzegovina in 1908?

_____ 4. Which TWO non-Balkan nations competed for dominance of the Balkans?

_____ 5. Which nation greatly regretted its loss of Alsace-Lorraine to Germany in 1870?

_____ 6. Which nation's heir to the throne was assassinated in 1914 by a Serbian nationalist?

_____ 7. Which nation was unified by Otto von Bismarck and later ruled by Kaiser Wilhelm II?

_____ 8. Which nation was the first to declare war in what would come to be called the Great War?

_____ 9. Which of the Great Powers did not have a large army by 1914?

_____ 10. Which nation did Otto von Bismarck believe was the greatest threat to peace in Europe?

B. Extended Response Briefly answer the following question on the back of this paper.

In your opinion, which was most important influence in setting the stage for World War I—nationalism, imperialism, militarism, or the alliance system? Explain.

Name _____   Date _____

A. Terms and Names If the statement is true, write "true" on the line. If it is false, change the underlined word or words to make it true.

Example: The <u>Russian</u> army's greatest asset was its numbers. _____*true*_____

Example: Because <u>France</u> had a huge population but little industry, its army suffered severe shortages of everything but soldiers. _____*Russia*_____

1. Under the Schlieffen Plan, Germany was to focus first on defeating <u>Great Britain</u>. _____

2. The battles of the Marne, the Somme, and Verdun were fought on <u>Austrian</u> soil. _____

3. Although <u>Japan</u> had been part of the Triple Alliance, it refused to join the Central Powers. _____

4. Trench warfare was the primary form of warfare used on the <u>Eastern Front</u>. _____

5. In the first weeks of the war, the <u>Allied Powers</u> included Great Britain, France, Russia, and Japan. _____

6. The territory between the trenches was known as "<u>no man's land</u>." _____

7. After Russia began mobilizing troops on its western border, <u>Serbia</u> declared war on Russia. Two days later, it also declared war on France. _____

B. Extended Response Briefly answer the following question on the back of this paper.
Why did a stalemate develop on the Western Front during World War I?

Name _____ Date _____

CHAPTER
13

Section 3

SECTION QUIZ   *A Global Conflict*

_____

A. Terms and Names Write the letter of the best answer.

_____ 1. In 1917, Germany returned to its policy of unrestricted submarine warfare, hoping to
    a. bring the United States into the war.
    b. force Russia to withdraw from the war.
    c. keep cargo ships from reaching Great Britain.
    d. destroy the British ships blockading German ports.

_____ 2. World War I was a "total war" in the sense that
    a. it brought great suffering to civilians.
    b. nations from all over the world were involved.
    c. new technologies played a large part in the war.
    d. the nations involved devoted all their resources to it.

_____ 3. The system of rationing was designed to limit
    a. civilian antiwar activities.
    b. production of luxury items.
    c. purchases of consumer goods.
    d. the number of men needed in the civilian work force.

_____ 4. The purpose of propaganda during World War I was to
    a. censor the press.
    b. inform the public.
    c. expose antiwar activity.
    d. influence public opinion.

_____ 5. The Zimmermann note, which pushed the United States to enter the war, exposed the German plan to
    a. make a truce with Russia.
    b. help Mexico regain U.S. territory.
    c. sink passenger ships without warning.
    d. plant German spies in the United States.

_____ 6. The armistice signed near Paris in November 1918 brought an end to
    a. World War I.
    b. Kaiser Wilhelm's rule.
    c. the Second Battle of the Marne.
    d. Russia's involvement in the war.

B. Extended Response Briefly answer the following question on the back of this paper.

Why did Russia withdraw from World War I? Why did the United States enter it?

SECTION QUIZ   *A Flawed Peace*

A. Terms and Names If the statement is true, write "true" on the line. If it is false, change the underlined word or words to make it true.

Example: The only major Allied nation that lost land after World War I was <u>Russia</u>.
_____ *true* _____

Example: After the war, the Ottoman Turks lost their former empire, retaining only what is today the country of <u>Lebanon</u>. _____ *Turkey* _____

1. <u>Woodrow Wilson</u> proposed the "general association of nations" that would later become the League of Nations._____

2. The right of nations to self-determination was a guiding principle of the <u>Treaty of Versailles.</u>_____

3. <u>Great Britain</u> was represented at the Paris Peace Conference by Georges Clemenceau. _____

4. All of Germany's territories in Africa and the Pacific were declared <u>colonies</u>, or territories to be administered by the League of Nations. _____

5. Agreement at the Paris Peace Conference was hindered primarily by strong differences of opinion between Woodrow Wilson and <u>David Lloyd George</u>._____

6. Article 231, also known as the "<u>war guilt</u>" clause, ordered Germany to pay huge war reparations to Allied nations._____

7. Two nations deliberately excluded from the League of Nations were Germany and <u>Russia</u>._____

B. Extended Response Briefly answer the following question on the back of this paper.
   What groups opposed the Treaty of Versailles and why?

CHAPTER 13

Form A

CHAPTER TEST *The Great War*

Part 1: Main Ideas
Write the letter of the best answer. (4 points each)

_____ 1. What is the policy of glorifying power and keeping an army prepared for war?
   a. nationalism   b. militarism   c. imperialism   d. patriotism

_____ 2. What region was referred to as the "powder keg" of Europe?
   a. the Middle-East   c. Austria-Hungary
   b. Alsace-Lorraine   d. the Balkan Peninsula

_____ 3. Who led Germany during the last decade of the 1800s and most of World War I?
   a. Otto von Bismark   c. Kaiser Wilhelm II
   b. Adolf Hitler   d. George Clemenceau

_____ 4. Which statement summarizes the Schlieffen Plan that Germany created to prepare
          for a two-front war?
   a. Attack France first, then Russia.
   b. Attack Russia first, then France.
   c. Send half of the army to France and half to Russia.
   d. Ally with Russia to fight France.

_____ 5. Why were Germany and Austria-Hungary known as Central Powers?
   a. because the war was fought on two fronts
   b. because of their combined armies
   c. because of their alliance in the war
   d. because of their location in the heart of Europe

_____ 6. Which nation's actions caused the United States to fight in World War I?
   a. Russia   c. Germany
   b. Mexico   d. Austria-Hungary

_____ 7. What did the war become once the participating countries began devoting all
          of their resources to the war effort?
   a. industrial war   c. total war
   b. world war   d. uncontrolled war

_____ 8. What action on November 11, 1918, brought World War I to an end?
   a. An armistice was signed.
   b. A surrender was given.
   c. A propaganda campaign was waged.
   d. The allies won a major battle.

_____ 9. What were the Fourteen Points?
   a. parts of the "war guilt" clause
   b. a plan for the postwar world
   c. the constitution of the League of Nations
   d. the terms of surrender offered to Germany

_____ 10. Who was forced to assume sole responsibility for the war under the Treaty of Versailles?
   a. Germany   c. Russia
   b. Austria-Hungary   d. Italy

Part 2: Map Skills

Write the letter of the best answer. (4 points each)

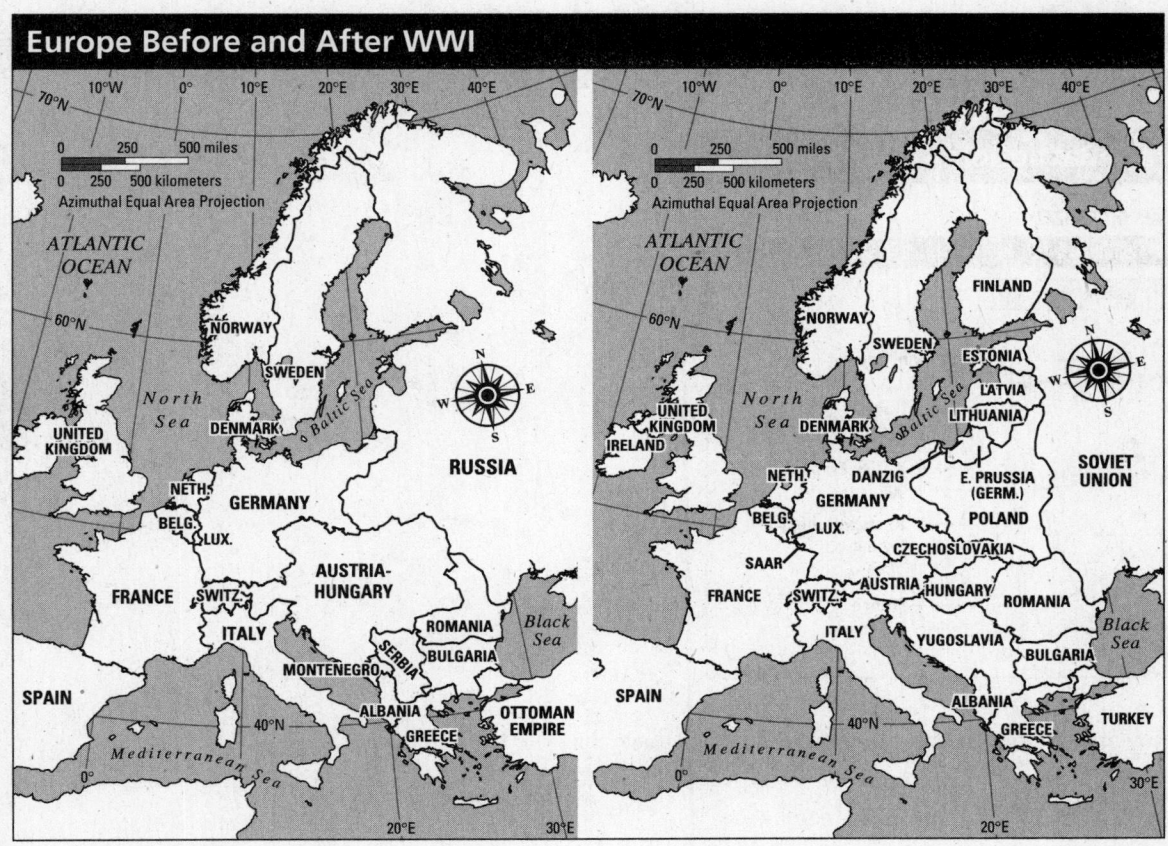

Europe Before and After WWI

_____ 11. Which of the following countries completely changed its name after World War I?
   a. Germany   c. Great Britain
   b. Romania   d. Ottoman Empire

_____ 12. How did the United Kingdom change after World War I?
   a. Ireland gained self-rule.
   b. Ireland was annexed by the United Kingdom.
   c. The United Kingdom established Poland and Finland.
   d. The United Kingdom was isolated from the rest of Europe.

_____ 13. From which country did Czechoslovakia, Poland, and Yugoslavia gain
independence?
    a. Germany   c. Bulgaria
    b. Austria-Hungary   d. Ottoman Empire

_____ 14. Around which body of water did the greatest number of new countries emerge
after World War I?
    a. North Sea   c. Black Sea
    b. Mediterranean Sea   d. Baltic Sea

_____ 15. After the war, which country had a province separated from it by states that had
gained independence?
    a. Poland   c. Russia
    b. Germany   d. Italy

Part 3: Interpreting Graphs

Write the letter of the best answer. (4 points each)

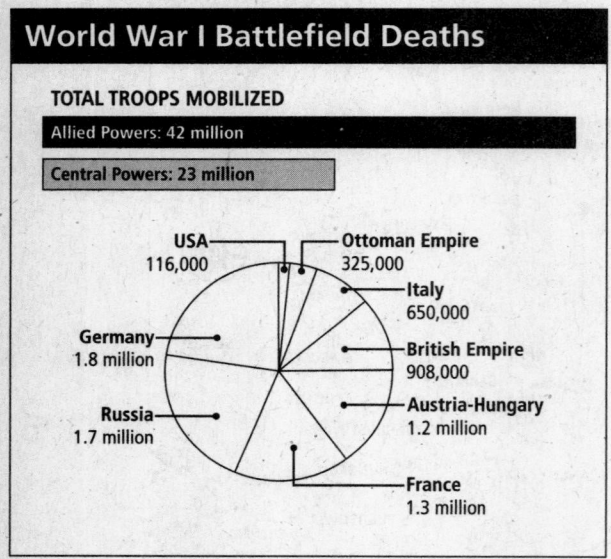

World War I Battlefield Deaths

TOTAL TROOPS MOBILIZED
Allied Powers: 42 million
Central Powers: 23 million

USA 116,000; Ottoman Empire 325,000; Italy 650,000; British Empire 908,000; Germany 1.8 million; Austria-Hungary 1.2 million; Russia 1.7 million; France 1.3 million

_____ 16. How many more troops did the Allied Powers have than the Central Powers?
    a. 19 million   c. 42 million
    b. 23 million   d. 65 million

_____ 17. Which nation lost the most troops?
    a. Russia
    b. France
    c. Italy
    d. Germany

_____ 18. Which countries each lost more than a million troops from battlefield deaths?
    a. USA, British Empire, France, Russia
    b. Austria-Hungary, France, Russia, Germany
    c. Ottoman Empire, Italy, France, Germany
    d. all of the above

_____ 19. Which country lost the smallest number of troops from battlefield deaths?
    a. Ottoman Empire
    b. British Empire
    c. USA
    d. France

_____ 20. How many troops did Russia lose, even though it pulled out of the war early?
    a. 1,700
    b. 17,000
    c. 1,700,000
    d. 17,000,000

Part 4: Extended Response

Answer the following questions on the back of this paper or on a separate sheet. (10 points each)

21. **Drawing Conclusions** What were the reasons for the extensive loss of life and property damage in World War I?

Think about:
- new technology
- military strategies
- spread of the war

22. **Analyzing Causes; Recognizing Effects** Why did the United States enter World War I, and what effect did its entry have on the war?

Think about:
- American sympathies
- German actions before America entered the war
- the state of the war before and after U.S. involvement

CHAPTER TEST   *The Great War*

Form B

Part 1: Main Ideas

Write the letter of the best answer. (4 points each)

_____ 1. Which countries made up Europe's Great Powers?
a. Germany and France
b. Great Britain, France, Germany, Austria-Hungary, Russia, and Italy
c. Great Britain and Germany
d. Great Britain, Austria-Hungary, Germany, Spain, Russia, Italy, and France

_____ 2. Why did Bismark seek alliances that later became the Triple Alliance?
a. to isolate France
b. to expand Germany's boundaries
c. to strengthen Germany's army
d. all of the above

_____ 3. Whay did Italy refuse to support its ally Germany?
a. It opposed the Treaty of Brest-Litovsk.
b. It accused Germany of starting the war.
c. It did not want to fight the United States.
d. It viewed the Schlieffen Plan as a poor strategy.

_____ 4. What did the Central Powers gain over Russia at the battle near Tannenberg?
a. Germany drove the Russians into full retreat.
b. German forces killed the czar.
c. Germany seized Russia's only port.
d. All of the above are true.

_____ 5. Which of the following was a goal of the Allies' Gallipoli campaign?
a. to gain access to Africa
b. to capture Sarajevo
c. to destroy Germany's U-boat fleet
d. to establish a supply line to Russia

_____ 6. What did the policy of unrestricted submarine warfare refer to?
a. Britain's policy to sink any ship in German waters without warning
b. Germany's policy to sink any ship in British waters without warning
c. the U.S. Navy's warning of the type of warfare the Central Powers could expect
d. Germany's decision to focus its resources on the waters surrounding Europe

_____ 7. Which of the following events occurred after the Americans joined the war?
a. Russia withdrew from the war.
b. The Bulgarians and the Ottoman Turks surrendered.
c. Britain and France recruited laborers from their colonies.
d. All of the above are true.

_____ 8. How did the Treaty of Versailles affect postwar Germany?
      a. It left a legacy of bitterness and hatred in the hearts of the German people.
      b. It stabilized the German economy and gave monetary aid to the nation.
      c. It left Germany in much the same state as it was before the war.
      d. It gave Germans the drive to rebuild their nation on a stronger foundation.

_____ 9. What was the American public's opinion about joining the League of Nations?
      a. The public thought that America should lead the League of Nations.
      b. The public generally supported the idea but wanted to play a smaller role.
      c. It supported the president and actively took part in the League of Nations.
      d. It believed that the United States should stay out of European affairs.

_____ 10. What impact did the war have on the economy of Europe?
      a. It drained the treasuries of Europe.
      b. It enriched the treasuries of the Allied Powers.
      c. It speeded the industrialization of Europe.
      d. It gave women an opportunity to become heads of companies.

Part 2: Map Skills

Use the map to choose the best possible answer. (4 points each)

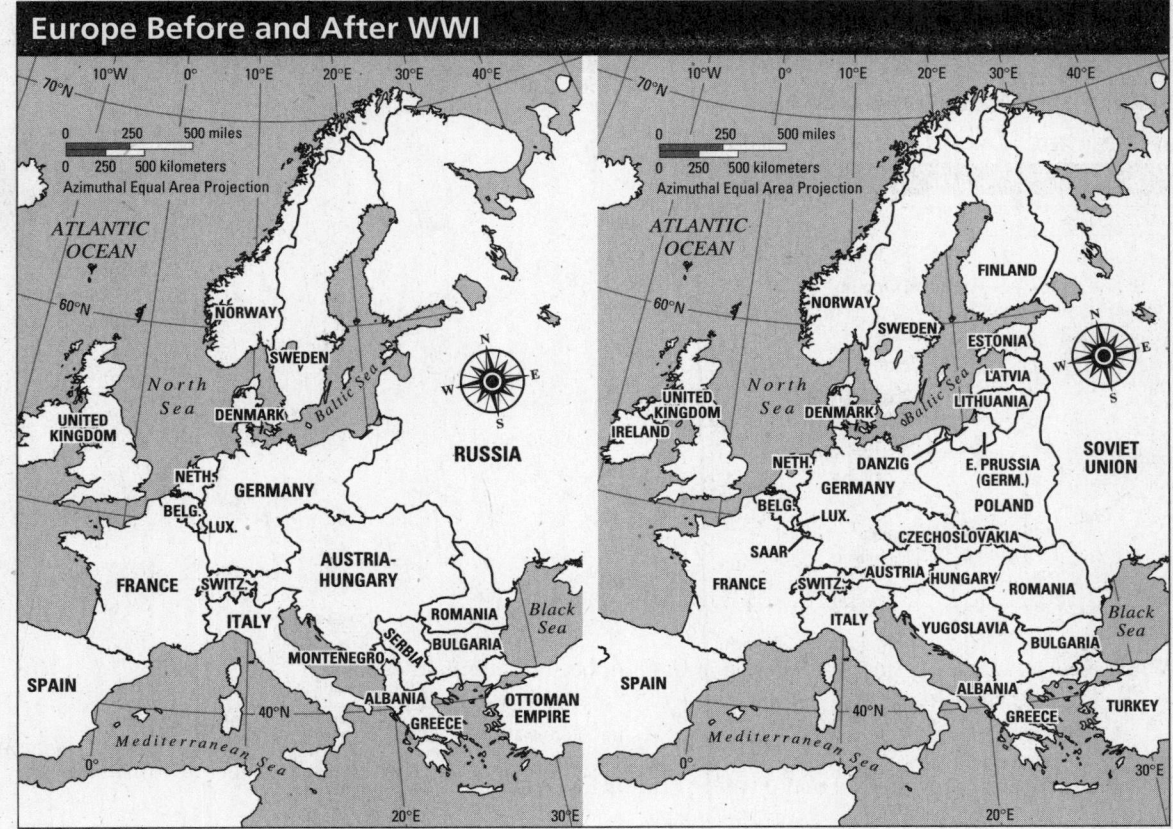

Europe Before and After WWI

_____ 11. What newly independent country emerged on the former Eastern Front?
      a. Czechoslovakia   c. Hungary
      b. Poland   d. Finland

_____ 12. What new state was created between France and Germany?
   a. Saar   c. Netherlands
   b. Belgium   d. Switzerland

_____ 13. Which of the following Allies gained territory?
   a. Belgium   b. France   c. Italy   d. Russia

_____ 14. What happened to the countries Montenegro and Serbia?
   a. They became part of Yugoslavia.
   b. The became part of Greece.
   c. Their people migrated to Germany.
   d. All their people died in the war.

_____ 15. What major difference might be present on the postwar map had Russia NOT
        pulled out of the war?
   a. It might still be known as Russia.
   b. It might have retained its western boundary.
   c. It might have gained Germany as a colony.
   d. All of the above are true.

Part 3: Interpreting Graphs

Write the letter of the best answer. (4 points each)

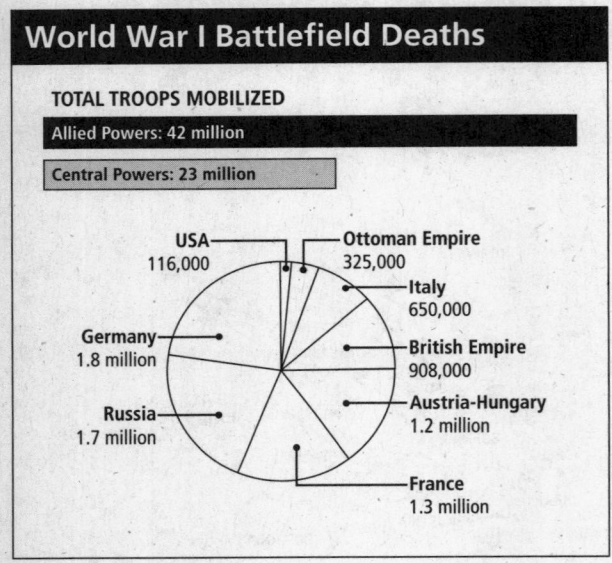

World War I Battlefield Deaths

TOTAL TROOPS MOBILIZED
Allied Powers: 42 million
Central Powers: 23 million

USA 116,000
Ottoman Empire 325,000
Italy 650,000
Germany 1.8 million
British Empire 908,000
Russia 1.7 million
Austria-Hungary 1.2 million
France 1.3 million

_____ 16. Which country was most similar to Russia in the number of battlefield deaths?
   a. Great Britain   c. Austria-Hungary
   b. France   d. Germany

_____ 17. How many more troops did the major Allied Powers lose than the major Central
        Powers?
   a. 875,000   c. 3,325,000
   b. 1,349,000   d. 4,674,000

_____ 18. What major Central Power lost the most troops?
     a. Germany
     b. British Empire
     c. Ottoman Empire
     d. Austria-Hungary

_____ 19. What was true of the combined losses of the United States, Italy, and the British Empire?
     a. They equaled the losses of France.
     b. They were less than the losses of France.
     c. They were greater than the losses of Russia.
     d. They were less than the losses of Russia.

_____ 20. Consider what you know about the two fronts of the war. What relationship existed between the battlefronts and the war deaths?
     a. The countries between the two fronts suffered the highest losses.
     b. The countries along the two fronts suffered the highest losses.
     c. The countries farthest from the two fronts suffered the highest losses.
     d. The location of the front had no effect on how high a country's losses were.

Part 4: Extended Response

Answer the following questions on the back of this paper or on a separate sheet. (10 points each)

21. **Recognizing Effects** What conditions did Russia face that caused its withdrawal from World War I, and what effect did its withdrawal have on the war?

Think about:
- battlefield deaths
- war supplies
- revolutionary uprising

22. **Analyzing Issues** What forces contributed to the spread of fighting in World War I from Europe to Asia and Africa?

Think about:
- the role of colonies
- the role of non-European nations
- the strategic reason for battles outside of Europe

CHAPTER
13

Form C

CHAPTER TEST   *The Great War*

Part 1: Main Ideas

Write the letter of the best answer. (4 points each)

_____ 1. What is the most probable link between militarism and imperialism?
   a. As a country gains colonies, its military grows to protect them.
   b. As a country's military expands, the country wants colonies to recruit troops.
   c. As a country's colonies grow, the military stages training exercises there.
   d. As the military expands, a country seeks colonies to prevent coups at home.

_____ 2. What key factor led to the formation of the Triple Alliance and the Triple Entente?
   a. Germany's desire to isolate France and Britain's desire to remain dominant
   b. Germany's hostility toward France and Britain's allegiance to France
   c. Bismarck's fear of France's army and Britain's fear of Germany's empire
   d. Germany and France's separate desires to gain control of the Balkans

_____ 3. What event in Sarajevo ignited the Great War?
   a. an ultimatum presented to Serbia in response to royal assassinations
   b. the assassination of Archduke Franz Ferdinand and his wife Sophie
   c. Austria's rejection of Serbia's offer and declaration of war on Serbia
   d. Russia's mobilization of troops along the Austrian border

_____ 4. What was significant in the Allied victory at the First Battle of the Marne?
   a. It prompted Great Britain to enter the war.
   b. It allowed Russia time to mobilize its army.
   c. It resulted in Germany's having to fight on two fronts.
   d. It stopped Germany from a planned invasion of France.

_____ 5. What was trench warfare intended to accomplish?
   a. to protect soldiers from enemy gun fire on the front lines
   b. to trap enemy soldiers in mud pits on the front lines
   c. to force enemy soldiers to pass through a "no man's land"
   d. all of the above

_____ 6. Which of the following was used to widen the war?
   a. attacks on African colonies
   b. the development of poison gas
   c. the use of propaganda
   d. the start of rationing

_____ 7. What gamble did Germany make before the United States entered the war?
   a. that a defeat of Russia would lead to a German victory in the war
   b. that the Gallipoli campaign would weaken the forces on the Western Front
   c. that unrestricted submarine warfare would defeat the United States
   d. that their blockade would defeat Britain before U.S. troops arrived

_____ 8. What impact did the Treaty of Brest-Litovsk have on Germany?
     a. It gave Germany the Russian army's aid against the Allies.
     b. It allowed Germany to focus all their efforts on the Western Front.
     c. Germany gained lands that were formerly part of Russia.
     d. All of the above are true.

_____ 9. How did the Allies respond to Wilson's vision for peace?
     a. Britain and France showed little sign of agreeing to Wilson's plan.
     b. Britain and France were concerned with strengthening their own security.
     c. Britain and France wanted to strip Germany of its war-making power.
     d. All of the above are true.

_____ 10. What actions led to the formation of new nations out of the Central Powers?
     a. Wilson's idea of self-determination that inspired revolutions in Europe
     b. military occupation of the defeated nations and redistribution of peoples
     c. provisions of peace treaties signed with the Central Powers
     d. a direction by the League of Nations to realign territories after the war

Part 2: Map Skills

Use the map to choose the best possible answer. (4 points each)

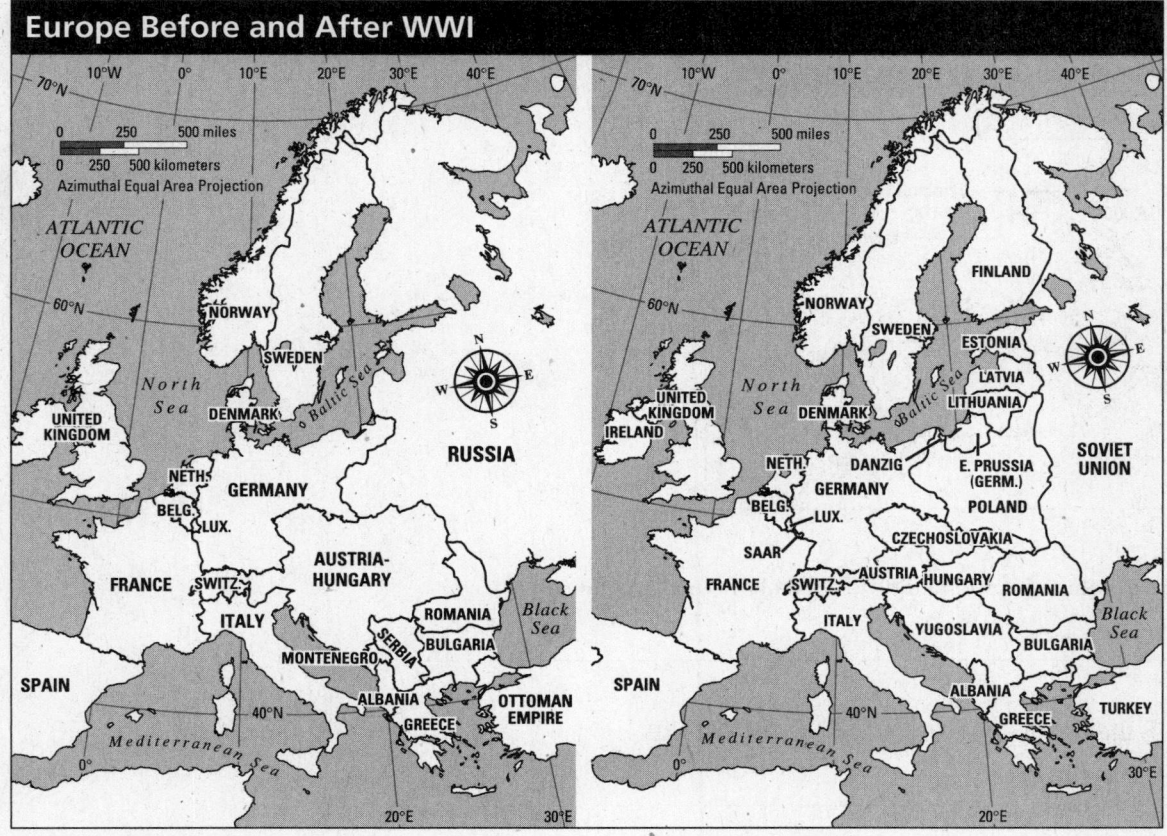

Europe Before and After WWI

_____ 11. Which of the following countries was NOT established on formerly Russian land?
     a. Poland   c. Lithuania
     b. Estonia   d. Czechoslovakia

_____ 12. Which of the Central Powers had its territory LEAST changed by the war?
         a. Austria-Hungary   c. Germany
         b. Bulgaria   d. Ottoman Empire

_____ 13. Which country was formed out of two Allied nations and part of a Central Power?
         a. Yugoslavia   c. Lithuania
         b. Romania   d. Czechoslovakia

_____ 14. What geographic reason might explain why, when Poland gained its independence after the war, it gained a strip of land that split Germany in two parts?
         a. to avoid barren land   c. to give it sea access
         b. to control the river   d. to divide Germany

_____ 15. Which of the causes of World War I most helped shape postwar borders?
         a. imperialism   c. militarism
         b. nationalism   d. the alliance system

Part 3: Interpreting Graphs – Constructed Response

Answer the following questions on the lines provided. (4 points each)

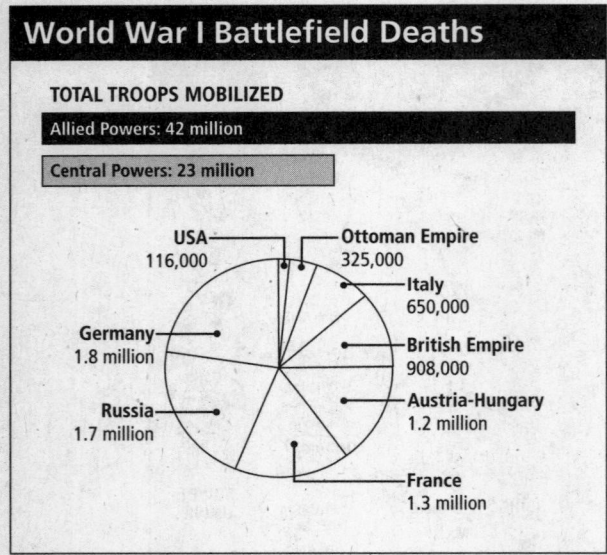

World War I Battlefield Deaths

TOTAL TROOPS MOBILIZED
Allied Powers: 42 million
Central Powers: 23 million

USA 116,000
Ottoman Empire 325,000
Italy 650,000
Germany 1.8 million
British Empire 908,000
Russia 1.7 million
Austria-Hungary 1.2 million
France 1.3 million

16. How many combined battlefield deaths did all the major combatants have?

_____

17. What were the combined deaths of the major Central Powers?

_____

18. What were the combined deaths of the major Allied Powers?

_____

19. Which side lost a higher percentage of its troops?

_____

20. How does the number of U.S. deaths compare to the other combatants, and why?

_____

Part 4: Extended Response
Answer the following questions on the back of this paper or on a separate sheet. (10 points each)

21. **Evaluating Decisions** What mistakes were made by the leaders who made the Treaty of Versailles?

22. **Synthesizing** World War I is considered a major turning point in history. How did the war change the nature of warfare, the map of Europe, and the outlook of modern society?

CHAPTER
14

SECTION QUIZ   *Revolutions in Russia*

Section 1

A. Terms and Names
Write the letter of the term or name that matches the description. A term may be used once or not at all.

a. soviet
b. Duma
c. pogrom
d. Rasputin
e. Karl Marx
f. Nicholas II
g. Bolsheviks

h. Mensheviks
i. V.I. Lenin
j. Alexander III
k. Bloody Sunday
l. World War II
m. Trans-Siberian
Railway

n. provisional
government
o. March Revolution
(1917)
p. New Economic
Policy (NEP)

_____ 1. This was Russia's first parliament.

_____ 2. He was the last Romanov czar of Russia.

_____ 3. He was the major leader of the Bolsheviks.

_____ 4. This is an event during the Revolution of 1905.

_____ 5. This was overthrown by the Bolshevik Revolution.

_____ 6. This group masterminded the revolution in November 1917.

_____ 7. This type of organized violence against Jews was encouraged by Alexander III.

_____ 8. This man's influence on Czarina Alexandra led a group of Russian nobles
to murder him.

_____ 9. This general uprising forced the czar to abdicate.

_____ 10. For Russia, this ended with the signing of the Treaty of Brest-Litovsk, which
cost Russia a large chunk of territory.

_____ 11. This was the influential local council of workers, peasants, and soldiers, formed
by revolutionaries in cities such as Petrograd.

_____ 12. After the assassination of this man's reform-minded father by revolutionaries,
he determined to strengthen "autocracy, orthodoxy, and nationality" in Russia.

B. Extended Response
Briefly answer the following question on the back of this paper.

Why did the Bolshevik Revolution succeed after earlier revolutions had failed?

CHAPTER 14

Section 2

SECTION QUIZ *Totalitarianism*
Case Study: Stalinist Russia

A. Terms and Names Write the letter of the best answer.

_____ 1. Under Joseph Stalin's command economy system, all economic decisions
were made by
    a. government officials alone.
    b. workers and government officials.
    c. members of the socialist realism movement.
    d. local soviets composed of workers, soldiers, and peasants.

_____ 2. The Soviet government decided to eliminate kulaks because of their strong
resistance to
    a. collective farming.
    b. the Five-Year Plans.
    c. religious persecution.
    d. censorship and propaganda.

_____ 3. All of the following were goals of the Five-Year Plans EXCEPT
    a. rapid industrial growth.
    b. a stronger national defense.
    c. the promotion of communism worldwide.
    d. the modernization of the Soviet economy.

_____ 4. Between 1934 and 1939, the Great Purge was a campaign to eliminate
    a. traditional religious beliefs.
    b. opposition to Stalin's power.
    c. opposition to the Communist Party.
    d. shortages of housing, food, and goods.

_____ 5. Which of the following is a weapon of totalitarianism?
    a. free elections
    b. uncensored mass media
    c. tolerant treatment of all ethnic groups
    d. police terror

B. Extended Response Briefly answer the following question on the back of this paper.

Identify one key trait of a totalitarian state. How did Stalin use the "weapons" of
totalitarianism to force that trait onto Soviet society?

CHAPTER
14

Section 3

SECTION QUIZ *Imperial China Collapses*

A. Terms and Names Write the letter of the term or name that answers the question. A term may be used more than once or not at all.

a. Germans
b. Japanese
c. Sun Yixian
d. Jiang Jieshi
e. Nationalists
f. Communists
g. Mao Zedong
h. Chinese civil war
i. May Fourth Movement

_____ 1. Who founded the Kuomintang?

_____ 2. Who was Sun Yixian's successor?

_____ 3. Which group was also known as the Kuomintang?

_____ 4. Which group was forced to go on the Long March?

_____ 5. Who was one of the founders of the Chinese Communist Party?

_____ 6. Which group attracted the support of China's peasants in the 1920s?

_____ 7. Who became the first president of the Nationalist Republic of China in 1928?

_____ 8. To whom did the Treaty of Versailles give territories and privileges in China?

_____ 9. Which group's 1937 invasion brought about an uneasy truce in China's civil war?

_____ 10. Which group joined with the Kuomintang in the 1920s to defeat the warlords?

_____ 11. What occurred in response to the treatment of China in the Treaty of Versailles?

_____ 12. Who became president of the Republic of China after the overthrow of the Qing Dynasty?

_____ 13. Which leader ordered the Shanghai massacre that nearly wiped out the Chinese Communists?

B. Extended Response Briefly answer the following question on the back of this paper.

What did both the Nationalists and the Communists want for China? How did what the Nationalists wanted for China differ from what the Communists wanted?

SECTION QUIZ # Nationalism in India and Southwest Asia

Section 4

A. Terms and Names Write the letter of the nation that answers the question. A nation may be used more than once.

a. Iran
b. India
c. Turkey
d. Saudi Arabia

_____ 1. Which nation was formerly known as Persia?

_____ 2. In which nation did the Salt March take place?

_____ 3. In which nation did the Amritsar Massacre occur?

_____ 4. Which nation was unified by Abd al-Aziz Ibn Saud?

_____ 5. Which nation's Congress Party endorsed civil disobedience?

_____ 6. Which nation's movement for independence was led by Mohandas K. Gandhi?

_____ 7. At the end of World War I, which nation was all that remained of the Ottoman Empire?

_____ 8. Before World War I, which nation was divided into British and Russian spheres of influence?

_____ 9. In which nation did Reza Shah Pahlavi embark on a program of modernization after seizing power?

_____ 10. Which nation's existence was threatened by an invasion of Greek soldiers after the end of World War I?

_____ 11. Which nation's nationalist revolt was triggered by Great Britain's post-war attempt to take control of the whole nation?

_____ 12. Which nation continued to be ruled strictly by Islamic law despite all of the changes it underwent in the postwar period?

_____ 13. In which nation did Mustafa Kemal embark on a program of modernization after becoming the republic's first president?

B. Extended Response Briefly answer the following question on the back of this paper.

Why did nationalist activity in India increase dramatically after the end of World War I?

CHAPTER TEST   *Revolution and Nationalism*

Part 1: Main Ideas

Write the letter of the best answer. (4 points each)

_____ 1. What did the pogroms that occurred in the late 19th-century Russia do?
    a. violently persecute Jews
    b. kill all the kulaks
    c. enlist the aid of foreigners
    d. establish a Communist council

_____ 2. Who were the Bolsheviks?
    a. soldiers in the White Army
    b. radical Russian Marxist revolutionaries
    c. members of the Duma, Russia's parliament
    d. followers of Rasputin

_____ 3. Who did China's peasants align themselves with in the 1920s?
    a. warlords   c. Qing Dynasty
    b. Nationalists   d. Communists

_____ 4. What were soviets under Russia's provisional government?
    a. labor unions
    b. local councils
    c. revolutionary leaders
    d. plans for redistributing land

_____ 5. What is a totalitarian state?
    a. a state in which the people have a direct say in their government
    b. a state in which the people elect representatives to the legislature
    c. a state in which the government controls every aspect of
       public and private life
    d. a state in which the working class is glorified and has the greatest voice
       in government

_____ 6. What was the purpose of the Soviet state's Five-Year Plans?
    a. foreign policy   c. social restructuring
    b. political reform   d. economic development

_____ 7. Who seized power from Persia's shah and changed the name of his country to Iran?
    a. Mustafa Kemal   c. Alexander Kerensky
    b. Reza Shah Pahlavi   d. Abd al-Aziz Ibn Saud

_____ 8. What did Sun Yixian's Revolutionary Alliance accomplish?
    a. defeating the Kuomintang
    b. overthrowing the last emperor
    c. spreading Communism in China
    d. controlling the rampaging warlords

_____ 9. Which group was known for taking a 6,000-mile journey known as the "Long March?"

      a. Chinese Communists, fleeing the Nationalists

      b. Chinese Nationalists, fleeing the Communists

      c. Chinese peasants, fleeing the Japanese invaders

      d. the Russian White Army, fleeing the Bolsheviks

_____ 10. Who led the famous protest known as the Salt March?

      a. Sun Yixian   c. Mao Zedong

      b. Mustafa Kemal   d. Mohandis K. Gandhi

Part 2: Map Skills

Write the letter of the best answer. (4 points each)

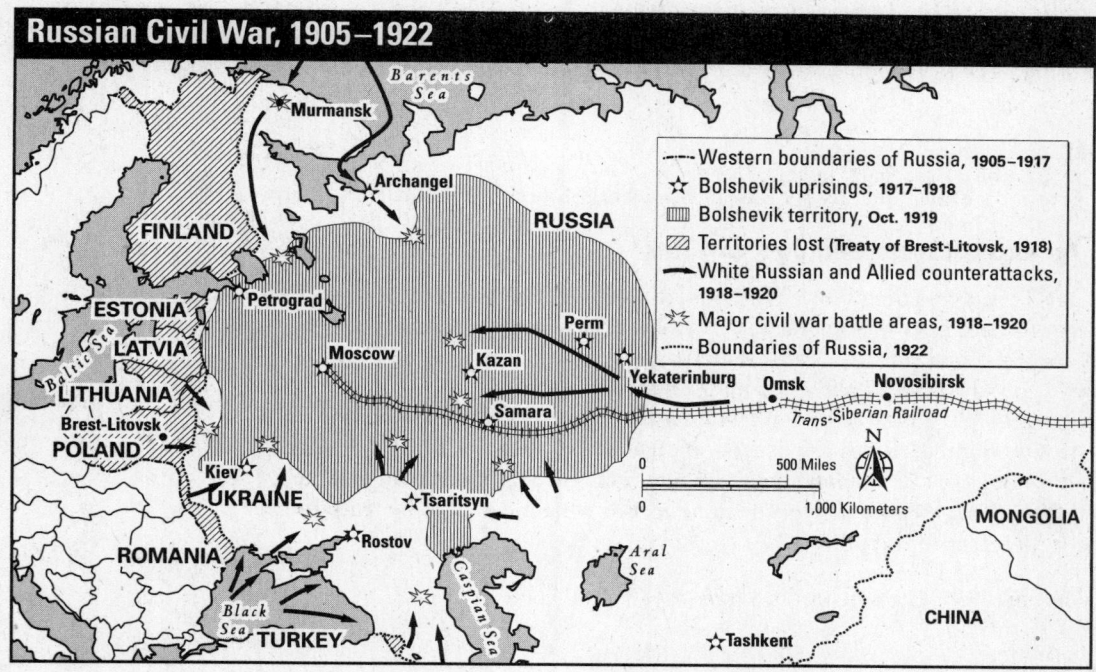

Russian Civil War, 1905–1922

Legend:
- ----- Western boundaries of Russia, **1905–1917**
- ☆ Bolshevik uprisings, **1917–1918**
- ▥ Bolshevik territory, **Oct. 1919**
- ▨ Territories lost **(Treaty of Brest-Litovsk, 1918)**
- → White Russian and Allied counterattacks, **1918–1920**
- ✸ Major civil war battle areas, **1918–1920**
- ⋯ Boundaries of Russia, **1922**

_____ 11. In or near which city did the westernmost civil war battle take place?

      a. Murmansk   c. Brest-Litovsk

      b. Petrograd   d. Archangel

_____ 12. According to this map, how many Bolshevik uprisings took place between 1917 and 1918?

      a. 6   b. 11   c. 16   d. 21

_____ 13. Which territories were lost under the Treaty of Brest-Litovsk?

      a. Finland, Estonia, Latvia, Lithuania, Poland

      b. Romania, Turkey, China, Mongolia

      c. Brest-Litovsk, Ukraine, Russia

      d. all of the above

_____ 14. Approximately how many miles apart are Petrograd and Moscow?

      a. 200   b. 350   c. 500   d. 650

_____ 15. Which bodies of water were used by the White Army and their allies?
        a. Barents Sea and the Caspian Sea
        b. Barents Sea and the Black Sea
        c. Black Sea and the Aral Sea
        d. all of the above

Part 3: Document Based Questions
Introduction

Historical Context: After fighting for the British Empire in World War I, Indians expected England to loosen its hold on the Indian subcontinent. When this did not happen, Mohandis K. Gandhi, an English-trained lawyer who had worked in South Africa, developed the principle of satyagraha, called civil disobedience in English. His campaign, in which millions of Indians engaged in civil disobedience in the face of unjust laws, eventually led to the independence of his nation. Gandhi was assassinated in 1948, just months after India gained her independence.

Task: Discuss how Mohandis K. Gandhi provided leadership to the Indian people as they struggled for independence.

A. Short Answer

Study each document carefully and answer the questions that follow. (4 points each)

Document 1: An excerpt from Gandhi's writings

Satyagraha, then, is literally holding on to Truth and it means, therefore, Truth-force. For the past thirty years I have been preaching and practicing Satyagraha. . . . Satyagraha differs from Passive Resistance as the North Pole from the South. The latter has been conceived as a weapon of the weak and does not exclude the use of physical force or violence for the purpose of gaining one's end, whereas the former has been conceived as a weapon of the strongest and excludes the use of violence in any shape or form. . . . [the] pursuit of truth did not admit of violence being inflicted on one's opponent but that he must be weaned from error by patience and sympathy. For what appears to be truth to the one may appear to be error to the other.

16. How does Gandhi define the concept of *satyagraha*?

_____

Document 2: Excerpt from Jawaharlal Nehru, first prime minister of India

And then Gandhi came. He was like a powerful current of fresh air that made us stretch ourselves and take deep breaths, . . . like a whirlwind that upset many things but most of all the working of people's minds. He did not descend from the top; he seemed to emerge from the millions of India, speaking their language and incessantly drawing attention to them and their appalling condition. Get off the backs of these peasants and workers, he told us, all you who live by their exploitation; get rid of the system that produces poverty and misery. Political freedom took new shape then and acquired a new content. . . . The essence of his teaching was fearlessness and truth and action allied to these, always keeping the welfare of the masses in view.

17. How did the "whirlwind" brought by Gandhi affect Indian people?

_____

Document 3: Cartoon by Bill Mauldin following the assassination of Dr. Martin Luther King, Jr.

"THE ODD THING ABOUT ASSASSINS, DR. KING, IS THAT THEY THINK THEY'VE KILLED YOU."

Source: "The odd thing about assassins" cartoon by Bill Mauldin. Reprinted with special permission from The Chicago Sun-Times, Inc. Copyright © 2001

18. Why are Martin Luther King and Gandhi shown together?

_____

B. Essay

19. Using information from the documents, your answers to the questions in Part A, and your knowledge of world history, write an essay that discusses how Mohandis K. Gandhi influenced both India and the world. Students may also cite quotes or visual descriptions from the documents and cite information they may recall from the chapter. (8 points)

Part 4: Extended Response

Answer the following questions on the back of this paper or on a separate sheet. (10 points each)

20. **Comparing and Contrasting** In what ways did Lenin and Stalin govern the Union of Soviet Socialist Republics? Consider what actions the two men took and what life under their dictatorships was like.

   Think about:
   - impacts on work and living
   - partial control vs. total control
   - lives of the peasants and kulaks

21. **Drawing Conclusions** How did India go about resisting foreign control after World War I? What do you think caused the independence movement to ultimately succeed?

   Think about:
   - Gandhi's strategy
   - economic weapons
   - world opinion

CHAPTER

14

Form B

CHAPTER TEST *Revolution and Nationalism*

Part 1: Main Ideas

Write the letter of the best answer. (4 points each)

_____ 1. How did czars Alexander III and Nicholas II deal with calls for reform?
- a. They immediately moved to enact reforms.
- b. They made a few reforms but not all.
- c. They resisted all efforts for reform.
- d. They appointed ministers to study reforms.

_____ 2. How did the Russo-Japanese war show the czar's weakness?
- a. His insults to the Japanese emperor caused the war.
- b. His poor military strategy prevented his generals from gaining territory.
- c. News of repeated losses sparked unrest and led to revolt during the war.
- d. All of the above are true.

_____ 3. Under the Treaty of Versailles, to whom did the Allies give Chinese territories to that had previously been controlled by Germany?
- a. Italy   b. Japan   c. India   d. Russia

_____ 4. Which event did NOT happen immediately after the Bolshevik Revolution?
- a. The workers took control of factories.
- b. Farmland was distributed among the peasants.
- c. A truce was signed with Germany.
- d. A totalitarian state was established.

_____ 5. Which of the following reflects the leader who was responsible for the Great Purge and the main group that was victimized by it?
- a. Lenin → the Mensheviks
- b. Jiang → the Kuomintang
- c. Jiang → members of the Communist Party
- d. Stalin → members of the Communist Party

_____ 6. What was started under Stalin to improve the Soviet Union's economy?
- a. industrial and agricultural revolutions
- b. Bolshevik and Communist revolutions
- c. socialist and totalitarian revolutions
- d. all of the above

_____ 7. How did the "May Fourth Movement" influence the formation of a Communist party in China?
- a. established the disillusionment of the Chinese people in their government
- b. planted the seeds of Communist ideology within the minds of intellectuals
- c. turned the people against Sun Yixian's beliefs in Western democracy
- d. all of the above

_____ 8. What was the result of China having a Nationalist government recognized by the world but a Communist party growing in the countryside?
   a. A social realist art campaign was created to uplift nationalist ideas.
   b. Nationalist troops and armed gangs wiped out the Communists.
   c. Civil war broke out between the two groups.
   d. Communist leaders were forced to work in labor camps.

_____ 9. How was the result of the nationalist movement in Saudi Arabia different from the results in Turkey and Iran?
   a. Saudi Arabia had a violent revolution, while the other countries did not.
   b. Turkey and Iran pursued modernization more than Saudi Arabia did.
   c. Saudi Arabia built a state on oil money, while the other two did not.
   d. All of the above are true.

_____ 10. What led Great Britain finally to grant India limited self-rule?
   a. continuous campaigns of civil disobedience by Indians
   b. a sharp drop in the British economy based in India
   c. a demonstration known as the "Salt March"
   d. worldwide demonstrations in support of India's independence

Part 2: Map Skills

Use the map to choose the best possible answer. (4 points each)

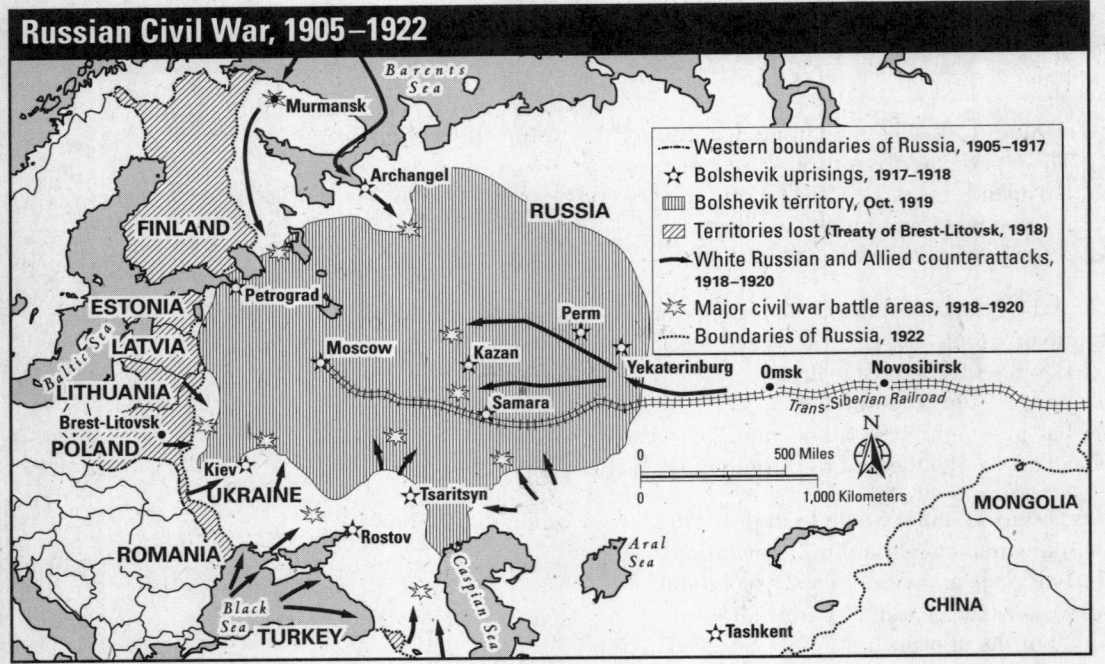

Russian Civil War, 1905–1922

_____ 11. Approximately how many miles from Moscow were all of the Bolshevik uprisings, except the one at Tashkent?
   a. within 300   c. within 1,000
   b. within 700   d. within 1,300

_____ 12. Which water route was used by Allied forces entering Russia from southeastern Europe?
        a. Black Sea   c. Caspian Sea
        b. Barents Sea   d. Aral Sea

_____ 13. By train, approximately how many kilometers are Moscow and Samara apart?
        a. 400   b. 600   c. 800   d. 1000

_____ 14. Which towns were in Bolshevik territory as of October 1919?
        a. Novosibirsk, Omsk, Tashkent, Rostov, Kiev, Perm
        b. Kiev, Tsaritsyn, Archangel, Murmansk, Brest-Litovsk
        c. Petrograd, Moscow, Samara, Kazan, Perm, Yekaterinburg
        d. Yekaterinburg, Moscow, Archangel, Murmansk, Brest-Litovsk

_____ 15. How might this map differ had the Treaty of Brest-Litovsk not been signed?
        a. The Bolsheviks would not control so much land.
        b. Finland, Estonia, Latvia, and Lithuania would not be separate from Russia.
        c. The Trans-Siberian Railway would not have been built.
        d. There would be no battles because the Russian Civil War would not have taken place.

Part 3: Document Based Questions

Introduction

Historical Context: After fighting for the British Empire in World War I, Indians expected England to loosen its hold on the Indian subcontinent. When this did not happen, Mohandis K. Gandhi, an English-trained lawyer who had worked in South Africa, developed the principle of satyagraha, called civil disobedience in English. His campaign, in which millions of Indians engaged in civil disobedience in the face of unjust laws, eventually led to the independence of his nation. Gandhi was assassinated in 1948, just months after India gained her independence.

Task: Discuss how Mohandis K. Gandhi provided leadership to the Indian people as they struggled for independence.

A. Short Answer

Study each document carefully and answer the questions that follow. (4 points each)

Document 1: An excerpt from Gandhi's writings

Satyagraha, then, is literally holding on to Truth and it means, therefore, Truth-force. For the past thirty years I have been preaching and practicing Satyagraha. . . . Satyagraha differs from Passive Resistance as the North Pole from the South. The latter has been conceived as a weapon of the weak and does not exclude the use of physical force or violence for the purpose of gaining one's end, whereas the former has been conceived as a weapon of the strongest and excludes the use of violence in any shape or form. . . . [the] pursuit of truth did not admit of violence being inflicted on one's opponent but that he must be weaned from error by patience and sympathy. For what appears to be truth to the one may appear to be error to the other.

16. What might Gandhi say is the major problem with someone who oppresses others or treats them unjustly?

_____

Document 2: Excerpt from Jawaharlal Nehru, first prime minister of India

And then Gandhi came. He was like a powerful current of fresh air that made us stretch ourselves and take deep breaths, . . . like a whirlwind that upset many things but most of all the working of people's minds. He did not descend from the top; he seemed to emerge from the millions of India, speaking their language and incessantly drawing attention to them and their appalling condition. Get off the backs of these peasants and workers, he told us, all you who live by their exploitation; get rid of the system that produces poverty and misery. Political freedom took new shape then and acquired a new content. . . . The essence of his teaching was fearlessness and truth and action allied to these, always keeping the welfare of the masses in view.

17. How did Gandhi's leadership differ from that of other leaders, according to Nehru?

_____

"THE ODD THING ABOUT ASSASSINS, DR. KING, IS THAT THEY THINK THEY'VE KILLED YOU."

Source: "The odd thing about assassins" cartoon by Bill Mauldin. Reprinted with special permission from The Chicago Sun-Times, Inc. Copyright © 2001

18. Why is Gandhi giving advice or comfort to Dr. King in this cartoon?

_____

B. Essay

19. Using information from the documents, your answers to the questions in Part A, and your knowledge of world history, write an essay that discusses how Mohandis K. Gandhi influenced both India and the world. Students may also cite quotes or visual descriptions from the documents and cite information they may recall from the chapter. (8 points)

Part 4: Extended Response

Answer the following questions on the back of this paper or on a separate sheet. (10 points each)

20. **Analyzing Issues** Do you think life for the average Russian citizen was better or worse under the totalitarian Soviet regime of the 1930s than it had been under the czars? Explain your answer.

    Think about:
    • class equality
    • religious freedoms
    • impacts on work and living

21. **Drawing Conclusions** What did Mohandis K. Gandhi's plan for achieving Indian independence require of the Indian people? Explain your answer.

    Think about:
    • passive resistance
    • anti-government demonstrations

CHAPTER
14

Form C

CHAPTER TEST *Revolution and Nationalism*

Part 1: Main Ideas

Write the letter of the best answer. (4 points each)

_____ 1. How did the reigns of Alexander III and Nicholas II help pave the way for revolution?
     a. They both upheld an autocratic government without reform.
     b. They supported rapid industrialization at the expense of the treasury.
     c. They instituted pogroms to weed out revolutionary thinkers.
     d. They saw to it that the poor were imprisoned for debts.

_____ 2. What impact did Russia's involvement in World War I have on the Russian government?
     a. It created a window for the Mensheviks to attempt a take over.
     b. It led to the establishment of the Duma as a voice for moderates.
     c. It revealed the weaknesses of czarist rule and military leadership.
     d. All of the above are true.

_____ 3. How did life change for Russians after the success of the Bolshevik revolution?
     a. Education became a public institution based on the Western model.
     b. Motherhood was no longer considered a patriotic duty.
     c. Russia was organized into several self-governing republics.
     d. All of the above are true.

_____ 4. Which of the following was NOT part of the transformation of the Soviet Union into a totalitarian state?
     a. Great Purge
     b. Five-Year Plans
     c. creation of the first soviets
     d. establishment of collective farms

_____ 5. Why did Chinese peasants align themselves with the Communists rather than the Nationalists?
     a. The Communists divided land among the farmers, while the Nationalists ignored their problems.
     b. The Nationalists relocated thousands of peasants in the Long March.
     c. The Nationalists were forcing China to industrialize through high taxes on farms.
     d. The Communists moved peasants to collective farms, where they prospered.

_____ 6. Who were the victims of the Shanghai Massacre, and who were their murderers?
     a. Chinese peasants were killed by a local warlord.
     b. Chinese Communists were killed by Chinese Nationalists.
     c. Chinese Nationalists were killed by the Chinese Red Army.
     d. Qing Dynasty officials were killed by the Revolutionary Alliance.

_____ 7. What event in 1937 halted the Chinese civil war?
        a. The Nationalists succeeded in wiping out the Communists.
        b. Chinese Communists began a 6,000 mile journey.
        c. The Japanese launched an all-out invasion of China.
        d. Chinese peasants aligned themselves with the Communists.

_____ 8. What promises were made to the Indian people in exchange for their service under Britain in World War I?
        a. complete and immediate independence
        b. repeal of the Rowlatt Act
        c. reforms that would eventually lead to self-government
        d. justice for the victims of the Amritsar Massacre

_____ 9. What influences created an environment for nationalism in Southwest Asia?
        a. nationalist ideas taught by Mustafa Kemal
        b. Communist propaganda campaigns out of China and Russia
        c. worldwide recognition of Gandhi's civil disobedience campaign
        d. the breakup of the Ottoman Empire and Western interest in the region

_____ 10. In which country did Nationalists lead a successful rebellion against its sultan and then reform the government with an emphasis on modernization?
        a. Syria   b. Turkey   c. China   d. Japan

Part 2: Map Skills

Using the map, place the letter of the correct answer next to each question. (4 points each)

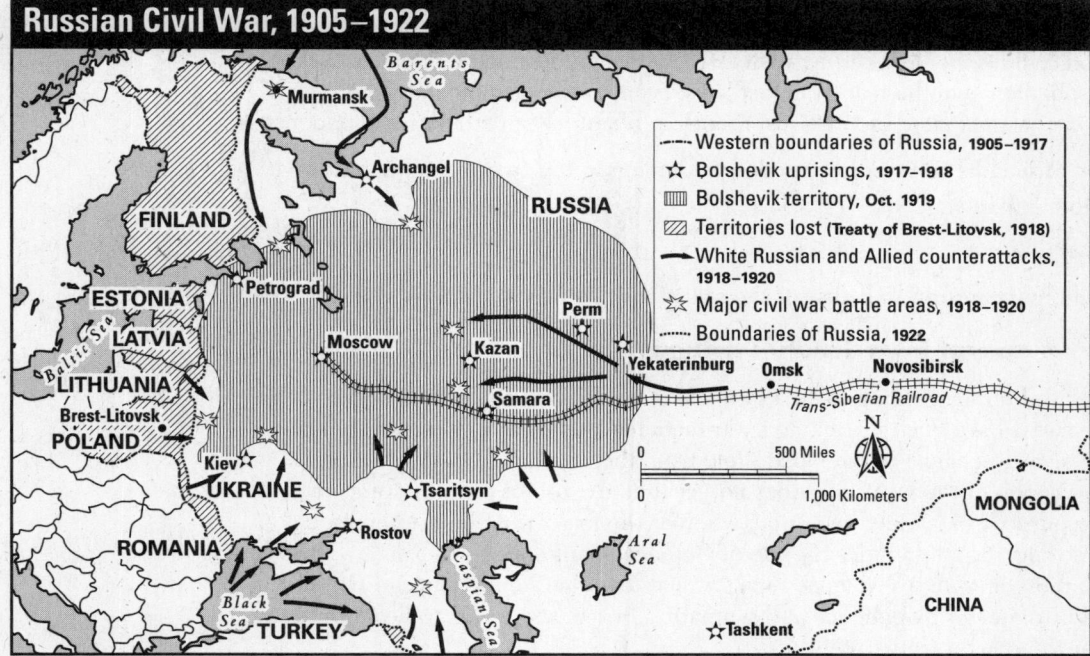

_____ 11. About how many miles from Moscow was the most remote Bolshevik uprising?
        a. 500   b. 1,000   c. 1,200   d. 1,700

_____ 12. From which direction(s) did most of the Allied attacks come from?
   a. north
   b. south and southwest
   c. east and southeast
   d. north and southwest

_____ 13. What area of the Bolshevik territory seems to have the most military activity?
   a. east of Moscow, south of Perm
   b. north of Moscow, west of Archangel
   c. west of Moscow, south of Petrograd
   d. south of Moscow, east of Poland

_____ 14. What was the goal of the battles north of Tsaritsyn and south of Kazan?
   a. to surround Samara
   b. to drive White Russians from Rostov
   c. to control the Trans-Siberian Railroad
   d. to control the Caspian Sea

_____ 15. Why was control of Archangel, Petrograd, and Rostov important?
   a. They were capitals of provinces.
   b. They were port cities.
   c. They surrounded Moscow.
   d. They were entry points for the Allied forces.

Part 3: Document Based Questions
Introduction

Historical Context: After fighting for the British Empire in World War I, Indians expected England to loosen its hold on the Indian subcontinent. When this did not happen, Mohandis K. Gandhi, an English-trained lawyer who had worked in South Africa, developed the principle of satyagraha, called civil disobedience in English. His campaign, in which millions of Indians engaged in civil disobedience in the face of unjust laws, eventually led to the independence of his nation. Gandhi was assassinated in 1948, just months after India gained her independence.

Task: Discuss how Mohandis K. Gandhi provided leadership to the Indian people as they struggled for independence.

A. Short Answer

Study each document carefully and answer the questions that follow. (4 points each)

Document 1: An excerpt from Gandhi's writings

Satyagraha, then, is literally holding on to Truth and it means, therefore, Truth-force. For the past thirty years I have been preaching and practicing Satyagraha. . . . Satyagraha differs from Passive Resistance as the North Pole from the South. The latter has been conceived as a weapon of the weak and does not exclude the use of physical force or violence for the purpose of gaining one's end, whereas the former has been conceived as a weapon of the strongest and excludes the use of violence in any shape or form. . . . [the] pursuit of truth did not admit of violence being inflicted on one's opponent but that he must be weaned from error by patience and sympathy. For what appears to be truth to the one may appear to be error to the other.

16. Which characteristic of Satyagraha distinguishes it from Passive Resistance, and what is the result of this distinction, according to Gandhi?

_____

Document 2: Excerpt from Jawaharlal Nehru, first prime minister of India

And then Gandhi came. He was like a powerful current of fresh air that made us stretch ourselves and take deep breaths, . . . like a whirlwind that upset many things but most of all the working of people's minds. He did not descend from the top; he seemed to emerge from the millions of India, speaking their language and incessantly drawing attention to them and their appalling condition. Get off the backs of these peasants and workers, he told us, all you who live by their exploitation; get rid of the system that produces poverty and misery. Political freedom took new shape then and acquired a new content. . . . The essence of his teaching was fearlessness and truth and action allied to these, always keeping the welfare of the masses in view.

17. What elements does Nehru say Gandhi combined in order to lead the people of India? How did this lead to a new shape for political freedom?

_____

Document 3: Political cartoon by Bill Mauldin

"THE ODD THING ABOUT ASSASSINS, DR. KING, IS THAT THEY THINK THEY'VE KILLED YOU."

Source: "The odd thing about assassins" cartoon by Bill Mauldin. Reprinted with special permission from The Chicago Sun-Times, Inc. Copyright © 2001

18. What do you think Gandhi means by his statement to Dr. King?

_____

B. Essay

19. Using information from the documents, your answers to the questions in Part A, and your knowledge of world history, write an essay that discusses how Mohandis K. Gandhi influenced both India and the world. Students may also cite quotes or visual descriptions from the documents and cite information they may recall from the chapter. (8 points)

Part 4: Extended Response

Answer the following questions on the back of this paper or on a separate sheet. (10 points each)

20. **Forming and Supporting Opinions** Why do you think communism and Communists gained widespread support in China during the 1920s and 1930s?

21. **Comparing** How were Joseph Stalin and Mohandis K. Gandhi different as national leaders? In your answer, discuss what they tried to accomplish, the methods they used, and their impacts on their countries.

Name _____   Date _____

CHAPTER
15
Section 1

SECTION QUIZ   *Postwar Uncertainty*

A. Terms and Names Write the letter of the term or name that best answers the question.
Not all terms and names will be used.

a. Helen Wills   g. Charles Lindbergh   m. Igor Stravinsky
b. Gertrude Stein   h. Friedrich Nietzsche   n. existentialism
c. Albert Einstein   i. Ernest Hemingway   o. stream of
d. Amelia Earhart   j. jazz   consciousness
e. Sigmund Freud   k. relativity
f. F. Scott Fitzgerald   l. surrealism

_____ 1. Who was the first person to successfully complete a solo, trans-Atlantic flight?

_____ 2. Who developed theories about the power of the part of the mind called the
            unconscious?

_____ 3. What is the name of the art movement that incorporates the concept of the
            unconscious mind?

_____ 4. Who is the "Lost Generation" writer who wrote the novel *The Great Gatsby*?

_____ 5. What is the name of the philosophy that rejects the idea of universal values?

_____ 6. What is the musical style that captured a sense of the new freedom of the
            postwar years?

_____ 7. James Joyce used this literary technique to present characters' thoughts and
            feelings.

_____ 8. What is the term for the relationship between the speed of light and the
            measurements of time and space?

_____ 9. Who developed the theory that the measurements of time and space can vary?

_____ 10. Who urged the idea of returning to the heroic values of pride, assertiveness,
            and strength?

B. Extended Response Briefly answer the following question on the back of this paper.

What effects did World War I have on the writers, painters, and musicians who worked
in the postwar years?

CHAPTER
15

Section 2

SECTION QUIZ *A Worldwide Depression*

___

A. Terms and Names Write the letter of the best answer.

_____ 1. In 1920, a dictatorship ruled
    a. Italy.
    b. Russia.
    c. Austria.
    d. Germany.

_____ 2. All of the following contributed to the weakness of the Weimar Republic EXCEPT
    a. uncontrollable inflation.
    b. a lack of democratic tradition.
    c. a large number of political parties.
    d. the implementation of the Dawes Plan.

_____ 3. The New Deal involved attempts to stimulate the American economy by
    a. lowering taxes.
    b. raising protective tariffs.
    c. increasing the minimum wage.
    d. increasing government spending.

_____ 4. All of the following increased during the Great Depression EXCEPT
    a. imports and exports.
    b. bank closings.
    c. unemployment.
    d. business failures.

_____ 5. During the global depression, war debts caused great suffering in
    a. France.
    b. Germany.
    c. Great Britain.
    d. the United States.

_____ 6. The Popular Front helped preserve democracy in
    a. China.
    b. France.
    c. Germany.
    d. Great Britain.

B. Extended Response Briefly answer the following question on the back of this paper.

What do you think President Franklin D. Roosevelt meant when he said that the only thing the United States had to fear was fear itself?

CHAPTER 15

Section 3

SECTION QUIZ *Fascism Rises in Europe*

A. Terms and Names Write the letter of the best answer.

_____ 1. All of the following embraced fascism EXCEPT
a. Juan Perón.
b. Adolph Hitler.
c. Benito Mussolini.
d. Paul von Hindenburg.

_____ 2. All of the following were common to both fascism and communism EXCEPT
a. a classless society.
b. a one-party system.
c. a disregard for individual rights.
d. supremacy of the state.

_____ 3. The title of Hitler's book *Mein Kampf* in English is
a. *Well-Being.*
b. *My Country.*
c. *My Struggle.*
d. *Master Race.*

_____ 4. By 1935, the only eastern European country that was still a democracy was
a. Poland.
b. Hungary.
c. Yugoslavia.
d. Czechoslovakia.

_____ 5. Hitler's main method for achieving *lebensraum* was to
a. attack Jews.
b. conquer other countries.
c. form a secret police force.
d. demand dictatorial power.

_____ 6. Nazism was the German form of
a. fascism.
b. socialism.
c. communism.
d. a coalition government.

B. Extended Response Briefly answer the following question on the back of this paper.

What political and social factors led to the fall of several European democracies in the 1920s and 1930s?

Name _____ **Date** _____

SECTION QUIZ *Aggressors Invade Nations*

CHAPTER 15

Section 4

A. Terms and Names Write the letter of the best answer.

_____ 1. All of the following countries took control of other countries' territory during the 1930s EXCEPT
   a. Italy.   c. Spain.
   b. Japan.   d. Germany.

_____ 2. Manchuria was invaded in 1931 by
   a. Italy.   c. Austria.
   b. Japan.   d. Germany.

_____ 3. All of the following joined the Axis Powers EXCEPT
   a. Italy.   c. Germany.
   b. Japan.   d. the Soviet Union.

_____ 4. A nonaggression pact with the Soviet Union in 1939 was signed by
   a. Spain.   c. Great Britain.
   b. Germany.   d. the United States.

_____ 5. The leader of the Third Reich was
   a. Adolf Hitler.   c. Benito Mussolini.
   b. Francisco Franco.   d. Emperor Hirohito.

_____ 6. During Spain's civil war, Francisco Franco was the leader of
   a. Spanish rebel troops.
   b. Spanish government troops.
   c. Socialist troops fighting against the rebels.
   d. republican troops supporting the government.

_____ 7. The Munich Conference was held to address the problems of a German threat to the nation of
   a. Poland.   c. Austria.
   b. Hungary.   d. Czechoslovakia.

B. Extended Response Briefly answer the following question on the back of this paper.

How were the effects of America's isolationism and Britain's policy of appeasement similar?

CHAPTER 15

CHAPTER TEST *Years of Crisis*

Part 1: Main Ideas

Write the letter of the best answer. (4 points each)

_____ 1. Whose theory of relativity replaced Newton's comforting belief in a world run by absolute laws of motion and gravity?
   a. Sigmund Freud   c. Charles Lindbergh
   b. Albert Einstein   d. F. Scott Fitzgerald

_____ 2. What were Franz Kafka, James Joyce, and F. Scott Fitzgerald all known for being?
   a. painters   c. novelists
   b. composers   d. philosophers

_____ 3. After World War I, most European nations had what type of government, if only temporarily?
   a. Fascist   c. Communist
   b. Socialist   d. democratic

_____ 4. What event marked the beginning of the Great Depression?
   a. the end of World War I
   b. the passage of the Dawes Plan
   c. the stock market crash of 1929
   d. the election of Franklin Roosevelt

_____ 5. What was one part of Roosevelt's New Deal program to fight the Depression?
   a. The stock market and banking system created their own reform council.
   b. Government agencies took over businesses and farms.
   c. Large public works projects helped to provide jobs.
   d. All of the above are true.

_____ 6. Il Duce was the title of which of the following leaders?
   a. Juan Péron   c. Haile Selassie
   b. Adolf Hitler   d. Benito Mussolini

_____ 7. Which German political party sought to overturn the Treaty of Versailles and combat communism?
   a. Socialist   c. Fascist
   b. Nazi   d. Republican

_____ 8. Which of the following was true of Germany, Italy, and Japan during the 1930s?
   a. All three successfully invaded other nations.
   b. All three had governments controlled by Fascists.
   c. All three signed nonaggression pacts with the Soviet Union.
   d. All three pledged to undo the decisions of the Versailles Treaty.

_____ 9. What term was used to identify the alliance of Germany, Italy, and Japan?
   a. Fascist Powers   c. Axis Powers
   b. Allied Powers   d. Central Powers

_____ 10. What was the goal of U.S. isolationists after World War I?
     a. that Nazi ties to other countries should be combatted
     b. that political ties to other countries should be avoided
     c. that foreign aid to other countries should be lessened
     d. that industrial ties to other countries should be ended

Part 2: Map Skills

Use the map to choose the best possible answer. (4 points each)

Expansion of Nazi Germany, 1933-1939

Legend:
- Germany in 1933
- Remilitarized, 1936
- Annexed, 1935-1939
- Conquered, September 1939

_____ 11. Which country did Germany conquer in September 1939?
     a. Poland   c. East Prussia
     b. Austria   d. Czechoslovakia

_____ 12. What did Germany do to the Rhineland?
     a. It annexed the Rhineland to Belgium.
     b. It surrendered the Rhineland to France.
     c. It remilitarized the Rhineland.
     d. The Rhineland became industrialized.

_____ 13. What happened to the Sudetenland?
     a. Germany invaded it.   c. It became independent.
     b. Germany annexed it.   d. Austria annexed it.

_____ 14. What happened to the rest of Czechoslovakia?
   a. It was annexed to Germany in 1939.
   b. It surrendered to Germany in 1939.
   c. It was remilitarized by Germany in 1939.
   d. It remained neutral.

_____ 15. In what key way are all of the shaded countries and regions related?
   a. They are all democratic states.
   b. They all have direct access to the Baltic Sea.
   c. They were taken over by Nazi Germany.
   d. They all border the Soviet Union.

Part 3: Interpreting Graphs

Write the letter of the best answer. (4 points each)

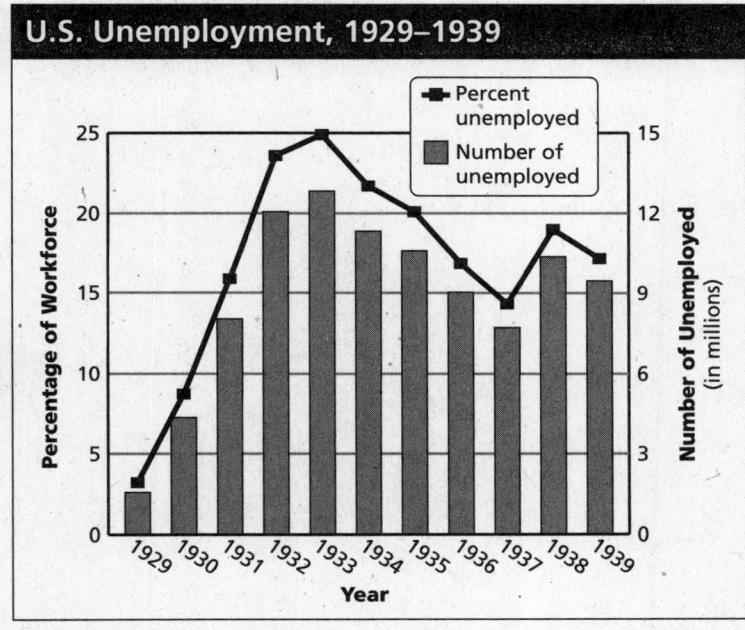

U.S. Unemployment, 1929–1939

_____ 16. What percentage of the workforce was out of work during the peak unemployment
   year?
   a. about 24 percent   c. about 22 percent
   b. about 25 percent   d. about 20 percent

_____ 17. What was the change in the workforce between 1933 and 1934?
   a. The percent of unemployed stayed the same.
   b. The percent of unemployed increased.
   c. The percent of unemployed decreased.
   d. The percent of employed decreased.

_____ 18. How many people were out of work during the peak unemployment year?
   a. about 10 million
   b. about 21 million
   c. about 12 million
   d. about 13 million

Name _____   **Test Form A** *continued*

_____ 19. How did the unemployment rate change between 1929 and 1930?
         a. It stayed about the same.
         b. It decreased by about 5 percent.
         c. It increased by about 5 percent.
         d. It increased by about 10 percent.

_____ 20. After the peak of unemployment, during which year did it reach its lowest rate again?
         a. 1929   b. 1930   c. 1931   d. 1937

Part 4: Extended Response

Answer the following questions on the back of this paper or on a separate sheet. (10 points each)

21. **Drawing Conclusions** What conditions and situations helped Fascists come to power in Germany and Italy in the 1920s and 1930s?

   Think about:
   • past political influences in both regions
   • growth of the Communist movement
   • anger and resentment during postwar years

22. **Recognizing Effects** How did technology change daily life after World War I?

   Think about:
   • advances in communication
   • advances in transportation
   • new forms of entertainment

© McDougal Littell Inc. All rights reserved.

268 UNIT 4, CHAPTER 15

CHAPTER TEST *Years of Crisis*

Form B

Part 1: Main Ideas

Write the letter of the best answer. (4 points each)

_____ 1. What is a main idea of the philosophy known as existentialism?
a. that one should find his or her own meaning in life
b. that one should make choices in life based on universal truth
c. that one should learn to delight in what is absurd and nonsensical
d. that one should consider the needs of the state above his or her own

_____ 2. Which of the following is NOT a painting style from the early 20th century?
a. cubism   c. existentialism
b. expressionism   d. surrealism

_____ 3. What effect did World War I have on the literature of the 1920s?
a. War stories became very popular.
b. Literature declined because many writers died in the war.
c. Writers expressed disillusionment about reason and progress.
d. Writers began to warn people about flaws in the Treaty of Versailles.

_____ 4. What effect did the Dawes Plan have on the economy of postwar Germany?
a. It saved Germany from an inflationary crisis and stabilized the economy.
b. It replaced German marks with the U.S. dollar as the nation's currency.
c. It introduced U.S. businesses into Germany, which provided jobs.
d. All of the above are true.

_____ 5. In the late 1920s, which of the following did NOT damage the U.S. economy?
a. soaring stock prices
b. a shortage of workers
c. an uneven distribution of wealth
d. a surplus of agricultural products

_____ 6. What caused Germans to start taking Adolf Hitler and his message seriously?
a. the threat of invasion by the Soviet Union
b. his skill at making speeches
c. the example of Mussolini's success in Italy
d. the economic crisis brought on by the Depression

_____ 7. Which of the following does fascism stress?
a. nationalism   c. individual rights
b. isolationism   d. a classless society

_____ 8. What was the policy of appeasement?
a. the British and French decision to give into aggression to keep peace
b. the move that Mussolini made to form an alliance with Germany
c. the U.S. desire to stay out of foreign affairs
d. the treaty between Germany and the Soviet Union to not fight each other

_____ 9. Why did Japan invade Manchuria?
        a. to revenge an ancient grudge
        b. to gain its iron ore and coal deposits
        c. to regain land lost in the Russo-Japanese War
        d. to obey the terms of the Kellogg-Briand Pact

_____ 10. What effect did the nonaggression pact between the Nazis and the Soviets have?
        a. It brought the United States out of its isolation.
        b. It allowed the Axis Powers to continue unchecked.
        c. It forced Britain and France to abandon the policy of appeasement.
        d. All of the above are true.

Part 2: Map Skills

Use the map to choose the best possible answer. (4 points each)

Expansion of Nazi Germany, 1933-1939

_____ 11. How did expansion affect the size of Germany?
        a. It grew slightly.   c. It roughly tripled.
        b. It roughly doubled.   d. It grew, then shrank.

_____ 12. How did the expansion into Poland differ from that of Austria?
        a. Poland was taken by force, whereas Austria was annexed.
        b. Austria was taken by force, whereas Poland was annexed.
        c. Austria was remilitarized with the Rhineland, whereas Poland was
           conquered.
        d. Poland was remilitarized with the Rhineland, whereas Austria was annexed.

_____ 13. What might be the effect of Nazi expansion toward France in 1936?
   a. France would be the next target for Nazi expansion.
   b. France would be forced to align itself with Germany.
   c. France would have an enemy army at its border.
   d. France would have to declare war on Germany.

_____ 14. Why would Czechoslovakia have been hard to defend against Germany in 1939?
   a. There were no natural boundaries.
   b. Its western half was surrounded by Germany.
   c. Germany had an alliance with the Soviet Union.
   d. Its capital city was on the border with Austria.

_____ 15. Why did Germany want northern Poland?
   a. It wanted the Vistula River.
   b. It wanted to join Lithuania with Germany.
   c. It wanted the southern coastline of the Baltic Sea.
   d. It wanted the Baltic Seaport of Danzig.

Part 3: Interpreting Charts

Write the letter of the best answer. (4 points each)

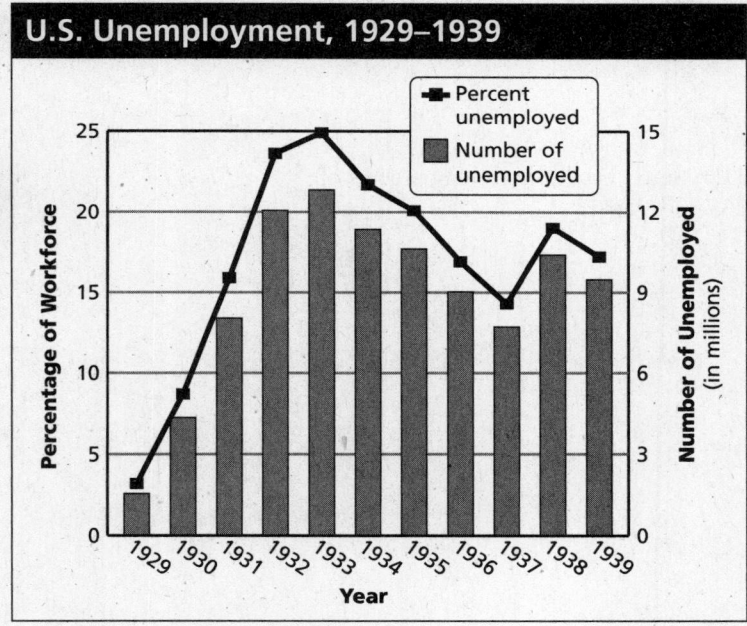

U.S. Unemployment, 1929–1939

_____ 16. During which years was the unemployment rate below 10 percent?
   a. 1929-1930   c. 1930-1937
   b. 1929-1937   d. 1937-1939

_____ 17. In which year was the percentage of unemployment nearly double that of the previous year?
   a. 1929   b. 1931   c. 1933   d. 1935

_____ 18. In what year did the gradual improvement in the Depression economy suffer a setback?
   a. 1933   b. 1935   c. 1938   d. 1939

_____ 19. Judging from this graph, how did Roosevelt's New Deal, which began in 1933, affect the Great Depression?
  a. It ended the Depression.
  b. It made the Depression worse.
  c. It eased the Depression slightly.
  d. It had no effect on the Depression.

_____ 20. What can be inferred about the United States over the course of the chart?
  a. During the years of 1929 to 1939, the U.S. job market was in a continuous slump.
  b. During the years 1929 to 1939, the unemployment rate generally rose and then fell.
  c. During the years 1929 to 1939, the economy grew slowly.
  d. All of the above are true.

Part 4: Extended Response

Answer the following questions on the back of this paper or on a separate sheet. (10 points each)

21. **Drawing Conclusions** What role did fear play in causing and prolonging the Great Depression?

Think about:
  • the stock market crash
  • customer bank withdrawals
  • overseas dependence on American aid

22. **Forming and Supporting Opinions** Why did the newly established democracies of Europe have trouble surviving in the years after World War I?

Think about:
  • past political experience
  • the economic situation
  • other political forces of the time

Name _____ Date _____

CHAPTER
15
Form C

CHAPTER TEST *Years of Crisis*

Part 1: Main Ideas

Write the letter of the best answer. (4 points each)

_____ 1. How did Sigmund Freud's ideas weaken faith in reason?
     a. He taught that mental illness was the normal human condition.
     b. He proposed absolute laws about the human mind.
     c. He believed that much of human behavior is irrational.
     d. He believed that much of human behavior is supernatural.

_____ 2. What impact did radio have after the war?
     a. It made movies lose popularity as Americans stayed home.
     b. It replaced newspapers as the major source of news.
     c. It allowed families to enjoy broadcasts of news, plays, music, and sports.
     d. All of the above are true.

_____ 3. Why did coalition governments usually prove unstable?
     a. They were based on the ideas of a minority political group.
     b. They were established by foreign governments.
     c. They were run by members of the aristocracy, whom no one trusted.
     d. They were alliances of several parties who disagreed on many policies.

_____ 4. Why did millions of Germans turn against the leaders of the Weimar Republic?
     a. They had signed the Treaty of Versailles.
     b. Their leadership led to the loss of the war.
     c. They were members of the Nazi party.
     d. The country was not ready for a democratic government.

_____ 5. What was the major cause of the collapse of the stock market?
     a. American businesses failed.
     b. More people bought stock than sold it.
     c. Stocks sold for more than they were worth.
     d. More stocks were sold than there were shares in companies.

_____ 6. What fear added to the appeal of fascism in Italy and Germany?
     a. a Communist revolution   c. foreign attack
     b. a loss of individual rights   d. all of the above

_____ 7. Why did Hitler blame the Jewish population for all of Germany's troubles?
     a. The Jewish people had aided Germany's enemies in World War I.
     b. Hatred of Jews, or anti-Semitism, was a key part of Nazi ideology.
     c. The Jewish population in Germany outnumbered the Nazi party.
     d. Jewish people held most of the prominent roles in the German government.

_____ 8. The Munich Conference came to symbolize the dangers of what?
     a. Communism   c. negotiation
     b. appeasement   d. militarism

_____ 9. What important role did Winston Churchill play during this period?
      a. He was prime minister of Great Britain.
      b. He was the British delegate at the Munich Conference.
      c. He warned that the policy of appeasement was a disaster.
      d. He suggested turning Danzig over to Germany.

_____ 10. In what way was Japan different from its allies Germany and Italy?
      a. It established a successful democracy.
      b. It was ruled by a hereditary aristocracy.
      c. It kept its economy prosperous throughout the Depression.
      d. It was ruled by militarists who kept the emperor in power.

Part 2: Map Skills—Constructed Response

Using the map, answer the questions below. You do not need to write complete sentences.
(4 points each)

Expansion of Nazi Germany, 1933-1939

11. What countries would have felt most threatened by the remilitarization of the Rhineland?

_____

12. How would you describe the relative location of the Sudetenland?

_____

13. In which direction did Nazi Germany have its greatest expansion?

_____

14. What did Germany gain by conquering Poland?

_____

15. Judging from the map, why did Hitler want to sign the nonaggression pact with Stalin in August 1939?

_____

Part 3: Interpreting Charts

Write the letter of the best answer. (4 points each)

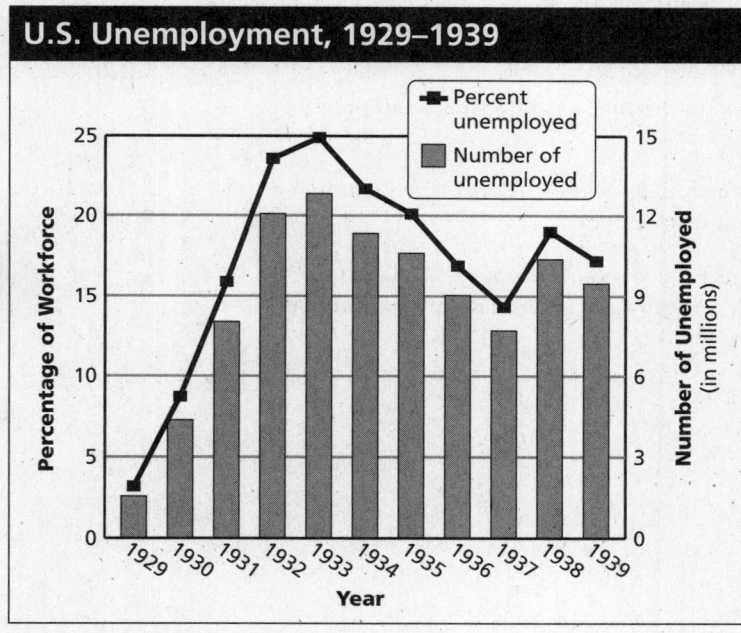

U.S. Unemployment, 1929–1939

_____ 16. What is true of the years 1932-1933?
  a. The unemployment rate was at its peak.
  b. The unemployment rate was at its lowest.
  c. The unemployment rate was unchanging.
  d. The unemployment rate was no problem.

_____ 17. From the beginning of the Depression to the year of highest unemployment, how much did the percentage of unemployment go up?
  a. about 3 percent
  b. about 15 percent
  c. about 22 percent
  d. about 35 percent

_____ 18. In what year was the percentage of unemployment nearly triple that of the
previous year?
   a. 1930
   b. 1932
   c. 1936
   d. 1940

_____ 19. Which year was an exception to the overall trend shown on the graph and why?
   a. 1929, because the rate would never be that low again
   b. 1933, because the increasing rate reached its climax
   c. 1935, because it was the lowest decrease over two years
   d. 1938, because the gradually dropping rate rose again

_____ 20. Assuming that a high unemployment rate indicates a depression, what conclusion
can you draw from this graph?
   a. The Great Depression ended in 1937.
   b. The Great Depression worsened in 1939.
   c. The Great Depression had not ended by 1939.
   d. The Great Depression eased significantly in 1936.

Part 4: Extended Response

Answer the following questions on the back of this paper or on a separate sheet. (10 points
each)

21. **Recognizing Effects** What were two ways in which the effects of World War I continued
to be felt in the decades that followed it? Explain your answers.

22. **Analyzing Motives** Why were Great Britain and France so eager to appease Germany?
Were the attitudes of the British and the French leaders reasonable? Explain your answer,
citing evidence from the chapter.

Name _____ Date _____

CHAPTER 16

Section 1

SECTION QUIZ *Hitler's Lightning War*

A. Terms and Names Write the letter of the best answer.

_____ 1. The Soviet Union signed a nonaggression pact in 1939 with
      a. Italy.
      b. Poland.
      c. Germany.
      d. Great Britain.

_____ 2. Great Britain and France entered World War II because of the invasion of
      a. Poland.
      b. Finland.
      c. Denmark and Norway.
      d. the Baltic States.

_____ 3. The Germans first successfully used the blitzkrieg in an attack on
      a. France.
      b. Poland.
      c. Finland.
      d. the Soviet Union.

_____ 4. Charles de Gaulle was the
      a. French general who negotiated France's terms of surrender.
      b. prime minister of France before World War II.
      c. prime minister of the puppet government in southern France during
         World War II.
      d. leader of the French government-in-exile and the Free French.

_____ 5. All of the following were advantages for the British in fighting the Battle of
    Britain EXCEPT
      a. radar.
      b. Enigma.
      c. British morale.
      d. superior numbers of aircraft.

_____ 6. The Atlantic Charter was a declaration of the right to freedom of
      a. trade.
      b. speech.
      c. the skies.
      d. economic self-determination.

B. Extended Response Briefly answer the following question on the back of this paper.

What were the military outcomes and important results of the German invasion of
France, the Battle of Britain, and the German invasion of the Soviet Union in 1941?

CHAPTER

16

Section 2

SECTION QUIZ *Japan's Pacific Campaign*

A. Terms and Names Write the letter of the best answer.

_____ 1. Why is Isoroku Yamamoto famous?
      a. ordering and overseeing the Bataan Death March
      b. leading the Japanese government during World War II
      c. breaking the Japanese secret code during World War II
      d. masterminding the Japanese naval strategy during World War II

_____ 2. Who went on the Bataan Death March, and why?
      a. Japanese soldiers, because they refused to surrender
      b. Allied prisoners of war, because the Japanese forced them to
      c. Allied soldiers, because it was essential to the success of the
         "island-hopping" strategy
      d. Chinese civilians, because they were forced off their land by the
         Japanese invasion

_____ 3. Which of the following events turned the tide of the war in the Pacific against
Japan and allowed the Allies to begin taking the offensive?
      a. Battle of Midway
      b. Battle of Guadalcanal
      c. Battle of the Coral Sea
      d. Doolittle's raid on Japan

_____ 4. Why were the Pacific islands attacked and seized during the Allied "island
hopping" chosen?
      a. They were isolated and uninhabited.
      b. They were farthest away from Japan.
      c. They were least heavily defended by Japan.
      d. They were former territories of the United States.

_____ 5. Who was the mastermind of the "island-hopping" strategy?
      a. Chester Nimitz
      b. James H. Doolittle
      c. Franklin Roosevelt
      d. Douglas MacArthur

B. Extended Response Briefly answer the following question on the back of this paper.

Why did Japan attack Pearl Harbor? What were some of the most important
consequences of the attack?

CHAPTER **16**

Section 3

SECTION QUIZ   *The Holocaust*

A. Terms and Names Answer the following questions on the lines provided.

1. What did Hitler incorrectly call the Germanic people he considered the "master race"?

   _____

2. What happened on *Kristallnacht?*

   _____

3. What was the first "solution" to the "Jewish problem," and why wasn't Hitler satisfied?

   _____

4. What is genocide?

   _____

5. What was the main goal of the "Final Solution"?

   _____

6. Identify two tools or tactics that were used to implement the "Final Solution."

   _____

7. Identify two groups other than Jews who were singled out for the "Final Solution."

   _____

8. What was Auschwitz?

   _____

B. Extended Response Briefly answer the following question on the back of this paper.

   Why do you think that an event as horrifying as the Holocaust was able to occur?

Name _____ Date _____

CHAPTER
16

SECTION QUIZ *The Allied Victory*

Section 4

A. Terms and Names Write the letter of the best answer.

_____ 1. Who was the supreme commander of the Western Allied forces in Europe?
      a. General George Patton
      b. General Erwin Rommel
      c. General Bernard Montgomery
      d. General Dwight D. Eisenhower

_____ 2. Which of the following occurred on D-Day?
      a. the Allied invasion of Italy
      b. the Allied invasion of France
      c. the Allied bombing of Hiroshima
      d. the Allied bombing of Nagasaki

_____ 3. What was the main target of the kamikazes?
      a. ships
      b. air bases
      c. ground troops
      d. civilian populations

_____ 4. Which of the following did Stalin repeatedly urge Churchill and Roosevelt to do in order to relieve German pressure on Soviet armies?
      a. invade Italy
      b. invade France
      c. invade Germany
      d. use atomic bombs

_____ 5. Which general led the victorious troops in the Battle of El Alamein?
      a. Erwin Rommel
      b. Friedrich von Paulus
      c. Bernard Montgomery
      d. Dwight D. Eisenhower

_____ 6. Why were thousands of Japanese Americans interned in relocation camps?
      a. their ancestry
      b. their need for protection
      c. their stated support of Japanese goals
      d. their unwillingness to aid the war effort

B. Extended Response Briefly answer the following question on the back of this paper.

In a paragraph, explain why any three of the following battles were particularly significant: the Battle of El Alamein, the Battle of Stalingrad, the invasion of Normandy, the Battle of the Bulge, and the Battle of Leyte Gulf.

CHAPTER **16**

SECTION QUIZ   *Europe and Japan in Ruins*

Section 5

A. Terms and Names Write the letter of the best answer.

_____ 1. Which of the following cities was NOT extensively damaged during the war?
  a. Paris, France
  b. Tokyo, Japan
  c. Warsaw, Poland
  d. Berlin, Germany

_____ 2. Which of the following nations paid the greatest price in terms of the number of lives lost during the war?
  a. Germany
  b. Soviet Union
  c. Japan
  d. France

_____ 3. In which of the following nations was the pre-war government allowed to return to power after the war?
  a. Belgium
  b. Japan
  c. Italy
  d. Germany

_____ 4. What group was tried at the Nuremberg Trials?
  a. Nazis
  b. Communists
  c. the Luftwaffe
  d. war criminals from all of the Axis Powers

_____ 5. Who led efforts to draw up the Japanese constitution?
  a. Hideki Tojo
  b. Harry Truman
  c. Emperor Hirohito
  d. Douglas MacArthur

_____ 6. Who organized and oversaw the demilitarization of Japan?
  a. U.S. Army
  b. U.S. Congress
  c. Diet of Japan
  d. emperor of Japan

B. Extended Response Briefly answer the following question on the back of this paper.

What were the social and economic conditions in Europe in the years immediately following World War II?

CHAPTER 16
Form A

CHAPTER TEST *World War II*

Part 1: Main Ideas

Choose the correct answer. (4 points each)

_____ 1. What prompted Great Britain and France to declare war on Germany?
   a. Soviet invasion of Finland
   b. German invasion of Poland
   c. German invasion of Czechoslovakia
   d. Soviet invasion of Poland

_____ 2. The German blitzkrieg was a military strategy that depended on what advantage?
   a. a system of fortifications
   b. "out-waiting" the opponent
   c. surprise and overwhelming force
   d. ability to make a long, steady advance

_____ 3. What crucial lesson was learned in the Battle of Britain?
   a. that Germany had a powerful airforce
   b. that Hitler's advances could be blocked
   c. that the RAF needed more planes
   d. that the British were inexperienced

_____ 4. What event occurred on the day described as "a date which will live in infamy"?
   a. attack on Pearl Harbor
   b. Battle of Guadalcanal
   c. bombing of Hiroshima
   d. signing of the Atlantic Charter

_____ 5. What was significant about the Battle of Midway?
   a. It turned the war in the Pacific against the Japanese.
   b. It marked the end of the war for the Japanese.
   c. It destroyed the whole of the Japanese navy.
   d. all of the above

_____ 6. Which of the following was the location of a Nazi extermination camp?
   a. Berlin
   b. Warsaw
   c. Auschwitz
   d. Dresden

_____ 7. Which of the following battles marked the final German offensive?
   a. Battle of the Bulge
   b. Battle of Stalingrad
   c. Battle of Leyte Gulf
   d. Battle of El Alamein

_____ 8. What caused the Japanese emperor to have reduced power after the war?
     a. the Allies' insistence
     b. the anger of the Japanese citizenry
     c. the distrust of the Japanese parliament
     d. the emperor's decision to reform the government

_____ 9. Where were atomic bombs dropped?
     a. Tokyo and Hong Kong
     b. Dresden and Berlin
     c. Hiroshima and Nagasaki
     d. Leyte Island and Midway

_____ 10. Which of the following was addressed by the Nuremberg Trials?
     a. the Holocaust
     b. the use of nuclear bombs
     c. the firebombing of Dresden
     d. the internment of Japanese-American citizens

Part 2: Map Skills

Using the map, write the letter of the correct answer next to each question. (4 points each)

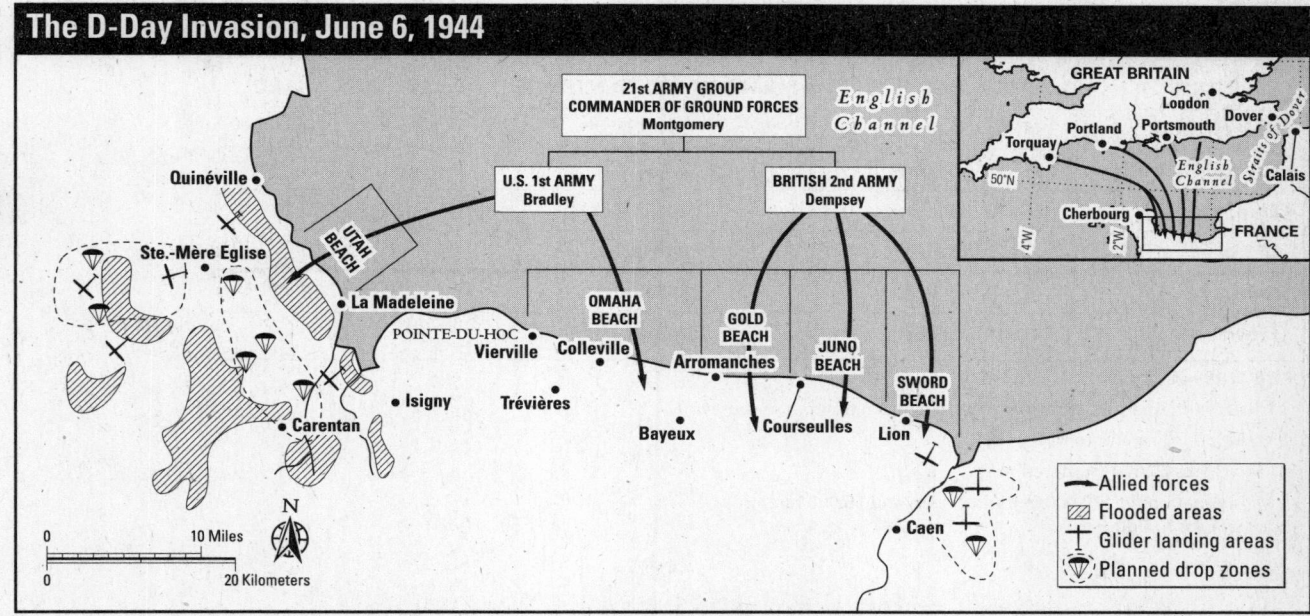

The D-Day Invasion, June 6, 1944

_____ 11. Which of these towns were British troops most likely to reach first?
     a. Caen
     b. Trévières
     c. Courseulles
     d. Carentan

_____ 12. Which of the following was an area targeted by the U.S. First Army?
     a. Gold Beach
     b. Sword Beach
     c. Juno Beach
     d. Omaha Beach

_____ 13. Which of the following officers did NOT command D-Day forces?
  a. Patton
  b. Bradley
  c. Montgomery
  d. Dempsey

_____ 14. How many beaches were targeted landing sites for forces coming from the water?
  a. one
  b. two
  c. four
  d. five

_____ 15. Which of the following was NOT a departure point in Great Britain?
  a. Torquay
  b. Portland
  c. London
  d. Portsmouth

Part 3: Interpreting Graphs

Using the chart, write the letter of the correct answer next to each question. (4 points each)

Costs of World War II: Allies and Axis

COUNTRY	DIRECT WAR COSTS	MILITARY KILLED/MISSING	CIVILIANS KILLED
United States	$288.0 billion*	292,131 **	--
Great Britain	$117.0 billion	271,311	60,595
France	$111.3 billion	205,707 ***	173,260 †
USSR	$93.0 billion	13,600,000	7,720,000
Germany	$212.3 billion	3,300,000	2,893,000 ††
Japan	$41.3 billion	1,140,429	953,000

  * In 1994 dollars.
 ** An additional 115,187 servicemen died from non-battle causes.
*** Before surrender to Nazis.
  † Includes 65,000 murdered Jews.
 †† Includes about 170,000 murdered Jews and 56,000 foreign
    civilians in Germany.

_____ 16. What was the direct war cost for the United States during World War II?
  a. $93 billion
  b. $150 billion
  c. $288 billion
  d. $312 billion

_____ 17. During World War II, how many German military personnel were killed or reported missing?
  a. 205,707
  b. 1,140,429
  c. 2,120,000
  d. 3,300,000

_____ 18. In which of the following countries were the most civilians killed during World War II?
      a. USSR
      b. Germany
      c. Japan
      d. Great Britain

_____ 19. Which of the following countries had the lowest direct war costs?
      a. Japan
      b. USSR
      c. France
      d. Great Britain

_____ 20. Which of the countries listed in the chart had the second lowest number of killed or missing military personnel?
      a. France
      b. Great Britain
      c. the United States
      d. Japan

Part 4: Extended Response

Answer the following questions. (10 points each)

21. **Drawing Conclusions** Why was D-Day such an important historic event?

    Think about:
    • wide reach of Axis Powers
    • the nature of the invasion
    • its immediate and long-term effects

22. **Recognizing Effects** How did World War II affect civilians around the world?

    Think about:
    • the Holocaust
    • the bombing of cities by several nations
    • the internment of Japanese Americans
    • civilian efforts to support the war

CHAPTER
16

Form B

CHAPTER TEST *World War II*

Part 1: Main Ideas

Write the letter of the best answer. (4 points each)

_____ 1. What was Hitler's prime reason for wanting to take Poland?
  a. He knew it would be a bargaining chip with the Soviet Union.
  b. He wanted the Polish Corridor and the port city of Danzig.
  c. He knew it would cause Great Britain and France to declare war.
  d. all of the above

_____ 2. Which of the following factors led to the fall of France to the Nazis?
  a. the fall of Dunkirk
  b. evacuation of the British forces
  c. the fall of Paris
  d. all of the above

_____ 3. What was the significance of the Atlantic Charter both during and after the war?
  a. It was signed on a ship in the Atlantic where the U.S. navy would soon enter an undeclared naval war with Germany.
  b. It established an alliance between Great Britain and the United States to oversee postwar peace.
  c. It upheld rights of free trade and choice of government, and it became the plan for postwar peace.
  d. It cut off trade with Axis Powers and established trade embargoes for the postwar era.

_____ 4. What did the Allies' strategy of "island hopping" in the Pacific involve?
  a. attacks on all Japanese-held islands
  b. attacks on all islands within 500 miles of Japan
  c. attacks only on islands that were not well-defended
  d. attacks only on islands that were Japanese strongholds

_____ 5. How did the Japanese try to build a Pacific empire?
  a. by attacking Pearl Harbor in a surprise raid
  b. by taking over U.S., British, and French territories
  c. by convincing native peoples to save "Asia for the Asians"
  d. by sponsoring Communist overthrow of colonial governments

_____ 6. How did *Kristallnacht* demonstrate Nazi persecution of Jews?
  a. Nazi troops attacked Jewish homes, businesses, and synagogues.
  b. A law passed on that day required Jews to wear yellow stars.
  c. That was the day the Nazis began large deportations of Jews.
  d. all of the above

_____ 7. What was the goal of Hitler's "Final Solution"?
     a. It was a process to divide up his territories among his generals.
     b. It was a system for winning the war before the Americans entered.
     c. It was a way to amass more soldiers for the invasion of Russia.
     d. It was genocide of people the Nazis considered inferior.

_____ 8. What combination led to the German defeat in the Battle of Stalingrad?
     a. Russian and British troops
     b. Russian troops and the Russian winter
     c. Russian and German fuel shortages
     d. Russian ground forces and American air strikes

_____ 9. Under the postwar constitution of Japan, who was the head of government?
     a. the emperor
     b. the leader of the diet
     c. a prime minister selected by the diet
     d. a prime minister selected by the emperor

_____ 10. What does the use of kamikaze pilots show about Japanese culture?
     a. They hated Americans enough to die killing them.
     b. They did not mind dying because they expected to lose the war.
     c. They valued national honor more than individual life.
     d. They were full of despair after the atomic bombs fell on Japan.

Part 2: Map Skills

Use the map to choose the best possible answer. (4 points each)

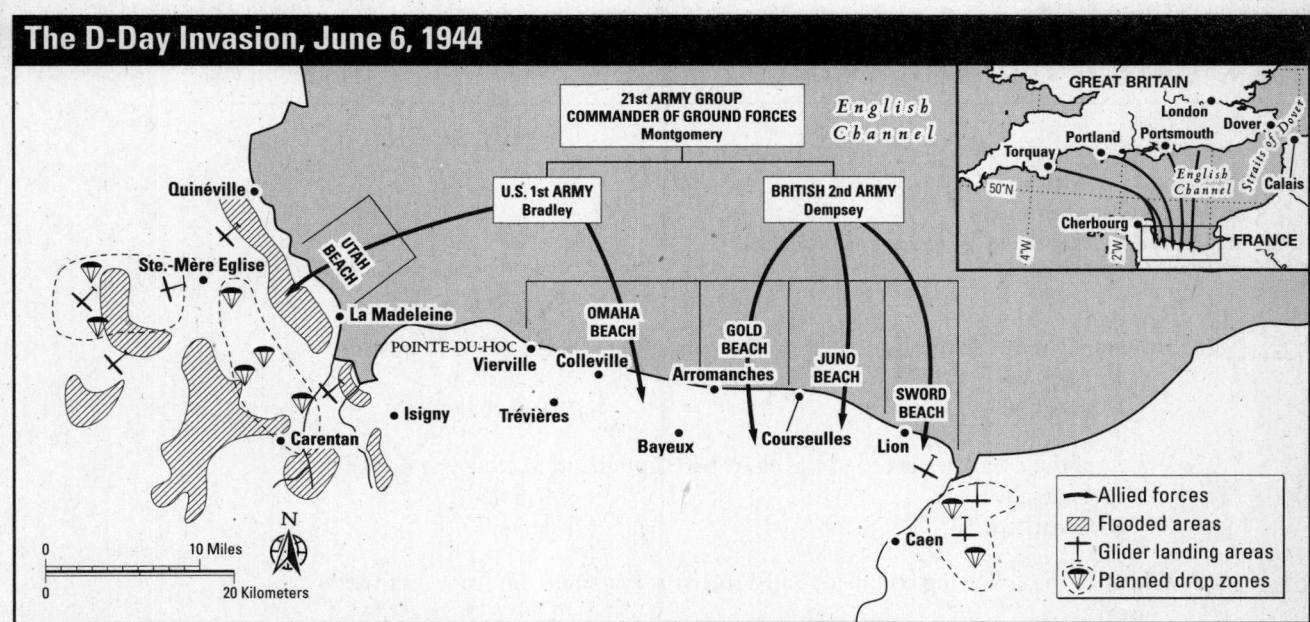

The D-Day Invasion, June 6, 1944

_____ 11. From where did the troops landing at Gold Beach cross the English Channel?
     a. Portland   b. Torquay   c. Cherbourg   d. Portsmouth

_____ 12. In which direction did the troops who landed at Gold Beach travel to reach their destination?
     a. northwest   b. west   c. south   d. southeast

_____ 13. How many drop zones also were glider landing areas?
        a. 2   b. 3   c. 7   d. 15

_____ 14. Which area seems most targeted for glider assault?
        a. the region north of Bayeux
        b. the region west of Sword Beach
        c. the region west of Utah Beach
        d. the region south of Omaha Beach

_____ 15. What made the D-Day invasion so hard to coordinate?
        a. Two armies were both commanded by one central figure.
        b. The attack areas were divided into two basic sections.
        c. It used a combination of air and land assaults.
        d. The base of operations was in Great Britain.

Part 3: Interpreting Charts

Write the letter of the best answer. (4 points each)

COUNTRY	DIRECT WAR COSTS	MILITARY KILLED/MISSING	CIVILIANS KILLED
United States	$288.0 billion*	292,131 **	--
Great Britain	$117.0 billion	271,311	60,595
France	$111.3 billion	205,707 ***	173,260 †
USSR	$93.0 billion	13,600,000	7,720,000
Germany	$212.3 billion	3,300,000	2,893,000 ††
Japan	$41.3 billion	1,140,429	953,000

Costs of World War II: Allies and Axis

  * In 1994 dollars.

  ** An additional 115,187 servicemen died from non-battle causes.

*** Before surrender to Nazis.

  † Includes 65,000 murdered Jews.

 †† Includes about 170,000 murdered Jews and 56,000 foreign
    civilians in Germany.

_____ 16. How many more Soviet soldiers than German soldiers were killed or missing?
        a. 7,300,000   c. 9,300,000
        b. 9,000,000   d. 10,300,000

_____ 17. Which of the countries listed in the chart had the second highest war costs?
        a. Germany   c. France
        b. Great Britain   d. Japan

_____ 18. Which of the following countries had 115,187 servicemen die from non-battle causes?
        a. Great Britain   c. Germany
        b. United States   d. Japan

_____ 19. What was the difference between the number of Jews and the number of foreign civilians killed in Germany?

      a. In Germany during World War II, 54,000 more Jews than foreign civilians were killed.

      b. In Germany during World War II, 84,000 more Jews than foreign civilians were killed.

      c. In Germany during World War II, 104,000 more Jews than foreign civilians were killed.

      d. In Germany during World War II, 114,000 more Jews than foreign civilians were killed.

_____ 20. What percentage of the civilians killed in France were Jews?

      a. 17.0

      b. 27.5

      c. 37.5

      d. 47.0

Part 4: Extended Response

Answer the following questions on the back of this paper or on a separate sheet. (10 points each)

21. **Analyzing Causes** What military strategies contributed to the Allied victory in World War II?

Think about:
- the war in Europe
- the war in Africa
- the war in the Pacific

22. **Recognizing Effects** What were the short and long-term effects of the invasion of Poland on Poland, Germany, the Soviet Union, Great Britain, and France?

Think about:
- the major reasons for the war
- effects on countries
- effects on people

CHAPTER

16

Form C

CHAPTER TEST *World War II*

Part 1: Main Ideas

Write the letter of the best answer. (4 points each)

_____ 1. What was the result of Germany's invasion of Poland?
      a. Soviet forces invaded Germany.
      b. Soviet forces came to Poland's defense.
      c. Britain and France declared war on Germany.
      d. Britain and France sued for peace with Germany.

_____ 2. How did the Lend-Lease Act benefit the United States?
      a. It enriched the U.S. economy through selling arms to the Allies.
      b. It lent the Allies American troops in exchange for European goods.
      c. It allowed the Allies to purchase food and medicine from the United States.
      d. all of the above

_____ 3. Which of the following did NOT motivate Japan to build an empire?
      a. Japan was overcrowded and faced shortages of raw materials.
      b. Japan wanted the rich European colonies of Southeast Asia.
      c. Japan took over Manchuria and later fought for the heartland of China.
      d. The emperor wanted a larger empire to suit his divine status.

_____ 4. What was the U.S. response to Japanese aggression in Southeast Asia in mid-1941?
      a. declare war on Japan
      b. cut oil supplies to Japan
      c. broke off peace talks with Japan
      d. began a boycott of Japanese-made products

_____ 5. How were the Holocaust and Hitler's "Final Solution" related?
      a. They were both terms used by the Germans to describe their plan for permanent removal of the Jewish population.
      b. Holocaust is the term for the genocide that resulted from the plan called the "Final Solution."
      c. The "Final Solution" was the plan Hitler meant to follow after the Holocaust was complete.
      d. The Holocaust and the "Final Solution" were not related.

_____ 6. How did civilians join in the war effort?
      a. scrap metal drives   c. rationing
      b. working in war industries   d. all of the above

_____ 7. What was the Allies' plan for victory over the Nazis?
      a. The Allies focused their forces on North Africa to keep control of the oil.
      b. The Allies would join forces on the Eastern Front and invade Germany.
      c. The Allies would fight Germany on two fronts to weaken it.
      d. The Allies instigated *Operation Torch* to burn key points in Germany.

_____ 8. Why were thousands of U.S. citizens put in internment camps during the war?

a. They were radioing helpful information to the Germans.

b. They were of Japanese descent and falsely labeled as enemies.

c. They were of German descent and falsely labeled as enemies.

d. They had known of the attack on Pearl Harbor in advance.

_____ 9. Why did President Truman agree to use the atomic bomb?

a. to punish Japan for Pearl Harbor

b. to revenge those who died in the Bataan Death March

c. to destroy weapons plants in Japan

d. to bring the war to the quickest possible end

_____ 10. Which of the following is NOT a reason for the high number of displaced persons after the war?

a. Border changes caused people to find themselves in the wrong country.

b. The United States deported thousands of Japanese-Americans to Japan.

c. Prisoners of war tried to return to their homelands.

d. Holocaust survivors searched desperately for missing loved ones.

Part 2: Map Skills

Use the map to choose the best possible answer. (4 points each)

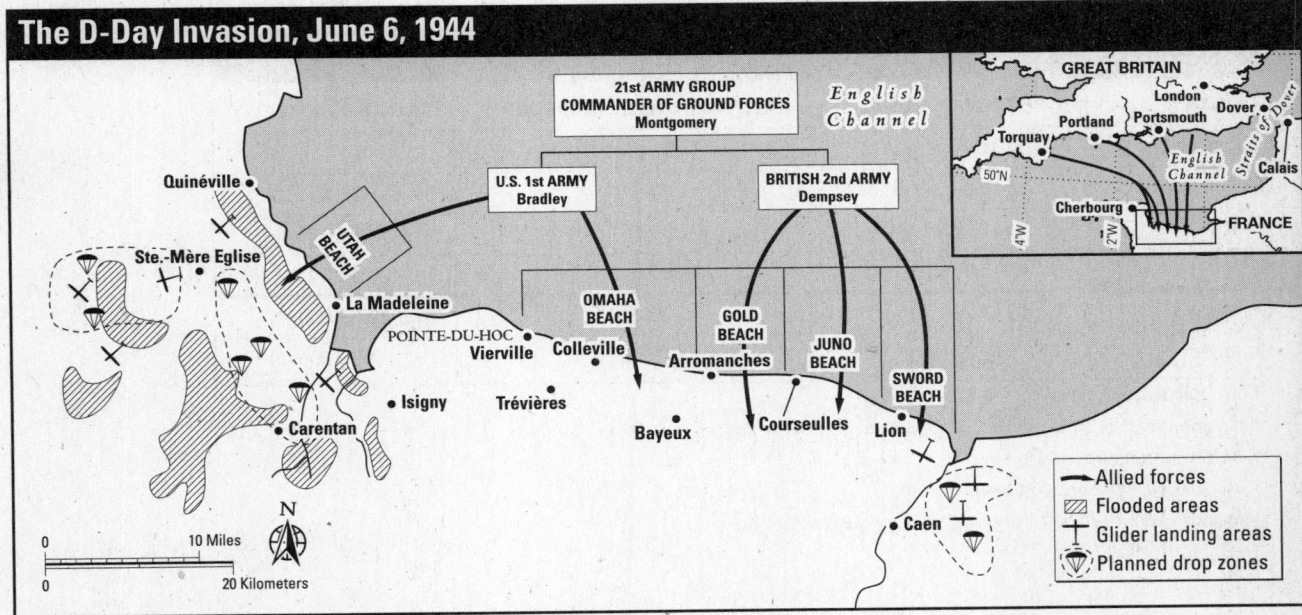

The D-Day Invasion, June 6, 1944

_____ 11. Which statement best describes the division of responsibility for beach landings?

a. The U.S. First Army demanded the most beachfront.

b. The British Second Army was given the most beachfront.

c. The assignment of beachfront was about evenly divided.

d. The assignment of beachfront was improperly divided.

_____ 12. How can the invasions east and west of Pointe-du-Hoc be contrasted?
       a. Four beaches were invaded on the east side as opposed to one on the west.
       b. The majority of gliders and airdrops occurred on the west side.
       c. The land to the west had many flooded areas, while the east was dry.
       d. all of the above

_____ 13. Which of the following did NOT occur during the D-Day invasion?
       a. The British Second Army landed at three beach sites, including Juno Beach.
       b. The Twenty-First group commander of ground forces was Montgomery.
       c. The U.S. First Army, under Dempsey, landed on two divided sites.
       d. Planned drop zones were organized in advance.

_____ 14. Approximately how many miles separate the westernmost drop zone from the easternmost drop zone?
       a. 52   b. 75   c. 80   d. 95

_____ 15. From which directions might the Germans advanced to stop the D-Day invasion?
       a. north and northeast   c. east and west
       b. south and southwest   d. west and east

Part 3: Interpreting Charts – Constructed Response

Answer the following questions on the lines provided. (4 points each)

Costs of World War II: Allies and Axis

COUNTRY	DIRECT WAR COSTS	MILITARY KILLED/MISSING	CIVILIANS KILLED
United States	$288.0 billion*	292,131 **	--
Great Britain	$117.0 billion	271,311	60,595
France	$111.3 billion	205,707 ***	173,260 †
USSR	$93.0 billion	13,600,000	7,720,000
Germany	$212.3 billion	3,300,000	2,893,000 ††
Japan	$41.3 billion	1,140,429	953,000

  * In 1994 dollars.
  ** An additional 115,187 servicemen died from non-battle causes.
  *** Before surrender to Nazis.
  † Includes 65,000 murdered Jews.
  †† Includes about 170,000 murdered Jews and 56,000 foreign civilians in Germany.

16. What was the difference between Allied and Axis civilian deaths?

_____

17. What percent of the civilians killed in Germany were Jews?

_____

18. Which of the countries listed in the chart does not include the number of military personnel killed or missing after surrender to Germany?

_____

19. What percent of the Axis direct war costs listed in the chart was spent by Japan?

_____

20. After the war, which two Allies might have had conflicting points of view about who gave the most to the war effort, and why?

_____

Part 4: Extended Response

Answer the following questions on the back of this paper or on a separate sheet. (10 points each)

21. **Analyzing Causes** What is one thing that Hitler or the Germans did that, in your opinion, was an important cause of Germany's defeat?

22. **Evaluating Decisions and Courses of Action** Was the United States right not to join the fight against Germany when Great Britain and France did? Explain your answer.

SECTION QUIZ *Cold War: Two Superpowers Face Off*

Section 1

A. Terms and Names Write the letter of the term or name that matches the statement. A term or name may be used more than once or not at all.

a. iron curtain   e. Cold War   i. U-2 incident
b. Warsaw Pact   f. United Nations   j. containment
c. NATO   g. Marshall Plan   k. *Sputnik I*
d. brinkmanship   h. *Apollo I*   l. Yalta agreement

_____ 1. This is an alliance between the United States, Canada, and ten Western European nations.

_____ 2. This is the name of the policy that aimed to prevent the spread of communism by blocking Soviet influence.

_____ 3. This term was used by Winston Churchill to represent the division between a mostly democratic Western Europe and a Communist Eastern Europe.

_____ 4. This names the first satellite to be launched into space by any country.

_____ 5. This was an alliance between the Soviet Union and its Eastern European allies.

_____ 6. This is an organization of nations set up after World War II, including both of the superpowers.

_____ 7. This was an alliance to which East Germany belonged but West Germany did not.

_____ 8. This is the policy of demonstrating willingness to engage in a war to protect national interests.

_____ 9. This is an economic aid package designed to give European nations the aid needed to rebuild after World War II.

_____ 10. This names a dispute between the Soviet Union and the United States that resulted from the shooting down of a spy plane.

_____ 11. This involved dividing Germany into sections controlled by the Soviet Union and the Western powers.

B. Extended Response Briefly answer the following question on the back of this paper.

What, in your opinion, were the positive results of the Marshall Plan?

Name _____ Date _____

CHAPTER 17

Section 2

SECTION QUIZ *Communists Take Power in China*

A. Terms and Names   Answer the following questions on the lines provided.

1. The Nationalists and Communists fought together against what nation during World War II?

   _____

2. Which side in China's civil war—the Communists or the Nationalists—had more support from the peasants?

   _____

3. Which side did the United States support with financial aid and weapons during the civil war?

   _____

4. What was the name of the island to which the Nationalist forces retreated at the end of the war?

   _____

5. What were the huge collective farms formed during the Great Leap Forward called?

   _____

6. What is the name of the campaign that was launched by China's leader in 1966 with the aim of restoring radical Communist values, and who was that leader?

   _____

B. Extended Response   Briefly answer the following question on the back of this paper.

   In your opinion, why did the Great Leap Forward fail?

CHAPTER 17

Section 3

SECTION QUIZ *Wars in Korea and Vietnam*

A. Terms and Names Write the letter of the term or name that best answers the question. A term or name may be used more than once or not at all.

a. Kim Il Sung
b. Ho Chi Minh
c. Harry Truman
d. Richard Nixon
e. Ngo Dinh Diem
f. Lyndon Johnson
g. Douglas MacArthur

h. Cambodia
 i. North Korea
 j. South Korea
k. North Vietnam
 l. South Vietnam
m. 17th parallel
n. 38th parallel

_____ 1. Which person was the original commander of the United Nations forces in the Korean War?

_____ 2. For which person was Saigon renamed following the fall of South Vietnam in 1975?

_____ 3. Which American publicly called for a nuclear attack on China as an extension of the Korean War?

_____ 4. Who was the leader of Communist North Vietnam?

_____ 5. In which country did the Khmer Rouge take control?

_____ 6. What was the border between North Korea and South Korea at the beginning of the Korean War?

_____ 7. Approximately where was the border set between North Korea and South Korea at the time of the cease-fire in the Korean War?

_____ 8. Who fired Douglas MacArthur?

_____ 9. In which country did the Vietcong do most of their fighting?

_____ 10. Which president called for the "Vietnamization" of the Vietnam War?

_____ 11. Who was the first leader of the anti-Communist government in South Vietnam?

_____ 12. Which country did the Soviet Union support during the Korean War?

B. Extended Response Briefly answer the following question on the back of this paper.

Do you think that the United States was justified in supporting the French imperialists who controlled Vietnam and, later, in supporting the corrupt government of South Vietnam? Explain.

CHAPTER
17

Section 4

SECTION QUIZ *The Cold War Divides the World*

A. Terms and Names Write the letter of the best answer.

_____ 1. During the Cold War, most Third World countries could have been accurately
described as being
    a. developing nations.
    b. established democracies.
    c. located in Eastern Europe.
    d. aligned with the United States.

_____ 2. During the Cold War, one of the nonaligned nations was
    a. Cuba.   c. Japan.
    b. India.   d. Poland.

_____ 3. The Bay of Pigs was a failed attempt to overthrow
    a. Fidel Castro.
    b. Fulgencio Batista.
    c. Anastasio Somozoa.
    d. Mohammed Reza Pahlavi.

_____ 4. The United States and the Soviet Union had a dangerous standoff over the
presence of Soviet missiles in
    a. Iraq.   c. Cuba.
    b. Iran.   d. Afghanistan.

_____ 5. Daniel Ortega was
    a. a U.S.-supported Nicaraguan dictator.
    b. a U.S.-supported El Salvadoran dictator.
    c. a leader of Contra forces in El Salvador.
    d. a Sandinista leader in Nicaragua.

_____ 6. Islamic revolutionaries held more than 60 Americans hostage for over a year in
    a. Iraq.   c. Turkey.
    b. Iran.   d. Afghanistan.

_____ 7. In 1979, the Soviet Union invaded
    a. Iraq.   c. China.
    b. Cuba.   d. Afghanistan.

B. Extended Response Briefly answer the following question on the back of this paper.

Think about Nicaragua, El Salvador, and Iran as examples of places where conflicts
occurred during the Cold War. What can you generalize about such conflicts? For
example, what was the government of such a nation typically like? What were typically
the goals of those who opposed that government? Why did the United States typically
support one side over the other?

SECTION QUIZ   *The Cold War Thaws*

A. Terms and Names   Write the letter of the best answer.

_____ 1. The goal of the Soviet policy known as destalinization was to
   a. purge the country of Stalin's memory.
   b. try to change the world's impression of Stalin.
   c. deny that Stalin had done what he was believed to have done.
   d. release satellite nations from political controls imposed by Stalin.

_____ 2. The Cuban missile crisis pitted Soviet leader Nikita Khrushchev against President
   a. Harry Truman.   c. John F. Kennedy.
   b. Richard Nixon.   d. Lyndon Johnson.

_____ 3. John F. Kennedy's immediate successor as U.S. president was
   a. Richard Nixon.   c. Jimmy Carter.
   b. Lyndon Johnson.   d. Ronald Reagan.

_____ 4. In the summer of 1968, forces from Warsaw Pact nations invaded
   a. China.   c. Afghanistan.
   b. Hungary.   d. Czechoslovakia.

_____ 5. The policy of détente was mainly intended to
   a. reduce Cold War tensions.
   b. restrict the spread of communism.
   c. call world attention to abuses of human rights.
   d. solidify U.S. relations with its economic allies.

_____ 6. The Strategic Defense Initiative (SDI) program was backed by
   a. Jimmy Carter.   c. Leonid Brezhnev.
   b. Ronald Reagan.   d. Nikita Khrushchev.

_____ 7. The first American president to visit Communist China was
   a. Jimmy Carter.   c. Richard Nixon.
   b. John F. Kennedy.   d. Lyndon Johnson.

B. Extended Response   Briefly answer the following question on the back of this paper.

What problems resulted from the Soviet attitude, expressed by Leonid Brezhnev, that the Soviet Union had the right to prevent its satellites from rejecting communism and the American attitude, demonstrated in Nicaragua, El Salvador, and Vietnam, that it had the right to prevent countries from becoming Communist?

CHAPTER 17   CHAPTER TEST   *Restructuring the Postwar World*

Form A

Part 1: Main Ideas

Write the letter of the best answer. (4 points each)

_____ 1. In the 1940s and 1950s, what did the region described as being "behind the iron
curtain" include?
   a. Soviet Union only
   b. Soviet Union and its satellite nations
   c. democratic nations of Western Europe
   d. German Democratic Republic, or East Germany

_____ 2. What was the purpose of the Truman Doctrine?
   a. to raise funds for Communist activities in Europe
   b. to create a Communist party in the United States
   c. to judge political parties that favored communism
   d. to support countries that rejected communism

_____ 3. What was the name of the alliance established by European Communist nations
in response to NATO?
   a. Iron Curtain
   b. Warsaw Pact
   c. Second World
   d. Union of Soviet Socialist Republics

_____ 4. Which two groups fought a civil war in China both before and after World War II?
   a. the peasants and the middle class
   b. the warlords and the emperor
   c. the nationalists and the Communists
   d. the socialists and the nationalists

_____ 5. During the Cultural Revolution, who were the "new heroes" of China?
   a. artists   c. intellectuals
   b. peasants   d. commune leaders

_____ 6. When did Chinese troops enter the war in Korea?
   a. when the UN voted to intervene
   b. when the fighting neared China's border
   c. when MacArthur's troops landed at Inchon
   d. when North Korean troops crossed the 38th parallel

_____ 7. What idea was the major justification for U.S. foreign policy during the Cold
War era?
   a. Vietnamization   c. nonaligned nations
   b. domino theory   d. Khmer Rouge

_____ 8. What were Third World countries?
        a. countries aligned with the United States and its allies
        b. countries aligned with the Soviet Union and its allies
        c. developing countries not aligned with the United States or Soviet Union
        d. countries with a gross national product higher than First and Second World
          countries

_____ 9. Which exiled leader led the religious opposition to Western influences in Iran?
        a. Ayatollah Ruholla Khomeini
        b. Shah Mohammed Reza Pahlavi
        c. Anastasio Somoza
        d. Fidel Castro

_____ 10. What was the Strategic Defense Initiative?
        a. a council created to create defense measures
        b. a failed operation to invade the Soviet Union
        c. a system to protect the United States against enemy missiles
        d. a program to weed out terrorist activity in the United States

Part 2: Map Skills

Using the map, place the letter of the correct answer next to each question. (4 points each)

The Warsaw Pact and NATO, 1955

_____ 11. What was the northernmost NATO member shown on this map?
      a. Turkey   c. Norway
      b. Ireland   d. United Kingdom

_____ 12. Name four Warsaw Pact countries that bordered NATO members.
   a. East Germany, Czechoslovakia, Bulgaria, Albania
   b. Portugal, Spain, France, Switzerland
   c. Turkey, Greece, Italy, Belgium
   d. Hungary, Poland, Romania, Spain

_____ 13. Which of the following Warsaw Pact countries shared a border with both a nonaligned country and a NATO member?
   a. Poland   b. Hungary   c. Albania   d. Romania

_____ 14. Which nonaligned countries lay between NATO and the Warsaw Pact?
   a. Sweden and Ireland   c. Spain and Switzerland
   b. Austria and Yugoslavia   d. France and Italy

_____ 15. Which group had the most coastline on the Mediterranean Sea?
   a. Warsaw Pact countries   c. nonaligned countries
   b. NATO members   d. all of the above

Part 3: Document Based Questions
Introduction

Historical Context: After World War II, revolution occurred in many places, including China, Cuba, and Vietnam. The United States became involved in the Vietnamese revolution to protect its interests in Southeast Asia and to keep Vietnam from becoming a Communist country. However, many Vietnamese wanted to reunite their country and fought hard, suffering tremendous numbers of casualties. As more and more American soldiers died and the United States was not able to secure a victory, Americans on all levels began to protest the war. The United States finally withdrew from Vietnam in 1973.

Task: Discuss the Vietnam War and its effect on the United States and Vietnam.

A. Short Answer

Study each document carefully and answer the questions that follow. (4 points each)

Document 1: "Who Am I?" by Tru Vu, a Vietnamese poet (translated by Nguyen Ngoc Bich)

I am neither a communist
nor a nationalist:
I am Vietnamese.
Is it not enough?
For thousands of years
that's what I've been:
Don't you think that's enough?
And Vietnam in flames
and mother who weeps
and youngsters who suffer
and all the terminology we use to kill each other!
O river
we stand on our respective banks
our fallen tears mingling.

16. Who do you think is speaking in this poem?

_____

Document 2: An excerpt from *In Retrospect* by President Johnson's secretary of defense Robert McNamara, from a report to Johnson in 1967

There may be a limit beyond which many Americans and much of the world will not permit the United States to go. The picture of the world's greatest superpower killing or seriously injuring 1000 noncombatants a week, while trying to pound a tiny backward nation into submission on an issue whose merits are hotly disputed, is not a pretty one. It could conceivably produce a costly distortion in the American national consciousness and in the world image of the United States—especially if the damage to North Vietnam is complete enough to be "successful."

17. What are noncombatants and why does McNamara talk about the war's effect on them?

_____

Document 3: Jules Feiffer cartoon from 1972

Jules Feiffer, *Village Voice*, June 4, 1972.

Source: Copyright © Jules Feiffer/Universal Press Syndicate.

18. Who do you think the three people on the television screens are, and why are they talking about the Vietnam War?

_____

B. Essay

19. Using information from the documents, your answers to the questions in Part A, and your knowledge of world history, write an essay that shows how the Vietnam War affected the United States and Vietnam over a long period of time. (8 points)

Part 4: Extended Response

Answer the following questions on the back of this paper or on a separate sheet. (10 points each)

20. **Drawing Conclusions** In what ways did the histories of the two superpowers affect their outlooks, goals, and fears about the postwar world? Support your answer.

    Think about:
    - their types of government
    - economic decline and recovery of both nations
    - impact of world wars on both nations

21. **Evaluating Decisions** What was at least one action that the United States should not have taken during the Cold War because its outcome had more negative effects than positive? Explain.

    Think about:
    - involvement in wars
    - support for foreign leaders
    - money spent on anti-Communist causes

CHAPTER
17

Form B

CHAPTER TEST   *Restructuring the Postwar World*

Part 1: Main Ideas
Write the letter of the best answer. (4 points each)

_____   1. Which European countries could receive aid through the Marshall Plan?
   a. any European country that needed it
   b. any European country that shared a border with iron curtain countries
   c. any European country that politically opposed the Soviet Union
   d. any European country that modeled its government after U.S. democracy

_____   2. What led the Soviets to blockade West Berlin?
   a. the formation of NATO
   b. a reunification of the three western zones of Germany
   c. Marshall Plan aid to West Germany
   d. the crash of a U2 spy flight over Soviet territory

_____   3. What event increased U.S. spending on education and technology?
   a. Cuban missile crisis
   b. establishment of the Warsaw Pact
   c. Chinese-Soviet treaty of friendship
   d. Soviet launching of a space satellite

_____   4. Which leader won China's civil war, and what name did he give to the country?
   a. Mao Zedong; People's Republic of China
   b. Jiang Jieshi; Republic of China
   c. the Dalai Lama; Tibet
   d. Zhou Enlai; New China

_____   5. What economic system was used to reshape China's economy after the civil war?
   a. laissez faire   c. social democracy
   b. communism   d. capitalism

_____   6. During the war in Korea, what did President Truman and Douglas MacArthur
   disagree strongly about?
   a. American involvement
   b. the use of nuclear weapons
   c. whether to attempt to cross the 38th parallel
   d. whether China posed a threat to South Korea

_____   7. Which of the following was NOT a tactic used by the superpowers during the Cold
   War to influence Third World nations?
   a. sponsored revolutions and counterrevolutions
   b. engaged in covert operations
   c. provided military aid and built schools
   d. threatened them with nuclear attack

_____ 8. Who were most of the Vietcong?
        a. pro-Communist South Vietnamese
        b. pro-Communist North Vietnamese
        c. anti-Communist South Vietnamese
        d. anti-Communist North Vietnamese

_____ 9. Why did the United States shift from a policy of brinkmanship to détente?
        a. The Soviet Union became a greater power.
        b. Nixon and Brezhnev signed the SALT I Treaty.
        c. The country needed to heal its internal conflicts over Vietnam.
        d. The U-2 crisis almost drew the United States into war.

_____ 10. How did the Cold War cause a change in U.S. policy toward Nicaragua?
        a. The United States gave aid to the Sandinistas but withdrew support when
           the Sandinistas aided Marxist rebels in El Salvador.
        b. The United States built a nuclear base there to deter Communists.
        c. The failed Bay of Pigs invasion ended U.S. military aid to Nicaragua.
        d. The Contra rebels in Nicaragua enlisted the aid of the Soviet Union, and
           the United States intervened to halt Communist support.

Part 2: Map Skills

Use the map to choose the best possible answer. (4 points each)

The Warsaw Pact and NATO, 1955

_____ 11. Which NATO member on this map is NOT primarily a European nation?
      a. Soviet   b. Sweden   c. Turkey   d. Portugal
          Union

_____ 12. Why was it relatively easy for the Soviets to cut off highway and rail traffic into West Berlin in 1948 and 1949?
      a. because Berlin was in the heart of East Germany
      b. because the Soviets had a superior military force
      c. because East Berlin did not oppose the Soviets
      d. all of the above

_____ 13. Which NATO members shared a common border with a nonaligned country?
      a. Bulgaria, Romania, Hungary, Portugal, France, Albania
      b. Netherlands, Italy, East Germany, Sweden, Austria, Yugoslavia
      c. Portugal, France, Italy, West Germany, Norway, Greece, United Kingdom
      d. United Kingdom, France, Belgium, Italy, Turkey, Denmark

_____ 14. What geographic feature is true of all the Warsaw Pact countries EXCEPT Albania?
      a. They all are in the northwestern part of Europe.
      b. They all border either the Black Sea or the Baltic Sea.
      c. They share a common border with another Warsaw Pact country.
      d. All of the above are true.

_____ 15. Which group controlled the LEAST territory in Europe?
      a. NATO members   c. nonaligned countries
      b. Warsaw Pact countries   d. none of the above

Part 3: Document Based Questions
Introduction

Historical Context: After World War II, revolution occurred in many places, including China, Cuba, and Vietnam. The United States became involved in the Vietnamese revolution to protect its interests in Southeast Asia and to keep Vietnam from becoming a Communist country. However, many Vietnamese wanted to reunite their country and fought hard, suffering tremendous numbers of casualties. As more and more American soldiers died and the United States was not able to secure a victory, Americans on all levels began to protest the war. The United States finally withdrew from Vietnam in 1973.

Task: Discuss the Vietnam War and its effect on the United States and Vietnam.

A. Short Answer

Study each document carefully and answer the questions that follow. (4 points each)

Document 1: "Who Am I?" by Tru Vu, a Vietnamese poet (translated by Nguyen Ngoc Bich)

I am neither a communist
nor a nationalist:
I am Vietnamese.
Is it not enough?
For thousands of years
that's what I've been:
Don't you think that's enough?
And Vietnam in flames
and mother who weeps
and youngsters who suffer
and all the terminology we use to kill each other!
O river
we stand on our respective banks
our fallen tears mingling.

16. What are three effects of the war described in the poem?

_____

Document 2: An excerpt from *In Retrospect* by President Johnson's secretary of defense Robert McNamara, from a report to Johnson in 1967

There may be a limit beyond which many Americans and much of the world will not permit the United States to go. The picture of the world's greatest superpower killing or seriously injuring 1000 noncombatants a week, while trying to pound a tiny backward nation into submission on an issue whose merits are hotly disputed, is not a pretty one. It could conceivably produce a costly distortion in the American national consciousness and in the world image of the United States—especially if the damage to North Vietnam is complete enough to be "successful."

17. What does McNamara fear in this excerpt? What does he mean by "an issue whose merits are hotly disputed"?

_____

Document 3: Jules Feiffer cartoon from 1972

Jules Feiffer, *Village Voice*, June 4, 1972.

Source: Copyright © Jules Feiffer/Universal Press Syndicate.

18. What happens to the figure watching the television from the first through the third panel? What does the cartoonist mean to suggest by this?

_____

B. Essay

19. Using information from the documents, your answers to the questions in Part A, and your knowledge of world history, write an essay that shows how the Vietnam War affected the United States and Vietnam over a long period of time. (8 points)

Part 4: Extended Response

Answer the following questions on the back of this page or on your own paper. (10 points each)

20. **Contrasting** How did the Cultural Revolution's concept of equality differ from the U.S. concept of equality stated in the "self-evident truth" that all people are created equal?

Think about:
- value of the individual as opposed to the group
- definition of equality
- methods of promoting equality

21. **Forming and Supporting Opinions** What do you think has prevented a third world war given the fact that World War I and World War II were only 20 years apart?

Think about:
- new types of weapons
- containment of regional wars
- the United Nations

CHAPTER TEST   *Restructuring the Postwar World*

Form C

Part 1: Main Ideas
Write the letter of the best answer. (4 points each)

_____ 1. Which of the following circumstances contributed to the breakdown of the alliance between the United States and the Soviet Union?
  a. Stalin's nonaggression pact with Hitler
  b. Stalin's unfulfilled promise of free elections
  c. Stalin's promise to aid in the war against Japan
  d. United States inclusion in the Security Council

_____ 2. What statement did Joseph Stalin make shortly after President Truman's succession?
  a. He said that communism and capitalism could not exist in the same world.
  b. He said that free elections could be held only if they benefited the Soviets
  c. He said that war between the United States and the Soviet Union was certain.
  d. all of the above

_____ 3. Which of the following worked together to produce similar goals?
  a. Truman Doctrine and containment
  b. NATO and the Warsaw Pact
  c. Marshall Plan and the iron curtain
  d. détente and brinkmanship

_____ 4. In what way did the existence of two Chinas intensify the Cold War between the United States and the Soviet Union?
  a. The People's Republic of China and the Soviet Union pledged to defend each other should the need arise.
  b. The United States and the Soviet Union fought to enlarge their spheres of influence in Asia, creating a divided Korea.
  c. The United States actively supported the Republic of China, and the Soviets did the same for the People's Republic of China.
  d. All of the above are true.

_____ 5. What were the long-term effects of the Cultural Revolution?
  a. establishment of communes where up to 25,000 people would live and work
  b. widespread chaos that closed down factories and threatened farm production
  c. dangerous border disputes between Communist China and the Soviet Union
  d. creation of the Red Guards, who acted as military police for Mao Zedong

_____ 6. What action did General MacArthur take during the Korean War that immediately led to his discharge?
        a. suggested that nuclear arms be used against North Korea
        b. was unable to stop the South Korean capital of Seoul from being captured
        c. attempted to use the press and Congress to go over the president's head
        d. allowed the Korean War to escalate to a war between China and the United States

_____ 7. What unexpected turn of events occurred in postwar Vietnam involving the United States?
        a. About 70,000 refugees settled in the United States.
        b. Communism remained the ruling political force in Vietnam.
        c. America expanded its trade embargo against the Vietnamese.
        d. Vietnam eventually accepted foreign investment from the United States.

_____ 8. How did the "Bay of Pigs" failure lead to the Cuban missile crisis?
        a. Khrushchev believed the United States was too weak to oppose Soviet expansion into Cuba.
        b. Kennedy announced a blockade of Cuba following the failure of the Bay of Pigs invasion.
        c. Castro protested his country's being used as a tool for the Cold War and asked Khrushchev to intervene.
        d. The Bay of Pigs troops were used to build the missile bases.

_____ 9. What was the primary goal for the Soviet Union's invasion of Afghanistan?
        a. to fight an indirect war with the United States
        b. to gain control of Middle Eastern oil supplies
        c. to reestablish the Communist regime in Afghanistan
        d. to cause the United States to boycott the 1980 Olympics

_____ 10. How did Brezhnev's leadership of the Soviet Union differ from that of Khrushchev?
        a. Khrushchev repressed dissent at home and abroad more than Brezhnev had.
        b. Brezhnev repressed dissent at home and abroad more than Khrushchev had.
        c. Brezhnev's policies were not as strongly felt on Eastern Europe as Khrushchev's.
        d. Khrushchev's policies were more directed toward Cuba than Brezhnev's had been.

Part 2: Map Skills

Use the map to choose the best possible answer. (4 points each)

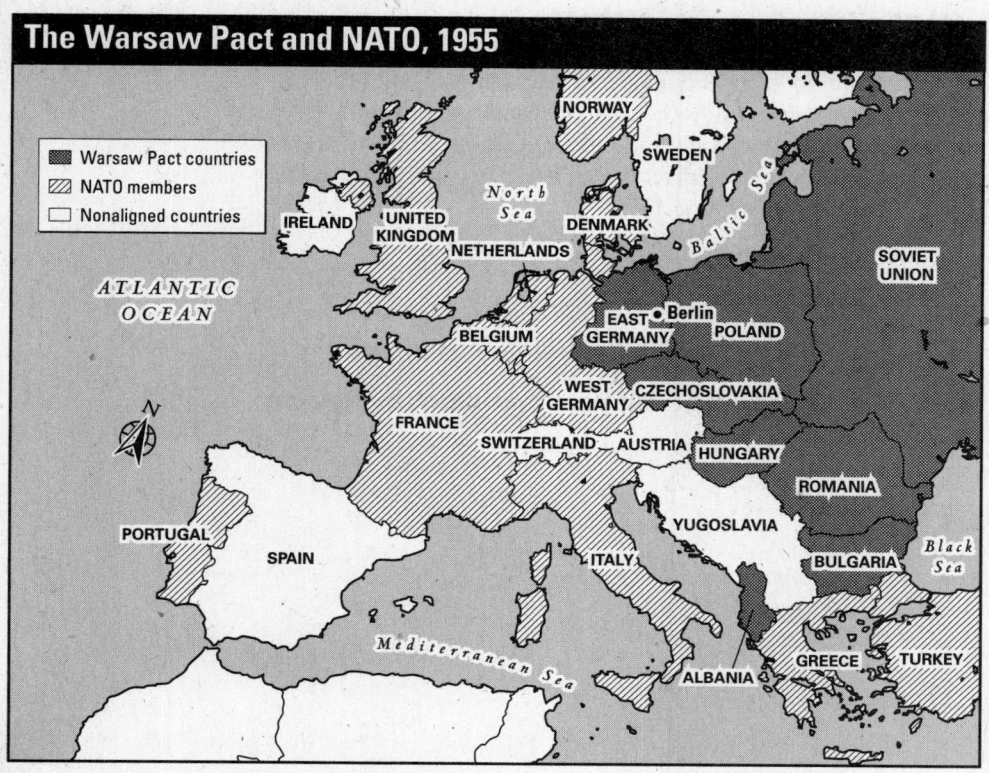

The Warsaw Pact and NATO, 1955

Legend:
- Warsaw Pact countries
- NATO members
- Nonaligned countries

_____ 11. Which country became divided due to Cold War influences?
    a. Spain   c. Austria
    b. Germany   d. United Kingdom

_____ 12. Which country on the map is the westernmost NATO member?
    a. Ireland   b. Portugal   c. Greece   d. Norway

_____ 13. Which body of water was most likely a site of Cold War tensions?
    a. Black Sea   c. North Sea
    b. Mediterranean Sea   d. Baltic Sea

_____ 14. Which neutral country would most fear being overrun if a shooting war broke out
    between NATO and Warsaw Pact countries?
    a. Ireland   b. Spain   c. Austria   d. Sweden

_____ 15. Why was an airlift needed to overcome the Soviet blockade of West Berlin?
    a. because West Berlin was too far from the nearest NATO member
    b. because Berlin was located well within the iron curtain
    c. because Berlin was a known Soviet stronghold
    d. because NATO members feared contact with the Soviets

Part 3: Document Based Questions
Introduction

Historical Context: After World War II, revolution occurred in many places, including China, Cuba, and Vietnam. The United States became involved in the Vietnamese revolution to protect its interests in Southeast Asia and to keep Vietnam from becoming a Communist country. However, many Vietnamese wanted to reunite their country and fought hard, suffering tremendous numbers of casualties. As more and more American soldiers died and the United States was not able to secure a victory, Americans on all levels began to protest the war. The United States finally withdrew from Vietnam in 1973.

Task: Discuss the Vietnam War and its effect on the United States and Vietnam.

A. Short Answer

Study each document carefully and answer the questions that follow. (4 points each)

Document 1: "Who Am I?" by Tru Vu, a Vietnamese poet (translated by Nguyen Ngoc Bich)

I am neither a communist
nor a nationalist:
I am Vietnamese.
Is it not enough?
For thousands of years
that's what I've been:
Don't you think that's enough?
And Vietnam in flames
and mother who weeps
and youngsters who suffer
and all the terminology we use to kill each other!
O river
we stand on our respective banks
our fallen tears mingling.

16. What do you think the poet is saying in the first three lines of the poem?

_____

Document 2: An excerpt from *In Retrospect* by President Johnson's secretary of defense Robert McNamara, from a report to Johnson in 1967

There may be a limit beyond which many Americans and much of the world will not permit the United States to go. The picture of the world's greatest superpower killing or seriously injuring 1000 noncombatants a week, while trying to pound a tiny backward nation into submission on an issue whose merits are hotly disputed, is not a pretty one. It could conceivably produce a costly distortion in the American national consciousness and in the world image of the United States—especially if the damage to North Vietnam is complete enough to be "successful."

17. Why does McNamara enclose the word *successful* in quotation marks?

_____

Document 3: Jules Feiffer cartoon from 1972

Jules Feiffer, *Village Voice*, June 4, 1972.

18. What happens to the figure watching TV in the final panel? How does this compare to the message being spoken on the television?

_____

B. Essay

19. Using information from the documents, your answers to the questions in Part A, and your knowledge of world history, write an essay that shows how the Vietnam War affected the United States and Vietnam over a long period of time. (8 points)

Part 4: Extended Response

Answer the following questions on the back of this paper or on a separate sheet. (10 points each)

20. **Synthesizing** What was the relationship between the nuclear arms race and the space race? Do you think the achievements in space travel and exploration would have been as remarkable without competition between the two superpowers? Explain.

21. **Analyzing Issues** What do you think accounts for the fact that American involvement in Korea was more direct and intense than its role in the civil war in China? Support your answer with details from the chapter.

CHAPTER 18

Section 1

SECTION QUIZ

The Indian Subcontinent Achieves Freedom

A. Terms and Names Write the letter of the name that matches the description. A name may be used more than once or not at all.

a. India
b. Pakistan
c. Kashmir
d. Sri Lanka
e. Bangladesh
f. Rajiv Gandhi

g. Indira Gandhi
h. Benazir Bhutto
i. Jawaharlal Nehru
j. Mohandas Gandhi
k. Lord Mountbatten
l. Muhammad Ali Jinnah

_____ 1. This nation was formerly known as East Pakistan.

_____ 2. This Congress Party leader was independent India's first prime minister.

_____ 3. This politician was twice elected prime minister of Pakistan but was removed from office in 1996.

_____ 4. The civil war between Tamils and others in this Buddhist-dominated country began in the early 1980s.

_____ 5. This Muslim League leader died shortly after becoming the first governor-general of independent Pakistan.

_____ 6. This former prime minister of India was assassinated by a Tamil terrorist in 1991 while campaigning for reelection.

_____ 7. This mostly Hindu country is the world's largest democracy.

_____ 8. This prime minister of India was assassinated by Sikh extremists in retaliation for ordering the attack on the Golden Temple.

_____ 9. Known as the Mahatma, or "Great Soul" of the Indian independence movement, this Congress Party leader was assassinated in 1948 by a Hindu extremist.

_____ 10. A cease-fire line established by the UN in 1949 left a third of this territory under Pakistani control and the rest under Indian control.

B. Extended Response Briefly answer the following question on the back of this paper.

What do you think Great Britain could—or should—have done to make the partition of India more efficient and less violent?

CHAPTER 18

Section 2

SECTION QUIZ *Southeast Asian Nations Gain Independence*

A. Terms and Names Write the letter of the term or name that best answers the question.
A term or name may be used more than once.

a. Suharto
b. Sukarno
c. Corazón Aquino
d. Aung San
e. Ferdinand Marcos
f. Aung San Suu Kyi
g. Great Britain
h. the Netherlands
i. the United States

_____ 1. Which imperialist nation colonized Burma (Myanmar)?

_____ 2. Which imperialist nation colonized Malaysia?

_____ 3. Which imperialist nation colonized Indonesia?

_____ 4. Which imperialist nation colonized Singapore?

_____ 5. Which imperialist nation colonized the Philippines?

_____ 6. Who proclaimed Indonesia's independence and named himself its first president?

_____ 7. Who put down an attempted coup in Indonesia and then seized power for himself?

_____ 8. Which Burmese pro-democratic leader won the Nobel Peace Prize in 1991 while under house arrest?

_____ 9. Which Burmese nationalists' army leader was killed by political rivals?

_____ 10. Who imposed an authoritarian regime in the Philippines and stole millions of dollars from the treasury before being forced into exile?

_____ 11. Which president of the Philippines left office after overseeing the ratification of a constitution and a shortening of military base leases?

_____ 12. Which leader turned Indonesia into a police state and frequently imposed martial law?

B. Extended Response Briefly answer the following question on the back of this paper.

Why do you suppose the leaders of newly independent nations in Southeast Asia tended to be repressive, corrupt, or both?

CHAPTER 18

Section 3

SECTION QUIZ *New Nations in Africa*

A. Terms and Names Write the letter of the term or name that matches the description. A term may be used once or not at all.

a. Ghana
b. Kenya
c. Congo
d. Algeria
e. Angola
f. FLN
g. MPLA
h. UNITA

i. Mau Mau
j. Negritude movement
k. Jomo Kenyatta
l. Leopold Senghor
m. Kwame Nkrumah
n. Ahmed Ben Bella
o. Mobutu Sese Seko

_____ 1. He became the first president of independent Kenya.

_____ 2. As a British colony, this nation was called the Gold Coast.

_____ 3. This was formed to celebrate African culture, heritage, and values.

_____ 4. This revolutionary group fought for and won Algeria's independence.

_____ 5. This former Belgian colony was named Zaire after its independence but took this name back again in 1997.

_____ 6. This first prime minister and later president-for-life of Ghana worked to promote African unity until he was overthrown in 1966.

_____ 7. This secret society was made up mostly of Kikuyu farmers determined to win back the lands seized by British settlers in Kenya.

_____ 8. This dictator of Zaire seized power in a bloodless coup in 1965 and was himself easily overthrown by opposition forces in 1997.

_____ 9. Independent Algeria's first prime minister and first president, he was overthrown after only two years.

_____ 10. This former Portuguese colony became a battleground in the Cold War when the Soviet Union and the United States took sides in its civil war.

_____ 11. This nation was once France's principal colony. In the early 1990s, civil war began after the ruling government rejected elections won by Islamic militants.

B. Extended Response Briefly answer the following question on the back of this paper.

In your opinion, is it fair to blame the European colonial powers for the violence that took place in Africa after they withdrew? Explain.

CHAPTER 18

Section 4

SECTION QUIZ *Conflicts in the Middle East*

A. Terms and Names Write the letter of the term or name that matches the description. A term may be used once or not at all.

a. PLO
b. intifada
c. Suez Crisis
d. Six-Day War
e. Yom Kippur War
f. Balfour Declaration

g. Golda Meir
h. Yasir Arafat
i. Anwar Sadat
j. Yitzhak Rabin
k. Hosni Mubarak
l. Menachem Begin

_____ 1. This is the name given to a 1917 letter from a British foreign secretary who seemed to make promises to both Zionists and Palestinians.

_____ 2. This occurred in 1956 when Egyptian president Gamal Nasser seized control of certain French and British business interests in Egypt.

_____ 3. This resulted in Israel's 1967 annexation of the Sinai Peninsula, the Golan Heights, Jerusalem, and the West Bank.

_____ 4. In 1978, this Israeli prime minister signed the Camp David Accords and agreed to return the Sinai Peninsula to Egypt.

_____ 5. This Egyptian president signed the Camp David Accords and recognized Israel as a legitimate state, enraging many Arabs.

_____ 6. This Egyptian president took office after the assassination of Anwar Sadat by Muslim extremists in 1981; he kept the peace with Israel.

_____ 7. In the 1970s and 1980s, this group's military wing conducted a violent campaign against Israel, which, in turn, bombed Palestinian towns thought to be the group's strongholds.

_____ 8. In the late 1980s, Palestinians began this "uprising," a campaign of civil disobedience that succeeded in putting international pressure on Israel.

_____ 9. This Palestinian leader took part in reaching the Oslo peace agreement.

_____ 10. This Israeli prime minister signed the Oslo peace agreement and was assassinated in 1995 by a Jewish extremist.

B. Extended Response Briefly answer the following question on the back of this paper.

Identify two key similarities and one key difference between the Camp David Accords and the Declaration of Principles signed after the Oslo peace talks.

Central Asia Struggles

CHAPTER 18
SECTION QUIZ

Section 5

A. Terms and Names Write the letter of the best answer.

_____ 1. What caused the emergence of nine independent nation states in Central Asia?
    a. the departure of Britain from Central Asia
    b. the collapse of the Ottoman Empire
    c. the departure of France from Central Asia
    d. the collapse of the Soviet Union

_____ 2. Which of the following make up the Transcaucasian Republics?
    a. Uzbekistan, Tajikistan, and Azerbaijan
    b. Armenia, Tajikistan, and Kazakhstan
    c. Armenia, Azerbaijan, and Georgia
    d. Georgia, Afghanistan, and Uzbekistan

_____ 3. Which of the following regions attempted to gain independence from Azerbaijan?
    a. the Hindu Kush region
    b. the Nagorno-Karabagh region
    c. the Kurdish region
    d. the Tian Shan region

_____ 4. Which of the following countries wanted access to the Indian Ocean through Afghanistan?
    a. Russia
    b. France
    c. Britain
    d. China

_____ 5. What is the name of the group that fought against the Soviet-supported government in Afghanistan?
    a. mujahideen
    b. Armenian Christians
    c. al-Qaieda
    d. Armenian Muslims

_____ 6. What is the name of the group that took control of Afghanistan in 1998?
    a. al-Qaida
    b. the Soviets
    c. the Taliban
    d. the Northern Alliance

B. Extended Response Briefly answer the following question on the back of this paper.

In Central Asia, which country has the best chance to build a solid economy? Why?

CHAPTER
18
Form A

CHAPTER TEST   *The Colonies Become New Nations*

Part 1: Main Ideas

Write the letter of the correct answer next to each question. (4 points each)

_____ 1. The dividing of India into two nations was referred to as
     a. the civil war.   c. the separation.
     b. the partition.   d. all of the above.

_____ 2. After gaining their independence, India and Pakistan fought a war over
     a. Kashmir.   c. New Delhi.
     b. Nepal.   d. East Punjab.

_____ 3. Pakistan began as a divided nation. Its east and west regions were separated by
     a. the Brahmaputra River.
     b. 1,000 miles of Indian territory.
     c. 500 miles of Afghan territory.
     d. the Krishna River.

_____ 4. After World War II, the greatest source of U.S.–Filippino conflict was
     a. U.S. trade relations with the Philippines.
     b. U.S. industrial interests in the Philippines.
     c. U.S. economic sanctions on the Philippines.
     d. U.S. military bases in the Philippines.

_____ 5. Which of the following is true of Burma's Aung San Suu Kyi?
     a. She is the daughter of a U.S. diplomat.
     b. She has been allowed to live freely.
     c. She has not won a Nobel Prize.
     d. She is active in the National League for Democracy.

_____ 6. French-speaking Africans and West Indians formed a movement to celebrate African culture, heritage, and values called
     a. Negritude.   c. Black Pride.
     b. African Peoples.   d. African Heritage.

_____ 7. The Mau Mau was
     a. a secret society that wanted to liberate Kenya from British rule.
     b. a Communist organization that wanted to rule Kenya.
     c. an alliance of tribes that wanted to liberate Kenya from French rule.
     d. an organization that wanted to set up a democratic government in Kenya.

_____ 8. The 1956 Suez Crisis began when
     a. the United States refused to give up control of the Suez Canal.
     b. the Soviet Union bombed the Suez Canal.
     c. Great Britain refused to make improvements to the Suez Canal.
     d. Egypt seized control of the Suez Canal.

_____ 9. The long-time dictator of the Congo (formally the Belgian Congo) was

      a. Mobutu Sese Seko.   c. Laurent Kabila.

      b. Jomo Kenyatta.   d. Ahmed Ben Bella.

_____ 10. In 1978, the Camp David Accords were signed by

      a. Anwar Sadat and Golda Meir.

      b. Anwar Sadat and Menachem Begin.

      c. Yasir Arafat and Yitzhak Rabin.

      d. Yasir Arafat and Menachem Begin.

Part 2: Map Skills

Using the map, answer the following questions. (4 points each)

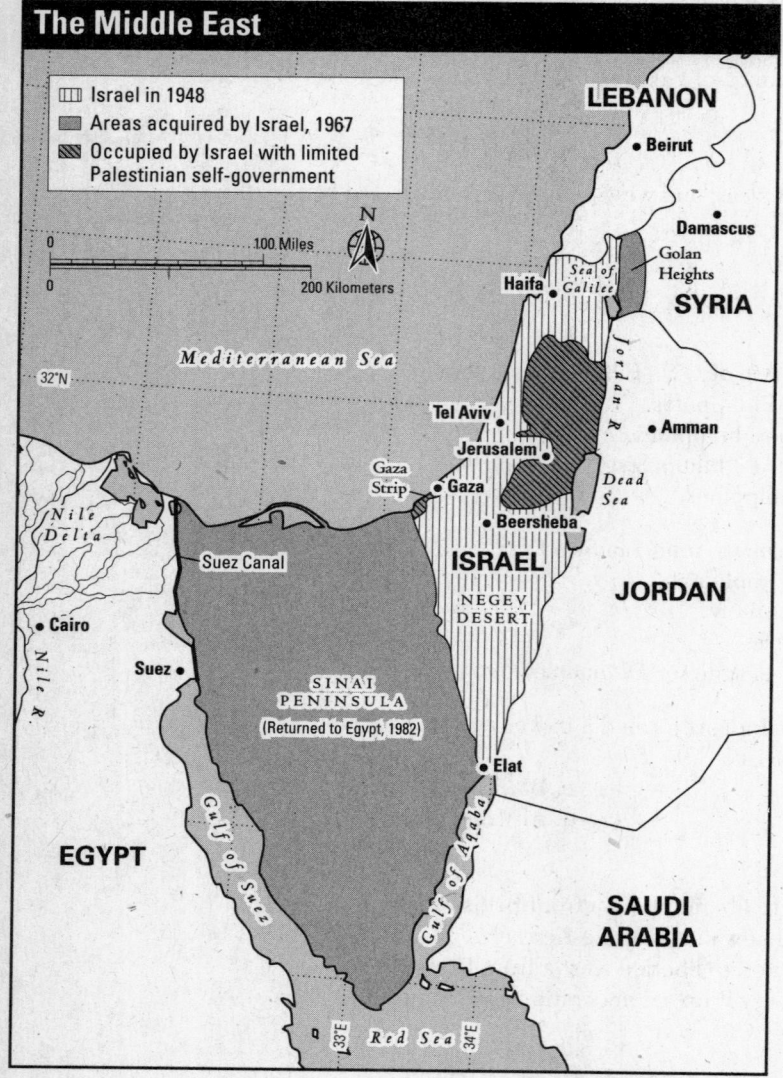

_____ 11. How many miles apart are Tel Aviv and Haifa?

      a. 40   b. 70   c. 85   d. 100

_____ 12. In 1967, which of the following did Israel acquire?
         a. the Nile Delta   c. the Golan Heights
         b. Syria   d. the Negev Desert

_____ 13. Which of the following covers the least area?
         a. the Sea of Galilee   c. the Gulf of Aqaba
         b. the Dead Sea   d. the Gulf of Suez

_____ 14. Which of the following borders the West Bank?
         a. Israel, the Sea of Galilee, and the Jordan River
         b. the Golan Heights, the Dead Sea, and the Jordan River
         c. Israel, the Dead Sea, and the Jordan River
         d. the Golan Heights, the Sea of Galilee, and the Jordan River

_____ 15. Which of the following cities is the furthest west?
         a. Beersheba   b. Jerusalem   c. Gaza   d. Haifa

Part 3: Interpreting Graphs

Using the graph, answer the following questions. (4 points each)

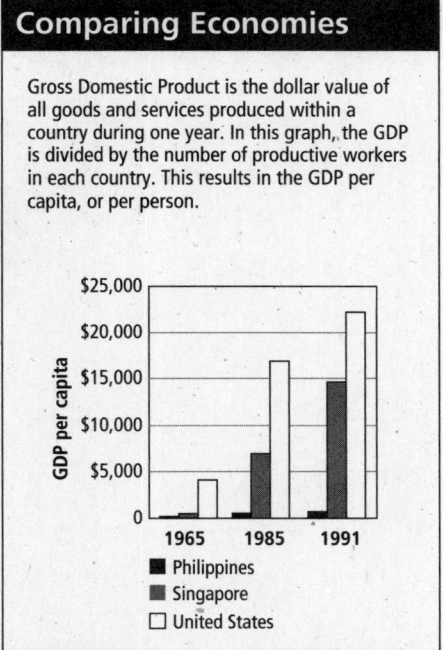

Comparing Economies

Gross Domestic Product is the dollar value of all goods and services produced within a country during one year. In this graph, the GDP is divided by the number of productive workers in each country. This results in the GDP per capita, or per person.

SOURCE: *World Statistics in Brief* (1978) and *World Statistics Pocketbook* (1995), published by the United Nations.

_____ 16. Approximately what was the GDP per capita of the United States in 1991?
        a. $6,000   b. $15,000   c. $22,000   d. $25,000

_____ 17. Which of the following had the lowest GDP per capita in 1985?
         a. Philippines
         b. Singapore
         c. the United States
         d. the Philippines and Singapore (about equal)

_____ 18. About how much did Singapore's GDP per capita increase from 1965 to 1985?
      a. $3,000   b. $6,000   c. $8,000   d. $10,000

_____ 19. About what was the Philippines' GDP per capita in 1965?
      a. $100   b. $1,000   c. $2,000   d. $5,000

_____ 20. In 1985, about how much higher was the GDP per capita in the United States than the GDP per capita in Singapore?
      a. $1,000   b. $5,000   c. $8,000   d. $10,000

Part 4: Extended Response

Answer the following questions on the back of this page or on your own paper. (10 points each)

21. **Recognizing Effects** What were some of the effects of the partition of India?

    Think about:
- the political effect
- the administrative effect
- the effect on Hindu and Muslim relations

22. **Analyzing Issues** After World War II, why was there conflict between the Israelis and Palestinians?

    Think about:
- effects of World War II
- the partition of Palestine
- Palestinian military action

Name _____ Date _____

CHAPTER
18
Form B

CHAPTER TEST *The Colonies Become New Nations*

Part 1: Main Ideas

Write the letter of the correct answer next to each question. (4 points each)

_____ 1. Which of the following two countries each had a civil war after independence?
        a. Pakistan and Angola   c. Pakistan and Israel
        b. India and Singapore   d. Angola and Singapore

_____ 2. Which of the following has caused much of the violence in Sri Lanka?
        a. a militant minority trying to overthrow a Communist regime
        b. a militant minority trying to achieve independence
        c. a militant majority trying to overthrow British rule
        d. a militant majority trying to achieve independence

_____ 3. How were the governments of Ferdinand Marcos and Mobutu Sese Seko similar?
        a. Both were elected into office.
        b. Both supported democracy.
        c. Both imposed strict authoritarian regimes.
        d. Both were forced out of office after a civil war.

_____ 4. The extremist Islamic group that seized control of Afghanistan during the 1990s
was known as the
        a. Taliban.
        b. Mau Mau.
        c. mujahideen.
        d. intifada.

_____ 5. Which of the following colonies became an independent city-state with a standard
of living far higher than any of its Southeast Asia neighbors?
        a. Burma   b. Malaysia   c. Indonesia   d. Singapore

_____ 6. Which of the following was influenced by communism?
        a. the political policy of Sukarno
        b. the Popular Movement for the Liberation of Angola
        c. the ideology of Aung San Suu Kyi
        d. all of the above

_____ 7. Which former colony of France was torn apart in the 1990s by a deadly civil war
between the government and Islamic militants?
        a. Ghana   b. Congo   c. Kenya   d. Algeria

_____ 8. Which of the following was NOT true of the intifada in the West Bank and
Gaza Strip?
        a. caused by Palestinian frustration about Israel
        b. involved attacks on Israeli soldiers
        c. involved boycotts and demonstrations by Palestinians
        d. caused Israel to declare war on Palestine

_____ 9. Which of the following resulted in the creation of an Israeli "buffer zone" consisting
of Jerusalem, the Sinai Peninsula, the Golan Heights, and the West Bank?
a. the first Arab-Israeli war   c. the Yom Kippur War
b. the Six-Day War   d. the Suez Crisis

_____ 10. Why did the UN fail in its plan to create a Palestinian State in the late 1940s?
a. The Palestinians objected to receiving only part of the Mandate of Palestine.
b. The new state of Israel immediately seized the territory for Palestine.
c. The Israelis did not agree on the borders for the Palestinian State.
d. The Palestinians could not agree on a government for the Palestinian State.

Part 2: Map Skills

Using the map, answer the following questions. (4 points each)

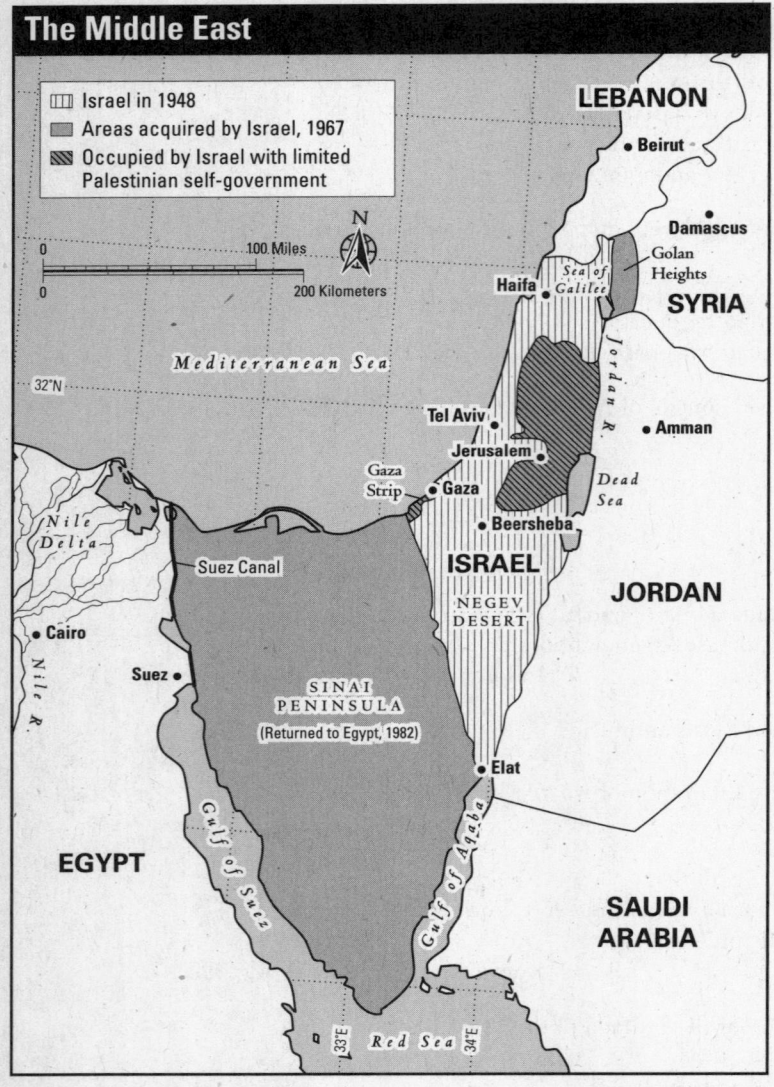

_____ 11. Which of the following cities provided Israel with access to the Red Sea?
a. Elat   b. Gaza   c. Suez   d. Amman

_____ 12. Which of the following cities probably had the highest potential for Arab and Israeli conflict?

    a. Cairo   b. Jerusalem   c. Haifa   d. Damascus

_____ 13. Which of the following areas acquired by Israel in 1967 did not come under Palestinian self-rule in 1994?

    a. the Gaza Strip   c. the Golan Heights
    b. the West Bank   d. all of the above

_____ 14. About how many hours would it take a plane flying at 200 miles per hour to travel from Haifa to Cairo?

    a. 1   b. 1.4   c. 2   d. 2.4

_____ 15. Which of the following separated the Gaza Strip from the West Bank?

    a. the Dead Sea   c. Israel
    b. the Sinai Peninsula   d. the Golan Heights

Part 3: Interpreting Graphs

Using the graph, answer the questions. (4 points each)

Comparing Economies

Gross Domestic Product is the dollar value of all goods and services produced within a country during one year. In this graph, the GDP is divided by the number of productive workers in each country. This results in the GDP per capita, or per person.

GDP per capita — 1965, 1985, 1991 — Philippines, Singapore, United States

SOURCE: *World Statistics in Brief* (1978) and *World Statistics Pocketbook* (1995), published by the United Nations.

_____ 16. How much did the GDP per capita of Singapore increase from 1965 to 1991?

    a. about $8,500   c. about $13,500
    b. about $10,000   d. about $15,500

_____ 17. Which of the following countries had the greatest economic growth from 1985 to 1991?
      a. the Philippines
      b. Singapore
      c. the United States
      d. Singapore and the United States (about equal)

_____ 18. In 1991, a citizen of which of the following countries would be least likely to own two TVs?
      a. the Philippines
      b. Singapore
      c. the United States
      d. the Philippines and Singapore (about equal)

_____ 19. What was the GDP per capita of the Philippines in 1985?
      a. about $500
      b. about $1,500
      c. about $2,500
      d. about $3,500

_____ 20. Which of the following probably had the highest export rate?
      a. the United States in 1965
      b. the Philippines in 1991
      c. Singapore in 1985
      d. Singapore in 1991

Part 4: Extended Response
Answer the following questions on the back of this page or on your own paper. (10 points each)

21. **Comparing and Contrasting** How were the 1978 Camp David Accords and the 1993 Declaration of Principles alike and different?

Think about:
- the way the meetings were held
- the participants of the meetings
- the results of the meetings

22. **Analyzing Motives** What motivated Aung San Suu Kyi to strive for democratic rule in Burma?

Think about:
- political conditions in Burma
- her ideological beliefs

Name _____   Date _____

CHAPTER **18**

Form C

CHAPTER TEST   *The Colonies Become New Nations*

Part 1: Main Ideas
Write the letter of the correct answer next to each question. (4 points each)

_____ 1. What influenced the independence movements of colonial countries?
   a. the spread of democratic ideas
   b. during World War II, the occasional defeat of Europeans by Japanese
   c. the expense of maintaining and governing distant colonies
   d. all of the above

_____ 2. Which of the following might have relocated after the partition of India?
   a. a Muslim in Pakistan   c. a Muslim in India
   b. a Hindu in India   d. a Sikh in Sri Lanka

_____ 3. Which of the following was caused by religious conflict?
   a. the civil war in Sri Lanka   c. the overthrow of Sukarno
   b. the assassination of   d. the U.S. invasion of
      Laurent Kabila   Afghanistan

_____ 4. What hindered the development of the Philippines after it gained independence?
   a. economic and political dependence on the United States
   b. the defeat of Ferdinand Marcos in 1986 election
   c. investments with the Japanese
   d. all of the above

_____ 5. Which of the following has contributed to Singapore's high standard of living?
   a. Singapore has one of the busiest ports in the world.
   b. Singapore has a Socialist economy.
   c. Singapore receives economic aid from the United Nations.
   d. Singapore defeated Malaya in a war.

_____ 6. During the late 1900s, how were the Philippines, Myanmar, and Algeria similar?
   a. They all established a democratic government.
   b. They all established a Communist government.
   c. They all had rulers who refused to accept the results of an election.
   d. They all had rulers who came to power through a political coup.

_____ 7. Which nation is part of the Central Asian Republics?
   a. Armenia
   b. Tajikistan
   c. Azerbaijan
   d. Georgia

_____ 8. In which of the followings ways were the Mau Mau and the PLO similar?
        a. Both fought for the liberation of their respective peoples.
        b. Both fought against a European colonial power.
        c. Both formed alliances with their opponents.
        d. Both objected to the partitioning of their country.

_____ 9. How were the assassinations of Yitzhak Rabin and Anwar Sadat similar?
        a. The assassins came from a rival ethnic group to the leaders.
        b. Each assassin came from an enemy government.
        c. Each assassin came from the leader's own religion.
        d. The assassins and leaders knew each other well.

_____ 10. How did the Declaration of Principles affect Palestinians living in Gaza in 1993?
        a. They were able to elect their own political representatives.
        b. They had to relocate to the West Bank.
        c. They received financial support from the United States.
        d. They boycotted Israel and all countries that support Israel.

Part 2: Map Skills

Using the map, answer the following questions. (4 points each)

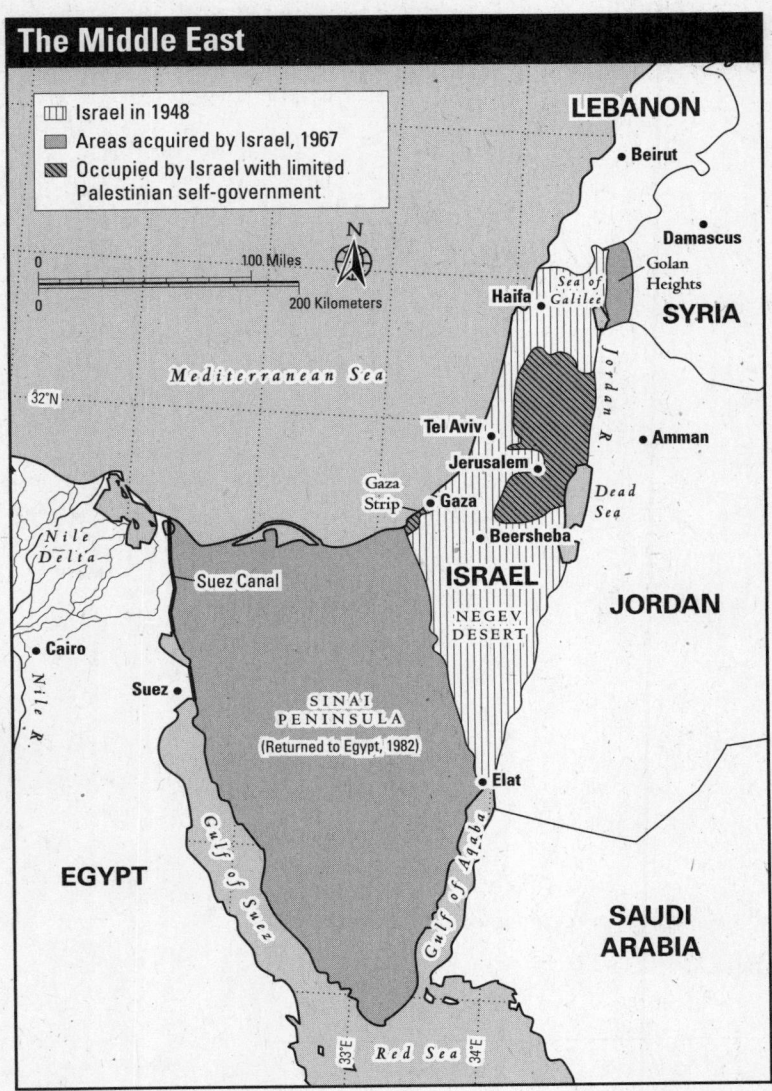

The Middle East

Israel in 1948
Areas acquired by Israel, 1967
Occupied by Israel with limited Palestinian self-government

LEBANON
• Beirut
• Damascus
Golan Heights
SYRIA
Haifa • *Sea of Galilee*
Mediterranean Sea
32°N
Tel Aviv •
Jerusalem •
Gaza Strip • Gaza
• Amman
Dead Sea
• Beersheba
Jordan R.
ISRAEL
NEGEV DESERT
JORDAN
Nile Delta
Suez Canal
• Cairo
Suez •
SINAI PENINSULA
(Returned to Egypt, 1982)
• Elat
EGYPT
Gulf of Suez
Gulf of Aqaba
SAUDI ARABIA
100 Miles
200 Kilometers
33°E *Red Sea* 34°E

_____ 11. Which country would govern a person living in the Sinai in 1980?

    a. Egypt   b. Israel   c. Syria   d. Jordan

_____ 12. For Arabs living in Haifa, which of the following countries would be the closest destination for migration to an Arab state?

    a. Egypt   b. Jordan   c. Syria   d. Lebanon

_____ 13. Where and when would a person most likely protest for Arab self-rule?

    a. the West Bank in 1996   c. the West Bank in 1989

    b. Egypt in 1992   d. Egypt in 1998

_____ 14. What has probably been the site of much Israeli and Syrian conflict?

    a. the West Bank   c. the Golan Heights

    b. the Sinai Peninsula   d. the Gaza Strip

_____ 15. Which region of Israel is probably the most sparsely populated?

   a. south   b. central   c. north   d. west

Part 3: Interpreting Graphs—Constructed Response

Using the graph, answer the questions. (4 points each)

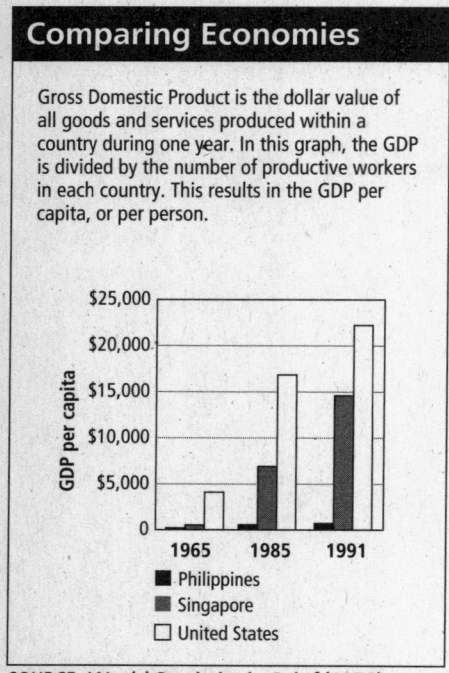

Comparing Economies

Gross Domestic Product is the dollar value of all goods and services produced within a country during one year. In this graph, the GDP is divided by the number of productive workers in each country. This results in the GDP per capita, or per person.

GDP per capita

$25,000
$20,000
$15,000
$10,000
$5,000
0

1965   1985   1991

■ Philippines
■ Singapore
□ United States

SOURCE: *World Statistics in Brief* (1978) and *World Statistics Pocketbook* (1995), published by the United Nations.

16. Of the countries listed in the graph, which had the highest percentage of skilled workers? Give a reason for your answer based on the graph.

   _____

17. Of the countries listed in the graph, which two were the most economically competitive? Give a reason for your answer based on the graph.

   _____

18. Of the countries listed in the graph, which probably exported the least manufactured goods? Explain your answer.

   _____

19. In 1991, would a citizen from the Philippines or Singapore be more likely to own a compact disc player? Give a reason for your answer based on the graph.

_____

20. Of the countries listed in the graph, which had the slowest economic development? Give a reason for your answer based on the graph.

_____

Part 4: Extended Response

Answer the following questions on the back of this page or on your own paper. (10 points each)

21. **Hypothesizing** After gaining independence, what were the challenges faced by African nations in establishing stable governments? Support your answer with examples from the text.

22. **Making Inferences** Oppressive regimes took over many of the countries of Southeast Asia after they gained independence. What are three reasons for this? Give examples from the text to support your answer.

Name _____ Date _____

A. Terms and Names Write the letter of the best answer.

_____ 1. The problems caused by developing Brasilia as a new capital city were mainly
a result of
   a. the cost of construction.
   b. excessive foreign influence.
   c. conflict over the city's location.
   d. Brazilians' resistance to change.

_____ 2. The land reform that the Brazilian government proposed involved
   a. forbidding foreign investment in the Amazon.
   b. combining small plots into large communal farms.
   c. converting large amounts of the rainforest to farm land.
   d. breaking up large estates to provide land grants for peasants.

_____ 3. During the recession that Brazil experienced in the early 1980s, business
activity
   a. boomed.
   b. leveled off.
   c. slowed down.
   d. grew slowly but steadily.

_____ 4. People's "standard of living" is measured by
   a. their level of contentment.
   b. the stability of their income.
   c. the extent of their civil liberties.
   d. the amount of goods they have.

_____ 5. The PRI in Mexico was, for more than 30 years, all of the following EXCEPT
   a. a force for political stability.
   b. the only legal political party.
   c. the controlling political party.
   d. the party affiliation of Mexico's president.

B. Extended Response Briefly answer the following question on the back of this paper.

Name one right or one responsibility that you think is critical to maintaining a
democracy. What makes it so important?

Name _____   Date _____

CHAPTER
19

Section 2

SECTION QUIZ   *The Challenge of Democracy in Africa*

A. Terms and Names If the statement is true, write "true" on the line. If it is false, change the underlined word or words to make it true.

Example: In its recent history, Nigeria has suffered from distrust and bitterness among its <u>ethnic</u> groups. _____*true*_____

Example: Many newly independent African nations faced difficulties because of a history of <u>Communist</u> rule. _____*colonial*_____

1. In Nigeria's short-lived <u>federal system</u>, power was shared by the central government and regional governments. _____

2. In 1966, a group of army officers overthrew the central Nigerian government in Lagos, abolished the regional governments, and declared a state of <u>civil</u> law. _____

3. Nigeria went to war in 1967 when Biafra attempted to <u>invade</u>. _____

4. Dissidents are people who <u>oppose</u> government policy. _____

5. <u>Desmond Tutu</u> was jailed for 27 years for his activities with the African National Congress but later became South Africa's president. _____

6. South Africa began moving toward significant political reform under the presidency of <u>F. W. de Klerk</u>. _____

7. In April 1994, South Africa held the first elections in which <u>women</u> were allowed to vote. _____

B. Extended Response Briefly answer the following question on the back of this paper.

Economic protests against apartheid ranged from multinational trade restrictions to the refusal of small companies, and even individuals, to invest in banks or corporations that did business in South Africa. Why do you suppose so many people and countries had such negative reactions to apartheid, and why did their economic protests work?

CHAPTER 19

Section 3

SECTION QUIZ   *The Collapse of the Soviet Union*

A. Terms and Names Write the letter of the best answer.

_____ 1. Before 1990, the most powerful policy-making body in the Soviet Union was
        a. the Politburo.
        b. the Parliament.
        c. the Supreme Soviet.
        d. the Central Committee.

_____ 2. The reforms that led to democratization of the Soviet Union were begun by
        a. Joseph Stalin.   c. Leonid Brezhnev.
        b. Victor Grishin.   d. Mikhail Gorbachev.

_____ 3. All of the following occurred in response to glasnost EXCEPT
        a. decreased censorship.
        b. the release of imprisoned dissidents.
        c. the privatization of small businesses.
        d. criticism of the government by the media.

_____ 4. The purpose of perestroika was to
        a. reduce criminal activity.
        b. revive the Soviet economy.
        c. allow a free exchange of ideas.
        d. open up the Soviet political system.

_____ 5. The end result of the August coup attempt was to increase the power of
        a. Boris Yeltsin.   c. Mikhail Gorbachev.
        b. the Soviet Union.   d. the State Committee.

_____ 6. Members of the Commonwealth of Independent States, or CIS, had all
    formerly been
        a. Russian colonies in   d. part of the Union
           Europe and Asia.   of Soviet Socialist
        b. so-called "satellites"   Republics.
           of the Soviet Union.
        c. Eastern European
           allies of the Soviet
           Union.

B. Extended Response Briefly answer the following question on the back of this paper.

Why do you suppose that allowing the free exchange of ideas led to the democratization of the Soviet Union?

Name _____ Date _____

CHAPTER
19
Section 4

SECTION QUIZ *Changes in Central andEastern Europe*

A. Terms and Names Write the letter of the best answer.

_____ 1. After the Communist Party in his nation lost power, Lech Walesa became the first freely elected leader of
   a. Poland.
   b. Hungary
   c. Romania.
   d. Czechoslovakia.

_____ 2. Although the group known as Solidarity eventually obtained wide public support and political power, it began as simply an organization of
   a. workers.
   b. radical reformers.
   c. political dissidents.
   d. frustrated shoppers.

_____ 3. Some European nations were hesitant to support the reunification of Germany because of fears that it would
   a. support communism.
   b. attempt to dominate Europe.
   c. require significant foreign aid.
   d. be politically unstable.

_____ 4. Vaclav Havel was elected president of
   a. Poland.
   b. Hungary.
   c. Romania.
   d. Czechoslovakia.

_____ 5. Yugoslavia was led from 1945 to 1980 by
   a. Lech Walesa.
   b. Helmut Kohl.
   c. Nicolae Ceausescu.
   d. Josip Tito.

_____ 6. The brutal policy of ethnic cleansing was most widely used against
   a. Slovenes.
   b. Bosnian Serbs.
   c. Bosnian Muslims.
   d. Croatia's Serbian minority.

B. Extended Response Briefly answer the following question on the back of this paper.

In your opinion, is the world a better place as a result of the changes in Central and Eastern Europe? Explain.

CHAPTER 19

Section 5

SECTION QUIZ   *China: Reform and Reaction*

A. Terms and Names Write the letter of the best answer.

_____ 1. The main purpose of the Cultural Revolution was to
     a. modernize the Chinese economy.
     b. strengthen ties with the Soviet Union.
     c. preserve revolutionary Communist values.
     d. increase China's technological capabilities.

_____ 2. The Chinese premier who made the first overtures toward establishing a more
open relationship with the West was
     a. Zhou Enlai.   c. Jiang Zemin.
     b. Mao Zedong.   d. Deng Xiaoping.

_____ 3. The program that Deng Xiaoping embraced and referred to as the "second
revolution" included the goals of the
     a. Cultural Revolution.   c. Great Leap Forward.
     b. First Five-Year Plan.   d. Four Modernizations.

_____ 4. The students who were killed in Tiananmen Square were protesting the
Chinese government's
     a. takeover of Hong Kong.
     b. lack of political freedom.
     c. imprisonment of the Gang of Four.
     d. abandonment of Communist values.

_____ 5. The government's response to the protest in Tiananmen Square resulted
in all of the following EXCEPT the
     a. arrests of thousands of dissidents.
     b. preservation of Deng Xiaoping's power.
     c. disruption of China's economic progress.
     d. massacre of hundreds of student demonstrators.

_____ 6. Mao Zedong, Zhou Enlai, and Deng Xiaoping were all
     a. strong supporters of the Cultural Revolution.
     b. political conservatives but economic moderates.
     c. political moderates but economic conservatives.
     d. participants in the war between Communists and Nationalists.

B. Extended Response Briefly answer the following question on the back of this paper.

The USSR abandoned communism in order to achieve economic growth. How did
China's path compare to that of the USSR, and what problems arose within China as a
result the path it took?

CHAPTER TEST   *Struggles for Democracy*

Form A

Part 1: Main Ideas

Write the letter of the best answer. (4 points each)

_____ 1. What prompted the Brazilian government to open up Brazil's political system?
a. The economy grew substantially.
b. The economy fell into a recession.
c. A new civilian president was elected.
d. Corruption charges were brought against the government.

_____ 2. Which of the following is NOT a basic practice needed for democracy to work?
a. free elections
b. constitutional government
c. citizen participation
d. a presidency

_____ 3. What happened after the Nigerian military promised to bring back civilian rule in 1993?
a. A civilian government was elected and began a program of gradual democratic reform.
b. Dissidents called for the military to stay in power to control ethnic conflict.
c. A popular leader was elected president, but then the military threw him in jail.
d. The military canceled the elections, and they were never held.

_____ 4. What was apartheid?
a. a South African policy separating the races
b. a policy of open discussion proposed by Gorbachev
c. an abrupt shift to free-market economics in Czechoslovakia
d. a gradual opening of the Soviet political system

_____ 5. Under which program did Gorbachev attempt to modify the economic structure of the Soviet economy by allowing some private enterprise?
a. glasnost   c. perestroika
b. shock therapy   d. modernization

_____ 6. What caused the two Germanys to reunify?
a. the fall of the Berlin wall
b. the fall of communism in East Germany
c. the crumbling economy of East Germany
d. Kohl's assurances that Germany had learned from the past

_____ 7. Who became the Russian Republic's first elected president?
a. Vaclav Havel   c. Mikhail Gorbachev
b. Egon Krenz   d. Boris Yeltsin

_____ 8. What was it called when Bosnian Serbs used violence to rid Bosnia of its Muslims?
    a. revolution   c. ethnic cleansing
    b. militarism   d. shock therapy

_____ 9. What did the Four Modernizations call for?
    a. progress in agriculture, industry, defense, and science and technology
    b. improvement in social structuring, education, political reforms, and wages
    c. an exploration of socialists' ideas to further the economy of China
    d. a revolution from China's educated youth to reform political policies

_____ 10. What led Chinese students to demand democratic reform?
    a. the visit by U.S. president Richard Nixon
    b. economic reforms that allowed Western ideas into China
    c. the breakup of the Soviet Union and election of Yeltsin
    d. the fall of the Berlin Wall and reunification of Germany

Part 2: Map Skills

Use the map to choose the best possible answer. (4 points each)

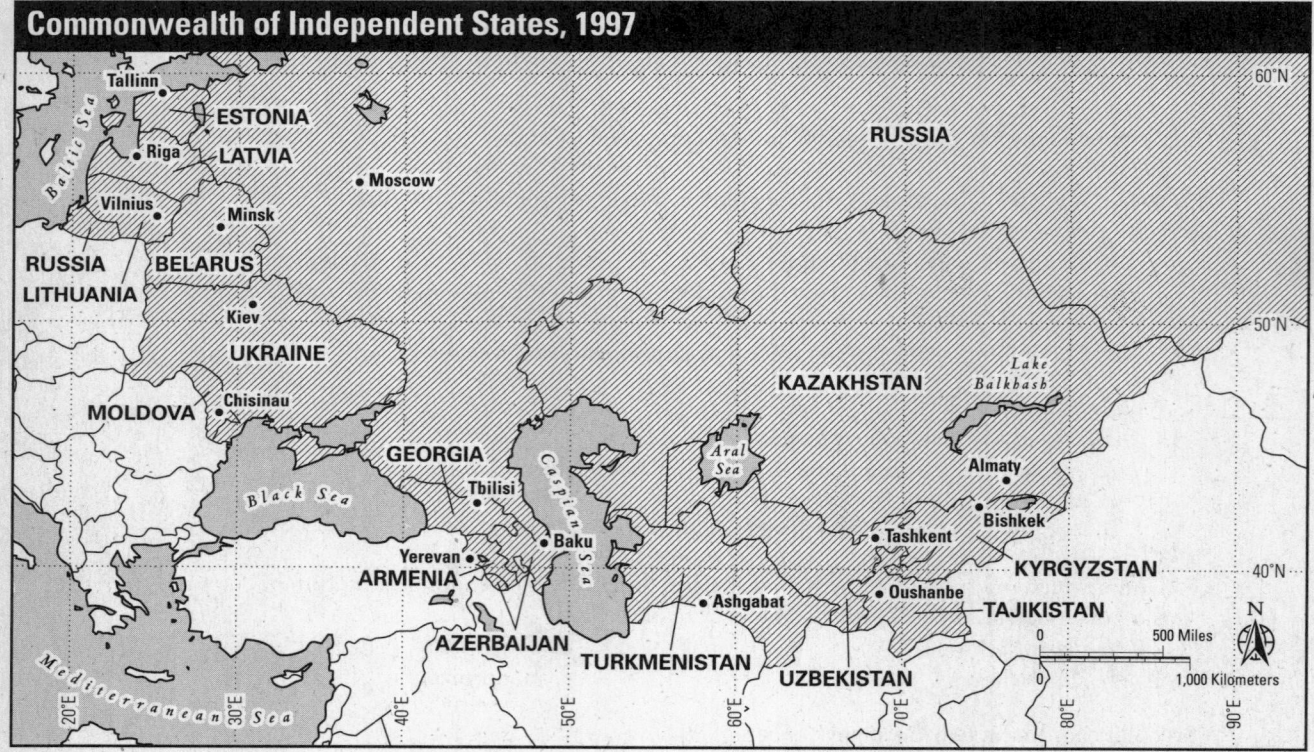

Commonwealth of Independent States, 1997

_____ 11. Which former Soviet republic shares a border with the greatest number of other
republics?
    a. Georgia   b. Kazakhstan   c. Russia   d. Ukraine

_____ 12. How many of the 15 republics border the Caspian Sea?
    a. four   b. five   c. six   d. seven

_____ 13. In which direction can Kiev be found from Moscow?
     a. east   c. northeast
     b. west   d. southwest

_____ 14. Along which body of water can Tallin be found?
     a. Aral Sea   c. Baltic Sea
     b. Black Sea   d. Lake Balkhash

_____ 15. Which republic has a small separate territory west of Lithuania?
     a. Russia   c. Latvia
     b. Belarus   d. Moldova

Part 3: Interpreting Political Cartoons

Write the letter of the best answer. (4 points each)

Source: Tony Auth, Philadelphia Inquirer. Copyright © 1989. Reprinted with permission of Universal Press Syndicate. All rights reserved

_____ 16. What is this cartoon about?
     a. the ill health of three political leaders
     b. the creation of the Soviet Union
     c. the collapse of communism
     d. a people's revolution

_____ 17. Who is the man on the far right dressed as a doctor?
   a. Lech Walesa
   b. Joseph Stalin
   c. Mikhail Gorbachev
   d. Deng Xiaoping

_____ 18. What belief about China was the cartoon expressing?
   a. that the Chinese government is in decline
   b. that the Chinese leader is going to die
   c. that Poland and the USSR will outlast China
   d. that communism is dead in China

_____ 19. According to the cartoon, in which country was communism likely to survive?
   a. Poland
   b. China
   c. Soviet Union
   d. all of the above

_____ 20. This cartoon was published June 7, 1989. Which of the cartoonist's predictions about communism were accurate?
   a. Communism did end in China.
   b. Communism did end in Poland.
   c. Communism did not end in the Soviet Union.
   d. All the predictions were accurate.

Part 4: Extended Response

Answer the following questions on the back of this paper or on a separate sheet. (10 points each)

21. **Analyzing Causes and Recognizing Effects** How did the changes encouraged by Mikhail Gorbachev lead to the breakup of the Soviet Union?

   Think about:
   • the effect of glasnost
   • the effect of perestroika
   • the effect of democratization

22. **Analyzing Issues** What are the four main practices needed for democracy to succeed? For each practice, name a country that is a successful or unsuccessful example, and explain briefly.

   Think about:
   • form of government
   • treatment of citizens
   • responsibilities of citizens

CHAPTER TEST **Struggles for Democracy**

CHAPTER 19

Form B

Part 1: Main Ideas
Write the letter of the best answer. (4 points each)

_____ 1. What prompted the generals of Argentina to step down and allow free elections?
    a. The military ousted Perón and drove him into exile.
    b. The military suffered a humiliating defeat over the Falkland Islands.
    c. They established a brutal dictatorship and hunted down political opponents.
    d. The government was known for pushing people out of airplanes.

_____ 2. Which of the following were obstacles to Latin American nations establishing democratic governments?
    a. powerful militaries   c. sharp class divisions
    b. single-crop economies   d. all of the above

_____ 3. Which of the following events did NOT contribute to the fall of the Berlin Wall?
    a. The governments of East and West Germany began to discuss reunification.
    b. The Hungarian government allowed East Germans to cross its border into Austria.
    c. The East German government closed its borders, sparking protests.
    d. Erich Honecker lost his authority and resigned as Communist Party boss.

_____ 4. Which of the following factors led to war among Nigerians?
    a. government opposition   c. martial law
    b. ethnic divisions   d. the federal system

_____ 5. Aside from trade restrictions, what was another way that foreign nations opposed South Africa's policy of apartheid?
    a. U.S. naval blockade of South Africa
    b. ejection of South Africa from the UN
    c. exclusion from the Olympic Games
    d. all of the above

_____ 6. What action did Poland accomplish successfully before any other nation?
    a. create a government of Communist and democratic leaders
    b. remove a Communist regime from office peacefully
    c. revive a crumbling economy under martial law
    d. establish a socialist party in a Communist country

_____ 7. What was significant about the outcome of the August coup in the Soviet Union?
    a. Gorbachev was released and was able to carry on with his reforms.
    b. The Communist Party disbanded in favor of constitutional government.
    c. The military crushed the protesters but sparked worldwide outrage.
    d. The Soviet people lost their fear and defended their freedoms.

_____ 8. What effect did the end of Communist rule have on Yugoslavia?
        a. Without communism as a unifier, ethnic hatred tore the country apart.
        b. Without communism acting to repress free speech, art began to flourish.
        c. Communists began using ethnic cleansing against democratic leaders.
        d. After the Communists fell, four republics peacefully gained independence.

_____ 9. What was the result of the student protest in Tiananmen Square?
        a. It weakened the Communist government and established democracy.
        b. It showed the students' poor education and embarrassed the country.
        c. The military arrested, killed, and wounded hundreds of protesters.
        d. The state used the media to misrepresent the protesters' cause.

_____ 10. What did China promise to do when it regained rule of Hong Kong?
        a. reestablish a Communist government
        b. respect the economic system and political liberties
        c. deport all non-Chinese people from the city
        d. establish a separate ruling party for Hong Kong

Part 2: Map Skills

Use the map to choose the best possible answer. (4 points each)

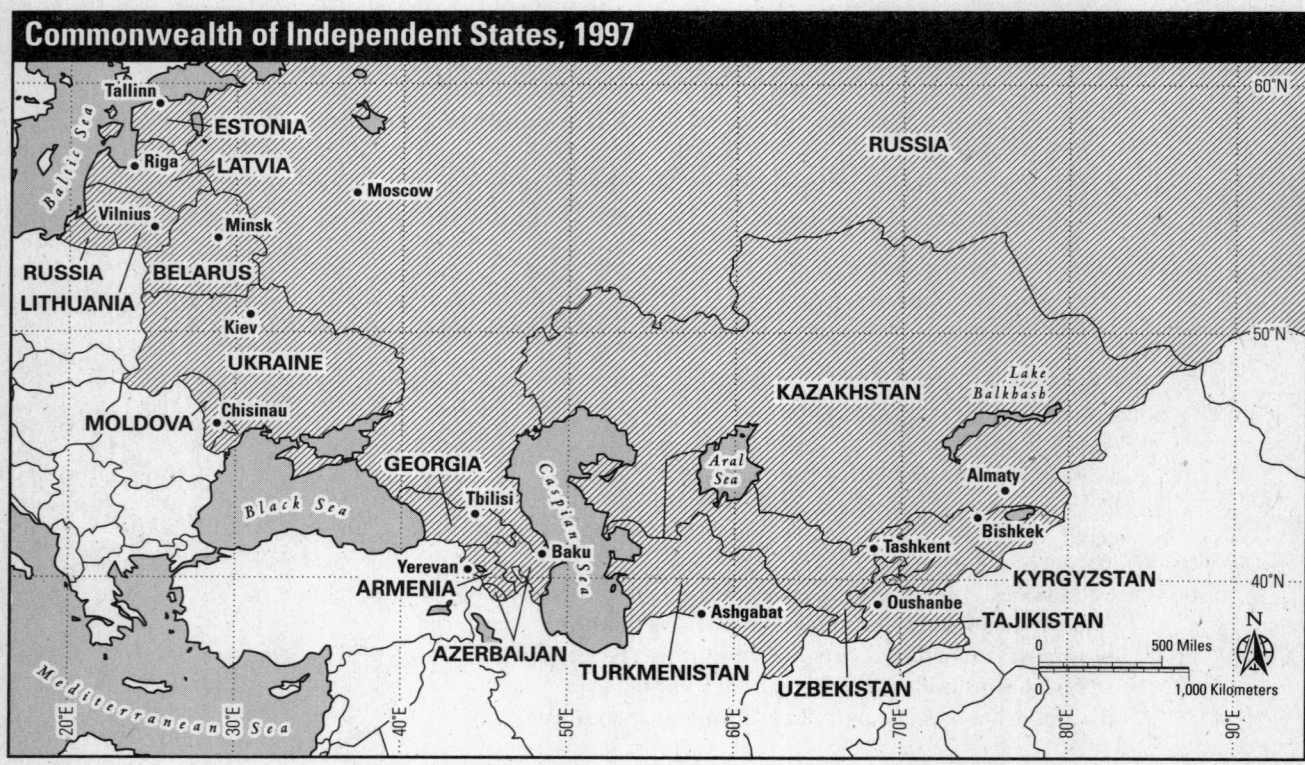

Commonwealth of Independent States, 1997

_____ 11. Which Soviet republic can be found at 60° E by 40° N?
    a. Tajikistan   c. Uzbekistan
    b. Kyrgyzstan   d. Turkmenistan

_____ 12. About how many miles is it from the Baltic Sea to Moscow on a direct route?
    a. 500   b. 700   c. 1,000   d. 1,500

_____ 13. In which republic can the southernmost city be found?
- a. Armenia
- b. Tajikistan
- c. Azerbaijan
- d. Turkmenistan

_____ 14. Which republic has the second largest land area?
- a. Ukraine
- b. Georgia
- c. Kazakhstan
- d. Turkmenistan

_____ 15. Which of the following republics does NOT have access to the Mediterranean Sea?
- a. Armenia
- b. Georgia
- c. Russia
- d. Ukraine

Part 3: Interpreting Political Cartoons

Write the letter of the best answer. (4 points each)

Source: Tony Auth, Philadelphia Inquirer. Copyright © 1989. Reprinted with permission of Universal Press Syndicate. All rights reserved

_____ 16. What message is the artist conveying by placing communism in a hospital?
- a. that communism is a system of checks and balances
- b. that communism is on the decline and in a critical state
- c. that Poland, China, and the USSR can save communism
- d. that history should view the collapse of communism sympathetically

_____ 17. According to the cartoon, in which of the three countries was communism most likely to fall?
- a. USSR
- b. Poland
- c. China
- d. all of the above

_____ 18. Who are the patients in the beds supposed to be?
          a. people dying from starvation under Communist rule
          b. the people of various Communist countries
          c. the Communist party of each labeled country
          d. the leaders of various Communist countries

_____ 19. What do the graphs on the patients' beds seem to portray?
          a. the erratic heartbeat of a Communist leader
          b. the ups and downs of popular support for communism
          c. the number of Communist leaders each country has had
          d. the health of communism in those countries

_____ 20. This cartoon was published three days after the incident at Tiananmen Square.
How did the cartoonist think that incident would affect China?
          a. It would lead to a government repression of protests.
          b. It would cause a backlash that would lead to the death of communism there.
          c. It would cause other Communist countries to help strengthen Chinese communism.
          d. It would cause Chinese Communists to go into hiding.

Part 4: Extended Response

Answer the following questions on the back of this paper or on a separate sheet. (10 points each)

21. **Identifying Problems and Solutions** What are some of the problems that arose in newly independent nations that experienced a long period of colonial rule? How have these problems made it difficult to establish and maintain a true democracy?

Think about:
- how borders were established
- economic strengths and weaknesses
- past and present systems of government

22. **Analyzing Causes and Recognizing Effects** How did the end of Communist rule affect the Soviet Union and its Central and Eastern European allies? Explain your answer.

Think about:
- the political changes
- the economic changes
- the loss of a strong, unifying force

Name _____ Date _____

Struggles for Democracy

Part 1: Main Ideas

Write the letter of the best answer. (4 points each)

_____ 1. Why is a stable economy closely tied to the success of democratic government?
     a. Economic opportunity gives citizens a stake in their country's future.
     b. Democratic governments depend on high tax revenues.
     c. Politicians have to raise millions of dollars to run free and open campaigns.
     d. A strong capitalist economy prevents Communist takeovers.

_____ 2. Which two Latin American countries in this chapter are most alike and why?
     a. Brazil and Mexico both had economies strongly influenced by oil prices.
     b. Brazil and Argentina were both ruled by military dictators before transitioning to democracy.
     c. Mexico and Brazil both signed the North American Free Trade Agreement.
     d. Mexico and Argentina each dominated by a single political party for much of the 20th century.

_____ 3. How did European colonists cause later conflicts in African nations?
     a. They manufactured goods that were useful only to the home country.
     b. They set up unbalanced economies based on one or two cash crops.
     c. They established boundaries that ignored ethnic and cultural divisions.
     d. They left the newly independent nations without any governments.

_____ 4. Which of the following is NOT a similarity in the way democracy has evolved in both the United States and South Africa?
     a. a movement that protested racial segregation
     b. the creation of a written constitution and bill of rights
     c. the end of a minority-controlled government
     d. the extension of voting rights to all races

_____ 5. How was the Soviet Union's foreign policy changed by Mikhail Gorbachev?
     a. He announced a policy of openness that promoted foreign investments.
     b. Arms control became one of Gorbachev's top priorities.
     c. He introduced perestroika, which let Soviet citizens move abroad.
     d. He signed a treaty that brought monetary aid from the United States.

_____ 6. What event caused Germany to rethink its role in international affairs?
     a. Germany's bankrupt economy
     b. re-election of Chancellor Helmut Kohl
     c. production of noncompetitive goods
     d. reunification of East and West Germany

_____ 7. Which force triggered the events that led to the collapse of the Soviet Union?
     a. environmentalism   c. capitalism
     b. nationalism   d. inflation

_____ 8. How were the breakups of Yugoslavia and Czechoslovakia different?
           a. Czechoslovakia broke into more separate republics than Yugoslavia did.
           b. Czechoslovakia broke apart only because of political differences while
              Yugoslavia broke apart because of ethnic differences.
           c. Czechoslovakia's breakup was peaceful; Yugoslavia's was violent.
           d. All of the above are true.

_____ 9. Which event began the process of opening up Chinese-American relations?
           a. Mao Zedong died in 1976.
           b. Deng Xiaoping decided to use capitalist ideas to help China's economy.
           c. Zhou Enlai invited an American table tennis team to tour China.
           d. President Nixon made a state visit to China.

_____ 10. Why was China's future uncertain after the death of Deng Xiaoping?
           a. Under Deng, China's strong economy produced enormous changes.
           b. Jiang Zemin, Deng's successor, had no military experience.
           c. Hard-line officials favored a shift away from Deng's economic policies.
           d. All of the above are true.

Part 2: Map Skills – Constructed Response

Answer the following questions on the lines provided. (4 points each)

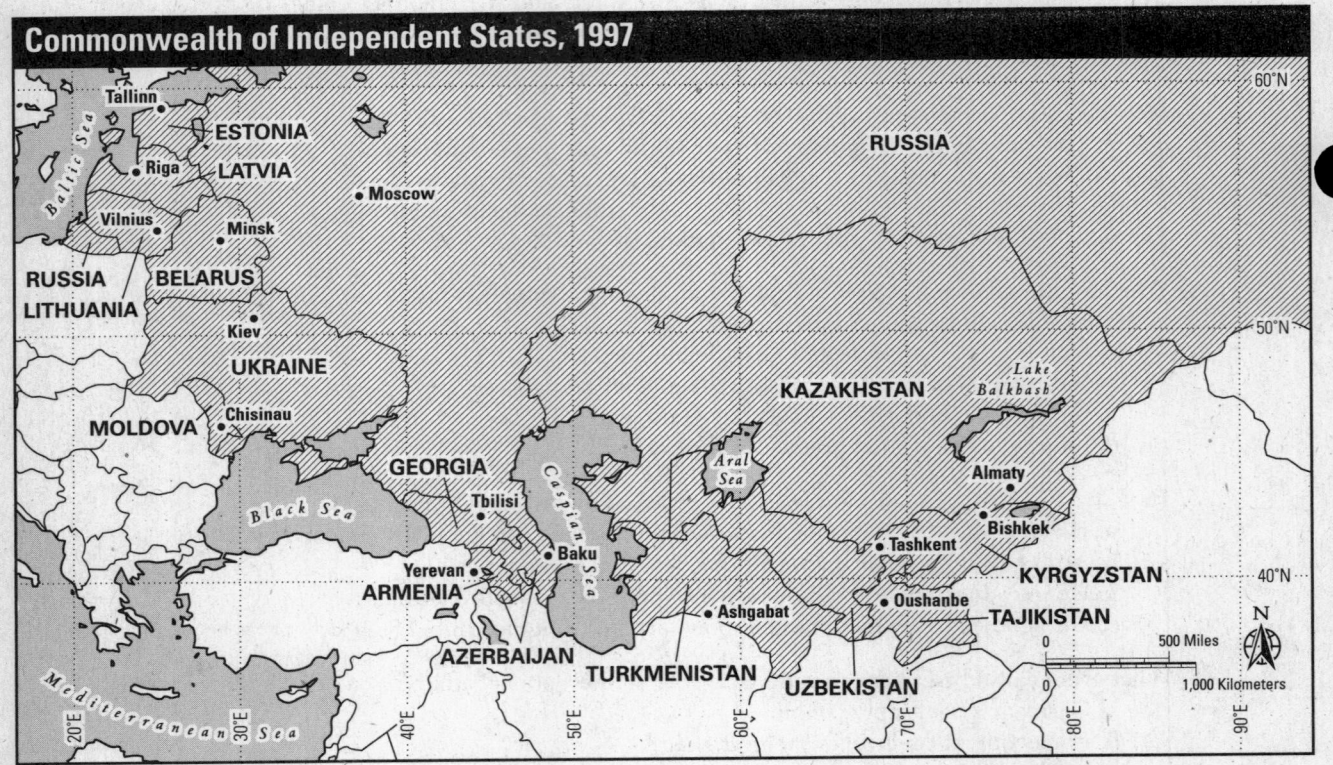

Commonwealth of Independent States, 1997

11. Judging from this map, which republic dominated the old Soviet Union?

_____

12. What characteristic do Lithuania, Latvia, and Estonia share?

_____

13. What geographic feature separates Azerbaijan from Turkmenistan?

_____

14. Which two republics have small territories separated from their main landholdings?

_____

15. What potential problems might happen in the republics that have territories that are
separate from their main landholding?

_____

Part 3: Interpreting Political Cartoons
Write the letter of the best answer. (4 points each)

**Source: Tony Auth, Philadelphia Inquirer. Copyright © 1989. Reprinted with permission of Universal Press
Syndicate. All rights reserved**

_____ 16. Who is the doctor by the USSR patient?
        a. Leonid Brezhnev
        b. Adolf Hitler
        c. Mikhail Gorbachev
        d. Richard Nixon

_____ 17. What is the doctor by the USSR doing?
        a. trying to save the Communist regime by treating its ills
        b. gearing up to take over the world and spread communism
        c. realizing that changes are imminent because the chart turns downward
        d. attempting to establish political ties with Poland and China

_____ 18. If the figure on the left is Lech Walesa, what is the best description of his actions?
        a. He is pounding the patient's chest to save him.
        b. He is jumping up and down in joy over communism's decline.
        c. He is trying to attract the attention of a doctor to get help.
        d. He is defending himself from Communists.

_____ 19. What is a possible meaning of the skeleton in the bed on the far left?
        a. the eventual death of communism
        b. countries that have already given up communism
        c. the lasting harm done by communism
        d. all of the above

_____ 20. This cartoon was published in 1989 right after Tiananmen Square. What conclusion can you draw from this fact?
        a. It was difficult in 1989 to foresee where current events would lead.
        b. By 1989, the experts knew where communism was most in trouble.
        c. By 1989, the cartoonist could see that Gorbachev's reforms were failing.
        d. In 1989, the United States had the most accurate information about China.

Part 4: Extended Response

Answer the following questions on the back of this paper or on a separate sheet. (10 points each)

21. **Drawing Conclusions** Why do you think the Soviet republics rejected the concept of unity and declared independence once the Communist Party lost control of the USSR?

22. **Synthesizing** The chapter states that democracy is always a "work in progress." Explain how four different countries discussed in the chapter illustrate this statement.

CHAPTER
20
Section 1

SECTION QUIZ *The Impact of Science and Technology*

A. Terms and Names Write the letter of the best answer.

_____ 1. NASA and the European space agency cooperated in the launch of the
        a. International Space Station.
        b. Hubble Space Telescope.
        c. first manned spacecraft.
        d. first spacecraft with an international crew.

_____ 2. The Internet was originally developed for use in
        a. international espionage.
        b. missile control.
        c. space exploration.
        d. scientific research.

_____ 3. The term "genetic engineering" refers to
        a. using extremely precise surgical techniques.
        b. selective breeding to emphasize certain traits.
        c. modifying the hereditary units in an organism.
        d. creating machines that can do the work of humans.

_____ 4. The successful cloning of an organism would, by definition, result in a new
organism that was
        a. unable to reproduce itself.
        b. genetically identical to the original.
        c. superior in at least one trait to the original.
        d. larger, stronger, and healthier than the original.

_____ 5. The "green revolution" was an effort to
        a. produce food more efficiently.
        b. use only natural fertilizers and pesticides.
        c. combine small farms into large businesses.
        d. increase the number of people engaged in farming.

B. Extended Response Briefly answer the following question on the back of this paper.

The word *outlook* can mean "attitude; way of thinking" or it can mean "what is likely
for the future; likely outcome." How have recent advances in science and technology
shaped both our attitudes and what is likely for us in the future?

CHAPTER
20

Section 2

SECTION QUIZ *Global Economic Development*

_____

A. Terms and Names Write the letter of the best answer.

_____ 1. A developed nation is usually LOWER than an emerging nation with respect to
     a. literacy.
     b. life expectancy.
     c. standard of living.
     d. political instability.

_____ 2. In the Persian Gulf War of 1991, 39 allied nations fought against the nation of
     a. Iran.
     b. Iraq.
     c. Kuwait.
     d. Saudi Arabia.

_____ 3. The term "global economy" refers to financial interactions that
     a. cross international borders.
     b. occur anywhere in the world.
     c. decrease one nation's dependence on another.
     d. are controlled or overseen by the United Nations.

_____ 4. The major cause of damage to the atmosphere's ozone layer is caused by
     a. acid rain.
     b. global warming.
     c. chlorofluorocarbons.
     d. the sun's ultraviolet rays.

_____ 5. A nation that opposed the principles of free trade would
     a. establish import taxes.
     b. import more products than it exports.
     c. refuse to trade with a particular nation.
     d. increase the price of an exported product.

_____ 6. A multinational corporation is one that
     a. produces products for export.
     b. operates in a number of countries.
     c. has stockholders from many nations.
     d. depends on the import of raw materials.

B. Extended Response Briefly answer the following question on the back of this paper.

Why might it be more difficult to successfully practice sustainable development in an emerging nation than in a developed nation?

CHAPTER 20

Section 3

SECTION QUIZ *Global Security Issues*

A. Terms and Names Write the letter of the best answer.

_____ 1. The purpose of the Nuclear Non-Proliferation Treaty can be found in its name, in which *proliferation* refers to the
   a. use of something.
   b. spread of something.
   c. prohibition of something.
   d. elimination of something.

_____ 2. Whose traditional homeland crosses the borders of Turkey, Iran, and Iraq?
   a. Croats
   b. Serbs
   c. Palestinians
   d. Kurds

_____ 3. What event do you think prompted the UN to issue the Universal Declaration of Human Rights?
   a. apartheid in South Africa
   b. the Holocaust in Europe
   c. the Cultural Revolution in China
   d. the civil rights movement in the United States

_____ 4. Which world region has suffered the most from the AIDS epidemic?
   a. Asia and the Pacific
   b. Latin America
   c. Sub-Saharan Africa
   d. Western Europe

_____ 5. Push factors of migration include lack of food due to drought, natural disasters, and
   a. gender inequality.
   b. nuclear proliferation.
   c. political oppression.
   d. political dissent.

B. Extended Response Briefly answer the following question on the back of this paper.

The UN's Universal Declaration of Human Rights established that all people possess certain civil rights. What rights do you think all people should have? Explain your answer.

CHAPTER 20

Section 4

SECTION QUIZ *Terrorism*
Case Study: September 11, 2001

A. Terms and Names Write the letter of the best answer.

_____ 1. The major goal of radical religious and cultural terrorist groups is the
destruction of
   a. government and religious buildings.
   b. what they consider the forces of evil.
   c. subway stations and shopping malls.
   d. all forms of government.

_____ 2. Why do government officials find the use of chemical and biological agents in
terrorist attacks particularly worrisome?
   a. because biochemical agents are relatively easy to acquire
   b. because it is impossible to guard against biochemical attacks
   c. because biochemical attacks inflict huge numbers of casualties
   d. because people fear biochemical attacks more than other terrorist
   attacks

_____ 3. Terrorism that involves politically motivated attacks on information systems
is known as
   a. virtual terrorism.
   b. cyberterrorism.
   c. narcoterrorism.
   d. biochemical terrorism.

_____ 4. Osama bin Laden used mountain hideouts in Afghanistan as a base of
operations for his global network of terrorists known as
   a. Islamic Jihad.
   b. FARC.
   c. Aum Shinrikyo.
   d. al-Qaeda.

_____ 5. One criticism leveled at the USA Patriot Act is that it
   a. allows the government to infringe on people's civil rights.
   b. provides too much protection for people's civil rights.
   c. focuses too heavily on aviation security.
   d. fails to address the issue of aviation security.

B. Extended Response Briefly answer the following question on the back of this paper.

Many governments have firmly stated that they do no and will not negotiate with
terrorists. Do you think this a practical approach to the problem of terrorism? Why
or why not?

CHAPTER 20

Section 5

SECTION QUIZ   *Cultures Blend in a Global Age*

A. Terms and Names Write the letter of the best answer.

_____ 1. The cultural trait LEAST likely to be significantly affected by popular culture is
    a. fads.
    b. slang.
    c. musical styles.
    d. religious beliefs.

_____ 2. The product most likely to be found in an American household is
    a. a telephone.
    b. a television.
    c. a personal computer.
    d. a videocassette recorder.

_____ 3. English is referred to as the "premier international language" because
    a. it is the most widespread of any language.
    b. it is the most scientifically precise language.
    c. more people speak English than any other language.
    d. languages all over the world contain some English words.

_____ 4. The definition of *materialism,* as the word is used in this chapter, is the
    a. "idea that everything consists of matter."
    b. "tendency to rely on physical proof rather than theory."
    c. "idea that matter, or the content, of something is more important than its form."
    d. "mindset of placing a high value on acquiring material possessions."

_____ 5. What methods might a country use to ensure that global popular culture does not overwhelm its national culture and traditions?
    a. set aside television broadcast time for national programming
    b. take Western television shows and rework them according to national culture and traditions
    c. strictly censor the mass media to keep out unwanted ideas
    d. all of the above

B. Extended Response Briefly answer the following question on the back of this paper.

What is one event in recent history that supports the idea that a nation can be deeply affected by events that occur far away? How does that event support this idea?

CHAPTER
20
Form A

CHAPTER TEST *Global Interdependence*

Part 1: Main Ideas
Write the letter of the best answer. (4 points each)

_____ 1. What was the first cooperative space venture between the United States and
the Soviet Union?
     a. the launching of *Sputnik I*
     b. the launching of the International Space Station
     c. the docking of American and Soviet spacecraft in 1975
     d. the American/Soviet crew that flew on *Soyez 28*

_____ 2. What tool, jointly designed and made by NASA and ESA, is observing objects in
the most remote regions of the universe?
     a. *Magellan*
     b. *International Space Station*
     c. *Pathfinder*
     d. Hubble Space Telescope

_____ 3. What was the original purpose of the Internet?
     a. shopping from home
     b. a national defense database
     c. "virtual" travel to distant places
     d. shared information about research

_____ 4. What do all developed nations have that emerging nations do not?
     a. transportation and business facilities for advanced production of
       manufactured goods
     b. an internationally recognized space program using cooperation between
       one or more countries
     c. a board of trade that exchanges multiple currencies in international markets
     d. a government body represented in the United Nations

_____ 5. What is included within the global economy?
     a. financial interactions among people that cross international borders
     b. financial interactions among businesses that cross international borders
     c. financial interactions among governments that cross international borders
     d. all of the above

_____ 6. What name is used for the concept of preserving the environment and conserving
resources while still meeting current economic needs?
     a. recycling
     b. free trade
     c. sustainable development
     d. green revolution

_____ 7. What was the main purpose of the Nuclear Non-Proliferation Treaty?
    a. to eliminate stockpiled nuclear weapons
    b. to prohibit the creation of new nuclear weapons
    c. to avoid the use of nuclear weapons as a first response
    d. to prevent the spread of nuclear weapons to other nations

_____ 8. Which document states that "All human beings are born free and equal in dignity and rights. . . . Everyone has the right to life, liberty, and security of person"?
    a. Universal Declaration of Human Rights
    b. Helsinki Accords
    c. *Progress of the World's Women*
    d. Declaration of Commitment on HIV/AIDS

_____ 9. What is meant by popular culture?
    a. the laws and provisions established by government to regulate civil liberties
    b. the ways in which the most famous members of a society present themselves
    c. cultural elements that reflect a group's common background and changing interests
    d. cultural practices no longer used by majority groups but still used by minority groups

_____ 10. What is meant by global interdependence?
    a. the elimination of international borders through use of the Internet and the sharing of information worldwide
    b. the idea that nations are dependent on other nations and affected by the actions of others far away
    c. the existence of multinational corporations that have branch offices worldwide and utilize native laborers
    d. the central influence of one nation on the world and the amount of change forced on others

Name _____

Part 2: Map Skills

Using the map, place the letter of the correct answer next to each question. (4 points each)

Trading Blocs in the Americas, 1997

a. North American Free Trade Agreement
b. Caribbean Community and Common Market
c. Central American Common Market
d. Andean Group
e. Southern Cone Common Market

_____ 11. Which is the largest trading bloc in terms of the land mass of the member countries?

_____ 12. Which trading bloc represents the most South American nations?

_____ 13. Which trading blocs have nations located at 0° latitude?

_____ 14. Which trading blocs include the southernmost countries?

_____ 15. Which trading bloc comes closest to representing an entire continent?

Part 3: Interpreting Graphs

Write the letter of the best answer. (4 points each)

_____ 16. Which pair had nearly identical economic
growth between 1980 and 1991?
   a. USA and Japan
   b. Japan and Singapore
   c. Singapore and Hong Kong
   d. Hong Kong and South Korea

_____ 17. Which pair's per capita gross domestic
product surpassed $20,000 by 1989?
   a. USA and Japan
   b. Japan and Singapore
   c. Singapore and Hong Kong
   d. Hong Kong and South Korea

_____ 18. Which country had the most dramatic
growth between 1985 and 1989?
   a. USA
   b. Japan
   c. Singapore
   d. South Korea

_____ 19. What is unusual about the data shown for
Hong Kong and South Korea?
   a. They both show constant ups and
downs.
   b. The both surpassed Singapore.
   c. There is no data before 1980.
   d. They both struggled with steady declines.

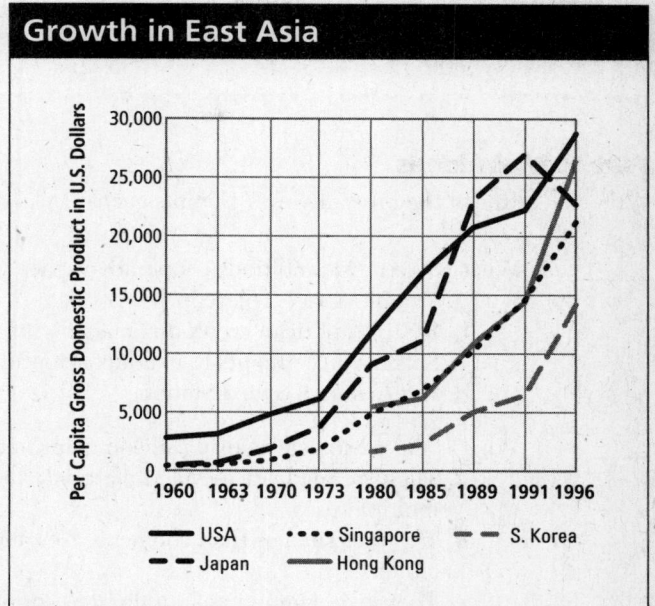

SOURCE: *United Nations World Statistics in Brief,*
1976, 1986, 1992, 1995

_____ 20. Which territory or nation began with the greatest per capita gross domestic
product overall but was surpassed by another?
   a. USA
   b. Japan
   c. Singapore
   d. Hong Kong

Part 4: Extended Response

Answer the following questions on the back of this page or on your own paper. (10 points each)

21. **Forming and Supporting Opinions** What technological advance made in the last few
decades do you think is the most important? Explain your choice.

Think about:
• worldwide communication
• biological and chemical research
• discoveries above and beyond Earth

22. **Analyzing Issues** What has been done for human rights since the end of World War II?

Think about:
• organizations committed to human rights
• continuing challenges to human rights

CHAPTER TEST *Global Interdependence*

20

Form B

Part 1: Main Ideas

Write the letter of the best answer. (4 points each)

_____ 1. What is the most ambitious cooperative space venture?
   a. Hubble Space Telescope
   b. Soviet/American crews on *Soyez* flights
   c. Space shuttle flights to conduct scientific experiments
   d. International Space Station

_____ 2. What is the advantage of using silicon chips in computers?
   a. They are made of recycled materials and can be reprogrammed for multiple uses.
   b. They are smaller than contact lenses and hold millions of microscopic circuits.
   c. They give computers an unlimited supply of power.
   d. They limitlessly expand the amount of memory a computer can handle.

_____ 3. What impact has technology had on the world's economy?
   a. It has created new industries in both Asia and the Western world.
   b. It has caused a depression in developing nations.
   c. It has created the need for a one-world currency.
   d. All of the above are true.

_____ 4. What is the difference between developed and emerging nations?
   a. Developed nations are industrialized, while emerging are in the process of industrializing.
   b. Emerging nations are industrialized, while developed are in the process of industrializing.
   c. Both are industrialized, but in emerging nations only one language is spoken and understood.
   d. Both are in the process of industrializing, but developed nations are further along.

_____ 5. Why was the World Trade Organization established?
   a. to abolish free trade practices by all nations
   b. to ensure that trade among nations flows as smoothly as possible
   c. to require free trade practices by all nations
   d. all of the above

_____ 6. What did the Persian Gulf War of 1991 reveal about international economies?
   a. that war does little to improve the economies of aggressor nations
   b. that without the resource of oil, international economies would fail
   c. that the economies of nations are globally linked
   d. that if Iraq had been successful, it would have developed an international economy

_____ 7. What has led nations to pursue collective security measures?
      a. divisions and tensions created by the Cold War
      b. proliferation of nuclear weapons around the world
      c. establishment of multinational regional trading blocs
      d. protection of global corporations

_____ 8. What was the immediate impact of the terrorist attack in the United States on September 11, 2001?
      a. It left Americans feeling vulnerable and afraid.
      b. It caused martial law to be temporarily enforced in the United States.
      c. It led to the creation of an international antiterrorism force.
      d. It permanently increased television news coverage of terrorist attacks.

_____ 9. What has been a lasting effect of European colonization in the Americas, Asia, and Africa?
      a. Western languages are spoken throughout the world.
      b. All nations have friendly relations with the West.
      c. More people speak English than any other language.
      d. all of the above

_____ 10. Which is an example of an action taken by a government to preserve cultural identity?
      a. relaxing national dress codes to foster individuality
      b. strictly censoring the mass media
      c. making English the official language of government
      d. using mass media to popularize foreign fashions

Part 2: Map Skills

Using the map, place the letter of the correct answer next to each question. (4 points each)

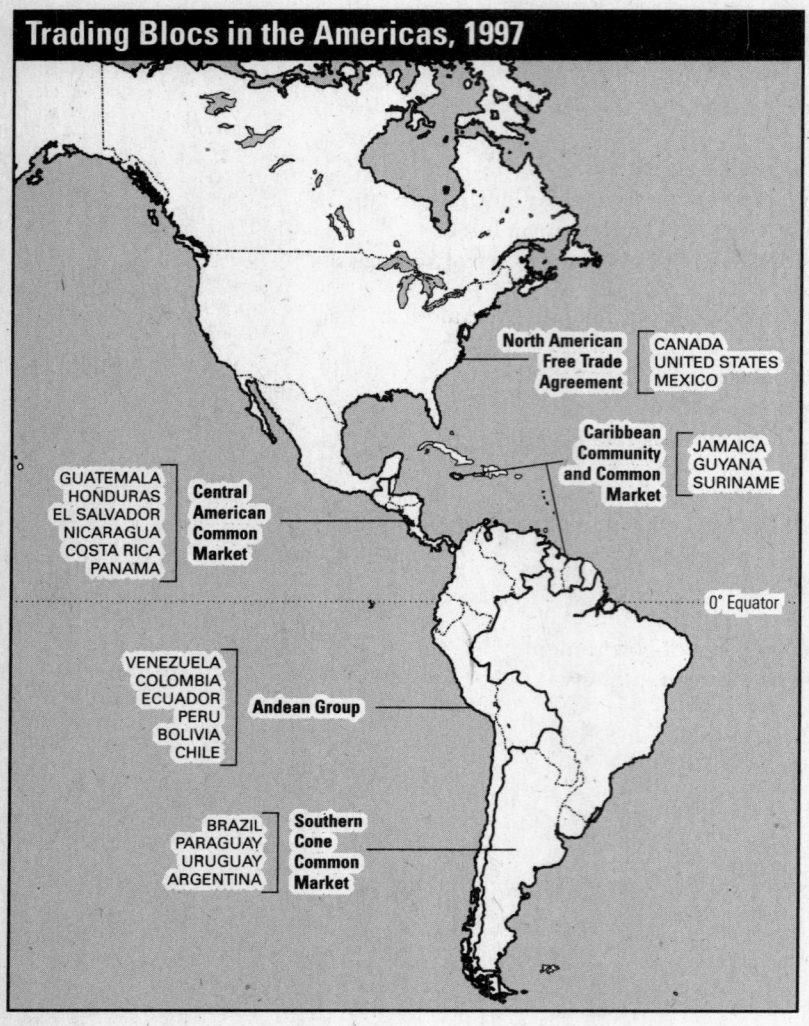

Trading Blocs in the Americas, 1997

a. North American Free Trade Agreement
b. Caribbean Community and Common Market
c. Central American Common Market
d. Andean Group
e. Southern Cone Common Market

_____ 11. Which trading blocs do NOT lie entirely within the Northern Hemisphere?

_____ 12. Which trading blocs have direct access to both the Pacific and Atlantic oceans?

_____ 13. Which trading bloc includes island nations?

_____ 14. Which trading blocs have nations in two hemispheres?

_____ 15. Which trading bloc includes both English and Spanish as the majority languages spoken?

Part 3: Interpreting Graphs

Write the letter of the best answer. (4 points each)

_____ 16. Which Asian territory or nation had the
steadiest rate of growth between 1973 and
1991?
   a. Japan
   b. Singapore
   c. Hong Kong
   d. South Korea

_____ 17. Which Asian territory or nation showed
the slowest rate of growth?
   a. Japan
   b. Hong Kong
   c. Singapore
   d. South Korea

_____ 18. Which Asian territory or nation had a
pattern of growth most like the USA?
   a. Japan
   b. Singapore
   c. Hong Kong
   d. South Korea

_____ 19. Which territory's or nation's per capita
gross domestic product surpassed $10,000
by 1989?
   a. USA and Japan
   b. USA, Japan, and Singapore
   c. USA, Japan, Singapore, and Hong Kong
   d. USA, Japan, Singapore, Hong Kong, and South Korea

_____ 20. Which nation probably had the highest standard of living in 1991?
   a. USA
   b. Japan
   c. Singapore
   d. South Korea

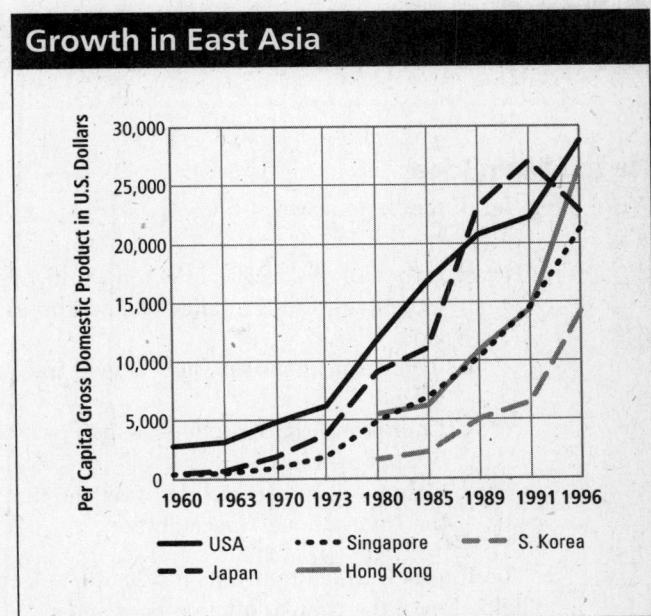

Growth in East Asia

SOURCE: *United Nations World Statistics in Brief,*
1976, 1986, 1992, 1995

Part 4: Extended Response

Answer the following questions on the back of this page or on your own paper. (10 points each)

21. **Recognizing Effects** What is one aspect of modern life that you think serves to increase
global competition or conflict? Explain your choice.

   Think about:
   • information technology
   • worldwide organizations
   • medical research and breakthroughs

22. **Comparing** What are the pros and cons of accepting ideas from another culture?

   Think about:
   • varieties of style, food, music, religion
   • cultural evolution v. loss of identity

CHAPTER 20

Form C

CHAPTER TEST *Global Interdependence*

Part 1: Main Ideas

Write the letter of the best answer. (4 points each)

_____ 1. How has the use of satellites affected worldwide communications?
    a. Communications satellites helped break down barriers created by the Cold War.
    b. Communications satellites helped transform the world into a "global village."
    c. Communications satellites helped pave the way for voyages of exploration by space probes.
    d. Communications satellites were the first step toward the development of the International Space Station.

_____ 2. The Internet, which transmits information electronically to remote locations, helped pave the way for home offices and
    a. free trade.
    b. globalization.
    c. telecommuting.
    d. virtual travel.

_____ 3. What negative consequence resulted from the green revolution?
    a. It sparked social interest groups to stage protests and riots.
    b. It led to a large surplus of nondegradable materials and waste.
    c. It introduced dangerous pesticides and chemical fertilizers.
    d. It created a climate of agricultural distress and famine in Asia.

_____ 4. What negative economic impact was felt by industrialized nations because of global development?
    a. Industries moved to emerging nations, raising unemployment in developed nations.
    b. The release of chemicals in manufacturing processes has destroyed the ozone layer.
    c. Iraq invaded Saudi Arabia in an attempt to control the oil supplies in that region.
    d. Nations increasingly have come into conflict over the management of water resources.

_____ 5. NATO, SEATO, and the Warsaw Pact are all examples of
    a. regional trade associations.
    b. nuclear non-proliferation treaties.
    c. military alliances.
    d. peace treaties.

_____ 6. What services does the UN provide to aid world peace?
      a. legislative advice, government reconstruction, and weapons
      b. language instruction and cultural adaptation skills
      c. a public forum, private meeting places, skilled mediators, and soldiers
      d. all of the above

_____ 7. What are the main reasons why people decide to immigrate to other nations?
      a. unstable political situations at home and prosperous economies abroad
      b. the lure of popular culture and a wealth of natural resources
      c. the establishment of regional trading blocs and alliances
      d. global warming and other environmental problems such as pollution

_____ 8. What impact has television and mass media had globally?
      a. It has caused terrorist groups to reduce their activity.
      b. It has helped to create a shared experience of current worldwide events.
      c. It has changed the way most people use their leisure time.
      d. It has made Texas the most sought–after destination to live.

_____ 9. What influence has the entertainment industry had on the world?
      a. It has given countries at war a way to view their enemy's movements.
      b. It has broadly educated the public about history.
      c. It has caused the radio broadcasting industry to cease operations.
      d. It has spread American popular culture across the world.

_____ 10. Which of the following is NOT an effect of non-Western ideas on the West?
      a. growth of Eastern religions such as Islam and Buddhism
      b. placing a high value on meditation and contemplation
      c. placing a high value on material possessions
      d. manners of dress and clothing style adapted from world cultures

Part 2: Map Skills – Constructed Response

Answer the following questions on the lines provided. (4 points each)

Trading Blocs in the Americas, 1997

11. Which trading bloc is NOT made primarily of Latin American nations?

    _____

12. Which trading blocs are entirely in tropical regions?

    _____

13. Which trading bloc includes nations that are separated by water?

    _____

14. Which of the trading blocs includes equatorial nations?

    _____

15. Which two trading blocs include the nations with the largest land mass?

_____

Part 3: Interpreting Graphs

Write the letter of the best answer. (4 points each)

_____ 16. During which years did the Asian nations experience their FASTEST growth?
   a. 1973 - 1980
   b. 1980 - 1985
   c. 1985 - 1989
   d. 1989 - 1991

_____ 17. Judging from this graph, which two territories or nations provided the highest standard of living during this period?
   a. USA and Japan
   b. Singapore and Hong Kong
   c. USA and Hong Kong
   d. Japan and Singapore

_____ 18. What was the approximate difference in per capita gross domestic product between the USA and Hong Kong in 1989?
   a. $5,000
   b. $10,000
   c. $15,000
   d. $20,000

_____ 19. Which of the following nations exhibited the most significant growth overall?
   a. Japan
   b. USA
   c. Singapore
   d. South Korea

_____ 20. Which nation lagged behind the others in economic growth?
   a. USA
   b. Japan
   c. Singapore
   d. South Korea

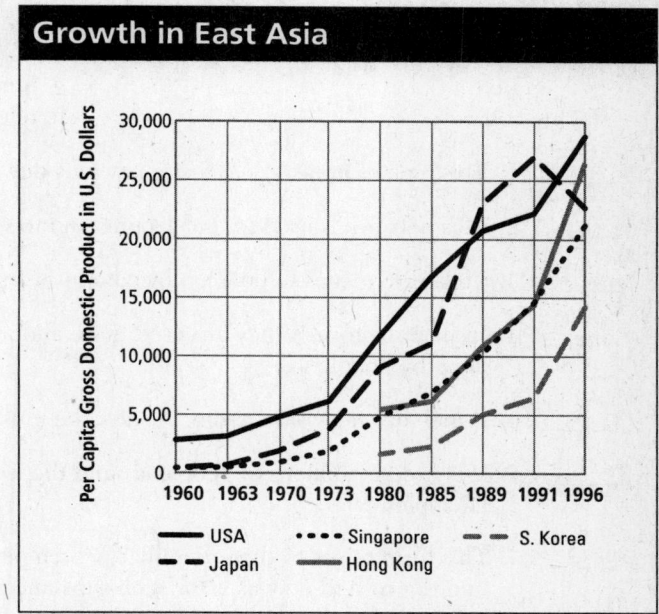

Growth in East Asia

SOURCE: *United Nations World Statistics in Brief,*
1976, 1986, 1992, 1995

Part 4: Extended Response

Answer the following questions on the back of this page or on your own paper. (10 points each)

21. **Comparing** How does global interdependence both improve and endanger security?

22. **Recognizing Effects** What effect has free trade had on the global economy and what measures have been taken to protect the process?

Technology Transforms Life

A. Terms and Names Write the letter of the term or name that best matches the description. A term or name may be used more than once or not at all.

a. the Internet   e. the mass media
b. robots   f. television
c. deep blue   g. e-mail
d. blue collar   h. telecommute

_____ 1. This type of industry has lost many jobs due to technology.

_____ 2. This network is used for chat rooms and to send electronic mail.

_____ 3. This term means to do a job by computer from home.

_____ 4. In manufacturing, they are used more and more to do jobs that were once done by people.

_____ 5. It includes television, radio, movies, the music industry, and the popular press.

_____ 6. It is used by billions of people around the world to watch events, such as the Olympics.

_____ 7. This term refers to the scientific research performed on biological substances in order to find new uses for such substances.

_____ 8. This machine is used to help diagnose illnesses.

B. Extended Response Briefly answer the following question.

What are some of the effects of mass media on culture?

EPILOGUE

QUIZ 2

Environmental Changes

A. Terms and Names Choose the correct answer.

_____ 1. Which of the following was involved in the largest oil spill in U.S. history?
      a. *Exxon Valdez*   c. the MOSOP
      b. UNICEF   d. Red Cross

_____ 2. The greenhouse effect might cause which of the following?
      a. oil spills
      b. global warming
      c. the pollution of rivers
      d. the destruction of the ozone layer

_____ 3. How much of the world's population has no access to clean water?
      a. one-tenth   c. one-fourth
      b. one-eighth   d. one-half

_____ 4. Which of the following could possibly be caused by the destruction of the rain forests?
      a. the extinction of many of the world's species of animals and plants
      b. an imbalance in the earth's environment
      c. an increase of the greenhouse effect
      d. all of the above

_____ 5. Automobiles cause which of the following?
      a. greenhouse gases
      b. soil erosion
      c. radioactive wastes
      d. the expansion of deserts

_____ 6. Which of the following is a renewable energy source?
      a. solar power   c. coal
      b. oil   d. all of the above

B. Extended Response Briefly answer the following question.

According to the text, what is a possible cause for global warming, and what has been done to limit this cause? Explain your answer.

Feeding a Growing Population

A. Terms and Names Choose the correct answer.

_____ 1. Overpopulation occurs when
   a. there are too many people for the transportation of an area to carry.
   b. there are too few people involved in manufacturing.
   c. there are too many people for the local natural resources.
   d. there are too few people involved in the service industries.

_____ 2. In the 1970s and 1980s in Africa, low rainfall helped cause
   a. a shortage of food supplies.
   b. widespread malnutrition.
   c. widespread famine.
   d. all of the above.

_____ 3. The green revolution has resulted in
   a. the development of high-yield plants, such as wheat and rice.
   b. the development of plants that do not need herbicides to protect them.
   c. the development of plants that do not need much irrigation.
   d. the development of inexpensive farming methods.

_____ 4. Critics fear that altering plant genes may accidentally
   a. create plants, such as the tomato, that ripen too quickly.
   b. create poisonous plants.
   c. create new disease-causing organisms.
   d. all of the above

_____ 5. When a country's economy improves, birth rates
   a. rise because of better health care for children.
   b. rise because women become pregnant more frequently.
   c. fall because overcrowded hospitals make health care worse.
   d. fall because women become pregnant less frequently.

_____ 6. When the literacy rate of women in a country increases, the birth rate usually
   a. increases.
   b. decreases.
   c. stays the same.
   d. fluctuates greatly.

B. Extended Response Briefly answer the following question.

What are some of the causes of famine in Africa? Explain your answer, using details from the text.

EPILOGUE

QUIZ 4

Economic Issues in the Developing World

A. Terms and Names If the statement is true, write "true" on the line. If it is false, change the underlined word or words to make it true.

Example: For economic growth to occur in a country, investment capital is

needed to pay for the construction of industries and <u>foreign embassies</u>.

_____ *infrastructure* _____

1. The industrialized nations have remained interested in the less-developed countries (LDCs) as sources of <u>manufactured</u> materials and as potential markets for goods. _____

2. For economic growth to occur in a country, qualified <u>managers</u> need to make sure that workers and materials are used efficiently. _____

3. When most colonized regions gained their independence after World War II, they had underdeveloped economies and weak <u>cultural</u> traditions. _____

4. Industrialized nations have tried to work with the LDCs by providing <u>political aid</u> through international organizations, such as the World Bank and the International Monetary Fund. _____

5. Most LDCs want multinational companies to invest in them because the multinationals do create <u>jobs</u>. _____

   _____

6. In Nicaragua, *maquilas* do <u>much</u> to contribute technology, capital, and infrastructure to the country. _____

   _____

7. <u>Grassroots</u> development calls for small-scale, community-based projects to help poor people lift themselves from poverty. _____

B. Extended Response Briefly answer the following question.

   How have grassroots programs helped LDCs? Give an example from the text.

Name _____   Date _____

Seeking Global Security

_____

A. Terms and Names Choose the correct answer.

_____ 1. What is terrorism?
    a. the use of violence against people or property to force changes in societies or governments
    b. the use of nonviolent protest to force changes in societies or governments
    c. the use of harsh diplomatic measures to force changes in societies or governments
    d. all of the above

_____ 2. The collapse of the Soviet Union led to which of the following?
    a. political instability in Yugoslavia only
    b. political instability in all underdeveloped countries in Asia
    c. political instability in France and Great Britain
    d. political instability in parts of the world the Soviets once controlled

_____ 3. The illegal sale of weapons has resulted in which of the following?
    a. the use of these weapons in regions with political, ethnic, or religious tensions
    b. enormous profits for arms dealers
    c. organized nonviolent protests against arms dealers
    d. all of the above

_____ 4. Which of the following is NOT a weapon of mass destruction?
    a. nuclear arsenals
    b. artillery
    c. poison gas
    d. bioweapons

_____ 5. Which of the following did U.S.-led forces invade in 2003?
    a. Iraq
    b. Iran
    c. Kuwait
    d. Yugoslavia

B. Extended Response Briefly answer the following questions.

What has helped terrorists to carry out their attacks? Base your answer on the text.

EPILOGUE

QUIZ 6

Defending Human Rights and Freedoms

A. Terms and Names Choose the correct answer.

_____ 1. The Universal Declaration of Human Rights defines
   a. human rights goals for democratic countries only.
   b. human rights goals for the world community.
   c. human rights goals for less-developed countries only.
   d. human rights goals for the European community.

_____ 2. The Universal Declaration of Human Right calls for
   a. free and fair elections.
   b. freedom of speech and religion.
   c. freedom from political terror.
   d. all of the above

_____ 3. All of the following are situations that often lead to human rights violations EXCEPT
   a. political dissent.
   b. ethnic conflicts.
   c. athletic competition.
   d. religious persecution.

_____ 4. In 1993, General Abacha took power during the chaos that erupted after
   a. the results of the Nigerian presidential election were wiped out.
   b. economic conditions in Nigeria got worse.
   c. extensive oil spills caused the death of many people.
   d. all of the above

_____ 5. Children in many parts of the world often work
   a. long hours for average pay.
   b. long hours for little or no pay.
   c. in dangerous conditions for high pay.
   d. in safe conditions for high pay.

_____ 6. In Europe, countries that were once part of the Soviet bloc have
   a. kept their political systems closed to improve their economies.
   b. kept their political systems closed to stop democratic elections.
   c. opened up their political systems to establish socialist governments.
   d. opened up their political systems to allow for democratic elections.

_____ 7. Throughout the world, women compared to men in the same region tend to be
   a. better educated.
   b. richer.
   c. poorer.
   d. more often employed.

B. Extended Response Briefly answer the following question.

Important trends in today's world provide reasons for hope for progress on human rights. What are some of these trends? Base your answer on the text.

EPILOGUE

Unresolved Problems of the Modern World

FORM A

Part 1: Main Ideas

Write the letter of the best answer. (4 points each)

_____ 1. What are the mass media?
  a. the abilities of a computer to think or to have artificial intelligence
  b. television, radio, movies, the music industry, and the popular press
  c. telecommuting or doing one's work from home on a computer
  d. increased trade between Europe and the United States

_____ 2. What is a technological advance that has impacted some workers' lives?
  a. factories that use robots in place of humans
  b. media censors that stop false information from being spread
  c. highly sophisticated machines that help in the diagnosis of illnesses
  d. television broadcasts that contribute to the loss of traditional cultures

_____ 3. What is the greenhouse effect?
  a. chemicals used to kill insects in farming
  b. the plentiful nature of earth's resources
  c. medical advantages gained from biotechnology
  d. a heat buildup caused by industrial pollution

_____ 4. What might be a solution for environmental problems?
  a. improved technology
  b. renewable energy resources
  c. government regulations
  d. all of the above

_____ 5. What causes overpopulation?
  a. the decreased amount of food availability worldwide due to wars
  b. the increased amount of food availability worldwide due to peaceful times
  c. too many people for the natural resources of an area to support
  d. too many people for a government to control

_____ 6. What is grassroots development?
  a. large-scale, government projects to help middle class people grow rich
  b. small-scale, community-based projects to help poor people escape poverty
  c. industrial sources of economic growth for less-developed countries
  d. the exploitation of workers by decreasing wages below standard limits

_____ 7. How can free trade improve the economies of less-developed countries?
  a. Free trade promotes commerce by removing taxes from trade.
  b. Free trade increases government revenue through high tariffs on imports.
  c. Free trade influences local corporations to expand overseas.
  d. Free trade directly funds community programs for poor people.

_____ 8. What is terrorism?
   a. a secret military group used to protect against threats of war and violence
   b. a traditional means for mass media to warn the public about danger
   c. the use of violence against people or property to force changes in society
      or government
   d. the use of legislation against people or property to force changes in society
      or government

_____ 9. In what way have nations tried to combat overpopulation?
   a. building exhaust-free cars
   b. improving the status of women
   c. discouraging couples from marrying
   d. encouraging greater use of the Internet

_____ 10. What is the purpose of the Universal Declaration of Human Rights?
   a. It defines human rights goals for the world community.
   b. It lists human rights violations against the world community.
   c. It states the ways for governments to deal with human rights violations.
   d. It supports people who use violence to fight human rights violations.

Part 2: Map Skills

Use the map to choose the best possible answer. (4 points each)

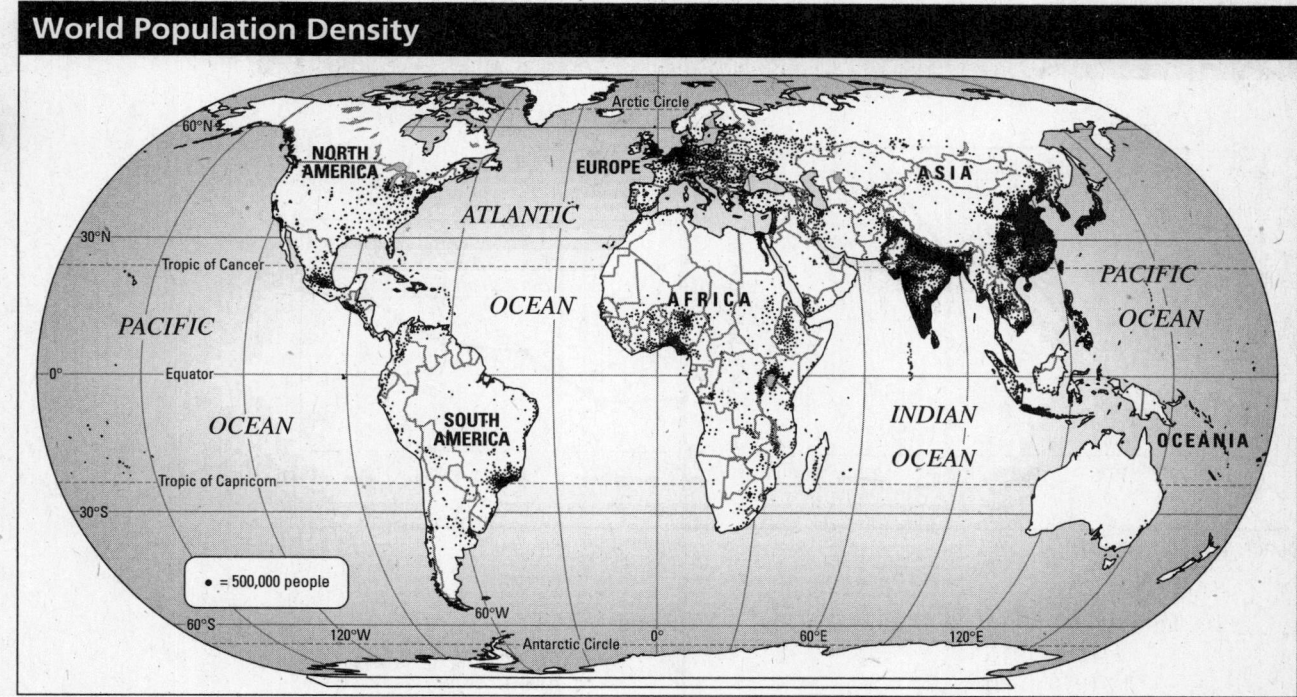

World Population Density

_____ 11. Which of the following continents has the greatest population density?
   a. North America   c. Africa
   b. South America   d. Asia

_____ 12. Which of the following is true about Oceania?
   a. The population density is equal to that in South America.
   b. The population density is less than the rest of the world.
   c. The population density is greater than the rest of the world.
   d. The population density the same as that in Europe.

_____ 13. Which of the following continents seems to have a fairly even and heavy distribution of its population over its entire land mass?
   a. Asia   c. North America
   b. Europe   d. South America

_____ 14. Along which latitude line do the densest populations seem to be?
   a. 60° N   c. 30° S
   b. 30° N   d. 60° S

_____ 15. What pattern describes the population density in North America?
   a. Population is equal in all portions of the continent.
   b. Population is greater in the far northern regions of the continent.
   c. Population is least in the southeastern region of the continent.
   d. Population is greatest in the southeastern region of the continent.

Part 3: Interpreting Graphs

Write the letter of the best answer. (4 points each)

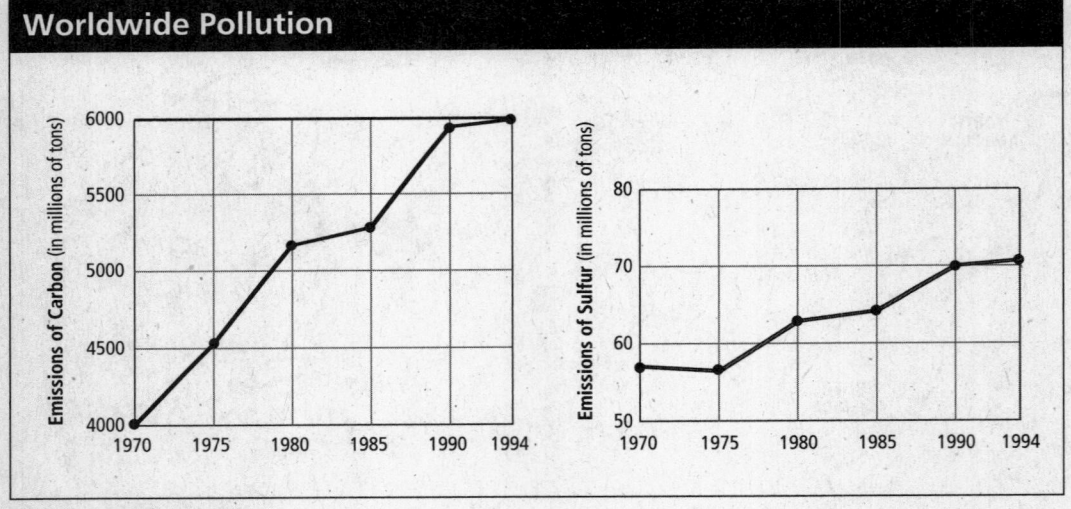

SOURCE: *Vital Signs,* 1997

_____ 16. During which years did sulfur decrease in emissions?
   a. 1970-1975   c. 1980-1895
   b. 1970-1980   d. 1990-1994

_____ 17. What was the approximate amount in tons of sulfur emissions in 1980?
   a. 63   c. 63,000
   b. 6,300   d. 63,000,000

_____ 18. What was the approximate increase in tons in carbon emissions between 1970 and 1975?

a. 600

b. 600,000

c. 600,000,000

d. 600,000,000,000

_____ 19. During which years was the increase in carbon and sulfur emissions the least?

a. 1975-1980

b. 1980-1985

c. 1985-1990

d. 1990-1994

_____ 20. How do the emissions of carbon and sulfur compare in any given year?

a. The emissions of sulfur are millions of tons more than carbon.

b. The emissions of sulfur are billions of tons more than carbon.

c. The emissions of carbon are millions of tons more than sulfur.

d. The emissions of carbon are billions of tons more than sulfur.

Part 4: Extended Response

Answer the following questions on the back of this paper or on a separate sheet. (10 points each)

21. **Comparing** What are the pros and cons of using renewable and nonrenewable energy resources? Explain your answer.

Think about:
- environmental damage
- technology and availability

22. **Recognizing Effects** What consequences might a country that commits human rights violations suffer? Explain your answer.

Think about:
- international reputation
- trade and economic development

EPILOGUE

Unresolved Problems of the Modern World

FORM B

Part 1: Main Ideas

Write the letter of the best answer. (4 points each)

_____ 1. What impact has technology had on the global economy?
     a. Computer-driven robots have replaced the manual laborer in factories throughout the world.
     b. Modern telecommunications allow trade, banking, and financial transactions to be done electronically.
     c. Less-developed countries have all been able to industrialize fully.
     d. The Internet has become the world's dominant form of entertainment.

_____ 2. What is a major advance in modern communications?
     a. e-mail
     b. iris identification
     c. *maquilas*
     d. bioweapons

_____ 3. What is an issue the world faces in reaching sustainable development?
     a. less-developed nations that receive no aid for environmental concerns
     b. developed nations who will not protect the environment and lose profit
     c. the lack of scientific studies in the proper use of tropical rainforest lands
     d. the severe pressure placed on water resources by large populations

_____ 4. What is the purpose of alternative fuel?
     a. to reduce air pollution   c. to battle forest fires
     b. to stop coal burning   d. to stop public smoking

_____ 5. How does rapid population growth affect the quality of life?
     a. Developed nations increase their labor force.
     b. Less-developed nations industrialize faster.
     c. Poverty rates rise and human health suffers.
     d. Poverty rates drop and human health improves.

_____ 6. Which of the following characterizes a less-developed country?
     a. no form of government   c. no natural resources
     b. not fully industrialized   d. a barter economy

_____ 7. Why do developed nations want less-developed nations to become strong and stable?
     a. to be sources of raw materials and potential markets for goods
     b. for the natural flow of migration and the sharing of labor forces
     c. so the funds in the IMF and the World Bank can be repaid
     d. so they can protect themselves from potential invaders

_____ 8. What effect did the September 11, 2001, terrorist attack on the United States
have on that country?
     a. widespread disease
     b. lower birth rates
     c. crop failures
     d. increased literacy

_____ 9. What keeps the market for weapons an active enterprise?
     a. wars among developed nations
     b. the need of developing nations to keep their weapons industries
     c. the huge revenues produced through weapons sales to developing nations
     d. the need for manufactured weapons to protect developing nations

_____ 10. Why should political dissent be allowed in a country?
     a. to give voice to different opinions over political issues
     b. to incite people to riots, revolutions, and counterrevolutions
     c. to allow people to release their anger in a vocal way
     d. to raise people's literacy rates

Part 2: Map Skills

Use the map to choose the best possible answer. (4 points each)

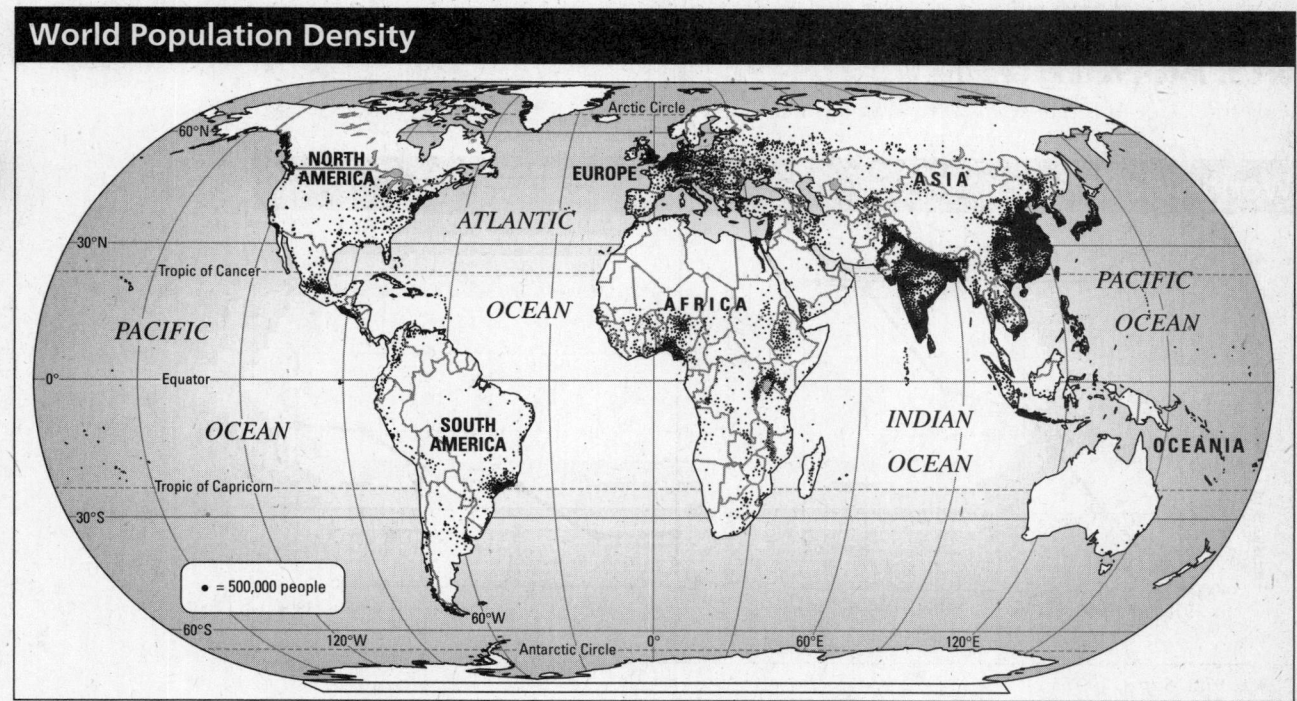

World Population Density

_____ 11. Which regions of Asia have the greater population densities?
     a. north and south   c. east and west
     b. north and west   d. south and east

_____ 12. How would you compare the South American region on the Tropic of Capricorn
with the same region in Africa?
    a. Population densities are less in South America than in Africa in that region.
    b. Population densities are greater in South America than in Africa in that
       region.
    c. Population densities are equal in South America and in Africa in that region.
    d. Neither continent has population densities in that region.

_____ 13. In which coastal region do the largest populations seem to live?
    a. western edge of Pacific Ocean
    b. western edge of Atlantic Ocean
    c. western edge of Indian Ocean
    d. southern region of Pacific Ocean

_____ 14. Which of the following seems to have almost no population density?
    a. Europe   c. Arctic Circle
    b. Oceania   d. North America

_____ 15. What might account for greater population densities on or near coastal regions?
    a. tropical climates
    b. beach communities
    c. tourism
    d. port cities

Part 3: Interpreting Graphs

Write the letter of the best answer. (4 points each)

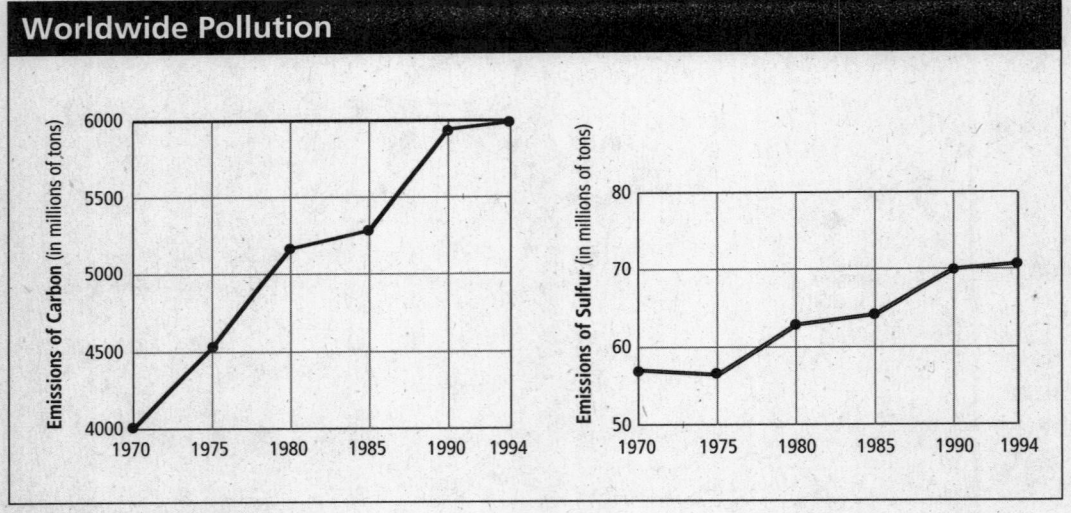

SOURCE: *Vital Signs,* 1997

_____ 16. Approximately how many more tons of sulfur emissions were there in 1980 than
in 1975?
    a. 6,000   c. 600,000
    b. 60,000   d. 6,000,000

_____ 17. What happened to the emissions of carbon and sulfur between the years of
        1990 and 1994?
        a. Both showed a minor decrease in emissions.
        b. Both showed a minor increase in emissions.
        c. Carbon showed a minor increase, and sulfur showed a decrease.
        d. Sulfur showed a minor increase, and carbon showed a decrease.

_____ 18. How would the approximate amount of carbon emissions in 1985 be compared
        with that of sulfur at the same time?
        a. 53,000 tons of carbon to 6,400 tons of sulfur
        b. 53,000,000 tons of carbon to 64,000 tons of sulfur
        c. 5,300,000 tons of carbon to 6,400,000 tons of sulfur
        d. 5,300,000,000 tons of carbon to 64,000,000 tons of sulfur

_____ 19. During which of the following five-year cycles did the emissions of carbon make
        its most dramatic increase?
        a. 1970-1975
        b. 1975-1980
        c. 1980-1985
        d. 1985-1990

_____ 20. What might account for the way the amount of emissions changed during the
        years 1990-1994?
        a. There was a worldwide economic slowdown.
        b. Industries began to use mostly solar and nuclear power.
        c. Industries burned ever-increasing amounts of fossil fuels.
        d. Stricter emission controls on automobiles went into effect.

Part 4: Extended Response

(10 points each)

21. **Analyzing Issues** What are some of the causes and possible solutions for famine in Africa?
    Explain your answer.

    Think about:
    • yearly climate patterns
    • impacts of civil unrest
    • aid from international groups
    • technological advances

22. **Identifying Problems** What are some of the difficulties and solutions for establishing
    economic growth in less-developed countries? Explain your answer.

    Think about:
    • worldwide groups that provide monetary support
    • large-scale companies with branches in other countries
    • small community-based programs

Name _____   Date _____

Unresolved Problems of the Modern World

Part 1: Main Ideas

Write the letter of the best answer. (4 points each)

_____ 1. How can mass media cause traditional ways to be abandoned?
    a. by the censorship of images and ideas
    b. by the spread of Western culture globally
    c. by popularizing alternate traditional cultures
    d. by the denigrating of the past

_____ 2. How has technology changed people's lives?
    a. through improvements in communications, economics, and medicine
    b. through mass media by the spread of popular culture
    c. by influencing traditional cultures to abandon old ways
    d. all of the above

_____ 3. What is a negative consequence of the reduction of the rain forest?
    a. the loss of animal and plant species and a reduced oxygen production
    b. reduced income from tourists and film companies who visit the rain forest
    c. reduced supply of hardwood for building
    d. all of the above

_____ 4. How have technology and industrialization created dangers to the global environment?
    a. through decreased demands for skilled laborers
    b. through increased demand for energy and resources
    c. by revealing peoples' similarities and differences
    d. by placing less emphasis on traditional ways

_____ 5. Which of the following is a reason for world hunger?
    a. increased industrialization
    b. forest depletion
    c. natural catastrophes
    d. bioterrorism

_____ 6. Why might free trade lead to more economic growth than protectionism would?
    a. Free trade attracts multinational corporations to establish branch offices.
    b. Free trade promotes commerce by making trade less expensive because it is not taxed.
    c. Protectionism encourages too much competition and chaos.
    d. Protectionism causes foreign companies to grow at the expense of local companies.

_____ 7. What might be the greatest fear about the proliferation of biological and chemical weapons?
    a. Urban criminals may use them instead of guns.
    b. Developed nations will begin to use them in war rather than conventional forces.
    c. Such weapons are easy to produce and distribute, making them more available to terrorist groups.
    d. Such weapons are difficult to make and distribute, increasing their value to terrorist groups.

_____ 8. What might have been the reason India chose not to sign the Non-Proliferation of Nuclear Weapons Treaty?
    a. India and Pakistan have been involved in wars since 1947.
    b. India and Pakistan have signed their own treaty.
    c. India believes nuclear weapons can have a beneficial effect.
    d. All of the above are true.

_____ 9. What human rights abuse do children of less-developed countries often suffer?
    a. eating a diet primarily of junk food
    b. performing dangerous work for long hours
    c. attending schools that teach out-dated information
    d. imprisonment for not obeying society's rules

_____ 10. What is a major way that human rights abuses have been remedied?
    a. Democratic rights and freedoms have been expanded in former Soviet bloc countries and South Africa.
    b. The United Nations has been successful in ceasing the abuse of children in all parts of the world.
    c. International organizations have dramatically improved women's lives in less-developed countries.
    d. The use of torture has been eliminated from the world.

Part 2: Map Skills

Use the map to choose the best possible answer. (4 points each)

World Population Density

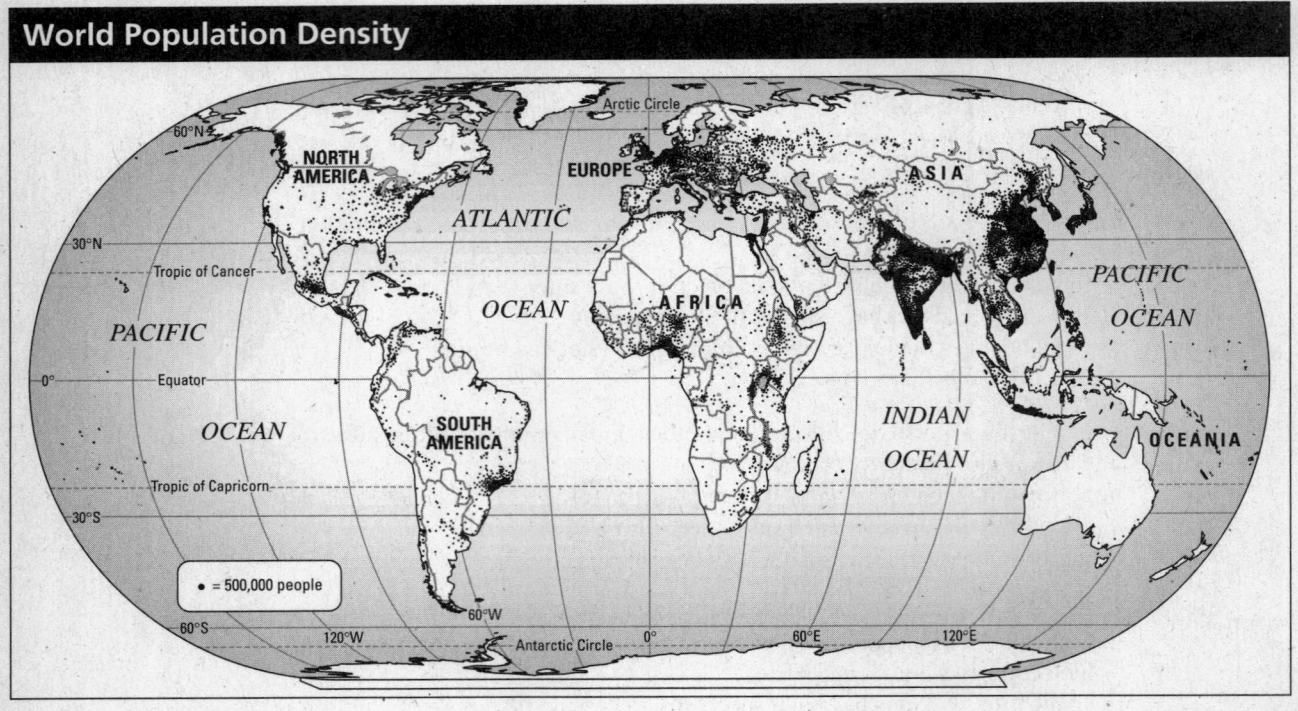

_____ 11. Which two continents seem to have similar population densities?
    a. Europe and Asia   c. North and South America
    b. Africa and Europe   d. Asia and North America

_____ 12. Which latitude region seems to have the largest population density?
    a. Equatorial   c. Tropic of Cancer
    b. Arctic Circle   d. Tropic of Capricorn

_____ 13. What common factor is present in every continent's northern region?
    a. The population density is less.
    b. The population density is more.
    c. They are part of the Arctic Circle.
    d. They are on the Equator.

_____ 14. Which statement describes population density from a global perspective?
    a. Population density is less on the Equator.
    b. Population density is greater on the Equator.
    c. Population density is greater north of the Equator.
    d. Population density is less north of the Equator.

_____ 15. What pattern is true as one moves west to east, starting in the Americas?
    a. The West has the greatest population density.
    b. The West has a greater population density than the East.
    c. Populations become less dense as one moves east.
    d. Populations become denser as one moves east.

Part 3: Interpreting Graphs – Constructed Response

Answer the following questions on the lines provided. (4 points each)

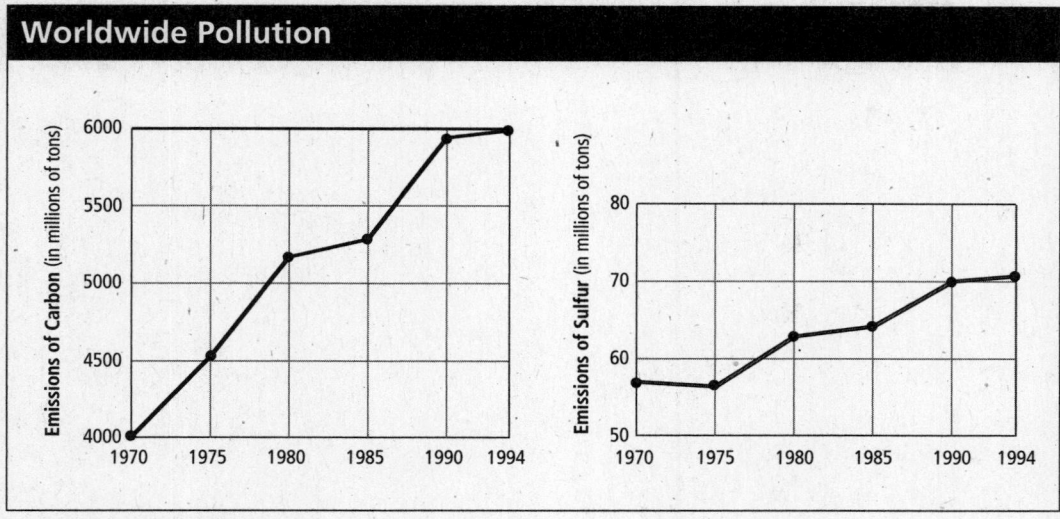

Worldwide Pollution

SOURCE: *Vital Signs,* 1997

16. Approximately how much more carbon was released in 1975 than sulfur?

_____

17. By what percentage did sulfur emissions decrease between 1970 and 1975?

_____

18. By what percentage did carbon emissions increase between 1975 and 1980?

_____

19. Judging only from the two graphs, which pollutant is the greater problem? Why?

_____

20. During which two periods did pollution controls seem to have an effect?

_____

Part 4: Extended Response

(10 points each)

21. **Identifying Problems** How has technology created a growing gap between developed nations and less-developed nations?

22. **Making Inferences** Why is international cooperation essential to combating terrorism?

Answer Key

Answer Key

Prologue: The Rise of Democratic Ideas
QUIZ 1

The Legacy of Greece and Rome

A. 1. i, f

2. d

3. g

4. b

5. e

6. c

7. k, l

8. h

9. j

10. a

B. A democracy that puts unreasonable limitations upon who is or is not a citizen is not unlike an aristocracy. If one group of people is denied the right to vote for reasons that cannot be justified, there is no guarantee that another group will not also unreasonably have their rights taken away. When those in power can control who gets to vote, they do not have to fear being voted out of office.

Prologue: The Rise of Democratic Ideas
QUIZ 2

Judeo-Christian Tradition

A. 1. c

2. a

3. a

4. c

5. d

6. b

7. c

8. b

B. The Renaissance encouraged people to find interest in matters outside the Church; the Reformation resulted from believers questioning the practices of the Church. Both movements challenged the Church's support of the status quo and its discouraging of independent thought.

Prologue: The Rise of Democratic Ideas
QUIZ 3

Democratic Developments in England

A. 1. e

2. g

3. a

4. h

5. b, n

6. c

7. j, m

8. d, f

9. k, l

10. i

B. The English people may have felt that they traded one authoritarian ruler for another. Cromwell, for example, had dissolved Parliament, which many British subjects thought may have been the only institution to protect them from a despotic ruler.

Prologue: The Rise of Democratic Ideas
QUIZ 4

The Enlightenment and Democratic Revolutions

A. 1. the consent of the governed

2. true

3. Parliament

4. Articles of Confederation

5. true

6. dictatorship

7. General Assembly

B. Yes, because of the Declaration of Independence, the leaders creating the new government should have recognized the equality of the peoples who lived in and near the new nation. No, the Native Americans had a culture so different from that of the Europeans that their participation in the new democracy would have caused the fragile experiment to fail.

The Rise of Democratic Ideas
TEST FORM A

Part 1: Main Ideas

1. c

2. d

3. a

4. c

5. b

6. d

7. c

8. a

9. d

10. b

Part 2: Map Skills

11. c

12. c

13. a

14. d

15. b

Part 3: Interpreting Charts

16. b

17. c

18. b

19. a

20. d

Part 4: Extended Response

21. Possible answers:

Possible responses should include the following points: The Reformation was about people challenging the authority of monarchs and popes, which indirectly contributed to the growth of democracy. Those that wanted to reform the Church protested against the abuses of power by the Church. By questioning the power of the Church, the people began to realize that they had a say in rules and how power was used. The protesters, or Protestants, also believed people had a direct relationship with God and that salvation was not necessarily only through the Church. They believed people could interpret the Bible for themselves and find an individual path to God, which helped bolster the importance of the individual. The Renaissance also emphasized the individual, and the idea of the individual would play a significant role in the democratic revolutions that followed. Finally, the Reformation also introduced individuals to reading when it called on people to read the Bible for themselves, a trend that exposed people to more than just religious ideas.

22. Possible responses should include the following points: The signing of the Magna Carta, the Glorious Revolution, and the English Bill of Rights all had a great impact on democracy. The Magna Carta was the first step in guaranteeing individuals certain rights. It contained certain important principles that limited the power of the English monarch and implied that monarchs could not rule in any way they chose but had to govern according to law. The Glorious Revolution is seen as the turning point in English constitutional history, as Parliament had established its right to limit the English monarch's power and to control succession of the throne. The constitution and the laws of the country now restricted the power of the ruler. The English Bill of Rights took the limiting of the monarch's power a step further. The Bill of Rights was a formal summary of the rights and liberties considered essential to the people. The monarch was forbidden to suspend laws, tax without the consent of Parliament, or to raise an army during peacetime without Parliament's approval. The Bill of Rights set an example for England's American colonies, and it would help give rise to democratic revolutions in America and France in the late 18th century.

The Rise of Democratic Ideas
TEST FORM B

Part 1: Main Ideas

1. natural laws
2. true
3. representative government
4. true
5. English Bill of Rights

6. Christian and Jewish
7. Catholic Church
8. true
9. true
10. the Soviet Union

Part 2: Map Skills

11. b
12. d
13. c
14. c
15. a

Part 3: Interpreting Charts

16. c
17. d
18. a
19. b
20. a

Part 4: Extended Response

21. Possible responses should include the following points: When Louis XIV died, he left the country in massive debt and with unresolved problems. Unrest grew during the reigns of his successors. For example, the clergy and monarchy didn't pay taxes, only the commoners paid taxes. Further, the peasants after two years of poor harvests, they were hungry and felt that neither their king nor nobility cared. In 1789, when Louis XVI's government was about to go bankrupt, he sought to raise taxes. The commoners felt that they were not fairly represented in the Estates-General, which Louis had called to raise taxes, so they formed the National Assembly. In the meantime, the people of Paris stormed the Bastille, and the French Revolution had begun. The French middle class and some nobles had become inspired by Enlightenment ideas and the American Revolution. The National Assembly adopted a Declaration of the Rights of Man, ended feudalism in France, drafted a constitution, reorganized the Catholic Church, and redistributed land. It disbanded in 1791 for the Legislative Assembly to take over, but this new assembly was not accepted. Other European countries with absolute monarchs feared the

spread of democratic ideas and together made war on France. The royal family was imprisoned, and the Reign of Terror followed. Finally, in 1799, a military leader, Napoleon Bonaparte, assumed control of France and set up a dictatorship.

22. Possible responses should include the following points: In 1215, after losing a costly war and attempting to raise taxes, King John faced a rebellion by nobles who drafted a document that would guarantee certain traditional political rights. The Magna Carta became a contract between the king and the nobles of England. It contained certain important principles that limited the power of the English monarch, and it implied that the monarch had to govern according to law. The Magna Carta had 63 clauses, two of which established basic legal rights for individuals. One stated that the king had to ask for a popular consent to levy taxes, and the other stated that a person had the right to a jury trial and to the protection of the law. Over the centuries, the Magna Carta has been extended to protect the liberties of all the English people. Because it was the first document to recognize the individual rights of the people, it was the first step in a democratic government in England. It was only the first step because the Magna Carta would need both the Glorious Revolution and the English Bill of Rights to complete the transition of English government from a monarchy to a constitutional monarchy.

The Rise of Democratic Ideas
TEST FORM C

Part 1: Main Ideas

1. a
2. b
3. b
4. d
5. c
6. b
7. a
8. d

9. a

10. b

Part 2: Map Skills—Constructed Response

11. 190 miles

12. Sparta couldn't be attacked by sea.

13. It was surrounded by water, which made trade easier.

14. It was largely uninhabited and probably uninhabitable.

15. It was a seaport that could be a center for trade. Its location at the mouth of the Dardanelles could also have enabled it to control access to the Sea of Marmara and Byzantium.

Part 3: Interpreting Charts

16. a

17. b

18. c

19. d

20. c

Part 4: Extended Response

21. Possible responses should include the following points: When the British government taxed the American colonies after the French and Indian War, the colonists protested. The colonists believed there should not be taxation without representation, and the American colonists were not represented in Parliament. Enlightenment thinker John Locke believed that all people had the right to life, liberty, and property, and that the power of the government came from the people and not from God. The colonists wanted to protect their economic and political rights, so they united and began to arm themselves against British oppression. The Declaration of Independence explained to King George III why the American colonists should be free of British rule. The ideas of the Enlightenment—especially Locke's ideas—strongly influenced the writers of the Declaration. After the war, the colonies existed as a new nation that was a loose federation. They soon realized that the government was too weak, as it could not collect taxes or pay war debt. In the summer of 1787, a group of American leaders met to write the Constitution. They wanted a stable government, but feared that too strong a government would grow tyrannical. To reach a balance, the framers first agreed to a representative government to ensure that the power to govern rested with the people, as advocated by Rousseau. Yet unlike Rousseau, they selected an indirect democracy. Second, the framers created a federal system—the powers of government would be divided between the central government and the state governments. Third, the framers set up a separation of powers based on the writings of Montesquieu. Power was divided among the executive, legislative, and judicial branches to prevent any branch from having too much power.

22. Possible Responses should include the following points: In the Glorious Revolution, Parliament established its right to limit the English monarch's power, and the rights and liberties of the people were formally recognized and protected. The monarch was now forbidden, among other things, to tax without the consent of Parliament. Also, people were assured the right to petition the king about their grievances against the government. Nearly 100 years later when the British government taxed the American colonies, the colonists protested that those taxes were a direct violation of their rights under the Bill of Rights. The colonists were not represented in Parliament and therefore should not be taxed. Therefore, since the king had failed to protect their rights, they believed they should rebel against his rule. The colonists felt they were being oppressed by the British government and that their economic and political rights were being violated. About the same time, the French citizens were going through a time of unrest—the government near bankruptcy and taxes being increased. The people began to rethink the structure of society and were impressed by the ideas of the social contract and freedom of speech. They were also inspired by the example of the Americans Revolution. The French people later began a revolution in order to balance inequities in French society, and the National Assembly created a document strongly influenced by the American Declaration of Independence. Without the Glorious Revolution and Bill of Rights, the American colonies might not have felt justified in rejecting King George III's rule. And many French Revolutionaries were inspired by the example of the American Revolution.

Chapter 1, Section 1
SECTION QUIZ

Italy: Birthplace of the Renaissance

A. 1. c

2. b

3. a

4. c

5. d

6. c

B. Possible answers:

a. The bubonic plague, which devastated Europe, left its survivors with a desire to enjoy life and made them question the traditional Christian teaching that one must endure suffering in this world and wait for reward in the next. It also brought economic changes that put more wealth in the hands of merchants and increased the wages of laborers.

b. Cities and towns had become more important as serfs left estates to seek more rewarding work. The growth of cities led to an increase in the exchange of ideas and a generally more intellectual climate.

c. The Ottoman Turks' conquest of Byzantium caused Byzantine scholars to leave that city and bring ancient Greek texts with them, making those texts available for study in Europe.

d. The rise of the merchant class made more money available to support the arts.

Chapter 1, Section 2
SECTION QUIZ

The Northern Renaissance

A. 1. a

2. b

3. d

4. b

5. a

6. c

B. Possible answers:

a. The printing press made the Bible available to many more people, decreasing people's reliance on the Church's interpretation of scripture.

b. It increased literacy. The availability of reading material made being able to read much more practical and desirable.

c. It increased people's knowledge of the world. Because printed material was much more widely available, ideas could spread more quickly.

Chapter 1, Section 3
SECTION QUIZ

Luther Leads the Reformation

A. 1. l

2. j

3. h

4. k

5. b

6. n

7. o

8. d

9. e

10. k

11. m

12. l

B. Possible answers:

a. Some princes may have stayed loyal to the pope because it seemed the safest thing to do. Others probably sincerely believed that the pope was God's messenger. Others may simply have wanted to align themselves wtih Charles V, who was strongly supportive of the pope.

b. Some princes may have opposed the pope due to a sincere belief in Luther's ideas, such as the concept of salvation through faith. Others undoubtedly longed for the local control that breaking with the Church seemed to offer them.

Opposing the pope gave them justification for seizing Church property.

Chapter 1, Section 4
SECTION QUIZ

The Reformation Continues

A. 1. d

2. b

3. c

4. a

5. b

6. d

B. Possible answers:

a. Calvinism was based on a strict set of doctrines that created a structured, orderly society.

b. Many people were willing to trade personal freedom for safety and life in what they saw as a moral society.

c. The Renaissance had many benefits over life in medieval society, but it also had its insecurities. The life in Geneva probably seemed safe and secure in contrast to life in many Renaissance cities.

d. It gave order to the new faith that Luther created.

e. Calvin taught his followers to enjoy the gifts of God.

Chapter 1
TEST FORM A

European Renaissance and Reformation

Part 1: Main Ideas

1. b

2. a

3. c

4. d

5. c

6. a

7. b

8. a

9. d

10. c

Part 2: Map Skills

11. b

12. c

13. d

14. b

15. c

Part 3: Document-Based Questions

A. (4 points each)

16. It is best to be both loved and feared, but these rarely come together.

17. To be a good man and a famous ruler, a person should read literature deeply and study it as a possible model of behavior.

18. to portray human hands realistically

B. (8 points)

19. Machiavelli's view of human nature is somewhat negative and cynical, emphasizing greed and self-interest. His viewpoint is thoroughly realistic; his advice is very pragmatic. Leonardo's drawing of hands reflects his concentration on a person's individuality. Even a person's hands are worthy of study. He strives for realistic portrayal. Aeneas Silvius values learning and the serious study of literature, philosophy, and jurisprudence. He believes people can learn the principles of a good life from the study of these materials, and he emphasizes study and hard work. In summary, the Renaissance view of humans was varied and diverse, emphasized complexity, saw both the positive and negative in human nature and behavior, but valued people.

Part 4: Extended Response

20. Possible responses should include the following points:

Movable type made it possible to set an entire page in block print. The printing press made it possible to run off many copies of a manuscript. The availability of multiple copies brought down the price of each book. A classical education was not required to read these "mass-produced" books because they were often written in or translated into the vernacular. Literacy increased and thus people became more educated and worldly.

21. *Possible responses should include the following points:*

In his 95 Theses, Martin Luther took a stand against the sale of indulgences. The Church sold indulgences in order to raise money. Indulgences were pardons, freeing people from performing assigned penalties for sin. Luther thought that the sale of indulgences gave the impression that people could buy their way into heaven. Similarly, Luther worried that people might believe they could be saved by doing good works. Luther insisted that only by faith in God's forgiveness could a person win salvation. He also insisted on the primacy of the Bible over Church traditions and the pope. Each individual could read and interpret the Bible without the pope or a priest to interpret it.

Chapter 1
TEST FORM B

European Renaissance and Reformation

Part 1: Main Ideas

1. true
2. Hundred Years' War
3. Constantinople
4. true
5. patrons
6. printing press
7. annul
8. true
9. Anglican Church
10. true

Part 2: Map Skills

11. b
12. c
13. a
14. c
15. b

Part 3: Document-Based Questions

A. (4 points each)

16. to be feared, because fear is supported by dread of pain and because, unlike love, a prince can rely on fear and control it

17. Aeneas Silvius recommends the study of literature because it offers models of how to live and a way of becoming a good man and a famous ruler.

18. respect for individuals; focus on humans; desire to portray people realistically.

B. (8 points)

19. Machiavelli's view of human nature is somewhat negative and cynical, emphasizing greed and self-interest. His viewpoint is thoroughly realistic; his advice is very pragmatic. Leonardo's drawing of hands reflects his concentration on a person's individuality. Even a person's hands are worthy of study. He strives for realistic portrayal. Aeneas Silvius values learning and the serious study of literature, philosophy, and jurisprudence. He believes people can learn the principles of a good life from the study of these materials, and he emphasizes study and hard work. In summary, the Renaissance view of humans was varied and diverse, emphasized complexity, saw both the positive and negative in human nature and behavior, but valued people.

Part 4: Extended Response

20. Possible answers should include the following points:

Rebellious—He stood up against Church authorities to openly oppose Church practices. Determined—He refused to be intimidated by threats. Controlled by conscience—He refused to recant, declaring that he was bound by his conscience. Inspiring—Many people were swayed by Luther's teachings; these followers eventually began a separate religious group. Unforgiving—His reaction to the peasant revolt was to urge German princes to show the peasants no mercy. Brilliant or innovative—He came up with theological ideas that overturned centuries of Catholic teaching.

21. Possible responses should include the following points:

The Middle Ages focused narrowly on the study of God, whereas the Renaissance focused broadly on the study of all aspects of humans. Medieval art portrayed stilted, one-dimensional religious scenes. Gothic cathedral architecture reached toward the heavens; stained-glass windows told religious stories. The medieval world was unified by Christian faith; Latin was the language of the Church. In contrast, Renaissance arts reflected the search for balance and harmony and a new appreciation for the human body. The use of perspective presented the world more realistically. As Renaissance interests became more secular, writers' use of the vernacular became common. The arts blossomed under the patronage of nobles and wealthy merchants, who saw in art the opportunity to enrich their lives.

Chapter 1
TEST FORM C

European Renaissance and Reformation

Part 1: Main Ideas

1. b
2. c
3. d
4. c
5. a
6. d
7. b
8. a
9. b
10. a

Part 2: Map Skills

11. 1541–1579
12. approximately 1,000
13. Ireland had adherants to three different religions. Moreover, although Roman Catholicism was the strongest, countries dominated by the other two religions were geographically very close.
14. The farther away from Rome, the more likely it was that a region would become Protestant. Rome was where the pope lived, and nearby lands remained more loyal or more easily controlled.
15. Anglican; it was created for political reasons, not from religious zeal.

Part 3: Document-Based Questions

A. (4 points each)

16. not loyal or trustworthy; pursuing self-interests; needing to be coerced

17. Silvius believes that humans can learn from literature, philosophy, and the law and that this learning can transform a person. Such a transformation cannot be earned by the dillitante who learns easily and quickly on a superficial level. To become a good person who leads a good life, a person must study hard and learn deeply. Humans do have this ability to develop themselves.

18. as important, beautiful, deserving of study

B. (8 points)

19. Machiavelli's view of human nature is somewhat negative and cynical, emphasizing greed and self-interest. His viewpoint is thoroughly realistic; his advice is very pragmatic. Leonardo's drawing of hands reflects his concentration on a person's individuality. Even a person's hands are worthy of study. He strives for realistic portrayal. Aeneas Silvius values learning and the serious study of literature, philosophy, and jurisprudence. He believes people can learn the principles of a good life from the study of these materials, and he emphasizes study and hard work. In summary, the Renaissance view of humans was varied and diverse, emphasized complexity, saw both the positive and negative in human nature and behavior, but valued people.

Part 4: Extended Response

20. Possible responses should include the following points:

Established leaders, such as the pope and the emperor of the Holy Roman Empire lost power when kings and princes used the Reformation as justification for ignoring the orders of the Church. Without the support of the local clergy and the peasants, the Church was unable to enforce its orders. Kings and local princes gained power by taking advantage of the Reformation to seize land and property and to assert their independence from the Church

and Emperor Charles V. The Reformation was widely seen as an opportunity to exert local control.

21. Possible responses should include the following points:

The Renaissance broke the unified religious world view of the Middle Ages. It emphasized the secular and the dignity of the individual. This outlook challenged the authority of the Roman Catholic Church. The invention of the printing press made possible the quick spread of new ideas; its ability to print multiple copies that were cheap greatly expanded literacy and the reading public. The fact that more people read the Bible caused them to form their own ideas about religion. In addition, the Church had grown ever more wealthy and worldly, as many Renaissance leaders had. This change evoked much criticism.

Chapter 2, Section 1
SECTION QUIZ

The Ottomans Build a Vast Empire

A. 1. d
2. b
3. d
4. c
5. c
6. a
7. a
8. e
9. b
10. d

B. Possible answers:

a. The ghazi were Turks who considered themselves warriors for Islam. They were similar to Christian knights in Europe. They belonged to military societies and followed a strict Islamic code of conduct. They carried out raids on "infidels" and fought in wars that expanded the Ottoman Empire.

b. The janissaries were part of an elite fighting force of slaves owned by the sultan. They came, as young Christian boys, from territories conquered by the Ottomans and

became Muslim through conversion. They fought in wars that expanded the Ottoman empire.

c. The janissaries were part of the devshirme system.

Chapter 2, Section 2
SECTION QUIZ

Cultural Blending CASE STUDY: The Safavid Empire

A. 1. c
2. d
3. d
4. a
5. c
6. c

B. Students could note that Shah Abbas

a. reformed the military.

b. punished political corruption and promoted competent officials.

c. established a period of peace by ensuring that the military and important government officials were loyal to him.

d. established relations with nations in Europe and Asia.

e. brought Chinese artisans to the Safavid Empire.

f. rebuilt the capital city of Isfahan and decorated it with monumental buildings, gardens, and broad boulevards.

Chapter 2, Section 3
SECTION QUIZ

The Mughals Empire in India

A. 1. g
2. j
3. a
4. e
5. c
6. i
7. b
8. a
9. h

B. Students could note that Akbar

a. was a defender of religious freedom.

b. abolished taxes on non-Muslims and adopted a fairer method of taxation similar to the U.S. graduated income tax.

c. increased the quality of government by opening government service to all of the peoples of the empire.

d. initiated policies that prevented the growth of a strong aristocracy at the expense of other groups in society.

e. conquered many lands, adding significantly to the wealth of the empire.

f. welcomed influences from many cultures, which encouraged the arts, literature, and architecture to flourish.

Chapter 2
TEST FORM A

The Muslim World Expands

Part 1: Main Ideas

1. a
2. d
3. i
4. c
5. e
6. h
7. g
8. j
9. f
10. b

Part 2: Map Skills

11. c
12. a
13. c
14. d
15. b

Part 3: Interpreting Graphs

16. c
17. d
18. d
19. b
20. d

Part 4: Extended Response

21. Possible responses should include the following points:

Shah Abbas helped create a Safavid culture that drew from the best of the Ottoman, Persian, and Arab worlds. He reformed the military by limiting the power of the redheads and creating two armies that would be loyal to him alone. He punished corruption severely and promoted officials who were competent and loyal. He established relations with Europe that helped industry and art to flourish. He brought Chinese artisans to the Safavid Empire. Artistic collaborations gave rise to artwork that beautified the mosques, palaces, and marketplaces of Isfahan.

22. Possible responses should include the following points:

Suleyman's military conquests led to the expansion of the Ottoman Empire. He treated non-Muslims as *millets*, or nations. This reduced conflict. He simplified the system of taxation and reduced government bureaucracy—bettering the lives of citizens and reducing the possibility of rebellion. As part of the system of *devshirme*, Christian boys were converted to Islam and trained as soldiers. The janissaries became the core of the Ottoman armies, forming a disciplined war machine that helped to conquer more territories and defend the empire. Art and literature flourished under Suleyman's rule. Both painters and poets looked to Persia and Arabia for models. Their works used these foreign influences to express original Ottoman ideas. Still, the decline of the Ottoman Empire had begun. Suleyman killed his ablest son and drove another in exile, leaving an incompetent son to inherit the throne. This weakened the Ottoman Empire, leading to its decline.

Chapter 2
TEST FORM B

The Muslim World Expands

Part 1: Main Ideas

1. a
2. b

3. c
4. b
5. d
6. a
7. b
8. c
9. a
10. d

Part 2: Map Skills

11. c
12. c
13. a
14. d
15. b

Part 3: Interpreting Graphs

16. c
17. b
18. c
19. d
20. a

Part 4: Extended Response

21. Possible responses should include the following points:

Shah Abbas established relations with European nations and invited Chinese artisans to the Safavid Empire. Industry and art flourished. Artistic collaborations gave rise to beautiful artwork that decorated the mosques, palaces, and marketplaces of Isfahan. Akbar was a Muslim who firmly defended religious freedom. Unlike Shah Abbas, who created an army of Christian janissaries, Akbar appointed Hindu Rajputs as officers. In Akbar's bureaucracy, natives and foreigners, Hindus and Muslims, could all rise to high office. Cultural mingling affected art, education, politics, and language. Mughal artwork reveals Persian, Western, and Hindu influences. Both Akbar and Shah Abbas welcomed cultural influences from conquered peoples, as well as influences from people outside their empires.

22. Possible responses should include the following points:

After Shah Jahan fell ill, Aurangzeb gained the throne by executing his older brother and placing his father in prison. Aurangzeb expanded the Mughal holdings through conquest, but the power of the empire weakened due to his oppression of the people. He rigidly enforced Islamic laws and policed his subjects' morals. He heavily taxed non-Muslims and dismissed Hindus from high positions of government. He banned the construction of new temples and had Hindu monuments destroyed. The Hindu Rajputs rebelled. Marathas formed a breakaway state and turned to guerrilla warfare. The Sikhs formed a breakaway state. Aurangzeb levied oppressive taxes to pay for wars against increasing enemies. By the end of his reign, he had drained the empire of its resources. His subjects felt little or no loyalty to him; millions had died in a famine while he was waging war. The power of local lords grew. After Aurangzeb's death, his sons fought a war of succession; but the next Mughal emperors were nothing but wealthy figureheads.

Chapter 2
TEST FORM C

The Muslim World Expands

Part 1: Main Ideas

1. b
2. d
3. c
4. b
5. a
6. b
7. d
8. c
9. a
10. c

Part 2: Map Skills—Constructed Response

11. Hungary, Tripoli, and Mesopotamia
12. Constantinople was on the Bosporus, and gaining control of the Bosporus could unify the territories of the Ottoman Empire. The Bosporus connected the Black Sea to other waterways.

13. They stretched further north, east, and west.
14. They stretched further south, east, and west.
15. The Ottomans conquered coasts, rivers, and other waterways to control trade and transportation.

Part 3: Interpreting Graphs

16. c
17. d
18. b
19. a
20. c

Part 4: Extended Response

21. Possible responses should include the following points:

Shah Abbas and Akbar both supported cultural blending. Abbas encouraged a great cultural and artistic age in the Safavid Empire. He reformed the Safavid military, borrowing methods from the Ottomans. He developed relationships with European nations and invited Chinese artisans to the Safavid Empire. Artistic collaborations gave rise to beautiful artwork that decorated the mosques, palaces, and marketplaces of Isfahan. As Akbar extended the Mughal Empire, he welcomed influences from the many cultures it included. This cultural mingling affected art, architecture, education, politics, and language. A new language, Urdu, developed. Akbar continued the tradition of Mughal miniatures—a style taught by Persian artists. Akbar firmly supported religious freedom, and he eliminated special taxes on non-Muslims. Hindu literature experienced a revival, and Akbar period architecture reflects Hindu themes. Students may name other rulers if they can provide evidence to support their opinions.

22. Possible responses should include the following points:

Akbar encouraged a great cultural and artistic age, whereas Aurangzeb's policies led to the decline of the Mughal Empire. Akbar was a genius at cultural blending. He tolerated other religions and levied fair taxes.

He removed the jizya, the tax against non-Muslims. Akbar encouraged art, language, and literature from other cultures in the Mughal court and lands. Aurangzeb oppressed his people. He rigidly enforced Islamic laws and appointed censors to police his subjects' morals. He outlawed the building of Hindu temples, and destroyed Hindu monuments. Akbar and Aurangzeb both believed in war. Akbar, however, appointed Rajputs as officers in the military, turning potential enemies into allies. Aurangzeb dismissed Hindus from high government positions, enraging them until they rebelled. Aurangzeb had to increase his taxes to pay for wars against increasing enemies. He doubled taxes on Hindu merchants; such unfair taxation encouraged further rebellion.

Chapter 3, Section 1
SECTION QUIZ

Europeans Explore the East

A.
1. a
2. c
3. c
4. d
5. b
6. c
7. d

B. Inspirations:

a. "God," that is, the belief that it was their duty to spread Christianity
b. "glory," that is, the desire for fame
c. "gold," that is, the desire for wealth for themselves and their nations' treasuries

What made the explorations possible:

a. The Europeans invented and borrowed technology, including the caravel and the magnetic compass, that made it possible for their ships to sail against the wind and to follow a course without using landmarks.
b. The Portuguese government gave strong support to the study of navigation and to overseas explorations.

c. Spain financed Columbus's voyage, believing it could help the Spanish control a trade route with the East.

Chapter 3, Section 2
SECTION QUIZ

China Limits European Contacts

A. 1. m

2. h

3. f

4. m

5. n

6. a

7. d

8. d

9. k

10. i

11. c

B. Possible answers:

a. Most Chinese were farmers.

b. Increased use of fertilizers and irrigation increased rice production.

c. Farmers began growing new crops, introduced from newly discovered lands.

d. The increase in the food supply improved nutrition.

e. Improvements in nutrition encouraged larger families.

f. The Chinese population increased dramatically and rapidly.

g. Males were valued much more highly than females.

h. Many female infants were killed.

i. Men dominated households and families.

j. Women worked in the home, in the fields, and sometimes outside of the home.

k. Women raised children and managed the family's finances.

l. Drama was a popular form of entertainment.

Chapter 3, Section 3
SECTION QUIZ

Japan Returns to Isolation

A. 1. a

2. c

3. b

4. a

5. c

6. a

7. a

B. Possible answers:

a. The "closed country policy" largely closed off foreign access to Japan.

b. For more than 200 years, Japan existed as a self-sufficient country with only one port (Nagasaki) remaining open to foreign (Dutch and Chinese) traders.

c. Due to the repression of Christianity and persecution of Christians, Christianity was virtually eliminated in Japan.

d. All Japanese were required to demonstrate faithfulness to Buddhism.

e. Japan remained free from European attempts to colonize or to establish a presence in Japan.

f. The Tokugawa Shogunate grew rich from its monopoly on foreign trade.

Chapter 3
TEST FORM A

An Age of Explorations and Isolation

Part 1: Main Ideas

1. c

2. b

3. a

4. b

5. b

6. d

7. c

8. b

9. a

10. c

Part 2: Map Skills

11. d

12. b

13. a

14. d

15. c

Part 3: Interpreting Time Lines

16. c

17. a

18. c

19. b

20. d

Part 4: Extended Response

21. Possible responses should include the following points: The main problem was technology. It wasn't until the 1400s that shipbuilders designed a new vessel, the caravel, which was sturdier than earlier vessels and had triangular sails that allowed it to sail effectively against the wind. Before the 1400s, European ships could not sail against the wind, making it nearly impossible for any European sea captain to sail 3,000 miles of ocean and return again. Europeans also improved their navigational techniques. Sailors began using the astrolabe, which was perfected by the Muslims, to determine their location at sea. Explorers also began using the magnetic compass, which was invented by the Chinese, to track their direction more accurately. The next problem they had to overcome was getting around the southern tip of Africa. Vasco da Gama reached the port of Calicut, on the southwestern coast of India in 1498, giving Portugal a direct sea rout to India.

22. Possible responses should include the following points: Agricultural improvements increased the amount and the variety of food produced by China's farmers, which led to improvements in nutrition. The Qing Dynasty introduced a long line of stable, competent rulers that created an era of peace and prosperity. The Qing Dynasty also prevented European powers from colonizing or otherwise dominating China. In Japan, the Tokugawa Shogunate

unified the country and imposed a period of peace. The growth of urban and commercial centers offered new opportunities for people, and arts and literature flourished. The Tokugawa Shogunate also prevented European powers from colonizing or otherwise dominating Japan.

Chapter 3
TEST FORM B

An Age of Explorations and Isolation

Part 1: Main Ideas

1. true
2. true
3. Indian Ocean
4. true
5. Chinese
6. true
7. Portuguese
8. Qing Dynasty
9. Christian
10. Muslims and Italians

Part 2: Map Skills

11. b
12. a
13. c
14. b
15. d

Part 3: Interpreting Time Lines

16. d
17. c
18. d
19. a
20. c

Part 4: Extended Response

21. Possible responses should include the following points: For Europeans, God, gold, and glory were the primary reasons for exploring new land. The Europeans believed it was their duty to convert non-Christians to Christianity. They also desired to become wealthy by dominating the trade of spices and other luxuries from Asia, and many of the European countries wanted to break the Italian-Muslim monopoly of trading Asian goods and wanted to find routes to Asia themselves. Finally, the explorers themselves risked their lives in order to serve their nations and achieve fame and wealth for both their nations and themselves. The Chinese desired international fame, and they desired to impress other peoples with their superiority and goods. They also wanted to find additional wealth and attract new tributaries.

22. Possible responses should include the following points: In China, the official policy was isolation, and only the government was allowed to conduct foreign trade. Later, under the Manchus, countries that wanted to trade with China had to follow certain rituals and rules. In reality, however, trade with Europeans flourished, and profit-minded merchants smuggled silk, porcelain, and other goods out of the country and into the hands of eager Europeans. While this had a ripple effect on those industries, China did not become a highly industrialized nation because the government did not support trading and taxed manufactured goods highly, while taxes on agriculture stayed low. The Chinese rulers acted in this way because they did not want European influences in China—such as missionaries trying to convert people to Christianity—and the idea of commerce offended China's Confucian beliefs. In Japan, trade with Europeans was first welcomed, as the Japanese were particularly interested in the Portuguese muskets and cannons. The Japanese even accepted the missionaries at first because they associated them with the European goods they wanted. Part of this acceptance also was because Japan had no central authority to contain the Europeans. Later, as Japan's rule centralized and the leaders became strong, Japan's borders were sealed to merchants and missionaries and a "closed country" policy was initiated. Only one port remained open, and only the Chinese and Dutch could trade through that port. Japan wanted to be a self-sufficient country and remain free of European attempts to colonize or establish their presence.

Chapter 3
TEST FORM C

An Age of Explorations and Isolation

Part 1: Main Ideas

1. b
2. c
3. b
4. d
5. b
6. c
7. a
8. d
9. b
10. a

Part 2: Map Skills

11. c
12. d
13. a
14. d
15. c

Part 3: Interpreting Time Lines—Constructed Response

16. The building of the Forbidden City was completed and exploration stopped.

17. It was a rivalry as shown by Dutch seizures of Malacca from Portugal.

18. Japan did not have a centralized rule so it was more focused on unifying the country than it was on new trade.

19. There was mistrust and hostility. The Europeans wanted to build up trade, even if they had to conquer Asian lands, while the Chinese wanted to be left alone.

20. It had finally unified, and it might have been concerned about the outside influences of merchants and missionaries.

Part 4: Extended Response

21. Possible responses should include the following points: The Europeans weren't content just to trade goods, they wanted to dominate their trading partners to get wealthy and to convert them to Christianity. Neither the Japanese or Chinese

were eager to deal with such interference, nor did they to feel the need to convert others to their religions. China also had an ancient and sophisticated civilization and viewed itself as self-sufficient and central to the world, therefore it didn't need to seek out others for trade because it didn't need anything. Also, the Japanese and Chinese were already trading with each other, and the goods from Europe might not have been as enticing to Asians as the goods from Asia were to Europeans. Finally, the Chinese has a long history of invasion that made them suspicious of foreigners and protective of their cultural traditions.

22. Possible responses should include the following points: Japan first encountered Europeans in 1543 when shipwrecked Portuguese sailors washed up on the shores of southern Japan. Merchants soon followed, and the Japanese were eager to expand their markets and receive the European goods. The daimyo were also welcoming and were particularly interest in the firearms and cannons. At this time, Japan lacked a strong central authority to contain the Europeans or to make any decisions about the pros or cons of trade. In China, however, the Ming Dynasty had been strong for more than a century by the time the first Europeans arrived. China believed itself to be the center of the world, and the emperor was quick to realize that along with trade came outside influences, which he did not welcome. Also, the government did not support commerce because it went against China's Confucian beliefs. Instead, agriculture was favored. Japan accepted the merchants and missionaries until the 1600s. By this time, Tokugawa Ieyasu had taken power in Japan and centralized it. The success of the European missionaries bothered him because they began to become involved in politics, and he feared an uprising. The strong leaders under Tokugawa did not like the introduction of European ideas and ways. By 1639, Japan sealed its borders and instituted a "closed country" policy. China, however,

did not change its attitude and continued its policy of isolation through the Qing Dynasty. The Dutch were the only Europeans to be allowed to trade with China because the Dutch were willing to kowtow and pay China gifts. The Chinese, however, felt that their country was self-sufficient, and they would remain isolated for centuries.

Chapter 4, Section 1
SECTION QUIZ

Spain Builds an American Empire

A. 1. Spanish colonists
2. true
3. west across the Atlantic Ocean
4. true
5. conquistadors
6. Aztec people of Mexico
7. true

B. Students who feel that natives could have successfully defended their civilizations could point out that

a. disease was probably the chief weapon the Spanish had. Greater suspicion of the first Spanish to arrive would have kept them at a distance and protected Native Americans from contagion.

b. if all of the Spanish had been killed, perhaps after tricking them into feeling safe as the Spanish did to the Incas, there might not have been later voyages, at least for quite awhile.

Students who feel that natives could not have successfully defended their civilizations could point out that

a. the Spanish had superior weaponry and, more importantly, disease.

b. once the Spanish had glimpsed the wealth available to them, no threat would have stopped them.

c. even if the first Spanish had not completely conquered these civilizations, they would have carried home to Spain tales of American wealth. Later Spanish voyages would have completed the destruction begun earlier.

Chapter 4, Section 2
SECTION QUIZ

European Nations Settle North America

A. 1. true
2. Jamestown
3. New France
4. Plymouth
5. true
6. King Philip's War
7. English (British)

B. Possible answers:

a. French; wealth; exploring, fur trading, and fighting wars to dominate North America.

b. English; wealth and religious freedom; searching for gold, farming tobacco, creating model communities (colonizing), and fighting wars to dominate North America.

c. Dutch; wealth; exploring, fur trading, building trading posts, colonizing, farming tobacco and sugar

Chapter 4, Section 3
SECTION QUIZ

The Atlantic Slave Trade

A. 1. Islam spread across Africa; and Muslims bought and sold non-Muslim prisoners-of-war as slaves.

2. In most African and Muslim societies, slaves had legal rights they did not have in the Americas.

In most African and Muslim societies, slaves had greater opportunities for social mobility than they did in the Americas.

In Muslim societies, slaves could occupy positions of power and authority. This was not the case in the Americas.

In African societies, slaves could escape bondage in a number of legal ways that were not available to slaves in the Americas.

3. Many Africans had built up immunity to some European diseases.

Many Africans were used to farming.

Because Africans had little chance of successful escape, they were unlikely to attempt it.

4. North America, New England, Northern colonies, or Southern colonies; West Indies or Caribbean Islands; England or Europe; Africa or West Africa.

5. sugar, coffee, tobacco, slaves, rum, molasses, furs, gold, firearms, gum, cotton.

6. Starting point: Africa (West coast of Africa); Ending points: West Indies, North America, South America

B. Possible answers:

a. Africa: African societies lost generations of their most able members; millions of African families were devastated by the loss of members; the firearms that were introduced encouraged conflict and chaos in Africa.

b. Americas: Africans provided the backbreaking labor on which the survival and prosperity of many colonies rested; knowledgeable Africans brought knowledge of agriculture; Africans introduced aspects of their cultures to the Americas; Africans contributed to the racial diversity of the Americas.

Chapter 4, Section 4
SECTION QUIZ

The Columbian Exchange and Global Trade

A. 1. true

2. private

3. founding colonies

4. after

5. east across the Atlantic Ocean

6. east across the Atlantic Ocean

7. exceeds (is greater than)

B. Possible answers:

a. Mercantilism was an economic theory and policy that held that a country's power depended mainly upon its wealth.

b. Colonies increased the wealth of the home country by providing gold and silver and other valuable raw materials that could not be found in the home country and by providing markets for the home country's goods.

Chapter 4
TEST FORM A

The Atlantic World

Part 1: Main Ideas

1. b

2. a

3. c

4. b

5. a

6. d

7. b

8. d

9. a

10. c

Part 2: Map Skills

11. a, b, d

12. b

13. c, d

14. a

15. a, b

Part 3: Interpreting Charts

16. b

17. c

18. d

19. a

20. c

Part 4: Extended Response

21. Possible answers should include the following points: The Spanish had superior weaponry, and the Aztec arrows were no match for Spanish rifles and cannons. The Spanish were also able to obtain the help of Native Americans by exploiting the resentment that many of them felt toward the Aztec. Finally, the Spanish unknowingly exposed the Native Americans to a wide variety of European diseases for which the

natives had no immunity. Many Aztecs died from these diseases or became too weak to fight the Spanish.

22. Possible responses should include the following points: England saw New Netherland as separating its northern and southern colonies. Therefore, England sent a fleet to New Netherland to drive the Dutch out of North America. When the fleet arrived, the Dutch surrendered peacefully. The Duke of York claimed New Netherland for England and renamed it New York. The English later wanted more land to suit its growing colonial populations. The English pushed further west into the continent, but by doing so, the English intruded on France's North American holdings. The English fought the French for the control of French lands in North America during the French and Indian War. The war became part of a larger conflict known as the Seven Years' War in which Britain and France—along with their European allies—battled for territorial and colonial supremacy in Europe and the West Indies. In North America, the British Army helped the British colonists defeat the French and forced the French to surrender most of their colonial holdings on the continent.

Chapter 4
TEST FORM B

The Atlantic World

Part 1: Main Ideas

1. Jamestown

2. Africa or West Africa

3. exports

4. the French and Indian War

5. Spanish

6. true

7. true

8. true

9. capitalism

10. true

Part 2: Map Skills

11. c

12. b

13. c

14. d

15. d

Part 3: Interpreting Charts

16. d

17. a

18. d

19. c

20. b

Part 4: Extended Response

21. Possible responses should include the following points: The Spanish conquistadors violently subdued the native population. Then priests were sent into the area. The Spanish colonized the area, and the Spanish settlers and priests lived among the conquered people and imposed their culture upon them. Spanish settlers and native women created a new group of peoples and a mixture of cultures. Though the Spanish lived among the natives, they also oppressed the native people in a variety of ways. For instance, they forced Native Americans to labor within the *encomienda* system and frequently whipped the laborers. One way the Spanish were able to suppress the natives was with their superior weapons. The Spanish also brought many diseases from Europe that the natives were not immune to, and millions of natives died because of these diseases.

22. Possible responses should include the following points: In most African and Muslim societies, enslaved people had some legal rights, which was not the case in the Americas. Enslaved people had greater opportunities for social mobility in African Muslim societies; they could occupy positions of power and authority. Enslaved persons did not have social mobility in the Americas, and they were treated as inferior humans.

Chapter 4
TEST FORM C

The Atlantic World

Part 1: Main Ideas

1. b

2. b

3. a

4. c

5. d

6. b

7. a

8. a

9. c

10. a

Part 2: Map Skills

11. c

12. a

13. b

14. a

15. a

Part 3: Interpreting Charts—Constructed Response

16. They exported rum, trade goods, and currency to Africa, which exported slaves and gold to the West Indies, and the West Indies exported enslaved Africans, coins, molasses, and sugar to New England, Philadelphia, and New York.

17. England imported salt, fruit, and wines from Spain and imported sugar, molasses, fruit, and bills of exchange for the West Indies. England then exported manufactured goods to New England, New York, and Philadelphia.

18. They worked the sugar plantations in the colonies, and sugar was one of the main exports from the southern colonies and the West Indies. The enslaved Africans were not only part of the trading triangle, but helped to produce some of the products that were traded.

19. It was made into coins in the West Indies.

20. because it involved three stages of trade and the routes formed a triangle

Part 4: Extended Response

21. Possible responses should include the following responses: Both the Dutch and the French were interested in using the resources of North America to gain wealth. Both countries explored North America and built sizable fur trades. France's North American empire was immense, but it was sparsely populated. A large number of colonists had no desire to build towns or raise families; they were interested in the economic activity of fur trading. The English, however, were more interested in establishing colonies. The English who colonized North America were interested in religious freedom. The English Puritans wanted to build a model community that would set an example for other Christians to follow. The family life in the colony helped to create a sense of order and ensured reproduction. The Dutch colony was slow to attract colonists, so it eventually opened its doors to a variety of people.

22. Possible responses should include the following points: Europe experienced increased economic activity. The joint-stock company was developed, allowing investors to gamble on a new colony for a small amount of money and share the risks and rewards. The joint-stock company became the model for modern business and the concept of the stock exchange. Capitalism grew and flourished, as did individual businesses. Many merchants became quite wealthy. There was a change from the wealth and power being held by the government, to the wealth and power being held by individuals. The increase of the overall money supply to the nations also led to inflation, or the increase in the price of goods. The economic policy of mercantilism also developed. This policy stated that a nation's wealth made it powerful, since wealth allowed nation to build navies and purchase goods. For a nation to become wealthy, it had to accumulate silver and gold. Spain, for instance, took a great deal of precious metals from the Americas.

Mercantilism also led nations to try to ensure that they sold more goods to other countries than they bought from other countries, therefore having a favorable balance of trade. Finally, the number of towns in Europe increased, and the merchant class rose in status and power.

Chapter 5, Section 1
SECTION QUIZ

Spain's Empire and European Absolutism

A. 1. true
2. Spanish
3. Dutch
4. the Netherlands
5. true
6. Catholicism
7. Spain

B. Possible answers:

a. An absolute monarch is a king or queen who claims the authority to rule without limits.

b. The belief in the divine right of monarchs gave religious authority to absolute monarchs and all of their actions. It held that God created the monarchy and that the monarch acted as God's representative on Earth. The absolute monarch, therefore, answered only to God.

c. Monarchs were driven by a constant state of crisis to impose order at any cost. To do so, they increased their own power and placed controls on all aspects of their subjects' lives.

Chapter 5, Section 2
SECTION QUIZ

The Reign of Louis XIV

A. 1. e
2. n
3. a
4. n
5. m
6. b
7. o
8. c

9. e
10. g
11. h
12. l
13. j

B. Possible answers:

a. Absolutism: the people came to prefer a strong monarch who could keep the peace; fed up with rebellious nobles, monarchs and their advisors adopted policies that severely weakened the nobility and made them more dependent on the monarch.

b. Skepticism: many intellectuals who witnessed the horror of the religious wars came to doubt churches that claimed to have the only correct set of beliefs and doctrines and to adopt skepticism, the idea that nothing can ever be known for certain.

Chapter 5, Section 3
SECTION QUIZ

Central European Monarchs Clash

A. 1. b
2. d
3. a
4. a
5. d
6. a

B. Possible answers:

a. Germany was devastated. Its population dropped, trade and agriculture were disrupted, and its economy ruined. As a result, Germany did not become a unified state until the 1800s.

b. The Hapsburg states of Spain and Austria were weakened.

c. France was strengthened.

d. German princes became independent of the Holy Roman Emperor.

e. The religious wars in Europe ended.

f. A new method of negotiating peace was introduced in which all participants met to settle the problems of the war and decide the terms of peace.

g. The modern state system was adopted in which Europe was divided into

independent states that were seen as equals and that could negotiate for themselves.

Chapter 5, Section 4
SECTION QUIZ

Absolute Rulers of Russia

A. 1. b
2. c
3. d
4. c
5. a
6. c

B. Students should recognize that Peter believed that westernization would make Russia stronger. Regarding westernization, students might also note that Peter

a. was fascinated by modern tools and machines.

b. wanted to compete with Europe both commercially and as a military power.

Regarding Peter's efforts to westernize Russia, students could note that he

a. introduced potatoes, which became a staple of the Russian diet.

b. started Russia's first newspaper.

c. raised the status of women.

d. ordered nobles to give up Russian styles for Western styles.

e. founded schools and made other efforts to advance learning.

f. fought a long war to take control of a warm-water port that would allow easier access to the West.

g. built St. Petersburg.

Chapter 5, Section 5
SECTION QUIZ

Parliament Limits the English Monarchy

A. 1. g
2. d
3. d
4. b
5. n

6. l

7. l

8. h

9. c

10. a

11. i

12. j

B. Possible answers:

a. Absolute monarchy came to a permanent end.

b. A constitutional monarchy was adopted.

c. The monarchy governed in partnership with Parliament.

d. The monarchy recognized legal limits on its power.

e. The monarchy couldn't suspend Parliament's laws.

f. The monarchy couldn't levy taxes without the consent of Parliament.

g. The monarchy couldn't interfere with freedom of speech in Parliament.

h. Citizens couldn't be penalized for petitioning the monarchy about grievances.

i. The cabinet system of government was adopted, helping to prevent government from coming to a standstill when Parliament and the monarchy disagreed.

Chapter 5
TEST FORM A

Absolute Monarchs in Europe

Part 1: Main Ideas

1. a

2. b

3. d

4. d

5. c

6. b

7. d

8. c

9. d

10. b

Part 2: Map Skills

11. b

12. b

13. d

14. c

15. d

Part 3: Interpreting Charts

16. c

17. c

18. b

19. c

20. a

Part 4: Extended Response

21. Possible responses should include the following points: The English were governed by a constitutional monarchy in which Parliament and the monarchy were equal partners in governing. The French were governed by an absolute monarchy in which most aspects of life fell under the centralized control of the king. In English government, the Bill of Rights limited the powers of the monarchy, and the cabinet system prevented government deadlock when the monarch and the Parliament disagreed. In France, the king depended upon the powerful intendants who collected taxes and administered justice. The French government also followed a policy of mercantilism. The lifestyle of the king in France was different, too, in that the king lived very elaborately, and court rituals and lifestyles were used to control the nobility. The monarch could not control the Parliament in England in the same manner. Finally, the English government backed Protestantism, while the French government backed Catholicism.

22. Possible responses should include the following points: Peter the Great worked to westernize Russia. He traveled to western Europe to learn about the culture. When Peter the Great returned to Russia, he changed many things to make the country more modern and westernized. He changed the laws to allow Russians to leave the country to study, whereas before they would be punished by death if they left. He wanted a better route to Europe, so he fought for land on the Baltic Sea and built St. Petersburg and moved the Russian capital there. Other changes were also made in Russia: The ruler became more "absolute" than ever; the Russian Orthodox church was brought under state control; the traditional nobility lost power and lower-ranking families rose to power (a way to ensure loyalty to the czar); the military was modernized; the status of women was improved, and they were allowed to attend social gatherings; potatoes became a staple in the Russian diet; and people adopted western styles and customs.

Chapter 5
TEST FORM B

Absolute Monarchs in Europe

Part 1: Main Ideas

1. d

2. a

3. d

4. b

5. c

6. b

7. a

8. a

9. b

10. d

Part 2: Map Skills

11. c

12. b

13. a

14. c

15. d

Part 3: Interpreting Charts

16. b

17. a

18. d

19. a

20. b

Part 4: Extended Response

21. Possible responses should include the following points: Russia's economy was different from that of western Europe. When Peter the Great came to power, Russia was still under the feudal system. Serfs were sold with the land, they could not run away and had no chance for freedom. In western Europe, serfs had the opportunity for freedom, which helped to create a middle class and allowed rulers to collect more taxes. Geographic barriers also kept Russians from learning about western Europe, and Russia looked to Constantinople for leadership rather than to Rome. Russia had religious differences as well; Russia had adopted the Eastern Orthodox branch of Christianity, while most western Europeans were Catholic or Protestant. After Peter the Great visited western Europe, he wanted to westernize and use western Europe as a model for change. Peter reduced the power of landowners, brought the Russian Orthodox Church under state control, and modernized the army. He also began the first newspaper, raised women's status, and ordered nobles to adopt western clothing, and he introduced the potato to the Russian diet. Peter's biggest change came with changing the location of the capital from Moscow to St. Petersburg. Peter believed it was important to have a better water route to Europe, so he fought Sweden to gain a piece of the Baltic coast. Once he gained control of the land, Peter sent Russian serfs to build a city, and then he forced nobles to leave Moscow to live in St. Petersburg. While most Russians were unhappy with the changes, Peter did make Russia a force to be reckoned with.

22. Possible responses should include the following points: In France, French nobles were ordered to take down their fortified castles, and French cities were not allowed to have walls. During Louis XIV's rule, the nobility were required to live at court, away from their families and homes, and they were totally dependent on the approval of the monarch. In many countries, the power of the middle class was increased by appointing members of the middle class to serve as government officials. The nobility were often excluded from the king's council. In Russia, the czar's secret police force hunted down and killed members of the nobility, and their lands were seized and distributed to others. Peter the Great reduced the power of great landowners by recruiting men from lower-ranking families and giving them positions of power and land. This act made these men loyal to Peter alone. In England, the monarchs regularly clashed with Parliament and dissolved Parliament. Oliver Cromwell abolished the House of Lords when he took over, and later sent the rest of the Parliament home and eventually ruled as a military dictator. In all of these cases, the rulers wanted to limit the powers of the nobility in order to have absolute rule. The rulers did not want to answer to anyone or to confer with anyone, so they limited the powers of the nobles in order to become more powerful themselves.

Chapter 5
TEST FORM C

Absolute Monarchs in Europe

Part 1: Main Ideas

1. a
2. b
3. c
4. a
5. d
6. b
7. c
8. a
9. b
10. a

Part 2: Map Skills—Constructed Response

11. Marston Moor, Naseby, and Edge Hill

12. They began with quite a bit of control, continued to hold onto it through December 1643, then began to lose control by 1644, and controlled very little land by the end of 1645.

13. They controlled the capital city of London all four years.

14. part of the southwest peninsula and part of the western shore

15. The Puritans had the advantage since they controlled the capital city of London. The Royalists controlled the southwest peninsula and the western shore, which were probably not as populated or modernized as London.

Part 3: Interpreting Charts

16. d
17. a
18. d
19. c
20. d

Part 4: Extended Response

21. Possible responses should include the following points: Central Europe developed its economy differently from western Europe. Central Europe kept the feudal system and did not allow serfs an opportunity to become independent and move to cities. Instead, central Europe kept serfs on the land and under control. By contrast, in western Europe, serfs often gained their freedom and moved to cities to become merchants, thus forming a middle class. The monarchs then taxed the middle class and used the money to build armies and reduce the influence of the nobility. In central Europe, a middle class didn't develop and the monarchy had fewer people to tax, making central European rulers financially weaker. By keeping the serfs under control, the nobility was able to remain powerful enough to control the monarchy. The nobility of central Europe used a variety of means to block the development of strong kings, such as in Poland where the monarch was allowed little income and no army.

22. Possible responses should include the following points: Charles I continually fought with Parliament, and in 1641, when Parliament passed laws limiting his powers, Charles tried to arrest the Parliament's leaders. The leaders escaped and soon a civil war broke out—between

those who opposed King Charles and those who supported him. In 1644, Oliver Cromwell finally defeated the supporters of Charles. Charles was brought up for trial on treason, sentenced to death, and beheaded. Cromwell then took over, eventually ruling as a military dictator. After Cromwell's death, the English people realized they were not happy with military government, and Parliament voted to restore rule to the monarchy with Charles II, heralding the Restoration. When Charles II died, James II became king but soon offended the English by flaunting his Catholicism. Fearing a line of Catholic kings, members of the Parliament invited the Protestants William of Orange and his wife Mary, James's older daughter, to overthrow James II. In this bloodless overthrow, called the Glorious Revolution, William and Mary agreed to rule with Parliament. The Parliament and the monarchs became partners in the rule of England, which made the government not an absolute monarchy but a constitutional monarchy. The cabinet was then introduced in order to act as the link between Parliament and the monarch, and the system remains in place today.

Chapter 6, Section 1
SECTION QUIZ

The Scientific Revolution

A. 1. k
2. e
3. d
4. f
5. l
6. j
7. h

B. Possible answers:

a. The Scientific Revolution introduced a completely new way of thinking about the natural world.

b. The Scientific Revolution was based upon careful observation and a willingness to question accepted beliefs. Previously, the vast majority of scholars and scientists simply

accepted the conclusions of ancient thinkers and church authorities.

c. The scientific method introduced a new approach to science. The old approach to science relied on ancient authorities, church teachings, and reasoning from abstract theories. The new approach (the scientific method) involved observation, experimentation, and the analysis and interpretation of data.

Chapter 6, Section 2
SECTION QUIZ

The Enlightenment in Europe

A. 1. f
2. h
3. c
4. g
5. a
6. b
7. d

B. Students could note that the Enlightenment

a. inspired the American Revolution.

b. inspired the French Revolution.

c. inspired other revolutionary movements.

d. popularized a belief in progress.

e. helped to convince people that human reason could solve social problems and reform society.

f. popularized a more worldly, less spiritual outlook on life.

g. encouraged people to question traditions and beliefs.

h. popularized individualism.

i. inspired people to use reason to judge right and wrong.

Chapter 6, Section 3
SECTION QUIZ

The Enlightenment Spreads

A. 1. a
2. h
3. d
4. c

5. a
6. b
7. d
8. d
9. g
10. e

B. Possible answers:

a. Enlightenment ideals of order and reason came to be reflected in the arts.

b. The baroque style gave way to the neoclassical style of art.

c. The ornate, detailed, grand style of art was replaced with a simple and elegant style that reflected a new emphasis on order and balance.

d. A new classical style of music also reflected the Enlightenment ideals of order and reason.

e. In literature, Enlightenment-era writers developed many of the features of the modern novel. The novel came to appeal to a wide middle-class audience.

Chapter 6, Section 4
SECTION QUIZ

The American Revolution

A. 1. b
2. c
3. c
4. b
5. a

B. Possible answers:

a. The Constitution reflected Enlightenment distrust of powerful central governments. It established three separate branches of government to provide a built-in system of checks and balances that would prevent any one branch from gaining too much power. It also set up a federal system that divides power between national and state governments.

b. The Bill of Rights also reflected the Enlightenment distrust of powerful central governments. It was added to the Constitution to protect the rights of individual citizens. It protects basic rights that Enlightenment thinkers considered essential, such as the freedom of speech and freedom of religion.

Chapter 6
TEST FORM A

Enlightenment and Revolution

Part 1: Main Ideas

1. b
2. c
3. a
4. c
5. b
6. c
7. d
8. c
9. d
10. c

Part 2: Map Skills

11. a
12. c
13. d
14. a
15. b

Part 3: Interpreting Charts

16. c
17. c
18. d
19. b
20. d

Part 4: Extended Response

21. Possible answers should include the following points: The scientific method begins with a problem or question arising from observation. Then the scientist forms a hypothesis, gathers data and tests the hypothesis, and analyzes and interprets the data to either confirm or disprove the hypothesis. Ancient authorities and church teachings are questioned by the scientific method. During medieval times, scholars relied on ancient authorities, church teachings, and common sense instead of experimentation and

scientific reasoning to explain the physical world.

22. Possible answers should include the following points: According to Locke, all people are born free and equal, with three natural rights—life, liberty, and property. The purpose of government is to protect these rights. If a government fails to do so, citizens have a right to overthrow it. All of these ideas influenced the Declaration of Independence. For example, the Declaration says, "all Men are created equal, . . . they are endowed by their Creator with certain unalienable Rights, that among these are Life, Liberty, and the Pursuit of Happiness."

Chapter 6
TEST FORM B

Enlightenment and Revolution

Part 1: Main Ideas

1. a
2. d
3. a
4. b
5. c
6. a
7. d
8. b
9. d
10. c

Part 2: Map Skills

11. a
12. c
13. b
14. b
15. d

Part 3: Interpreting Charts

16. d
17. a
18. c
19. d
20. d

Part 4: Extended Response

21. Possible answers should include the following points: The Enlightenment concept of nature viewed the natural as being good and reasonable. According to this concept, there were natural laws of economics and politics just as there were natural laws of motion. In support of this concept, an answer could mention that nature follows a certain order that is good, because it supports life and is reasonable because it follows principles. Similar to nature, economics and politics have cycles and patterns that can be described in terms of laws. To refute this concept, an answer could argue that the natural world seems chaotic and that good and bad events happen indifferently. Therefore, what is natural is not always good or reasonable. Also, the principles of economics and politics can change. Because of this, they are not based on objective, natural laws. Other arguments that support or refute the Enlightenment concept of nature are acceptable if they are well supported.

22. Possible answers should include the following points: Catherine the Great realized that the legal system in Russia was oppressive, especially for the peasants. She probably thought that granting the peasants more freedom would make them more content and perhaps even more productive. She also may have been drawn to a more reasonable way of governing that did not rely on brute force. The ideas of the philosophes showed her a way to achieve the reform she desired. However, Catherine the Great's plan backfired when the peasants rebelled. Her fear that she might lose her power overwhelmed any desire she had for reform. As a result, she crushed the rebellion, won the support of the nobles, and suppressed the Enlightenment ideas that she had been promoting.

Chapter 6
TEST FORM C

Enlightenment and Revolution

Part 1: Main Ideas

1. c

2. a

3. b

4. c

5. d

6. b

7. a

8. d

9. c

10. b

Part 2: Map Skills

11. d

12. c

13. b

14. b

15. d

Part 3: Interpreting Charts—Constructed Response

16. The literate middle class was strongly influenced by Enlightenment ideas. Because they were educated, this portion of the middle class was exposed to various works by Enlightenment writers and discoveries by scientists.

17. Enlightenment ideas were spread by written materials (works by the philosophes), word-of-mouth (the salon), and political reforms (enlightened despots).

18. They both overthrew established authority and replaced it with a new approach.

19. The willingness to question assumptions, to dispute established authority, and to use reason to discover truths were ways that the Scientific Revolution influenced the philosophes.

20. American colonists felt oppressed by the British monarchy. Enlightenment ideas questioned the old forms of government, such as monarchies, and presented new and more just forms of government as an alternative.

Part 4: Extended Response

21. Possible answers should include the following points: Enlightenment ideas emphasized reason, balance, and order. These traits are reflected in the simple, elegant style of neoclassical architecture. The works of composer Wolfgang Amadeus Mozart also show elegance and balance. In addition, Enlightenment ideas stressed invention and discovering new ways of doing things. These qualities are clearly seen in the works of composer Ludwig van Beethoven who began new trends in music. New approaches were also being discovered in literature by novelists Samuel Richardson and Henry Fielding. They both developed many of the features of the modern novel.

22. Possible answers should include the following points: Locke stressed that the government's power comes from the consent of the people. This concept is reflected in the representative government with limited powers of the U.S. Constitution. Montesquieu believed in the separation of powers into executive, legislative, and judicial branches of government. He also felt that each branch should act as a check on the other branches. The separation of powers and the "checks and balances" system are also seen in the Constitution. Rousseau's idea of the people directly forming a democracy influenced the part of the Constitution that deals with the election of the president and Congress. Beccaria held that the accused should have rights and should not be tortured. Voltaire believed in freedom of speech and religion. These ideas are found in the Bill of Rights, which protects the rights of the accused, prohibits cruel punishment, and protects the rights of freedom of speech and religion.

Chapter 7, Section 1
SECTION QUIZ

The French Revolution Begins

A. 1. g

2. f, e, a

3. d, b, c

4. i, h

5. k

6. c, b

7. e, l

B. Answers will vary. Students might make points similar to the following:

a. The meeting of the Estates-General was a signal in that it was forced upon the king.

b. The establishment of the National Assembly proclaimed an end to the absolute monarchy.

c. The Tennis Court Oath showed that the National Assembly was determined to succeed.

d. The storming of the Bastille showed that the peasant class would defend Paris against the king's troops.

e. The king's departure from Versailles, which was forced by a crowd of protestors, showed that Louis did not have the support or the power he had once had.

Chapter 7, Section 2
SECTION QUIZ

Revolution Brings Reform and Terror

A. 1. e

2. c

3. b

4. a

5. d

6. g

7. h

8. j

9. i

10. l

11. k

B. Answers will vary. Students might make points similar to the following:

a. The radicals in power needed a way to control their enemies within France—both the peasants who disapproved

b. of what they were doing and rival

c. revolutionaries.

d. Ruling by terror gave these radicals a way to dispose of opposition.

e. Robespierre and his followers wanted to wipe out every trace of the monarchy and nobility.

f. Once put in motion, the activities of the Reign of Terror became impossible to control as fear grew.

g. Fearful for their own safety, revolutionaries turned on each other. Those who did not fully support the most radical revolutionaries became victims themselves.

h. The Committee of Public Safety operated without any controls.

i. Robespierre's fellow revolutionaries had to organize against him in order to end the Reign of Terror, which was a difficult and dangerous thing to do since failure would have meant death for any participants.

Chapter 7, Section 3
SECTION QUIZ

Napoleon Forges an Empire

A. 1. true

2. true

3. public schools

4. emperor

5. true

6. Trafalgar

B. Answers will vary. Students might make points similar to the following:

a. He was seen as a savior of the republic for his role in dispersing a group of royalists.

b. He was a military genius who saved France from the threat of Austrian troops.

c. He was extremely well-liked by the soldiers he led and inspired patriotism and heroism.

d. France had suffered many years of chaos, and he was the type of leader who could restore order.

e. Many of his initial efforts as emperor created needed reforms that were appreciated by the people.

Chapter 7, Section 4
SECTION QUIZ

Napoleon's Empire Collapses

A. 1. h

2. a

3. h

4. b, d

5. e

6. k, i

7. f

8. c, g

B. Answers will vary. Students might make points similar to the following:

a. Quest for power. He was never satisfied with the power he had and saw the way of obtaining more as involving the conquest of more and more territory.

b. Pride. His refusal to accept failure when events did not go according to plan led to huge and costly losses (as in his attempt to establish the Continental System and his insistence on waiting for a peace offer from Czar Alexander that never came).

c. Conceit. He felt he was capable of anything, regardless of the odds against him.

d. Selfishness. He sacrificed thousands and thousands of soldiers' lives to further his often impossible goals.

Chapter 7, Section 5
SECTION QUIZ

The Congress of Vienna

A. 1. d

2. d

3. c

4. a

5. a

B. Possible answers: Valuable:

a. It managed to establish a true balance of power among European nations. This enabled the nations of Europe to maintain peaceful relationships for many years.

b. Its actions kept France from becoming either too strong and overpowering other countries or too weak and becoming overpowered.

c. The basic fairness of its settlements kept individual nations from harboring resentments.

Harmful:

a. By restoring monarchies based on "legitimacy," it may have simply delayed the inevitable interest in true democracy.

b. The foreign control it established in certain countries helped to create growth of nationalistic sentiments in those countries, which eventually led to revolutions.

Chapter 7
TEST FORM A

The French Revolution and Napoleon

Part 1: Main Ideas

1. d

2. c

3. c

4. b

5. a

6. d

7. b

8. b

9. c

10. d

Part 2: Map Skills

11. b

12. c

13. d

14. e

15. a

Part 3: Interpreting Time Lines

16. b

17. b

18. c

19. d

20. c

Part 4: Extended Response

21. Possible responses should include the following points: Despite the fact that most of France's wealth belonged to the two privileged Estates, the people of the Third Estate paid most of France's taxes.

Approximately half of their income went to pay taxes. The other two Estates, made up of clergy and rich nobles, paid almost no taxes. As a result, when the cost of bread rose, urban workers and peasants went hungry. Moreover, the Third Estate could do little about their situation because the First and Second Estates could always outvote them. As a result, it had little to lose. The bourgeoisie, who were merchants and artisans, were well-educated and sometimes wealthy, but had no political power. They believed in the Enlightenment ideals of liberty and equality. They led the way for change by demanding a representative government.

22. Possible responses should include the following points: Napoleon's invasion of Russia in 1812 was his most disastrous mistake of all and led to his downfall. The Russian czar, Alexander I, refused to be lured into an unequal battle. Instead, he pulled back his troops toward Moscow. He practiced a scorched-earth policy by burning grain fields and slaughtering livestock. This meant that when Napoleon's troops arrived, they had nothing to eat. When Napoleon and his Grand Army finally entered Moscow in September, they found it burning. Napoleon kept his troops in the ruined city for five weeks waiting for the czar to make a peace offer. The offer never came. By the middle of October it was too late to advance farther and almost too late to retreat. Napoleon ordered his starving army to retreat. In early November, it began to snow; his army was not prepared for a Russian winter. Of approximately 420,000 soldiers, only 10,000 survived.

Chapter 7
TEST FORM B

The French Revolution and Napoleon

Part 1: Main Ideas

1. a
2. b
3. a
4. d

5. b
6. d
7. c
8. c
9. b
10. c

Part 2: Map Skills

11. b
12. c
13. c
14. c
15. a

Part 3: Interpreting Time Lines

16. a
17. b
18. d
19. b
20. b

Part 4: Extended Response

21. Possible responses should include the following points: Napoleon's most urgent task upon taking power was to stabilize the economy—one of the main causes of the Revolution. He did this by setting up an efficient, fairer tax-collection system and establishing a national bank. He also dismissed corrupt officials. To insure that future government officials had training, he established government-run public schools or *lycées*. Napoleon signed *a concordat* with the Pope, spelling out a new relationship between church and state. In short, the church would no longer have control in national affairs. Napoleon thought that his greatest work was his comprehensive system of laws. Although the Napoleonic Code had flaws, it did provide France with a comprehensive set of laws. All of these actions help to stabilize France.

22. Possible responses should include the following points:

a. In 1806 Napoleon ordered a blockade against Great Britain in order to destroy Britain's commercial and industrial economy. However, other nations defied the blockade and Britain formed its own. With its stronger navy, Britain was better able to make its blockade work.

b. Because Portugal ignored the French blockade, Napoleon sent an army through Spain into Portugal in 1808. When the Spanish protested, Napoleon replaced the Spanish king with his own brother. Bands of peasant guerrilla fighters struck at the French armies for five years.

c. In 1812 Napoleon invaded Russia. Alexander I pulled his troops back toward Moscow instead of fighting and destroying everything in their wake. Thus, Napoleon's troops found ruins instead of provisions. When Napoleon finally arrived in Moscow, he found it burning. After futilely waiting five weeks for the czar to make a peace offer, Napoleon ordered his starving army to retreat. In November, it began to snow on an army unprepared for a Russian winter. Of approximately 420,000 soldiers, only 10,000 survived.

Chapter 7
TEST FORM C

The French Revolution and Napoleon

Part 1: Main Ideas

1. d
2. a
3. c
4. b
5. c
6. c
7. d
8. b
9. d
10. b

Part 2: Map Skills

11. a
12. c

13. b

14. d

15. c

Part 3: Interpreting Time Lines—Constructed Response

16. 11 years

17. Napoleon's loss of 400,000 men in Russia enabled France's enemies to defeat it in Leipzig in 1813.

18. He did not give up easily.

19. Because Portugal disregarded the blockade, Napoleon invaded it.

20. He wanted to be free from conflicts in other continents in order to conquer Europe. He needed money to fight wars.

Part 4: Extended Response

21.

a. Possible responses for "more economic" should include the following points: Despite the fact that most of France's wealth belonged to the two privileged Estates, the people of the Third Estate paid most of France's taxes. Approximately half of their income went to pay taxes. The other two Estates, made up of clergy and rich nobles, paid almost no taxes. As a result, when the cost of bread rose, urban workers and peasants went hungry. The peasant class, desperate for food, initiated the early events in the Revolution. They deeply resented Louis XVI and Marie Antoinette for their extravagance during a time when France was suffering from a severe economic crisis. The class system had severe economic ramifications and was both firmly entrenched and deeply resented by the Third Estate.

b. Possible responses for "more political" should include: The Third Estate could do little about its situation because the First and Second Estates could always outvote them. As a result, it had little to lose. The bourgeoisie, merchants and artisans who were well-educated and not poor, believed in the Enlightenment ideals of liberty and equality. These ideas

were tied much more closely to politics than to economics. Moreover, many of the radical leaders of the Revolution did not suffer from economic hardships. The bourgeoisie led the way for change by demanding a representative government. If the Third Estate had enjoyed a fair share of political power, the events that led to the French Revolution would never have occurred.

22. Possible responses might include the following points: The French were desperate to have social and political order restored. The revolutionaries' enemy had been the economic, social, and political system know as the Old Regime, and the idea of an absolute monarchy frightened them more than the idea of a monarchy itself. Moreover, the people were used to being governed by a monarchy. And there was no system for establishing who would be in power and how those people would be chosen. Perhaps, had Louis been a different and more popular leader, he might never have lost either his crown or his head. Napoleon was the type of leader the French wanted and believed they needed—strong and charismatic. Napoleon was seen as a savior of the republic for turning back the royalists. Napoleon had brought about many reforms.

Chapter 8, Section 1
SECTION QUIZ

Latin American Peoples Win Independence

A. 1. f

2. h

3. j

4. c

5. i

6. b

7. k

8. e

9. d

10. b

11. a

12. i

B. Possible answers:

a. Of those who had something to gain from independence, this group was the best educated and most familiar with Enlightenment ideas.

b. Many had military training, compliments of Spain.

c. Even though members of this group led privileged lives in comparison to others, they had reason for complaint and felt that the injustice they suffered was severe.

d. Being well-educated, members of this group probably thought they were capable of running their country without help from Spain.

Chapter 8, Section 2
SECTION QUIZ

Europe Faces Revolutions

A. 1. c

2. a

3. c

4. d

5. b

6. d

B. Possible answers:

a. Most of the leaders of Europe were members of the nobility. These people had nothing to gain from constitutional governments and strongly opposed their establishment.

b. The revolutionaries who overthrew monarchies or the old order were often unable to unify and retain the power they had seized.

c. The republican government in France was split into factions regarding the extent of reform, which led to violent conflicts and exhausted the French people.

d. Without a workable political system, a stable economic system, and experienced leaders, it would be virtually impossible for any revolutionary government to survive.

Chapter 8, Section 3
SECTION QUIZ

Nationalism CASE STUDY: Italy and Germany

A. 1. d

2. c

3. a

4. a

5. c

6. c

B. Students should recognize that nationalism is still a powerful force today and is involved in major conflicts around the world. Students could note such points as the following.

a. Not many years ago, nationalism was behind the breakup of the Soviet Union. Nationalistic feelings currently influence the establishment of independent nation-states within that region and serious conflicts within and between them.

b. In the Middle East, Palestinians battle for a homeland against Israel, itself a nation-state that has strong nationalistic sentiment.

c. In Northern Ireland, Catholic revolutionaries struggle against what they see as British domination of what should be their own nation.

Chapter 8, Section 4
SECTION QUIZ

Revolutions in the Arts

A. 1. c

2. b

3. d

4. a

5. d

6. b

7. a

B. Possible answers:

a. One major idea in romanticism was the beauty of nature, which seemed irrelevant in a highly industrialized society.

b. Romanticism dealt with things that were beautiful, fanciful, and noble.

Industrialization had effects that were none of those.

c. As Europe became more industrialized, the living and working conditions of the lower classes became worse. It became harder for artists and writers to look at things with a romantic point or view.

Chapter 8
TEST FORM A

Nationalist Revolutions Sweep the West

Part 1: Main Ideas

1. b

2. c

3. a

4. c

5. d

6. a

7. c

8. b

9. a

10. b

Part 2: Map Skills

11. c

12. b

13. a

14. e

15. d

Part 3: Document-Based Questions

A. (4 points each)

16. No. Bolívar believed that the federal system of government was a difficult one to run successfully and required skills that Latin Americans lacked.

17. He has gained independence for many Latin American countries and has given them the freedom to choose their own governments.

18. Indians; Peninsulares

B. (8 points)

19. Possible answers should include the following points:

Democracies were difficult to establish in Latin America for several

reasons. The oppressive Spanish rule did not allow Latin Americans to be trained in government. In his Jamaican Letter, Bolívar stated: "[Spain] has kept us in a sort of permanent infancy with regard to public affairs." Because of this, Latin Americans lacked the skills needed to effectively run a democracy. Also, Latin Americans were oppressed for hundreds of years; many of them knew no other way of life. The sudden change to democracy must have been a difficult adjustment. In addition, after an old regime fell there was usually a political vacuum that was often unstable. In an attempt for security, many people tried to fill this vacuum with a "new" government that was similar to the old one. San Martín, in his farewell address, showed repulsion toward this tendency when he stated: "I am also disgusted with hearing that I wish to make myself a sovereign." Another problem is clearly shown by the pie graph. The vast majority of Latin Americas were poor; Africans and Native Americans (about 62 percent of population) made up the lowest part of society. The split between the haves and the have-nots was extreme. Such a split built unrest and resentment among the population and made it difficult for a stable democracy to take hold. Education for the people as a whole was vital for democratic governments in Latin America to be successful. People needed to be given the skills and knowledge necessary to effectively participate in a democracy. Also, education was needed to close the gap between the haves and have-nots by providing training that enabled people to get better paying jobs. Strong leadership that was dedicated to democratic ideals was also important. Such leadership promoted education, insured that an oppressive government would not replace the old regime, and attempted to close the economic gap.

Part 4: Extended Response

20. Possible responses should include the following points: In the first half of the 1800s, the three groups that struggled to gain a political advantage in European societies were the conservatives, the liberals,

and the radicals. Usually wealthy property owners and members of the nobility, the conservatives argued for protecting the traditional monarchies of Europe. In certain cases conservatives approved of constitutional monarchies. Mostly middle-class business leaders, the liberals wanted to give more power to elected parliaments, but only to parliaments in which the educated and the landowners could vote. Radicals favored drastic change to extend democracy to the people as a whole.

21. Possible responses should include the following points: Influenced by nationalism, the Hungarians pressured Emperor Francis Joseph to split the Austro-Hungarian Empire in half, so he declared Austria and Hungary independent states. However, Francis Joseph made himself ruler of both. Nationalist disputes continued to plague this empire for more than 40 years. Finally, after World War I, Austria-Hungary crumbled into separate nation-states. With the Russian Empire, the ruling Romanov dynasty was determined to maintain iron control over the diverse groups within the empire. However, their severe policy of Russification—imposing Russian culture on all the ethnic groups in the empire—strengthened nationalist feelings. Weakened by nationalism, this empire could not withstand the double shock of World War I and the Communist revolution. The last Romanov czar gave up his power in 1917.

Chapter 8
TEST FORM B

Nationalist Revolutions Sweep the West

Part 1: Main Ideas

1. c
2. a
3. c
4. d
5. d
6. b
7. a
8. c
9. d
10. b

Part 2: Map Skills

11. c
12. a
13. a
14. b
15. b

Part 3: Document-Based Questions

A. (4 points each)

16. The oppressive Spanish regime kept Latin Americans in a sort of permanent infancy.

17. San Martín has mixed feelings about the future of democracy in Peru. If Peruvians place their trust in this form of government, they will succeed with it. However, if they doubt this type of government, they will fail.

18. Peninsulares, Creoles, Mulattos, Mestizos, and Africans

B. (8 points)

19. Possible answers should include the following points:

Democracies were difficult to establish in Latin America for several reasons. The oppressive Spanish rule did not allow Latin Americans to be trained in government. In his Jamaican Letter, Bolívar stated: "[Spain] has kept us in a sort of permanent infancy with regard to public affairs." Because of this, Latin Americans lacked the skills needed to effectively run a democracy. Also, Latin Americans were oppressed for hundreds of years; many of them knew no other way of life. The sudden change to democracy must have been a difficult adjustment. In addition, after an old regime fell there was usually a political vacuum that was often unstable. In an attempt for security, many people tried to fill this vacuum with a "new" government that was similar to the old one. San Martín, in his farewell address, showed repulsion toward this tendency when he stated: "I am also disgusted with hearing that I wish to make myself a sovereign." Another problem is

clearly shown by the pie graph. The vast majority of Latin Americas were poor; Africans and Native Americans (about 62 percent of population) made up the lowest part of society. The split between the haves and the have-nots was extreme. Such a split built unrest and resentment among the population and made it difficult for a stable democracy to take hold. Education for the people as a whole was vital for democratic governments in Latin America to be successful. People needed to be given the skills and knowledge necessary to effectively participate in a democracy. Also, education was needed to close the gap between the haves and have-nots by providing training that enabled people to get better paying jobs. Strong leadership that was dedicated to democratic ideals was also important. Such leadership promoted education, insured that an oppressive government would not replace the old regime, and attempted to close the economic gap.

Part 4: Extended Response

20.

a. Possible responses should include the following points: A student who disapproves of Bismark's realpolitik should point out that his approach disregarded democratic ideals and thereby the will of the people by ignoring the German parliament. His lack of ideals allowed him to stage "incidents" to gain public support. His alternate version of a telegram that has Wilhelm I insult the French ambassador shows this. In addition, Bismarck would run over anyone or any country that got in his way. This approach resulted in many wars, such as the Seven Years' War, which caused much loss of life.

b. A student who approves of Bismark's realpolitik should point out that, although his approach was sometimes harsh, Bismarck succeeded in unifying Germany and greatly enhancing this country's wealth and influence. Rulers throughout history have practiced shrewd political tactics; Bismarck was just very good at it. He created tensions between

Holstein and Schleswig that resulted in a German military victory over Austria and the annexation of more German territory. Bismarck was also able to bridge the division between German Protestants and Catholics (which had often resulted in violent conflict) by again using political cunning. He manufactured an "incident" between Germany and France that united German Protestants and Catholics against the French.

21. Possible responses should include the following points:

Romantic literature often dealt with supernatural events. Also, the beauty of nature was frequently emphasized; the poems of Byron, Shelley, and Keats depicted the mystery and splendor of nature. In addition, this literature often had main characters who were in some way different from normal people. *Frankenstein* had a prominent character who was a monster. A common goal of romantic literature was to portray an ideal that was sought after but was not completely obtainable. The hero in *The Sorrows of Young Werther* desired the love of a virtuous young woman but was unable to attain this love. In contrast, realistic literature showed life as it was. *The Human Comedy* by Balzac portrayed the lives of over 2,000 people from all levels of French society, and the works of Zola exposed harsh working conditions in small shops, factories, and coal mines. The main characters in this literature were usually common people, such as the working poor in the novels of Charles Dickens. The goal of realistic literature was to depict real life as accurately as possible and, often, to expose unfair or oppressive conditions. By showing the misery of many French workers, the works of Zola spurred reforms of labor laws and working conditions.

Chapter 8
TEST FORM C

Nationalist Revolutions Sweep the West

Part 1: Main Ideas

1. a
2. b
3. c
4. d
5. d
6. c
7. d
8. a
9. a
10. b

Part 2: Map Skills

11. c
12. b
13. c
14. a
15. d

Part 3: Document-Based Questions

A. (4 points each)

16. More successful—because it involved a monarchy and therefore was somewhat similar to Spanish rule. Latin Americans would not have needed to make as big of an adjustment. Less successful—because if it was used, Latin Americans would be more likely to regress into complete control by a monarchy.

17. A successful military leader, such as San Martín, was adored by much of the population. Because Latin Americans were familiar with monarchies and not democracy, they might ignore democratic ideals and ask the leader to be king or emperor.

18. The people (Native Americans, Africans, Mestizos, Mulattos, and Creoles) who were oppressed by Spanish control greatly outnumbered the people (Peninsulares) who benefited from Spanish control.

B. (8 points)

19. Possible answers should include the following points:

Democracies were difficult to establish in Latin America for several reasons. The oppressive Spanish rule did not allow Latin Americans to be trained in government. In his Jamaican Letter, Bolívar stated: "[Spain] has kept us in a sort of permanent infancy with regard to public affairs." Because of this, Latin Americans lacked the skills needed to effectively run a democracy. Also, Latin Americans were oppressed for hundreds of years; many of them knew no other way of life. The sudden change to democracy must have been a difficult adjustment. In addition, after an old regime fell there was usually a political vacuum that was often unstable. In an attempt for security, many people tried to fill this vacuum with a "new" government that was similar to the old one. San Martín, in his farewell address, showed repulsion toward this tendency when he stated: "I am also disgusted with hearing that I wish to make myself a sovereign." Another problem is clearly shown by the pie graph. The vast majority of Latin Americas were poor; Africans and Native Americans (about 62 percent of population) made up the lowest part of society. The split between the haves and the have-nots was extreme. Such a split built unrest and resentment among the population and made it difficult for a stable democracy to take hold. Education for the people as a whole was vital for democratic governments in Latin America to be successful. People needed to be given the skills and knowledge necessary to effectively participate in a democracy. Also, education was needed to close the gap between the haves and have-nots by providing training that enabled people to get better paying jobs. Strong leadership that was dedicated to democratic ideals was also important. Such leadership promoted education, insured that an oppressive government would not replace the old regime, and attempted to close the economic gap.

Part 4: Extended Response

20.

a. Possible responses should include the following points: Nationalism was inspired by ideals of freedom and self-government and strove to achieve these ideals despite opposition. Nationalistic ideals were reflected in much of the art and literature of romanticism. Beethoven's "Ninth Symphony" celebrated freedom, dignity, and triumph. The brothers Jakob and Wilhelm Grimm collected fairy tales that emphasized German history and a sense of national pride. Writers penned stories that portrayed mythical rebels or leaders, such as the legendary King Arthur. In addition, romantic literature often emphasized the struggle to attain an ideal.

b. During the early 18th century, industrialism was spreading throughout much of Europe. However, much romantic art and literature seemed to be a reaction against industrialization. Some artists sought to escape industrialization by emphasizing the beauty in nature. For example, artist John Constable depicted the peaceful, English countryside, and poet William Wordsworth honored nature as the source of truth and beauty. Other writers saw the horrific side of industrialization. Mary Shelley's Gothic novel *Frankenstein* weaved a tale about a monster created (or manufactured) from the body parts of dead human beings, thus revealing the possible dangers of science and technology.

21.

a. Possible responses should include the following points: Nationalistic movements that were successful had strong leadership. Simón Bolívar and José de San Martín spearheaded the independence of Spanish South America, and Otto von Bismarck was the driving force behind the unification of Germany. All of these men were strong leaders who inspired loyalty. Also, the leaders of successful nationalistic movements often used shrewd political skills. Otto von Bismarck devised plans that led to the unification of Germany and Camillo di Cavour formed

well-chosen alliances to assist with the unification of Italy. In addition, the support of the people was crucial for the success of nationalistic movements. Volunteers flocked to support Giuseppe Garibaldi and his Red Shirts as they liberated southern Italy. Bismarck realized that it was necessary to win the support of Catholics in southern Germany and manufactured a war with France to gain this support.

b. Many nationalistic movements failed because the revolutionaries did not successfully unite themselves or their nations. In Vienna, an unruly mob of liberals clashed with the police and eventually forced Metternich to resign. However, this group of nationalists failed to unite and was later overthrown by conservatives. In 1848, a Paris mob overturned a monarchy and established a republic. But the new government began to fall apart immediately; the radicals soon split into factions. Bloody battles broke out in the Parisian streets. This disunity was caused by a lack of strong leadership and ineffective political skills. Soon the movement lost the support of the French citizens. As a result, the republic failed.

Chapter 9, Section 1
SECTION QUIZ

The Beginnings of Industrialization

A. 1. a
2. b
3. c
4. d
5. b
6. c

B. Possible answers:

a. Modern agricultural techniques

b. Abundant food supplies

c. Increasing population

d. High demand for food and goods

e. Large population of workers

f. Extensive natural resources

g. Expanding economy

h. Highly developed banking system

i. Encouraging business climate for investors

j. Availability of bank loans

k. Increasing overseas trade

l. Economic prosperity

m. Climate of progress

n. Political stability

o. Positive attitude

Chapter 9, Section 2
SECTION QUIZ

Industrialization Case Study: Manchester

A. 1. a
2. d
3. c

B. Possible answers:

a. Benefitted the most: entrepreneurs. They made a great deal of money, led basically pleasant lives enjoying the benefits of industrialization and what it made available to them, and occupied a comfortable social position as part of the new middle class.

b. Benefitted the least: children of the poor. They were forced to risk their lives working under dangerous conditions in factories and mines for very long hours at very low wages.

Chapter 9, Section 3
SECTION QUIZ

Industrialization Spreads

A. 1. textile
2. true
3. slowed
4. the United States
5. true
6. widening
7. Japan

B. Possible answers:

a. British secrecy about the new industrial technology

b. Disruptions caused by wars such as the War of 1812, the French Revolution, and the Napoleonic wars

c. Political division

d. Economically isolated populations

e. Scattered resources

f. The existence of certain types of social structures

g. Geographic obstacles to transportation

h. Lack of natural resources

Chapter 9, Section 4
SECTION QUIZ

An Age of Reforms

A. 1. a

2. d

3. b

4. b

5. b

6. c

B. Possible answers:

a. Laissez-faire capitalists believed that a free-market economy benefitted society as a whole; Marxists believed that a free-market economy harmed workers and benefitted only the middle- and upper-classes.

b. Laissez-faire capitalists believed that if the government allowed free trade, capitalism would prosper; Marxists believed that if the government allowed free trade, the capitalist economy would eventually destroy itself.

c. Laissez-faire capitalists believed that a permanent underclass would always be poor; Marxists believed that the underclass was neither permanent nor necessarily destined to be poor.

d. Laissez-faire capitalists were in favor of private ownership of the means of production (property); Marxists were in favor of public ownership of the means of production (property).

Chapter 9
TEST FORM A

The Industrial Revolution

Part 1: Main Ideas

1. b

2. d

3. a

4. b

5. b

6. c

7. c

8. d

9. a

10. d

Part 2: Map Skills

11. a

12. d

13. a

14. c

15. b

Part 3: Interpreting Charts

16. b

17. c

18. a

19. a

20. b

Part 4: Extended Response

21. Possible responses should include the following points:

Factors of production existed in Great Britain that did not exist to the same degree elsewhere in Europe. The included modern agricultural techniques, abundant food supplies, a high demand for consumer goods, a large population of workers, extensive natural resources (waterways, coal, iron ore, harbors), an expanding economy, a highly developed banking system, and political stability. Also, Great Britain did not have the geographical barriers, such as mountains that blocked transportation, that prevented some European nations from industrializing.

22. Possible responses should include the following points:

Economically: Business people invested in the manufacture of new inventions. Britain's highly developed banking system also contributed to the country's industrialization. People were encouraged by the availability of bank loans to invest in new machinery and expand their operations. Growing overseas trade, prosperity, and a climate of progress increased the demand for goods. Politically: Though Britain took part in many wars during the 1700s, none of these occurred on British soil. Their military and political successes gave the British a positive attitude. Parliament passed laws that protected business and aided expansion. Socially: The middle class grew dramatically as some members became as wealthy as the aristocracy. Child labor laws were passed to protect children from being overworked in factories. Laws were passed to keep women and children from working in underground mines. Also, the workday of women and children in factories was limited to ten hours a day.

Chapter 9
TEST FORM B

The Industrial Revolution

Part 1: Main Ideas

1. d

2. a

3. c

4. c

5. b

6. d

7. d

8. c

9. d

10. d

Part 2: Map Skills

11. d

12. c

13. b

14. a

15. d

Part 3: Interpreting Charts

16. d

17. a

18. b

19. a

20. b

Part 4: Extended Response

21. Possible responses should include the following points:

Great Britain had undergone an agricultural revolution that resulted in abundant food supplies and population growth. A high demand for consumer goods emerged as well as an available workforce to produce them. England was rich in natural resources such as waterways, coal, iron ore, and harbors. Great Britain was experiencing a prosperous and expanding economy boosted by a highly developed banking system. The country was politically stable and was experiencing a period of progress and optimism.

22. Possible responses should include the following points:

The idea of communism promised a better future to factory workers, who led extremely difficult lives. It placed a higher value on workers than on other groups in society. It seemed to make heroes out of workers who were used to being taken advantage of and being looked down on. Also, most factory workers were exploited in the way that Marx said they were. This truth seemed obvious to any factory worker of the time.

Chapter 9
TEST FORM C

The Industrial Revolution

Part 1: Main Ideas

1. d

2. a

3. d

4. c

5. a

6. d

7. a

8. a

9. c

10. c

Part 2: Map Skills

11. It allowed for the efficient transport of goods, materials, and people across vast distances.

12. It effectively linked northern Washington to southern California as well as the major east/west routes across the plains.

13. They were probably used to carry raw materials from ports, farms, and mines to places of production.

14. There was much many more miles of railroad in the East, probably due to Midwest factories and ports on the East Coast.

15. Geographic features such as mountains, deserts, and canyons, and rivers would have made western expansion difficult as well.

Part 3: Interpreting Charts

16. b

17. d

18. b

19. b

20. c

Part 4: Extended Response

21. Possible responses should include the following points:

Many members of the middle-class profited from the free-market system. The lack of government regulations meant that factory owners could set the pace of production and factory specific standards for their laborers. They enjoyed a comfortable standard of living and had hopes of increasing their wealth. Capitalism and the free-market economy worked well for the middle-class and also expanded it dramatically.

22. Possible responses should include the following points:

The system had as its goal the production of wealth, not the betterment of society. It was based on the assumption that the poor will always be poor and, in fact, needs this to be true so that labor remains cheap. If the production of wealth was the measure of success, then complete reliance on the free-market system worked well. However, if social welfare was the measure of success, then complete reliance did not work well. In Britain, the free-market system helped those who were already doing well to do better. It failed to help those who needed help the most such as workers and their families. The system kept workers from being able to live decent lives. It encouraged child labor, failed to provide for the safety of workers, and made family life difficult because of the lengthy work day.

Chapter 10, Section 1
SECTION QUIZ

Democratic Reform and Activism

A. 1. a

2. d

3. c

4. c

5. b

6. b

7. d

B. Possible answers:

a. The French had an extremely bloody and violent history during and since the revolution.

b. The French government had taken a variety of forms, none of which had lasted.

c. The need to avoid further divisions had become overwhelmingly clear.

Chapter 10, Section 2
SECTION QUIZ

Self-Rule for British Colonies

A. 1. a

2. d

3. a

4. d

5. c

6. a

7. d

B. Possible answers:

a. Their behavior was similar.

b. In all three cases, settlers virtually ignored the rights of the native peoples, setting up colonies.

c. In all three cases, settlers eventually expanded their settlements to the point that they had moved native peoples off the most desirable land.

d. In all three cases, settlers destroyed native populations and cultures.

Chapter 10, Section 3
SECTION QUIZ

War and Expansion in the United States

A. 1. d

2. a

3. c

4. c

5. a

6. b

7. c

B. Possible answers:

a. Lincoln believed that the proclamation would help to save the Union.

b. It decreased European sympathy for the South and made it less likely that European nations would assist the Southern war effort.

c. It allowed Union armies to free slaves in areas they conquered.

Chapter 10, Section 4
SECTION QUIZ

Nineteenth-Century Progress

A. 1. g

2. d

3. h

4. a

5. c

6. f

7. f

8. b

9. a

10. i

11. e

12. g

13. a

14. j

B. Possible answers:

a. More people had become literate.

b. Improved communications made books, newspapers and magazines cheaper and more plentiful.

c. Shorter work days gave people more leisure time to engage in reading and pursuing other forms of entertainment.

d. Motion pictures had wide appeal.

e. Spectator sports grew in popularity.

Chapter 10
TEST FORM A

An Age of Democracy and Progress
Part 1: Main Ideas

1. c

2. c

3. d

4. b

5. d

6. d

7. d

8. b

9. c

10. b

Part 2: Map Skills

11. c

12. b

13. a

14. c

15. a

Part 3: Document Based Questions

A. (4 points each)

16. laws contrary to the expressed wishes of the people, and by unconstitutional means enforced them

17. establish their own state

18. It suggested that women were held back from competing equally with men by not having the right to vote.

B. (8 points)

19. In the early 1800s as nations began to prosper through industrialization and to grow more urbanized, people became aware that the laws enacted when their nations were formed were not going to remain effective in light of the changing times. Merchants, business owners, and the middle class required a greater say in their countries' politics because the people they had elected to represent them were not governing in the their best interests. In other parts, of the world entire communities, like the Jewish people, sought the most basic right of having a their own state. Women in the United States and Great Britain began reform movements for suffrage, the right to vote. In addition, by 1890, several industrial countries had already enacted universal male suffrage. These reform movements would have sweeping effects over time as people the world over would struggle for equal rights and greater freedoms. In some instances, those freedoms would be achieved, such as those in "The Great Charter." Women's suffrage and the establishment of a Jewish state both came about much later. World history continues to demonstrate that reform movements are a vital part of the evolution of nations and the world, because it is through them that politics and rights change for the betterment of societies.

Part 4: Extended Response

20. Possible responses should include the following points:

It was according to Lord Durham's report on the status of Upper and Lower Canada that he believed the two divisions should be reunited as one province and that the province should be self governing in its domestic matters. It wasn't until 1867, when Nova Scotia and New Brunswick joined the province of Canada, that it became the Dominion of Canada. Canada's first prime minister, John MacDonald, quickly expanded Canada westward to the Pacific Ocean by purchasing lands and persuading frontier territories to join the Canadian Union. MacDonald was also instrumental in the construction of the transcontinental railroad, which helped to unite the distant parts of the dominion. Like many Canadians, the colonists of Australia and New Zealand wanted to rule themselves, yet remain in the British Empire. During the 1850s, the colonies in both Australia and New Zealand became self-governing and created parliamentary forms of government. In 1901, the Australian colonies were united under a federal constitution as the Commonwealth of Australia. In the 1900s, both Australia and New Zealand became dominions. The people of both dominions went on to pioneer a number of political reforms. The secret ballot, also known as the Australian ballot, was first used in Australia in the 1850s. In 1893, New Zealand became the first nation in the world to give full voting rights to white women. These were small steps but their effects would be felt and reflected throughout the world in time.

21. Possible responses should include the following points:

The invention of the radio and telephone.This allowed for faster and more direct communication. Henry Ford's development of the Model T allowed middle-class people to purchase and use automobiles, which radically changed personal transportation. Hygiene improved significantly due to discoveries by Pasteur and Lister that linked germs to disease and infection, which allowed surgery to be performed more safely. Mass culture developed based on magazines, newspapers, and books. The motion picture industry began. Music halls and vaudeville became popular. The phonograph brought musical performances into the home. Electricity was harnessed to provide light and the power to run machinery. The study of human psychology developed the concept of the unconscious.

Chapter 10
TEST FORM B

An Age of Democracy and Progress

Part 1: Main Ideas

1. b
2. d
3. a
4. b
5. c
6. b
7. c
8. c
9. b
10. c

Part 2: Map Skills

11. b
12. a
13. d
14. c
15. a

Part 3: Document Based Questions

A. (4 points each)

16. They believe that if representation in Parliament is denied, then they should not have to pay the taxes that support the Parliament.

17. Their ethnicity and religious beliefs give them common characteristics, but just as there are American Jews and European Jews, it is by their historic role in history as a people blighted by other nations and regimes that has united them.

18. The female character is in a rowboat fighting the current, while the male character is in a sailboat, with the word "votes" on the sail, comfortably navigating the sea because of the advantage afforded him by having suffrage.

B. (8 points)

19. In the early 1800s as nations began to prosper through industrialization and to grow more urbanized, people became aware that the laws enacted when their nations were formed were not going to remain effective in light of the changing times. Merchants, business owners, and the middle

class required a greater say in their countries' politics because the people they had elected to represent them were not governing in the their best interests. In other parts, of the world entire communities, like the Jewish people, sought the most basic right of having a their own state. Women in the United States and Great Britain began reform movements for suffrage, the right to vote. In addition, by 1890, several industrial countries had already enacted universal male suffrage. These reform movements would have sweeping effects over time as people the world over would struggle for equal rights and greater freedoms. In some instances, those freedoms would be achieved, such as those in "The Great Charter." Women's suffrage and the establishment of a Jewish state both came about much later. World history continues to demonstrate that reform movements are a vital part of the evolution of nations and the world, because it is through them that politics and rights change for the betterment of societies.

Part 4: Extended Response

20. Possible responses should include the following points:

The telephone allowed people communication across vast areas. The electric light bulb changed the very way people lived by greatly extending the period of time in a day when work could be done or leisure time enjoyed. The automobile changed how and where Americans could live. Students may come up with other ideas and offer compelling reasons for their choices.

21. Possible responses should include the following points:

Australia and New Zealand were both home to convicts from Great Britain, except there was an established penal colony on Australia and some escapees then went to New Zealand. Slowly colonization grew in Australia, including settlers who chose to go there to begin new lives as mostly sheep farmers and wool exporting became its biggest business. New Zealand's growth happened more slowly because the Maori, native population, wanted their land rights respected in exchange for not interferring with British colonization. Both countries had problems assimilating with their native populations. In Australia, the Aborigines were completely displaced from the beginning by the British people. On New Zealand the British government respected the Maori's land rights at first, but those rights deteriorated over time as more settlers arrived needing land. Both colonies wanted to establish self-rule and created parliamentary forms of government, but they remained part of the Commonwealth.

Chapter 10
TEST FORM C

An Age of Democracy and Progress

Part 1: Main Ideas

1. d
2. b
3. c
4. d
5. b
6. b
7. a
8. d
9. b
10. a

Part 2: Map Skills

11. b
12. c
13. c
14. d
15. b

Part 3: Document Based Questions

A. (4 points each)

16. The government rules the land with absolute power leaving the common people to feel as if they are enslaved rather than free.

17. enough people united under a single purpose with the knowledge and capital to govern themselves

18. Men wanted to keep the huge advantage afforded them by suffrage, even though they saw that the lack of the vote caused women to struggle and fall behind.

B. (8 points)

19. In the early 1800s as nations began to prosper through industrialization and to grow more urbanized, people became aware that the laws enacted when their nations were formed were not going to remain effective in light of the changing times. Merchants, business owners, and the middle class required a greater say in their countries' politics because the people they had elected to represent them were not governing in the their best interests. In other parts, of the world entire communities, like the Jewish people, sought the most basic right of having a their own state. Women in the United States and Great Britain began reform movements for suffrage, the right to vote. In addition, by 1890, several industrial countries had already enacted universal male suffrage. These reform movements would have sweeping effects over time as people the world over would struggle for equal rights and greater freedoms. In some instances, those freedoms would be achieved, such as those in "The Great Charter." Women's suffrage and the establishment of a Jewish state both came about much later. World history continues to demonstrate that reform movements are a vital part of the evolution of nations and the world, because it is through them that politics and rights change for the betterment of societies.

Part 4: Extended Response

20. Possible responses should include the following points:

Captain Alfred Dreyfus was one of the few Jewish officers in the French army and was accused of selling military secrets to Germany. He was found guilty on false evidence and served time in jail. Once it was discovered that Dreyfus had been framed by other army officers, public opinion became divided over the matter. Many army leaders, nationalists, clergy, and anti-Semitic groups refused to reopen the case because they feared the reputation of the entire army would be effected. The writer Emile Zola published a letter in a popular French paper entitled *J'accuse* in which he denounced the army for covering up the scandal. Zola also was imprisoned for a year over his views, but in the end his letter garnered the support that eventually won Dreyfus his freedom and innocence. Therefore, the Dreyfuss Affair shed light on the problems of anti-Semitism, corruption in the army, lack of free speech, and judicial malpractice.

21. Possible responses should include the following points:

Manifest destiny played a part in advancing democratic progress for certain individuals, but also played a role in hindering democratic progress for others. Manifest Destiny was an idea that justified the U.S. claim to control North America from the Atlantic to the Pacific. It allowed settlers to have plenty of space in which to set up homes and establish towns across the country. However, it also gave the United States an excuse for the displacement of many tribes of Native Americans. Segregation was another hindrance to democratic progress. It was a policy that separated blacks and whites in most situations, and caused blacks to be treated as inferior to whites. Emancipation was probably the most beneficial policy to the advancement of democracy for all. Emancipation brought freedom to slaves in the Confederacy and led to the Fourteenth and Fifthteenth Amendments, which extended the right of citizenship to all Americans, black or white, and guaranteed former slaves the right to vote. The African-American community would continue to fight discrmination in Northern states as well, and it would be decades before they made more progress achieving equal status with whites.

Chapter 11, Section 1
SECTION QUIZ

The Scramble for Africa

A. 1. Dutch
2. true
3. European
4. support *or* justify *or* defend

5. mineral

6. British

7. true

8. Boers (Dutch/Dutch settlers/Afrikaners)

B. Motives include:

a. desire to gain new markets for manufactured goods

b. desire to obtain raw materials necessary for manufacturing

c. desire to improve their economies

d. greed

e. nationalism

f. desire to Christianize, "civilize," and Westernize foreigners

Reasons for success include:

a. superior technology (i.e., steam engine, railroads, cable, steamships)

b. superior weapons (i.e., Maxim gun)

c. use of quinine to prevent malaria

d. lack of African unity

e. playing of rival groups of Africans against each other

Chapter 11, Section 2
SECTION QUIZ

Imperialism Case Study: Nigeria

A. 1. b

2. c

3. a

4. a

5. b

B. Students could note that the British

a. used both diplomatic and military means to control the area.

b. persuaded local rulers to sign treaties of protection.

c. gained control of the Nigerian palm oil trade.

d. sought and received a protectorate over part of Nigeria at the Berlin Conference.

e. claimed Nigeria as a colony.

f. appointed local officials to keep order in Nigeria.

Chapter 11, Section 3
SECTION QUIZ

Europeans Claim Muslim Lands

A. 1. d

2. a

3. a

4. b

5. c

B. Possible answers:

a. Russian goods had to pass through Ottoman lands to reach the Mediterranean Sea.

b. Russia desperately wanted to gain Ottoman land on the Black Sea to obtain free passage to the Mediterranean Sea for its goods.

c. To fulfill this need, Russia declared war on the Ottoman Empire.

d. To prevent Russia from gaining more Ottoman lands, Britain and France joined forces with the Ottoman Empire to defeat Russia.

Chapter 11, Section 4
SECTION QUIZ

British Imperialism in India

A. 1. b

2. a

3. a

4. b

5. d

B. Possible answers:

a. India was referred to as Britain's "jewel in the crown" because India was the most valuable of all Britain's colonies.

b. India's value as a colony had mainly to do with the size of its territory and population. India was a major supplier of raw materials for British industry, and its large population provided a huge potential market for British goods.

Chapter 11, Section 5
SECTION QUIZ

Imperialism in Southeast Asia

A. 1. a

2. c

3. a

4. b

5. a

6. b

7. d

8. d

B. Positive results:

a. The economies of Southeast Asian countries grew.

b. New roads, harbors, and rail systems linked areas and improved communication and transportation, although these benefits were largely confined to the European population.

c. Education in Southeast Asia improved.

d. Health of Southeast Asians improved.

e. Sanitation in Southeast Asia improved.

f. Areas of Southeast Asia were unified for the first time.

g. Southeast Asia became more racially and ethnically diverse.

Negative results:

a. The introduction of foreign racial and ethnic groups into Southeast Asia led to conflicts.

b. The development of the cash-crop system endangered the ability of Southeast Asians to provide enough food for themselves.

c. Local leaders and governments lost power.

Chapter 11
TEST FORM A

The Age of Imperialism

Part 1: Main Ideas

1. b

2. i

3. g

4. j

5. c

6. a

7. d

8. h

9. e

10. f

Part 2: Map Skills

11. d

12. b

13. d

14. b

15. c

Part 3: Interpreting Charts

16. c

17. d

18. c

19. a

20. b

Part 4: Extended Response

21. Possible responses should include the following points:

After the Industrial Revolution, European nations wanted new markets and raw materials to improve their economies. Feelings of nationalism also drove competition for colonies. Many Europeans believed that they were superior to other peoples because they had advanced technology. This racism was linked to Social Darwinism, which applied Charles Darwin's ideas about evolution and "survival of the fittest" to social change. Christian missionaries also pushed for expansion. They believed that European rule would end slavery. Africans did not have European technology—such as the Maxim gun. They were forced to rely on outdated weapons. The invention of the steam engine allowed Europeans to travel upstream into the interior of the African continent. Other inventions, such as railroads, cables, and steamships, allowed close communication between the colony and its existing nation. Quinine protected Europeans against malaria. Africans' huge variety of languages and cultures discouraged unity. Wars fought between ethnic groups over land, water, and trade rights prevented a unified stand. Europeans played rival groups against each other.

22. Possible responses should include the following points:

The British completed the world's third largest railroad network in India, which enabled India to develop a modern economy. It also brought unity to the connected regions. A modern road network, telephone and telegraph lines, dams, bridges, and irrigation canals helped India to modernize. Sanitation and public health improved. Schools and colleges were founded, and literacy increased. British troops cleared central India of bandits and put an end to local warfare. Still, the British oppressed India. British policies called for India to produce raw materials for British manufacturing and to buy British finished goods. Indian competition with British finished goods was prohibited. The British held much of the political and economic power, and they restricted Indian-owned industries such as cotton textiles. The emphasis on cash crops resulted in a loss of self-sufficiency for many villagers; it reduced food production and caused famines in the late 1800s. The increased presence of missionaries and the outspoken racist attitude of most British officials threatened Indian traditional life. Indians were made second-class citizens in their own country, and even Indians with a European education faced discrimination. They were barred from top posts in the Indian Civil Service. Indian workers were paid less than Europeans for the same jobs.

Chapter 11
TEST FORM B

The Age of Imperialism

Part 1: Main Ideas

1. a
2. c
3. b
4. a
5. d
6. c
7. b
8. d
9. c
10. b

Part 2: Map Skills

11. c

12. a

13. c

14. b

15. d

Part 3: Interpreting Charts

16. d

17. b

18. c

19. b

20. a

Part 4: Extended Response

21. Possible responses should include the following points:

Gossip spread among the sepoys that the cartridges of their new rifles were sealed with beef and pork fat. Soldiers had to bite off the seal to use the cartridges. As Hindus consider the cow sacred, and Muslims do not eat pork, Hindus and Muslims were outraged. When 85 sepoys refused to accept the cartridges, the British placed them in jail. The next day, the sepoys rebelled. They marched to Delhi, where they were joined by Indian soldiers stationed there. They captured Delhi, and the rebellion spread. The British sent troops to help the East India Company fight the sepoys. The Indians could not unite against the British due to weak leadership and serious divisions between Hindus and Muslims. Hindus did not want the Mughal Empire restored. Most of the princes and maharajas who had made alliances with the East India Company did not take part in the rebellion. The Sikhs, who had conflicts with the Mughals, remained loyal to the British. As a result, the mutiny failed.

22. Possible responses should include the following points:

The ethnic groups who lived in Nigeria were different in language, culture, and religion. Europeans did not consider this when they divided Africa amongst themselves at the Berlin Conference of 1884–1885. The Hausa-Fulani were Muslim and accustomed to a strong central government. The Igbo and Yoruba peoples followed traditional religions and relied on local chiefs. Lacking enough troops to govern the area, Britain turned to indirect rule. The British relied on local administrations and chiefs to keep order. Indirect rule worked well in northern Nigeria, where the Hausa-Fulani were accustomed to centralized government. It did not work as well elsewhere. Igbo and Yoruba chiefs resented having their power limited by the British.

Chapter 11
TEST FORM C

The Age of Imperialism

Part 1: Main Ideas

1. c

2. d

3. b

4. c

5. b

6. c

7. d

8. a

9. b

10. c

Part 2: Map Skills—Constructed Response

11. South America; it was colonized by Spain and Portugal previously and then gained independence.

12. about 2,750 miles

13. Britain colonized a nearly solid band of land in eastern Africa running from the north to the south.

14. They're the only British holdings that extend far north. They're the only holdings that extend farther north that Britain. Canada was larger than the area of any other colony.

15. Britain held lands across the globe, in many different time zones. The sun would always be shining in some portion of the British Empire.

Part 3: Interpreting Charts

16. a

17. c

18. d

19. a

20. b

Part 4: Extended Response

21. Possible responses should include the following points:

The two nations were Siam and Ethiopia. In Ethiopia, Menelik II exploited the rivalries between colonial powers intent on taking over his country and built up a large arsenal of modern weapons. These tactics enabled Ethiopia to remain free of foreign spheres of influence and defeat Italy in battle. King Mongkut and his son Chulalongkorn modernized Siam and skillfully promoted the country as a neutral zone between French and British colonies. Siam started schools, reformed the legal system, and reorganized the government. The government built its own railroads and telegraph systems and ended slavery. Modernization enabled the country to defend itself from colonial powers.

22. Possible responses should include the following points:

Africans lost control of their land and their independence. Many died of diseases such as smallpox. They also lost thousands of people who resisted the Europeans. Famines resulted from the substitution of cash crops for subsistence agriculture. Africans also suffered a breakdown of traditional cultures. Traditional authority figures were replaced, and homes and property were transferred with little regard to their importance to local people. Men were forced to leave villages to support themselves and their families. Contempt for traditional culture and admiration of European life undermined stable societies and caused identity problems. The artificial boundaries that combined or unnaturally divided groups left a troublesome political legacy. Long-term rival chiefdoms were sometimes united (such as in Nigeria), and kinship groups were sometimes split between colonies. These boundaries continue to create problems for the nations that evolved from these colonies. The positive effects of colonialism were the reduction of local warfare, improved sanitation, and the introduction of hospitals and schools. African products came to be valued on the international market, and African colonies gained some infrastructure. However, this benefited European business interests—not Africans' lives. Overall, imperialism is generally considered to have been more negative than positive.

Chapter 12, Section 1
SECTION QUIZ

China Resists Outside Influence

A. 1. c

2. h

3. b

4. j

5. f

6. k

7. d

8. i

9. g

10. e

B. Possible answers:

a. Although the world changed a great deal during the 19th century, the Chinese government failed to adapt to this changing world or to respond to changing conditions in China.

b. Many Chinese were so unhappy with China's favoritism toward foreigners that they rebelled against the government.

c. China had not responded well to external pressures from foreign powers.

d. The government had largely ignored internal problems, such as the scarcity of food for the expanding population and widespread opium addiction.

Chapter 12, Section 2
SECTION QUIZ

Modernization in Japan

A. 1. a

2. d

3. d

4. b

5. a

6. d

7. b

B. Possible answers:

a. How: by adopting and adapting aspects of Western civilization, such as a centralized government, a disciplined military, and a system of universal public education

b. How: by industrializing (building railroads, increasing coal production, building factories, expanding traditional Japanese industries, and developing modern industries)

c. Why: in order to gain the strength necessary to maintain its independence and to compete with imperialistic European nations

Chapter 12, Section 3
SECTION QUIZ

U.S. Economic Imperialism

A. 1. true

2. Britain

3. Spanish-American War

4. true

5. true

6. European nations'

7. gain independence

B. Possible answers:

a. An unequal distribution of land and the system of peonage meant that most Latin Americans lived lives of poverty and hardship with little hope for improvement.

b. Most countries were ruled by dictators (caudillos) and most Latin Americans lacked a voice in government.

c. Most nations suffered from political instability.

d. Foreign imports discouraged the development of industry.

e. Latin American nations borrowed money at high interest rates. When the governments were unable to repay those loans, foreign lenders were able to take over many Latin American industries.

Chapter 12, Section 4
SECTION QUIZ

Turmoil and Change in Mexico

A. 1. l

2. k

3. c

4. d

5. h

6. f

B. Possible answers:

a. Breakup of large estates: rich landowners kept most other Mexicans in a cycle of debt and poverty.

b. Minimum wage for workers: most of Mexico's population was very poor. A minimum wage law would allow these poor workers to feed families, educate children, and produce better citizens.

Chapter 12
TEST FORM A

Transformations Around the Globe

Part 1: Main Ideas

1. f

2. e

3. c

4. b

5. a

6. j

7. d

8. i

9. h

10. g

Part 2: Map Skills

11. b

12. c

13. b

14. d

15. b

Part 3: Document-Based Questions

A. (8 points each)

16. Lin Zexu thought the trading of opium was wrong. The opium brought into China by merchants had spread throughout the provinces and was poisoning many of the Chinese people.

17. John Hay was worried that Germany might impose, in its sphere of influence in China, higher harbor dues on ships from other countries.

18. France; Russia

B. (8 points)

19. Possible answers should include the following points:

China was a self-sufficient country with little interest in trading with the West. In a letter to Queen Victoria, Lin Zexu stated that China was willing to completely stop trade relations with the West. However, China knew that European powers wanted to trade with their country. To prevent conflict and to turn a profit, the Chinese agreed to trade. But when opium was brought by Britain into China and began to be used extensively, the Chinese protested to the British, as shown by Lin Zexu's letter. China's pleas to stop the opium trade went unanswered by Britain. The Opium War of 1839 soon followed and China was defeated. By the end of the 19th century, Britain, France, Germany, Russia, and Japan took economic control of regions, called spheres of influence, within China. These spheres of influence could have put American traders and the Chinese government at a strong disadvantage. The next step of the European powers could have been the colonization of China, which would have completely shut out American trade in that country and strengthened European control over the Chinese. Eventually, the United States established the Open Door Policy, which stated that China's doors be open to merchants of all nations. The policy also stated that the Chinese treaty tariff should apply to all goods "landed or shipped" within the spheres of influence and that the Chinese government should collect the duties and that, within their spheres, European powers should not levy higher harbor dues on vessels of another nationality than on its own vessels. The Open Door Policy protected both American trading rights in China and China's freedom from colonization.

Part 4: Extended Response

20. Possible responses should include the following points:

Emperor Mutsuhito decided that the best way to oppose imperialism was to adopt new ways. In the Meiji era, the period of "enlightened rule." Japanese statesmen went to Europe and North America to observe foreign ways. The Japanese admired Germany's strong centralized government and used its constitution as a model for their own. They modernized their military using the militaries of Germany and Britain as models. Japan adopted the U.S. system of universal public education. In addition, the emperor supported industrialization. Railroad lines were built, and coal production grew, along with shipbuilding and the weapons industry. Japan began to pursue a course of imperialism, attacking China and then Russia over Korea. Japan finally annexed Korea.

21. Possible responses should include the following points

Throughout the late 1840s and early 1850s, Juárez worked to start a liberal reform movement called *La Reforma*. Redistribution of land, separation of church and state, and increased educational opportunities were among its goals. Beginning in 1847, Juárez served as governor of the state of Oaxaca. After a period of exile, Juárez was elected president in 1861 and, after a brief time of French rule, was reelected president in 1867. He promoted trade, built railroads, and set up a national education system. A supporter of democratic ideals, Juárez's rallying cry was: "Liberty, Order, and Progress." In contrast, Porfirio Díaz came to power by ousting the president in the mid-1870s. During the Díaz years, elections were meaningless. He offered land, power, or political favors to anyone who supported him. His policies reversed many of Juárez's reforms. Díaz did not support democratic ideals. Instead of "Liberty, Order, and Progress" Díaz's motto was just "Order and Progress." Díaz did expand railroads, build banks, and stabilize the currency, but his methods were very harsh.

Chapter 12
TEST FORM B

Transformations Around the Globe

Part 1: Main Ideas

1. a
2. c
3. d
4. c
5. b
6. d
7. b
8. a
9. c
10. b

Part 2: Map Skills

11. b
12. d
13. b
14. c
15. a

Part 3: Document-Based Questions

A. (4 points each)

16. Apparently, Lin Zexu thought that China was very self-sufficient. He mentions that the Chinese had many goods that Europeans want but the Europeans do not have goods that are valuable to the Chinese. This implies that the Chinese have what they need.

17. European powers could use their spheres of influence to interfere with U.S. trade in China. For example, Germany might interfere with U.S. "treaty ports or vested interests" located in the German sphere.

18. Great Britain. Great Britain's sphere of influence extended along the Chang Jiang River, which flows through the interior of China.

B. (8 points)

19. Possible answers should include the following points:

China was a self-sufficient country, with little interest in trading with the West. In a letter to Queen Victoria, Lin Zexu stated that China was willing to completely stop trade

relations with the West. However, China knew that European powers wanted to trade with their country. To prevent conflict and to turn a profit, the Chinese agreed to trade. But when opium was brought by Britain into China and began to be used extensively, the Chinese protested to the British, as shown by Lin Zexu's letter. China's pleas to stop the opium trade went unanswered by Britain. The Opium War of 1839 soon followed and China was defeated. By the end of the 19th century, Britain, France, Germany, Russia, and Japan took economic control of regions, called spheres of influence, within China. These spheres of influence could have put American traders and the Chinese government at a strong disadvantage. The next step of the European powers could have been the colonization of China, which would have completely shut out American trade in that country and strengthened European control over the Chinese. Eventually, the United States established the Open Door Policy, which stated that China's doors be open to merchants of all nations. The policy also stated that the Chinese treaty tariff should apply to all goods "landed or shipped" within the spheres of influence and that the Chinese government should collect the duties and that, within their spheres, European powers should not levy higher harbor dues on vessels of another nationality than on its own vessels. The Open Door Policy protected both American trading rights in China and China's freedom from colonization.

Part 4: Extended Response

20. Possible responses should include the following points:

During the reign of Emperor Mutsuhito, Japan took many steps toward modernization. It sent statesmen to Europe and North America to study foreign ways. The Japanese improved their army and navy, pursued industrialization, and set up a strong centralized government. All of these changes strengthened Japan's status as a world power. Further, Japan won both the Sino-Japanese and Russo-Japanese wars, establishing itself as a military and imperial power. In contrast, China's status as a world power was hindered by a lack of modernization. In the 19th century, the country made slow progress toward industrialization. The rest of the world knew its weak military technology. Instead of conquering other countries as Japan did, China was subject to foreign interference. In addition, the government of China was riddled with corruption. Eventually, in 1905, Chinese officials were sent to Europe and the United States to study the operation of different governments. This occurred decades after Japan sent statesmen abroad to learn about the West.

21. Possible responses should include the following points:

In 1823, President James Monroe issued the Monroe Doctrine stating that the American continents should not be colonized by any European power. Cuba was still a colony of Spain. Backed by the Monroe Doctrine, the United States in 1898 decided to help the Cubans fight for independence. The ensuing Spanish-American War lasted for four months; the Spanish lost. One reason for U.S. interest in Cuba was that the United States had many business holdings in this country. In fact, economic interests were a major reason for U.S. involvement in Latin America. The United States had large investments in Central and South America. To protect these interests, President Roosevelt issued a corollary to the Monroe Doctrine, giving the United States the right to be "an international police power" in the Western Hemisphere. The United States gained a huge economic advantage through the building of the Panama Canal. The canal greatly improved ship transportation for the United States and countries around the world. The United States received tolls from ships passing through the canal.

Chapter 12
TEST FORM C

Transformations Around the Globe

Part 1: Main Ideas

1. d

2. b
3. b
4. c
5. a
6. d
7. c
8. a
9. b
10. c

Part 2: Map Skills

11. c
12. d
13. a
14. b
15. c

Part 3: Document-Based Questions

A. (4 points each)

16. China used force to stop the opium trade. Apparently, the opium situation in China had reached a crisis point. Lin Zexu's statement: "imagine how many people opium has killed!" implies this. Also, China was willing to use extreme measures, such as stopping trade with Britain.

17. China was probably pleased with John Hay's document. He supported China's right to collect tariff duties. Also, by seeking assurances that Germany would not over-extend its control in China, Hay implied that the U.S. did not want European powers to colonize this country.

18. Great Britain. Besides having large spheres of influence within China, Britain also had extensive colonies along the south and southwest borders of China.

B. (8 points)

19. Possible answers should include the following points:

China was a self-sufficient country with little interest in trading with the West. In a letter to Queen Victoria, Lin Zexu stated that China was willing to completely stop trade relations with the West. However, China knew that European powers wanted to trade with their country. To prevent conflict and to turn a profit, the Chinese agreed to trade.

But when opium was brought by Britain into China and began to be used extensively, the Chinese protested to the British, as shown by Lin Zexu's letter. China's pleas to stop the opium trade went unanswered by Britain. The Opium War of 1839 soon followed and China was defeated. By the end of the 19th century, Britain, France, Germany, Russia, and Japan took economic control of regions, called spheres of influence, within China. These spheres of influence could have put American traders and the Chinese government at a strong disadvantage. The next step of the European powers could have been the colonization of China, which would have completely shut out American trade in that country and strengthened European control over the Chinese. Eventually, the United States established the Open Door Policy, which stated that China's doors be open to merchants of all nations. The policy also stated that the Chinese treaty tariff should apply to all goods "landed or shipped" within the spheres of influence and that the Chinese government should collect the duties and that, within their spheres, European powers should not levy higher harbor dues on vessels of another nationality than on its own vessels. The Open Door Policy protected both American trading rights in China and China's freedom from colonization.

Part 4: Extended Response

20. Possible responses should include the following points:

For centuries, the rulers of China resisted change. Attempts at reform were often put down. In 1898, when Emperor Guangxu attempted sweeping political, educational, and military changes, the Dowager Empress Cixi suppressed his efforts. Because of this lack of reform, China had many economic and political problems. Most of the peasants were very poor, and the government was riddled with corruption. The internal strife within China made it vulnerable to foreign influences. Further, China's industrialization was slow. When the Chinese did attempt to manufacture gunboats and rifles, they hired foreigners to run the arsenals. These outsiders imported both raw materials and factory machinery. This contributed to a trade imbalance for China and a lack of quality control. As a result, China's economy was greatly weakened. A third reason for China's vulnerability to the West was its weak military. This was clearly demonstrated during by China's defeat during the Opium War of 1839.

21. Possible responses should include the following points:

Both China and Latin America were dominated by authoritarian rule. For example, except for the brief success of the Taiping Rebellion, the Qing Dynasty ruled China. During the 19th century, authoritarian rulers such as Santa Anna and Porfirio Díaz also controlled Mexico. Latin America was also run by a series of strongmen known as caudillos. In both China and Latin America, attempts at reform proved short-lived. Guangxu's attempted reforms in China were blocked by the Dowager Empress Cixi. And in Mexico, Porfirio Díaz undid many of the reforms of Benito Juárez. Both China and Latin America had undeveloped economies that relied primarily on agriculture. Most of the Chinese people were farmers or peasants. The population was increasing rapidly, but the food production barely increased. As a result, hunger was widespread. The rebel Hong Xiuquan promised that all Chinese people would share in China's vast wealth and no one would live in poverty, but his rebellion was short-lived. Nineteenth century Mexico was also primarily agricultural. A few wealthy landowners controlled a vast amount land; the large majority of people were poor peasants who were landless. Unequal land distribution was also a serious issue elsewhere in Latin America.

Chapter 13, Section 1
SECTION QUIZ

Marching Toward War

A. 1. c, d, g

2. a, f, h

3. h

4. c, h

5. d

6. h

7. f

8. h

9. g

10. d

B. Answers will vary regarding what was most responsible for setting the stage for World War I. Any of the four general causes can be supported, but each should include points similar to the following.

a. Nationalism: It led to all of the other causes by creating intense economic competition, territorial disputes, and various nations' determination to dominate the others. It encouraged a dangerous arms race as these nations believed that they needed powerful military forces in order to be truly great. It was a Serbian nationalist who assassinated the heir to the throne of Austria-Hungary and led that nation to declare war.

b. Imperialism: It created a situation in which rivalry over colonies pushed nations to the brink of war. Imperialism had caused the original problems in the Balkans, the "powder keg" of Europe.

c. Militarism: The possession of strong standing armies and stockpiles of weapons made many nations feel ready for war. This war-readiness allowed nations to mobilize quickly, and the war had actually started before other plans for settling the dispute between Austria-Hungary and Serbia could be fully explored.

d. The alliance system: It divided the Great Powers into two rival camps, neither of which was very stable. However, a dispute between any two member nations could draw all of them into war, which is precisely what happened. Without the alliance system, Austria-Hungary and Serbia would have been forced to work out their problems without involving other nations.

Chapter 13, Section 2
SECTION QUIZ

Europe Plunges into War

A. 1. France

2. French

3. Italy

4. Western Front

5. true

6. true

7. Germany

B. Possible answers:

a. When the Germans were defeated at the Battle of the Marne, they were unable to carry out their plan for a quick defeat of France.

b. Because Russia was invading Germany on the east, many German troops were moved from the Western Front to the Eastern. This kept Germany from being able to overwhelm the Allies along the French border.

c. The style of fighting (trench warfare) that took place on the Western Front encouraged stalemate. Fighting from trenches made it easier to defend territory than to advance. Both sides could defend their positions but neither could move forward significantly.

Chapter 13, Section 3
SECTION QUIZ

A Global Conflict

A. 1. c

2. d

3. c

4. d

5. b

6. a

B. Students could say that Russia left the war because

a. its army was continually short of supplies.

b. its civilian population was in desperate need of products that were being used by the army.

c. its army, after having lost millions of men, refused to fight any longer.

d. a revolution brought to power a government that didn't support Russian participation in the war.

Students could say that the United States entered the war because

a. Germany's policy of unrestricted submarine warfare resulted in the sinking of U.S. ships.

b. many Americans were angered by the Zimmerman note in which Germany promised to help Mexico regain U.S. lands.

c. many Americans felt a strong bond with Britain.

d. the United States had economic ties with Allied nations.

Chapter 13, Section 4
SECTION QUIZ

A Flawed Peace

A. 1. true

2. Fourteen Points

3. France

4. mandates

5. Georges Clemenceau

6. true

7. true

B. Germany: felt bitterness and resentment due to war guilt clause; Mandated territories: felt that their desires for independence had been ignored; Japan and Italy: gained less territory than they sought; United States: opposed joining the League of Nations and becoming more involved in European affairs.

Chapter 13
TEST FORM A

The Great War

Part 1: Main Ideas

1. b

2. d

3. c

4. a

5. d

6. c

7. c

8. a

9. b

10. a

Part 2: Map Skills

11. d

12. a

13. b

14. d

15. b

Part 3: Interpreting Graphs

16. a

17. d

18. b

19. c

20. c

Part 4: Extended Response

21. Possible responses should include the following points:

World War I was fought on a scale such as no other war before it. Large industrialized countries aligned themselves on both sides of the battlefield. New technologies such as war planes, tanks, submarines, and automated gunfire had devastating effects on all parties involved, and instead of delivering a fast-moving war, these instruments simply killed huge numbers more effectively. The war was fought over vast areas of land, and many people and places were wiped out in its destructive path. Soldiers fought in trenches, which became known as trench warfare, to escape enemy gun fire on the front lines but found themselves as open targets in between the trenches as they attempted to move forward or were forced back. What began as a war in Europe slowly spread over the world as European colonies were called in to aid in their colonizers. Japan entered the war to fight for its colonies in China and the Pacific. The United States had at first stayed clear of the war under a policy of isolationism. Then Germany sank three American ships, and America intercepted a message sent to Mexico stating that Germany would aid it in regaining land lost to the United States in exchange for its aid in the war.

22. Possible responses should include the following points:

The United States entered the war because Germany's unrestricted submarine warfare threatened U.S. shipping. Germany sent Mexico the Zimmerman note offering to help Mexico regain lands lost to the United States, which angered the United States and made its citizens feel directly threatened. U.S. sympathies tended to lie with the Allies due to long-term loyalties to Britain and economic ties to other Allied nations. Americans might have feared living in a world dominated by Germany, and by 1917, it looked like it could happen. Fortunately, the entry of the United States tipped the balance in the Allies' favor. The addition of millions of fresh American soldiers allowed the Allies to launch a counterattack against weary German troops and to steadily advance toward Germany.

Chapter 13
TEST FORM B

The Great War

Part 1: Main Ideas

1. b

2. a

3. b

4. a

5. d

6. b

7. b

8. a

9. d

10. a

Part 2: Map Skills

11. b

12. a

13. c

14. a

15. b

Part 3: Interpreting Graphs

16. d

17. b

18. a

19. d

20. b

Part 4: Extended Response

21. Possible responses should include the following points:

Russia had lost an enormous number of soldiers in the war. A lack of supplies kept the Russian army in a state of constant need. Consequently, Russia's devoting its limited supplies to the army kept its civilian population in a state of desperation. The Russian army, exhausted and hopeless, refused to continue to fight. Revolutions brought to power a government that wanted no part of the war. Russia's withdrawal from the war allowed the Central Powers to win the war on the Eastern Front, to send nearly all of its forces to the Western Front, and to launch a final massive attack on the Allies on the Western Front.

22. Possible responses should include the following points:

Peoples outside of Europe, such as the Ottoman Turks and the Japanese, took sides in the war. The Allies brought the fighting to Southwest Asia in attempting to take the Ottoman capital of Constantinople, control the Dardanelles, and establish a supply line to Russia. Japan attacked Germany's colonial possessions in China and the Pacific, while England and France attacked Germany's African colonies. The British and French recruited the peoples of their Asian and African colonies for the war effort.

Chapter 13
TEST FORM C

The Great War

Part 1: Main Ideas

1. a
2. c
3. b
4. c
5. a
6. a
7. d

8. b

9. d

10. c

Part 2: Map Skills

11. d

12. b

13. a

14. c

15. b

Part 3: Interpreting Graphs – Constructed Response

16. 7,999,000

17. 3,325,000

18. 4,674,000

19. Central Powers

20. U.S. deaths were much lower due to their late entry into the war.

Part 4: Extended Response

21. Possible responses should include the following points:

Allowing the desire for revenge to control a peace treaty is ultimately unsuccessful. Forcing one nation to accept all the blame for a war that was actually started by another is neither fair nor practical. The war guilt clause led not only to bitterness in Germany but, because it required huge reparations of Germany, also led to severe economic problems. A peace treaty should address the problems that caused a war or they may occur again. All of the nations that have been involved in a war should be involved in the decisions laid out in the treaty. If a major world power does not support a treaty, the terms of said treaty are not on firm ground. A world peacekeeping body is a necessary safeguard against future wars. Such a body must have real power and authority and the support of all the major world powers.

22. Possible responses should include the following points:

World War I was different from previous wars in many ways. New forms of warfare emerged such as trench warfare. Soldiers would lie for weeks in trenches dug in parallel lines along the front and utilize mini attacks to attempt to gain ground

on their enemy. At the same time, as troops made their way between trenches, the enemy would open fire. New weapons like machine guns, tanks, and airplanes gave both sides enormous destructive power, a trend that has continued to the present. There were great losses of life, homes, businesses, and land. Entire communities were destroyed. Industry boomed with manufacturing of war-making materials, and women took on a greater role in the workforce. When the war ended, huge reparations were made by the Central Powers in which their territory and colonies were stripped. New and independent states were formed that completely changed the face of the European continent. The tragedy drained the treasuries of Europe leaving the continent in an economic decline. It also destroyed a large part of a generation. The war's legacy left a feeling of disillusionment that was reflected in the art and literature of the time.

Chapter 14, Section 1
SECTION QUIZ

Revolutions in Russia

A. 1. b
2. f
3. i
4. k
5. n
6. g
7. c
8. d
9. o
10. k
11. a
12. f

B. Possible answers:

a. The Revolution of 1905 was more a political demonstration than an actual revolution, but it prepared the way for the Bolsheviks by sparking further unrest and weakening Nicholas's rule.

b. The March Revolution in 1917 forced Nicholas to abdicate but failed to establish a strong government. The decision of Kerensky's provisional government to keep fighting in World War I caused conditions in Russia to worsen.

c. Lenin's return from exile gave the Bolsheviks a powerful and ruthless leader.

d. The Bolsheviks gained control of several powerful soviets.

e. In November 1917, the Bolsheviks acted quickly to seize power and dispose of the provisional government.

f. The Bolsheviks immediately ended Russian involvement in the war and focused on domestic problems.

g. The Bolshevik Red Army won the civil war with their opponents' White Army.

h. The Bolsheviks were able to restore peace, revive the economy, restructure the government, and institute certain reform policies.

Chapter 14, Section 2
SECTION QUIZ

Totalitarianism CASE STUDY: *Stalinist Russia*

A. 1. a

2. a

3. c

4. b

5. d

B.

Stalin imposed a dictatorship on Soviet society by crushing opposition and forcing obedience. He did this by

a. taking command of the Communist Party and forcing his chief rival, Trotsky, into exile.

b. instituting a command economy, taking control of workers' lives, and forcing peasants onto collective farms.

c. using police terror and violence to stop civilian riots, to purge the Communist Party of anyone who threatened his power, and to destroy the kulaks and others who resisted his policies.

d. relying on indoctrination and propaganda to promote the Communist Party, atheism and other Communist values, and his own image and achievements.

e. censoring artists and assuming control of all means of communication.

f. persecuting members of the Russian Orthodox Church and other religious groups and trying to replace religious teachings with Communist ideals.

Chapter 14, Section 3
SECTION QUIZ

Imperial China Collapses

A. 1. c

2. d

3. e

4. f

5. g

6. f

7. d

8. b

9. b

10. f

11. i

12. c

13. d

B. Possible answers:

a. Both groups wanted an independent, strong China.

b. In addition, the Nationalists claimed to want a modern society, a democratic government, and economic security for all Chinese.

c. In addition, the Communists claimed to want a Communist government and economy based on Lenin's Soviet model. Land redistribution and a more powerful, revolutionary peasantry.

Chapter 14, Section 4
SECTION QUIZ

Nationalism in India and Southwest Asia

A. 1. a

2. b

3. b

4. d

5. b

6. b

7. c

8. a

9. a

10. c

11. a

12. d

13. c

B. Possible answers:

a. During the war, the British government asked for Indian aid in the war effort in return for promised reforms that would lead to Indian self-government. More than a million Indians enlisted in the British army.

b. Indian troops returning from the war expected Britain to make good on its promises. However, Britain made no move to advance Indian independence.

c. Britain responded to increased protests for self-rule by passing a restrictive law that only helped to convince more Indians of the need for independence.

d. The Amritsar Massacre changed millions of Indians from loyal British subjects into nationalist revolutionaries.

Chapter 14
TEST FORM A

Revolution and Nationalism

Part 1: Main Ideas

1. a

2. b

3. d

4. b

5. c

6. d

7. b

8. b

9. a

10. d

Part 2: Map Skills

11. c

12. b

13. a

14. d

15. b

Part 3: Document Based Questions

A. (4 points each)

16. He defines it as "truth-force," or holding on to the truth.

17. The whirlwind caused many things to change, mostly the way people thought.

18. because both men fought for civil rights using civil disobedience

B. (8 points)

19. Gandhi led a movement for independence from Britain through a campaign of satyagraha, or civil disobedience, which forbade protesters to act with violence toward any attacker or provocation; Gandhi and his followers came to believe that their oppressors should be led to the truth of their wrong actions through patience and non-violence, that violence was never justified even to gain a good end; Gandhi's campaign opened the eyes of many, both in India and elsewhere, to the pain suffered by people in an unjust system. His teachings were tied to the daily lives of masses of people; he influenced others worldwide, including Dr. Martin Luther King, Jr., a leader in the U.S. Civil Rights Movement; Gandhi was assassinated.

Part 4: Extended Response

20. Lenin established a mixture of capitalism and free enterprise, allowing some small factories and businesses to be privately owned; Stalin developed a command economy that controlled every aspect of economic life and banned private ownership of farms, factories, or businesses. Lenin's government redistributed land to the peasants; Stalin established collective farms that took the land back and kept it under state control. Although both

governments were dictatorships, Lenin's interfered much less in the daily lives of the citizens. Life under Lenin involved less terror and oppression than life under Stalin. Although an agricultural revolution under Stalin made certain types of food more plentiful, this progress came at a huge cost to the peasants forced to work on collective farms and to the kulaks who were murdered or shipped to Siberia.

21. Possible responses should include the following points: Muslims and Hindus founded groups to fight for independence. These groups often worked together. Under Gandhi's leadership, the independence movement adopted a program of civil disobedience and nonviolent noncooperation, which gained worldwide attention and support. Indians hurt Britain economically by refusing to buy British cloth and by refusing to carry on their normal work on railroads and in factories. Some Indian nationalists rioted and used violence to protest British rule. Indian boycotts and strikes took an enormous financial toll on Britain. Worldwide attention was focused on the movement, and sympathies lay with the protestors. Britain did not want to look bad in the eyes of the world by responding violently to nonviolent protests. The movement had a strong and charismatic leader in Gandhi.

Chapter 14
TEST FORM B

Revolution and Nationalism

Part 1: Main Ideas

1. c
2. c
3. b
4. d
5. d
6. a
7. d
8. c
9. b
10. a

Part 2: Map Skills

11. c

12. a

13. d

14. c

15. b

Part 3: Document Based Questions

A. (4 points each)

16. Gandhi believes that a person who oppresses another does not know the truth.

17. Gandhi's leadership seems to come from the reality and the needs of the people, or from the bottom up rather than from the top down.

18. Dr. King, a follower of Gandhi who used the strategy of civil disobedience in the U.S. Civil Rights Movement, had just been assassinated. Gandhi had also been assassinated years earlier.

B. (8 points)

19. Gandhi led a movement for independence from Britain through a campaign of satyagraha, or civil disobedience, which forbade protesters to act with violence toward any attacker or provocation; Gandhi and his followers came to believe that their oppressors should be led to the truth of their wrong actions through patience and non-violence, that violence was never justified even to gain a good end; Gandhi's campaign opened the eyes of many, both in India and elsewhere, to the pain suffered by people in an unjust system. His teachings were tied to the daily lives of masses of people; he influenced others worldwide, including Dr. Martin Luther King, Jr., a leader in the U.S. Civil Rights Movement; Gandhi was assassinated.

Part 4: Extended Response

20. Possible responses should include the following points:

    Better: A citizen who embraced communism had a chance to reap some rewards for his or her work. The state-controlled economy, with collective farms and state-owned businesses, would at least reduce the gap between rich and poor. The economy was successfully developed by Stalin's

Five-Year Plans. The nation greatly increased its production of wheat, which would have made food more plentiful. Women were encouraged to get an education and to work in professional areas, such as medicine.**Worse:** Under totalitarianism, the government controlled every aspect of life. People had no choice about what work to do, how to do it, where to live, or how to live. People were not safe anywhere. There was no such thing as truly private communication. Family members were turned against one another by the state's determination to uncover any indication of disloyalty. No incident of rebellion was tolerated. Peasants who objected to collective farming were crushed. The secret police had enormous power. Even events outside a person's control could result in his or her being arrested. Millions of citizens were killed. Although the Jews had been victimized, terrorized, and persecuted under the czars, Stalin extended this persecution to members of all religions.

21. Possible responses should include the following points:

Time. Gandhi's plan required time to work. For example, his boycott of British cloth required Indians to spend time making their own cloth. The Indian people had to learn to live without certain creature comforts, while making do with what they had. Boycotts of British goods were an important part of Gandhi's strategy. However, the conscious choice not to use British goods also had an effect on Indians lives as their demonstrations were considered illegal by the government and often met with military opposition. Gandhi's plan didn't allow protesters to fight back when attacked. It took a supreme amount of courage for these people to actively use civil disobedience and knowingly suffer the consequences. Gandhi's plan required the Indian people to forgive the British and to treat them as friends no matter what the British did.

Chapter 14
TEST FORM C

Revolution and Nationalism

Part 1: Main Ideas

1. a
2. c
3. c
4. c
5. a
6. b
7. c
8. c
9. d
10. b

Part 2: Map Skills

11. b
12. b
13. a
14. c
15. b

Part 3: Document Based Questions

A. (4 points each)

16. Satyagraha does not allow for violence to achieve an end, but Passive Resistance does allow for violence. This difference leads to the strength of Satyagraha and the weakness of Passive Resistance.

17. Nehru says that Gandhi allied action to a combination of fearlessness (or courage) and truth. The political freedom that flowed from this was the effect of the actions of millions of people, rather than single leaders or representatives.

18. Assassins think they have killed the ideas and influence of a person when they have only killed the person.

B. (8 points)

19. Gandhi led a movement for independence from Britain through a campaign of satyagraha, or civil disobedience, which forbade protesters to act with violence toward any attacker or provocation; Gandhi and his followers came to believe that their oppressors should be led to the truth of their wrong actions through patience and non-violence,

that violence was never justified even to gain a good end; Gandhi's campaign opened the eyes of many, both in India and elsewhere, to the pain suffered by people in an unjust system. His teachings were tied to the daily lives of masses of people; he influenced others worldwide, including Dr. Martin Luther King, Jr., a leader in the U.S. Civil Rights Movement; Gandhi was assassinated.

Part 4: Extended Response

20. Possible responses should include the following points:

The Chinese people had a long history of being victimized by their leaders. The Qing dynasty had neglected the growing problems in China, especially the hardships suffered by its poor, and discontent had reached a boiling point. The Kuomintang and Sun Yixian were unsuccessful in unifying the country. Sun Yixian's successor abandoned the principles of democracy and ruled as a dictator. Civil war broke out as local warlords grabbed power. Again, the peasants were the major victims. The Chinese were deeply angered that the Treaty of Versailles gave Chinese territory to Japan. Many people, especially young intellectuals, began to believe that communism offered more hope for the future than did Western forms of government. Sun Yixian was rebuffed by Western governments, who would provide no assistance. The Russian government led by Lenin wanted to expand communism in the world and provided aid to the Chinese Communists. Jiang Jieshi's corrupt government did not address the needs of China's poor and its rural peasants. Mao Zedong skillfully gathered support for the Communists among the peasants.

21. Possible responses should include the following points:

Stalin and Gandhi were as different as night and day. Stalin formed a totalitarian government that controlled every aspect of public and private life. He ruled Russia with an iron fist using police terror, indoctrination, and propaganda. One of Stalin's major goals was to boost the Soviet economy, and he was successful in this but at a great price to his people. He created

Five–Year Plans that set impossibly high quotas for steel, coal, oil, and electricity. To reach these targets, the government restricted the production of consumer goods, so the people suffered severe shortages. Stalin also beefed up agricultural production with collective farms on which hundreds of families worked collectively to produce food for the state. Resistance was met with violence and almost an entire class of people called the kulaks were executed. Gandhi, on the other hand, used his experience as a lawyer in South Africa, and developed the principle of satyagraha within the bounds of the law. This principle would become known as civil disobedience around the world. It also became the "strong arm" of the Indian people and their guiding force in all demonstrations against the British government in opposition to British rule. Gandhi's campaign was eventually successful, but it also came with a price to the Indian people. Boycotts against British goods also meant that the Indian people often had to go without basic necessities which effected their health and well-being. In demonstrations, the Indian people were unable to defend themselves against violent attacks from the British under Gandhi's principle of satyagraha. Gandhi did not fight for complete control of his country, nor did he want it. He fought for the Indian people to gain independence for all and for all to reap the rewards of a democracy.

Chapter 15, Section 1
SECTION QUIZ

Postwar Uncertainty

A. 1. g

2. e

3. l

4. f

5. n

6. j

7. o

8. k

9. c

10. h

B. Possible answers:

a. Many writers suffered from despair, disillusionment, and alienation, which was reflected in their work.

b. The work of writers and painters reflected their uncertainties about the power of reason and the meaning of life.

c. Many writers, painters, and musicians broke with the traditions of the past and abandoned the restrictions imposed by old structures.

d. Surrealism, stream-of-consciousness writing, and jazz were embraced as new ways to explore and express ideas.

Chapter 15, Section 2
SECTION QUIZ

A Worldwide Depression

A. 1. b

2. d

3. d

4. a

5. b

6. b

B. Possible answers:

a. Roosevelt was probably referring to the panic that hastened the collapse of the stock market and the failure of many banks.

b. Fear can keep people from taking logical and constructive steps, so people's fears during the Depression contributed to the severity of the crisis.

c. The United States possessed the ability to pull out of the economic slump. It had industrial development, good farms, a willing and skillful work force. All that stood in the way of reversing the slump was a lack of confidence.

d. Reversing the effects of the Depression would require that both the government and the citizens stop acting and reacting out of fear.

Chapter 15, Section 3
SECTION QUIZ

Fascism Rises in Europe

A. 1. d

2. a

3. c

4. d

5. b

6. a

B. Possible answers:

a. These countries lacked strong democratic traditions.

b. They suffered from severe economic problems and the social unrest that accompanied those problems.

c. Their citizens feared continued unrest and saw strong leadership as the only way to prevent it.

d. There were strong leaders who were ready and willing to take advantage of the situation, take power, and crush any opposition to their rule.

Chapter 15, Section 4
SECTION QUIZ

Aggressors Invade Nations

A. 1. c

2. b

3. d

4. b

5. a

6. a

7. d

B. Possible answers:

a. Both policies were attempts to avoid war.

b. Both policies allowed the countries involved to avoid having to confront Hitler and his aggression.

c. Both policies relied on the idea that what was happening at a distant location in the world would not happen closer to home.

d. Both policies were dangerously shortsighted.

e. Both policies were ultimately unsuccessful.

f. Both policies backfired in that Fascist aggression might have been stopped sooner and more easily if it had been confronted.

Chapter 15
TEST FORM A

Years of Crisis

Part 1: Main Ideas

1. b
2. c
3. d
4. c
5. c
6. d
7. b
8. a
9. c
10. b

Part 2: Map Skills

11. a
12. c
13. b
14. a
15. c

Part 3: Interpreting Graphs

16. b
17. c
18. d
19. c
20. d

Part 4: Extended Response

21. Possible responses should include the following points:

The countries that became ruled by Fascist governments had little historical experience with democracy. There were few systems in place to deal with the problems caused by economic depression and the resulting social unrest. Germany suffered enormously as a result of losing World War I, and its people were bitter and angry. Both Germany and Italy feared that communism might take hold as a result of inflation and unemployment. They felt that only a strong government could protect their nations from this threat. Hitler and Mussolini were both enormously skillful at manipulating public opinion. Germans blamed their postwar government for the difficulties they faced as a result of the Treaty of Versailles. Italians were angry about failing to gain territory after World War I.

22. Possible responses should include the following points:

The radio, which was invented before the war, really developed during the war. Commercial radio stations appeared in the United States and government-owned stations in Europe. The automobile benefited from many wartime innovations and improvements. Cars gave people the ability to travel longer distances and affected where they lived and worked. Airplanes also had their place in the war and expanded their reach after the war. The idea of international travel by air became an objective. There were also new forms of entertainment, including radio plays and movies.

Chapter 15
TEST FORM B

Years of Crisis

Part 1: Main Ideas

1. a
2. c
3. c
4. a
5. b
6. d
7. a
8. a
9. b
10. b

Part 2: Map Skills

11. b
12. a
13. c
14. b
15. d

Part 3: Interpreting Charts

16. a
17. b
18. c
19. c
20. b

Part 4: Extended Response

21. Possible responses should include the following points:

Panicked selling of stock helped to cause the collapse of the stock market. Panicked withdrawing of savings from struggling banks caused bank failures when the banks had insufficient funds to honor withdrawal attempts. This hastened the partial collapse of the banking system. Panic by American bankers resulted in demands for repayment of foreign loans, which could not be hastily repaid and helped to cause severe economic crises in other countries. The loss in American jobs resulted in high protective tariffs and the resultant lowering of imports. This backfired, making European countries impose their own tariffs. World trade dropped sharply, which further hurt industry and increased unemployment.

22. Possible responses should include the following points:

Many citizens of the new democracies had little experience with representative government. For generations, kings and emperors had ruled Germany and Austria-Hungary. Even in France and Italy, whose parliaments existed before World War I, the large number of political parties made effective government difficult. In these countries, it was almost impossible for one party to win enough support to govern effectively, and because the parties disagreed on so many policies, coalitions seldom lasted very long. Frequent changes in government made it hard for democratic countries to develop strong leadership and move toward long-term goals. Further, the Depression caused severe economic problems. In some countries, inflation was rampant. People wanted strong leaders who promised prosperity, even if they were not democratic. Finally, anger over the Treaty of Versailles and leaders who stirred up nationalist feelings also helped many Europeans to accept dictators.

Chapter 15
TEST FORM C

Years of Crisis

Part 1: Main Ideas

1. c
2. c
3. d
4. a
5. c
6. a
7. b
8. b
9. c
10. d

Part 2: Map Skills—Constructed Response

11. the Netherlands, Belgium, Luxembourg, and France

12. It is an outlying area of Czechoslovakia that shares common borders mostly with Germany and Austria.

13. east

14. vast territory, reunification with East Prussia, and the port of Danzig

15. to prevent the Soviet Union from feeling threatened by the conquest of Poland in September 1939 and possibly fighting Germany

Part 3: Interpreting Charts

16. a
17. c
18. a
19. d
20. c

Part 4: Extended Response

21. Possible responses should include the following points:

The war spread the developments of technological and scientific advances, such as the use of the airplane and radio communications, that permanently changed the world. The United States made huge loans to European countries devastated by the war, which created a dependence on the American economy and made the effects of the American stock market collapse felt worldwide. The attitude of the returning soldiers and the other young people who lived through the war was different from their parents' attitudes. More open to change, they brought about drastic changes in society and culture. The effects of both the war and the terms of the treaty that ended it were devastating to Germany and largely contributed to its determination to regain power through aggression. Many Americans became determined to follow an isolationist policy in order to avoid future foreign conflicts. This helped to create a situation in which Germany, Italy, and Japan were unchallenged in their preliminary aggression against other nations.

22. Possible responses should include the following points:

Students who say yes should note that Britain and France had both undergone severe economic problems and were not eager to become involved in costly and dangerous international problems. Both countries had suffered greatly because of World War I and did not want to become involved in another war. Each hoped that Germany would be satisfied and that their own countries would remain safe. No one could have foreseen how determined Germany was to rule the world. British and French leaders' first responsibility was to their own nations and people, who were not ready for war and who were not, at that time, actually threatened. Students who say no might state that Germany had proven its aggressiveness in World War I. Germany had broken its promises to renounce war. It was entirely

unreasonable to expect Germany to suddenly start honoring promises. By failing to take a stand against German aggression, the British and French were encouraging more aggression.

Chapter 16, Section 1
SECTION QUIZ

Hitler's Lightning War

A. 1. c
2. a
3. b
4. d
5. d
6. a

B. Possible answers:

a. France: battle won by Germany; British army forced to flee the continent; German victory convinced Mussolini to join with Germany; northern France occupied by Germany; puppet government established in southern France.

b. Britain: Germany was ultimately unsuccessful; great deal of destruction and loss of life in London; British resistance persuaded Hitler to stop bombing and to give up plan to invade Britain; British morale boosted; Allies learned that Hitler's advances could be blocked.

c. Soviet Union: invasion deflected at tremendous cost to USSR; enormous loss of life on both sides; enormous destruction to Soviet lands and cities.

Chapter 16, Section 2
SECTION QUIZ

Japan's Pacific Campaign

A. 1. d
2. b
3. a
4. c
5. d

B. Students could say that Japan attacked Pearl Harbor because

a. the U.S. was threatening to prevent Japan from fulfilling its empire-building goals in Southeast Asia.

b. the U.S. Pacific fleet was stationed at Pearl Harbor.

c. Japan perceived the U.S. Pacific fleet as a potential threat.

In addition, students could say that the attack on Pearl Harbor

a. sank or damaged nearly the entire U.S. Pacific fleet.

b. killed or wounded thousands of Americans.

c. led the United States to declare war on Japan.

d. allowed Japan early victories in carrying out its empire-building plan.

Chapter 16, Section 3
SECTION QUIZ

The Holocaust

A. 1. Aryans

2. Nazis attacked Jewish homes, businesses, and synagogues across Germany and murdered Jews.

3. Emigration, but there weren't enough countries willing to take enough Jews.

4. the systematic killing of an entire people

5. to protect the so-called racial purity of the Germans ("Aryans")

6. Students should include two of the following: mass murder, concentration camps, death camps, hard labor, starvation, medical experimentation, gas chambers

7. Students should include two of the following: Roma, Poles, Russians (Soviets, Communists), homosexuals, the insane, the disabled, the incurably ill

8. extermination camp (death camp, concentration camp)

B. Possible answers:

a. There was a long history of anti-Semitism in Europe.

b. The war distracted people from paying attention to the Holocaust.

c. Death and suffering were commonplace during the war.

d. People were terrified of opposing the Nazis. As long as the persecution was happening to someone else, many chose not to react.

e. It was difficult for people to believe that something as horrifying as the Holocaust could actually be happening. Absolute evil is a difficult thing for normal people to imagine.

f. By conquering most of Europe, Nazi Germany was able to do as it liked with the peoples of Europe.

g. The Nazis proceeded in gradual steps, each more devastating than the former. By the time they embarked on their "Final Solution," it was very difficult to successfully oppose their plans and very easy for them to round up Jews.

Chapter 16, Section 4
SECTION QUIZ

The Allied Victory

A. 1. d

2. b

3. a

4. b

5. c

6. a

B. Possible answers:

a. The Allied victory in the Battle of El Alamein forced the German army to begin its retreat from North Africa.

b. The Soviet victory in the Battle of Stalingrad forced the German army onto the defensive in Eastern Europe.

c. The Allied invasion of Normandy forced the German army onto the defensive in Western Europe. It also enabled the Allies to liberate many nations on the continent, including France.

d. The damage inflicted on the German army in the Battle of the Bulge was so extensive that, from then on, the German army could do little but retreat.

e. The damage inflicted on the Japanese navy during the Battle of Leyte Gulf

was so extensive that the Japanese navy was eliminated as a fighting force in the war.

Chapter 16, Section 5
SECTION QUIZ

Europe and Japan in Ruins

A. 1. a

2. b

3. a

4. a

5. d

6. a

B. Answers could include such details as the following:

a. Hundreds of cities were reduced to rubble.

b. Farmland, factories, and transportation systems were damaged or destroyed.

c. Millions of refugees were stranded away from home.

d. There was insufficient housing, clean water, electricity, and so on.

e. The interruptions to agriculture caused by the war resulted in food shortages and starvation.

f. Widespread illness and disease plagued the region.

g. There was widespread unemployment and poverty.

h. Family members, separated during the war, searched desperately for each other.

Chapter 16
TEST FORM A

World War II

Part 1: Main Ideas

1. b

2. c

3. b

4. a

5. a

6. c

7. a

8. a

9. c

10. a

Part 2: Map Skills

11. c

12. d

13. a

14. d

15. c

Part 3: Interpreting Graphs

16. c

17. d

18. a

19. a

20. b

Part 4: Extended Response

21. Possible answers should include the following points:

Most of Europe was occupied by Axis forces. There was no way to free the nations of Europe except by invading them. The millions of Allied forces fighting in Europe were in desperate need of relief. The Russians had been holding out against the Germans for years, losing millions of soldiers in the effort. They were pushing the Germans from the east, but it was necessary to launch an Allied attack on a second front to provide the Russians some relief. The D-Day invasion landed enormous numbers of Allied troops in a single day. The huge assault drove the Germans from the coast and allowed the Allies to gain a crucial foothold. Except for the Battle of the Bulge, the war in western Europe after D-Day had the Allies on the offensive and the Germans on the defensive. Gradually, the Allies were able to push into Germany itself.

22. Possible answers should include the following points:

The mass slaughter of civilians, especially Jews, took place in Germany and its conquered territory from about 1933 to 1942. In the initial stages, thousands of refugees fled their homes and emigrated to neighboring lands and distant countries. Those who could not get

out or chose not to go were later isolated into overcrowded ghettos. Many of these were later killed. In the United States, Japanese Americans suffered because of a program of internment and loss of property, because they were considered a threat to the country. It lasted from 1941 to 1946. Also, any number of cities were assaulted by bombing raids during the war and had civilian populations that were dislocated from their homes or died. The atomic bombs dropped on Japan had devastating and lasting effects on the populations in Hiroshima and Nagasaki. Thousands of people were killed by the enormously destructive power of these bombs and many more touched by the lasting effects of radiation. Lastly, many citizens supported the war effort by buying bonds, taking part in scrap drives, working in war-related industries, and rationing scarce items.

Chapter 16
TEST FORM B

World War II

Part 1: Main Ideas

1. b

2. d

3. c

4. c

5. b

6. a

7. d

8. b

9. c

10. c

Part 2: Map Skills

11. a

12. d

13. a

14. c

15. c

Part 3: Interpreting Charts

16. d

17. a

18. b

19. d

20. c

Part 4: Extended Response

21. Possible responses should include the following points:

The joint effort of the Allied forces was a main factor in ending the war. In Africa, German forces were well dug in. The British forces had no alternative but to stage an assault from the front. Meanwhile, additional Allied troops, mostly Americans, landed in Morocco and Algeria. They effectively caught the Germans in between and ended that part of the German offensive. In Europe, the Allies were building a secret force in Great Britain that they would use to attack the Germans in France. British, American, French, and Canadian troops fought their way onto a 60-mile stretch of beach in Normandy. Within three months the Allies had liberated France, Belgium, Luxembourg, and much of the Netherlands. In the meantime, the Soviets invaded from the east so that Germany was squeezed from two directions. Germany's unconditional surrender was not far off, however; there was still the war in the Pacific to be dealt with. The Allies began with retaking the Philippines, which they had been forced to surrender earlier in the war. The Japanese attempted to destroy the American fleet and had to use almost their entire naval fleet to do so. It was a gamble the Japanese lost disastrously, leaving them with just their army and kamikaze pilots. Iwo Jima and Okinawa signaled an end to fighting off the Japanese mainland. The final push came in the form of two atomic bombs. Hiroshima and Nagasaki's devastation brought surrender from the Japanese on September 2. The war had ended.

22. Possible responses should include the following points:

Poland ceased to exist as an independent nation for the duration of the war. Hundreds of thousands of Poles eventually died in the Holocaust. Germany gained half of Poland's territory and initially gave the other half to the Soviet Union. Britain and France declared war on Germany. The surrender of France and the Battle of Britain came soon after. Those events pulled much of the world into the war as well. Germany also turned on its ally and invaded the Soviet Union.

Chapter 16
TEST FORM C

World War II

Part 1: Main Ideas

1. c
2. a
3. d
4. b
5. b
6. d
7. c
8. b
9. d
10. b

Part 2: Map Skills

11. c
12. d
13. c
14. a
15. b

Part 3: Interpreting Charts – Constructed Response

16. The Allied countries had 4,107,855 more civilians killed than the Axis countries.
17. 5.9%
18. France
19. 16.3%
20. the USSR because it lost the most people and the United States because it spent the most money

Part 4: Extended Response

21. Possible responses should include the following points:

Germany made the serious mistake of violating its nonaggression pact with Russia. If the Germans had not invaded Russia, they would have saved the lives of hundreds of thousands of German soldiers. In addition, they would not have had

to fight on two fronts and might have persuaded Russia to join the war against the Allies. Hitler's narrow-mindedness and lack of trust in his officers made it difficult to provide practical leadership. He refused to let his troops retreat from Stalingrad, and refused to learn from Germany's mistakes in World War I. Hitler's persecution of the Jews caused him to devote manpower and resources to the plan to wipe out an entire race, a plan that did nothing for the German war effort. The Germans continually underestimated their enemies. They underestimated the Russians, the Russian winter, and the resistance capabilities and determination of the British and the Americans.

22. Possible responses should include the following points:

Students who say yes may note that at that point, it was a European war that had little to do with the United States. No Axis Power had yet attacked America. Britain and France were fighting to protect themselves; it was not America's responsibility to protect them. The United States had suffered from being pulled into World War I despite not having been involved in the problems that caused it. Students who say no may note that the United States had a moral responsibility to fight Nazism and anti-Semitism and a practical need to defend its economic allies. The United States bore as much responsibility for stopping Hitler's aggression as Britain and France did. Hitler's actions clearly showed that he would never stop unless forced. The United States could never have peacefully coexisted with a Nazi Empire controlling all of Europe. It also should have realized immediately that an eventual attempt to do so was the only alternative to joining the war.

Chapter 17, Section 1
SECTION QUIZ

Cold War: Two Superpowers Face Off

A. 1. c
2. j

3. a
4. k
5. b
6. f
7. b
8. d
9. g
10. i
11. l

B. Possible answers:

a. European nations that had been devastated by World War II benefitted enormously from the financial aid. Many countries were able to rebuild, to end starvation, to provide jobs, and to do the other things necessary to recover from the war.

b. The financial aid provided by the plan helped stabilize European politics.

c. The plan worked to contain communism, which insulated the U.S. from the problems that could easily have developed if former allies had come under Soviet control.

d. Countries aided by the plan became indebted to the U.S.

Chapter 17, Section 2
SECTION QUIZ

Communists Take Power in China

A. 1. Japan
2. the Communists
3. the Nationalists *or* the anti-Communists
4. Taiwan *or* Formosa
5. communes
6. the Cultural Revolution; by Mao Zedong

B. Possible answers:

a. People could see little reason to work tirelessly when they did not directly benefit from their work. As appealing as the idea of working for "the common good" is, people tend to want to benefit themselves and their loved ones through their work.

b. People do not respond well to being forced to do things.

c. Whenever people are forced to behave in certain ways, other people have to spend their time making sure this happens.

d. The program was not well-planned.

e. China was insufficiently industrialized.

f. People were not happy. They disliked the impersonality of the program, the communal atmosphere, and the governmental control over their lives. It is difficult to have a successful program when it is not supported by those it is supposedly designed to benefit.

g. Many people died resisting the takeover of their land.

h. There were serious crop failures.

Chapter 17, Section 3
SECTION QUIZ

Wars in Korea and Vietnam

A. 1. g

2. b

3. g

4. b

5. h

6. n

7. n

8. c

9. l

10. d

11. e

12. i

B. Students who feel that the U.S. was justified might include such points as the following:

a. The French were U.S. allies. They were being fought by Communists.

b. The U.S. had adopted a well-publicized policy of containment.

c. The North Vietnamese were being supported by Communist regimes. If the U.S. provided no support, South Vietnam's struggle to resist a Communist takeover was doomed.

d. Corrupt as the South Vietnamese leader was, his policies were not

hostile to U.S. interests, while Ho Chi Minh's were.

Students who feel that the U.S. was not justified might include such points as the following:

a. People in any nation have a right to political self-determination.

b. The French had colonized the region. They had no rights to it, and the U.S. had no right to take their side against people subjected to their imperialism.

c. The war was a regional conflict of warring factions within another country. It did not put U.S. security at stake.

d. The South Vietnamese leader was a dictator.

e. The South Vietnamese people were not clearly the victims of North Vietnamese aggression. Many South Vietnamese were involved in the rebellion.

Chapter 17, Section 4
SECTION QUIZ

The Cold War Divides the World

A. 1. a

2. b

3. a

4. c

5. d

6. b

7. d

B. Possible answers:

a. The conflict typically involved an attempt to overthrow an established dictator.

b. The dictator had typically ruled with little concern for the poor and powerless in his nation.

c. The rebels typically wanted to oust the government and replace it with one more sympathetic to the people's needs.

d. The dictator typically received U.S. support to prevent the spread of communism and/or to protect U.S. economic interests.

Chapter 17, Section 5
SECTION QUIZ

The Cold War Thaws

A. 1. a

2. c

3. b

4. d

5. a

6. b

7. c

B. Possible answers:

a. Neither attitude allowed for political self-determination.

b. Each attitude required the superpower to interfere, which led to or increased armed conflicts and loss of life.

c. Neither attitude could be successfully imposed over the long haul.

d. Both attitudes required considerable financial expenditures and risk.

e. Both attitudes increased the hostility between the superpowers and, therefore, raised the level of Cold War tensions.

Chapter 17
TEST FORM A

Restructuring the Postwar World

Part 1: Main Ideas

1. b

2. d

3. b

4. c

5. b

6. b

7. b

8. c

9. a

10. c

Part 2: Map Skills

11. c

12. a

13. c

14. b

15. b

Part 3: Document Based Questions

A. (4 points each)

16. A Vietnamese patriot—perhaps, but not necessarily a soldier.

17. Noncombatants are civilians—people who do not go into combat—or non-military people, or people who are not soldiers who can defend themselves, etc. McNamara is concerned that the deaths of thousands of Vietnamese civilians each month make the United States look bad in the eyes of the world.

18. The three figures are Presidents Kennedy, Johnson, and Nixon, and they are talking about the Vietnam War because the war took place mostly during their administrations.

B. (8 points)

19. The Vietnam War involved several American presidential administrations and an entire generation of American fighting men; Vietnamese Communists and nationalists were willing to lose hundreds of thousands of their own citizens each year in order to reunify their country; this resistance caused the United States to question its role in Southeast Asia and to wonder how its continued presence there would look to the world and to people at home; Americans who were boys when the war began grew up to be old enough to fight by the time the United States was forced to withdraw from Vietnam. A long-term effect on the United States was a reluctance to become involved in other countries' struggles. A long-term effect on Vietnam was the defeat of the South, reunification, and Communist rule.

Part 4: Extended Response

20. Possible responses should include the following points:

The United States had a history of strong democracy and a generally successful capitalist economy. Therefore, it believed that democracy and capitalism should be the basis for European nations and developing countries alike. The United States had generally been protected, at least until the nuclear age, from attack by aggressive

enemies. It sat between two oceans and had friendly relations with its neighbors to the north and south. It did not have the same fears of invasion that the Soviet Union had. The United States could better afford the money it had spent on World War II than could the Soviet Union. Even though the United States was recovering from the Depression, it did not deplete its raw materials during the war and did not need to rebuild. Therefore, it did not need to take over other countries for their raw materials. In contrast, the Soviet Union had no history of democratic rule. The country had a history of being repeatedly invaded. Therefore, it felt the need to protect itself and its thousands of miles of borders by establishing a buffer zone of nations it could control. The Soviet Union was impoverished by World War II and believed it needed to obtain raw materials and industrial equipment from other countries.

21. Possible responses should include the following points:

Some students will name the U.S. involvement in the Vietnam War. The war resulted in a tragic loss of life and did not accomplish the American goals for that region. Others might cite the U.S. support for the shah of Iran. Although the shah tried to modernize his nation, he did not alleviate poverty, and he was eventually overthrown despite U.S. support. U.S.-Iran relations might be more productive and mutually beneficial today if Iran did not have reason to resent the United States. Some might mention the U.S. support of Jiang Jieshi who was ineffective and corrupt and lost the war. The United States wasted millions of dollars in propping him up and endangered relations with China for many years by insisting that Nationalist China (Taiwan) was the "real China" and that Jiang Jieshi was its legitimate leader.

Chapter 17
TEST FORM B

Restructuring the Postwar World

Part 1: Main Ideas

1. a

2. b

3. d

4. a

5. b

6. b

7. d

8. a

9. c

10. a

Part 2: Map Skills

11. c

12. a

13. c

14. c

15. c

Part 3: Document Based Questions

A. (4 points each)

16. Vietnam in flames; weeping mothers; suffering children

17. He fears that continuing the war, with its high death toll, will make the United States look bad in the eyes of the world, and will cause trouble at home. In the quote, he means that people challenge the reasons for the U.S. involvement in Vietnam, or think the reasons do not have merit.

18. The figure starts out as a boy and grows into a young man old enough to become a soldier. Finally, he is contained in a casket. The cartoonist means to suggest that the war dragged on throughout a boy's passage from child to adult to death from the war itself.

B. (8 points)

19. The Vietnam War involved several American presidential administrations and an entire generation of American fighting men; Vietnamese Communists and nationalists were willing to lose hundreds of thousands of their own citizens each year in order to reunify their country; this resistance caused the United States to question its role in Southeast Asia and to wonder how its continued presence there would look to the world and to people at home; Americans who were boys when the war began grew up to be

old enough to fight by the time the United States was forced to withdraw from Vietnam. A long-term effect on the United States was a reluctance to become involved in other countries' struggles. A long-term effect on Vietnam was the defeat of the South, reunification, and Communist rule.

Part 4: Extended Response

20. Possible responses should include the following points:

The U.S. belief in equality had (and has) to do with the equal value of human beings and their equal rights and opportunities. The Chinese Communist goal during the Cultural Revolution seems to have involved a concept of sameness. Everyone became "equal" by being the same and doing the same things. This "equality" meant that no one should have more, know more, or do more than anyone else. The American concept of equality reflects the idea that each individual matters, and all individuals have equal value. The Cultural Revolution concept seemed to reflect the idea that individuals do not matter in and of themselves, but what matters are the group and the "common good." The American concept of equality has very little to do with income, except perhaps in terms of everyone's having a theoretical opportunity to increase wealth; in contrast, while the Cultural Revolution's concept had much to do with equality of income and financial status.

21. Possible responses should include the following points:

The establishment of the United Nations, with both superpowers as members, has provided a forum for communication. World leaders and common citizens alike are aware that the development of nuclear weapons has made all-out war synonymous with the destruction of civilization and the end of life as we know it. Also, wars in which the superpowers have become involved have remained regional, partially because many uninvolved nations have chosen not to escalate the conflict to a global scale.

Chapter 17
TEST FORM C

Restructuring the Postwar World

Part 1: Main Ideas

1. b
2. a
3. a
4. d
5. b
6. c
7. d
8. a
9. c
10. b

Part 2: Map Skills

11. b
12. b
13. a
14. c
15. b

Part 3: Document Based Questions

A. (4 points each)

16. The speaker identifies with being a native of the Vietnamese people, who have lived in Vietnam for thousands of years. They do not want anyone placing other labels on them. Many Vietnamese, like the poet, would be willing to fight to protect their people and identity from those who wanted to force them into other ways of life labeled "communist" or "nationalist."

17. He uses quotes to call attention to the word. In order to be successful in Vietnam, he feels the United States would have to destroy the country, or kill many of its inhabitants. He wonders what kind of success this would look like to the world.

18. He lies dead because of the war. The speeches on the television have been trying to convince listeners that the Vietnam War is being waged in such a way that Americans will not need to keep dying in it, and the casket shows this goal failed.

B. (8 points)

19. The Vietnam War involved several American presidential administrations and an entire generation of American fighting men; Vietnamese Communists and nationalists were willing to lose hundreds of thousands of their own citizens each year in order to reunify their country; this resistance caused the United States to question its role in Southeast Asia and to wonder how its continued presence there would look to the world and to people at home; Americans who were boys when the war began grew up to be old enough to fight by the time the United States was forced to withdraw from Vietnam. A long-term effect on the United States was a reluctance to become involved in other countries' struggles. A long-term effect on Vietnam was the defeat of the South, reunification, and Communist rule.

Part 4: Extended Response

20. Possible responses should include the following points:

Rockets and missiles were originally developed as methods for delivering bombs. However, technology for both races was basically the same. Advances in "rocket science" were applicable to both races. It was probably the weapons race that drove the space race. If Americans fell behind in the space race, the U.S. would be vulnerable because the Soviets would be able to deliver intercontinental ballistic missiles to the United States, and the United States would be unable to retaliate. Fear and suspicion were powerful motivators. Competition between the Soviets and the Americans probably greatly increased the speed with which advances were made. Soviet successes with Sputnik shocked the U.S. into devoting tremendous resources to making advances in space travel and exploration. Cooperation between the superpowers might have had even better results than competition, but hostilities between the nations made cooperation impossible at first.

21. Possible responses should include the following points:

The Chinese civil war occurred directly after World War II. The U.S.

was probably unwilling to commit troops to another foreign conflict so soon. American involvement in Korea was part of UN intervention. Direct U.S. involvement was justified by international approval. The Chinese civil war was probably not seen at the time as directly threatening to other nations. However, by the time North Korea invaded South Korea, Truman and others had adopted the domino theory, which stated that if one nation fell to Communist control, nearby nations would soon fall too. The situation in China involved warring philosophies and differing goals for the nation but was not clearly a problem of one regional group. China was one nation; Korea at the time of the conflict was two. China had to be viewed as an internal struggle for power; Korea involved one nation's aggression against another. The conflict in Korea was clearly a result of North Koreans' use of aggressive tactics to impose their political system on South Koreans.

Chapter 18, Section 1
SECTION QUIZ

The Indian Subcontinent Achieves Freedom

A. 1. e
2. i
3. h
4. d
5. l
6. f
7. a
8. g
9. j
10. c

B. Possible answers:

a. The British House of Commons could have granted a longer period of time for the two new nations to prepare for partition and independence.

b. British officials could have assisted in the division and reorganization of courts, militaries, civil service, and so on.

c. The British military could have supervised the movement of people so as to minimize violence.

d. Britain could have tried to resolve religious conflicts instead of using the Muslim League-Congress Party division to strengthen its own authority.

e. Britain could have been less imperialistic in previous decades. If it had prepared India for independence by gradually granting greater self-rule, the administrative problems, at least, might have been lessened.

Chapter 18, Section 2
SECTION QUIZ

Southeast Asian Nations Gain Independence

A. 1. g
2. g
3. h
4. g
5. i
6. b
7. a
8. f
9. d
10. e
11. c
12. a

B. Possible answers:

a. The colonial governments had tended to be repressive and sometimes corrupt. When the colonies achieved independence, the rulers who came to power established governments like those they had known under imperialism.

b. The colonies had been dependent on the colonial powers and were unprepared for self-government. People in the new nations, accustomed to having little or no power, were easy prey for ambitious leaders.

c. The new nations included many diverse ethnic and religious groups and rival political factions. Indonesia and Malaysia were spread across hundreds of miles of sea, making it especially hard for these groups and factions to work together to oppose corrupt, repressive leaders.

d. Except when their own economic and military interests were involved, the colonial powers paid little attention to affairs in the new nations. Corrupt and repressive leaders felt they could do as they pleased.

Chapter 18, Section 3
SECTION QUIZ

New Nations in Africa

A. 1. k
2. a
3. j
4. f
5. c
6. m
7. i
8. o
9. n
10. e
11. d

B. Possible answers:

a. No. People are responsible for their own actions. Although they did little to help Africans develop their governments and economies, the Europeans cannot be held responsible for violence carried out by Africans.

b. Yes. The Europeans established borders in Africa to serve their own purposes, exploited its resources, and did little to help its people develop their economies and governments. Enemy peoples were forced together, and allied peoples were separated. Nationalism was on the rise and Communist influence was spreading. It must have been obvious to the Europeans that their departure would be followed by chaos and violence. Before France and Portugal pulled out, they contributed to the atmosphere of violence by using troops to oppose independence movements.

Chapter 18, Section 4
SECTION QUIZ

Conflicts in the Middle East

A. 1. f
2. c
3. d
4. l
5. i
6. k
7. a
8. b
9. h
10. j

B. Possible similarities:

a. Both negotiations involved Israel and one of its Arab enemies.

b. Both negotiations were conducted in isolation outside the Middle East.

c. In the Accords, Israel returned Israeli-occupied territory to Egypt. In the Declaration, Israel gave the Palestinians self-rule in Israeli-occupied territories.

d. Both negotiations were unpopular with right-wingers in each country or group.

e. Following each negotiation, a signer was assassinated by an extremist from his own nation.

Possible differences:

a. The Accords ended hostilities between Israel and Egypt. The Declaration has not yet resolved conflicts between Israelis and Palestinians.

b. At Camp David, the two sides were publicly invited to negotiate; although they met privately, there was pressure to produce results. At Oslo, the two sides met secretly, and their agreement was a surprise to the public.

c. In the Accords, Israel returned Israeli-occupied territory to Egypt. In the Declaration, Israel did not give the Palestinians territory, just

limited self-rule in Israeli-occupied territories.

Chapter 18, Section 5
SECTION QUIZ

Central Asia Struggles

A. 1. d
2. c
3. b
4. a
5. a
6. c

B. Azerbaijan. This country is located among the oil fields of the Caspian Sea. As a result, it has the best chance to build a solid economy based on the income from oil and oil products.

Chapter 18
TEST FORM A

The Colonies Become New Nations

Part 1: Main Ideas

1. b
2. a
3. b
4. d
5. d
6. a
7. a
8. d
9. a
10. b

Part 2: Map Skills

11. b
12. c
13. a
14. c
15. c

Part 3: Interpreting Graphs

16. c
17. a
18. b
19. a
20. d

Part 4: Extended Response

21. Possible Answer:

Possible answers should include the following points: The partition divided India into two nations, mostly Hindu India and mostly Muslim Pakistan. The administration of the courts, the military, the railways, and the police had to be divided between the two countries. Hindus and Sikhs in Pakistan and Muslims in India soon found themselves minorities in a hostile nation. Many of these people decided to move. During the summer of 1947, 10 million people were migrating in the Indian region. Muslims killed Hindus and Sikhs who were moving into India. Hindus and Sikhs killed Muslims who were headed into Pakistan. In total, an estimated 1 million died. During the following decades, conflicts erupted between India and Pakistan over the territory of Kashmir. Eventually, a truce line was set up between the Indian and Pakistani areas of Kashmir.

22. Possible answers should include the following points: After World War II, the UN decided to partition Palestine into a Palestinian state and a Jewish state. This division outraged the Arab states. They objected that the UN did not have the right to partition a country without considering the wishes of the majority of its people. The United States and many countries in Europe felt sympathy for the Jews because of the Holocaust. The day after Israel proclaimed itself a state, six Arab states invaded the new country. This war ended within months in a victory for Israel. However, several more wars took place in the following decades, and Israeli-Palestinian conflict continues to this day.

Chapter 18
TEST FORM B

The Colonies Become New Nations

Part 1: Main Ideas

1. a
2. b
3. c
4. d

5. d

6. b

7. d

8. d

9. b

10. a

Part 2: Map Skills

11. a

12. b

13. c

14. b

15. c

Part 3: Interpreting Graphs

16. c

17. b

18. a

19. a

20. d

Part 4: Extended Response

21. Possible answers should include the following points: In 1978, Carter invited Egyptian president Anwar Sadat and Israeli prime minister Menachem Begin to Camp David. There Sadat and Begin discussed in secret the issues dividing their two countries. After 13 days of negotiations, Carter announced that Egypt recognized Israel as a legitimate state. In exchange, Israel agreed to return the Sinai Peninsula to Egypt. The meeting that led to the Declaration of Principles was also secretive; it was held in Europe (Oslo). The Israelis and the Palestinians were the two countries that negotiated. Eventually, Israeli Prime Minister Yitzhak Rabin and Palestinian leader Yasir Arafat signed the Declaration of Principles. This agreement granted the Palestinians self-rule in the Gaza Strip and the West Bank. The Camp David Accords involved an exchange of concessions between Israel and Egypt. The Declaration of Principles primarily involved Israeli concessions to the Palestinians.

22. Possible answers should include the following points: She wanted to overturn the repressive government that had dominated Burma for many

years. From 1962 to 1988, this country was ruled by the oppressive regime of General Ne Win. Although Ne Win stepped down, the military continued to rule Burma. In addition, Aung San Suu Kyi was probably inspired by the democratic ideals of freedom. She refused to stop her democratic activities in Burma and was imprisoned for six years because of them.

Chapter 18
TEST FORM C

The Colonies Become New Nations

Part 1: Main Ideas

1. d

2. c

3. a

4. a

5. a

6. c

7. b

8. a

9. c

10. a

Part 2: Map Skills

11. b

12. d

13. c

14. c

15. a

Part 3: Interpreting Graphs—Constructed Response

16. The United States. The apparently high GDP of this country required a high number of skilled workers.

17. Singapore and the United States. Both countries had large and similar increases in GDP per capita.

18. The Philippines. This country had a very low GDP per capita in all three years, which means it manufactured a low amount of goods. Because of this, the Philippines had few manufactured goods to export.

19. Singapore. Because Singapore probably produced more goods, CD players would be more available.

20. The Philippines. This country had the least growth in GDP per capita.

Part 4: Extended Response

21.

a. Possible answers should include the following points: Economic problems were a major challenge faced by African nations in establishing stable governments. Kwame Nkrumah, the first prime minister of Ghana, attempted many development plans and economic projects, such as new roads, new schools, and expanded health facilities. However, the expense of the programs undermined the economy of his country and strengthened the opposition. Eventually, the military seized control of Ghana. In Algeria, efforts to modernize and industrialize were undermined when oil prices plunged in 1985-1986. Unemployment and unfulfilled promises of the revolution led to riots in 1988 against the secular government.

b. Political conflict has also contributed to the instability of governments in Africa. After a country overthrows a regime and gains independence, a political vacuum often results. During this period, many factions usually try to take power. In Angola, for example, a civil war raged after the country gained independence from Portugal. The Communist MPLA fought against the UNITA, which was assisted by South Africa and the United States.

c. A third challenge to the establishment of stable governments in Africa has been oppressive leadership. The harsh rule of Mobutu Sese Seko in Zaire caused many armed rebellions and ethnic clashes. The leader of Kenya, Daniel Moi, faced more and more opposition to his one-party rule. Under him, university strikes and protests resulted in the deaths of some students.

22. Possible answers should include the following points: Communism had a strong effect on many of

the countries of Southeast Asia. Leaders who were influenced by this ideology often imposed authoritarian rule. In Burma, General Ne Win set up a repressive military government with the goal of making the country a socialist state. Also, the colonial powers left Southeast Asia countries ill prepared for democracy. The Dutch resisted native Indonesians attempts to acquire a higher education and thereby the necessary political skills needed to participate effectively in a democracy. After Indonesia gained independence, President Sukarno attempted to guide this diverse nation in a parliamentary democracy. Unfortunately, this attempt failed. In 1965, a military coup attempted to take over the government. It was suppressed by a general named Suharto who seized power for himself and imposed authoritarian rule. A third reason was a disregard for the democratic rule of law. Ferdinand Marcos was elected president of the Philippines in 1965 but imposed an oppressive regime. Although the constitution limited Marcos to eight years in office, he got around this restriction by imposing martial law from 1972 to 1981.

Chapter 19, Section 1
SECTION QUIZ

Democracy

A. 1. a
2. d
3. c
4. d
5. b

B. The protection of individual rights is critical to maintaining a democracy. Fair and equal treatment of all citizens is a basic democratic principle. If some citizens are unjustly denied a right, other citizens cannot be certain that that right is, or will be, secure for them. Further, unfairly denying rights to some individuals means denying the contributions they might have made to all of society. A legislature may not be representative if many citizens

choose not to vote, but it cannot be representative if some citizens are not allowed to vote.

Chapter 19, Section 2
SECTION QUIZ

The Challenge of Democracy in Africa

A. 1. true
2. martial
3. secede
4. true
5. Nelson Mandela
6. true
7. all races *or* blacks

B. Possible answers:

a. Individuals protested apartheid because it was so obviously unfair for the small white minority to rule over, and deny rights to, the large black majority.

b. Individual customers and citizens pressured businesses and governments to join the protest.

c. Many Americans learned about both apartheid and the effectiveness of economic protest during the civil rights movement.

d. Trade restrictions and economic protests succeeded because they had the greatest effect on the white South Africans who controlled most of the nation's wealth.

Chapter 19, Section 3
SECTION QUIZ

The Collapse of the Soviet Union

A. 1. a
2. d
3. c
4. b
5. a
6. d

B. Possible answers:

a. The more freedom the Soviet people had, the more they wanted.

b. Glasnost allowed people to read, see, hear, and discuss more freely ideas that totalitarianism had tried to keep from them.

c. Increased exposure to ideas and ways of life outside the USSR made people want change in their own lives.

d. The freedom to complain publicly about economic conditions led Gorbachev to introduce perestroika—economic reforms that gave individuals more rights and responsibilities for their own economic well-being.

e. Pressure to open the political system to reform was an inevitable result of granting social and economic freedoms.

Chapter 19, Section 4
SECTION QUIZ

Changes in Central andEastern Europe

A. 1. a
2. a
3. b
4. d
5. d
6. c

B. Students who believe that the world is a better place could say that

a. more people live under democratic governments than ever before.

b. the process that led to the breakup of the Soviet Union was involved in ending Soviet domination of Eastern European nations and, consequently, brought down the totalitarian regimes in those nations.

c. the changes allowed people to make choices about economic and political systems governing their lives.

Students who believe that the world is not a better place could say that

a. millions of people still live under Communist and/or totalitarian regimes.

b. economic and political instability and continuing ethnic and cultural

---

conflicts in formerly Communist nations could lead to problems both domestically and globally.

c. the changes resulted in severe ethnic conflicts and brutal policies of ethnic cleansing in several new nations.

Chapter 19, Section 5
SECTION QUIZ

China: Reform and Reaction

A. 1. c
2. a
3. d
4. b
5. c
6. d

B. Regarding China's path, students could make points similar to the following:

a. Chinese leaders, like those in the USSR, turned to capitalist ideas to help the economy. They gave individuals more economic freedoms and invited foreign investment and tourism.

b. Unlike the Soviets, Chinese leaders maintained strict control over political freedoms, including those of speech, press, and assembly.

Regarding problems that arose, students should note some of the following:

a. a conflict between certain Western ideas and Communist values

b. the physical conflict that resulted when Deng Xiaoping refused to consider political reform and instead crushed the massive student protest at Tiananmen Square

c. a widening gap between the rich and poor

d. a widespread belief that Communist officials were corrupt

e. increasing pressure from the West to ensure basic human rights

f. increasing pressure from Communist hard-liners to shift away from economic reforms

g. a populace that had become more difficult to rule because of its increasing prosperity and exposure to Western values

Chapter 19
TEST FORM A

Struggles for Democracy

Part 1: Main Ideas
1. b
2. d
3. c
4. a
5. c
6. b
7. d
8. c
9. a
10. b

Part 2: Map Skills
11. c
12. a
13. d
14. c
15. a

Part 3: Interpreting Political Cartoons
16. c
17. c
18. d
19. c
20. b

Part 4: Extended Response
21. Possible responses should include the following points:

Gorbachev's reforms reversed totalitarian policies that had rewarded silence and discouraged individuals from acting on their own. Glasnost encouraged a free flow of ideas and information and allowed public criticism of government economic policies. Perestroika gave local farm and factory managers greater authority and allowed individuals to own small private businesses. Democratization loosened the Communist Party's control on society and politics. Citizens turned to other reformers who promised faster and even greater changes. Communist hard-liners tried to undo Gorbachev's reforms, but their August coup resulted in the

collapse of the Communist Party. Nationalist groups that had been demanding self-rule now declared independence.

22. Possible responses should include the following points:

Free elections are one practice and require more than one political party and universal suffrage. For a long time, Mexico was an example of a country with only one significant political party, but this has recently changed. South Africa used to be a country that denied suffrage to the majority, but in 1994, it held its first all-race election. Citizen participation is an important practice. China is an example of a country that represses free speech, thus squelching citizen participation. Gorbachev's policy of glasnost was an example of a leader trying to increase citizen participation. Support for majority rule and minority rights is another crucial practice. Nigeria and the former Yugoslavia are examples of countries that have persecuted their minorities. In contrast, South Africa's new bill of rights protects all racial groups. Finally, constitutional government is a crucial practice to make democracy work. China has failed to move toward constitutional government. East Germany gave up one-party rule and joined in a constitutional government when it reunified with West Germany. Students may cite other examples for each practice as long as they cite details from the chapter.

Chapter 19
TEST FORM B

Struggles for Democracy

Part 1: Main Ideas
1. b
2. d
3. a
4. b
5. c
6. b
7. d
8. a
9. c

10. b

Part 2: Map Skills

11. d

12. c

13. d

14. c

15. a

Part 3: Interpreting Political Cartoons

16. b

17. c

18. c

19. d

20. b

Part 4: Extended Response

21. Possible responses should include the following points:

European powers created colonial borders that threw rival ethnic groups together. As a result, many former colonies suffered from having multiple ethnic conflicts. They often did not share a national identity, which could bind them together. The lack of modern industry, transportation, and communication systems further complicated the transition for former colonies. A heavy dependence on one or two products of export while importing almost everything else hurt the economies of the countries. Often the middle class was very small, and the work force was unskilled and illiterate. This adversely affected community life and disrupted families by forcing them to split up in order to survive. In addition, the leaders of these countries were unfamiliar with working under democratic laws and processes and would often rely on the military to keep order. These problems contributed to the difficult transition to democracy as rival ethnic groups fought each other for power. The unbalanced economies tended to promote political and social instability.

22. Possible responses should include the following points:

Some economic problems in the Soviet Union, such as industrial

inefficiency, resulted from decades of central planning and other similar policies. In some of the Central and Eastern European allies there were also economic problems of inflation and unemployment caused by shock therapy and other efforts to make a quick shift to capitalism. Ethnic and cultural conflicts in Yugoslavia exploded when totalitarian rule ended. Political crises, such as in Chechnya and Czechoslovakia, also resulted from ethnic and cultural differences as well as the desire for self-rule. In Russia and Poland, social crises such as rising crime rates were caused by economic hardships and underfunded, inexperienced civilian police. In addition, personal fear and insecurity was compounded by all of these issues and left many people uncertain of the future.

Chapter 19
TEST FORM C

Struggles for Democracy

Part 1: Main Ideas

1. a

2. b

3. c

4. c

5. b

6. d

7. b

8. c

9. c

10. d

Part 2: Map Skills – Constructed Response

11. Russia

12. They all lie on the Baltic Sea.

13. The Caspian Sea.

14. Russia and Azerbaijan

15. Russia might attack Belarus and Lithuania to reunify with its other territory; similarly, Azerbaijan might attack Armenia.

Part 3: Interpreting Political Cartoons

16. c

17. a

18. b

19. d

20. a

Part 4: Extended Response

21. Possible responses should include the following points:

The collapse of communism in Eastern Europe inspired or increased the desire for independence in the Soviet republics. Some of the republics had been independent states before their annexation by the Soviet Union. Even in republics that had never known independence, nationalist feelings created a strong desire for self-rule. In addition, Gorbachev's reforms had provided a taste of democracy, and people throughout the USSR wanted more freedom. People resented party leaders in Moscow who had controlled nearly every aspect of life in the USSR for decades. The August 1991 coup attempted by Communist hard-liners (the State Committee) sparked anger against the party. The military's refusal to support the hard-liners suggested that it would refuse to enforce Soviet unity if the republics declared independence.

22. Possible responses should include the following points:

Brazil evolved from a monarchy to a republic (controlled by the aristocracy) to a dictatorship to a democracy, which was overturned by a military coup. Democracy was re-established in the 1980s. Mexico set up constitutional government in 1917, but democracy was limited because one political party dominated the country until the 1990s. Now, multi-party democratic rule is developing. Argentina has a long history of being ruled by either a dictator or the military, but in the 1980s and 1990s, the country seemed to establish democratic government. South Africa nominally had a constitutional government, but it denied rights to the black majority. In response to domestic and international protests, the government allowed an all-race election. Nelson Mandela was elected, and South Africa adopted a new constitution and bill of rights. Poland had an anti-Communist movement for decades. The government banned Solidarity (an activist union) and declared martial law. An economic crisis led to additional protests, free elections, and the peaceful overthrow of Communist rule. Mikhail Gorbachev introduced many reforms to the USSR, including glasnost (openness) and democratization (a gradual opening of the political system). These reforms triggered a hard-line Communist crackdown, but this backfired. The Soviet people defied the party and demanded their rights. Soon after, the Soviet Union broke apart, and republican governments were established. Students may name other countries as examples if they provide supporting details.

Chapter 20, Section 1
SECTION QUIZ

The Impact of Science and Technology

A. 1. b
   2. d
   3. c
   4. b
   5. a

B. Answers could note that advances in science and technology have shaped our attitudes by

a. making it clear that we live in a world community. Views of Earth from space, instantaneous communication made possible by satellites, television, the Internet, and so on, have made us sharply aware that we all inhabit the same world. They have also put people in touch, made the unfamiliar familiar, and made us aware that all people are more alike than they are different.

b. changing the problems we face and making us aware of how huge those problems are. Recent developments in science and technology have resulted in, or contributed to, such problems as the threat of nuclear war and many of the dangers to the environment.

c. making the problems we face solvable, or seem to be solvable. For example, genetic engineering could wipe out horrible diseases and make it possible to grow food without dangerous chemicals.

Answers could note that advances in science and technology have shaped what is likely for us in the future by

a. increasing the possibilities for worldwide cooperation through better communication.

b. increasing life spans and health.

c. creating serious problems with the environment.

d. developing ways to solve serious problems with the environment.

e. creating new problems never imagined in the past, such as ethical questions about cloning.

Chapter 20, Section 2
SECTION QUIZ

Global Economic Development

A. 1. d
   2. b
   3. a
   4. c
   5. a
   6. b

B. Possible answers:

a. Emerging nations need to grow economically much more quickly than developed nations. When there is not enough food to feed the existing population and there are not enough jobs, economic growth seems more important than environmental protection.

b. Emerging nations do not have the same scientific and technological resources available. Whereas a developed nation might be able to use solar power to run a factory, an emerging nation might need to burn wood or coal.

c. Emerging nations have become manufacturing sites for the industries of developed nations. Manufacturing requires using vast amounts of

energy and can pose great threats to the environment.

d. Emerging nations often suffer from political instability. Sustainable development is difficult in an unstable environment.

Chapter 20, Section 3
SECTION QUIZ

Global Security Issues

A. 1. b
   2. d
   3. b
   4. c
   5. c

B. Possible responses should include the following rights:

a. rights to life, liberty, and personal security; these are the basic human rights on which all other rights depend.

b. right to free speech; all people should be free to say what they think without fear of reprisal.

c. rights to religious freedom; everyone should have the right to follow the religion of their choice.

d. rights to political equality; everyone should have the right to choose their own political representatives and to participate in government.

e. rights to economic opportunity; everyone should have the right to earn a decent living.

f. rights to health; everyone should be able to enjoy a decent standard of health.

Chapter 20, Section 4
SECTION QUIZ

Terrorism Case Study: September 11, 2001

A. 1. b
   2. a
   3. b
   4. d
   5. a

B. Students who feel that the policy is practical could make such points as the following:

a. It does terrorists no good to kill people or to destroy property if they cannot accomplish their main goal, which is to change a government's policy.

b. If terrorists are unsuccessful in meeting their goals, they will abandon their tactics.

c. Negotiation encourages terrorism by giving terrorists a reason to continue their activities.

d. There are other methods available to people who want to change policy.

e. Give a terrorist an inch, he or she will take a mile.

f. Terrorists are not trustworthy.

Students who feel that the policy is impractical could make such points as the following:

a. The victims of terrorism are almost always innocent and should not be sacrificed.

b. Governments usually do negotiate, regardless of their stated policy, and it is foolish to pretend otherwise. No one is really fooled.

c. It is much easier to state such a policy than it is to follow it.

Chapter 20, Section 5
SECTION QUIZ

Cultures Blend in a Global Age

A. 1. d

2. b

3. a

4. d

5. d

B. Answers will vary widely. A model answer for the Gulf War follows.

a. Although it occurred thousands of miles from the U.S., Americans were deeply affected by Iraq's invasion of Kuwait.

b. Threats of an interruption to the world's supply of oil threatened people in every nation dependent on foreign sources of oil.

c. The war that resulted from this event took soldiers from America and many other nations to a location far from home and brought death and injury to many of them.

Chapter 20
TEST FORM A

Global Interdependence

Part 1: Main Ideas

1. c

2. d

3. d

4. a

5. d

6. c

7. d

8. a

9. c

10. b

Part 2: Map Skills

11. a

12. d

13. d,e

14. d,e

15. a

Part 3: Interpreting Graphs

16. c

17. a

18. b

19. c

20. a

Part 4: Extended Response

21. Possible responses should include the following points:

1. The Internet—it makes enormous amounts of information instantly available, increases communication, allows interaction with people all over the world, increases possibilities for flexible working situations, and encourages the sharing of knowledge. 2. Genetic engineering—it offers hope to people with genetic disorders, may result in cures for previously incurable diseases, and may greatly aid in agriculture. 3. The space shuttle—it has led to a wide range of scientific experiments, cooperation with neighboring nations, and may make it possible for ordinary citizens to travel in space.

22. Possible responses should include the following points:

The UN established and ratified the Universal Declaration of Human Rights which stated that all people are born free and equal in dignity and rights, and that everyone has the right to life, liberty, and security of person. Later, the Helsinki Accords addressed issues of freedom of movement and freedom to publish and exchange information. Although both the declaration and the accords are nonbinding, many people around the world have become committed to ensuring that basic human rights are respected. The UN and other nonprofit organizations, like Amnesty International, work to track and publicize human rights violations. The women's rights movement addressed such issues as employment discrimination and equal salary in the United States. In non-Western countries, it further addressed issues of women being denied access to education and being victims of violence and abuse in times of war.

Chapter 20
TEST FORM B

Global Interdependence

Part 1: Main Ideas

1. d

2. b

3. a

4. a

5. b

6. c

7. a

8. a

9. a

10. b

Part 2: Map Skills

11. d,e

12. a,c,d

13. b

14. d,e

15. a

Part 3: Interpreting Graphs

16. b

17. d

18. b

19. c

20. b

Part 4: Extended Response

21. Possible responses should include the following points:

Student responses will vary widely and the following should not be considered an inclusive list. The Internet has become a tool for information sharing all over the world and can be used to spread political and social propaganda, which can spark unrest. Genetic engineering has opened the doors to new modes in medical research and a competitive race to find cures for terminal diseases. World trading blocs tie regions of the world together on an economic level and an increase or decrease in one region can effect the others as well. Global security may raise issues of conflicting security needs among nations. Popular culture has the ability to spread ideas based on temporary trends that may or may not have beneficial effects on the world.

22. Possible responses should include the following points:

People's lives can be substantially enriched by accepting ideas from other cultures. New ideas allow for growth, change, and make life more interesting. Some examples might be the benefits people in the West have found from the meditative techniques in some Eastern religions; many Chinese people are working for greater democratization because of exposure to Western ideas; life is more varied due to exposure of foreign foods, music, fashions, etc. However, accepting too many ideas from other cultures could cause a group to lose its own identity. A culture could be weakened by replacing what has traditionally been important to it with untested new ideas and methods of doing

things. What may be meaningful and practical for one culture will not necessarily work for another. The ideas that have stood the test of time in a culture have done so because they have evolved within that culture as it developed.

Chapter 20
TEST FORM C

Global Interdependence

Part 1: Main Ideas

1. b

2. c

3. c

4. a

5. c

6. c

7. a

8. b

9. d

10. c

Part 2: Map Skills – Constructed Response

11. North American Free Trade Agreement

12. Central American Common Market and Caribbean Community and Common Market

13. Carribean Community and Common Market

14. Andean Group and Southern Cone Common Market

15. North American Free Trade Agreement and Southern Cone Common Market

Part 3: Interpreting Graphs

16. c

17. a

18. b

19. a

20. d

Part 4: Extended Response

21. Possible responses should include the following points:

It increases security in that nations dependent on each other, for raw

materials, manufactured products, etc., are more hesitant to go to war with each other. However, economic interdependence endangers security by encouraging nations not to meet all of their own needs, such as depending upon the Middle East for oil. Security is increased by making the nations and peoples of the world more familiar with each other. Familiarity and understanding tend to encourage friendly relations. This, in turn, decreases the chance of war. Security is increased by making the nationalities of the world aware that we are all on the same planet. This encourages cooperation in combating those perils that threaten all of us, such as environmental dangers and the depletion of nonrenewable resources. Lastly, global interdependence endangers security by subjecting every nation to what could be shortsighted or rash decisions by other nations that can have a ripple effect on the world.

22. Possible responses should include the following points:

Many national leaders have felt that economic cooperation among countries worldwide is the key to peace and prosperity. The idea of free trade, which is the elimination of trade barriers and tariffs among nations, has been addressed through a variety of forums. An agreement known as GATT (General Agreement on Tariffs and Trade) has been one such forum where these issues have been addressed. Over the years, a general lowering of protective tariffs and an expansion of free trade, region by region, has expanded the global marketplace. By 1995, the WTO (World Trade Organization) was established to supervise free trade. Another organization now known as the EU (European Union) has brought about the integration of many European countries under the umbrella of a single form of currency, unrestricted travel between member countries, and highly improved trading. Consequently, other trading blocs have emerged across the globe such as the North American Free Trade Agreement (NAFTA), Asia-Pacific Economic Cooperation (APEC), Latin American Free Trade Agreement (LAFTA), and more. Multinational corporations, freer world travel, and regional trading blocs today tie nations together economically. Economic ripples can be felt around the world if a particular region suffers; therefore it is in the global markets best interest to promote programs to protect the economic security of world nations. These collective efforts have done a great deal in expanding the awareness and cooperation of people across the globe.

Epilogue
QUIZ 1

Technology Transforms Life

A. 1. d
2. a
3. h
4. b
5. e
6. f
7. g
8. c

B. Possible answers should include the following points: Because the mass media now reach around the world, they are able to spread images, ideas, and fashions from one country to another. These ideas or trends can travel from developed countries to undeveloped countries or vice versa. In addition, through the use of television, billions of people can watch the same event, such as the Olympics. However, mass media may cause deep changes in traditional cultures. Old ways may be lost because of the spread of new images, ideas, and fashions through the media. In some cases, people experience a loss of identity because they lose a sense of their culture or what defines them as people.

Epilogue
QUIZ 2

Environmental Changes

A. 1. d
2. b
3. c
4. d
5. c

6. a

B. Possible answers should include the following points: The greenhouse effect is a possible cause for global warming. Much industrial pollution comes in the form of gases, such as carbon dioxide. These gases—sometimes called greenhouse gases—are the exhaust from factories and automobiles. They create a kind of ceiling—like the roof of a greenhouse—that traps heat near the earth's surface. This buildup of heat near the earth's surface causes a gradual warming of the earth's atmosphere. To combat this problem, the industrialized nations have called for limits on the release of greenhouse gases.

Epilogue
QUIZ 3

Feeding a Growing Population

A. 1. c
2. d
3. a
4. c
5. d
6. b

B. Possible answers should include the following points: In Africa, changes in climate have played a major role in creating famine. In the 1970s and 1980s, low levels of rainfall (compared to the previous two decades) caused food supplies to run short. As a result, thousands of Africans died of starvation. In addition, wars in Africa have contributed to famine. In the early 1990s, Somalia was having a civil war that disrupted food production. Thousands of Somalis died of starvation. High African birth rates made the famine problem even worse. Food supplies were getting smaller while populations were getting larger.

Epilogue
QUIZ 4

Economic Issues in the Developing World

A. 1. raw
2. true
3. political

4. financial aid
5. true
6. little
7. true

B. Possible answers should include the following points: Grassroots programs usually focus on helping individuals and communities to improve their lives. For example, microcredit programs give small loans—often less than $100—to individuals as seed money to enable them to begin small-scale businesses and lift themselves from poverty. Organizations, such as the World Bank and multinational corporations, run microcredit programs.

Epilogue
QUIZ 5

Seeking Global Security

A. 1. a
2. d
3. d
4. b
5. a

B. Possible answers should include the following points: Weapons of mass destruction have worsened the threat that terrorism poses to international security. For example, in 1995, the Aum Shinrikyo cult in Japan released sarin gas into the Tokyo subway. In addition, modern transportation and communications enable terrorists to cross borders, commit terrorist acts, and escape to friendly nations.

Epilogue
QUIZ 6

Defending Human Rights and Freedoms

A. 1. b
2. d
3. c
4. a
5. b
6. d
7. c

B. Possible answers should include the following points: Rising levels of education are providing people with the skills to exercise their political rights and improve their lives. Modern communications networks are helping human rights organizations to investigate and report on human rights abuses. In addition, today's mass media can make people instantly aware of abuses in almost any part of the world. Other reasons for optimism include the political changes that have occurred in Eastern Europe and South Africa. Beginning with Poland in 1989, one country after another threw off its old regime and turned to a democratic form of government. In 1991, the Soviet Union came to an end and, in the same year, the republic of Russia held its first free presidential election. And in 1994, South Africa held its first universal election, in which people of all races could vote.

Unresolved Problems of the Modern World
TEST FORM A

Part 1: Main Ideas

1. b
2. a
3. d
4. d
5. c
6. b
7. a
8. c
9. b
10. a

Part 2: Map Skills

11. d
12. b
13. b
14. b
15. d

Part 3: Interpreting Graphs

16. a
17. d
18. c
19. d

20. d

Part 4: Extended Response

21. Possible responses should include the following points:

Eighty percent of the earth's energy supply now comes from nonrenewable sources, such as coal and oil. These resources are often cheaper to use, but they cannot be replenished. Most of this energy is consumed by developed countries. Although these nations account for just 25 percent of the world's population, they use 75 percent of the energy consumed worldwide. Using nonrenewable energy sources has many environmental effects. The burning of wood and coal emits greenhouse gases. Cutting down trees leads to soil erosion and the expansion of deserts in some areas. Renewable resources, such as wind, water, and solar power can be replenished. At present, these sources are more costly to use. However, in the future, improved technology and inexpensive ways to use these resources may lead to reduced air pollution and fewer greenhouse gases. Solar power can be used to heat homes in the winter and to power battery operated instruments. Turbines use flowing water to produce power. And wind is being used in the form of windmills to produce electricity in homes, communities, and some cities.

22. Possible responses should include the following points:

When the basic human rights of citizens, such as those stated in the Universal Declaration of Human Rights, are violated in a country, it can suffer severe consequences internationally. A country that becomes known for treating its people unfairly might suffer from trade embargoes placed against it by countries that do not want to be associated with the offending nation or do not want to support their actions. Also, human rights abuses committed in a country can give the offending nation a bad reputation in the media, which will display their abuses for the world to see. The issue can have an adverse effect on tourism, corporate sponsorship from multinational companies, and even support from

international organizations like the UN, the World Bank, or the IMF. There are also independent organizations that monitor human rights violations worldwide, such as Amnesty International and Americas Watch. These help to improve conditions in the offending countries and even save lives.

Unresolved Problems of the Modern World
TEST FORM B

Part 1: Main Ideas

1. b
2. a
3. d
4. a
5. c
6. b
7. a
8. c
9. c
10. a

Part 2: Map Skills

11. d
12. b
13. a
14. c
15. d

Part 3: Interpreting Graphs

16. d
17. b
18. d
19. b
20. d

Part 4: Extended Response

21. Possible responses should include the following points:

Some African nations face severe food shortages. Natural factors, such as the weather, and human actions, such as civil war, have caused these shortages. Changes in the climate have played a major role in creating famine. During the 1950s and 1960s, rainfall was plentiful. The rain helped produce good crops and steady economic growth for many African nations. In the 1970s and 1980s, rainfall fell to typically low levels. In many areas, food supplies ran short. Ethiopia confronted severe famines in the 1980s and 1990s because of drought. Tens of thousands of Ethiopians died of starvation. Many others endured malnutrition and disease. In addition to droughts, wars have contributed to famine. Somalia was touched by the same drought that affected Ethiopia, but Somalia was also having a civil war that disrupted food production. Thousands died of starvation. More than a million refugees fled the nations. The reduction in food supply caused by drought and war created deep problems for many African nations. While agriculture declined, the prices for many African exports fell as well. High African birth rates made these problems even worse. International organizations such as the Red Cross often try to send humanitarian aid. However, in the case of Somalia, members of the warring factions demanded bribes from the aid organization. Consequently, little of the aid reached the starving masses. Scientists are also doing their part in the fight against famine through the development of advanced agricultural methods. Their successes, known as the green revolution, have helped to boost food production greatly. Also, genetic research has played a growing role in which scientists alter plant genes to produce new plants that are more productive and resistant to pests and disease.

22. Possible responses should include the following points:

Industrialized nations have tried to work with less-developed countries by providing aid through international organizations, such as the World Bank and the International Monetary Fund (IMF). The World Bank provides loans for large-scale development projects. The IMF offers emergency loans to countries in financial crisis. International agencies can play an important role in development, but they also have drawbacks. The World Bank, for example, might fund a

project that it considers worthy, such as a large dam. But the project may do little to help the people of a country. The IMF has been criticized for setting harsh financial conditions for countries receiving IMF loans. For instance, the IMF might require a country to cut its government spending drastically. Another source of economic growth for less-developed countries is investment by multinational corporations. These giant companies build factories in countries where the costs of labor and materials are low in order to increase their profits. They often bring jobs, investment capital, and technology to nations that need them. Yet some of these companies have been criticized for exploiting workers and harming the environment in their host countries. Another approach to economic development is grassroots development. These are small-scale, community-based projects that help poor people lift themselves from poverty. Grassroots development responds to community needs and can help raise standards of living while still preserving local customs.

Unresolved Problems of the Modern World
TEST FORM C

Part 1: Main Ideas

1. b
2. d
3. a
4. b
5. c
6. b
7. c
8. a
9. b
10. a

Part 2: Map Skills

11. c
12. c
13. a
14. c

15. d

Part 3: Interpreting Graphs – Constructed Response

16. 4,543,000,000 tons
17. 2% decrease
18. about 14%
19. carbon, because the amount of emissions is so much higher than sulfur
20. 1980-1985 and 1990-1994

Part 4: Extended Response

21. Possible responses should include the following points:

High-tech workplaces are found mainly in industrialized countries, such as the United States, Japan, and the countries of Western Europe. This technological imbalance has given rise to a new kind of economic imperialism in which the industrialized nations dominate less-developed countries. This problem occurs because technology helps the developed countries become economically stronger than the less-developed countries. This economic strength gives the developed countries a great deal of control over economic aid and investment in less-developed countries. Technology also gives the developed nations better military equipment with which to influence the behavior of the less-developed countries.

22. Possible responses should include the following points:

The threat of terrorism has spread to more and more places around the globe. A number of terrorist groups posses chemical and biological weapons, which are relatively easy to produce and use. The terrorist attack on the World Trade buildings was the first time hijacked planes had been used as weapons of mass destruction. The nature of terrorism is not as clear as that of war where one country or people engages in a prolonged conflict with another. Terrorist groups often act on their own initiative for reasons that may be against their own government. They may be supported by foreign or domestic governments, popular

opinion, or even private resources.
Therefore, the only effective way
that they can be combated is through
global cooperation of governments.
In the wake of the terrorist attacks
on the United States, President Bush
called on world governments to aid
the United States in a global crusade
to wipe out all forms of terrorism
wherever it may be. The ultimate
success of this enterprise will be
dependent upon the cooperation of
world governments to see it through
to its conclusion.